GLOBAL LOGISTICS

New Directions in Supply Chain Management

FIFTH EDITION

Edited by **Donald Waters**

London and Philadelphia

Publisher's note

First published in 1988
Revised edition 1990
Second edition 1994
Paperback edition 1995
Third edition 1999
Fourth edition 2003
Fifth edition 2007

First published in Great Britain in 2007 by Kogan Page Limited

120 Pentonville Road
London N1 9JN
United Kingdom
www.kogan-page.co.uk

525 South 4th street #241
Philadelphia PA 19147
USA

ISBN-10 0 7494 4813 X
ISBN-13 978 0 7494 4813 4

British Library Cataloguing-in-Publication Data

A CIP record for this book is available from the British Library.

Library of Congress Cataloging-in-Publication Data

Global logistics : new directions in supply chain management / [edited by] Donald Waters. -- 5th ed.
p. cm.
Title of 4th ed.: Global logistics and distribution planning.
Includes bibliographical references and index.
ISBN 0-7494-4813-X
1. Physical distribution of goods. 2. Business logistics--Management. I. Waters, C. D. J. (C. Donald J.), 1949-

HF5415.6.G55 2006
658.7--dc22

2006017281

Typeset by Saxon Graphics Ltd, Derby
Printed and bound inGreat Britain by MPG Books Ltd, Bodmin, Cornwall

Contents

Figures

Tables

Contributors

Julian Allen is a research fellow at the Transport Studies Group, University of Westminster, where his major research interests are urban freight transport and logistics, and the impact of manufacturing and retailing techniques on logistics and transportation systems. He lectures and conducts research on freight transport and logistics and has published a number of papers, reports and chapters in books.

Grzegorz Augustyniak has an MA from the Warsaw School of Economics (SGH), where he is currently an assistant professor in the Department of Management Theory. He is coordinator of a student exchange programme within the Community of European Management Schools, and is deputy director of the Polish–Japanese Management Centre.

Until 1998 he was a faculty member of the Department of Logistics at SGH and held visiting positions at Carleton University, the University of Calgary, the University of Minnesota and the University of British Columbia. He has been a consultant to many companies in manufacturing and distribution, and is currently working on improving productivity and quality in Poland.

Colin Bamford is professor of transport and logistics at the University of Huddersfield. His interest in transport issues originated in the early 1970s when he was one of Ken Gwilliam's researchers at the University of Leeds. At Huddersfield he has been responsible for the development of a pioneering suite of undergraduate courses in transport and logistics management. More recently he has been involved in setting up a new distance-learning training programme for logistics managers in Hungary. He has written many articles and supervised research on a variety of supply chain management topics and published textbooks in the field of transport economics.

Adrian Beesley is the head of product development for DHL Exel Supply Chain within its consumer sector. Before this he was director of the Academy of Logistics and director of client operations at BAX Global, covering EMEA solutions and business development. He has been a senior research fellow with the University of Warwick's Manufacturing Group, where he worked on a number of projects for leading companies in the area of time compression. During this time he developed time-based process mapping for supply chain re-engineering. Adrian started his career as a management trainee for Unilever, and his other experiences include director of DLR Consulting in the Far East, senior consultant at Price Waterhouse, and company logistics manager for B&Q.

Alan Braithwaite is a visiting lecturer in supply chain management at Cranfield School of Management, and chairman of LCP Consulting, a specialist supply chain and logistics consultancy. He has a first degree in chemical engineering from the University of Birmingham and a Master's in business studies from the London Business School. His early career was spent as a production manager and industrial engineer in the food industry with Lyons and Heinz. He then worked in the furniture industry as managing director of a subsidiary of Christie-Tyler plc before moving to consulting. Over the last 30 years he has consulted with more than 300 companies around the world and developed and implemented innovative supply chain solutions. He is a recognized educator and author in his specialization.

Michael Browne is the Exel professor of logistics at the University of Westminster. During the past five years he has been the head of the Transport Department and the course leader for the Master's programme in European logistics. He is the director of research activities in freight transport and logistics, where recent projects include research on distribution in European cities, potential energy savings from sustainable logistics strategies and forecasting future trend in logistics. Michael works on studies for the European Commission, Department for Transport, the Research Councils and commercial organizations, and represents the university on many external committees and boards. He is assistant editor of the journal *Transport Reviews* and is a member of the editorial boards of the *Journal of International Logistics* and *Supply Chain Forum*.

Simon Chan is a research member of the Logistics Management Research Centre, Hong Kong Baptist University, and is a PhD candidate at the Department of Finance and Decision Sciences. He earned his Bachelor degree in business administration (information systems management) from the same university. His research interests are enterprise resource planning systems, information systems and technologies application, logistics and supply chain management. He has published research papers in a number of international conferences, journals and book chapters, and is active in several academic and professional bodies.

Garland Chow is an associate professor in the Faculty of Commerce and Business Administration at the University of British Columbia (UBC). His interests span transport economics, logistics, supply chain management and services management, and current research includes work on the logistics services industry, prediction of bankruptcies in transport firms and a book on motor carriers. His paper (co-authored with Trevor Heaver) 'Logistics performance, definition and measurement' won the *International Journal of Physical Distribution and Logistics Management*'s best paper prize. Garland is coordinator of the UBC supply chain specialization and a national director of the Canadian Association of Logistics Management.

Martin Christopher is professor of marketing and logistics at Cranfield School of Management, UK. His work in the field of logistics and supply chain management has gained international recognition. He has published widely, and his recent books include *Logistics and Supply Chain Management* and *Marketing Logistics*. Martin is also co-editor of the *International Journal of Logistics Management* and is a regular contributor to conferences and workshops around the world.

At Cranfield, Martin chairs the Centre for Logistics and Transportation, and is an emeritus fellow of the Institute of Logistics, on whose council he sits. In 1988 he was awarded the Sir Robert Lawrence Gold Medal for his contribution to logistics education.

Jacques Colin is professor of management science at the Université de la Méditerranée, Aix–Marseille, France. At the Faculty of Economic Sciences and Business Administration, he is director of the CRET-LOG (Centre de Recherche sur le Transport et la Logistique), which is the main French research and teaching centre devoted to logistics. He is a specialist in logistics, and more specifically his interests lie in the study of logistics and supply chain management strategies developed by major companies (in industry, distribution and third-party logistics sectors), and in the effects of logistics growth on land planning and sustainable development. He has carried out many research projects for government bodies. He is also a consultant for companies such as IBM, SNCF, OTIS, SAGA and ELF. He has published widely, with more than 160 publications since 1980.

Andrew Cox is professor and director of the Centre for Business Strategy and Procurement at Birmingham University's Business School. This centre undertakes research in all aspects of business strategy, supply chain management and procurement competence.

Andrew has a major grant from the EPSRC to undertake a research project into critical assets in supply chain management. This involves working closely with a number of major UK companies on the development of audit tools for strategic and operational alignment. He has also worked as a consultant for the EU, HM Treasury and DTI, and for a range of multinational firms based in

Europe and the United States, emphasizing the evaluation of existing strategy, operational practice, procurement and supply competence. Andrew has written on a wide range of topics related to procurement and business strategy.

Robert Duncan is a director of B & C Business Services Limited and operates as an independent consultant in the field of supply chain management. He has over 35 years of global supply chain management experience as both an executive and a consultant in many industry sectors. Robert has particular expertise in the area of outsourced supply chain resources. His recent work has been in the areas of supply chain process improvement and the use of IT to support those process changes within both outsourced and in-house supply chain environments. Robert has contributed to a number of publications and conferences relating to supply chain management.

Dag Ericsson was formerly professor of e-logistics at the University of Skovde, Sweden, and is now a professor at the University of Boras, where he specializes in the implementation of integrated logistics in manufacturing industry.

He was the pioneer and developer of the Swedish concept of materials administration and supply chain management, and has written several books including *Purchasing: Concepts and tools, Materials Administration/Logistics, Supply Chain Management* and *Virtual Integration with IT as an Enabler*.

In his recent research and consulting, Dag focuses on the interface between technology, management, organizational effectiveness and efficiency. He is especially concerned with renewal processes and organizational restructuring enabled by technological development. He works with most of the global Swedish companies – and several international companies – bridging the gaps between business, technology and executive education.

Nathalie Fabbe-Costes is professor of management science at the Université de la Méditerranée, Aix–Marseille, France, and a senior researcher at the CRET-LOG (Centre de Recherche sur le Transport et la Logistique), teaching strategy, logistics, supply chain management and management information systems. She is also director of their Master's and PhD programmes in management logistics and strategy. Her major fields of interest include: 1) logistics as a global and complex intra- and inter-organizational management concept, a structured function within companies, and an increasing component of firms' strategy; and 2) logistics information and communication systems as part of supply chain management and company strategy. She has written more than 120 publications since 1984 and has been the co-author or coordinator of more than 15 books.

John Fernie is professor of retail marketing and head of the School of Management and Languages at Heriot-Watt University, Edinburgh. He has written and contributed to numerous textbooks and papers on retail management, especially in the field of retail logistics and the internationalization of retail formats. He is editor of the *International Journal of Retail and Distribution Management*, and received the award of Editor of the Year in 1997, in addition to Leading Editor awards in 1994, 1998 and 2000. He is on the editorial board of several marketing and logistics journals. He is an active member of the Institute of Logistics and Transport and the Chartered Institute of Marketing in the UK as well as holding office in the American Collegiate Retail Association. He is a member of the Logistics Directors Forum, a group of leading professionals in supply chain management and logistics in the UK.

David Grant is a lecturer in logistics at Heriot-Watt University, Edinburgh, where his research interests focus on customer service and satisfaction, service quality, relationships, integration of logistics and marketing, and logistics in SMEs. He obtained his PhD at the University of Edinburgh, and his doctoral thesis received the James Cooper Memorial Cup from the Chartered Institute of Logistics and Transport (UK). He has over 35 publications in various refereed journals, books and conference proceedings, and is a member of the Council of Supply Chain Management Professionals, the UK Logistics Research Network, the NOFOMA Nordic logistics researchers group, and the UK Higher Education Academy.

Trevor Heaver is professor emeritus at the Faculty of Commerce and Business Administration at the University of British Columbia (UBC). He is a past chairman of the World Conference on Transport Research and immediate past president of the International Association of Maritime Economists. He specializes in transport policy, maritime economics, logistics and supply chain management. He still lectures at UBC, but has recently been a visiting professor at the University of Antwerp – UFSIA, the University of Sydney, Australia and the University of Stellenbosch, South Africa. His current research and publications deal with issues of corporate strategy and service integration in international transport and logistics.

Peter Hines is professor of supply chain management and director of the Lean Enterprise Research Centre at Cardiff Business School. He holds an MA in geography from Cambridge University and an MBA and PhD from the University of Cardiff. Peter followed a successful career in distribution and manufacturing industry before joining Cardiff Business School in 1992. He initially led the Materials Management Unit and now leads the interdepartmental Innovative Manufacturing Research Centre and the Lean Enterprise Research Centre. He has undertaken extensive research into the supply chain and has pioneered a number of key concepts, methods and applications in Europe, including: supplier associations (now involving over 800 European firms), value stream mapping and network sourcing. He has written or co-written several leading books. Peter is also chairman of S A Partners.

Chris Lonsdale first taught at the University of Hull in 1992. In 1993, he moved to the University of Birmingham, Department of Political Science and International Studies and the Institute for Local Government Studies. He moved to Birmingham University's Business School in 1994 and is a senior lecturer in the Centre for Business Strategy and Procurement, the school's supply chain management group. He received his PhD in 1995, and from 1997 to 2001 was the programme director of the MBA (strategy and procurement management). In 2000, he was awarded honorary membership of the Chartered Institute of Purchasing and Supply.

Kirstie McIntyre is the waste electronics and electrical equipment (WEEE) programme manager for HP in the UK. Her responsibilities cover all issues concerning the implementation of the European WEEE directive into UK law. She liaises with government, industry partners and peers, and supply chain members, as well as business customers and consumers on implementation of end-of-life directives and the take-back and recycling of HP's products. Kirstie has worked for a number of years in the strategic development of end-of-life programmes for various companies in the electronics sector . She has an engineering doctorate in environmental technology and has published widely on sustainability and supply chain issues.

Alan McKinnon is professor of logistics in the School of Management at Heriot-Watt University, Edinburgh. A graduate of the universities of Aberdeen, British Columbia and London, he has been researching and teaching in the fields of freight transport and logistics management for over 20 years and has published extensively on these subjects. He has been an adviser to several government departments and committees, and consultant to numerous public and private sector organizations on a range of logistics-related topics. He is a fellow of the Institute of Logistics and Transport.

Helen Peck is a senior lecturer at the Resilience Centre, Cranfield University. She joined Cranfield in 1983, from a major UK clearing bank. Initially employed in the university's library and information service, she transferred to the academic staff of Cranfield School of Management in 1989, where she completed her PhD. From early 2001 she has been at the forefront of Cranfield University's government-funded programme of research into all aspects of supply chain-related risk and resilience. Her publications include the UK Department for Transport-sponsored report *Creating Resilient Supply Chains: A practical guide* and numerous academic papers and practitioner journal articles. She is also co-editor and author of several books and an award-winning writer of management case studies.

Stephen Rinsler is a director of Bisham Consulting, focusing on the strategic and operational supply chain audits, procurement, inventory and outsourcing consultancy practices. He is chairman of the Chartered Institute of Logistics and Transport, honorary professor of engineering and logistics at the Nanjing University, China, and a visiting fellow in supply chains and procurement at Cranfield University. He is commissioned as a major in the Engineer and Logistics Staff Corps, and is a liveryman of the Worshipful Company of Carman and a freeman of the City of London. He actively lectures and writes on logistics and supply chain management.

Stephen started his management career in Unilever in factory planning. After roles in distribution and procurement, he worked in Van den Bergh Foods Ltd as chief buyer and company supply chain manager. After a spell at NFC Europe Ltd as services director he became a consultant, and an interim procurement director with his main client, Storehouse. Then he joined Volt Europe Ltd as managing director of the temporary recruitment administration and procurement outsourcing division.

Stephen was educated at Bristol University, has attended the Advanced Management Programme at Wharton Business School, Pennsylvania, and is currently studying mathematics with the Open University.

Donna Samuel is a senior research associate who lectures in purchasing and supply chain management in the Cardiff Business School. As a member of the Lean Enterprise Research Centre, Donna has undertaken a series of research projects on supply chain integration and lean supply. She has published in books and academic journals such as the *Journal for Retail Distribution Management*. She is a qualified member of the Chartered Institute of Purchasing and Supply (CIPS) and a member of the Institute of Learning and Teaching in Higher Education (ILTHE).

Joe Sanderson is a research fellow at the Centre for Business Strategy and Procurement at the University of Birmingham. He is currently working on a project to map the structural characteristics of supply and value chains in a range of service and industrial sectors. He has a BA in politics from the University of Hull and is writing his doctoral thesis on the regulatory and organizational drivers of procurement efficiency in the UK utilities after privatization. His principal research interests are in international business and supply management, power in supply chains, and the impact of national, regional and international regulation on procurement practices.

Philip Schary is professor emeritus at the College of Business at Oregon State University, where he taught marketing and business logistics. He has been a visiting professor at Cranfield School of Management, Copenhagen and Aarhus Schools of Business in Denmark, and the University of New South Wales in Australia. He has also lectured in Chile and China. He holds an MBA from UC Berkeley and a PhD from UCLA in business economics. He has written widely in professional journals and serves as editorial reviewer for journals in logistics management. He has authored or co-authored several books in the area.

Xinping Shi is the director of the Logistics Management Research Centre, and associate professor in the Department of Finance and Decision Sciences, Hong Kong Baptist University. He has taught widely on business management subjects to BBA, MBA and EMBA students, and has supervised PhD graduates in information system and logistics and supply chain management. His research interests include logistics and supply chain management, decision making in organizations, enterprise resource planning, knowledge management, and international business negotiations. He has published widely, is the guest professor of logistics management at the College of Logistics, Beijing Normal University (Zhuhai), consults, and is an independent director of logistics firms in Hong Kong and China.

Lars Stemmler is a senior project manager with BLG Consult GmbH, and a member of the BLG Logistics Group, Bremen, Germany. Prior to joining BLG he worked in various functions for Deutsche Schiffsbank AG, a leading ship financier, and for the Oldenburg Chamber of Industry and Commerce. He teaches as guest professor at postgraduate level at a number of universities. In this function he is about to join the World Maritime University at Malmo. Lars holds a PhD in economics and received an MSc in logistics from Cranfield University.

Remko van Hoek is a professor in supply chain management at the Cranfield School of Management, and is also managing director of the Operations Management Roundtable at the Corporate Executive Board, based in Washington, DC. He has worked at the University of Ghent, Belgium, the Erasmus University, Rotterdam, the Netherlands (where he headed a supply chain management research institute), and the Rotterdam School of Management. He is the European editor of the *International Journal of Physical Distribution and Logistics Management*, and is on the editorial board of several leading journals. He has published widely, and has won awards for his research into logistics. He has worked with companies such as Dow, Johnson and Johnson, Schenker BTL and Nedlloyd, and is an adviser to various government bodies and organizations.

James Wang is an associate professor in the Department of Geography, University of Hong Kong. He received his Bachelor in Economics from the People's University of China, MPhil from the University of Hong Kong, and PhD from the University of Toronto. Currently he is a council member and chairman of the China Development Committee and the Transport and

Logistics Policy Committee, the Chartered Institute of Logistics and Transport (HK). His research area is transport geography, with special interests in port development and transportation in China. He has published widely and is on the editorial board of the *Journal of Transport Geography*.

Donald Waters is a graduate of the universities of Sussex, London (Imperial College) and Strathclyde. He worked in the UK as a systems analyst, operational researcher and consultant before joining the University of Strathclyde. In 1986 he moved to Canada to become professor of finance and operations management at the University of Calgary. Since returning to Europe, he has continued to use his specialized knowledge of operations and supply chain management, combining work with international companies and visiting appointments at universities. He runs Richmond, Parkes and Wright, a private group whose interests are in management research, analysis and education. He has written a number of successful books, focusing on aspects of logistics and operations management.

Glyn Watson is a research fellow at the Centre for Business Strategy and Procurement at the University of Birmingham. His research interests include the supply chain, supply chain typologies and supply chain management. Prior to joining the centre he did research in the broad area of integration and on European business issues.

Allan Woodburn is a senior lecturer in freight and logistics in the Transport Studies Group at the University of Westminster. He is involved in a range of teaching and research activities, and his specific areas of interest include freight transport planning and operations (particularly rail freight), and transport policy. Allan was previously a lecturer at Napier University, where, in 2000, he completed his doctorate, examining the role for rail freight within the supply chain. He has also worked for Colin Buchanan and Partners, doing consultancy in freight transport, logistics and strategy.

Preface

The first edition of *Global Logistics and Distribution Planning: Strategies for management* appeared in 1988. Since then the whole field of logistics has changed. Even since the last edition in 2003, the subject has continued to develop at a remarkable pace. Not long ago, logistics would hardly be mentioned in the long-term plans of even major companies; now its strategic role is recognized in almost every organization. There are many reasons for this change. Communications and information technology are offering new opportunities; world trade is growing; new markets and sources of materials are developing; relative costs of services and materials are changing; and there is increasing concern for the environment.

Logistics has responded to these changes – and played a major role in accomplishing some of them. As a result it has evolved into a single, integrated function that is responsible for all aspects of material movement. With this broad view, logistics includes all the activities that are needed to ensure a smooth journey of materials from original suppliers, through supply chains and on to final customers.

This fifth edition of the book builds on the success of earlier editions and follows the same general format. It is not an encyclopedia of logistics that gives an exhaustive review of every aspect of this broad subject. Instead it is a forum in which a number of key issues are addressed. It focuses on areas that are of particular current interest, and emphasizes changes that have occurred in recent years. These areas include the wider integration of logistics, the growing importance of logistics strategies, improving communications and technology, risk, customer satisfaction and the importance of global operations.

The contributors are acknowledged experts in their fields, and they give authoritative views of current thinking. This does not, of course, mean that they present the *only* view, and we hope that the material will encourage informed discussion.

This new edition has been completely rewritten. To keep the book's contemporary focus we have removed some of the previous chapters and replaced them by new ones. The remaining chapters have all been rewritten and updated to maintain their relevance to an international readership. In this way, the book continues to evolve, discussing a broad range of current topics and views, but keeping within a reasonable length.

The book will appeal to everyone with an interest in the broader aspects of logistics. This includes academics and students doing a variety of courses with some logistics content. It also includes logistics professionals, consultants and managers from different backgrounds who want an appreciation of current thinking on the supply chain. It is especially important for these non-specialists to realize the growing importance of logistics, and the way that it crosses organizational and disciplinary boundaries. The long-term success of every organization depends on its ability to deliver products to customers – and this is precisely the role of logistics.

James Cooper edited the first two editions of this book – and I must agree with his summary of the pleasures of editing the contents:

> In my role as editor, I have already had the opportunity to read the thoughts and ideas expressed in each of the chapters. Indeed, one of the greatest pleasures of being editor was to be *the first* to enjoy the riches of the chapters as they converged into this book. I now leave it to new readers to explore the chapters that follow, in the anticipation that they too will benefit, both professionally and personally, from the wealth of knowledge and expertise that they contain.

Donald Waters

1

Trends in the supply chain

Donald Waters, Richmond, Parkes and Wright

Definitions

Every organization delivers products to its customers. These products are traditionally described as either goods or services, but this distinction is misleading and it is fairer to view every product as a complex package – or offer – that includes both goods and services. For example, Toyota manufacture cars, but they also give services through warranties, after-sales service, repairs and finance packages; McDonald's supply a combination of goods (burgers, cutlery, packaging, etc) and services (when they sell food and look after the restaurant); Vodafone offer telephone services, but they also provide equipment, documents and other hardware. A better view of products has a spectrum, at one end of which are products that are predominantly goods (such as cars and washing machines) and at the other end are products that are predominantly services (such as insurance and education). In the middle are products with a more even balance, such as restaurants and hospitals.

At the heart of an organization are the operations that create and deliver its products. So we can view an organization as taking a variety of inputs (the raw materials, people, equipment, information, money and other resources), doing operations (the manufacture, serving, transport, selling, training, etc) and creating outputs (especially the products that it passes to customers) (Waters, 2002). This view highlights the flow of materials from suppliers, through operations and on to customers. The materials are everything that the organization uses – both tangible (raw materials, work in progress, finished goods, spare parts, etc) and intangible (information, money, knowledge, etc).

Materials generally move through several tiers of suppliers on their journey from initial suppliers into an organization; and they move through several tiers of customer on their journey out of the organization and on to final customers. All the organizations from the initial supplier to the final customer form a supply chain. In practice, there are complex relationships between organizations, so a supply chain is likely to appear as a network of interacting entities.

Logistics is the function responsible for all movements of materials through the supply chain. To summarize two key definitions (Waters, 2003):

- A *supply chain* is the series of activities and organizations that materials – both tangible and intangible – move through on their journeys from initial suppliers to final customers.
- *Logistics* is the function responsible for moving materials through their supply chains.

Not surprisingly, there are variations on these definitions. Some people say that there are differences between 'logistics' and 'supply chain management' – typically arguing that logistics is concerned with an individual organization while supply chain management (SCM) considers the whole chain. But this is not a meaningful distinction, and we will use the terms interchangeably. This view is supported by the Council of Supply Chain Management Professionals (2006), who describe logistics as the function that 'plans, implements and controls the efficient, effective forward and reverse flow and storage of goods, services and related information between the point of origin and the point of consumption in order to meet customers' requirements'. In a similar vein, the Chartered Institute of Logistics and Transport (1998) says that:

- 'Logistics is the time related positioning of resources or the strategic management of the total supply-chain.'
- 'The supply-chain is a sequence of events intended to satisfy a customer. It can include procurement, manufacture, distribution and waste disposal, together with associated transport, storage and information technology.'

Logistics costs

The broad function of logistics embraces a series of related activities, including procurement, transport, receiving, warehousing, inventory management, materials handling, order processing, distribution, recycling, location decisions, information processing, and other related functions. These activities exist – at least to some extent – in every organization. Christopher (1986) emphasizes their importance, saying that 'Logistics has always been a central and essential feature of all economic activity.' Shapiro and Heskett (1985) confirm that 'There are few aspects of human activity that do not ultimately depend on the flow of goods from point of origin to point of consumption.' A survey by Deloitte & Touche in Canada (Factor, 1996) showed that 98 per cent of companies considered supply chain management to be either 'critical' or 'very important'.

Despite its importance, it took a long time for logistics to get the attention it deserves. Traditionally organizations put all their effort into making products – and then considered the movement and storage of materials as an unavoidable overhead or clerical chore. In 1962 Drucker described physical distribution as 'the economy's dark continent' and said that this formed 'the most sadly neglected, most promising area of... business'.

By the 1970s it was clear that logistics was expensive – but few organizations could say precisely how expensive. Ray (1976) noted that 'The whole area [of logistics costing] is clouded with ad hoc approaches and untidy accounting procedures, to which there appears little underlying systematic ideology.' Little (1977) agreed, saying that 'Identifying logistics costs through accepted accounting statements in the firm is very misleading.' Managers started to identify the 'total cost' of logistics, and by the 1980s surveys – for example, Ray, Gattorna and Allen (1980), Firth *et al* (1980), McKibbin (1982) and Delaney (1986) – suggested that logistics generally account for 15–20 per cent of costs. However, in 1994 Hill could still say that 'many distributors are unaware of the costs of the distribution service they provide'.

At a national level, the gross domestic product of the United States is $12 trillion a year, so $2.4 trillion might be spent on logistics, with half of this for transport (US Census Bureau, 2006). The UK government says that wholesale and retail trades contribute more than 12 per cent of the GDP, with transport and storage contributing another 4.5 per cent (Office of National Statistics, 2006). This suggests that overall logistics costs might be considerably higher than survey estimates – supporting an earlier estimate by Childerley (1980) that logistics accounted for 32.5 per cent of the UK GDP.

Development of logistics

When managers started to recognize its importance, logistics developed very quickly. By 1996, Deloitte & Touche found that over 90 per cent of organizations were currently improving their supply chain or planning improvements within the next two years (Factor, 1996). This pace continues, with pressures for change including:

- recognition that logistics is an essential function that must be managed properly;
- realization that decisions about the supply chain have a strategic impact on performance;
- appreciation of the high cost of logistics and the opportunity for major savings;
- growing emphasis on customer satisfaction – and recognition that this depends on logistics;
- increasing competition for both users and providers of logistics;
- new types of operations – such as just-in-time, total quality management, flexible operations, mass customization, lean operations, time compression, virtual organizations, etc;
- sustained growth of international trade – and free trade areas such as the European Union and North American Free Trade Agreement;
- improved communications allowing electronic data interchange (EDI), B2B, B2C and e-commerce;
- more technology with vehicle telematics, intermodal systems, identification and tracking systems, improved vehicle design, etc;
- integration of operations and organizations through strategic alliances, partnerships and collaboration;
- changing patterns of power in the supply chain with large organizations dominating certain areas and setting industry standards;
- organizations concentrating on their core operations and outsourcing logistics to third parties;
- organizations focusing on the whole process of satisfying customer demand, rather than simply making products;
- increasing concerns over risks to supply chains and their ability to respond;
- growing concern about environmental damage and changing attitudes towards pollution, waste, traffic congestion, road building, etc;
- changing government policies on the ownership, regulation, use, responsibilities and cost of transport.

Approach to integration

Initially, organizations responded to these pressures by looking for improvements to the separate activities of logistics – procurement, inventory control, transport, warehousing, materials handling, packaging, and so on. But it soon becomes clear that these are not separate activities that can be handled in isolation – and any change to one activity inevitably affects the others. Planned improvements to procurement have consequences for inventory management; changes in packaging affect material handling; changes to transport affect warehousing, and so on. This means that organizations can only get the best results by considering all aspects of material movement in a single, coordinated flow through the supply chain. This leads to a broad and inclusive view of logistics, with all related activities combined into a single integrated function.

In practice, it is difficult to achieve this integration. The usual approach develops over time, with one department slowly taking over all aspects of ordering and receiving raw materials, and another department taking over all aspects of delivering finished products to customers. Many organizations stop when they reach this stage, so they have two functions: 1) *materials management*, aligned with production and concerned with the inward flow of raw materials and their movement through operations; and 2) *physical distribution*, aligned with marketing and concerned with the outward flow of finished goods. But this still leaves an artificial break in an essentially continuous function. The obvious next step is to complete the *internal integration* of logistics by combining the two into a single function responsible for all material movement into, through and out of the organization.

If each organization only looks at its own logistics, there are still unnecessary boundaries between them, disrupting the flow of materials and increasing costs. So the next step has *external integration* to merge logistics along the supply chain and remove these boundaries. This recognizes that all organizations along a particular supply chain share the same objective – which is satisfied final customers – and they should cooperate to achieve this aim. Competitors are not other organizations within the same supply chain, but are organizations in other supply chains. As Christopher (1996) says, 'supply chains compete, not companies', and he adds that 'Most opportunities for cost reduction and/or value enhancement lie at the interface between supply chain partners' (1999). So the aim of an integrated supply chain is to improve overall efficiency and reduce overall costs – rather than have each organization working independently and pushing costs and inefficiencies to other parts of the chain.

The benefits from integrating logistics along the supply chain include:

- common objectives for all parts of the supply chain;
- genuine cooperation to achieve these objectives;
- sharing information and highlighting important features;
- faster and more flexible responses to customer demands;
- replenishment and movements triggered by actual demands;
- lower stocks;
- less duplication of effort, information, planning, stocks, etc;
- improved efficiency and productivity;
- easier planning;
- less uncertainty, errors and delays;
- elimination of activities that add no value for customers.

Levels of integration

Now we have three levels of integration. The first has logistics as separate activities within an organization; the second has internal integration to bring them together into a single function; the third has external integration, where organizations look beyond their own operations and integrate more of the supply chain. Decker and van Goor (1998) give a different view, with four levels of physical integration, information integration, control integration and infrastructure integration.

Higher levels of integration allow a supply chain to work together, with 'quick response' or 'efficient customer response' (ECR) allowing final customer purchases automatically to send a message back through the chain and trigger a response from upstream suppliers. When a customer buys a pair of jeans in a clothes shop, the EPOS (electronic point of sales) system sends a message back to the wholesaler to say that the stock needs replenishing, then back to the manufacturer to say that it is time to make another pair of jeans, then back to suppliers to say that they should deliver materials to the manufacturer, and so on. The result is 'a focus on the consumer, the development of partnership relationships between retailers and their suppliers, and an increased integration of the components of the supply-chain' (Szymankiewicz, 1997). Hutchinson describes ECR as 'meeting consumer wishes better, faster and at less cost', and he adds, 'Is there anybody, wishing to remain in business, who believes that his or her company should not be striving to meet the wishes of the customer of their products and services better, faster and at less cost?' (quoted in O'Sullivan, 1997).

By 1997 a survey by P-E Consulting found that 57 per cent of companies had moved to some form of integrated supply chain. Significantly, more than 90 per cent of companies expected an increase in integration over the next three years, with a quarter of companies moving to 'fully integrated' systems (although it was not clear what this actually meant). At the same time, though, Szymankiewicz (1997) noted that 'In the grocery sector ECR is often regarded as an established way of doing business... [but] overall there is more talk than action.' This note of caution is well founded, as in 2003 Poirier and Quinn noted that most organizations were still working on internal integration and were moving towards external integration – but only 10 per cent had made significant progress. They concluded that 'Only a comparatively small percentage of companies have evolved to the more advanced stages of supply chain management.' For a variety of reasons – ranging from an unwillingness to share information to a lack of appropriate technology – most organizations are still missing this opportunity both to raise customer service and to lower costs.

Logistics strategy

With logistics as a single integrated function, it is clear that some of its decisions have a strategic importance – such as the design of supply chains, sourcing policies, alliances with suppliers, methods of procurement, relations with customers, modes of transport, location of facilities, size of operations, use of technology, recycling policies, and so on. These decisions form a part of the logistics strategy – which consists of all the long-term goals, plans, policies, culture, resources, decisions and actions that relate to the supply chain.

To design a successful logistics strategy, managers need to understand and balance the competing demands of:

1. *Higher strategies*, including the mission, corporate and business strategies that set the context for logistics.
2. *Business environment*, which includes all external factors that affect logistics, but which managers cannot control. These include customers, market conditions, available technology, economic conditions, legal restraints, competitors, shareholders, interest groups, social conditions, political conditions, and so on.
3. *Internal features*, which are factors within the organization that managers can control. These include customer relations, employee skills, finances, products, facilities, technology used, suppliers, resources available, etc.

By definition, managers have virtually no control over the external environment, so they adjust the internal features of logistics to work within this fixed environment. When they do this well, there is said to be good 'strategic fit' between logistics and their environment. Stacey (2002) says that 'organizations are successful when they intentionally achieve internal harmony and external adaptation to their environment'. In practice, this means that organizations build on their strengths to develop distinctive features that give a sustainable competitive advantage. Prahalad and Hamel (1990) describe the activities that an organization does particularly well as its 'strategic competencies'.

Selznick (1957) established the principle that an organization can only succeed by doing key activities better than competitors – or maybe doing completely different activities (which Porter (1996) summarizes as 'choosing to perform activities differently or to perform different activities than rivals'). So logistics managers must run their supply chains more efficiently than competitors, or else they must find some service that competitors are not offering. This is in line with Porter's (1985) two generic strategies of *cost leadership* (giving the same, or comparable, products at a lower price) and *product differentiation* (giving products that customers cannot find anywhere else).

In logistics, these two generic strategies are phrased as 'lean' and 'agile'. Essentially, a lean strategy aims for the lowest possible costs with efficient flows of materials that eliminate waste, minimize stocks, reduce lead times, use fewer resources, employ fewer people, remove duplicated effort, eliminate non-value-adding operations, and so on. This brings benefits to the whole supply chain. For example, lower transport costs allow organizations to work over a wide geographical area, and manufacturers in the Pacific Rim can deliver goods anywhere in the world at prices that compare with domestic companies. Although this seems a sensible approach, lean logistics can put too much emphasis on costs, and not have the flexibility to deal with rapidly changing conditions. An alternative agile strategy stresses customer satisfaction by responding quickly to changing conditions – perhaps triggered by increasing competition, more sophisticated customers, changing customer requirements, variable demand, unforeseen conditions, natural disasters, or many other factors. Agility often appears as a short lead time, so that customers do not have to wait for products, and suppliers do not have products hanging around and clogging the supply chain.

At first sight it seems difficult to reconcile the aims of lean and agile logistics. One minimizes costs, and sees customer service as a constraint; the other maximizes customer service, and sees costs as a constraint. In practice, the two policies are not necessarily distinct. For example, when a supplier improves its EDI links with customers, it can both reduce costs and increase customer service – becoming both leaner and more agile. Evans and Powell (2000) conclude that 'lean and agile are not mutually exclusive, they both have their merits, but also limitations, especially if an individual aspect is taken, in isolation, to the extreme'.

There are other, more specific strategies for logistics – including time-based strategies (which deliver products quickly to customers), high-productivity strategies (which use resources fully), value-added strategies (which maximize added customer value), diversification or specialization strategies (which define the width of product ranges), growth strategies (which aim for economies of scale), globalization strategies (which buy, store and move materials in a single, worldwide market), environmental protection strategies (which focus on sustainable operations, renewable resources, recycling, etc), and a whole range of others.

Logistics managers often face similar pressures, and they respond by adopting similar strategies. The results appear as identifiable trends in the industry. We have already mentioned one of these, where logistics managers have responded to pressures for better efficiency by increasing integration of their supply chains. There are several other trends in the industry, which we can demonstrate by examples related to:

- improved communications and e-business;
- globalization;
- satisfying more demanding customers;
- responding to changes in the business environment.

Improved communications and e-business

When a company buys something, it typically has to generate a description of the product, search for suppliers, request a price and conditions, issue a purchase order, negotiate details, organize transport, discuss special conditions, organize finance, arrange payment, and so on. In the past, this needed a lot of paperwork, which made even the simplest transaction complicated, expensive and time-consuming. More recently, technology has revolutionized these communications, replacing onerous manual operations by automated electronic ones. EDI appeared in the 1990s, and by 1997 around 2,000 companies in the UK routinely used it for procurement (Stafford-Jones, 1997). Electronic purchasing – moving through intranet, extranet and internet models – brought instant access to any supplier irrespective of location, available at any time, with a transparent market, low entry costs and low transaction costs.

Electronic trading mushroomed, with e-mail followed by e-business, e-commerce, e-trading, e-retail, e-logistics – and soon 'e-anything'. This has developed in two main directions – B2B (business-to-business), where one business buys materials from another business, and B2C (business-to-customer), where a business sells directly to a final customer. By 2002 around 83 per cent of UK suppliers used B2B (MRO Software, 2001), with worldwide B2B trade valued at over US $2 trillion (Gartner Group, 2006). A typical index of e-retail value had risen from 100 in July 2000 to 1,357 by 2004 (IMRI, 2004). However, it is difficult to put a reliable value on electronic trade as there are many variations of 'e-business'. Is it a transaction where every stage is completed through the internet, one that is initiated by a website, or one where even a single activity is done over the internet? Figure 1.1 shows two views of the value of global electronic trade (Forrester, 2006; Gartner Group, 2006).

The benefit of e-business is its standard formats for instant communication between systems. This does not just improve purchasing, but it allows completely new types of logistics, with the emphasis moved from physical materials to information. For example, organizations traditionally held safety stock to allow for uncertain demand – but an alternative is to replace forecasts by instant information about actual demand, and replace stocks by information of where to find products with short lead times. The ultimate aim – which remains a theoretical target – is to pass information to completely flexible operations, which have production batches of one, and zero lead time.

Improved communications are the enablers of supply chain integration. They are the means by which organizations can exchange information – both internally and externally. Internally, they track individual packages using bar codes, magnetic stripes and radio frequency identification (RFID); they monitor vehicles through telematics; they control warehouses through automatically

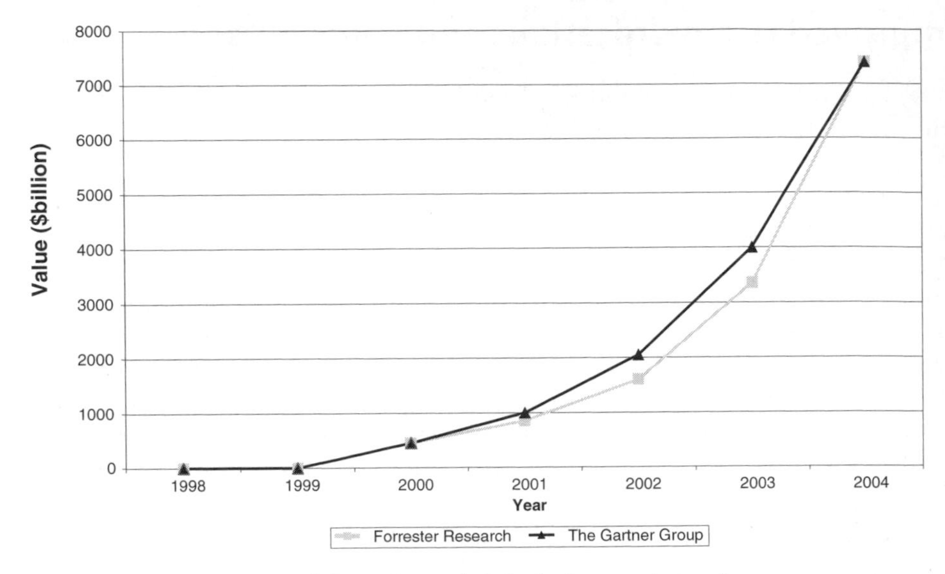

Figure 1.1 Estimates of the value of global electronic trade

guided vehicles; they monitor transactions and plan operations – and a host of other functions. Externally, they allow vendor-managed inventory (VMI), collaborative planning, forecasting and replenishment (CPFR), synchronized material movement through the whole supply chain, payments by electronic fund transfer (EFT), roadside detectors to monitor traffic conditions and route vehicles around congestion – and so on. Realistically, it is difficult to find an area of logistics that is not affected by improved communications.

Globalization

E-business allows organizations around the world to communicate as if they are physically close – so physical distances become less significant, and organizations can become global in outlook. They can broaden their supplier and customer bases to buy, transport, store, manufacture, sell and distribute products in a single worldwide market.

Many factors encourage global operations, including:

- *Cost differences.* Organizations can reduce their overall costs by moving operations to the regions where they can be done least expensively. Then manufacturing is moved to China, call centres to India, R&D to Europe, and so on.
- *Growing demand in new markets.* As developing regions become more prosperous, foreign companies recognize the opportunities in these new markets.

- *Economies of scale.* Many manufacturing operations depend on – or work best with – stable, large-scale production. The best size for this is often larger than demand from a single market.
- *Greater demands from customers.* As customers become more demanding, local suppliers may not be able to meet their requirements, so they look further afield to find the best sources.
- *Convergence of market demands.* Different markets are increasingly accepting the same products – or at least products with minor differences in finishing. This effect (which Ohmae (1985) calls 'Californianization') allows companies to sell the same products in virtually any country.
- *Removal of trade barriers.* Free trade areas – such as the European Union and North American Free Trade Agreement – specifically encourage international trade.
- *Changing logistics.* Better logistics makes international trade easier. For example, containerization and intermodal transport make the movement of goods easier, faster and cheaper.
- *Specialized support services.* Many organizations concentrate on their core competencies and outsource logistics to third-party specialists. The outsourced operations are in locations determined by other organizations, and may not be in the host country.
- *Improved communications among consumers.* Satellite television, the web and other communication channels have made customers more aware of products from outside their local regions.
- *Improved communications in business.* As we have seen, developments in information systems make it as easy to do business on the other side of the world as in the next town.

Leontiades (1985) says that 'One of the most important phenomena of the 20th century has been the international expansion of industry. Today, virtually all major firms have a significant and growing presence in business outside their country of origin.' Perhaps half of the trade between industrialized countries is accounted for by transfers between subsidiaries of the same company (Julius, 1990). In the United States a third of exports are sent by US companies to their overseas subsidiaries, and another third are sent by foreign manufacturers back to their home market.

By 2004 around $9 trillion of merchandise was moved around the world each year, with $21 trillion of commercial services (see Figure 1.2) (WTO, 2005).

Because the rationalized operations and supply chains of global operations bring such obvious benefits, it is easy to imagine that this is an automatic movement. In practice, of course, there can be serious barriers. Sometimes there are simply problems with product design – with different regions demanding different types of product, products not lending themselves to global operations, or customers simply not viewing them favourably.

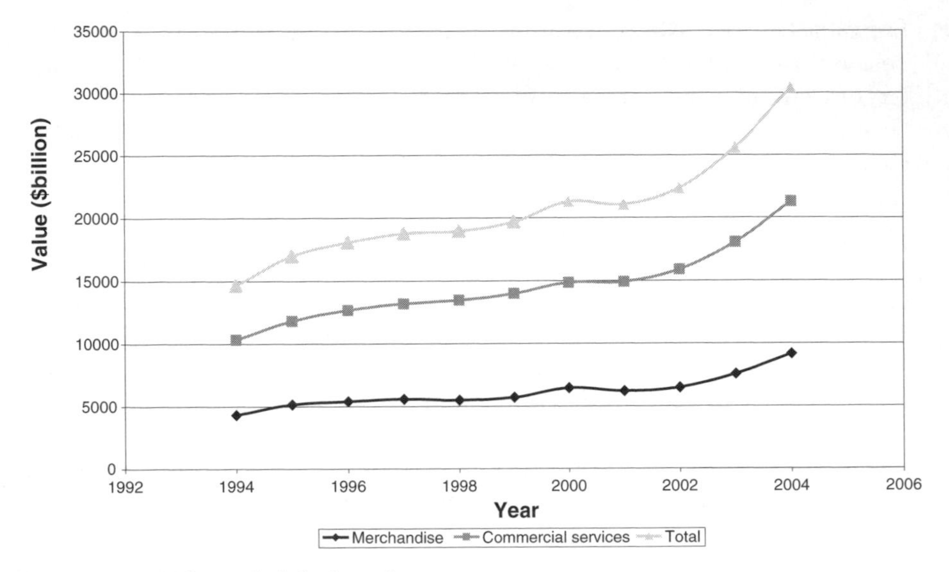

Figure 1.2 Value of global trade

Sometimes there is demand, but practical difficulties make it impossible to deliver – such as protectionist government policies, problems at national frontiers, inadequate infrastructure, missing technical skills, or other cultural and economic differences. Companies adopt various structures to minimize these problems, with the main choices of working nationally, internationally, multinationally or globally. Essentially, a national company only works within its home market and exports to other organizations in foreign countries; an international company has a centre in one country, from which it controls the activities of subsidiary divisions in other countries; a multinational consists of connected, but largely independent, companies in different countries; a global company sees the world as a single market and works in the locations that are most effective and efficient. These descriptions are really too rigid, and many organizations respond to local conditions, practices and demands. This gives a looser 'transnational' structure that includes many different types of operation – and still gives a unified culture for the whole organization.

Satisfying more-demanding customers

The internet allows customers to access suppliers all around the world in a transparent market where they can compare deals and conditions. So they inevitably become more demanding – looking for more choice, lower prices, shorter lead times, accurate fulfilment, better value, and a generally better experience. Logistics managers have to respond by designing the best services they can – and this means knowing what their customers want, building on their capabilities to design operations that satisfy customers, monitoring performance to see that they are achieving their aims, and continually looking for improvements.

Central to the idea of monitoring and improving performance is some kind of measurement – and there are a huge number of possible measures for logistics. Rushton (1994) lists measures commonly used by grocery retailers, ranging from cost as a percentage of company sales to overtime hours as a percentage of total hours. Lennox (1995) lists measures of customer service, starting with the proportion of items supplied at first demand, the number of order-pick errors, availability of back orders, proportion of orders satisfied in full, amount of damage – and continuing down to lead time, courtesy of staff, ease of ordering, etc.

Managers have to choose measures of performance that relate to significant factors in their operations. So there would be no point in, say, an insurance company monitoring the cost of rail freight. Another problem is separating the performance of logistics from both other internal operations and external influences. For example, late deliveries at customers might be caused by poor logistics – but they might also be caused by poor demand forecasts, or production problems, roadworks, traffic congestion, ferry operators on strike, or a whole range of other factors that logistics managers cannot control or even influence. Logistics provides the final link between suppliers and customers, so it often gets blamed for faults in other parts of the system.

The point of measuring performance is to see if predefined targets are being met. Some of these targets are absolute values – such as no accidents or customer complaints – but most are arbitrary values that managers decide are demanding but achievable. The most widely used sources for targets are performance actually achieved in the past, performance achieved by comparable operations within the organization, performance achieved by competitors or other organizations, benchmarks from the industry's best performers, negotiated and agreed targets, industry standards, and absolute standards such as zero defects.

Normally, these targets are continually made more demanding to encourage the improvements that are essential if a business is to remain competitive. But where should logistics managers look for improvements? In practice, there is no shortage of suggestions. All managers face a constant stream of 'new ideas' for improving operations, and the main difficulty is sifting through these to see which might bring real benefit, which are old ideas disguised in new words, and which are – at best – a waste of time. Most of the suggestions are supported by anecdotal evidence to show how they have improved the performance of particular companies. Unfortunately, this evidence is presented to support a specific viewpoint and is not based on objective analyses – so it can be difficult for managers to identify ideas that will work in their own organization. There is no doubt that total quality management (TQM), for example, has brought huge benefits to many organizations (Deming, 1986) – but it might not work in a particular company. Re-engineering has been hugely influential, but Hammer (1996) says that 75 per cent of organizations using it do not get the expected benefits. Even well-established methods can be questioned, with Braithwaite (1996) describing material requirements planning (MRP) as 'Too big, too slow and too inflexible… it is essentially obsolete and waiting to die.'

The best advice is to take a rational approach to improvement, such as the following steps:

1. Make everyone aware that to remain competitive changes are continually needed to the supply chain.
2. Examine current operations, identify their aims, see how well they achieve these and identify problem areas and weaknesses.
3. Use benchmarking and other comparisons to identify potential improvements.
4. Design better procedures using the knowledge, skills and experience of everyone concerned.
5. Discuss the proposals widely, make adjustments, negotiate agreements, and get people committed to the new methods.
6. Design a detailed plan for implementing the improvements.
7. Prepare for the new methods – making necessary changes to the organization's structure, systems, facilities, etc; establishing milestones; giving appropriate training; setting challenging but achievable goals; making it clear how goals can be achieved.
8. Have a specific event to start the new methods.
9. Monitor and control progress, checking that milestones are achieved, giving support and encouragement, updating plans, and continuing discussions about progress, problems, adjustments, etc.
10. Accept that the new methods are only temporary, and continually look for further improvements.

The search for improvements has led to many changes in logistics practices. There are far too many of these to list, but we can illustrate the scope by some widely used methods:

- *Postponement.* Traditionally, manufacturers moved finished goods out of production and stored them in the supply chain until needed. When there are many variations on a basic product, this gives high stocks of similar products. Postponement moves almost-finished products into the chain, and delays completion, final adjustment or customization until the last possible moment. You can imagine this with a manufacturer of electrical equipment that keeps stocks of standard products and only adds the transformers, cables and instructions needed for a particular market when they are about to be shipped, or 'package-to-order', where a company keeps a product in stock, but only puts it in a box written in the appropriate language when it is about to ship an order.

- *Factory gate pricing.* One way to coordinate the flow of materials in a supply chain is for a key player to take over management of logistics. As retailers are increasing their power, they want more control of logistics. With factory gate pricing, a single organization – often a retailer – takes responsibility of delivery from the factory gate through to the final customer.
- *Cross-docking.* Traditional warehouses move materials into storage, keep them until needed, and then move them out to meet demand. Cross-docking coordinates the supply and delivery, so that goods arrive at the receiving area and are immediately transferred to the loading area and put on to delivery vehicles. There may be some sorting, breaking bulk, merging and consolidation of materials at the warehouse – but no storage. These activities can be done at a simple transfer point, so the aim is to remove the warehouse completely and have 'stock on wheels'. A related arrangement uses 'drop-shipping', where warehouses do not keep stock themselves, but coordinate the movement of materials directly from upstream suppliers to downstream customers.
- *Direct delivery.* More customers are buying through the web or finding other ways – such as mail order or catalogues – of buying directly from manufacturers or earlier tiers of the supply chain. This 'disintermediation' has the benefits of reducing lead times, reducing costs to customers, having manufacturers talking directly to their final customers, allowing customers access to a wider range of products, and so on.
- *Small deliveries.* Some methods – such as just-in-time and agile and direct deliveries – inevitably lead to smaller, more frequent deliveries. This suggests some movement away from large trucks and into smaller delivery vehicles – which are inherently less efficient. However, it has spurred the growth of parcel delivery services such as FedEx, UPS and DHL – and it has encouraged operators to look for efficiencies, such as round-the-clock deliveries to unattended destinations, better planning of deliveries, and higher vehicle utilization.
- *Increasing vehicle utilization.* For a variety of reasons – such as unbalanced demand, composition of the vehicle fleet, characteristics of the vehicles and loads, poor coordination, etc – vehicles spend a proportion of their time travelling empty or with partial loads. Methods for reducing this include backhauls (where delivery vehicles find loads for their return journeys), reverse logistics (returning goods for repair, reuse or recycling), freight forwarding (where loads from several companies are combined), and more efficient schedules (perhaps with regular routes). To some extent these measures counteract the move to smaller loads, but after continuous improvements for almost half a century the overall productivity of the UK's transport fleet peaked in 1999 and is now stable or even falling (Department for Transport, 2005).

Responding to changes in the business environment

The above examples – along with many others – show how managers are making direct improvements to logistic operations. But they also have to respond to more general business trends, such as the outsourcing of non-core activities and the growing power of retailers. Again, we cannot list even a fraction of these responses, but can give some examples:

- *Outsourcing.* Organizations often benefit from concentrating on their core operations and outsourcing peripheral activities to specialists. These peripheral activities might be anything from cleaning and catering through to accounting, legal services and information processing. Logistics is a particularly popular function for outsourcing, with specialist service providers taking over part, or all, of the material movement and storage. This use of third-party logistics (3PL) has the usual benefits of lower fixed costs, expert services, combined work to give economies of scale, flexible capacity, lower exposure to risk, increased geographical coverage and guaranteed service levels. Sometimes the administration of several 3PL contracts gets so complicated that another company is used to manage it – giving fourth-party logistics (4PL). Almost 60 per cent of Fortune 500 firms outsource some logistics (Eye for Transport, 2005). In the EU the outsourced logistics market was valued at €176 billion by 2004, and this was forecast to rise to 45 per cent of all logistics expenditure by 2008 (Datamonitor, 2004). Unfortunately, outsourcing does not inevitably give the level of service that companies would like (Richards, 2006).
- *Fewer suppliers.* Traditionally, organizations have used a large number of suppliers, to encourage competition, ensure that they get the best deal, and guarantee continuing deliveries if one supplier runs into difficulties. However, increasing cooperation within a supply chain – particularly strategic alliances – encourages organizations to look for a small number of the best suppliers and work exclusively with them. This inevitably reduces the number of suppliers used, as illustrated by Rank Xerox, which reduced its suppliers from 5,000 to 300, while Ford moved from 4,000 to 350 (Lamming, 1993).
- *Concentration of ownership.* Large companies can get economies of scale and efficient operations, so a few large companies often dominate industries (with examples like supermarket chains and transport companies). Continuing benefits mean that these large companies tend to grow at the expense of smaller rivals. The result is a continuing concentration of ownership, with the largest organizations setting standards that others strive to match.
- *Movement of power to retailers.* Historically, most power in the supply chain was with manufacturers – in the way that Toyota is still the focal

organization in its supply of cars. Several trends – including the outsourcing of manufacturing to low-cost regions and global sourcing – have moved the power in many supply chains. In particular, the retailer is often the key player, being the company that makes the link to the final customer.

- *Mass customization.* Many trends in manufacturing have direct links to logistics, with obvious examples of just-in-time operations and shorter life cycles. Some of these effects are brought together into the general heading of 'mass customization', which is the ability to personalize products to meet individual customer demands. The aim is to combine the benefits of mass production with the flexibility of customized products – with B2C giving direct communications between a final customer and a manufacturer, and supply chains that can move materials reliably and quickly. Dell is a pioneer of mass customization, collecting customer orders through its website, building a computer for each specific order, and working so closely with suppliers that 'virtual integration' gives the impression that they are all part of the same company. Similar movements towards a '3DayCar Programme' suggest 'that 80% of cars in the UK could be built to order by 2010' (Holweg, Judge and Williams, 2001).
- *Increasing environmental concerns.* There is growing concern about air and water pollution, energy consumption, urban development, waste disposal and other aspects of environmental damage. It is fair to say that logistics does not have a good reputation for environmental protection – demonstrated by the emissions from heavy lorries, noisy and inefficient vehicles, use of green-field sites for warehouses, calls for new road building, use of extensive packaging, oil spillage from tankers, inefficient operations wasting energy, and so on. But logistics is clearly moving towards greener practices. One aspect of this is reverse logistics, which includes the collection and recovery of end-of-life products, and return and reuse of packaging. There is a growing recognition that careful management can bring both environmental protection and lower costs.
- *Risk management.* Managers are increasingly aware that they have to assess risk – both natural and artificial – and plan their actions either to avoid risk or to mitigate the effects. As supply chains become longer, there is inevitably more chance of disruption, and logistics managers have to take a proactive approach.

Conclusions

- Logistics is the function responsible for moving materials through supply chains – where a supply chain is the series of activities and organizations that materials move through on their journeys from initial suppliers to final customers.

- In recent years organizations have begun to appreciate the importance of logistics – and recognize it as an essential function, with a clear impact on strategic performance.
- There are many pressures on logistics, and managers respond by continual change. A key result is that logistics has developed into a single integrated function, first within organizations and then along the broader supply chain.
- The long-term direction of logistics is defined by a logistics strategy. Two common themes refer to lean and agile strategies – but there are many other aspects of strategy. These can be illustrated by:
  - improved communications and e-business, which change the way that logistics work, putting the emphasis on information flows, and creating new opportunities for e-business;
  - globalization, with growing international trade – encouraged by many factors – and more organizations working internationally through extended supply chains;
  - satisfying more-demanding customers, which means that logistics managers must continually monitor and improve their operations to remain competitive;
  - responding to changes in the business environment, as there are many broad trends that affect logistics.

References

Braithwaite, A (1996) MRP – partially discredited solution in decline, *Logistics Focus*, **4** (4), pp 5–6

Chartered Institute of Logistics and Transport in the UK (CILT) (1998) *Members' Directory*, CILT, Corby, www.ciltuk.org.uk

Childerley, A (1980) The importance of logistics in the UK economy, *International Journal of Physical Distribution and Materials Management*, **10** (8)

Christopher, M (1986) *The Strategy of Distribution Management*, Heinemann, Oxford

Christopher, M (1996) Emerging issues in supply chain management, Proceedings of the Logistics Academic Network Inaugural Workshop, Warwick University

Christopher, M (1999) Global logistics: the role of agility, *Logistics and Transport Focus*, **1** (1)

Council of Supply Chain Management Professionals (CSCMP) (2006) Publicity material from CSCMP, Oak Brook, IL, www.cscmp.org

Datamonitor (2004) European logistics market maps 2004, Datamonitor, London

Decker, H and van Goor, A (1998) Applying activity-based costing to supply chain management, Proceedings of the 1998 Logistics Research Network Conference, Cranfield University
Delaney, RV (1986) Managerial and financial challenges facing transport leaders, *Transportation Quarterly*, **40** (1), p 35
Deming, WE (1986) *Out of the Crisis*, MIT Centre for Advanced Engineering, Cambridge, MA
Department for Transport (2005) *Transport Statistics Great Britain*, Stationery Office, London
Drucker, P (1962) The economy's dark continent, *Fortune*, April, p 103
Evans, B and Powell, M (2000) Synergistic thinking: a pragmatic view of 'lean' and 'agile', *Logistics and Transport Focus*, **2** (10), pp 26–32
Eye for Transport (2005) Survey of outsourcing: the latest trends in using 3PL providers, www.eyefortransport.com
Factor, R (1996) Logistics trends, *Materials Management and Distribution*, June, pp 17–21
Firth, D *et al* (eds) (1980) *Distribution Management Handbook*, McGraw-Hill, London
Forrester (2006) Report on eBusiness, Forrester Research Paper, Cambridge, MA
Gartner Group (2006) *Worldwide B2B Internet Commerce*, Gartner Group, Stamford, CT
Hammer, M (1996) *Beyond Reengineering*, Harper Collins, New York
Holweg, M, Judge, B and Williams, G (2001) The 3DayCar challenge: cars to customer orders, *Logistics and Transport Focus*, **3** (9), pp 36–44
IMRI (2004) *E-retail Sales Index*, Interactive Media in Retail Group, London
Julius, DA (1990) *Global Companies and Public Policy*, Royal Institute of International Affairs, London
Lamming, R (1993) *Beyond Partnership: Strategies for innovation and lean supply*, Prentice Hall, London
Lennox, RB (1995) Customer service reigns supreme, *Materials Management and Distribution*, January, pp 17–22
Leontiades, JE (1985) *Multinational Business Strategy*, DC Heath, Lexington, MA
Little, WI (1977) The cellular flow logistics costing system, *International Journal of Physical Distribution and Materials Management*, **7** (6), pp 305–29
McKibbin, BN (1982) Centre for Physical Distribution Management national survey of distribution costs, *Focus on Physical Distribution*, **1** (1), pp 16–18
MRO Software (2001) *Supplying the Goods*, MRO Software, London
Office of National Statistics (2006) *UK National Accounts*, Stationery Office, London, www.statistics.gov.uk
Ohmae, K (1985) *Triad Power: The coming shape of global competition*, Free Press, New York
O'Sullivan, D (1997) ECR – will it end in tears?, *Logistics Focus*, **5** (7), pp 2–5

P-E Consulting (1997) *Efficient Customer Response: Supply chain management for the new millennium?*, P-E Consulting, Surrey

Poirier, CC and Quinn, FJ (2003) A survey of supply chain progress, *Supply Chain Management Review*, September/October

Porter, ME (1985) *Competitive Advantage*, Free Press, New York

Porter, ME (1996) What is strategy?, *Harvard Business Review*, November–December, pp 61–79

Prahalad, CK and Hamel, G (1990) The core competencies of the corporation, *Harvard Business Review*, May–June, pp 79–91

Ray, D (1976) Distribution costing, *International Journal of Physical Distribution and Materials Management*, **6** (2), pp 73–107

Ray, D, Gattorna, J and Allen, M (1980) Handbook of distribution costing and control, *International Journal of Physical Distribution and Materials Management*, **10** (5), pp 211–429

Richards, G (2006) *Client Satisfaction with 3PL Suppliers*, Burman Group, London

Rushton, A (1994) Monitoring logistics and distribution operations, in *Logistics and Distribution Planning*, 2nd edn, ed J Cooper, Kogan Page, London pp 280–298

Selznick, P (1957) *Leadership in Administration*, Harper & Row, New York

Shapiro, RD and Heskett, JL (1985) *Logistics Strategy*, West Publishing, St Paul, MN

Stacey, RD (2002) *Strategic Management and Organizational Dynamics*, 4th edn, Financial Times Prentice Hall, London

Stafford-Jones, A (1997) Electronic commerce: the future with EDI, *Logistics Focus*, **5** (9), pp 9–10

Szymankiewicz, J (1997) Efficient customer response: supply chain management for the new millennium?, *Logistics Focus*, **5** (9), pp 16–22

US Census Bureau (2006) *Statistical Abstract of the US*, US Census Bureau, Washington, DC, www.census.gov

Waters, D (2002) *Operations Management*, Financial Times Prentice Hall, Harlow

Waters, D (2003) *Logistics: An introduction to supply chain management*, Palgrave Macmillan, Basingstoke

World Trade Organization (WTO) (2005) *International Trade Statistics*, World Trade Organization, Geneva

2

New directions in logistics

Martin Christopher, Cranfield School of Management

In recent years there has been a growing recognition that the *processes* whereby we satisfy customer demands are of critical importance to any organization. These processes are the means by which products are developed, manufactured and delivered to customers and through which the continuing service needs of those customers are met. The logistics concept is the thread that connects these crucial processes and provides the basis for the design of systems that will cost-effectively deliver value to customers.

Accompanying this recognition of the importance of process has been a fundamental shift in the focus of the business towards the marketplace and away from the more inwardly oriented production and sales mentality that previously dominated most industries. This change in orientation has necessitated a review of the means by which customer demand is satisfied – hence the dramatic upsurge of interest in logistics as a core business activity.

The emergence of the value-conscious customer

Recession in many markets, combined with new sources of competition, has raised the consciousness of customers towards value. 'Value' in today's context does not just mean value for money – although that is certainly a critical determinant of the purchase decision for many buyers – but it also means perceived benefits. Customers increasingly are demanding products with added value, but at lower cost, and hence the new competitive imperative is to seek out ways to achieve precisely that.

Michael Porter (1980, 1985) was one of the first commentators to highlight the need for organizations to understand that competitive success could only come through cost leadership or through offering clearly differentiated products or services. The basic model is illustrated in Figure 2.1. Porter's argument was that a company with higher costs and no differential advantage in the eyes of the customer was in effect a commodity supplier with little hope of long-term success unless it could find a way out of the box. His prescription was that the organization should seek to become either a *low-cost producer* or a *differentiated supplier*.

However, in reality it is not sufficient to compete only on the basis of being the lowest-cost supplier. The implication of this is that a competitor in the bottom right-hand corner has to compete on price – if a company is only a cost leader, how else can it compete? Competing solely in terms of price will merely reinforce the customer's view that the product is a commodity – the very thing the company wishes to avoid. On the other hand, a strategy based upon differentiation will make it possible to compete on grounds other than price. Whilst value for money will always be an issue, the aim is to increase customers' perception of the value they are receiving and hence their willingness to pay a higher price.

Organizations create value for their customers either by increasing the level of 'benefit' they deliver or by reducing the customers' costs. In fact customer value can be defined as follows:

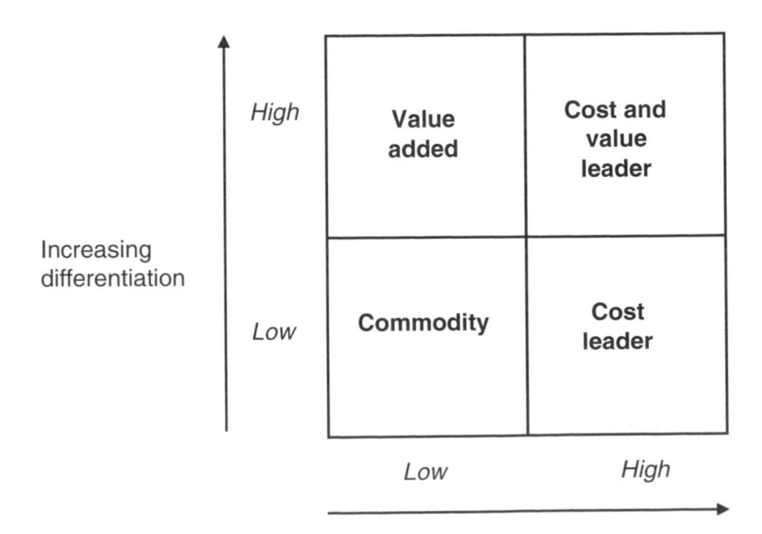

Figure 2.1 The competitive options

$$\text{Customer value} = \frac{\text{Perceived benefits}}{\text{Total cost of ownership}}$$

Perceived benefits include the tangible, product-related aspects as well as the less tangible, service-related elements of the relationship.

The key point to note is that these benefits are essentially perceptual and that they will differ by customer. The 'total cost of ownership' reflects all the costs associated with the relationship, not just the price of the product. Hence the customer's cost of carrying inventory, ordering costs and other transactions costs all form part of this total cost concept.

Because logistics management, perhaps uniquely, can impact upon both the numerator and the denominator of the customer value equation, it can provide a powerful means of enhancing customer value.

An argument that is being heard more frequently is that logistics is a *core capability* that enables the firm to gain and maintain competitive advantage. More and more the view is expressed (Stalk, Evans and Shulman, 1992) that it is through capabilities that organizations compete. These capabilities include such processes as new product development, order fulfilment, marketing planning and information systems. There can be little doubt that companies that in the past were able to rely upon product superiority to attain market leadership can no longer do so, as competitive pressure brings increasing technological convergence. Instead these companies must seek to develop systems that enable them to respond more rapidly to customer requirements at ever lower costs.

Logistics and supply chain management

Logistics management is essentially an integrative process that seeks to optimize the flows of materials and supplies through the organization and its operations to the customer. It is essentially a planning process and an information-based activity. Requirements from the marketplace are translated into production requirements and then into materials requirements through this planning process.

It is now being recognized that, for the real benefits of the logistics concept to be realized, there is a need to extend the logic of logistics upstream to suppliers and downstream to final customers. This is the concept of *supply chain management*.

Supply chain management is a fundamentally different philosophy of business organization and is based upon the idea of partnership in the marketing channel and a high degree of linkage between entities in that channel. Traditional models of business organization were based upon the notion that the interests of individual firms are best served by maximizing their revenues and minimizing their costs. If these goals were achieved by disadvantaging another entity in the channel, then that was the way it was. Under the supply chain management model the goal is to maximize profit through enhanced competitiveness in the final market – a competitiveness that is achieved by a lower cost to serve, achieved in the shortest time-frame possible. Such goals are only attainable if the supply chain as a whole is closely coordinated in order that total channel inventory is minimized, bottlenecks are eliminated, time-frames compressed and quality problems eliminated.

This new model of competition suggests that individual companies compete not as company against company, but rather as supply chain against supply chain. Thus the successful companies will be those whose supply chains are more cost-effective than those of their competitors.

What are the basic requirements for successful supply chain management? Figure 2.2 outlines the critical linkages that connect the marketplace to the supply chain.

The key linkages are between procurement and manufacturing, and between manufacturing and distribution. Each of these three activities, while part of a continuous process, has a number of critical elements.

Procurement

Typically in the past, supply management has been paid scant attention in many companies. Even though the costs of purchases for most businesses are the largest single cost, procurement has not been seen as a strategic task. That view is now changing, as the realization grows that not only are costs dramatically impacted by procurement decisions and procedures but also that innovation and response-to-market capability are profoundly affected by supplier relationships.

The philosophy of *co-makership is* based upon the idea of a mutually beneficial relationship between supplier and buyer, instead of the more traditional adversarial stance that is so often encountered. With this partnership

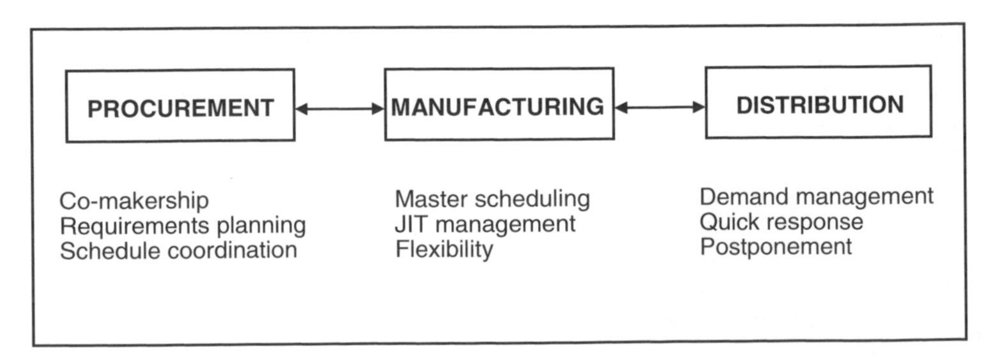

Figure 2.2 Critical linkages in the supply chain

approach, companies will identify opportunities for taking costs out of the supply chain instead of simply pushing them upstream or downstream. Paperwork can be eliminated, problems jointly solved, quality improved and information shared. By its very nature, co-makership will often involve longer-term relationships, but with fewer suppliers.

A fundamental feature of this integrated approach to supply chain management is the adoption of some form of alignment and synchronization of the customer's and the supplier's processes.

The aim should be to view your suppliers' operations as merely an extension of your own. Companies like Nissan, in their UK manufacturing facility, have developed closely linked systems with all of their suppliers so that those suppliers have full visibility not only of the production schedule at Nissan's Washington plant, but also of the real-time sequence in which cars are moving down the assembly line. By the use of electronic data interchange (EDI) and open communications, Nissan has been able to reduce lead times, eliminate inventories and take costs out of the supply chain. Other companies may have introduced similar JIT systems, but often, in so doing, have added to their suppliers' costs, not reduced them.

Manufacturing

There has been much talk of 'lean' manufacturing over the last decade (Womack, Jones and Roos, 1990). The idea of leanness in this sense is that wasteful activities are reduced or eliminated and that value-creating processes are performed more quickly. However, just as important as leanness is agility. Agility is a wider supply chain concept that is more concerned with how the firm responds to changes in marketplace requirements – particularly requirements for volume and variety. Leanness is undoubtedly a desirable feature of a supply chain unless it leads to a misplaced emphasis on manufacturing costs. It may be preferable, for example, to incur a cost penalty in the unit cost of manufacture if it enables the company to achieve higher levels of customer responsiveness at less overall cost to the supply chain.

The key word in manufacturing in today's environment is *flexibility* – flexibility in terms of the ability to produce any variant in any quantity, without significant cost penalty, has to be the goal of all manufacturing strategies. In the past, and even still today, much of the thinking in manufacturing was dominated by the search for economies of scale. This type of thinking led to large mega-plants, capable of producing vast quantities of a standardized product at incredibly low unit costs of production. It also has led many companies to go for so-called 'focused factories', which produce a limited range of products for global consumption.

The downside of this is in effect the possibility of hitting the 'diseconomies' of scale: in other words, the build-up of large inventories of finished product ahead of demand, the inability to respond rapidly to changed customer requirements and the limited variety that can be offered to the customer. Instead of economies of scale, the search is now on for strategies that will reduce total supply chain costs, not just manufacturing costs, and that will offer maximum flexibility against customer requirements. The goal must be 'the economic batch quantity of one', meaning that in the ideal world we would make things one at a time against known customer demands.

One of the lessons that the Japanese have taught us is that the route to flexibility in manufacturing does not necessarily lie through new technology, eg robotics, although that can help. A lot can be achieved instead through focusing upon the time it takes to plan, to schedule, to set up, to change over and to document. These are the classic barriers to flexibility and if they can be removed then manufacturing can respond far more rapidly to customer requirements. In a factory with zero lead times, total flexibility is achieved with no forecasts and no inventory! Whilst zero lead times are clearly an impossibility, the Japanese have shown that impressive reductions in such lead times can be achieved by questioning everything we do and the way in which we do it.

Distribution

The role of distribution in the supply chain management model has extended considerably from the conventional view of the activity as being concerned solely with transport and warehousing. The critical task that underlies successful distribution today is *demand management*.

Demand management is the process of anticipating and fulfilling orders against defined customer service goals. Information is the key to demand management: information from the marketplace in the form of medium-term forecasts; information from customers, preferably based upon actual usage and consumption; information on production schedules and inventory status; and information on marketing activities such as promotions that may cause demand to fluctuate away from the norm.

Clearly, while forecasting accuracy has always to be sought, it must be recognized that it will only rarely be achieved. Instead the aim should be to reduce our dependence upon the forecast by improved information on demand and by creating systems capable of more rapid response to that demand. This is the principle that underlies the idea of *quick response* logistics.

Quick response logistics has become the aim for many organizations, enabling them to achieve the twin strategic goals of cost reduction and service enhancement. In essence, the idea of quick response is based upon a replenishment-driven model of demand management. In other words, as items are consumed or purchased, this information is transmitted to the supplier and this immediately triggers a response. Often more rapid, smaller consignment quantity deliveries will be made, the trade-off being that any higher transport costs will be more than covered by reduced inventory in the pipeline and at either end of it, yet with improved service in terms of responsiveness. Clearly information technology has been a major enabling factor in quick response logistics, linking the point of sale or consumption with the point of supply.

A further trend that is visible in distribution is the search for *postponement* opportunities. The principle of postponement is that the final configuration or form of the product should be delayed until the last possible moment. In this way maximum flexibility is maintained, but inventory minimized. The distribution function takes on a wider role as the provider of the final added value. For example, at Xerox the aim is not to hold any inventory as finished product but only as semi-finished, modular work in progress, awaiting final configuration once orders are received. Similarly, at Hewlett Packard, products are now designed with 'localization' in mind. In other words products will be designed for modular manufacture but with local assembly and customization to meet the needs of specific markets. In this way economies of scale in manufacturing can be achieved by producing generic products for global markets whilst enabling local needs to be met through postponed configuration.

What is apparent is that distribution in the integrated supply chain has now become an information-based, value-added activity, providing a critical link between the marketplace and the factory.

The new competitive framework: the four Rs

We began this chapter with a brief review of how today's customer is increasingly seeking added value and how logistics management can provide that value. In the past, the primary means of achieving competitive advantage were often summarized as the 'four Ps' – product, price, promotion and place. These should now be augmented with the 'four Rs' – reliability, responsiveness, resilience and relationships – and logistics strategies need to be formulated with these as the objectives. Let us briefly examine each in turn.

Reliability

In most markets and commercial environments today, customers are seeking to reduce their inventory holdings. Just-in-time practices can be found in industries as diverse as car assembly and retailing. In such situations it is essential that suppliers can guarantee complete order-fill delivered at agreed times. Hence a prime objective of any logistics strategy must be reliability.

Making logistics systems more reliable means that greater emphasis must be placed upon process design and process control. The processes that are particularly germane to logistics are those to do with order fulfilment and supply chain management. Because traditionally these processes have been managed on a fragmented, functional basis they tend to have a higher susceptibility to variability. These processes are typified by multiple 'hand-offs' from one area of functional responsibility to another and by bottlenecks at the interfaces between stages in the chain. One of the benefits of taking a process view of the business is that it often reveals opportunities for simplification and the elimination of non-value-adding activities so that reliability inevitably improves.

One of the main causes of unreliability in supply chain processes is performance variability. Recently, the use of so-called 'Six Sigma' methodologies has been adopted to reduce that variability. Six Sigma is the umbrella term applied to a range of tools that are designed to identify the sources of variability in processes and to reduce and control that variability.

Responsiveness

Very closely linked to the customers' demands for reliability is the need for responsiveness. Essentially this means the ability to respond in ever-shorter lead times with the greatest possible flexibility. Quick response, as we have seen, is a concept and a technology that is spreading rapidly across industries. For the foreseeable future, speed will be a prime competitive variable in most markets. The emphasis in logistics strategy will be upon developing the means to ship smaller quantities, more rapidly, direct to the point of use or consumption.

The key to time compression in the logistics pipeline is through the elimination or reduction of time spent on non-value-adding activities. Hence, contrary to a common misconception, time compression is not about performing activities faster, but rather performing fewer of them. The old cliché 'Work smarter, not harder' is particularly relevant in this context.

As Hammer and Champy (Hammer, 1990; Hammer and Champy, 1993) have pointed out, many of the processes used in our organizations were designed for a different era. They tend to be paper-based, with many – often redundant – manual stages. They are sequential and batch-oriented rather than parallel and capable of changing quickly from one task to another. Even though eliminating or reducing such activities may increase cost, the end result will often be more cost-effective. For example, shipping direct from factories to end customers may be more expensive in terms of the unit cost of transport compared to shipping via a regional distribution centre, but time spent in the distribution centre is usually non-value-adding time.

Resilience

Today's supply chains are more complex and vulnerable to disruption than ever before. In many cases, as a result of outsourcing and the increasingly global nature of supply chains, the likelihood of interruption to product and information flows has increased significantly.

Identifying, mitigating and managing supply chain risk is now a critical requirement to ensure business continuity. The idea of resilience in the context of supply chain management is that supply chains need to be able to absorb shocks and to continue to function even in the face of unexpected disruption.

The paradox is that in many cases because companies have adopted 'lean' strategies and reduced inventories and, often, capacity there is little 'slack' left in their systems. Resilient supply chains will typically incorporate strategic buffers at the critical nodes and links in their networks. These buffers could be in the form of inventory or capacity, possibly shared with competitors.

As uncertainty in the business environment continues to increase, organizations need to adopt a more systematic and structured approach to supply chain risk management. One way in which this can be achieved is by creating a supply chain continuity team whose job is to audit risk across the supply chain and to develop and implement strategies for the mitigation of any identified risk.

Relationships

The trend towards customers seeking to reduce their supplier base has already been commented upon. The concept of 'strategic sourcing' is now receiving widespread support. Strategic sourcing is based on the careful selection of suppliers whom the customer wishes to partner. The benefits of such an approach include improved quality, innovation sharing, reduced costs and the integrated scheduling of production and deliveries. Underlying all of this is the idea that buyer–supplier relationships should be based upon partnership. More and more companies are discovering the advantages that can be gained by seeking out mutually beneficial, long-term relationships with suppliers. From the suppliers' point of view, such partnerships can prove formidable barriers to entry to competitors. Once again, companies are finding that logistics provides a powerful route to the creation of partnerships in the marketing channel. Logistics management should be viewed as the thread that connects the inbound and outbound flows of channel partners.

A good example of logistics partnership is the growing use of 'vendor-managed inventory' (VMI). The underlying principle of VMI is that the supplier rather then the customer assumes responsibility for the flow of product into the customer's operations. Thus instead of the customer placing orders on the vendor – often at short notice – the vendor can directly access information relating to the rate of usage or sale of the product by the customer. With this information the supplier can better plan the replenishment of the product with less need to carry safety stock. In effect, VMI enables the substitution of information for inventory in the supply chain.

The challenge to marketing and strategic planning in any business is to construct a corporate strategy that specifically builds upon logistics as a means to achieving competitive advantage through a much stronger focus on the four Rs. It is still the case that many organizations have not fully understood the strategic importance of logistics and hence have not explicitly tailored logistics into their corporate strategies and their marketing plans.

The organizational challenge

One of the most significant changes in recent years has been the way in which we think of organization structures. Conventionally, organizations have been 'vertical' in their design. In other words, businesses have organized around functions such as production, marketing, sales and distribution. Each function has had clearly identified tasks and within these functional 'silos' or 'stovepipes' (as they have been called) there is a recognized hierarchy up which employees might hope to progress. Figure 2.3 illustrates this functionally oriented business.

The problem with this approach is that it is inwardly focused and concentrates primarily on the use of resources rather than upon the creation of outputs. The outputs of any business can only be measured in terms of customer satisfaction achieved at a profit. Paradoxically, these outputs can only be realized through coordination and cooperation *horizontally* across the organization. These horizontal linkages mirror the materials and information flows that link the customer with the business and its suppliers. They are in fact the *core processes* of the business. Figure 2.4 highlights the fundamental essence of the horizontal organization.

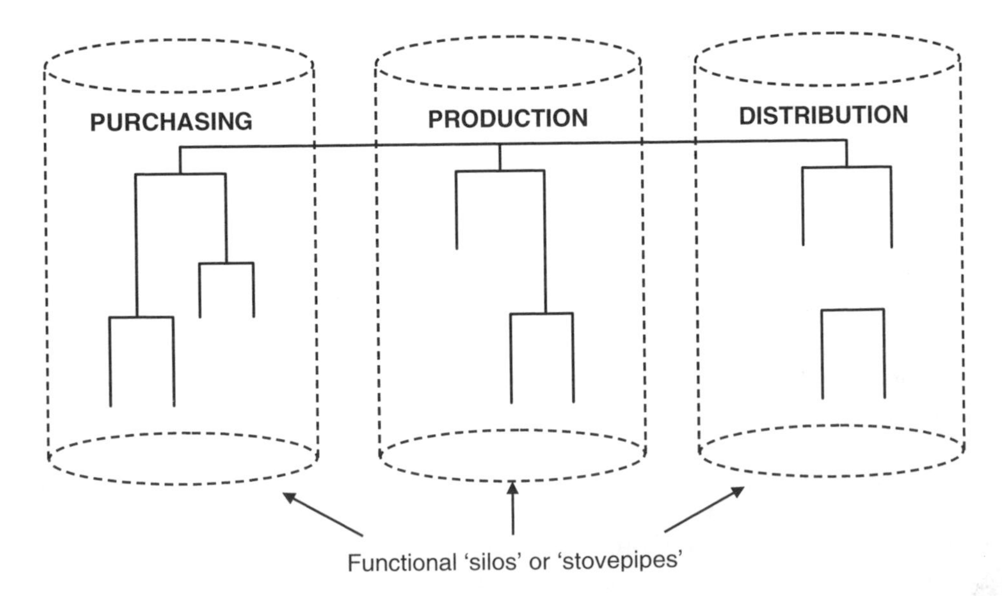

Figure 2.3 The vertical/functional organization

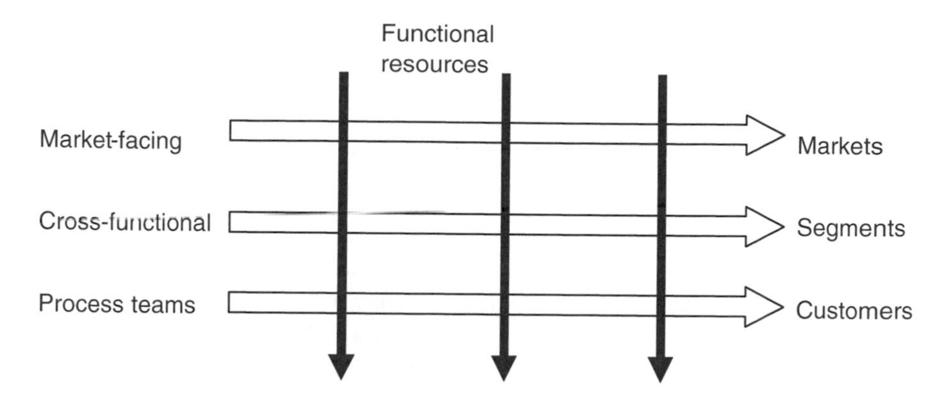

Figure 2.4 The horizontal/process organization

In the horizontal organization, the emphasis is upon the management of processes. These processes, by definition, are cross-functional and include new product development, order fulfilment, information management, profitability analysis and marketing planning.

The justification for this radically different view of the business is that these processes are in effect 'capabilities' and, as we have observed, it is through capabilities that the organization competes. In other words, the effectiveness of the new product development process, the order fulfilment process and so on determines the extent to which the business will succeed in the marketplace.

How does a conventionally organized business transform itself into a market-facing, process-oriented organization? One of the major driving forces for change is the revolution that has taken place in information technology and systems enabling the supply chain linkage to become a reality. More and more, the business will find itself organizing around the information system. In other words the processes for capturing information from the marketplace (forecasts, anticipated requirements, customer schedules and orders) will be linked to the processes for meeting that demand.

It is no coincidence that companies that have installed the new generation of 'enterprise resource planning' (ERP) systems have also been at the forefront of the change from vertical to horizontal organizational structures. These systems enable entire supply chains to become truly demand-driven through the use of shared information. They open up new and exciting opportunities to create true end-to-end pipeline management and the achievement of the ultimate business goal of high service to customers at less cost.

Summary

- Businesses in all types of industries are placing far greater emphasis on the design and management of logistics processes and the integration of those processes upstream and downstream with those of suppliers and customers.
- The business of the future will undoubtedly be market-driven, with logistics processes providing a critical means for achieving corporate goals.
- It will be a highly coordinated network of outsourced flows of materials and supplies, integrated through an information system that reaches from the ultimate consumer to the far end of the supply chain.
- The era of logistics and supply chain management, which many have predicted for some time, seems finally to have arrived.

References

Hammer, M (1990) Re-engineering work: don't automate, obliterate, *Harvard Business Review*, July/August pp 104–12

Hammer, M and Champy, J (1993) *Reengineering the Corporation*, HarperCollins, New York

Porter, M (1980) *Competitive Strategy*, Free Press, New York

Porter, M (1985) *Competitive Advantage*, Free Press, New York

Stalk, G, Evans, P and Shulman, LE (1992) Competing on capabilities: the new rules of corporate strategy, *Harvard Business Review*, March/April pp 56–68

Womack, J, Jones, D and Roos, D (1990) *The Machine that Changed the World*, Macmillan, London

3

Formulating logistics strategy

Nathalie Fabbe-Costes and Jacques Colin,
Université de la Méditerranée, Aix–Marseille

Why formulate logistics strategies?

Commercial and industrial organizations can be thought of as systems of operational processes structured and regulated by a set of functions that can become strategic. They are currently the object of intense environmental pressures. Never have these been so diverse, disrupting previous equilibriums and calling for rapid and coherent responses (as shown in Figure 3.1).

The multiplicity of corporate responses implies coordination and integration in a clearly defined strategy. Indeed, only through the use of strategy can this 'art of using information obtained in operating, integrating it, quickly formulating plans of action and having the ability to gather a maximum of certainties in order to confront the uncertain' (Morin, 1990) overcome the extreme environmental instability that appears to be characterizing the new millennium. Strategy enables companies to formulate and achieve their objectives, allowing them to take advantage of opportunities as they arise, while remaining in tune with their environment.

An essential priority today is an understanding of logistics and supply chain management (SCM). Logistics – defined as the control of the physical flow of materials and goods by the related virtual information flow that a firm sends, transfers and receives – is an organizational function that can conserve and improve the flexibility and reactivity of the firm to its environment.

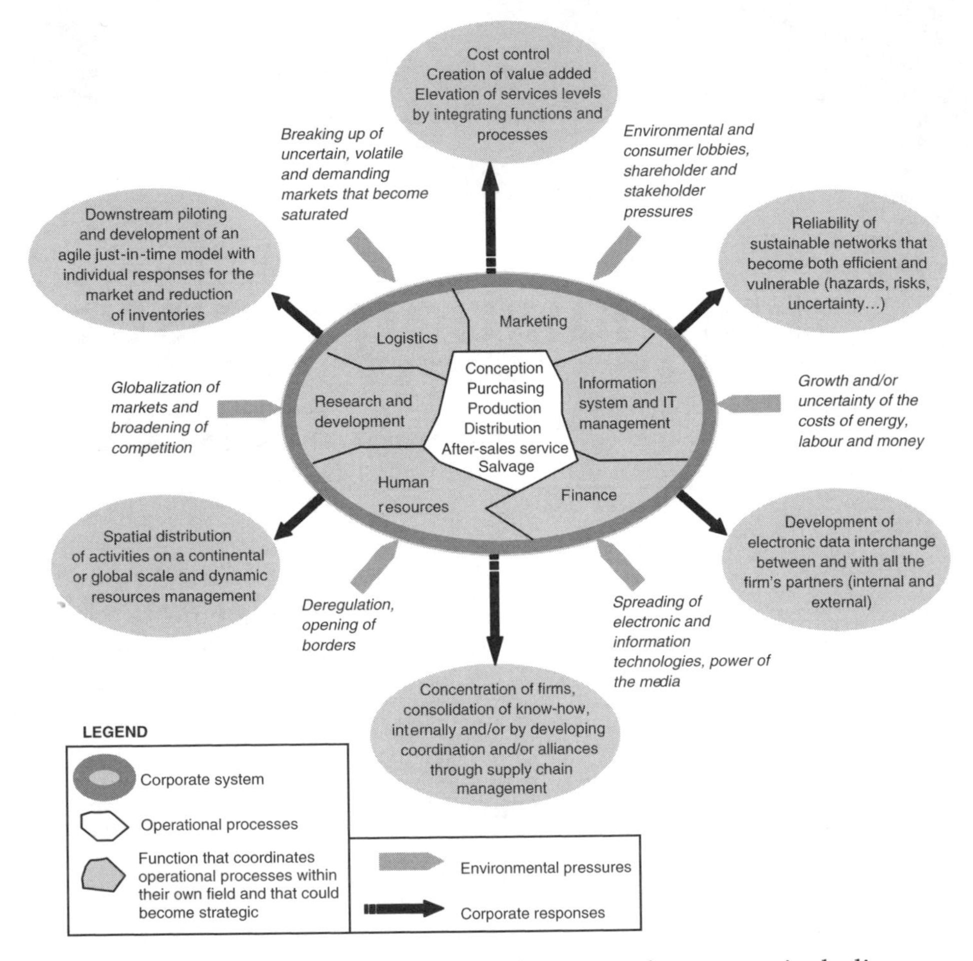

Figure 3.1 Corporate responses to environmental pressures including logistics dimensions

Logistics also leads companies to think about the whole supply chains they are involved in, and to try to improve both their own performance and the performance of the broader process. Firms now try to develop a collaborative approach within supply chain management, defined as 'a network of firms interacting to deliver product or service to the end consumer, linking flows from raw material supply to final delivery' (Ellram, 1991). More precisely, 'supply chain management is the integration of key business processes from end user through original suppliers that provide products, services, and information that add value for customers and other stakeholders' (Lambert, Cooper and Pagh, 1998).

To satisfy its ideal objectives of continuity (preventing stock-out) and fluidity (limiting overcapacity), logistics has progressively left behind its original operational role, which was a combination of transport, handling and warehousing operations. The concept of a supply chain enables firms to control the information flow from downstream to upstream, and to optimize (in terms of cost and level of service) the whole physical movement that is initiated by demand pull. The field of logistics has, therefore, considerably broadened (as illustrated in Figure 3.2) and it has become one of the most significant driving forces for organizational change.

The process-oriented perspective of logistics – that cuts across the traditional vertical functions of the organization – has been a powerful stimulator for change. This movement began early in the 1990s, contributing to a broad approach of process-based management (Davenport and Short, 1990; Hammer, 1990) that was often combined with ideas such as lean management (Womack, Jones and Roos, 1990), total quality management (Shiba, Graham and Walden, 1993) and time-based competition (Stalk and Hout, 1990). In the mid-1990s firms took a re-engineering perspective and considered that most processes had to be completely redesigned – thinking differently about the design/manufacturing/distribution/after-sales service/recycling process, with a complete redefinition of partners' role as well as a reconfiguration of information systems. For many companies, logistics became a key process and a strategic capability (Stalk, Evans and Shulman, 1992). Logistics was not just a tool for the global strategy of a company, but also the source of innovative new strategies.

Logistics has now become a far-reaching 'total' intra- and inter-organizational approach, which is both transverse and very ambitious, and where

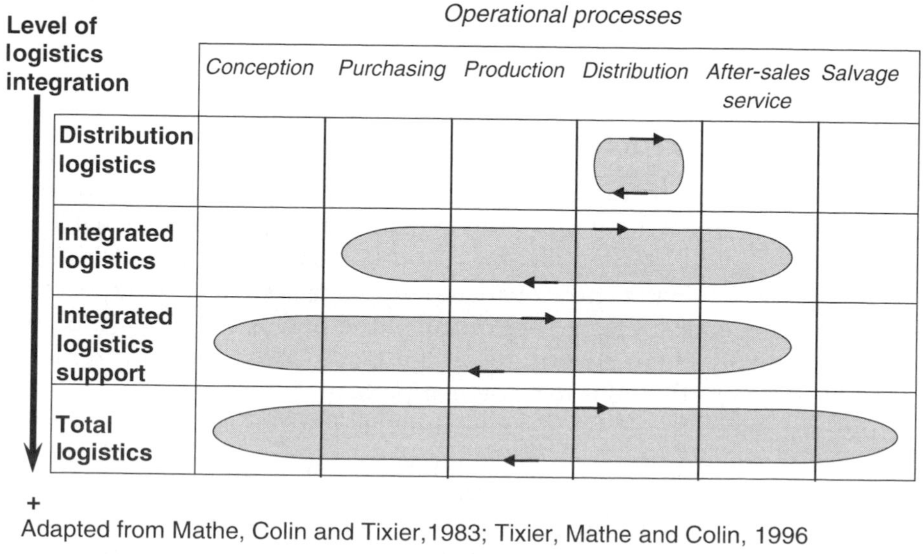

Adapted from Mathe, Colin and Tixier,1983; Tixier, Mathe and Colin, 1996

Figure 3.2 Evolution of the field of action of logistics

skills are applied at the interfaces between the various operational processes (see Figure 3.2). Its main role is to synchronize physical flows, and it is in permanent interaction with all the classic functions of a firm, forming an active interface between the firm and its environment. In practice, the aim of logistics and supply chain management is to optimize the three flows involved in supply chains: 'the flow of goods from sources to end-consumers, the flow of funds to satisfy the market needs at minimum costs, the flow of information to respond to customer requirements efficiently and effectively' (European Commission, 1999).

It is paradoxical that, while the environmental pressures shown in Figure 3.1 are not specific to logistics, the same cannot be said about the responses that firms in most sectors must make. The design of their responses conceals options that imply a logistics approach. For challenges that are not specifically logistic, the firm designs solutions and strategies that are, or that become, based on logistics (see Cohen and Roussel (2005) for examples).

The profound transformations that have taken place in the structure of firms, as well as the extension of their activities, have confirmed the need for a strategic approach to logistics. Its aim is to give a better response to consumers and to control the areas where the firm operates, the timing of these operations, their value creation and, finally, the inherent risks involved in the firm's choices.

How can we identify the strategic projects in which logistics can play a key role? To answer this question in a creative way, we have to propose an innovative approach to strategy formulation.

A conceptual approach to formulating logistics strategy

From logistics Strategy to strategic Logistics

The classic approach to formulating a logistics strategy begins with the firm's overall strategy and then defines the logistics strategy that will enable it to reach its objectives. Logistics is thus conceived as a functional support system and a tool for achieving the global strategy; logistics strategy appears as a subset of the overall strategy. The control of the flow of materials and goods along the supply chain constitutes a key factor for success in numerous domains, which justifies this top-down approach.

However, logistics also opens new strategic lines of action. To formulate these new lines, we have to reverse the classic approach, to think strategic Logistics (sL) rather than logistics Strategy (lS).

strategic Logistics consists of imagining and developing strategic actions that would be impossible without strong logistics competence. From being a key factor for success, logistics is becoming a fully competitive advantage –

and even a means to change the rules of the strategic game for an industry, or to adopt new game strategies (Buaron, 1981). This viewpoint makes it necessary to think about logistics at the time the overall strategy is being designed, and to foresee how, in certain cases, it can be the foundation of overall strategic action. In line with resource-based theories (Métais, 2004), logistics is one of the strategic capabilities likely to lead to innovative corporate and/or inter-organizational strategies.

The two interrelated perspectives of logistics and strategy shown in Figure 3.3 lead to very different results, and to company projects that are also very different. However, it should be noted that they do not exclude each other, but correspond to distinct consequences. Principal differences are summarized in Table 3.1.

The determining factor for reversing our perspective is the maturity of the perception of logistics as a cross-functional and deliberately open-ended management domain in the firm, and as a proactive interface with external partners in the supply chain, through a cross-organizational and agile approach. Thus, the interactive loop between strategy and logistics is generally initiated by a request from strategy to logistics, historically centred on the control (reduction) of logistics costs.

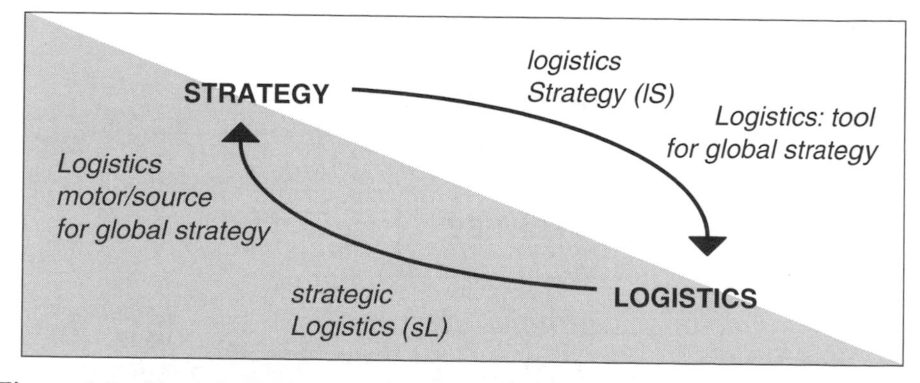

Figure 3.3 From logistics Strategy to strategic Logistics

Table 3.1 Main differences between logistics Strategy and strategic Logistics

	logistics Strategy	**strategic Logistics**
Perception of logistics role	Strategy support	Strategy foundation
Effects on organization	Improvement, evolution	Change, transmutation
Effects on the industry	Key success factor	New rules inductor

The experience, know-how and systems developed in logistics then retroact on the strategy, becoming the instigator of its (re)formulation, enabling the firm to differentiate itself by logistics services, or even diversifying in logistics activities. It also increases the flexibility and agility of companies to redesign their network within a supply chain management (SCM) process.

Finally, strategic Logistics formulations emerge from this iterative strategy/logistics loop, which becomes a 'progress spiral' (Martinet, 1983) for the firm. The purpose of this loop is to have a logistics organization that is adapted to the firm's objectives (lS – with logistics fitting strategy) and to be able to identify, exploit or even create opportunities for the firm (sL – where strategy is *intentionally* built on logistics). This loop also encourages learning in both strategic and logistics domains. In particular, it encourages the development of strategic Logistics competencies that are necessary for strategic Logistics.

Logistics competence: a strategic resource and capability

Logistics depends on three interrelated dimensions of competence: action, expertise and knowledge (Fabbe-Costes, 1997). Figure 3.4 illustrates the interrelationship between the three dimensions of competence. An upward arrow

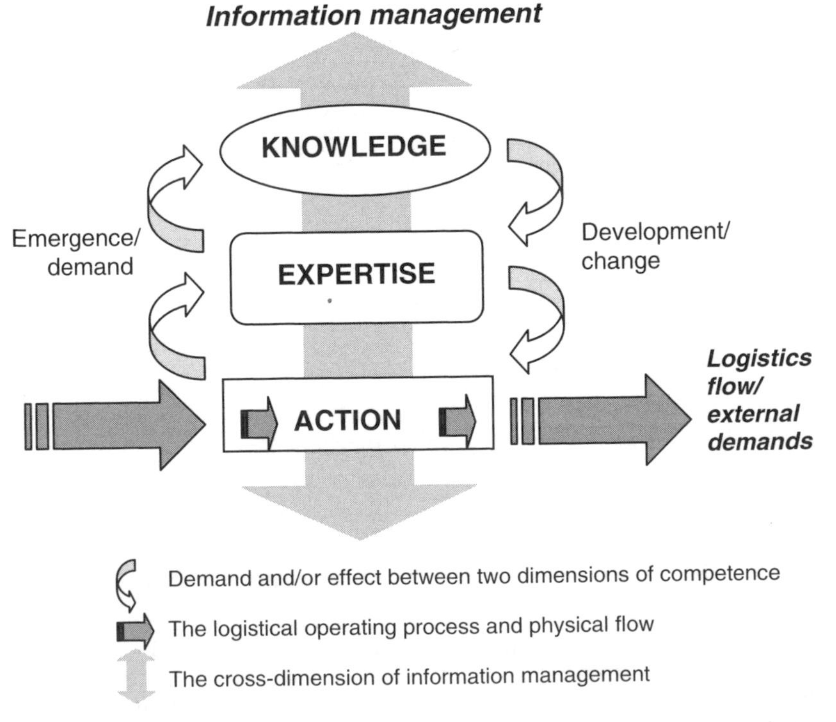

From Fabbe-Costes, 1997

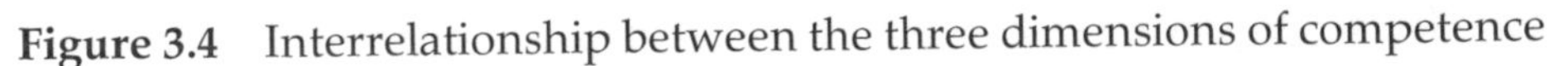

Figure 3.4 Interrelationship between the three dimensions of competence

signifies a demand from a lower dimension, while a downward arrow represents the effect of higher-level knowledge on expertise and, in turn, operating procedures and processes.

Action relates to the way in which logistics processes are actually performed. Expertise relates to all the resources directly associated with the action, including methods, procedures, organizational routines, technologies and engineering. They strongly influence the quality, efficiency, durability and reliability of the logistics process and are a major source of competitive advantage. Knowledge represents the highest level of abstraction in logistics management. It is high-level information that must be collected, assessed and assimilated while formulating strategy. It incorporates the experience of senior managers, and the general management culture of the business. Knowledge is a key factor to survival, evolution and adaptation; it compels companies to invest in high-level management skills and in research and development – and to try to convert everything that is experienced and perceived by people in the company and in the logistics network into knowledge. Intrinsic to the development of logistics competence is information management. The need for effective collection, communication and processing of information exists at each level. The information collected, created and memorized at each tier enriches strategic decision making and can encourage new strategic directions.

Towards logistics Strategy formulation

The strategic formulation of logistics can be expressed by three classic concepts of strategy: the profession, the mission and the objectives. In concrete terms, to formulate a logistics Strategy, managers define:

- the ranges of movement that it produces and how it produces them (technologies, know-how, organization);
- to whom they are directed (internal or external clients) and the needs that they satisfy;
- the kind of performance it aims at and the targeted level of that performance.

Consequently, this formulation can identify several sectors of logistics activity, or 'logistics business units', which are more or less synergistic. Among them, some can be considered as supports for the firm's overall strategy (lS perspective), while others can be drivers of its strategy (sL perspective).

Formulation is then oriented to the choice of logistics business units and the associated organizational solutions to adopt in order to reach defined objectives. As a transversal function of coordination for all stages of movement and for the management of both internal and external interfaces, logistics can only be efficient if it is linked internally with the other functions and if it coordinates externally with the other companies of the supply chain. The options chosen for logistics must be congruent with those in the domains of marketing, finance, information systems, manufacturing and human resources. Ideally, logistics Strategy should be combined with the other strategies, and strategic Logistics should use the levers that other functions present.

At present, information-system management is certainly the domain that has the strongest synergy with logistics. The coincidence of the emergence of strategic Logistics and strategic informatics is certainly not accidental. It can be explained by the overlapping of physical and informational flows (the piloting and monitoring concept), to which we can associate financial flows. It could also be explained by the transversality and the outward view of logistics and information communication systems, as well as by the dynamic character of the management processes that they support. In addition, the control and traceability of physical and informational flow develops and supports the flexibility and adaptability that is now indispensable. Information and communication systems, supported by new technologies, become a cornerstone of logistics management, and each firm looks for a better integration of information systems (Fabbe-Costes, 2002). Most companies try to develop inter-organizational information systems 'supporting cooperative, intraorganizational and interorganizational, functional teams' (Konsynski, 1993).

The formulation of logistics Strategy also deals with make-or-buy decisions. The decision to subcontract or, on the contrary, to (re)integrate logistics activities is contingent on several factors. First, it depends on the situation of the logistics supply industry at the time the question arises. It also depends on the shipper's perception of the relative risks and benefits of the two options. Moreover, this dilemma usually only arises when a shipper is conducting a strategic review of its logistical system. Discussions with European shippers have revealed that some logistics operations are more likely to be kept in-house, or reintegrated, than others (Fabbe-Costes and Colin, 1995). The choice is a burning issue for shippers when they consider operations that:

- directly concern customer services – the more an operation affects the shipper's customer, the more it is seen to be sensitive, confirming that logistics has become a strategic marketing element for many manufacturing and retailing companies;
- require the handling of information thought to be 'strategic' – usually pertaining to customers and/or cost structure and/or core expertise;
- can be considered 'critical' in the shipper's logistics process (in terms of their service and/or logistics costs) or, more precisely, operations in which security is more important than flexibility;
- do not require a large amount of new investment, particularly those for which physical or information systems have already been set up within the company;

- offer a rapid rate of return on investment in logistics assets;
- require highly specific investment and that logistics service providers – especially those providing mainly shared-user services – find difficult to run profitably;
- do not require staff with a different culture from that already prevailing in the company;
- require highly specific skills, not available from a logistics supplier.

The strategic (or non-strategic) character of a logistics organization provides information on the originality and confidentiality required for the necessary know-how, the expected reliability and agility of the processes, and the significance of the planned organization. In the cases of delegated operations or organizations, it defines the means required to ensure control and to improve relationships. It, therefore, creates networks of complementary skills and ensures their consistency.

Illustrated typology of possible logistics strategies

To illustrate the conceptual approach to strategy formulation for logistics, we have selected case studies of distributors, manufacturers and logistics firms (also called logistics service providers or third-party logistics companies). They represent a variety of strategies. Our typology (presented in Table 3.2) contains seven classic, generic strategies and considers strategic formulations from both perspectives described in Figure 3.3. The generic strategies are in

Table 3.2 Typology of logistic Strategies and strategic Logistics

Generic strategy	logistics Strategy	strategic Logistics
Cost leadership	Reduce logistics costs	Reduce overall costs with logistics
Differentiation	Quality of logistics service	Logistics factor of differentiation
Innovation	Logistics support for innovation	Logistics as a source/ motor for innovation
Alliance	Logistics as a means of alliance	Logistics as a source/ motor for alliance
Profession expansion	Logistics as a support for new profession integration	Logistics as a new profession
Mission expansion	Logistics as a support for extension	Logistics in order to win new clients
Diversification	Use of logistics synergies	Diversifying through or in logistics

line with those proposed by Ansoff (1965) and Porter (1985). Wiseman (1985) has discussed these with relation to informatics strategy formulation.

Some strategies correspond to actions conceived – at least initially – to maintain the existing domain of activity (cost leadership and differentiation), while others move to new domains of activity (expansion and diversification), and alliances and innovation allow for both.

Cost leadership

logistics Strategy: reduce costs that are specific to logistics

- **Becton-Dickinson**, a multinational firm in the medical sector, centralized its stock in a single European site in order to reduce its inventory level and the costs of invested capital.
- **Carrefour**, a French hypermarket chain, stopped supplying its outlets directly from suppliers' warehouses. To reduce costs in the supply chain, retail stores get deliveries from cross-docking facilities operated by logistics suppliers. Carrefour also decided to eliminate stocks of clothes, garments and shoes in its 215 French hypermarkets, replacing them by a single stock in a 220,000-square-metre warehouse operated by a logistics provider. Each outlet's inventory has decreased from some months or weeks of sales to a few days. At the same time, each outlet has daily deliveries (one outlet = one truck) from the warehouse, so the range of products is individually linked to local weather and fashion trends.

strategic Logistics: through logistics, reduce overall costs

- **Décathlon**, a French sport equipment retailer, has a network of continental, multi-regional and local warehouses and cross-docking sites. These allow it to reduce purchasing costs considerably through the company's ability to stock massive quantities that it imports, or buys on promotion from suppliers. They also allow the cheapest quick response to outlets' requirements.
- **Casino**, a huge French retailer, does not process any inventories of ultra-fresh products. At noon, stores send their orders to the central informatics system. After consolidation, orders are transmitted at 2 pm to the provider, Yoplait. Then Yoplait delivers at 5 am the next day to Casino's local warehouses, which are cross-docking sites that sort the goods for delivery to stores by 4 pm. **Carrefour** also uses such a continuous replenishment programme with some of its suppliers: with Lever, one of these suppliers, its stocks fell from 27 days to 7 days.
- In the automobile industry, logistics control external flows by reducing the number of suppliers, thereby reducing supply costs. **Renault** now has 150 'optima' suppliers who are registered to deliver just-in-time, with stricter certification than ISO norms. Qualitative and quantitative checks on delivery are totally eliminated.

Differentiation

logistics Strategy: improve the quality of the logistics service

- By rationalizing their logistics, **Becton-Dickinson**, **Hewlett-Packard** and many others have improved their performance in terms of quality of service, availability of products, complete deliveries, guaranteed delivery times and their ability to customize products.
- **Philips-Eclairage** has a highly automated central warehouse in Paris that allows it to deliver to clients every day. As wholesalers no longer have to hold more stock than they need between deliveries, they choose to be preferentially supplied by Philips.
- **Radiall**, a supplier of cables and connectors for many industries, had a problem giving an efficient service to some strategic customers. To survive in a very competitive industry, they decided to differentiate their logistics process to give an appropriate response to strategic customers. Now they run two logistics processes and offer a high-standard service to strategic clients.

strategic Logistics: permit an increased differentiation

- **PSA** and **Renault** have developed just-in-time logistics to feed very flexible production lines that are capable of assembling vehicles that conform exactly to client specifications. The Renault Clio, for instance, can be delivered with options for air-conditioning, power steering, 80 different motors, 20 different gearboxes and five different bodies – a total of 32,000 combinations, without taking into account the range of paintwork and other options. In 2001, PSA sold 3.1 million cars representing 2.1 million different 'references' – a reference being a model that is assembled in a factory according to the options required by an end customer.
- Since November 1994 **Federal Express** has been offering customers a tracking/tracing service. Shippers can know the location of their parcels upon request to the website (http://www.fedex.com). The number of enquiries increased tremendously, reaching 10,000 a day in 1998.
- **Hewlett-Packard** uses its strong logistics competencies to survive and develop in the competitive European PC industry. It completely restructured its logistics processes and can provide customers with a multi-channel distribution system with different levels of logistics service and product customization.

Innovation

logistics Strategy: logistics as a support for innovation, logistics innovation

- **La Redoute** is a French mail-order firm whose promise of a two-day delivery service has enlarged its market. This commercial innovation (which has since been widely copied) depends on strong integration of physical and information flows – and on automation of the sorting centre created by the French postal service.

- To exchange logistics information with its suppliers, the European automobile sector has set up an electronic data interchange (EDI) network – **Galia/Odette** – which genuinely supports the just-in-time model of production planning. Thanks to EDI, the different actors of the automotive industry (car manufacturers, suppliers and logistics providers) share information related to the whole design, planning, production and delivery process – and can dynamically monitor the supply chain. This integration is now developing upstream to better link second and third tiers to the first one, with the Alpha project launched by Galia in October 2004.
- Providing any US customer with highly customized trousers within 48 hours was the innovation foreseen by **Levi's USA**. To achieve this objective, it based a new service on an order-collecting website where you can design your own product, a flexible and computerized cutting and assembly service that produces every unit upon request, and alliance with an express parcel delivery service. To ensure success, it had to redesign its overall supply chain, including the management of stocks, close link between physical and information flows, and use of new technology.

strategic Logistics: logistics as a source or motor for innovation

- In the early 2000s, **Geodis** – a French third-party logistics company with six business lines related to transport and logistics – wanted to innovate, and in particular to design 'packaged logistics solutions'. By identifying, mapping and sharing logistics expertise and knowledge among the group, they could build innovative multi-business offers that exploit transfers and synergies. Thanks to their knowledge from this logistics project (launched mid-2002) they could also improve their consulting offer.
- Most assembly manufacturers (such as electronic equipment industries) use their logistics competencies, combined with powerful inter-organizational information systems, to develop postponement (to differentiate products as late as possible in the supply chain) and to minimize stocks with vendor-managed inventory (VMI) and collaborative planning, forecasting and replenishment (CPFR). This use of demand pull is more likely to initiate product innovations that satisfy customers.
- As a major organizational and logistics innovation, efficient consumer response (ECR) is now being jointly developed by both industrial and retailer partners in the same supply chain. It enables the two partners to save as much as 5 per cent of the value of the goods. The systematic sharing of logistics information reduces the average inventories held by each partner. This joint work becomes a driving force for the two partners to enhance their cooperation far beyond the field of logistics.

Alliance

logistics Strategy: logistics as a means of alliance

- By negotiating a 'logistics charter' with its suppliers (signed in 1986), the **PSA Automobile Group** sought to stabilize and perpetuate its client–supplier relationships. This logistics charter identifies the rights and duties of suppliers in terms of delivery requirements transmitted by PSA factories. Members of this network become very interdependent, to the point where the car maker transfers its skills to the suppliers (concepts for new parts, quality control at the source, etc). Some suppliers are no longer 'part suppliers' but have become 'function suppliers' (for example, tightness supplier as opposed to rubber joint supplier) and are genuine members of the external supply chain of PSA.
- Logistics is a powerful factor for integration in **Renault** and **Nissan** since their alliance in 1999. Many logistics synergies (related to supply, cross-manufacturing and international transport, as well as to best practice exchanges) reinforce the alliance between the two companies.

strategic Logistics: logistics as a source/motor for alliance

- By developing its own powerful, centralized logistics system, dedicated to the stores operated by independent members, the French distribution group **Intermarché** has placed them in a position of total dependence on the group.
- A branch of **Geodis** designs and operates advanced warehouses and is specialized in the synchronized delivery of parts to factories using just-in-time. It is associated with transport partners (inside and outside the Geodis Group), allowing it to respond to all invitations to tender made by automobile and aeronautical manufacturers. Its expertise in logistics gives a competitive advantage to maintain sustainable partnerships with car makers and first-tier suppliers.
- **Geodis** and **SITA** have created a joint venture – **Valogistic** – that specializes in waste electrical and electronic equipment (WEEE) and products from the automotive repair and maintenance business. This operates at a European level and pools logistics skills and networks of the two companies.

Expansion by profession

logistics Strategy: logistics as a support for integration

- Integrators (formerly messenger services) have become express delivery services by integrating various activities – air transport, sorting, and pre- and post-routeing, all of which are coordinated and controlled by very powerful communication and information systems.

- **André**, a French shoe distributor (a chain of both urban shops and specialized supermarkets), strengthened by its logistics organization, has taken over the ready-to-wear clothing chains of Kookai and Caroll. Renamed the **Vivarte Group**, it manages 15 trade names in the shoe and clothes sector in Europe. Logistics is a core business of the group, delivering to the group's 2,566 outlets.

strategic Logistics: logistics as a new profession

- The integrators (**Fedex**, **DHL**, etc) are developing a service in the management of spare parts and/or high-value items for e-commerce that are located near to their hubs and are ready to be delivered through their global networks. They can deliver their customers' goods globally, with orders received late in the evening delivered early the next morning.
- For **Otis**, **Dassault**, **Eurocopter** and others, after-sales logistics has now become a source of revenue – sometimes with profits higher than the original product sales.
- Reverse logistics is growing and logistics companies like **Geodis** develop specific offers for many sectors (automotive, electronic, etc).
- **Tesco** uses its outlets to prepare home deliveries of orders collected from its websites, giving its customers two channels to buy products. Order preparing and delivering are new logistics competences for Tesco.

Expansion by mission

logistics Strategy: logistics as a support for extension

- **SKF**, **Aventis**, **IBM**, etc can only ensure their internationalization by entrusting European subsidiaries with specialized factories, and by including them in a complex logistics network composed of central and national warehouses that are in constant contact.
- To succeed in its global strategy, and to promote the international distribution of its many products, **Danone International Brands** built an international information system to link its commercial subsidiaries spread around the world, and logistics units that supply the products when and where required. Since 2001, a B2B site with a customer relationship management (CRM) application links with Danone's enterprise resource planning (ERP), strengthening relations with the network of importers/distributors and giving information about the status of orders.

strategic Logistics: logistics in order to win new clients/customers

- **Continent**, a French hypermarket chain that now belongs to **Carrefour**, supplies its new Greek stores in Salonika and Athens with the same logistics tool it uses for its stores in the south of France.

- The organization of the **Philips-Eclairage** central warehouse in France enables it to serve neighbouring customers in Luxembourg, Italy and Spain.
- Informatics printer manufacturers such as **Lexmark** – which gets higher margins from consumables than from the machines themselves – are encouraged to collect empty ink cartridges to avoid competition from companies specializing in refilling the cartridges. They are quickly developing alliances with third-party logistics specialized in gathering scrap and salvaging end-of-life items.
- Thanks to its logistics differentiation, **Radiall** can develop rapidly in the car industry it defines as a new strategic client.

Diversification

logistics Strategy: the use of logistics synergies

- Numerous road haulage firms have specialized in particular traffic or goods that present homogeneous logistics characteristics: **TFE** (Transport Frigorifiques Européens) for fresh products; **Salvesen** for frozen products; **DHL** and **UPS** (Germany) for deliveries in dense urban zones; **ACR/ Kuehne & Nagel**, **Norbert Dentressangle Logistics** and **DHL Exel** for supplying large distribution chains.
- To support its diversification strategy and benefit from synergies, **Geodis** develops competence mapping in the group and encourages cross-exchanges of logistics experience and knowledge.
- Automobile makers, with their great capacity to mobilize the resources of their suppliers, are becoming vehicle designers (imagining more attractive combinations of components for the client) and assemblers (by just-in-time converging of everything needed to assemble the specific vehicle ordered by a customer).

strategic Logistics: diversifying through or in logistics

- By exploiting its automated warehouse, **Philips-Eclairage** diversified into a parcel delivery service with daily deliveries to all clients, anywhere in France – to the point where it now sells more logistics services than electric equipment. The company delivers articles made by other manufacturers, provided they are not in direct competition with its own products.
- **Laphal**, a medium-size French pharmaceutical laboratory, has developed its logistics skills and assets, and recently decided to offer its logistics services to other pharmaceutical SMEs. They can manage international distribution to wholesalers, hospitals and community pharmacies. Laphal also has a logistics joint venture in Singapore, is expanding in Asia – and is now considered a third-party operator.

- **Telemarket**, a subsidiary of the Monoprix–Galeries Lafayette distribution group with strong logistics know-how, has offered a home-delivery service since 1987, with appointments made with Parisian customers who order by phone or over their web shop (www.telemarket.fr). These customers are obviously different from those who shop in the Monoprix stores in city centres.

Strategic action itineraries in logistics

The above examples provide evidence that, on the one hand, firms do not centre their strategy on logistics alone (informatics and marketing, in particular, are always implicitly if not explicitly associated), while, on the other hand, they do not strictly aim for a single result (differentiation, for example). In reality, the generic strategies illustrated separately in the previous section are not only dependent, but are also more generally combined. Hence, three strategic action 'itineraries' can be detected:

1. The firm aims at a principal strategy and obtains other advantages from 'spin-offs'. The firm discovers in retrospect that other strategies are possible thanks to the first strategic move. The resulting itinerary is an emergent one that was not foreseen.
2. The firm deliberately aims at several strategies that may be spread out in time but are conceived as being interdependent. The resulting itinerary is a deliberate one that was designed before the first strategic move.
3. Once the firm has aimed at one or several strategies and has built a new logistics system, it discovers that it can 'rebound' and, from that point on, build a new strategy with different aims. In this case, the firm designs its strategic itinerary by steps (Avenier, 1997), combining emergent and deliberate moves. This kind of itinerary needs special attention to the learning processes and a strategic mobility in the whole company and its partners. Sometimes, the 'rebound path' can be foreseen, but there is too much uncertainty to risk a combined strategic itinerary from the beginning. The first strategy is then an intermediary one that will reveal (or not) the feasibility of the overall strategy.

For each of these itineraries, we present various options, followed by several examples. Here we have used the abbreviations lS (logistics Strategy) and sL (strategic Logistics) to identify the perspectives adopted by the firm.

The possible spin-offs from a strategic move (see Figure 3.5)

- André (now Vivarte), by expanding through professions (with lS) that were in large part founded on logistics and commercial abilities, found

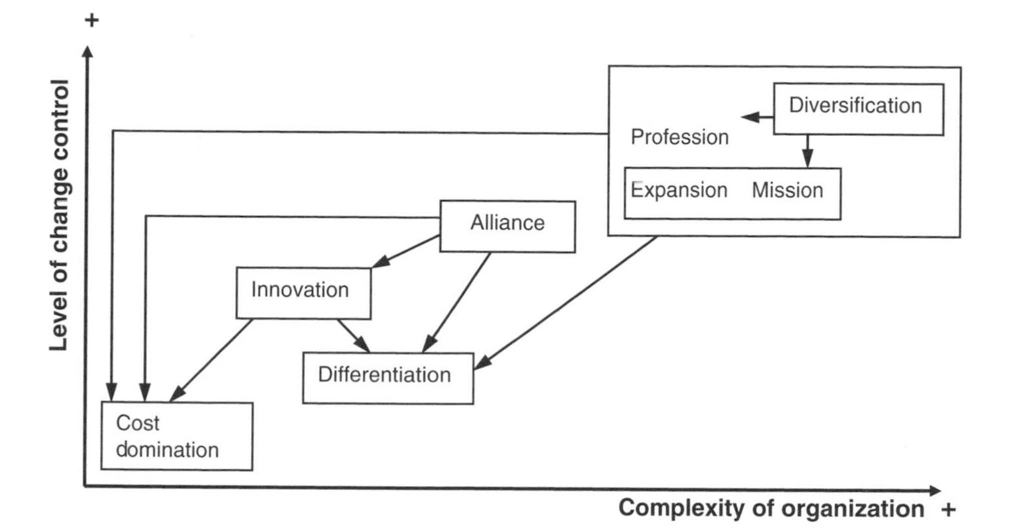

Figure 3.5 Possible spin-offs from a strategic move

logistics synergies in its distribution networks in order to reinforce its cost domination (lS).

- Tracking and tracing services – a logistics innovation (lS) developed by a growing number of express delivery services – at first constituted a differentiation approach (sL), attempting to obtain a modern image without great cost. By making transfers more reliable (increased control of risks), such technologies make it possible to reduce the level of the consignee's inventory and therefore its costs (sL), while at the same time reducing production cycles (as in IBM). The most dynamic express delivery services now integrate such technologies into their commercial approach and thus rebound by expanding their mission (sL).
- Diversifying in logistics as a new profession (sL) permits Laphal to look for logistics cost reduction (sL) that will benefit its own products.

It should be noted that spin-offs are always in the direction of decreasing organizational complexity and towards a lower level of change. Because spin-offs are not foreseen, they are not automatic and, in any case, are of less intensity than when strategic moves are deliberately played in a combined manner. To succeed in such an opportunistic approach, firms need to develop their vigilance and reactivity to catch any opportunity induced from the first strategic move.

Combination of articulated strategic moves (see Figure 3.6)

- In distribution, the intention of a firm to equip itself with its own and/or subcontracted logistics corresponds to a combination of deliberate logistics

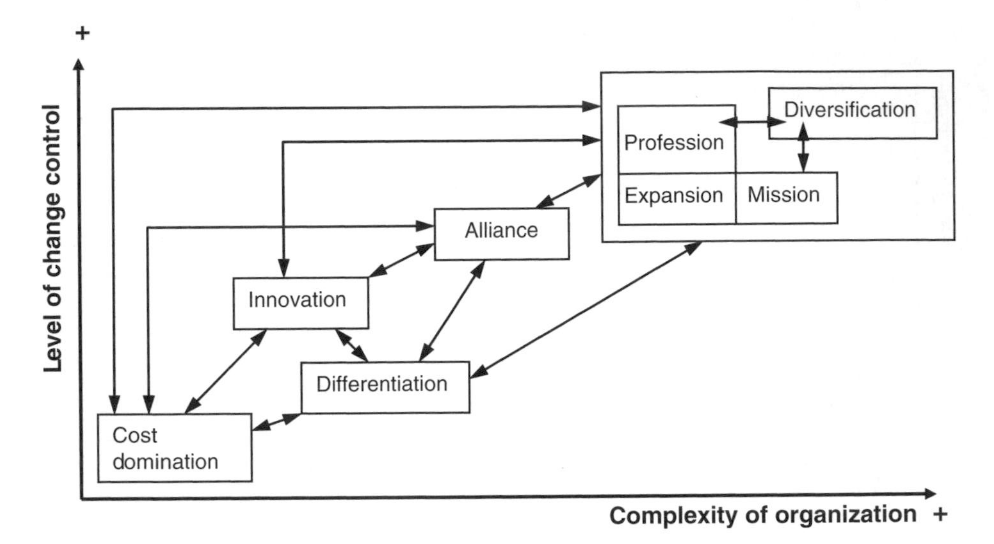

Figure 3.6 Possible combinations of articulated strategic moves

moves – reduction of direct logistics costs (lS) (Carrefour) and overall supply costs (sL) (Auchan and Intermarché); the will to differentiate (Auchan); the desire to make alliances (sL) (Intermarché) or to permit geographic expansion (sL) (Continent), or even to open up to diversification (sL) (Telemarket). Monoprix-Telemarket is an example of a firm that has more or less implemented all of these strategic dimensions, and others will follow the same path.

- The development of continuous replenishment programmes shared by manufacturers and retailers (Casino and Yoplait, Carrefour and Lever) and the development of ECR give a combination of cost domination (sL), innovation (sL) in the domain of information management, and vertical alliance (sL).
- Integrators, with their knowledge of complementarities and alliances (sL) (UPS), have sought to integrate operations (lS). Certain firms (DHL, TNT) offer their networks to dispatch parts between industrial sites working with just-in-time. This corresponds to a strategy of diversification (sL) from their original trade.
- For companies such as Hewlett-Packard, differentiation (lS) is always combined with a powerful cost reduction objective (lS) that was generally the first step of the combined itinerary.
- Hewlett-Packard's logistics strategy for PCs (sL) is efficient because they accepted the 'channel assembly' business model to transfer part of the assembly to selected resellers (lS). Then multi-channel differentiation (sL) had to be combined with alliances (lS) with channel partners.

- Levi's express customized service was a combination of innovation (lS) both on the offer and on the process, differentiation (sL) through the service, and expansion by mission (sL).
- The Tesco web offer based on outlets as logistics assets looks like Levi's strategic combination but with profession expansion (the web customers are the same as classic outlet customers).
- When Geodis launched its knowledge management project, the objective was to innovate (sL) but also to differentiate from competitors (lS), and to support its mission expansion (lS).

The combination itinerary deliberately aims at several strategies that are conceived as being interdependent. In certain cases, the implementation is synchronized, and in other cases it may be spread out in time – but the resulting itinerary is always designed before the first strategic move. This level of strategic maturity is not yet widespread, which explains why most firms rebound by making iterative improvements based on experiences during the strategic process.

Rebounding with new strategic moves (see Figure 3.7)

- At the end of the 1980s, with a major investment of €100 million (lS) in an automated distribution warehouse, Philips-Eclairage initially sought to differentiate itself from its competitors (lS). With its acquired experience, it then took over the distribution of materials complementary to, or different from, its range and made by other manufacturers. Can it be said that this diversification (sL) has transformed Philips-Eclairage into a

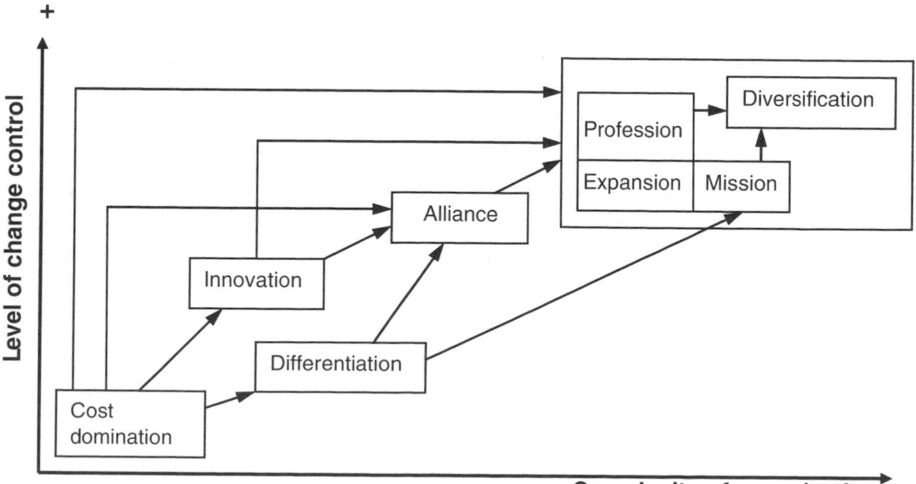

Figure 3.7 Rebounding with new strategic moves

logistics distribution firm? Where are the margins – in the sale of products, or the sale of logistics services? In fact, a second rebound has led the firm to geographic expansion (sL) by delivering to customers in regions beyond France.

- The automobile industry (PSA, Renault) has operated a complex combination of logistics approaches – overall cost reduction through logistics (sL), differentiation (sL), innovation in logistics EDI (lS), alliances with logistics suppliers and parts suppliers (sL) and expansion by internationalization (lS). On the strategic level, starting with logistics synergies (lS), a diversification phase can lead the firm to make a radical change in paradigm. With their strong logistics skills, the car makers are becoming conceivers and assemblers, able to offer either very differentiated ranges of cars or, on the contrary, very standardized vehicles.
- The logistics supplier Geodis developed know-how for advanced warehouses and just-in-time deliveries by first following an innovation approach (lS) and then by alliances founded on logistics (sL). Then it rebounded on diversification (sL) by proposing to its customers – car makers – that it perform assembly operations in its advanced warehouses for parts that it already managed. It assembles certain parts (eg bumper, lights and electric system) and delivers them directly to the production lines as required. It was a logistics supplier, and became a parts supplier.
- Thanks to its differentiated logistics service (lS), Radiall could expand into the car industry (sL) and compensate for decreasing activity in the telecommunications sector.
- For Geodis, the Valogistics joint venture with SITA (sL) is probably a first step towards expansion into European-wide operations (lS) and expansion of profession (sL) into reverse logistics and associated activities.

It should be noted that the possibilities illustrated in Figure 3.7 are not as numerous as those given in Figure 3.6, as the moves are not intended to be linked together from the beginning. It should also be noted that there is a strong difference between this kind of itinerary and the one illustrated by Figure 3.5. Here, firms capitalize on the experience acquired when 'acting' their first move, and they reformulate their strategy, exploiting new information, experience and competence. This explains why the first kind of itinerary (Figure 3.5) goes from complex strategies to simple ones, and the third one (Figure 3.7) gives an opportunity to increase complexity.

Conclusions

The formulation of logistics strategies is almost always complex. First, considering the relationship between logistics and strategy, there are two types of approach: reactive fit (logistics Strategy, lS) and active intent (strategic

Logistics, sL). Second, there is strong overlap with strategies formulated by other functions in the firm. Third, it is expressed by simple or multiple strategic moves. The way firms build strategic itineraries is another factor explaining the variety of logistics strategies: firms can either deliberately combine strategic moves, or rebound iteratively in new directions and take advantage of spin-offs that were unexpected. There can, therefore, be no a-priori rules for the formulation of logistics strategies.

The analysis in this chapter shows this complexity, and seems to be a good tool for the formulation of strategies – supported by or founded on logistics – that can develop on several levels. From this point of view, we can say that logistics and supply chain management now constitute a privileged area in strategic management, a point of view also developed by Cohen and Roussel (2005). At the least, logistics offers new ways of thinking about strategy. Because it motivates and supports organizational change, it also offers new frames for piloting managerial action in a strategic way. That is why logistics and supply chain management are now such an important strategic issue.

Summary

- Firms formulate their strategies in response to intense environmental pressures.
- Logistics is an essential element of that strategy.
- The field of logistics has become progressively broader and is now very far-reaching.
- A trend from the perspective of logistics Strategy to that of strategic Logistics is apparent, representing a source of competitive advantage and/or new strategies.
- A variety of generic strategies can be identified.
- Formulation of logistics strategies must also take into account the way of linking strategic moves, the so-called itineraries.

References

Ansoff, I (1965) *Corporate Strategy*, McGraw-Hill, New York

Avenier, MJ (ed) (1997) *La stratégie 'chemin faisant'*, Economica, Paris

Buaron, R (1981) New-game strategies, *McKinsey Quarterly*, Spring, pp 24–40

Cohen, S and Roussel, J (2005) *Strategic Supply Chain Management: The 5 disciplines for top performance*, McGraw-Hill, New York

Davenport, T and Short, J (1990) The new industrial engineering: information technology and business process redesign, *Sloan Management Review*, **31** (4), Summer, pp 11–27

Ellram, LM (1991) Supply chain management: the industrial organisation perspective, *International Journal of Physical Distribution and Logistics Management*, **21** (1), pp 13–22
European Commission (1999) *Transport and Logistics in Europe*, European Commission and PricewaterhouseCoopers, Belgium
Fabbe-Costes, N (1997) Information management in the logistics service industry: a strategic response to the reintegration of logistical activities, *Transport Logistics*, **1** (2), pp 115–27
Fabbe-Costes, N (2002) Le pilotage des supply chains: un défi pour les systèmes d'information et de communication logistiques, *Gestion 2000*, Jan–Feb, pp 75–92
Fabbe-Costes, N and Colin, J (1995) Strategies developed by logistics suppliers facing the temptation for shippers to reintegrate logistics operations, 7th World Conference on Transport Research, 16–21 July 1995, Sydney, Australia
Galia website, www.galia.com
Hammer, M (1990) Reengineering work: don't automate, obliterate, *Harvard Business Review*, **68** (4), July–Aug, pp 104–12
Konsynski, BR (1993) Strategic control in the extended enterprise, *IBM Systems Journal*, **32** (1), pp 111–42
Lambert, DM, Cooper, MC and Pagh, JD (1998) Supply chain management: implementing issues and research opportunities, *International Journal of Logistics Management*, **9** (2), pp 1–18
Martinet, A C (1983) *Stratégie*, Vuibert Gestion, Paris
Mathe, H, Colin, J and Tixier, D (1983) *La logistique*, Dunod, Paris
Métais, E (2004) *Stratégie et ressources de l'entreprise: théorie et pratiques*, Economica, Paris
Morin, E (1990) *Science avec conscience*, new edn, Le Seuil-Points, Paris
Porter, M (1985) *Competitive Advantage*, Free Press/Macmillan, New York
Shiba, S, Graham, A and Walden, D (1993) *A New American TQM: Four practical revolutions in management*, Productivity Press/Center for Quality Management, Cambridge, MA
Stalk, G and Hout, T (1990) *Competing against Time: How time-based competition is reshaping global markets*, Free Press, New York
Stalk, G, Evans, P and Shulman, L (1992) Competing on capabilities: the new rules of corporate strategy, *Harvard Business Review*, Mar–Apr, pp 57–69
Tixier, D, Mathe, H and Colin, J (1996) *La logistique d'entreprise: vers un management plus compétitif*, Dunod, Paris
Wiseman, C (1985) *Strategy and Computers*, Dow Jones/Irwin, New York
Womack, J, Jones, D and Roos, D (1990) *The Machine that Changed the World*, Harper Perennial, New York

Agile supply chain operating environments – avoiding implementation pitfalls

Remko van Hoek, Cranfield School of Management

Summary

Agile capabilities in the supply chain are needed now more than ever before – but not everywhere. This chapter develops a categorization for operating environments, and shows how this can be used to assess the viability of an agile supply chain for meeting contingencies in supply and demand. Further to that, this chapter offers ways to avoid pitfalls in implementing agile capabilities in the supply chain.

Introduction

There is no shortage of strategic opportunities for using supply chains and supply chain capabilities to achieve competitiveness and to achieve faster, more profitable company growth. There is a shortage of companies that achieve full potential and develop and leverage all needed supply chain capabilities. For almost a decade now the benefit of creating a more agile and responsive supply chain has been widely accepted. Recently, however, the head of the supply chain of a major European manufacturer told me: 'We have realized the need to become more agile for years and have tried several things but do you have any suggestions for how we can actually accomplish higher levels of agility?'

The point is clear: there has been a more-or-less clear vision of the benefits of creating an agile supply chain going back to Harrison, Christopher and van Hoek (1999) defining it in terms of responsiveness to markets based upon the dimensions of market sensitivity, virtual integration, process integration and network integration (as shown in Figure 4.1). This vision has been widely cited and reinforced since as a key competitive ambition and supply chain best practice aspiration (for example, Christopher (2004) and Lee (2004)). However, there has been a shortage of studies and cases of companies actually turning the vision or ambition into reality, let alone tools that they use to do so – and the theoretical argument in the references mentioned above is not sufficiently helpful in that respect.

So we now know that the market turbulence of the 1990s was only a start, and that continuing uncertainty makes the responsiveness that comes from agile supply chains a more valuable consideration than ever before. The key word here is 'consideration'. If there is one rule in supply chain management, it is that 'There is no universal solution to all operating circumstances.' So the key questions for this chapter become: 1) where to implement agile capabilities, or 'Which operating environments most favour an agile supply chain?'; and 2) how to approach implementation of agile capabilities.

The first part of this chapter introduces contingencies or operating factors that help answer the first question. It incorporates these factors into a more comprehensive description that shows when a supply chain should focus on

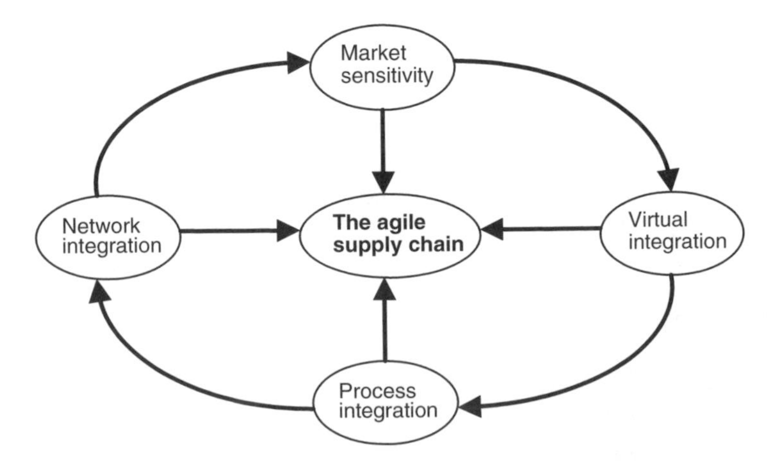

Figure 4.1 Theoretical framework for creating the agile supply chain

agility, leanness and other options. The second part of this chapter will introduce four pitfalls that companies commonly find themselves in and through which – despite good intentions and efforts to improve agility and responsiveness – they achieve anything but that. Instead they underperform by driving practice away from the agile vision and generating cost of complexity with little value return.

Operating circumstances requiring agility

Factors previously introduced include demand volatility, product variety, forecastability and 'fashion-type' short life cycles and fast delivery. Van Hoek and Harrison (2001) introduced demand and supply characteristics as dimensions impacting the relevance of agile versus alternative approaches (see Figure 4.2).

The relevance of factoring in demand and supply characteristics lies in the notion that creating the agile supply chain is about linking supply capabilities to demand requirements. In this respect, demand and supply 'characteristics' may be too general a term. There is an underlying dynamic between the two dimensions: supply abilities are to be created in response to demand requirements. Then one may think of the two dimensions as 'demand' indicating the viability of agility, and 'supply' indicating the feasibility of agility.

Responding to demand with a short lead time is a relevant feature of responsiveness to demand – but it also is a relatively basic one. It certainly does not capture a comprehensive set of responsiveness enhancers. When considering relevant agile capabilities, additional operating contingencies should be included. The remainder of this section will discuss demand and

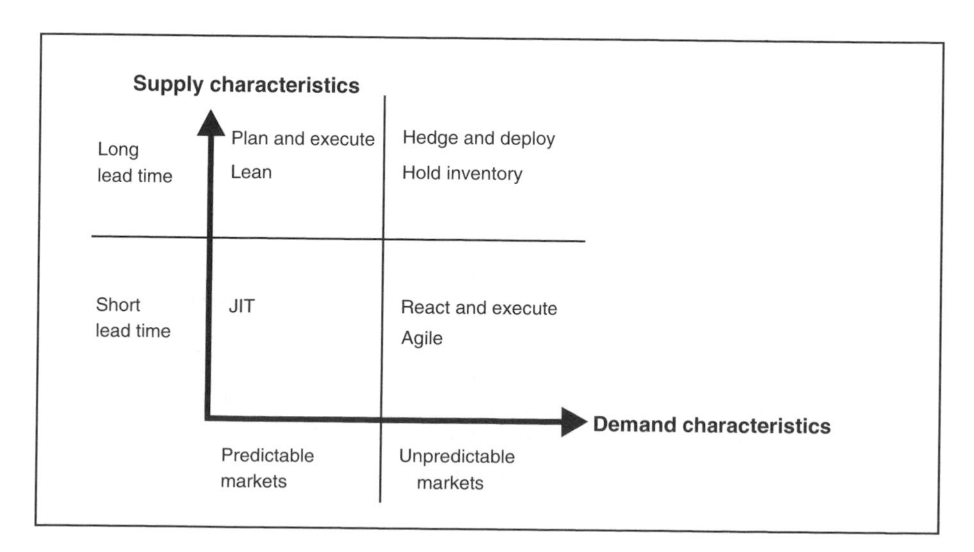

Figure 4.2 Leanness and agility under demand and supply conditions

supply contingencies to be included in the categorization for operating environments.

Demand contingencies

Returning to lead times, the length of response time is predominantly a relative measure. When developing a cross-industry categorization for operating environments, the absolute length in weeks, days or hours may be less relevant than the relative length. Lead-time tolerance is often the most relevant factor, as it captures leeway that supply chains have in responding to demand. It also incorporates the fact that reliability of delivery may be more important than absolute lead time. A lead-time tolerance, therefore, contains both a speed and a reliability element.

'Forecastability' of demand is a better measure than predictions of market conditions because it is more closely linked to supply chain management capabilities. Market conditions are generally very difficult to predict at the detailed level (of individual SKUs, for example), but that does not mean that companies cannot forecast demand relatively accurately. More important from the contingency point of view is the fact that forecastability includes a supply chain management requirement of aligning mid- to longer-term capacity decisions to demand, rather than the hard-to-predict market conditions. Of course, one might argue that an ultimately responsive system removes the need to forecast, but this is more of a theoretical perspective than a realistic one. Irrespective of the supply chain's responsiveness to actual orders, companies still have to forecast for mid- to longer-term factors, including advance orders to suppliers, long-cycle-time production processes and capacity-building plans.

Demand for a product is rarely stable, but contains peaks and troughs. It is traditionally difficult to accommodate this variance in demand across a given time period, because every supply chain has a limited capacity and other constraints, such as maximum order volumes or limits on the availability of expensive slack capacity. However, there are two underlying features here: 1) the difference between the peaks and troughs of demand; and 2) the frequency with which up- and downswings occur.

For the latter, a standard seasonal pattern may have just one peak (in the summer for garden furniture, for example), whereas the fashion industry may have a minimum of six or eight seasons. Retail promotions may have peaks every other week. These seasonal swings in demand may be significant, with peak demands often accounting for 60 to 70 per cent of total demand.

Figure 4.3 shows an operationalization of the above three demand contingencies – lead-time tolerance, forecastability and variance in volume.

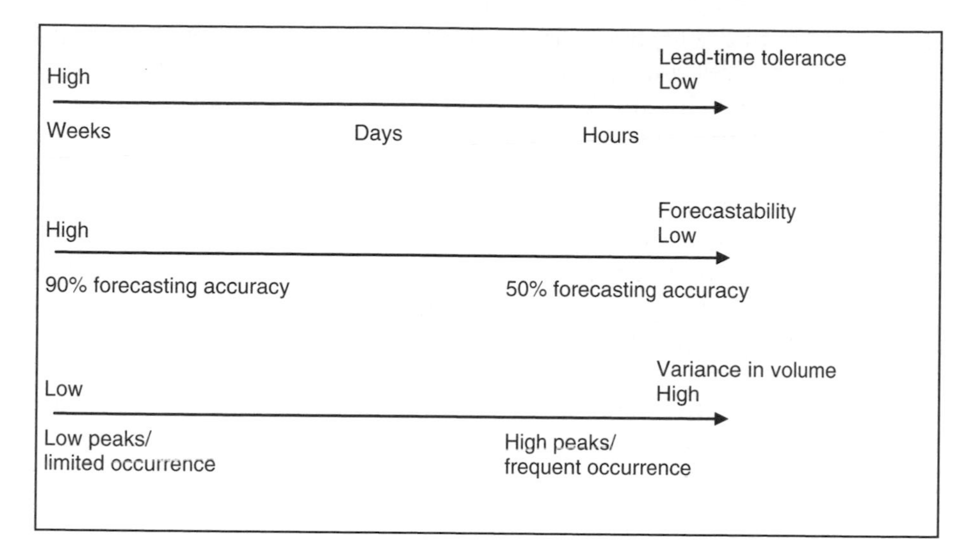

Figure 4.3 Demand contingencies impacting the viability of an agile supply chain

Supply contingencies

What are key supply contingencies that impact the feasibility of creating an agile supply chain? It is in this area that most gaps in current knowledge exist, as most of the publications on agile supply chains focus on the relevance of the approach itself in modern markets. Given the strength of this argument in favour of agility, and its importance in the current uncertain economic landscape, it is time to move beyond this basic view and consider the four layers (at least) of supply contingencies – or requirements for an agile supply chain.

'Postponement' has been widely identified as a mechanism that can support the creation of responsive supply. Delaying inventory allocation in the supply chain creates hedging options for responding to demand. This logistics postponement (delaying time and place functionality decisions) is helpful in the distribution segment of the supply chain but ultimately only offers partial responsiveness. It still assumes that stocks of finished goods build in anticipation of unknown demand, with all the risks of stock-outs still largely in place. Stock-outs generally have a very high cost in agile environments. It is for this reason that 'form postponement' is used – to delay the specification of final form and function of products until the last moment. Many companies do this by delaying packaging, labelling, adding documentation or product peripherals. Extending postponement into manufacturing, assembly, module manufacturing, etc may help create the greater flexibility required for agility.

Associated with the need for form and function customization is the manufacturing and engineering principle of 'design variance' across products and product lines. In order to achieve levels of customization beyond the appearance of products, designs may have to vary beyond packaging – even beyond modules and into components and more basic features of design. This creates obvious design, manufacturing, sourcing and inventory complexities that have to be dealt with in agile operating environments. This contingency also shows how creating an agile supply chain requires more than revising logistics and distribution management – but it can have an impact all the way back to product design. The impact on suppliers and trading partners is discussed as part of the next contingency.

'Supply chain partner modularity' specifies the extent to which individual companies participating in the creation of an agile supply chain will have to align operations through the redesign of management practices and interfaces for the flow of goods and information. Some examples may help clarify this. Traditional sourcing and contract logistics has a buy–sell approach that suggests interfaces limited to a transactional level. JIT sourcing has more extensive interfaces with the sharing of demand data and alignment of operations. Integrated contract manufacturing, in which a third party controls the majority of build and make operations, extends the interface beyond aligned supply into integrated form and functionality creation. Fourth-party logistics is similar to this, with a third party taking over the organization and coordination of the entire flow of goods, information and management for the entire logistics function, based around tightly structured interfaces. These approaches lead to a modular supply chain in which boundaries between partners are blurred and players are all orchestrated around real demand and service to the end customer.

It is important to note here that this contingency is not limited to upstream suppliers, but also involves the downstream trading partners between the company and the end customer. This is traditionally a hard set of interfaces – compared with upstream suppliers who are paid for their supply efforts, giving companies an obvious lever in the structuring of these interfaces. The implication of agile reasoning, however, is that downstream partners and direct customers can also encourage alignment around this approach. Then channel interfaces should be structured around end-customer demand contingencies. Service to the end customer gives the key to this; it is an objective that all supply chain players share and where there is significant unification in purpose and objectives.

This brings us a final contingency, which is the 'supply chain scope'. In order completely to meet the standards demanded for customization, modularity and partner integration, the scale or scope of supply chain involvement may be significant. It goes far beyond traditional views, and develops one-to-one interfaces that extend into a 'value chain'. A value chain is a sequence of one-to-one interfaces leading up to a customer, while a supply chain has many-to-many interfaces and interconnections, which must be dynamically rearranged around key processes and players in response to real demand. A network approach is far more appropriate here.

Figure 4.4 shows an operationalization of the above four supply contingencies – postponement, design variance, partner modularity and supply chain scope.

The categorization for operating environments

Figure 4.5 shows a categorization for operating environments based on the contingency factors introduced in the previous section. In the categorization a number of alternative approaches to agility are mentioned. The first consideration is to distinguish A, B, C products – based on Pareto analysis. Here A products (accounting for 80 per cent of volume and 20 per cent of orders) are more standardized, and the greater forecastability, lower volume variance and lower customization make them more suited to lean approaches. B products are more variable and more suited to agility.

Efficient consumer response (ECR) and quick response (QR) are generally better in environments where demand requirements particularly impact delivery and distribution, but have less effect on upstream operations. Mass customization is generally better in environments with modest to significantly

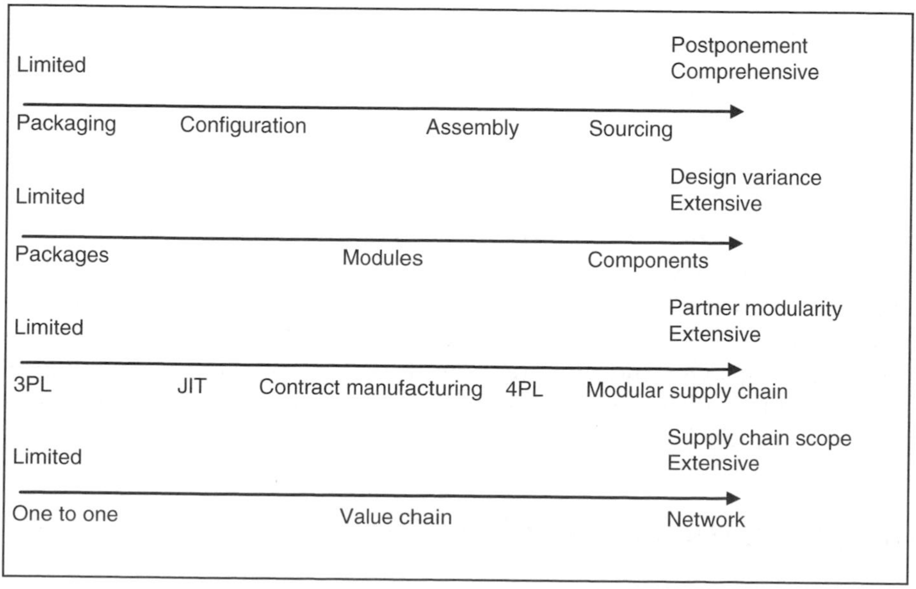

Limited — Postponement Comprehensive

Packaging → Configuration → Assembly → Sourcing

Limited — Design variance Extensive

Packages → Modules → Components

Limited — Partner modularity Extensive

3PL → JIT → Contract manufacturing → 4PL → Modular supply chain

Limited — Supply chain scope Extensive

One to one → Value chain → Network

Figure 4.4 Supply contingencies impacting the feasibility of an agile supply chain

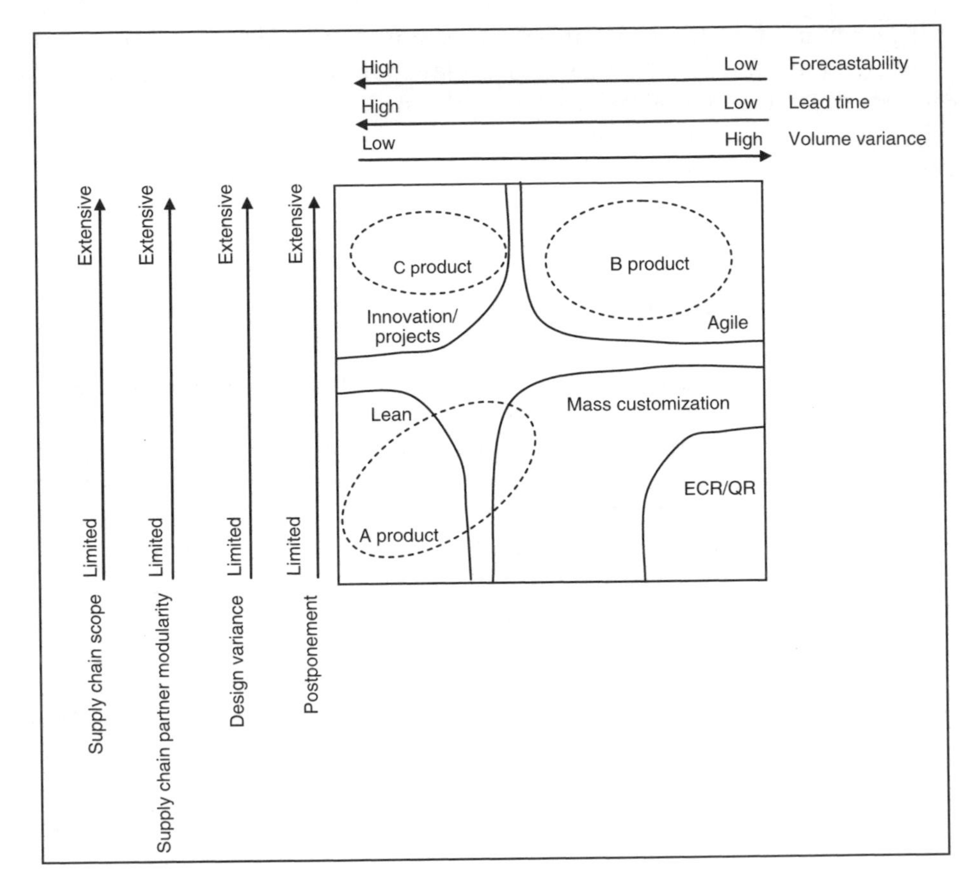

Figure 4.5 Categorization of operating environments

challenging demand, which can be met with medium postponement and customization.

Agility is positioned near project environments. This is the right place from a supply contingency point of view, but is not so good from a demand contingency point of view. For example, in environments of innovation and single projects, lead-time leeway is often significantly bigger.

With contingencies and operating environments considered, the question that remains is: how to avoid pitfalls in implementing agility? This is the focus of the next section.

Mitigating the minefield of pitfalls

Figure 4.6 conceptualizes the 'minefield' of creating the agile supply chain. If all goes well companies accomplish the four central dimensions of the agile supply chain as introduced in the previous section. However, lacking practical

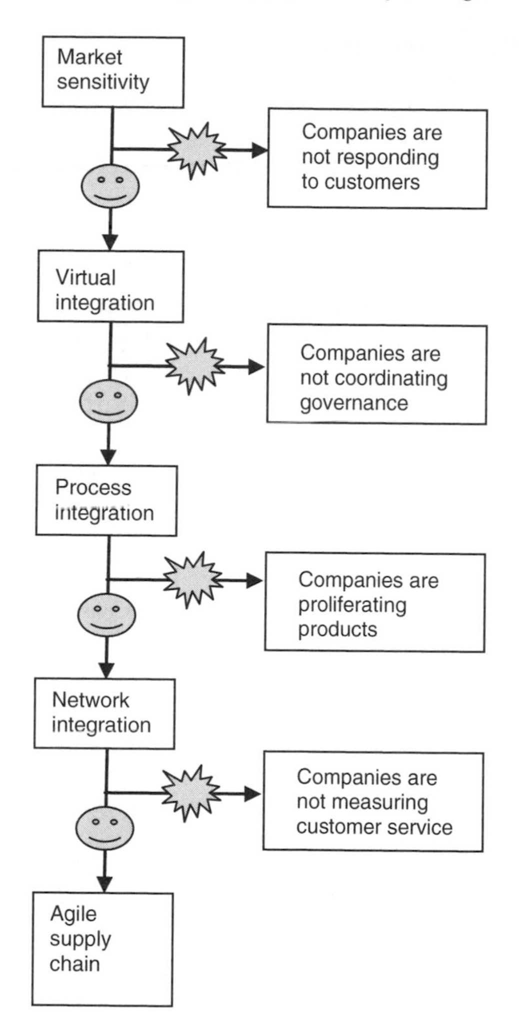

Figure 4.6 The minefield of creating the agile supply chain

guidance and experience there are pitfalls at every step of the way and companies can be found to be:

- not actually responding to the customer as opposed to creating market sensitivity;
- not coordinating governance, which allows for too much or too little responsiveness as opposed to virtual integration;
- proliferating product in meaningless and valueless areas because of failures in process integration; and
- despite a coming focus on service, not actually measuring that, leading to failed network integration.

Poor response to customers

It is common practice for companies to measure customer service in multiple ways. Customer satisfaction is the most widely used measure. However, there are several challenges with customer satisfaction measurement and surveys:

- Average scores hide extremes at the end (problems and excellence).
- What opinions and strategies are behind subjective measures?
- Who is speaking? There are many different voices within the customer organization.
- What is the value of individual responses averaged out (innovators, key accounts, marginal accounts)?
- There may be a lack of clear implications for service (what does a 3.75 mean in comparison to a 3.95 score?)

In response to these challenges, companies like GE, Honeywell and the Ford Motor Company have developed voice of the customer (VOC) processes. These aim to go beyond customer satisfaction measurement by crafting a more comprehensive exchange with selected customers.

Typical features of this exchange include:

- senior-manager-to-senior-manager meetings to avoid leaving the exchange to revenue-pressured situations, to signify commitment and to elevate the conversation;
- expansion of the interaction to an ongoing exchange to drive beyond measurement at specific points in time only and to establish sustained improvement and alignment;
- involving additional functions including logistics and engineering and multiple contacts on the customer side in order to broaden the exchange into a bi-directional learning and alignment opportunity;
- establishing joint improvement initiatives to turn the exchange into more than a listening exercise, including so-called 'At the customer, for the customer' teams.

The key distinctions between voice of the customer processes and customer satisfaction measurement are:

- It is based upon conversations, not surveys, which helps capture the story behind the survey scores and teach more about what actually drives scores.
- It is not the task of the customer service department but often starts with a senior executive sponsor talking to a customer peer and is followed by cross-functional work groups at a management and executive level

working together on improving responsiveness and process alignment where that matters to the customer.

- It is ongoing, not a point measurement, as initial conversations are followed up with reviews of process improvements.
- It is customer-centric as opposed to measuring average market performance scores.
- It captures multiple inputs from the customer not just a single respondent; this is important because there are many voices of the customer and it matters who is talking.
- It is linked to action, with project teams deployed 'at the customer, for the customer'; hence the outcomes of the review are not internalized but used as a basis for customer-focused action.
- It actually improves customer relations through improved learning about the customer, relationship development and resource investments to address service issues, and improvement opportunities.

Overall, voice of the customer leads to much better market sensitivity as opposed to running the risk of misguided interpretation of limited channels for capturing market input with no tie to actual customer-centric improvements.

Governance not supporting virtual integration

Agility requires the ability to be able to respond to local market requirements and opportunities. But this does not mean that companies should not aim at leveraging skills and capabilities across the regions in which they operate – let alone avoiding reinventing the wheel across parts of the organization. In the terminology of Bartlett and Goshal (1989), local responsiveness and global efficiency need to be integrated into a network organization that is a virtually integrated entity, despite operating in multiple locations and regions.

Most often, however, companies tend towards either local responsiveness or strong global standardization and organization. Hewlett-Packard used to be in the former camp. At one point, for example, they found that there were dozens of similar B2B efforts under way across the company with – at best – informal coordination between teams. Rightfully, HP did not respond with (what would have been intuitive to many) a centralization of efforts and control. Instead, they developed a distributed governance approach that allowed for local responsiveness but leveraged lessons learned for the company and avoided duplication of effort.

In order to find a way to balance proliferation of businesses and divisions, high divisional autonomy and complexity in organization, operations (including redundant operations) and key support processes such as procurement and customer support, HP launched a supply chain governance council. The charter that its executive committee set was to implement pan-company efficiency initiatives and uncover supply chain-based revenue opportunities. Specific goals included: to establish and drive a coordinated approach to investments pertaining to opportunities that have a pan-enterprise scope and impact and supporting executive awareness of key initiatives to avoid reinventing the wheel.

This means that the council explicitly does not get involved with initiatives that are specific to an individual business or region; it does not centrally control supply chain governance but it does support larger initiatives from which many parts of the organization can and should benefit. It also provides senior management with a method for supporting and steering direction on most important opportunities and directions.

Four key operating rules at the council are:

- mandated senior participation;
- focus on enterprise-wide initiatives;
- driving initiative development through divisional sponsorship;
- funding initiatives from divisional budgets.

The latter two are particularly interesting, as they help avoid creating a corporate-centre approach that can dictate without the businesses caring or paying for it.

Keys to success in a governance approach like this one include:

- Avoiding layering a governance council on top of existing structures. If it generates more governance, this not only could conflict with existing structures but might enhance bureaucracy rather than agility.
- Keeping it simple and crisp. The governance council serves the purpose of ensuring more agility for the company as opposed to just agility locally. In order to accomplish that, there should be minimal procedures and rules.
- Ensuring that what is purely local should remain local. If there is no benefit to leveraging a particular initiative to the global or corporate level, keep it local.

Meaningless product proliferation

A particular area of concern when it comes to process integration is product proliferation. Because of process misalignment between several parts of the supply chain, companies often end up proliferating products driven by internal misalignment rather than the market. How this often happens is: R&D want to innovate and expand product ranges, and sales want to create more opportunities to sell, while the supply chain and operations want to avoid margin reductions from cost of complexity in operations. A lack of process integration leads to uncontrolled efforts disconnected from market opportunity.

New products are created hoping that this will aid in growing the business by offering more revenue opportunities. In theory this improves the ability to respond to customer demand. In reality, however, companies typically get a lot of product proliferation wrong and end up creating too many products that do not sell, adding cost and needless complexity into their supply chain.

One company found that the bottom 25 per cent of products generated less than 1 per cent of revenue and were actually unprofitable, reducing the company's overall profit. Another company saw its SKU count double in two years, with SKU growth far outpacing revenue growth, resulting in a reduction of volumes per product, and return on investment in designing and marketing products – while mushrooming the cost of warehousing. While all of this was happening, the supply chain was left to cope with the consequences, with the business not really owning any responsibility for SKU management. One warehouse manager of this company said: 'When I meet people from the business I ask them how many SKUs they have in the warehouse. They never get it right and always underestimate.'

To summarize, common flags for product proliferation include:

1. growth of SKU count outpacing revenue growth;
2. SKUs that do not meet revenue and volume thresholds for generating return on design, marketing and shipping;
3. SKU management not being distributed across the business, and no accountability for or even transparency of SKU proliferation in the business.

Additional complexity flags can be found in warehouse and sales including:

- *warehouse flags:*
  - ongoing order and shipment size reduction;
  - a constant need for more stock locations in the warehouse;
  - night shifts and rush shipments outside seasonal peaks;
- *sales flags:*
  - a catalogue that is as thick as the *Yellow Pages*, running the risk of confusing customers;
  - more products than any salesperson could every carry;
  - special SKUs being added based upon special (key-)customer requests, events or market opportunities but perhaps not being removed after the event.

Faced with a lot of the unwelcome consequences of SKU proliferation outlined above, Company A, a consumer products company, reduced its SKU count by 30 per cent over three years while growing the company and adding new products, breaking away from flag 1. It did so by actively managing to avoid flags 2 and 3. The company initiated an SKU management effort – introduced by the CEO – with a mandate that 50 per cent of SKUs that did not meet revenue thresholds would be cut each quarter. The reason for the target being 50 per cent and not 100 per cent was that new products were being developed in the market that might not have been completely successful, there were products that did not perform steadily every quarter (because of seasonality, for example), and it left the business some autonomy in making cut decisions. Key to this approach was that it established SKU management as an ongoing discipline. A lot of companies do one-off efforts, but, as a manager from Company A says: 'Without sustaining the management focus, SKU count is likely to creep back up in no time. You cannot expect behaviour to just change without ongoing focus and accountability.'

In order to accomplish this accountability, SKU count was elevated to one of the measures on the global dashboard that was reviewed monthly by the senior executive team. Additionally, a so-called 'glide-path' was established. This was a set of SKU reduction targets on a time line. In addition to sustaining the focus on – and accountability for – SKU reduction, incorporating the SKU count on the dashboard also removed decisions from the executive level. The supply chain team dedicated a person to the SKU effort and this person created transparency to the business about the SKU count, flagged SKU levels when they were not on the glide-path and offered help in reducing the SKU count. Because senior management owned the outcomes of the effort at the dashboard level, the supply chain team was positioned as aiding the business rather than being seen negatively. Furthermore, it removed discussion about the effort from the executive level. According to the senior supply chain executive, this is important because otherwise 'You end up with emotion involved at this level, resulting in endless discussion instead of focused action.'

Incorrect measurement that focuses responsiveness wrongly

All companies include customer service in some form in their performance measurement system. However, almost all operationalize this measurement internally, leading to responsiveness that is misguided and focused wrongly – not being directly and fully on customers. In particular, most companies measure delivery service in one or multiple ways based upon their internal definition of success. Typically the measures focus on how reliably and fast the company delivered against the timetable it put forward. This misses the point, as this timetable might not be aligned with the customers' needs. So companies are not tracking responsiveness to customer need at all. The better way is to ask customers for their desired delivery window and measure execution against that customer-defined measure of success. General Electric realized this when it presented high delivery-reliability scores from its own measurement to customers and received a negative reaction. In short, customers reacted that performance was not at all good by their measurement, which considered the time when they needed deliveries to take place.

GE changed its measurement set towards what it calls span measurement. Span stands for the range of delivery around customer-requested due dates. Essentially, the company now measures, across all deliveries globally, how close it was to the delivery date the customer requested when ordering. In its plastics business the company brought span down from 30 days to just a few days – meaning that every customer can depend upon GE delivering any product, anywhere in the world, when the customer asks for it, with a maximum variation of a few days.

Experience from GE suggests the value of several actions to improve the measurement for agility:

- Share measurement dashboards with customers, and aim to measure your performance using the measures customers use to measure your company.
- Do not measure against your own measures of success, but ask the customer what defines success.
- Hold all parts of the supply chain accountable against the customer-defined measure of success, so that there is no escape from market sensitivity.

Enhancing the vision of agility

This chapter has offered practical findings from aspiring practitioners, several years of research and dozens of case studies. As valuable a starting point as the theory surrounding the vision of creating an agile supply chain is, it is still only vision-centred. The experiences and cases presented in this chapter show where the vision can be supplemented, thereby enhancing the theoretical framework presented in Figure 4.1. Figure 4.7 captures the particular axioms identified and visually displays the enhanced agile supply chain theoretical framework.

Conclusion and reflections

This chapter has attempted to offer additional insight into the questions of where and how to consider developing agile capabilities in the supply chain. The identification of operating environments that favour – or disfavour – the agile supply chain gives a more realistic chance of successful implementation. Avoiding the implementation pitfalls will further increase the likelihood of success.

As one of the authors of the original agile supply chain vision I would like to apologize to the head of the supply chain mentioned at the start of this chapter. I hope that this contribution will be more helpful and make up for the shortcomings of the original vision.

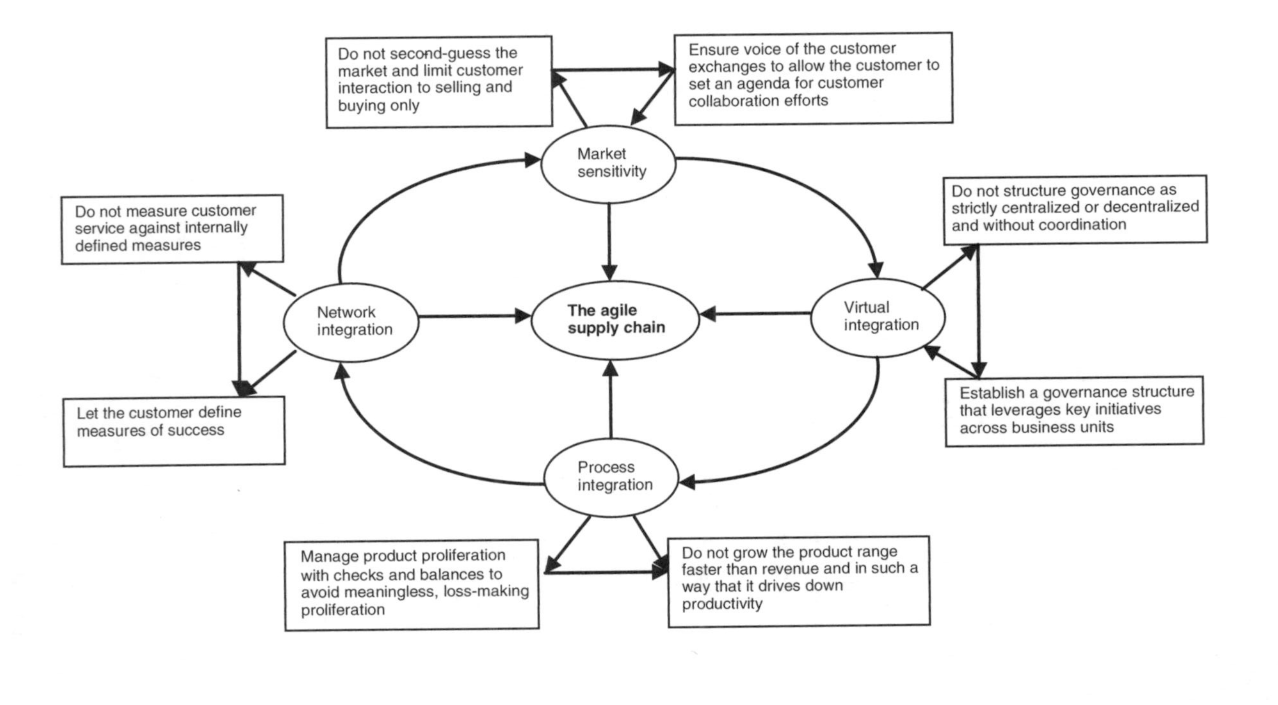

Figure 4.7 Enhanced agile supply chain theoretical framework

References

Bartlett, CA and Goshal, S (1989) *Managing Across Borders*, Harvard Business School Press, Boston, MA

Christopher, MC (2004) Supply chains: a marketing perspective, in *Understanding Supply Chains*, ed S New and R Westbrook, pp 69–108, Oxford University Press, Oxford

Harrison, A, Christopher, MC and van Hoek, RI (1999) *Creating the Agile Supply Chain*, Institute of Transport and Logistics, Corby

Lee, H (2004) The Triple-A supply chain, *Harvard Business Review*, Oct

van Hoek, R and Harrison, A (2001) Editorial, Special issue: *Creating the Agile Supply Chain, International Journal of Physical Distribution and Logistics Management*, **31** (4), pp 231–34

5

Time compression in the supply chain

Adrian Beesley, DHL Exel Supply Chain

This chapter explores the 'time compression' approach to business process improvement in the supply chain. The concept and strategic relevance of this approach was first published in the West in the early 1990s, and it still offers good potential and a fresh approach to achieving competitiveness through re-engineering. The rate of adoption of time compression (TC) has been slow and this is partly because the approach requires the total commitment of the whole business from the top downwards. Coupled with this is the fact that change within any organization is always challenging, particularly when it involves difficult decisions in one department or function to benefit another, for the good of the whole company and even the broader supply chain. Supply chain objectives and their relation to time compression implementation strategies are touched on, coupled with explanations of achievable benefits and case studies.

Time compression

Over 200 years ago Benjamin Franklin stated that 'Time is money' and this was reiterated in 1990 by Stalk and Hout claiming that 'time is the last exploitable resource'. Today time is still largely ignored by many companies because of enduring approaches that create inertia in organizational structures and associated business processes. Managers have always used time to manage their operations, but control has usually been limited to a segment or business function within the supply chain. For example, in the past, time was used for work study and human performance measurement, but it is usually associated with long-established and outdated business processes. Moreover this approach – and even some modern approaches – focuses purely on the value-adding elements of business processes, which often account only for 5 per cent (sometimes referred to as the business process velocity) of total process time. This emphasis on just the value-add time tends to focus on making people work faster – often with a risk to quality, safety and ultimately livelihoods as competitiveness starts to become an issue.

There is another problematical dimension to these approaches in that the time-based implications of individual actions only recognize one side of a 'trade-off' that may have holistic implications for the broader supply chain. Examples include companies that manage capacity and cost through applications and frameworks such as traditional accounting, functional budgeting, manufacturing resource planning (MRPII) and even enterprise resource planning (ERP). The resultant scope of thinking is usually constrained by not recognizing how time, stock, resource and service interrelate with each other along the supply chain. Using time as a measure creates a deeper understanding of a total holistic business process, thereby providing scope for optimization and a pragmatic approach to change. The use of time in this context is directly linked with competitiveness – and this is the meaning of the 'time compression' (TC) approach.

Time compression and competition

Womack, Jones and Roos's landmark work within the automotive sector in 1990 pointed out that competition had become more aggressive and customers were more demanding, so there is a constant need for a new source of competitiveness. In 1991, Reich went further and demonstrated the general applicability of this statement in a global context across many industrial sectors. Global competitive forces are placing increasing pressures on markets and supply chains. Demand for increasing service, product performance and variety across supply chains that extend across the globe creates new demands and challenges.

The TC approach is one route to addressing these demands and improving the design, balance and flexibility of the supply chain. If this approach is combined with a focus on customers who operate in markets that are time-sensitive, then a further dimension is added to TC. Stalk and Hout in 1990 make the comment that 'the world is moving to increased variety with better levels of service and faster levels of innovation. For suppliers that operate and service these sectors, time based competition is of significant advantage.'

A survey conducted by the European Logistics Association in 2004 identified factors that are increasing the complexity of supply chains (see Figure 5.1). This highlights the continuing trend to source products from outside traditional

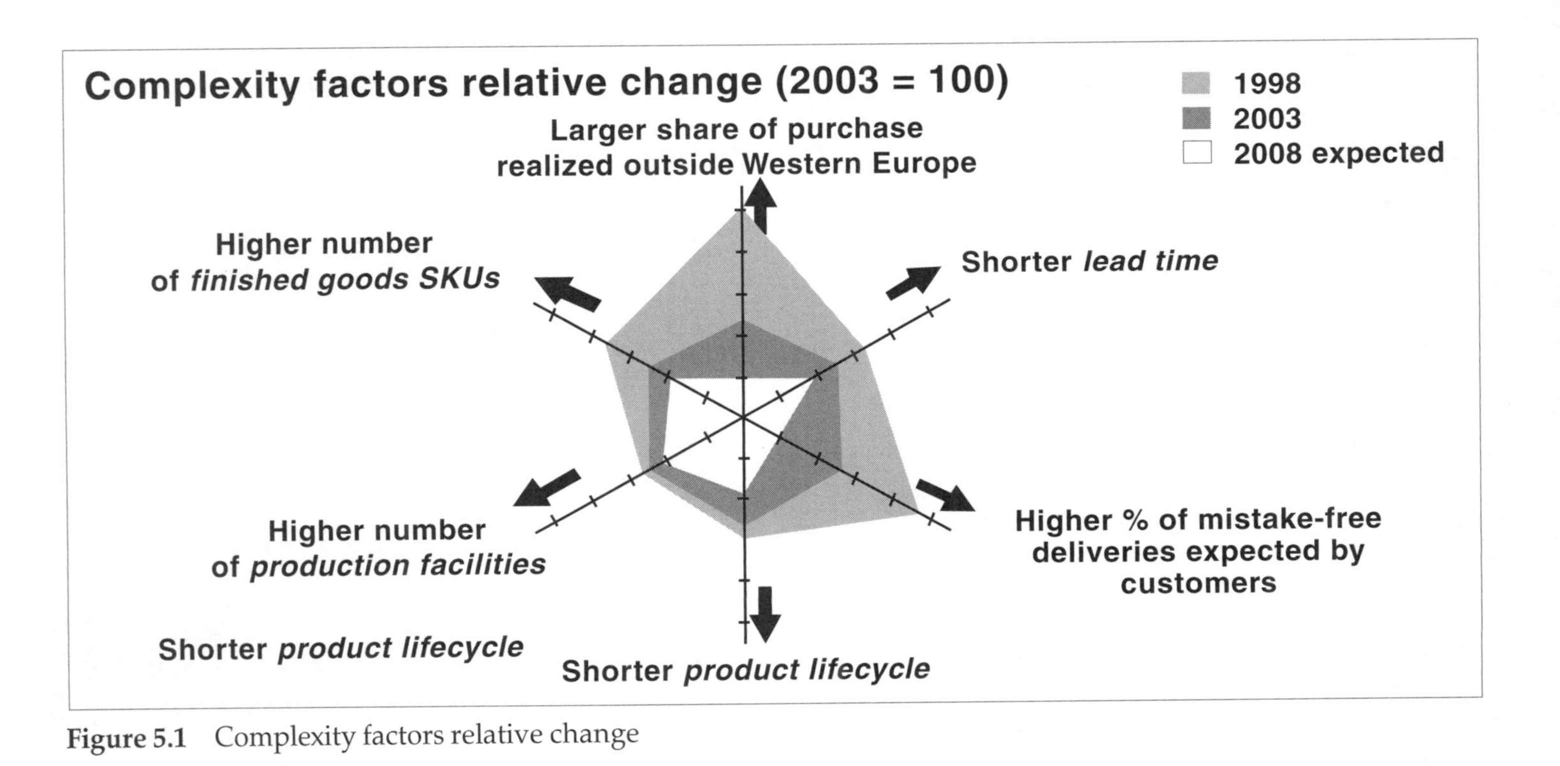

Figure 5.1 Complexity factors relative change

supply markets and this is coupled with the concerns and demands for mistake-free deliveries. Despite the presence of these two significant factors, the increase in SKUs will continue, as will demand for shorter lead times.

As a result, cycle times are a key consideration for most companies in the West. However, it is interesting that the more holistic approach offered by TC remains an opportunity for many companies. This is borne out by the content of numerous requests for quotations directed to third-party logistics providers over the past decade. The majority of these tend to focus on cost reduction, often with little or no consideration for the attainment of holistic supply chain benefits.

The question is why some major corporations seem to ignore, or do not directly engage with, this approach. The answer may lie in the fact that the use of TC to some extent relies on viewing the supply chain as a business process that can be designed and managed, ie the original concept of supply chain management (SCM). Some commentators such as Lamming (2002) consider the idea of managing the supply chain as a holistic entity to be totally impractical. He considers SCM to be a flawed concept because it has been around since 1982 and industry is still having difficulty with implementing and mastering this area of potential competitiveness. This may explain the reason why some of the more insular approaches to business improvement still dominate company key objectives. This debate will no doubt continue irrespective of whether SCM or, say, network management is the approach for the future.

What is time compression?

The key aspect for the use of time is that it is not necessarily about being faster or the fastest. Quality is paramount to competitiveness and compromising, say, quality for speed is not the primary objective. A TC approach focuses on how companies use time to deliver a sustainable fast response to customer needs, through business processes that are organized around a strategic time-based focus. The concept is about strengthening the holistic supply chain structure to achieve time-based objectives with tactical decisions made at the correct level to enable the speed of response.

The term 'time compression' was originally introduced by New in 1992, and in its most basic form relates to the reduction of the time consumed by business processes through the elimination of non-value-adding process time. Value-add processes are defined as entities that transform inputs into outputs that are of value to the customer, that they are willing to pay for (or negate their costs) and that involve no correction or rework (ie they are right first time). Some processes may be identified as producing very little added value and this may highlight the need to totally re-engineer them.

One of the reasons why the approach is important relates to the levels of time compression that can be achieved across business processes. Within, for example, a typical UK manufacturing company, at least 95 per cent of the process time is accounted as non-value-adding. This well-established statistic is supported in the UK by the University of Warwick's Time Compression Programme (1995) and in the USA by Barker (1994). Consultants (SUCCESS, 2004) confirm that these sorts of value-add statistics still hold true, making the approach powerful as well as relevant in today's business environment.

If this statistic is viewed in the context of a typical supply chain, as little as 0.01 per cent of time adds value. However, New (1992) demonstrated that all these percentages require qualification on two counts. First, a large proportion of the non-value-adding time is due to product queuing, so the value-adding percentage is a function of how much is being pushed through the supply chain at a particular time. Even if a particular supply chain is grossly inefficient, but has only one order during a particular period, the actual value-adding time is high because of minimal queuing. A second consideration is that inventory should add value and is, therefore, usually included in the overall value-adding percentage. Consequently a view has to be taken on how much of the inventory element of the pipeline – usually measured in days or hours of throughput cover – is actually adding value. The amount of value added by inventory is intrinsically linked to the process cycle times, as well as demand throughput levels and predictability.

The statistics do, however, show the immensity of the opportunities for companies and their associated supply chains – and they differ significantly from any perceived opportunity that might be available from, say, a cost-based approach.

Time compression can be achieved using any one or a combination of seven strategies identified by Carter, Melnyk and Handfield (1994) and these can be applied from company level through to the total supply chain. They are summarized as:

- *simplification:* removing process complexity that has accumulated over time;
- *integration:* improving information flows and linkages to create integrated information flows and operations;
- *standardization:* using generic best-practice processes – and standardized components, modules and information protocols;
- *concurrent working:* moving from sequential to parallel working;
- *variance control:* monitoring processes and detecting problems at an early stage so that corrective action can be taken to avoid quality- and time-related waste;
- *automation:* applied to improve the effectiveness and efficiency of entities and activities within the supply chain;
- *resource planning:* allocating resources in line with SCM best practice, for example planning by investigating bottleneck activities and considering use of multi-skilled workforces to provide resource flexibility.

These strategies should ideally be utilized in the sequence in which they appear. However, depending on a particular supply chain or company situation, various stages and combinations may be more pragmatically deployed to account for changes that are already – or about to be – in place. Through the use of these strategies TC can directly achieve increases in value-add time and help to contribute to objectives associated with fundamental principles of SCM and best practice.

Putting aside the debate surrounding the merits of SCM, a brief description of the nature of the key SCM principles and how they relate to time is given in Table 5.1. It can be argued that these principles hold true irrespective of whether a company is using a holistic approach to SCM, or a more focused approach.

The time compression approach – competitive advantage

The time compression approach can be applied at two levels – firstly, as a holistic approach in the context of the above principles, and secondly, as a competitive market focus. The former can be regarded as an internal time focus of the key supply chain processes that lie on, or close to, the critical path of the business process. The latter is the supply chain's external time that is of direct value to the customer. Both are interdependent and have outcomes that are strategically significant.

Referring to business strategy, Ohmae (1965) states that competitiveness relates to three basic elements: the customer, the competition and the company. There must be differentiation between the elements of value and cost if competitiveness is to emerge. A TC approach addresses these two sources of differentiation in a specific way. The first objective must be the elimination of non-value activities, ie waste, thereby maximizing the value created in the supply chain. The removal of non-value activities in turn gives rise to a cost advantage, hence forming the basis of cost differentiation. Tersine and Hummingbird (1995) state that 'managing time is the mirror image of managing quality, cost, innovation and productivity. Reducing wasted time automatically improves the other measures of performance in a multiplier fashion.' If, however, companies go for the reverse and apply cost reduction initiatives without a reference to the time-based implications, additional costs may be incurred elsewhere in the supply chain. An example relating to inventory positioning demonstrates this point. At the outset of a cost-reduction initiative it might be argued that upgrading a warehouse management system (WMS) will deliver cost advantages. It may, for example, reduce product storage and retrieval times, and drive cost reductions associated with resource utilization. However, a time-based examination of the

Table 5.1 SCM principles relating to time

	Nature of the principle	**Useful attributes of a time compression approach**
The principle of end-user focus	Long-term supply chain profitability is dependent on the end (ultimate) user being satisfied. This acts as the focus for all supply chain design, development and process engineering.	Time compression requires that the end user is identified as the principal anchor point. This provides the focus for all time-based parameter measurement across the supply chain.
The principle of horizontal boundary definition	Different end-user needs are more competitively satisfied by channels (horizontally defined routes or workflow) designed and engineered ideally across the supply chain from a logistics service perspective.	Time defines the principal characteristics of the logistically distinct channels and service needs. The time compression approach provides a good diagnostic and basis for redesign.
The principle of vertical boundary definition	Boundaries of ownership and control (dividing the chain vertically) should be positioned to suit the needs of the end user according to best practice and make–buy theory.	The consumption of non-value time highlights where ownership and general boundary issues exist and require adjustment.
The principle of inventory positioning	The positioning, levels and characteristics of inventory are best determined in a total supply chain context to suit end-user needs in line with stock and postponement theory.	Time and cost provide a good deterministic framework with cycle time as a fundamental driver of stock positioning, levels and service. 'Value-add stock' is a time-based diagnostic.
The principle of control over demand dynamics	Understanding and levels of control over demand dynamics are best achieved by having a holistic supply chain perspective. The principal basis is through information integration and the use of best-practice relationship management.	Time measures the problem and time compression tackles the root causes of demand dynamics.
The principle of cooperation and coordination	The attainment of the above principles requires cooperation and coordination between supply chain participants. For this to work effectively each supply chain participant must have self-defined and motivating objectives based on trust and some common business aspirations.	Time provides a common and trustworthy metric across the supply chain that highlights the opportunities and issues.

holistic business process asks whether the particular segment of the supply chain could operate on a just-in-time or a make-to-order basis. This total supply chain perspective may remove or displace the stock point – and hence the requirement for a WMS. In addition, if process times are compressed in other parts of the supply chain, the economic structure of the supply system may change the appropriate locations for inventory stock points, and the short-term cost savings associated with the proposed warehouse system could be negated by a new inventory regime. If the new WMS is still installed, the associated payback demands may impose an inappropriate constraint preventing future supply chain optimization – with ramifications in terms of cost, service levels, flexibility and agility.

The time compression approach – cost advantage

Cost reduction generally occurs as a direct result of the removal or compression of non-value-added time. This time compression can result in a number of cost savings associated with the removal of fixed and variable overheads (such as rent and management), direct costs (such as labour and materials) and working capital. Other cost savings depend on the nature of the compression, perhaps minimizing risk in the decision process by making relevant information available earlier in the process. The reduction – or even removal – of a rework activity can result from process change such as compression of information queues. These improvements can also have ramifications downstream and upstream in the chain, by reducing or removing expediting activities that are in place to deal with ongoing inadequacies.

The cost implications of compressing time are extensive and complex – but rarely absent. This is why the prescribed approach is to focus on time that directly affects the service a supply chain can offer, without the complications of identifying every cost 'trade-off'. In the past, this cost-based focus has been encouraged by the use of performance measures linking profit margins with cost. With the TC approach there may be a requirement to determine cost values associated with the processes, to assist with evaluation and project prioritization. Generally, the time-based implications of any proposal are easy to comprehend and quantify, because the length of time consumed by the process is proportional to the costs (New, 1992).

The SUCCESS programme, a joint university and industry initiative, developed a toolkit called supply chain time and cost mapping (SCTCM) to combine time-based process mapping with process cost analysis. The former highlights opportunities using value-add analysis (see Figure 5.2) and the latter translates and attributes functional costs to processes. SCTCM has the benefit of showing how time, value-add and cost interrelate along the supply chain. This can be useful for prioritizing projects, analysis and gaining buy-in to the TC approach. However, the benefits have to be weighed against the

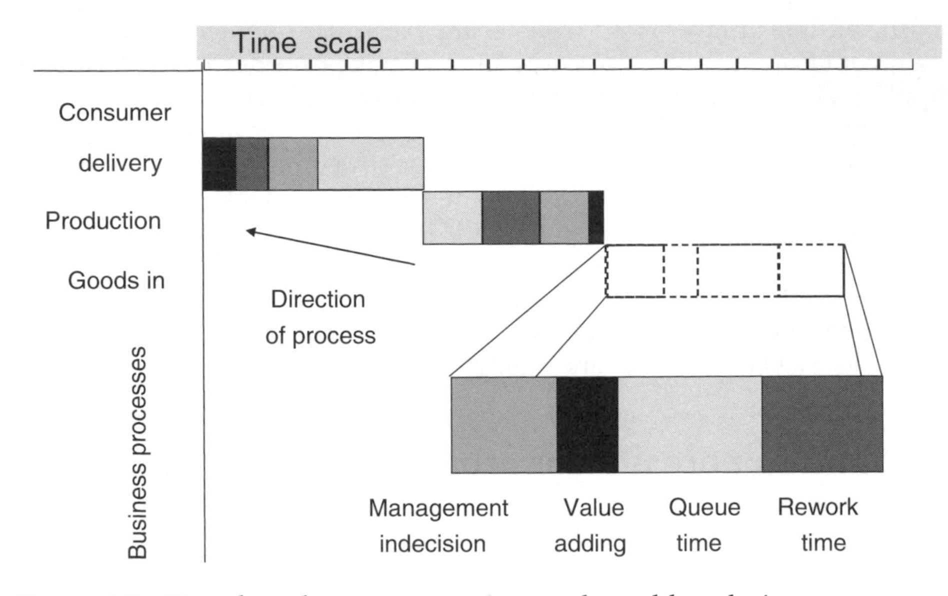

Figure 5.2 Time-based process mapping – value-add analysis

need to collect vast quantities of cost data and the risk of prolonging total project duration. It may also be an issue when the cooperation of process owners and operators is required, because it can then be perceived as a cost-cutting exercise. As a consequence, using these individuals to help with data collection, analysis and solution design may be challenging. However, SCTCM is a positive recent development that keeps TC on the re-engineering agenda.

The time compression approach – quality advantage

The achievement of time compression requires a quality-based approach. This can be viewed from two perspectives of quality. First, TC demands that product quality matches customer needs. Anything less obviously has strategic market implications, such as a loss of customers and goodwill. This adds unnecessary time in the sales, marketing and manufacturing, which have to rectify or replace the product or customers. An investigation of these time-wasting activities can, therefore, highlight possible root causes of problems that may be founded in quality issues. Time, therefore, provides the focus for quality improvement.

The above complements the second dimension of quality, where it is important not just for the customer but also for the company. This is the total quality management (TQM) approach, which also focuses on waste elimination. One key issue with TQM programmes is that they have been known to lose impetus because of a lack of focus. A lot of evidence demonstrates the need for a holistic approach to provide a focus for TQM to operate effectively (Mallinger,

1993). A TC approach provides this because it uses a simple measure that is visible to the total supply chain and not just a small isolated segment. It can thus link and integrate all of the elements of a TQM approach using the key metric of time. An example of this might be a focus on the time taken to make critical decisions that constrain an order or product batch being processed. Typically sales and operations meetings to match demand and production may represent this process constraint, as illustrated in Figure 5.3. By implication the lapse time of these meetings sits on the critical path of any supply chain process. The majority of this time is non-value-add and therefore provides a focus for addressing the total quality of all activities that interplay with the process. Examples include the major quality-related aspects such as having systems to produce accurate and timely information, through to more routine but easily underestimated aspects

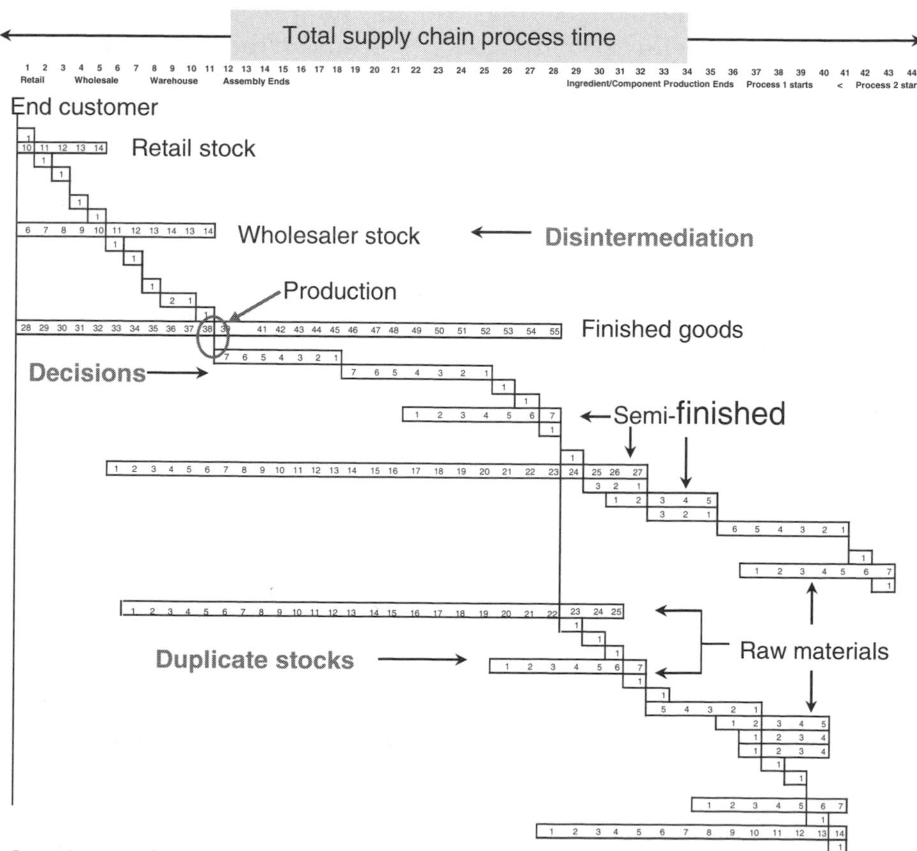

Figure 5.3 Time-based process map of an entire supply chain

such as people attending meetings on time, effective communications and proper prioritization of tasks and activities.

Figure 5.3 shows the key processes in a supply chain, with value analysis revealing that the parts shown in bold (duplicate stocks, decisions and disintermediation) are key issues. The longest process time in this example was the decision-making process, which takes 14 days and is the largest element of the finished goods lead time.

The time compression approach – technology advantage

Technology should not be applied purely for reasons associated with what is on offer or mimicking the competition. Its application must take account of the individual circumstances of the business and its customer needs – and then ensure a competitive differentiation. A focus on the time-based impact of the application of technology will help steer a company to this goal. Examples of technologies that can achieve TC are numerous, and some of the more notable developments (Barker and Helms, 1992) include computer numerically controlled (CNC) machines, robotics, computers in manufacturing (CIM) – and logistics-related examples such as the WMS application mentioned earlier. All of these reduce time for individual activities, but the time-based impact must be considered holistically in order to check that the technology is appropriate for the supply chain. A key point is that many automated systems cannot cope with high levels of demand variation, largely because the technology is designed to exacting functional specifications. A TC approach provides a focus for the application of technology when the seven strategies identified by Carter, Melnyk and Handfield (1994) are addressed in a carefully considered sequence. This usually considers the low- or non-technology strategy before moving to state-of-the-art automated solutions, such as computerized material handling and control, or the various forms of ERP. This approach ensures that the application of technology is strategically significant as well as delivering tactical productivity gains.

The time compression approach – customer focus

Different product and market sectors have different service needs. The most appropriate way to meet these needs is through channels that are specifically designed to have distinct logistical capabilities. The alternative is to push everything through the same channel – with the result that some customers are overserved while others are underserved. This has an adverse effect on costs, customer goodwill and ultimately sustainable profitability.

Figure 5.4 illustrates four generic supply categories for relating logistics channels to different product and market segments (adapted from FhG ISI, 1993). This shows that products with a volatile demand pattern and low complexity require flexible supply operations to minimize risk. An agile approach is required so that the business process can respond rapidly to new customer requirements in a market that is populated by 'fast follower' competitors enabled by low product complexity. Conversely, products that have more stable and predictable demand are usually in more cost-focused supply situations demanding lower unit costs through tighter management control and probable large economies of scale.

There are, therefore, two basic supply approaches – one where a business must be agile (for example, a high-fashion garment supply chain) and a second one lean (for example, commodity products such as industrial chemicals). A range of products lie between these extremes and may require a mix of both approaches. Quadrant 1 represents super-value goods such as aircraft. These are highly complex items sold into markets with some uncertainty and influenced by fluctuating business cycles – and, therefore, requiring process agility. However, some lean approaches will be required to

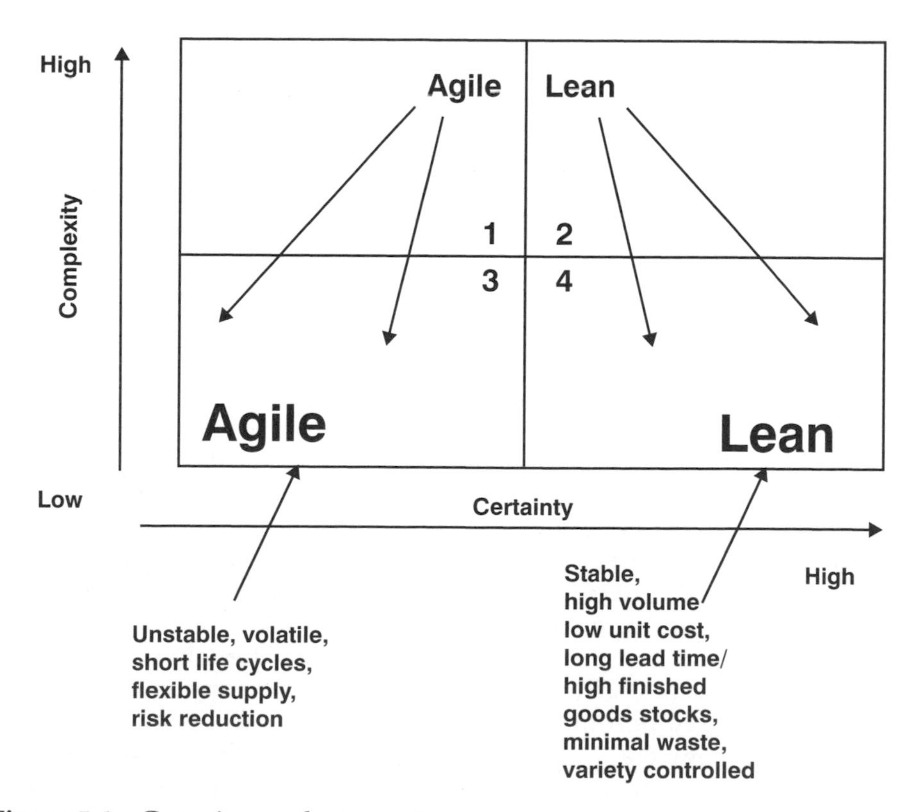

Figure 5.4 Generic supply strategies

underpin the longer-term investments in a supply market that has the time to evolve and apply competitive pressure. Quadrant 2 is the converse of quadrant 1, as it is characterized by FMCG products, which generally sell to more consistent market conditions, giving high competition – and the need for a lean cost focus. This, however, is mixed with some need for agility in areas linked with product development and innovation.

Benefits of time compression

There are two categories of TC benefit. The first is internal time consumed within the organization, which has an indirect impact on the customer. The second is external time, which relates to all aspects of time that have direct impact upon the customer, such as lead time from a stock. The net effect of internal time improvements has ramifications on external time-based benefits through cost and service interrelationships.

Internal time benefits in most manufacturing facilities, such as cycle-time reductions, give work-in-progress reductions and productivity increases. Stalk and Hout (1990) claim empirically that, for every halving of cycle times and doubling of work in process turns, productivity increases 20 to 70 per cent. A halving of manufacturing lead time using the same number of people reduces costs by 50 per cent. These changes are reflected in the return on assets where increases of 80 per cent are possible, with 45 per cent less cash required to grow the company at an equivalent rate.

Generally, the longer the elapsed time in the supply chain, the greater the risk of under- or over-forecasting demand. This results in the use of speculation stock for future customer needs (Mather, 1992). If, for example, a fashion-associated product has to be ordered from the Far East nine months in advance, then the risk of forecasting error is high. Consequently, the potential costs of markdowns are high where large stocks of inventory are held; and conversely, where minimal stocking or understocking occurs, the opportunity cost of lost sales and goodwill is substantial. The key point for TC is that, if lead times are compressed, not only is cycle stock reduced, but the period over which forecasting has to be performed reduces – and the shorter the period, the better the forecast accuracy. The better the forecast accuracy, the less demand variance will exist and the less buffer or safety stock is required. Less overall demand for inventory means that less has to be produced and supply processes can respond more promptly.

The internal benefits provide scope to assist the external benefits of TC. The primary aspect to consider is the consequence of compressing customer lead times and the opportunity to increase business turnover and possibly prices. Stalk and Hout (1990) infer that customers of time-based suppliers are willing to pay more for their products for both subjective and economic reasons:

- The customer needs less stock (cycle and buffer).
- The customer makes decisions to purchase nearer the time of need, thereby reducing risk.
- There is a reduction of cancelled/changed orders, with less time available and less need to change.
- There is an increase in the velocity of cash flow.

The factors influencing risk have an implication on market share. By being faster and more reliable than the competition, market share can be increased. A time-compressed supplier can use its flexible delivery system to supply increased variety to the customer in the form of increased style and/or technological sophistication. If this is delivered with a response advantage, the time-compressed supplier will attract the most profitable customers. Conversely, competitors will be forced to service the customers who are prepared to wait and, as a consequence, be prepared to pay less for the product. Generally, time-compressed suppliers appear to grow at three or four times the rate of their competitors, three times faster than overall demand, with twice the level of profitability. When the slower competitors decide to become time-based they must do so from the disadvantaged position of having to incur the costs of regaining market share.

Experience from the University of Warwick's Time Compression Programme (TCP) has shown that the general price and market share advantage must be considered in the context of the local market and the logistical characteristics of the product being supplied. For example, in the UK during the 1990s the spectre of cheap overseas sources became a reality, and TC enabled companies such as H&R Johnson to optimize their business processes and retain market share for ceramic tile products, rather than gain a specific price advantage. However, some price advantage can be achieved in time-sensitive market segments such as high-fashion products, where process time from design to full-volume production gives a sustainable strategic differentiation over competitors.

Demand acquisition methods such as customer relationship management help predict, define and place new customer demands at suppliers with short times. The need to respond to this level of rapidly communicated customer transparency has become the new competitive frontier. Companies that do not adjust their business processes fast enough will quickly lose ground to competitors. Agility coupled with lean is the key, with a focus on the use of TC as an enabler of process delivery and reinvention.

Examples of the application of time compression

Many companies in the United States, Japan and Europe use a TC approach, either as an open policy or as something philosophically buried within the strategic mix (Stalk and Webber, 1993). Table 5.2 illustrates results from a number of TCP projects.

Time compression of a global supply chain

The following case study has been compiled from a number of projects to demonstrate a diverse range of applications within one example. The hybrid example demonstrates a combination of TC strategies, focused on a number of the supply chain principles. The principles addressed are in **bold** and the strategies are denoted in *italics*.

The example considers a major Western retailer sourcing from a low-cost manufacturing nation. Two categories of product are considered. The first is a product group that has stable demand but a low margin, owing in part to intense competition. This might be, for example, wall fixings such as screws and nails, and requires a lean supply chain to capitalize on the stable demand and underpin a low-cost solution. In contrast, a fashion product such as women's skirts has less stable demand, with more scope for higher margins as

Table 5.2 Results from a sample of TCP projects

Company	Scope of the project	Compression achieved	Strategic significance of the improvement
H&R Johnson	Customer lead times.	Two weeks to two days.	To counter competitive import products and retain a strategic segment of the market.
Massey Ferguson	Process time.	Reduced by 20 per cent/	To reduce cost of inventory by compressing cycle times via a manufacturing cell.
British Airways	Warehouse link removed.	Two days' compression.	To maximize on aircraft flying hours, reduce inventory costs and increase asset utilization by moving into a contract market.
Fairey Hydraulics	Component arrears.	50 per cent reduction.	Retain market share and reduce inventory costs.
GKN Hardy Spicer	Inbound logistics.	Reduced by 85 per cent.	Reduce raw material and operating costs to maintain competitiveness.
CV Knitwear	Time to develop product.	Reduced by 50 per cent	To meet the customer's time-based requirement for an increased number of ranges each year. Customer retained.

there is – in the short term – limited competition from product replicas or substitutes. To cope with the higher demand variability, the fashion product supply chain must have the ability to react to change by fast product replenishment or product reinvention. The supply chain has to be agile rather than lean, with emphasis on risk mitigation rather than cost minimization.

This form of product categorization enables supply chain design (or re-engineering) based on the **end-user focus**, which is highlighted by the need for different levels of flexibility and costs. These end-user demands translate into logistical requirements that can be met by specific logistic (**horizontal**) **channels** design. A key aspect in the design of any channel is the **inventory positioning**, and this depends on supply and demand variability, coupled with lead times. These factors suggest appropriate types of inventory, held in specific quantities at strategic locations within a channel. An example of an agile channel has inventory held close to the retailer, but in semi-finished form – thereby postponing final assembly at a location with a short lead time, and low risk exposure. Products designed using *standardized* components and modules lend themselves to postponement.

The majority of supply chains are owned by different legal entities (such as companies) and also under the influence of different organizations (such as departments and employees). These entities interact with each other and create areas of focus and specialization along the supply chain, as well as constraints and check points (eg for quality or *variance control*) at the various interfaces (**vertical boundaries**). The operation of any channel is strongly influenced by the position of these vertical boundaries and the influence that they exert on the supply chain. The boundaries must, therefore, be designed and negotiated into the channel after considering the make–buy decision, and best-practice outsourcing and process design. In our two-channel example, a key question is who should own the inventory. Often the weakest channel partner is left with the cost of ownership, but in an agile or lean supply chain the suppliers may own inventory in the retail store. This might be for good, logical reasons of control and focus in a retailer that has to consider thousands of other product lines.

Ownership of the inventory, the process or the company entity is a major concern, and hence the focus on conflict resolution in supply chains, with aspirations to partnership. At a more generic level, some form of **cooperation and coordination** is always required between various interfaces along the supply chain. System-based exchange of information and data has transformed the way supply chains can operate. For example, systems (generically a form of *automation*) allow rapid transfer of data globally along supply chains. For practical purposes this is usually instantaneous (*concurrent working*) and *integrated* with interconnecting process links. In our agile channel example, retail sales information can be made available to the supplier on the other side of the world. The supplier can respond accordingly and authorize any replenishment orders on behalf of the retailer. This form of linkage alleviates the effects of **demand dynamics** where time delays in the supply of information along the chain create uncertainty, causing suppliers to perform non-value-adding tasks and incur unnecessary costs.

The final aspect of this example considers the inbound flow of materials to support manufacturing operations. There is a tendency to focus on parts of the supply chain that directly affect customers, to the exclusion of the inbound supply chain. However, there is often scope to investigate and map the entire inbound supply chain and consolidate it into **horizontal channels**, and to **simplify** the flows using a unified approach to handling raw materials. In the example of fixings, the metal rods, chemicals and other materials all arrived at the factory through a range of different channels, some with direct delivery through a carrier network, some supplied in bulk to the factory warehouse, some supplied from a vendor's regional warehouse – or a combination of all three through a range of providers. An equal level of complexity and variety existed to support the range of information flows and communications. Typically these supply arrangements and associated communication complexities arise for historical reasons and establish themselves over a period of time.

The inbound supply chain sustains manufacturing, but often no one can identify the logistical cost, as this is hidden within the procurement cost. And the complexity of the channels makes service level agreements difficult to manage, giving rise to safety stocks and non-value-add cost. The inbound supply chain can be mapped from a time, cost and value-add perspective. Horizontal channels of supply are identified, and possibly a neutral third-party logistics provider is given responsibility for delivery. This consolidates flows and gives a new focus on the factory as a customer of logistics services and not just a product manufacturer. Resource allocation in terms of inventory, transport, warehouse and IT capacity is designed into the solution on the basis of balanced service and cost.

Conclusion

Time, as a measure, is strategically significant for business. The potential for time compression in most businesses is very significant – with non-value-add time in most processes of at least 95 per cent. The commercial benefits are wide and include increased market share, price, productivity and innovation, together with reduced levels of commercial risk.

TC gives a mechanism for addressing most aspects of business strategy, and overarches the key objectives associated with in-company logistics and managing the broader supply chain. Six principles aligned with the latter have been identified and linked to a time-based approach. To identify and achieve TC objectives, tools such as time-based process mapping have been developed and coupled with a strategic re-engineering framework.

The approach supports a new source of competitiveness for time-sensitive markets and, as a focusing criterion, it enables one company or supply chain to be compared with another in terms of the internal and external benefits of time. This can provide the impetus for change and improvement. Even in markets that are not time-sensitive, it is difficult to argue that benefits cannot be acquired from TC. The approach does, however, require a top-down commitment – and for full impact a lead organization within a supply chain needs to drive the initiative. This becomes a challenge where trust is an issue, and there is the need for an unbiased hand to guide, arbitrate and have a stake in the process.

Looking towards the future, companies must blend leanness with agility in order to respond to at least two key challenges. The first is to ensure that supply chains are designed, operated and evolved to meet and drive end-user needs. The second is to manage the supply chain in a dynamic commercial environment that is making network management – rather than supply chain management – a challenging reality. The TC approach's simplicity and transparency across company and functional boundaries provides a good platform for meeting these challenges.

References

Barker, B and Helms, MM (1992) Production and operations restructuring: using time based strategies, *Industrial Management and Data Systems*, **92** (6), pp 3–7

Barker, RC (1994) The design of lean manufacturing systems using time-based analysis, *International Journal of Operations and Production Management*, **14** (11), pp 86–96

Carter, CR, Melnyk, PL and Handfield, SA (1994) *Identifying Sources of Cycle Time Reduction*, Quorum, Westport, CT

European Logistics Association (ELA)/AT Kearney (2004) *Excellence in Logistics*, ELA, Brussels

Fraunhofer Institut fur Systemtechnik und Innovationsforschung (FhG ISI) (1993) *Factory for the Future*, FhG ISI, Karlsruhe

Lamming, R (2002) Lecture to Thames Valley Supply Chain Network Group

Mallinger, M (1993) Ambush along the TQM trail, *Journal of Organisational Change Management*, **6** (4)

Mather, H (1992) Design for logistics, *Production and Inventory Management Journal*, **33** (3)

New, CN (1992) The use of throughput efficiency as a key performance measure for the new manufacturing era, Cranfield School of Management, BPICS Conference

Ohmae, K (1965) *The Mind of the Strategist*, Penguin, Harmondsworth

Reich, RB (1991) *The Work of Nations*, Simon & Schuster, New York

Stalk, G and Hout, TM (1990) *Competing against Time*, Free Press, New York

Stalk, G and Webber, AM (1993) Japan's dark side of time, *Harvard Business Review*, July–Aug
SUCCESS (2004) The route to success, *Project Manager's Handbook*, Cranfield University, Cranfield
Tersine, RJ and Hummingbird, EA (1995) Lead-time reduction: the search for competitive advantage, *International Journal of Operations and Production Management*, **15** (2), pp 36–53
University of Warwick (1995) Time Compression Programme conference: Profit from Time Compression, Birmingham International Convention Centre
Womack, J, Jones, D and Roos, D (1990) *The Machine that Changed the World*, Harper Perennial, New York

Strategic supply chain management: the power of incentives

Glyn Watson, Chris Lonsdale, Andrew Cox and Joe Sanderson,
University of Birmingham

The study of supply chain management is the study of incentives. Supply chain managers and their vendors are competitors as well as collaborators. The mutual gains from trade bring the parties together in the first place. Additional benefits accruing from closer collaboration can keep them working together thereafter. However, the value generated from the exchange process must be distributed and this is what makes buyers and sellers competitors as well as collaborators. Consequently, the function of the supply chain manager is to ensure that the interaction between the buying and the selling organization generates as much value-add as possible – but that the value-add passes to his or her organization, rather than being retained within the organization of the vendor. In order to achieve this, the supply manager must be skilled at crafting the incentive structures that will modify the behaviour of the vendor in ways that are consistent with the interests of the buying organization. It is for this reason that the study of supply chain management is the study of incentives.

This chapter divides into three sections. The first section deals with the incentive issue itself by establishing its central importance to supply managers. The second section focuses on the topic of outsourcing. Under certain circumstances it will be impossible for the supply manager to incentivize its vendor effectively. Having such activities outside the boundary of the organization, therefore, not only threatens to inflate the costs of the buyer but may also undermine the firm's revenue streams. Knowing where to draw the boundary of the firm is integral to the development of supply chain competence. Once the boundary has been drawn the supplier has to be managed. Supplier management is the subject of the third and final section. Here it is suggested that effective supplier management has as much to do with the management of demand as it does the management of supply. Therefore, the third section divides into three parts. It begins with some generalized comments before turning to the topic of demand management and the consolidation of spend. In the final part of the final section, the subject of the suppliers themselves receives attention. Here, questions both of governance and of contractual management are covered.

Incentivization and the process of exchange

All exchange involves elements both of cooperation and of competition. Assuming that the concerned parties have voluntarily agreed to the deal, the very act of signing a contract is a cooperative activity. The vendor (or seller) is getting something that he or she wants – cash – while the buyer is getting something that he or she wants – the products and services supplied by the vendor. However, the cooperative aspects of an exchange can (and frequently do) go beyond this. Buyers and sellers can actively work together to streamline the contracting process and/or adapt or develop the vendor's products and services so that they more closely match the requirements of the buyer. The creation of such value-adding relationships has today become a staple of supply chain management.

Buyers and sellers are also in competition, however. While both sides gain from a trade (else why trade in the first instance?), it is not necessary for both sides to gain equally for a trade to take place. For the buyer, the aim is to get value for money from a deal. If the buyer is a rational agent this means maximum value for money. Every time he or she is able to negotiate the price down a notch, the value for money that is obtained increases. Of course, for the vendor, passing value to its customers means smaller profits. Economists refer to the contested ground that exists between the two parties to a trade as the surplus value. Surplus value is the difference between the value that the customer places on the vendor's products (ie the customer's utility function) and the supplier's costs of production. That portion of the contested ground that passes to the customer is said to be the consumer surplus, while that which is retained by the vendor is the producer surplus (see Figure 6.1).

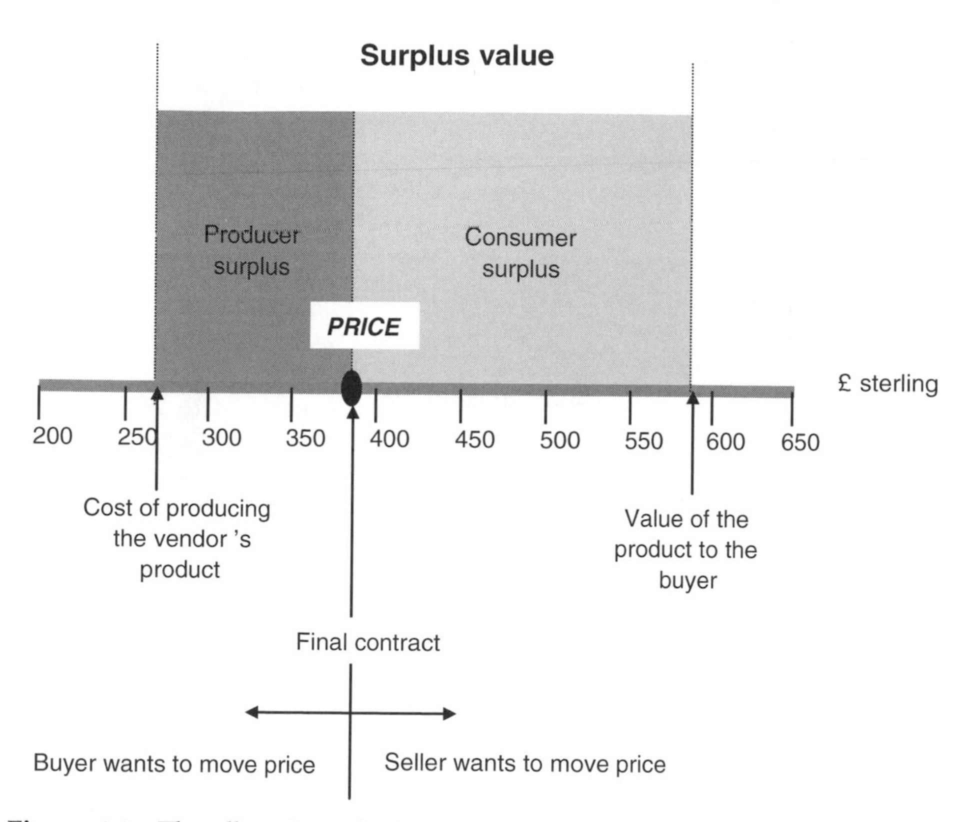

Figure 6.1 The allocation of value in an exchange

Even when buyers and sellers increase the cooperative element of an exchange by actively working together to add value to the relationship, the competitive element remains – so cooperative relationships can be adversarial or non-adversarial. This is because the fruits of the cooperation (in the form of either lower production costs for the vendor or a higher valuation of the vendor's products on the part of the customer) have to be divided up (see Figure 6.2). If, for example, the effect of collaboration is to reduce the supplier's costs by £100 a unit, there would be an issue about whether the vendor should pass all of the savings on to the customer or whether it should retain some of them in the form of higher profits. Alternatively, if the supplier invests £100 in developing its products and as a result increased the value to the customer by £200, should the vendor raise its prices by £100 to cover just the cost of the investment, or by the full £200?

What determines who wins out in this competitive process is the *incentive* structures that underpin the exchange relationship. Take, for example, the vendor that finds itself in a highly competitive market where its many customers are free to pick and choose where they buy their goods and services. Such a context forces the vendor into a Dutch auction in which it is forced

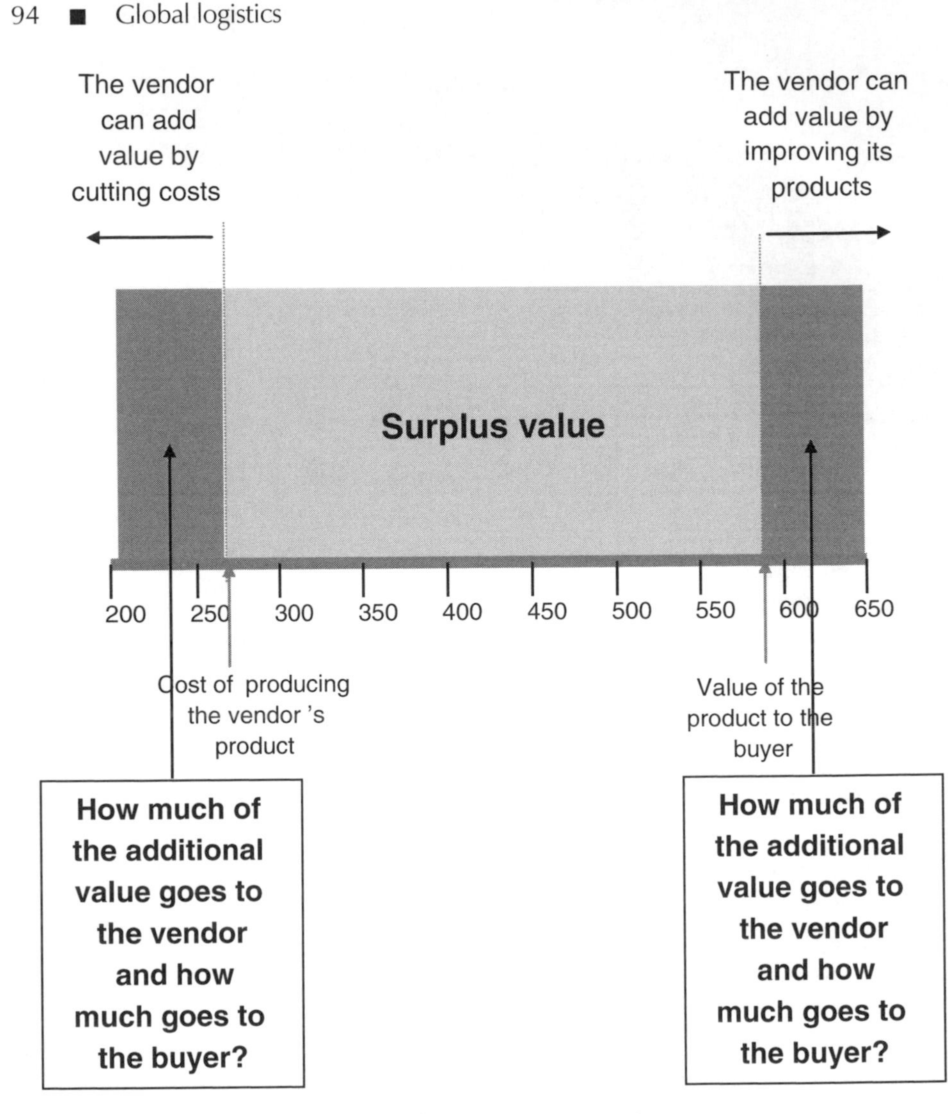

Figure 6.2 The generation of value-add in an exchange

constantly to drop its prices to buy its customer's business. In such a situation, the surplus value is bound to pass to the consumer. Compare that to a situation in which a particular customer has invested heavily in the vendor's technologies, even building the value proposition that it offers its own customers around the technologies of a particular supplier. This happened in the case of the PC market, where PC manufacturers fell over themselves to advertise the fact that their machines had an 'Intel inside'. In the end, it became impossible for PC manufacturers to compete unless they were able to make this boast. Unfortunately, this had the effect of handing enormous leverage over to Intel and as a result the surplus value passed from the consumer to the producer.

Consequently, much of supply management is reduced to a game between poachers and gamekeepers in which the vendor assumes the role of the poacher (trying to 'steal' its customers' scarce financial resources), while the procurement manager assumes the role of the gamekeeper, in trying to stop them. What follows is a cat-and-mouse game in which through a combination of guile and the development of distinctive capabilities the vendor attempts to close markets, while the procurement manager responds in kind with a range of counter-strategies, designed to stop its vendors by keeping its supply markets contested. To the victor go the spoils. Power (formally defined as the ability of one party adversely to affect the interests of another) and the pursuit of power are at the heart of the exchange process (Lukes, 1974; Cox, Sanderson and Watson, 2000; Cox *et al*, 2002).

To some it might appear that the competitive elements of an exchange have been overstated. While it is true that some people in life are maximizers (ie they are always looking for the highest possible return from a deal), critics would argue that most people are in fact happy just to satisfice (ie obtain a settlement that provides them with a deal that they can live with). If two people cooperate on a venture, then generally speaking those people are happy to split the proceeds. This may or may not be true: it is hard to say. What is true, however, is that such an approach is sub-optimal and imprudent. That satisficing is sub-optimal should be self-evident. The fact that it is also imprudent needs further elaboration.

The issue of prudence arises in a number of contexts. Firstly, it puts the profitability and even the survival of a firm at risk. The reason that firms come into business in the first instance is to make a return for shareholders. While it is true, as a number of resource-based writers have observed, that markets are often heterogeneous (ie they are capable of supporting laggards as well as world-beaters), it is not true that markets are infinitely forgiving of the weak (Peteraf, 1993). Firms that fall too far behind the competitive frontier are on borrowed time. Firms that forget about the competitive elements of an exchange, however, risk seeing their costs rise and falling behind the competitive frontier.

The second problem with cooperation and trust is that it demonstrates an unwarranted confidence in the capacity and willingness of others to reciprocate. Many firms that acquire leverage are happy to use it. Even those that do not possess a structural advantage may attempt to use guile instead, where they think it will pay off for them. Furthermore, denials that this is not true cannot be taken at face value (Williamson, 1985). The thing about people is that very few of them are honest all of the time. One only has to reflect on one's own experience to see that this is true.

According to business economists, economic agents are not simply self-interested but they pursue this self-interest with guile – not all of the time, but sufficiently often that opportunism is a fact of commercial life. What permits the existence of opportunism is two things: 1) a lack of honesty (obviously); and 2) a lack of transparency between buyers and sellers. Economists distinguish between public and private information (Molhow, 1997). Information is regarded as public if it involves something that is widely known. Information is regarded as private when access to it is restricted. When 'restriction' means that one side in an exchange knows something that the other side does not, then an information asymmetry is said to exist. It is information asymmetry that permits dishonesty to pay.

Business opportunism exists in a number of forms, but for buyers the three guises in which it is most common are adverse selection, moral hazard and hold-up. Adverse selection is *ex ante* opportunism or misrepresentation that arises prior to the signing of a contract. Shorthand definitions of the concept might revolve around buying a 'lemon' or being sold a 'turkey'. The scope for adverse selection varies but is more common under some circumstances than others. Commentators often distinguish between search, experience and credence goods. Search goods are products that allow buyers to make systematic comparisons prior to a purchase. They are normally tangible products like chairs, pens or iron ingots. Experience goods, by contrast, are products that can only be evaluated subsequent to purchase. Typically, they include services like cinemas or restaurants. However, the category can also include tangible products like cars or records. The final category of good is the credence good. Credence goods defy easy evaluation, even after consumption. They include intangible services such as advertising, consultancy or medical services. What makes evaluation so hard usually comes down to a difficulty with attributing blame or success. For example, a piece of professional advice might have been responsible for a commercial disaster. However, the blame might lie with some other concomitant factor. The point is, where pre-contractual evaluation of a product is difficult – either because evaluation is inherently difficult or because the buyer lacks the resources or expertise to undertake it – the buyer is open to the risk of adverse selection. Experience goods and credence goods, by definition, are difficult to evaluate prior to purchase.

If adverse selection involves being suckered before a contract is signed, moral hazard and hold-up involve being suckered once a party has signed on the dotted line. Moral hazard is concerned with shortfalls in effort. For example, prior to an agreement, a consultancy company might promise to dedicate its best staff to the task of servicing the client and set its costs accordingly. Unbeknown to the client, however, once the contract has been secured, the work is passed down to junior colleagues whose time is charged out at inflated rates. Alternatively, moral hazard may involve charging a client for materials that were never used or that were used but came from another job and had been paid for by another client.

Hold-up occurs as a result of an extended association with a supplier, where the terms of the association cannot be fully specified in advance and where the association requires one of the parties to incur significant sunk and/or switching costs. Over time the full requirements of the relationship are revealed, and this combination of factors allows the non-dependent party to renegotiate the terms of the deal in ways that are most favourable to it. The existence of high sunk and switching costs may also support blatantly opportunistic behaviour in which the non-dependent party even reneges on its promises that are covered by legal agreement. The calculation here is that any benefit that can be obtained through legal redress will be insufficient to compensate for the damage to, or loss of, the relationship.

Regardless of the form that opportunism takes, the potential for it means that firms must always be aware of the competitive nature of any trade. Even if a customer is honest and believes in giving the other party a fair break, the customer cannot be sure that the other side is operating according to the same code. Because a trade always involves some private information, we just don't know what we don't know – and what we don't know might turn out to be quite important. One of the essential elements of procurement and supply chain competence, therefore, centres on the capacity of buyers to ensure that their vendors offer a good deal (or at least keep to the terms of the deal that has been agreed).

Incentivization and the outsourcing dilemma

Nowhere are the issues of competition between buyers and sellers more acute than in respect to outsourcing. This is evidenced by the fact that so many outsourced contracts go wrong. One survey found that in only 5 per cent of cases did outsourcing prove to be an unqualified success (Lonsdale and Cox, 1998). Most respondents indicated that it was something of a curate's egg – that is, good in parts. Thirty-nine per cent of respondents in the survey said that their outsourced contracts were simultaneously moderately successful and moderately unsuccessful. Of course, this may have something to do with the way in which the contracts were managed. Such is the scale of disappointment, however, that it suggests that something deeper than simply poor contracting is at work.

On the face of it the decision to outsource should not be particularly problematic. It should involve a simple cost comparison between the expenses associated with undertaking the activity in-house as opposed to the expenses associated with contracting it out. For example, the size of the firm's requirement might be insufficient to cover the fixed costs associated with production in an efficient fashion. Under these conditions, sourcing externally, from a firm that can amortize its fixed costs more efficiently, might make eminent sense. Alternatively, a particular activity might suffer from a lack of effective managerial oversight. Managerial time within the firm is a scarce resource and most of it tends to be devoted to the firm's key activities. Residual activities tend to get overlooked and production suffers as a result. It is this thinking that underpins much of the core competence writing. If your firm can't do something well, find another firm that can.

Outsourcing tends to go wrong, however, because it exposes the firm to either a strategic or a contractual risk. Strategic risk arises if the firm outsources its competitive differentiator. Within strategy, there are three types of differentiation: cost leadership, product differentiation and niche production (Porter, 1980). In each case the firm is attempting to break the relationship between cost, price and profit in order that it might earn a sustained producer surplus. In a competitive marketplace, the consumer's ability to pick and choose between alternative vendors drives the firm's prices down towards the marginal cost of production. This is the last thing that a firm wants.

With cost leadership the firm is attempting to profit by developing a uniquely efficient production process that is difficult for its competitors to imitate, through the creation of *ex post* barriers to entry. So long as the firm is able to stave off competitive imitation it can afford to drop its prices below those of its competitors and still make a higher return. With product differentiation, the firm is attempting to develop a superior utility proposition for the customer. The idea here is that, when people comparison-shop and realize that the firm's products are better than those of its competitors, they will be prepared to pay a premium for the product that offers the higher utility. Again its ability to sustain its producer surplus and turn it into a rent is contingent upon its capacity to hinder or retard competitive imitation. Finally, niche production also seeks to target the customer's utility. This it achieves, however, not by creating relatively superior products but by servicing segments of a marketplace that nobody else is particularly interested in.

Being able to differentiate competitively is so valuable to the firm – and indeed is what strategy is all about – that firms must be able to protect those resources and capabilities that generate the differentiation in the first place. However, if the firm outsources such a resource or capability, then the odds are that it will end up paying the rent to its supplier that it should be earning for itself.

Outsourcing can also expose the firm to significant contractual risk. Again, this involves surplus value passing to the vendor, rather than being retained by the consumer. Sustaining the performance of a vendor depends upon a firm's ability to monitor or motivate the vendor. Monitoring becomes more difficult after a competence has been outsourced because either the staff who used to manage the activity move on to the supplier's payroll, or else they are lost from the equation altogether. Once the organization lacks the resource, or at least a resource that is sufficiently qualified to exercise proper oversight, the supplier starts to renege on its commitments.

Avoiding the risks of hold-up in an outsourced relationship involves maintaining motivational incentive. Such motivation might take the form of a carrot (bonuses for good performance) or a stick (the cancellation of the contract if the performance is poor). But in order for the incentive structure to work, the threat of sanctions as a last resort must be credible. This means being able to monitor the supplier to see if it is complying with the terms of the deal, and having the ability to punish the supplier (by invoking penalties or by threatening exit) if it is not.

The tasks that the firm has to perform, therefore, concern being able to spot those transactions for which there is significant scope for opportunism and being able to craft safeguards against the risk. Where contractual safeguards cannot properly be introduced, then the firm would probably be better to retain the competence within the organization, rather than to outsource it.

Hold-up is always a problem with outsourced contracts because effective monitoring is always an issue. However, sometimes the risks are particularly acute. Contracting that takes place in a highly volatile or uncertain environment is difficult because it raises the issue of renegotiation. Buyers attempt to draft contracts in as complete a fashion as possible, but when an environment is particularly volatile, specifying all the terms of an agreement in advance is likely to prove next to impossible. This in itself need not present a difficulty unless the firm becomes locked in to its outsourced provider. If this happens the supplier may choose to renegotiate on terms that benefit it, rather than its customer (Williamson, 1985).

As indicated in the preceding section, contractual lock-in occurs if the contract requires the buyer to make some form of highly specialized investment in the relationship. The investment might take the form of time. An organization that has spent months negotiating and implementing an outsourced relationship might be reluctant to write off all this hard work – especially if re-sourcing means repeating the effort with no greater chance of success next time around. Alternatively, firms might have made substantial and non-fungible investments in specialized training or equipment, otherwise known as asset-specific investments (Williamson, 1985). Less creditably, though, firms are often reluctant to call time on a poorly performing supplier if the managers who negotiated the contract have a significant investment of reputation in the deal. Calling a halt to the affair means admitting that they got it wrong and nobody likes doing that. Whatever the form of the lock-in, the effect is the same: the firm loses its capacity to impose costs on the vendor and thus its ability to impose discipline.

Of course, just because an outsourced contract presents the firm with a risk, it does not follow that the risk cannot be managed and that outsourcing should not take place. One strategy often pursued by firms involves unbundling a contract. This means separating out those elements that pose a risk from those that do not. The highly risky elements are retained in-house and only the less risky elements are outsourced. The supplier may even be asked to post a bond or share the costs of the dedicated investments, as a sign of its good faith (ie to show that its word of honour and commitment to the relationship are credible).

Incentivization and supplier management

Outsourcing requires the firm to understand what it is that allows it to leverage its customers (in the case of strategic outsourcing) and what it is that allows its 'potential' suppliers to exploit it (in the case of both strategic and tactical outsourcing). Effective relationship management is about reversing things by understanding what it is that allows the firm to control and leverage its suppliers. The question is to what end? This is where we are required to reintroduce the subject of surplus value.

The first question that the firm must ask itself is whether the relationship should include a value-added element. Many commentators would argue yes, citing the benefits that often flow from extending the cooperative elements of a trade. Lean thinking, for example, highlights the seven supply chain wastes that often plague buyer–supplier relationships. These relate to overproduction, unnecessary inventory, waiting, motion, transportation, defects and inappropriate processing (Hines *et al*, 2000). Yet, just because extended cooperation might potentially generate additional value, it does not mean that it will, or that the buyer will be the main beneficiary if it does. Four factors play a part in determining the buyer's calculation about whether cooperation is worthwhile: the upfront investment, the potential pay-off, power and risk. Creating a value-adding relationship requires an investment, even if only in terms of the time and managerial effort that it involves. The first thing that the firm must ensure is that the expected payback matches the upfront investment. No firm is going to spend a lot of time developing its supplier of toilet rolls. The improvement for the buyer is likely to be minuscule compared with the effort.

What complicates the calculation is that both the investment and return may be hard to determine *ex ante*. Take defence contractors. Suppliers of defence equipment work closely with their customers (governments) to ensure that the weapons that they develop are the ones that the customer wants and needs. The industry, however, is notorious for the delays in introducing new equipment and the cost overruns. In a number of instances the additional cost that the customer ends up committing itself to runs into billions of pounds. When the equipment finally arrives, it may be too late to be useful. It may not even work properly. Consequently, there is the issue of which party takes the risk and which party obtains the reward. This is a question of power. A simple example will illustrate the nature of the calculation that the buyer faces.

Take two firms: a buyer (A) and its supplier (B). B proposes to A that an upfront investment of £50 is capable of yielding cost savings of £200. In other words, the additional surplus value that has been created through the cooperation comes to £150. If A exercises leverage over B it will probably think that cooperating is a good idea. As it has the power it will probably insist that B takes all of the upfront risk, agreeing to cover B's costs only if the initiative pays off. This is a no-lose situation for A. If, however, A and B are interdependent, then the calculation becomes more complex. B will probably insist that A shares both the investment and the reward. This means that A must invest £25 (half the £50 cost) to get a payback of £100 (half the £200 cost savings). This leaves it with a net gain of £75 (£100 savings less the £25 costs). Once again cooperating makes sense – although the pay-off for the buyer is smaller than in the first example. What if the costs are fixed but the gains are far from certain? Say, for example, there was only a 25 per cent chance of a successful outcome. Under these circumstances the firm would be investing £25 to get a 25 per cent of £100 return. The cost–benefit calculation here is finely balanced (£25 cost less £25 return equals zero). Change the parameters again (eg increase the upfront investment by £1) and the initiative may cease to make commercial sense. This is why power is so important to all relationships: it affects the pay-off structures of buyers and sellers and thus over-determines the management of the relationship. It decides which side takes most of the risks and which side extracts most of the rewards. Furthermore, the same calculation pertains whether the firm is thinking in a dyadic or a wider supply chain context.

The second set of operational issues confronting organizations, therefore, relates to how they acquire or maintain a power advantage over suppliers. Buyers are aware that vendors segment their customer base. One simple segmentation (which nonetheless is still widely used) involves the vendor categorizing customers on the basis of the size of the customer's business and the difficulties associated with servicing it. The attempt here is to determine the overall profitability of a specific contract to the vendor's business. Obviously, what the buyer is looking for is large contracts that are easy (ie cheap) to service. What they are not looking for is low-value, costly and therefore nuisance business. This is why the procurement functions within many organizations have created commodity councils aimed at rationalizing specific items of spend so as to maximize their attractiveness, value or leverage to supply markets in general and to specific vendors in particular. The hope here is that, if the buyer can select a supplier that is competent and whose interests dovetail with the buyer's objectives, then the buyer will get a better deal.

Incentives and the consolidation of demand

However, creating this congruence is easier said than done. Operationally, the key to effective supply management is usually effective demand management, but as often as not a supply manager will experience considerable difficulty in getting the managers in other functions to recognize this point. In order to source effectively it is essential that buying organizations develop appropriate specifications, avoid unnecessary, last-minute changes to specification, create regular patterns of demand, and ensure that as little buying as possible takes place outside of the organization's commercial rules. Most importantly, however, it is essential that organizations do not unnecessarily fragment spend, thereby spreading their demand across an artificially large number of suppliers. The reason for this is twofold. First, it raises transaction costs – substantially in some instances. Second, it reduces the potential leverage that the organization has over its suppliers. And, as has already been indicated, generally speaking the weaker the leverage, the poorer the deals.

Of course, a certain level of fragmentation will always arise. For one thing, different business units within an organization often have very different missions and as a consequence have very different supply requirements. Additionally, when attempting to consolidate demand, organizations are often confronted by legacy issues. Standardizing demand may offer only a false economy if it is accompanied by significant write-off costs. Finally, organizations have to balance the short-term gains that may arise from obtaining volume deals with the long-term risk that they may become overly dependent on a particular supplier. Over time, this dependence may translate into higher prices and poorer service. Together, these factors combine to create what we can describe as a 'natural level of fragmentation' (Lonsdale and Watson, 2005). This natural level can be defined as the point at which any further consolidation results in a 'net reduction in organizational performance/welfare, notwithstanding any commercial gains that might have accrued from the consolidation initiative'. Where exactly this point lies will vary by commodity, organization and time.

Furthermore, where that point lies will often be one of the major areas of dispute between supply managers and their internal clients. This is because issues of consolidation are as much political issues as they are technical ones. There are a number of reasons why an internal client may not recognize that there are benefits to be obtained from consolidation. First, there is the issue of functional culture. Managers from different departments are usually functional specialists. Their specialisms may be largely commercial (as in the case of sales or purchasing) or largely operational (as in the case of HRM or production). Alongside the specialized knowledge that resides in a department there is often also a strong functional culture. This culture reflects the training of staff but it also reflects the management priorities of particular departments. For example, because a production manager's performance is measured in terms of faults or downtime, he or she is likely to be particularly sensitive to anything that might spoil or interrupt output. Such sensitivity may be justified, if what is being proposed poses a real threat to operational sustainability. For example, it would be ridiculous for an oil company to attempt to save a couple of thousand pounds on industrial valves if the downside risk was several hundred thousand pounds in lost production if a valve fails. However, a natural sensitivity can easily become an unnatural oversensitivity. The same production manager may refuse to participate in an initiative that will save £60,000 because there is an infinitesimal chance that the new product might fail.

Second, there is the principal–agent problem. Principal–agent problems arise because managers – and indeed all employees – have divided loyalties.

For example, managers have a loyalty to the organization that pays their wages. For many commentators, this loyalty constitutes (or should constitute) the manager's primary loyalty. In practice, however, managers also develop loyalties for those around them, and particularly departmental colleagues. And, less creditably, managers also have loyalties to their own interests (Milgrom and Roberts, 1992). Where firm or department and personal priorities conflict, it is often the firm's priorities that are sacrificed.

This is significant from the perspective of a consolidation programme because, although such a programme is intended to benefit the organization as a whole, it does not necessarily follow that consolidation will benefit all departments equally (or at all), or that the initiative will be without cost (or indeed that these costs will be evenly distributed). It is relatively easy for managers to sign up to a consolidation programme if the supplier that will get most of the business is the one they are already using, and the price being offered represents an improvement. It is less clear, however, that managers would be enthusiastic if the new deal is more expensive, or if it involves the termination of a relationship that is particularly valued.

Regardless of whether the dissent arises because mangers have failed to understand the advantages of the initiative or because they understand the advantages for the organization but are anxious to avoid the costs to their department (or them personally), such dissent is likely to make implementation problematic. Faced with such opposition, organizations have one of four options. Option one involves taking the path of least resistance and doing nothing. Options two, three and four all require the organization to confront the problem. Option two involves persuasion, demonstrating to the manager concerned that any fears are exaggerated or unfounded and setting them against the very obvious benefits. This may or may not work. However, it is most likely to work where a hostile manager has misunderstood the issues involved. It is less likely to work when a manager understands the issues and realizes that the initiative is not in his or her particular interest. Under these circumstances, the supply manager may pursue option three – coercion. Coercion involves the threat of sanctions or the use of the organization's authority structures to override the opposition of the hostile party. The limitation of this strategy, however, is that the procurement function often sits towards the bottom of the organization's hierarchy, and the procurement manager lacks the clout to make credible threats. Furthermore, more senior colleagues may prove reluctant to intercede on the procurement manager's behalf if it involves confronting one of the organization's more powerful constituencies. Option four, therefore, is bribery. Bribery involves compensating a manager for the costs of participation. It is perhaps not surprising if a manager does not want to get involved in a consolidation programme if all of the benefits flow to the centre. However, if some of the benefits can be passed back to the manager, then the initiative may appear to be more worthwhile.

Incentives and the management of suppliers

The final set of operational issues facing supply managers concerns the management of the chosen vendor itself. Supply management involves two issues: relationship management and contracting. Relationship management concerns how the buyer and seller are going to interact on a day-to-day basis. Is the association between the two essentially going to be an arm's length one, or is something closer going to be called for? If the firm has opted to pursue a value-adding relationship then presumably close interaction is required. The contracting parties will need to trade information, mutually adapt their processes, etc, so the maximum value-adding potential is achieved. At the same time, relationship management will also involve managing the tensions that exist between the two. Some forms of cooperation, for example, might be deemed neutral in the sense that they add value to the relationship without disturbing the commercial balance within it. Other forms of cooperation, however, are far from neutral. For example, if the buyer calls for the supplier to open its books, then the buyer is acquiring a considerable advantage over its supplier in that it now knows just how much money the supplier is making from the deal. Bother buyers and sellers, therefore, want to manage the relationship so that it adds value but does not tip the balance of power the wrong way.

In contrast to relationship management that tends to contain a value-adding element as well as a controlling element, contracts are primarily about control. They are about specifying in a legally binding way the manner in which buyers and suppliers are to work together, ie who is responsible for doing what. They are also about specifying (again in a legally binding way) the outputs of the relationship – what the supplier is expected to deliver, what the buyer is expected to pay and which party owns the rights to any exploitable technologies or processes should they emerge from the association.

Conventional contracts take two main forms: tight and flexible (Williamson, 1985). The shift from tight to flexible contracts tends to occur as the risk within the relationship increases. Risk, in this context, has a very specific meaning. It refers to events that can be foreseen but that have a probability of occurring of less than one but greater than zero. Where the probability is one or zero (ie the outcome is certain), this means that an element of a deal can be specified (or ignored) with total confidence. This allows the parties to use a tight contract. For example, if an organization requires laptops for a hundred employees, it is relatively easy for it to specify when it wants the machines, what it will pay and what level of after-sales support it will need.

By contrast, where there is a lack of clarity surrounding particular aspects of the deal, but where the lack of clarity falls within clearly defined limits (ie where the probability is between one and zero), the parties may seek to include a flexible element to the contract to take account of this ambiguity. This allows the requirement/reward relationship to be adjusted in a predictable way. For example, an organization requiring the development of a new piece of software may know what is needed but may not know how long it will take to develop the new product. Because the organization is aware, however, that the main variable driving cost will be the labour hours required to develop the software, the terms of the contract are set out to reflect the range of potential effort levels.

However, some events are genuinely uncertain in the sense that they were not or could not have been anticipated prior to reaching the original agreement. Such events may range from occasional but devastating acts of God (or people) to the more mundane. For example, many IT agreements are entered into before the requirement has been properly worked out. Under such circumstances it is simply not possible to draft a contract flexible enough to take account of all future possibilities. In the place of contracts, therefore, firms must use relational agreements. The purpose of such agreements is to provide a structured framework within which the terms of a deal can be re-negotiated as the future becomes clear.

Although a buyer–supplier relationship may largely consist of one of these control mechanisms, on occasion it can contain elements of all three. For example, short-term, arm's length relationships tend to call for tight contracts but may include a subsidiary element. Longer-term arm's length relationships tend to require the flexible element to increase. Long-term cooperative relationships (whether they are adversarial or non-adversarial) tend to call for all three.

Of course, while contracts aim to serve as instruments of control, whether in fact they succeed in this function depends on the *ex post* power balance. As we saw in our discussions on outsourcing and contractual risk, if the buyer loses his or her power then the contract may not be worth the paper that it is written on. As the political philosopher Thomas Hobbes once put it, 'contracts without the sword are but empty breath'. In the case of a tight or flexible contract the threat of the courts is only credible if they can be accessed at relatively low cost and if plaintiffs believe that they have a good chance of winning. Where fault is ambiguous or where an agreement has been poorly drafted, then the use of a contract as an incentive mechanism will start to break down. The reluctance to use this mechanism may then be further eroded by the fear that, if a plaintiff fails to make an effective case, the plaintiff will also be saddled with the costs. In addition, the party may also have to manage a disintegrating relationship while a replacement is found – assuming that one can be found in a timely manner.

In the case of relational agreements, where there may be no contract or at least where the terms of the contract do not cover the issues in question, the courts may not be an option at all. Neither might be the termination of the agreement. This is because the incidence of significant sunk and switching costs in arrangements that are likely to require a relational agreement tends to be quite high. Observers like Williamson (1985) generally recommend that parties look to mechanisms like the posting of hostages, which can be forfeited should the relationship collapse, as a way of maintaining some control. And, if such arrangements cannot be agreed upon, they would advise that either the organization look for a different vendor or else they should consider the possibility of vertical integration.

Conclusion

Exchange takes place in the first instance because it is mutually profitable. Closer forms of cooperation occur because they can increase this level of profitability. However, mutually profitable exchange is not the same as equally profitable exchange. Buyers and sellers are competitors as well as collaborators. Consequently it is important for supply chain managers to understand the following things. First, they must understand when it is not sensible to exchange (that is, when exchange imposes unacceptable levels of strategic and contractual risk). Second, they must also understand (when it is sensible to exchange) how to craft the incentive structures that will maximize the return to their organizations. Obviously, such structures need to cover relationships between buyer and supplier. However, they are also needed to regulate relationships within the organization. This is because poor demand management can have significant knock-on effects. Consequently, managers within an organization need to be encouraged (through the threat of sanction or the promise of reward) to engage in activities designed to maintain the organization's control over its external environment. At root, therefore, the study and practice of supply chain management is the study of managerial and contractual incentives.

References

Cox, A, Sanderson, J and Watson, G (2000) *Power Regimes*, Earlsgate Press, Boston, UK
Cox, A *et al* (2002) *Supply Chains, Markets and Power*, Routledge, London and New York
Hines, P *et al* (2000) *Value Stream Management*, Pearson, Harlow
Lonsdale, C and Cox, A (1998) *Outsourcing: A business guide to risk management tools and techniques*, Earlsgate Press, Boston, UK
Lonsdale, C and Watson, G (2005) The internal client relationship, demand management and value for money: a conceptual model, *Journal of Purchasing and Supply Management*, **11**, pp 159–71
Lukes, S (1974) *Power: A radical view*, Macmillan, London
Milgrom, P and Roberts, J (1992) *Economics, Organization and Management*, Prentice-Hall, New Jersey
Molhow, I (1997) *The Economics of Information*, Blackwell, Oxford
Peteraf, M (1993) The cornerstones of competitive advantage: a resource-based view, *Strategic Management Journal*, **14**, pp 179–91
Porter, M (1980) *Competitive Strategy*, Free Press, New York
Williamson, O (1985) *The Economic Institutions of Capitalism*, Free Press, New York

7

The development of supply chain relationships: a multi-lens approach

Peter Hines and Donna Samuel, Cardiff Business School

The last few decades have witnessed the rise of research into supply chain management and relationships within it. However, in many cases previous research has taken a single-lens approach to understanding and explaining what is happening as well as in subsequently developing solutions. The research reported here seeks to take a multi-lens approach to relationships in the supply chain using a complete farm to retail food supply chain as an instrumental case.

Introduction

Several authors have recently argued that, although supply chain management (SCM) has received a good deal of attention in the literature since the early 1980s, the concept is still not particularly well understood (Croom, Romano and Giannakis, 2000; Cigolini, Cozzi and Perona, 2004; Dubois, Hulthen and Pedersen, 2004). A case in point is integration through buyer–supplier or supply chain relationships (for instance, van Donk and van der Vaart, 2004). Specifically, the majority of current approaches tend to address the subject from a single perspective or lens.

A number of different perspectives have been taken in the literature, including power (Cox, 2001c; Christiansen and Maltz, 2002), trust (Sako, 1992; Simons *et al*, 2004) and risk (Rousseau *et al*, 1998; Zsidisin, 2003). Each of these variables has merit, but they are, on an individual basis, rarely the only variable that is at play. A few authors have attempted to link two of these three variables together, for example power and trust (Ramsay, 1996) or risk and trust (Das and Teng, 2001).

Building on this perspective, we propose a more pluralist multi-lens research view where a single instrumental case is viewed from a range of explanatory perspectives (Stake, 1998). In addition, it is our belief that, in some cases, there may be other variables at play that have not yet been sufficiently explored in the supply chain literature.

Our first research aim is, therefore, to understand how these different variables impinge and to explain the actions of actors within a supply chain. Linked to this, our second aim is to explore which of these might be more important in shaping the actions of each actor. Our third question seeks to understand whether there are any other important variables in addition to power, trust and risk. If indeed there is a more complex set of explanatory variables at play, our fourth research aim will investigate how such a level of understanding might be used to help the actors to improve their supply chain through better relationships.

The vehicle for exploring these aims is a longitudinal case centred on an Australian food processing firm.

A review of the existing literature

The idea of forming cooperative rather than adversarial relationships with suppliers made an appearance in the literature several decades ago (Farmer and Macmillan, 1978). Since then the idea has re-emerged under a variety of names including: co-makership (Merli, 1991); reverse marketing (Leenders and Blenkhorn, 1988); supplier alliances (Burdett, 1992) and partnership sourcing (DTI/CBI/PS, 1998). Variations have also appeared within the marketing domain under the title of relational or relationship marketing (Evans and Laskin, 1994) as well as within the strategic management field as strategic alliances. At the same time, the idea of cooperative relationships has been extended from immediate suppliers to encompass the wider supply chain (Macbeth, Baxter and Neil, 1989) and coupled with ideas borrowed from Japanese automotive and lean production literature (Womack, Jones and Roos, 1990; Lamming, 1993; Hines, 1994; Womack and Jones, 1996).

Ramsay (1996) argues that the majority of the academic literature emerged from an outright attack on the traditional, adversarial approach to supplier relationships with the assumption that collaboration and partnerships are the sine qua non of successful supplier relationship management. This latter view of relationship management has been supported by influential bodies in the UK such as the Confederation of British Industry (CBI) and the Department of Trade and Industry, which provided the initial support funding for Partnership Sourcing Ltd (PSL). However, evidence from many practitioners is that the term 'partnership' has been somewhat overused, often inappropriately where little real change has occurred (McIvor, Humphreys and McAleer, 1998).

The traditional purchasing-based view of SCM was to leverage the supply chain to achieve the lowest initial purchase prices whilst assuring supply, and was characterized by: multiple suppliers; supplier selection based primarily on purchase price; arm's length negotiations; formal short-term contracts; and centralized purchasing. A more contemporary view of SCM, heralded by some as the 'new paradigm' (Speckman, Kamauff and Myhr, 1998), redefines SCM as a process for designing, developing, optimizing and managing the internal and external components of the supply system, including material supply, transforming materials and distributing finished products or services to customers, that is consistent with overall objectives and strategies. The essence of SCM is as a strategic weapon to develop a sustainable competitive advantage by reducing investment without sacrificing customer satisfaction (Lee and Billington, 1992). While managers have long acknowledged the importance of getting closer to their key customers, the logic has now been extended to the upstream supply chain so that close ties with key suppliers are also seen as important (Helper, 1991). Speckman, Kamauff and Myhr (1998) conceptualize the transition from traditional open-market negotiations to collaboration as a continuum (see Figure 7.1), noting that the cooperation

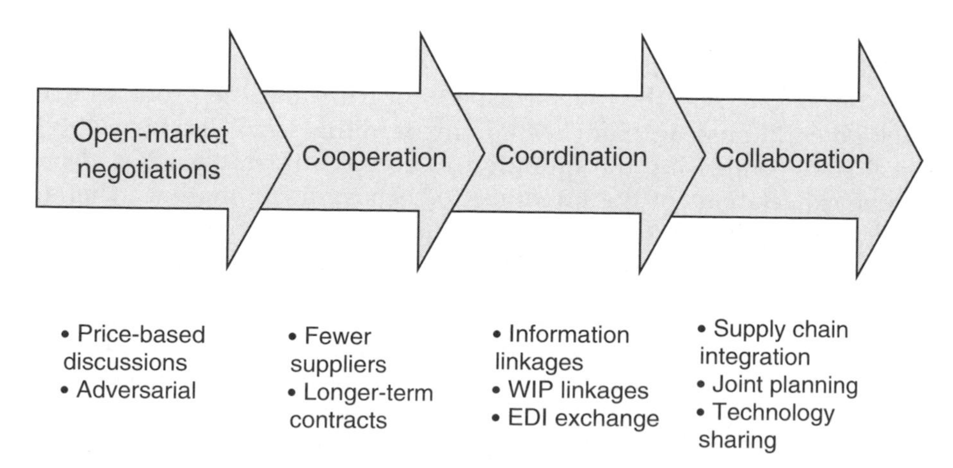

Source: Speckman, Kamauff and Myhr, 1998

Figure 7.1 The key transition from open-market negotiations to collaboration

and coordination stages are necessary but not sufficient to reap the benefits of effective collaboration.

Collaboration, then, is seen by many as an integral facet of an SCM strategy (Bhote, 1987; Kapoor, 1988; Anderson and Narus, 1990; Ellram, 1990; Speckman and Sawhney, 1995). This popular view is not without its critics, and a balanced approach to collaboration gives a picture of the determinants of successful SCM. Speckman, Kamauff and Myhr (1998) note that the road from open-market negotiations to collaboration is a long one and should not by travelled by every buyer–seller relationship.

Many authors have advocated a portfolio approach to supplier relationships management (Kraljic, 1983; Cox, 1996; Olsen and Ellram, 1997; Bensaou, 1999). Whilst the arm's length approach is now subject to criticism because of its focus on short-term cost reduction, it is often proposed under certain conditions: in commodity markets, with multiple suppliers, low asset specificity and little market uncertainty where the market serves as a control mechanism to ensure competitive prices (Schary and Skjøtt-Larsen, 2001).

However, much industrial purchasing does not meet these market characteristics, and here collaboration is usually presented as the obvious alternative. SCM demands a business transformation in which managers attempt to mitigate uncertainty and exploit opportunity through the creative use of both suppliers and customers by evaluating who best supplies value and then leveraging that expertise or capability through the entire supply chain. Speckman, Kamauff and Myhr (1998) note that this requires sharing what once might have been considered proprietary information, relinquishing control to others in the supply chain and trusting that your supply chain partners will act in your best interest. Trust clearly emerges throughout the literature as a key issue determining the success or otherwise of supply chain collaboration efforts.

However, trust is an ambiguous and complex phenomenon. Depending on their discipline and the problems they have been studying, many researchers have concentrated on the diverse aspects of trust and the process of trust development. Rousseau *et al* (1998) define it in this way: 'Trust is a psychological state comprising the intention to accept vulnerability based upon positive expectations of the intentions or behaviour of another.' Therefore trust is a psychological state, not a behaviour.

Economists have also recognized the nebulous nature of trust:

> Trust and similar values, loyalty or truth telling are examples of what an economist would call 'externalities'. They are goods; they are commodities; they have real practical value; they increase the efficiency of the system, enable you to produce more goods or more of whatever values you hold in high esteem. But they are not commodities for which trade on the open market is technically possible or even meaningful.
>
> (Arrow, 1974, cited in Smeltzer, 1997)

In recent years a number of authors have suggested classifications of trust (Mollering, 1998), but Bachmann (2001) comments that it is doubtful whether these classification schemes lead very far in coming to grips with the phenomenon. Sako (1992), for example, distinguishes between arm's length contractual relations (dominant in the West) and obligational contractual relations (dominant in the East) and conceptualizes three forms of trust: contractual trust (the mutual expectation that promises of a written or verbal nature will be kept), competence trust (the confidence that a trading partner is competent to carry out a specific task) and goodwill trust (commitments from both parties that they will do more than is formally required). He observes that goodwill trust is far more prevalent in Japanese buyer–supplier relationships and that it cannot be achieved without the presence of the other two types first. Simons *et al* (2004) identify the absence of trust as a key inhibitor to supply chain collaboration in the food industry. Stjernstrom and Bengtsson (2004) and Johnston *et al* (2004) suggest that relationships benefit from increasing trust. Hines (1996) argues that trust is an outcome (rather than a cause) of successful supply chain collaboration in Japan and that it is a set of other variables that lead to high-trust supplier relations. Similarly, Rousseau *et al* (1998) state that both risk and interdependence are necessary conditions for trust.

Many authors have identified that the primary role of trust in inter-organizational relationships is to mitigate risk. Das and Teng (2001) contend that trust and control are two principal antecedents of risk. Ring and Van de Ven (1992) argue that varying levels of risk and reliance on trust will explain the governance structures of transactions. Zsidisin (2003) highlights the lack of grounded definitions of risk within the context of supply. Kraljik (1983) discusses risk in terms of supply market complexity and incorporates supply scarcity, the pace of technology and/or materials substitution, entry barriers, logistics cost or complexity and monopoly or oligopoly conditions. Harland, Brenchley and Walker (2003) define supply risk as one of 11 risk types and adopt Meulbrook's (2000) definition of supply risk as being something that 'adversely affects inward flow of any type of resource to enable operations to take place'.

Zsidisin (2003), in accordance with other studies investigating risk definitions (Pablo, 1999), finds that supply risk is a multifaceted concept that differs according to industry (aerospace firms, for example, are more likely to understand risk in terms of threats to customer life and safety) but that the most widely held definition of supply risk focuses on understanding how risk affects a purchasing firm's ability to meet its customer requirements. Critical of previous efforts to address risk management in the absence of a grounded definition of risk, Zsidisin (2003) offers the definition, 'Supply risk is defined as the probability of an incident associated with inbound supply from individual supplier failures of the supply market occurring, in which its outcomes result in the inability of the purchasing firm to meet customer demand or cause threats to customer life and safety.'

Other authors argue that trust within buyer–supplier relations can be explained by another underlying factor, specifically power. Ramsay (1996) says that partnership formation involves a process of give and take. The supplier may expect increased order security, improved forward order cover and reduced uncertainty, whilst the buyer hopes to achieve improved supply continuity and a better match between the supplier's sale specification and the buyer's own specification, as well as reduced long-term costs. Ramsay (1996) says that 'In a genuine partnership, each party makes a commitment to the other and modifies its behaviour to more closely match the other's requirements. Each also becomes more dependent on the other – and thus both loses and gains power.' He also adds that for the majority of smaller companies the effort to form partnerships will frequently be met by supplier indifference or resistance – and the strategy itself is high-risk, high-cost and necessarily involves purchasers in an undesirable net loss of power. Cox (2001c) also argues that there will be only some power conditions that will be conducive to collaboration and that they will be in situations of buyer dominance or where power is equally distributed between buyer and seller to create interdependence.

Cox (2001a, 2001b) suggests that practitioners map the dominant power regimes in which they are located in order to formulate an understanding of which strategy – either proactive supplier selection (or traditional arm's length approaches) or proactive supplier development (more contemporary collaborative approaches) – is most suitable. However, any attempt to do so will reveal that power is itself a multifaceted concept and therefore subject to various interpretations. Power, most commonly viewed as market leverage, forms another determinant factor to effective supply chain collaboration.

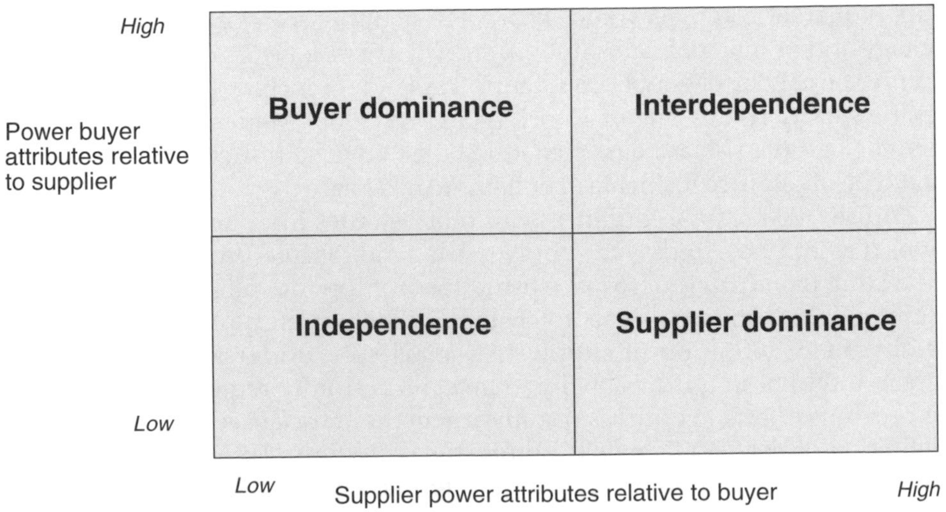

Source: Cox, 2001c

Figure 7.2 The power matrix

Methodology

The choice of research methodology is dependent upon the set of research questions under consideration and the state of knowledge (Pettigrew, 1990). Following Ahlstrom and Karlsson (2000) in deciding the most appropriate approach, consideration was made of:

- The focus, which was the process of improving a given supply chain and the relationships within it, particularly between a food processor and seven single or group entities. The study of processes is best served using longitudinal research (Kimberly, 1976).
- The fact that the study concerned change and adoption of new relationship sets. It was best to study this as it happened in their natural field settings (Van de Ven and Poole, 1995), as it is hard to establish cause and effect from retrospective research (Leonard-Barton, 1992).
- The fact that longitudinal cases of change are rare and as such the research was of an exploratory character.

It was necessary to spend a significant amount of time in field research to provide the depth of understanding necessary for subsequent theory building (Sofer, 1961). As such it was only possible to study a single supply chain – and this choice does limit the ability to generalize from this research.

The study began with the focal company's commitment to a lean supply chain initiative. The case study was undertaken from August 2003 (before the start of the initiative) until May 2005 (when the initiative developed past its original scope).

Instrumental case: the Perfect Pineapple Supply Chain Programme

Background

The Perfect Pineapple Supply Chain Programme was initiated in late 2003 and involved an Australian canned pineapple supply chain stretching from growers, through transport links and a processing plant, to a major retailer (see Figure 7.3). The supply chain also involved three key suppliers of cans, cartons and pallets.

The programme centred on a company processing 110,000 tonnes of fresh pineapple every year through a single facility. The majority of processed fruit is canned either in slices (or rings), pieces, cut (small pieces), crush, or pulp for juice.

The company was set up as a cooperative in 1946, and is owned by about 700 fruit and vegetable growers – with the majority of shares held by 171

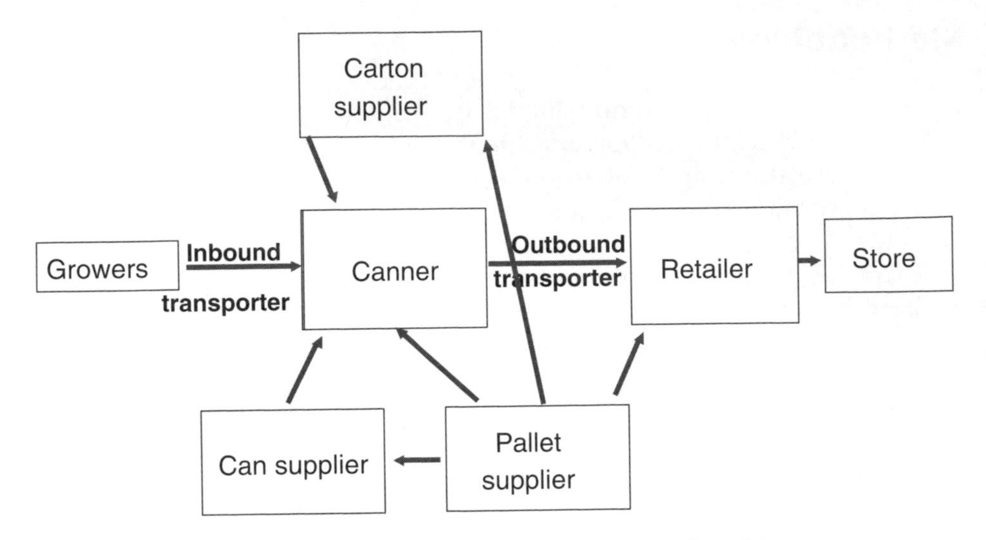

Figure 7.3 The Perfect Pineapple Supply Chain membership

pineapple growers. The company is Australia's largest grower-owned fruit and vegetable processor, with pineapple products representing 20 per cent of turnover. The market for these products is largely domestic and is dominated by Australia's two major supermarkets, who control 80 per cent of the market – one of whom took part in this study. The recent history of Australian supermarkets has been one of consolidation and emulation of overseas best practice and, in common with other markets, power in the Australian food industry seems to reside at the retailer, with relationships in the supply chain generally exhibiting low levels of trust (Sadler and Hines, 2002; Simons *et al*, 2004).

The retailer involved in the work was in the process of establishing a new supply chain strategy including:

- the development of a primary freight system, which is an Australian version of factory gate pricing (IGD, 2002; Potter *et al*, 2003) involving retailer-controlled collection, cross-docking and revised distribution centre configuration;
- store-friendly one-touch replenishment involving a streamlined material and information flow in the supply chain with the ideal of touching product only once between point of manufacture and checkout (Jones and Simons, 2000);
- vendor to store shelf end-to-end process efficiency and integration;
- the development of supplier relationships;
- delivery of cultural change and breakdown of functional silos.

At the start of the programme, there was limited evidence that the retailer had succeeded in implementing this new strategy.

The programme

In late 2002 the processor started a programme of manufacturing change under the a newly appointed general manager. The first year (step 1 of Figure 7.4) involved a series of improvement initiatives at the main manufacturing site. This included value stream mapping and a series of smaller improvements to internal and external information flows.

During this period it became apparent that many of the issues and problems faced by the company were the result either of actions taken by other organizations or of a lack of complete supply chain coordination. In addition, the company was suffering rapidly declining profits, reporting its first ever loss in 2003. At the same time, its major customers were increasing shelf space to imported product, including canned pineapple from the Philippines. As a result it was decided to widen the scope of the programme to encompass the wider supply chain. Focusing on canned pineapples, the programme was christened the Perfect Pineapple Supply Chain Programme.

Step 2 of the programme brought together senior executives from the different firms involved to establish what the supply chain looked like and what the programme could achieve, and to gain a commitment from the companies to take part in the programme. During this meeting the major issues facing the supply chain became clear. The managing director of the processor commented on the pressure exerted by retailers, particularly in terms of costs. This was particularly relevant as the company was losing market share to overseas competitors whose product retailed at 30 per cent lower prices. It would be difficult for the company to absorb these reduced margins – so they put pressure on growers, who had not received an increase

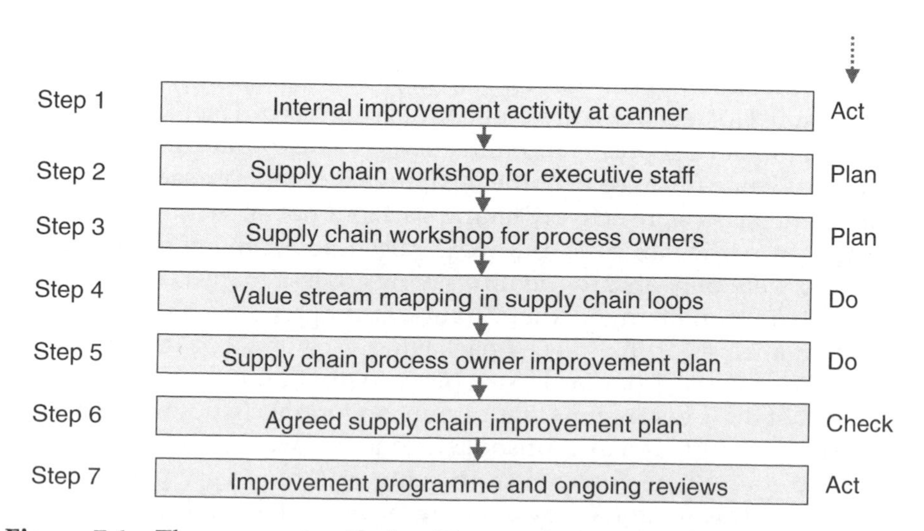

Figure 7.4 The seven-step Perfect Pineapple Supply Chain Programme

in price for their pineapples for nearly 10 years. The managing director concluded with the view that the only way forward was to work together as a team for everyone's mutual benefit. This view was generally accepted, but there was concern that some – primarily the retailer – would gain more than others, or even at the expense of the other participants.

The meeting included an exercise to map the whole supply chain. This showed that no one had a good picture of the complete supply chain, and few could describe the operations within their own business in great detail. The meeting also developed an ideal future state – as well as the barriers to getting there. These barriers included capital shortages, problems in changing culture, skilled people to make the change, the older age of growers, the lack of integrated IT, and the processor's lack of an explicit strategy.

Step 3 was to bring together the supply chain's process owners, or operational staff. This was done shortly after step 2, with meetings following a similar path to those of the executive group, except that less time was spent discussing what was required and more on how it might be done. A far more detailed map of the supply chain was developed, and with it the real problems began to emerge. Agreement was reached to undertake a more detailed analysis of the supply chain in five loops involving cross-company groups. The loops were a downstream loop (post-manufacture), a canning loop, an upstream fruit loop (up to delivery of pineapples) and two loops for the cans and cartons respectively. The result of this step was an agreed outline plan for each loop. These plans were presented back to the executive group.

Step 5 had discussions among the executive group of the findings and recommended projects – and how these could be developed into a workable plan. The view of the retailer was that they were keen to develop a new, closer relationship with suppliers – but would do so only in a step-by-step approach and only with like-minded firms.

The discussions quickly identified short-term gains of A$3–4 million, although further analysis showed that the true benefits could be of the order of A$20 million. However, two areas of concern emerged. The first was that it was difficult to plan a supply chain transition, as a new strategic plan for the processor was being finalized over the next three months. The second was the fact that all the firms were actively taking part, but not all seemed to be fully committed. In particular, concerns were raised about the can and carton makers who were only able to identify savings of less than A$100,000 each. However, they soon changed their stance and agreed a strategic review involving an analysis of the type of packaging used and how this might be changed – for example, from cardboard boxes to plastic bins.

As a result of these discussions, various uncomfortable issues were brought to the surface, and hidden and unspoken concerns were shared. The result was that the atmosphere changed from being unsure to very positive. This positive feeling was reinforced by a strong plan involving all the respective firms in its delivery. The top level of this plan is shown in Figure 7.5.

	Ease	Timing	Team							
			Retailer	Transp Out	Canner	Transp In	Growers	Pallet Supply	Carton Supply	Can Supply
Customer Integration		ST/LT	✓	✓	✓			✓		
Align consumer demand project 10 to 8 days SOH @ Retailers DCs	2	ST	✓	✓	✓					
Smoothing material flow (all product) transport / primary freight / packaging	5	LT	✓		✓			✓		
Consumer trends (alignment Canner/retailer)	2	ST	✓		✓			✓		
Internal Integration		JDI/LT	✓		✓		✓			
Avoid shift work with supply modification / analysis	3	JDI			✓					
Cost benefit of unsweetened from concentrate	2	JDI			✓					
Nitrate management	2	JDI			✓					
SKU rationalisation	4	JDI/ST	✓		✓		✓			
Align fruit intake to sales demand	4	LT			✓		✓			
Remove nightshift requirement / asset utilisation	3	LT			✓					
Rationalise of process lines	5	LT			✓					
Reduction of on-the-job training of seasonal staff	3	LT			✓					
Reducing premium paid for casual labour	3	LT			✓					
Remove inefficiency in low-volume period	3	MT			✓					
Grower Integration		JDI/LT			✓	✓	✓			
Increase sugar levels through quality-based payment system (QBPS)	4	JDI/LT			✓		✓			
Review grower rationalisation	5	LT			✓	✓	✓			
Feasibility study of sourcing supply options aligned to customer requirements	4	LT			✓		✓			
Packaging Integration		JDI/LT			✓			✓	✓	✓
Five-day carton inventory project	2	JDI/ST			✓				✓	
Electronic Receipting	3	JDI/ST			✓				✓	
PLI (Product, leadership & Innovation) Generic carton cost feasibility project: reduce SKUs	3	MT/LT			✓			✓	✓	
Can guage project (all products)	2	ST			✓					✓
Tin Coating	2	MT			✓					✓
PLI - Product, Leadership & Innovation	3	MT/LT			✓			✓		✓
EDI - Receipting	3	JDI/ST			✓					✓
Forecast Accuracy	4	LT			✓					✓
Enablers		JDI/ST			✓					
Develop & Communicate Short - Long Term Strategy for Pineapples	3	JDI/ST			✓					
Continued costing and profit potential	3	ST			✓					
Confirm targets & current state	2	JDI/ST			✓					

JDI = Up to 3 months
ST = Up to 6 months
MT = Up to 18 months
LT = Up to 5 years

Figure 7.5 The Perfect Pineapple Supply Chain plan

Since this point the group has continued implementing the plan and has already gained benefit of several million dollars. As a result, the processor has decided to extend the scope of the work to include a further loop – namely a beetroot loop, which represents a further 15 per cent of turnover. This step is a prelude to the development of further loops (for example, for baby food raw material ingredients, and fruit or fruit concentrate for fruit juice). It was also decided that once these further loops were in place (in late 2005) the extended group of companies (ie members of the Perfect Pineapple group and members of the new loops) would come together periodically and take on the shape and dynamics of a true supplier association (Hines, 1994).

Explanation and discussion

To explain what was happening within this case, a simple two-phase development model is presented, primarily in terms of changes at a macro level to the risk and trust that the food processor had developed with (but also to some degree between) members of the Perfect Pineapple Supply Chain Programme.

Phase 1 explanation

During the early stages of the work the processor was attempting to gain commitment by increased knowledge transparency, starting to increase competence levels and attempting to set up a common-destiny relationship set. In the process they were seeking to move away from historical contractual relationships (or what Sako (1992) terms a contractual trust relationship) that carried a varied but generally low level of trust and resulted in a high level of risk for all involved (phase 1 in Figure 7.6).

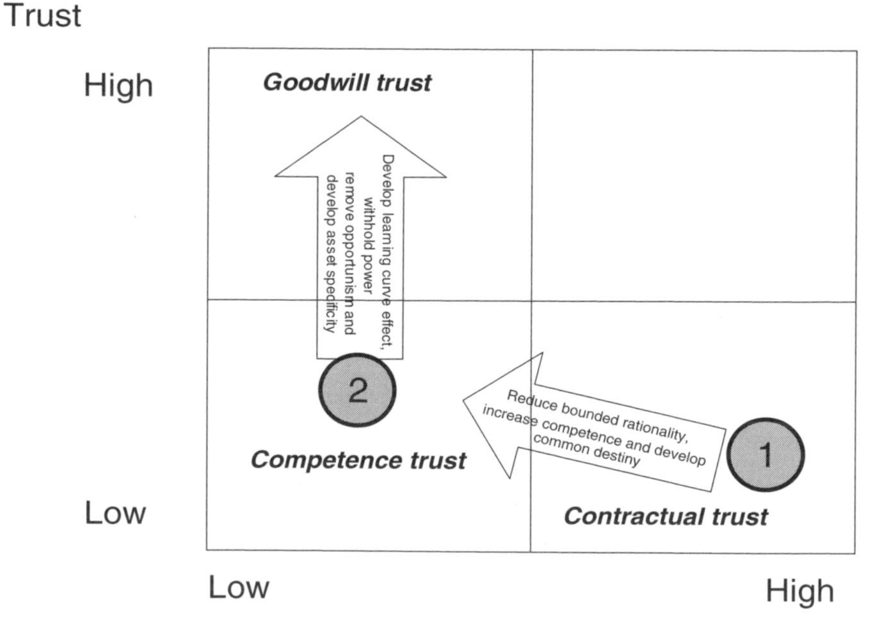

Figure 7.6 An explanatory model of the Perfect Pineapple Supply Chain Programme

Specifically, they were creating an open forum for exchange of views and information. This process involved identifying common (or not common) issues, concerns and visions for the supply chain, as well as the mapping of the complete chain by cross-company groups. This mapping also increased the individual and collective competence of the group, both in their own area and in the remainder of the supply chain. As a result, various individuals could see the bigger picture and the roles of others in improvement projects. In addition, this increase in individual and collective competence was likely to increase costs for new supply chain entrants, increasing barriers to entry and reducing risk for the present firms.

In this phase, senior staff from the processor went out of their way to develop a sense of common destiny, both by working to develop common measures across the supply chain and by creating an environment where mutually beneficial plans could be developed by teams from across the supply chain. Further commitment was sought with the full involvement of the retailer, but it was not yet possible to achieve the full commitment of all – particularly the packaging firms.

Phase 2 explanation

During the second phase of activity (steps 6 and 7), the processor was attempting to increase trust, having gone a significant way to reducing risk for all those involved. This second phase involved the development of learning effects, withholding power, and the removal of opportunistic behaviour – and ultimately was leading towards increased asset specificity. In terms of the explanatory model, the processor was seeking to move beyond competence trust to achieve goodwill trust, with firms doing more than their explicitly stated commitments (phase 2 in Figure 7.6).

Staff at the processor worked hard to ensure that a place in the improvement work could be found for all of the firms. In addition, they developed an approach that was sustainable, as it was not focused on quick wins, but a longer approach of at least three years' duration. Even at the early stages of the work they held informal discussions about developing the programme into a supplier association programme.

The second phase also involved the development of withheld power with a common set of metrics and attention paid to the fact that all the firms involved needed to see some benefit from the work. An example of the withheld power was the 'quiet word' to packaging firms when they appeared not to be giving their full commitment. They got reassurance that their involvement would benefit their firms and lead to a longer-term relationship with greater profit potential to all involved.

The second phase of activity moved the relationship set from a competence-based trust to the start of a goodwill trust where individual actors are starting to do things for the common good of the group rather than their individual benefit. This type of two-phase development has proved to be beneficial to the firms involved, but it may not be suitable in all other environments. It was appropriate here because the environment involved:

- regular repeated transactions (with daily or weekly orders);
- the willingness to hold back from explicit power relationships and the use of 'withheld power';
- an agreed common benefit in working together;
- a specific non-commodity product;
- appropriate outside facilitation to make concerns explicit.

Discussion: adding two more variables

In this case all the firms to a greater or lesser degree took an active and positive role in improvement. In addition, the relationship between the focal food processor and all the other firms improved – as did many of the relationships between the firms. And there are clear explanations for some of the activities and relationships when we view the case through the three different lenses of trust, risk and power.

However, we also concluded that, although each of these lenses is important, even together they are insufficient to explain the behaviour set. As a result of these observations, we would like to suggest two further interlinked factors that determined the success of collaboration in this case and may well have an importance in other instances. These are the type of ownership and corporate governance (and resultant governance structure), and the individual employee commitment or engagement.

Corporate governance is concerned with the decision made by senior executives of a firm and the impact of their decision on various stakeholder groups and therefore refers to the relationship between the board and the firm. Bradley (2004) comments that the search for the link between returns and governance is the Holy Grail for many practitioners and academics in the field of corporate governance, and that an ever-growing amount of evidence now exists to suggest that these links do not exist. Nonetheless we would argue that the corporate governance does influence management's approach to control versus commitment in the workplace.

Walton (1985) identifies these two opposing approaches to a company's human capital and points out the key challenges in moving from one to another. We would suggest that the firm's progress in this regard is likely to impact the individual's predisposition to supply chain collaboration's success. Lucy, Bateman and Hines (2004) coin the term 'employee engagement', highlighting its importance to the success of any change initiative. Indeed, their research suggests that people's degree of engagement is likely to be influenced by a range of personal and corporate objectives that may not be at all obvious at first sight to the casual observer. Supply collaboration invariably involves the reshaping of supply chain partners' patterns of behaviour and therefore demands a high commitment – a function of corporate governance – initially from the leading partner and subsequently from all parties involved.

Applying five lenses to the case

In order to understand the dynamics and relationships within the case study, it is useful to review the five determinant factors discussed earlier (power, risk and trust) and in the last section (ownership and governance structures, and commitment) and see how these have impacted on each of the participating firms. Before doing this, it is useful to explore how a single-lens perspective may give a misleading or incomplete impression of reality. In order to illustrate the point, we will take the example of a single power lens as advocated by Cox (2001a, 2001b, 2001c).

Using a development of Cox's power regime approach we can develop a power map for the physical movement of product (Figure 7.7), with the width of the arrows proportional to the cash flows, and the figures in circles representing the total business turnover of each firm. Following Cox (2001a), the symbols represent:

< buyer having power over supplier
> supplier having power over buyer
= interdependence
0 independence

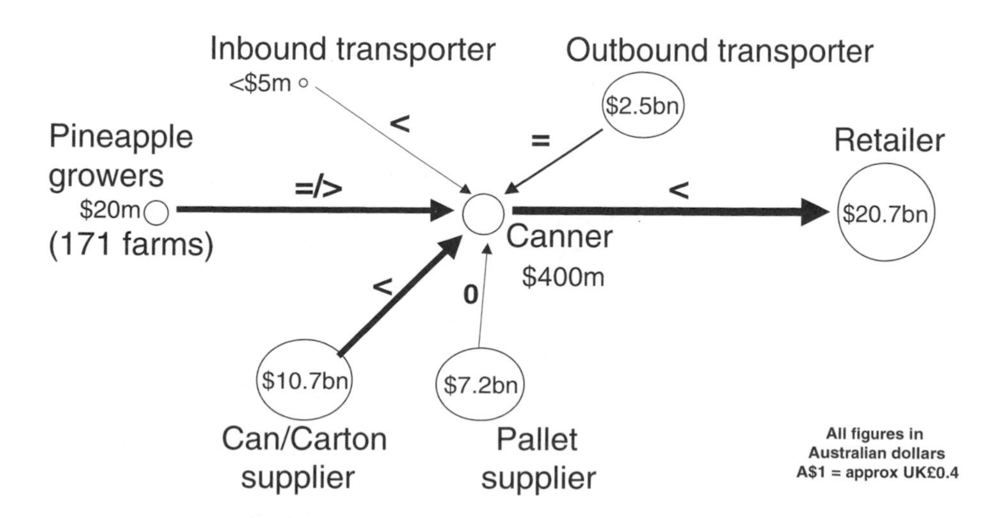

Figure 7.7 Power regimes within the Perfect Pineapple Supply Chain

The retailer holds power over the processor, primarily owing to size and ability to switch to cheaper imported product. The processor holds power over the can and carton maker as well as its inbound transporter. The processor has a relatively interdependent relationship with the outbound transporter and, owing to their low reliance on each other, a relatively independent relationship with the pallet supplier. The processor appears to hold power over the growers, but the governance structures between the two mean that the processor is owned largely by the pineapple growers.

It should be possible to interpret where successful supply chain relationships and development are possible, and where existing power regimes would preclude their effectiveness. According to Cox, a supply chain approach will only work where there is buyer dominance or buyer–supplier interdependence. So we can predict that the processor will be able to encourage the transport firms and packaging suppliers actively to take part, but find it very hard to engage the other firms. However, a different picture emerged. In gaining agreement and commitment to the programme, various difficulties appeared, which could not completely, or even largely, be explained by existing power regimes.

As the programme of activities aligned closely with the retailer's strategic objective, the retailer was enthusiastic about the programme. In addition, the growers were enthusiastic because it was ultimately to their benefit for the processor to produce a better financial result. The other company that showed the greatest enthusiasm was the outbound transporter. However, this owed little to the interdependence it enjoyed with the processor, and more to the perceived threat and risk that it felt in potentially losing business.

In addition, the inbound freight firm was not brought fully into the initiative in the early stages – but this was more to do with the commitment levels of the individuals involved, and once the discussions became more operational there was a much higher level of personal engagement. The pallet firm similarly did not take a very active part – but the reason appeared to be that improvements to the supply chain would probably reduce the number of pallets required. It also seemed that the packaging suppliers were only paying lip service to the work and were offering only marginal benefits. Their lack of involvement can be explained in two ways: firstly, the individuals involved saw little in the work in terms of career development; secondly, and more importantly, they did not trust the processor because of a history of adversarial price reduction demands.

The reactions and involvement of the different companies were sensible and indeed logical from their perspective. However, their responses cannot adequately be explained simply through a power lens. By viewing each company through each of the five lenses – power and dependency, risk, trust, ownership and governance structures, commitment – their behaviour can be both understood and explained (see Figure 7.8).

In reality, each of the five variables had some influence on individual firms' behaviours and how engaged they were (highly engaged firms are shown in

	Power and dependency	Risk	Trust	Ownership and governance structures	Commitment
Retailer ✓	Power over canner and outbound transporter	Little risk	Traditional arm's length, starting to use new close relationship language	Publicly quoted	High at senior levels, medium at process owner level
Outbound transporter ✓	Interdependence with canner	Risk of losing distribution contract in retailer's primary freight initiative	Good relationship with retailer and canner	Publicly quoted	High at each level
Canner ✓	Power over packaging suppliers and inbound transport	Losing market share to imported product	Good relationship with all players, sometimes arm's length with growers	Historically keeps grower directors in the dark	High at each level, skills gaps at process level
Inbound transporter	Dependent on canner	Risk of reduced pineapple business	Close relationship to canner	Family owned	Low at first as strategic discussion at too high a level to engage
Growers ✓	Strategically over canner	Risk of canner losing market share	Love–hate relationship with canner	Own / direct canner but historically kept in the dark operationally	High at both levels
Pallet supplier	Independence from canner	Risk of new technology in one-touch replenishment	Good relationships	Publicly quoted	Medium
Can supplier	Dependent on canner	Risk of losing business	Playing the negotiating game	Publicly quoted	Initially low
Carton supplier	Dependent on canner	Risk of losing business	Playing the negotiating game	Publicly quoted	Initially low

Figure 7.8 Involvement and influences in the Perfect Pineapple Supply Chain Programme

Figure 7.8 with a ✓) but in each case one variable was pre-eminent in shaping the behaviour. The pre-eminent variable for each firm is shown by a black box against the relevant variable. During the study it was possible to: 1) see how each less engaged firm could be brought on-side more readily and quickly; and 2) understand what was motivating the highly engaged firms and try to ensure that this factor was built upon to sustain the firm's positive role. In addition, it should be possible to repeat the multi-lens assessment periodically, as inevitably some of the variables will change in importance and weighting.

Conclusion

Returning to the research questions

We have attempted to address four questions. The first sought to understand how three well-established variables (power and dependency, trust and risk) impinge and explain the actions of actors within a supply chain. It has been shown that each of these lenses has proved helpful in understanding the motivation of behaviour. However, we have demonstrated that none of them, on their own, can adequately explain the behaviour of any one of the actors.

Linked to this first question, the second question was to explore which of the three variables might be more important in shaping the actions of each actor. The analysis presented in Figure 7.8 shows that each of these variables was the single most important factor in explaining some behaviour. Power and dependency was most important for the pallet supplier, risk was most important for the outbound transporter and the canner, and trust (or lack of it) was most important for both can and carton suppliers.

Our third question sought to understand whether there are any other important variables in addition to power, trust and risk. It was clearly established that it was not possible – in this particular case – to explain the behaviour of the firms using the three variables. We found two additional factors that were pre-eminent in explaining behaviour in at least one of the firms involved. These were the ownership and governance structures (most important for the growers) and personal commitment (most important for the retailer).

The last research question was contingent on there being a complex set of explanatory variables at play – which there did indeed prove to be. Gaining a more detailed understanding of the different variables at play might improve supply chain management through better relationships and more effective improvement activities. This was achieved in two ways. First, an explanatory model was developed (Figure 7.6) to supplement our description of what was happening within the case; second, a framework was constructed (Figure 7.8) that summarizes the impact of the different variables on each of the actors, and shows which was most important in influencing behaviour. We found that only a deep understanding of the actors would yield a full picture of all the different causes and effects.

Managerial lessons

This research has perhaps three important managerial lessons. The first is that taking a simple 'everything can be explained by one variable' approach was not appropriate in this study. This was highlighted by showing how using a single lens – power – led to a poor understanding of what might be occurring. Although this may be appropriate in rare examples, we believe that such a single-lens approach is very limited – and quite dangerous, as inappropriate solutions may be generated.

The second managerial lesson is that a multi-lens approach helps ensure that a better understanding is developed, which can lead to further stages of analysis and solution development. In this case the most appropriate five lenses were power and dependency, risk, trust, ownership and governance structures, and commitment. As a result an explanatory model was presented, which may prove a useful framework for establishing closer long-term relations within a supply chain setting, particularly where:

- there are regularly repeated transactions;
- there are (or could be) common goals;
- stronger actors are willing to withhold power for the good of the whole supply chain;

- products or services are in some way bespoke or unique;
- there is appropriate outside facilitation to make concerns explicit.

However, a caveat is that the five variables used here may not be the most important variables in all other cases – although they may provide a useful starting place for a discussion.

The final managerial lesson is that, either on a one-off occasion or better still on a periodic basis, using a framework such as Figure 7.8 to help understand and explain the behaviour of actors is likely to be the first step in developing a better and more sustainable set of relationships, which will result in a more effective supply chain.

References

Ahlstrom, P and Karlsson, K (2000) Sequences of manufacturing improvement initiatives: the case of delayering, *International Journal of Operations and Production Management*, **20**, pp 1259–77

Anderson, J and Narus, J (1990) A model of distributor firm and manufacturer firm working partnerships, *Journal of Marketing*, **54**, January, pp 42–58

Bachmann, R (2001) Trust, power and control in trans-organisation relations, *Organisation Studies*, **22** (2), pp 337–67

Bensaou, M (1999) Portfolios of buyer–supplier relationships, *Sloan Management Review*, **40** (4), pp 35–44

Bhote, RK (1987) *Supply Management: How to make US suppliers competitive*, American Management Association Membership Publications Division, New York

Bradley, N (2004) Corporate governance scoring and the link between corporate governance and performance indicators: in search of the Holy Grail, *Corporate Governance*, **12** (1), pp 8–10

Burdett, JO (1992) A model for customer–supplier alliances, *Logistics and Information Management*, **5** (1), pp 25–31

Christiansen, PE and Maltz, A (2002) Becoming an interesting customer: procurement strategies for buyers without leverage, *International Journal of Logistics*, **5** (2), pp 177–95

Cigolini, R, Cozzi, M and Perona, M (2004) A new framework for supply chain management, *International Journal of Operations and Production Management*, **24** (1), pp 7–41

Cox, A (1996) Relational competence and strategic procurement management, *European Journal of Purchasing and Supply Management*, **2** (1), pp 57–70

Cox, A (2001a) Managing with power: strategies for improving value appropriation from supply relationships, *Journal of Supply Chain Management*, **37** (2), Spring, pp 42–47

Cox, A (2001b) Supply chain and power regimes: toward an analytical framework for managing extended networks of buyer and supplier relationships, *Journal of Supply Chain Management*, **37** (2), Spring, pp 28–35

Cox, A (2001c) Understanding buyer and supplier power: a framework for procurement and supply competence, *Journal of Supply Chain Management*, **37** (2), Spring, pp 8–15

Croom, S, Romano, P and Giannakis, M (2000) Supply chain management: an analytical framework for critical literature review, *European Journal of Purchasing and Supply Chain Management*, **6**, pp 67–83

Das, TK and Teng, BS (2001) Trust, control and risk in strategic alliances: an integrated framework, *Organisation Studies*, **22** (2), pp 251–84

Department of Trade and Industry (DTI)/Confederation of British Industry (CBI)/Partnership Sourcing (PS) (1998) *Partnering for Profit*, Profile Pursuit, London

Dubois, A, Hulthen, K and Pedersen, A (2004) Supply chains and interdependence: a theoretical analysis, *Journal of Purchasing and Supply Management*, **10**, pp 3–9

Ellram, L (1990) The supplier selection decision in strategic partnerships, *Journal of Purchasing and Materials Management*, Fall, pp 8–14

Evans, JR and Laskin, RL (1994) The relationship marketing process: a conceptualisation and application, *Industrial Marketing Management*, **23**, pp 439–52

Farmer, D and Macmillan, K (1978) The benefits of reducing opportunism in buyer–supplier relationships, *Purchasing and Supply Management*, May, pp 10–13

Harland, C, Brenchley, R and Walker, H (2003) Risk in supply networks, *Journal of Purchasing and Supply Management*, **9** (2), pp 51–62

Helper, S (1991) How much has really changed between US auto makers and their suppliers?, *Sloan Management Review*, **32** (4), Summer, pp 15–29

Hines, P (1994) *Creating World-Class Suppliers: Unlocking mutual competitive advantage*, FT Publishing, London

Hines, P (1996) Network sourcing: a discussion of causality within the buyer–supplier relationship, *European Journal of Purchasing and Supply Management*, **2** (1), pp 7–20

Institute of Grocery Distribution (IGD) (2002) *Backhauling and Factory Gate Pricing: Evolution or revolution?*, IGD Business Publications, Watford

Johnston, D *et al* (2004) Effects of supplier trust on performance of cooperative supplier relationships, *Journal of Operations Management*, **22**, pp 23–38

Jones, D and Simons, D (2000) Towards perfect customer fulfilment, *Logistics Focus*, October, pp 45–50

Kapoor, V (1988) Becoming a just in time vendor, *Quality Progress*, **21** (6), June, pp 56–59

Kimberly, J (1976) Issues in the design of longitudinal organizational research, *Sociological Methods and Research*, **4** (3), pp 321–47

Kraljic, P (1983) Purchasing must become supply management, *Harvard Business Review*, **61** (5), pp 109–17

Lamming, R (1993) *Beyond Partnership: Strategies for innovation and lean supply*, Prentice Hall, London

Lee, H and Billington, C (1992) Managing supply chain inventory: pitfalls and opportunities, *Sloan Management Review*, **33** (3), Spring, pp 65–73

Leenders, MR and Blenkhorn, DL (1988) *Reverse Marketing: The new buyer–supplier relationship*, Free Press, New York

Leonard-Barton, D (1992) The factory as a learning laboratory, *Sloan Management Review*, **34** (1), pp 23–28

Lucy, J, Bateman, N and Hines, P (2004) *Achieving Pace and Sustainability in a Major Lean Transition*, 11th European Manufacturing and Operations Association (EUROMA) Conference Proceedings, Brussels, pp 815–24

Macbeth, D, Baxter, L and Neil, G (1989) Not purchasing but supply chain management, *Purchasing and Supply Management*, November, pp 30–32

McIvor, R, Humphreys, P and McAleer, W (1998) European car makers and their suppliers: changes at the interface, *European Business Review*, **98** (2), pp 87–99

Merli, G (1991) *Co-makership: The new supply strategy for manufacturers*, Productivity Press, Cambridge

Meulbrook, L (2000) Total strategies for company-wide risk control, *Financial Times*, 9 May, p 308

Mollering, G (1998) Trust across borders: relative rationality and relative specificity in the context of international cooperation and emerging markets, Paper presented at the Academy of International Business Annual Conference, London, 3–4 April

Olsen, RF and Ellram, LM (1997) A portfolio approach to supplier relationships, *Industrial Marketing Management*, **26** (2), pp 101–13

Pablo, AL (1999) Managerial risk interpretations: does industry make a difference?, *Journal of Managerial Psychology*, **14** (2), pp 92–107

Pettigrew, A (1990) Longitudinal field research on change: theory and practice, *Organization Science*, **1** (3), pp 267–92

Potter, A *et al* (2003) Modelling the impact of factory gate pricing on transport and logistics, Proceedings of the 8th International Symposium of Logistics, Seville, Spain

Ramsay, J (1996) The case against purchasing partnerships, *International Journal of Purchasing and Materials Management*, **3** (4), Fall, pp 13–19

Ring, PS and Van de Ven, AH (1992) Structuring cooperative relationships between organisations, *Strategic Management Journal*, **13**, pp 483–98

Rousseau, DM *et al* (1998) Not so different after all: a cross discipline view of trust, *Academy of Management Review*, **23** (3), pp 393–405

Sadler, I and Hines, P (2002) Strategic operations planning process for manufacturers with a supply chain focus: concepts and a meat processing application, *Supply Chain Management: An international journal*, **7** (4), pp 225–41

Sako, M (1992) *Prices, Quality and Trust: Inter-firm relations in Britain and Japan*, Cambridge University Press, Cambridge

Schary, PB and Skjøtt-Larsen, T (2001) *Managing the Global Supply Chain*, 2nd edn, p 185, Copenhagen Business School Press, Copenhagen

Simons, D *et al* (2004) *Making Lean Supply Work in the Food Industry*, Conference proceedings, Sixth International Conference on Chain and Network Management in Agribusiness and the Food Industry, The Netherlands, pp 111–17

Smeltzer, L (1997) The meaning and origin of trust in buyer–supplier relationships, *International Journal of Purchasing and Materials Management*, **33** (1), Winter, pp 40–49

Sofer, C (1961) *The Organization from Within: A contemporary study of social institutions based on a sociotherapeutic approach*, Tavistock Publications, London

Speckman, R and Sawhney, K (1995) Towards a conceptual understanding of the antecedents of strategic alliances, in *Business Marketing: An interaction and network perspective*, ed D Wilson and C Mollen, pp 157–92, Kent Publishing, Boston, MA

Speckman, R, Kamauff, J and Myhr, N (1998) An empirical investigation into supply chain management: a perspective on partnerships, *Supply Chain Management*, **3** (2), pp 53–67

Stake, R (1998) Case studies, in *Strategies of Qualitative Inquiry*, ed N Denzin and Y Lincoln, pp 88–90, Sage, California

Stjernstrom, S and Bengtsson, L (2004) Supplier perspectives on business relationships: experiences from six small suppliers, *Journal of Purchasing and Supply Management*, **10**, pp 137–46

Van de Ven, A and Poole, M (1995) Explaining development and change in organizations, *Academy of Management Review*, **20** (3), pp 510–40

van Donk, DP and van der Vaart, T (2004) Business conditions, shared resources and integrative practices in the supply chain, *Journal of Purchasing and Supply Management*, **10**, pp 107–16

Walton, R (1985) From control to commitment in the workplace, *Harvard Business Review*, March/April, pp 77–84

Womack, J and Jones, D (1996) *Lean Thinking*, Simon & Schuster, New York

Womack, J, Jones, D and Roos, D (1990) *The Machine that Changed the World*, Maxwell Macmillan, New York

Zsidisin, G (2003) A grounded definition of supply risk, *Journal of Purchasing and Supply Management*, **9**, pp 217–24

8

Demand flow leadership and the evolution of management concepts

Dag Ericsson, University of Skovde

Management concepts come and go. Some rise, explode and fall back like fireworks. Some remain like the North Star brightly shining and serving as guidelines for navigation on the stormy seas of management. The first major issue, then, is to learn how to distinguish between fads and lasting, innovative concepts. The next issue is to find out how to implement concepts; what kind of methods and tools we need; how to educate to change mindsets; and what the best way is to design the transformation process.

One way to distinguish between concepts and the rest is to use a holistic approach and see how the bits fit together to create a new pattern. When Taylor wrote about scientific management, he observed and summarized things that were happening in research and practice. He established a theory – or a frame of reference – for the emerging industrial society. One reason for the success of scientific management was the obvious need for a new paradigm to guide the transition from handicraft to industrial manufacturing.

Today there is a need for a new paradigm for the shift from the industrial to the digital society. It is obvious that 'something is trying to happen'. There are islands of rethinking and new frames of reference popping up in the ocean of business strategy and management. What is needed is a holistic frame of reference that can help bridge the troubled waters separating those islands.

Demand chain management (DCM) is an important new business model to help with this. Electrolux, one of the world's leading appliance companies, has created its own version of DCM, called demand flow leadership – and these words are carefully chosen. Demand means consumer-centric, with all activities based on consumer insight. Flow suggests an even, steady, uninterrupted and quality-assured value stream – as opposed to a chain of sequential, connected links. Leadership refers to the fact that the demand flows are not organizational units that have to be managed. Demand flows are processes where leaders can emerge anywhere in the value network. Their efforts have to be supported by executives with a vision of what can be achieved.

Visions and tools

Man is limited not so much by his tools as by his visions.

(Christopher Columbus)

The evolution of management concepts is influenced by several things. One of the most important is executive vision, which is important for identification and application of relevant methods and tools. Another is new tools, which create new possibilities. Information and communication technology (ICT) is a major trigger for renewal – and also a major enabler in the transition from the old industrial to the new digital world. The availability of new ICT tools is increasing rapidly, and the trick is to know which ones to use and for what purpose – with implementation driven by business needs and not by technology availability.

External developments also have to be analysed and classified in order of importance. External opportunities and threats should be transformed into action and internal adaptation – triggering internal rethinking and restructuring. Increasing global competition puts heavy stress on proaction rather than reaction – and it is important to identify trends early and benefit from them. For example, identification of emerging consumer needs, and efforts to turn market volatility from a threat to an opportunity are two of the major goals of DCM.

A lot of today's thinking has its roots far back in history, but visions that earlier could not be reached because of lack of efficient tools can now be realized. The next issue, then, asks how new concepts should be implemented to create lasting change. To get a better understanding of this it is worth looking back in history, to learn from experience and see how lasting management concepts have developed over time.

The evolution of management concepts

In order to look forward we have to look back.

(Winston Churchill)

The diffusion of a concept like DCM follows the usual S-shaped curve, with early adopters and laggards. It is also clear that there will never be complete implementation in any sample of companies, as the concept simply does not fit all conditions (Towill, 1997). We can see this in the development of other management concepts. In 1981, I described the development of production, sales and marketing orientation to provide a background to the evolving materials flow concepts (Ericsson, 1981) (see Figure 8.1). I wanted to show how concepts build on each other and develop partly in response to problems created by an old concept. The best parts of the old concept remain and are refined, while the flaws are removed. There is a considerable overlap in time, with laggards still introducing a new concept while early adopters are leaving for an even newer concept. Intense, global competition makes it more and more dangerous to lag behind, as concept life cycles – like product life cycles – get shorter over time.

Production orientation

In the early 1900s, production orientation developed as a natural response to increasing demand for industrial goods. Scientific management focused on the production process and the possibility of increasing productivity through rationalization. Taylor's frame of reference and the availability of new methods and tools hastened development and accelerating growth.

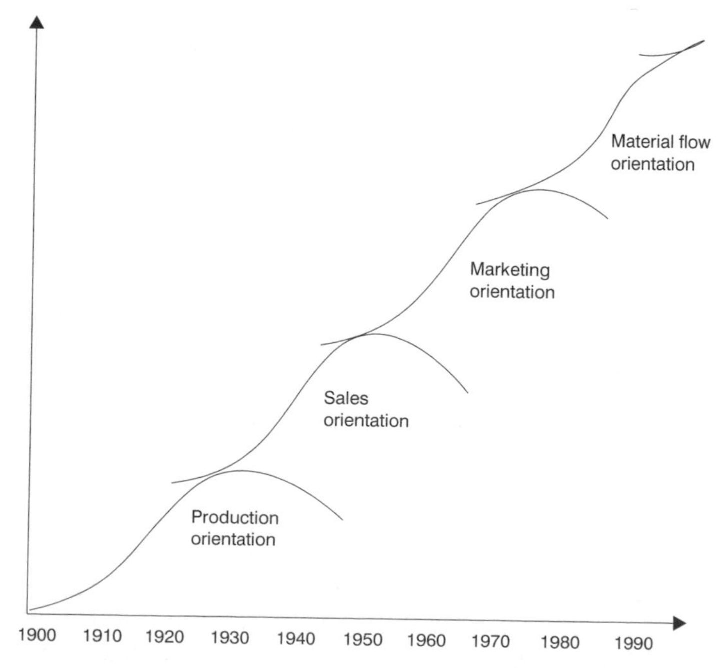

Source: Ericsson, 1981

Figure 8.1 The development of four major management concepts over time

Keith (1959) summarized the management philosophy of Pillsbury for the years 1891 to 1930, saying, 'Our task is to grind flour of high quality and to sell it. However, it is important that the business idea is built on the availability of wheat and water-power – not the availability and closeness of growing markets or the demand for better and cheaper flour.' Such a narrow view causes problems when productivity increases and getting rid of the product becomes a problem. Early writers observed this and pointed to the demand market as the major problem. In 1915 Shaw wrote, 'Even if we are still on the threshold to all the possibilities offered by increasing productivity, the development has already surpassed existing distribution systems. We have to find markets for the products we can manufacture. The most important issue today is to systematically study distribution in the same way as we have been studying manufacturing.' Despite this, laggards still stuck to production orientation until the 1950s and 1960s.

Sales orientation

In the 1920s, the view of sales orientation evolved, with Borsodi (1929) summarizing the change of focus by saying, 'The days are gone when the recipe for big profit simply was manufacturing, more manufacturing – and even more manufacturing! The distribution age is here.' Then Pillsbury's philosophy changed to: 'As a flour producing company with many different products for the consumer market, we need a first class sales force to get rid of all the products we can produce at a good price' (Keith, 1959).

The sales orientation was sufficient in a seller's market, when demand is higher than supply. However, when the situation was reversed, a change of mindset was needed. The sales orientation was successively replaced by a marketing orientation.

Marketing orientation

A 'new marketing concept' was launched in the early 1950s – with authors making a distinction between the old production and sales concepts and the new marketing concept. It was stressed that marketing is consumer-centric and focuses on analysis, planning, product development and profitability – and not only sales volume.

Pillsbury's philosophy changed again to: 'Today marketing in our company is seen as the function that plans and executes sales – the whole way from idea generation, through development and sales to the customer. Marketing starts and ends with the consumer… the marketing department leads all company resources in the transformation of the idea to a product and the product to a sales agreement' (Keith, 1959). This statement could have been written today, with the major difference that we now have the tools to carry it through. The focus had shifted from production to marketing, from the products we can manufacture to the products the consumer really wants and from the company to the market.

But the new marketing concept started to create its own problems, most of which came from too far-reaching customer orientation with focus on service and delivery – without any deeper analysis of the concepts and the consequences. Scattered remedies were popping up, but most of these were fads rather than cures. They generally demanded more flexibility and smaller batch sizes in manufacturing, while focusing on delivery lead times – and gave higher inventory, transportation and handling costs. The lack of a theoretical framework and a common language resulted in tension and conflicts between marketing and manufacturing – and increasing struggles for power. These problems initiated the development of the materials flow orientation, when it became clear that the problems could only be solved with a more holistic approach.

Materials flow orientation

In the early 1960s the materials flow approach started to spread in Sweden. It grew rather slowly to the end of the 1960s, and then took off when the concept of materials administration was developed through close collaboration between universities and major industrial companies such as Volvo, SKF, Atlas Copco, Sandvik and Astra. The approach was called materials administration because it was a much broader and more strategic concept than logistics at that time (see Ericsson, 2003). In particular, materials administration (MA) was defined as 'Planning, development, coordination, organization, control and review of the materials flow from raw materials supplier to the ultimate user' (Ericsson, 1969b).

The concept focused the need for integrated management of the inflow, throughput and outflow. From the start, MA stressed coordination and the strategic aspects of effective materials flows, but it also emphasized that implementation had to start internally with synchronization of purchasing, production and physical distribution on an operational and tactical level (see Figure 8.2). The internal structuring of the company must increase cooperation and synchronization of activities in different departments.

The focus on internal processes was the starting point for the implementation, but it was clear that internal efficiency was not enough, and links with suppliers and customers also had to be improved and coordinated. The first step was to improve cooperation on the supply side. Supplier development and evaluation, stockless buying, systems contracting and co-makership became key words in this development (Ericsson, 1969c).

The next step was to increase cooperation with first-tier customers. Early writers on marketing focused on consumer markets, but now the interest in industrial marketing – and hence in industrial buying – increased (Ericsson, 1969a).

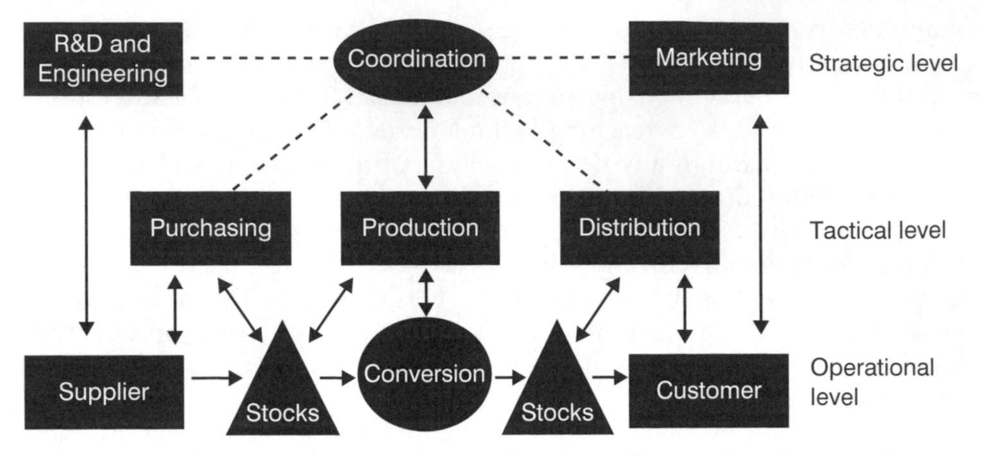

Figure 8.2 The MA concept with coordination of internal and external flows and processes

The term 'control' in the definition of MA refers to the use of developing computer tools for managing materials flows. Initial steps focused on operational and tactical levels in the company, but soon the strategic aspects of MA came into focus – not only for directly flow-related functions such as purchasing, production and physical distribution, but also with marketing and R&D and engineering.

Phases in the development of the materials administration/ logistics concept

The early development of the concept shows a typical growth curve: a rather slow start with acceleration in the early 1970s, as shown in Figure 8.3 (Ericsson 1981, 2003; Green, 1989).

The first generation of logistics – the total-cost-oriented one – came as a response to increasing need for a holistic view on costs. The functional and silo-oriented approach that had evolved as a consequence of the division of labour had gone too far. By the 1950s this approach had started to show major weaknesses – trade-offs between functions and departments were hard to achieve and sub-optimization was a major threat. Luckily, some new methods and tools were appearing to solve the problem, such as operational research models and emerging computer technology. So the first generation of materials administration/logistics was born in 1969 as a response to problems and needs – and the increasing availability of effective tools.

The vision is 'to create an even, steady, uninterrupted and quality assured flow from raw materials supplier to the ultimate user' (Ericsson, 1969b). This was a guiding statement of the ideal situation when all members of the flow

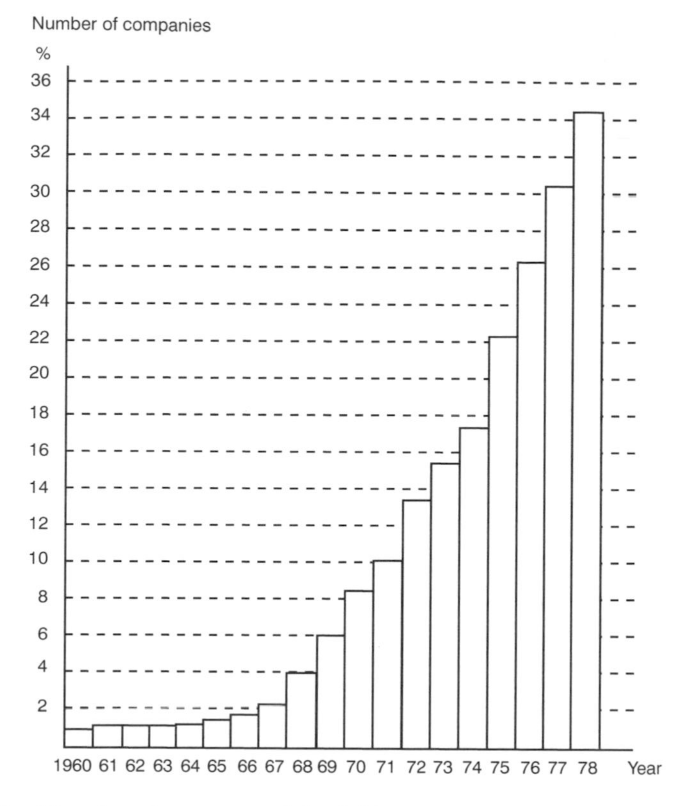

Figure 8.3 The development of the MA concept

think and act as one. This vision is very close to Towill's (1997) concept of the 'seamless supply chain'.

External conditions changed again with rapid growth in the 1960s replaced by zero growth of the 1970s. The problem was then to gain a bigger share of a non-growing cake. The solution was the second generation of logistics – the revenue-oriented one – based on logistics as a means of competition. One of the ways of increasing sales was to increase the local presence with sales outlets and warehouses close to the customer. The number of warehouses and number of items exploded – with the capital tied up in inventory creating new challenges. This triggered the third generation of logistics – the profitability-oriented one – that was born in the 1980s.

During the late 1980s and the early 1990s the need for more and better integration both internally and externally increased – but communication and integration tools were developing fast. Business process re-engineering and time-based management caught on and, if properly applied, could serve as a basis for effective and efficient use of new ICT tools.

The fourth and fifth generations of logistics – respectively the time and process one and the IT-based one – were born. They served as the launching pad for increased and improved integration in supply chains. They also pointed to the need to focus on inter-organizational processes, rather than on institutions in the chain. Different definitions of SCM illustrate this change of focus (Cooper, Lambert and Pagh, 1998). The implementation of SCM was enabled and facilitated by two important toolboxes that were developed in the 1990s – business resource management and e-logistics.

Business resource management

In the 1980s, the need for deeper integration and synchronization of processes across functional areas became urgent. In order not to get stuck in traditional functional or departmental silos, the focus was on interdepartmental resources and processes. This holistic view was called business resource management (BRM) (Ericsson, 1990). It had its roots in classical management literature, where the four main resources were 'men, materials, machines and money' – with information as a major new resource. The aim was to create a framework for integration of resources, flows and processes.

BRM is a broad, holistic management approach, and soon it became evident that it also could be used as a basis for inter-organizational process management. The focus on resources, flows and processes was an excellent starting point for process-oriented SCM and DCM.

E-logistics

BRM is a forerunner of the broadening of the logistics concept into e-logistics – which is a toolbox for improving inter-organizational relations. It was a response to the increasing interdependence between logistics and ICT.

The evolution of the logistics concept illustrates the interplay between visions and tools. In the early history of logistics development, tools were lagging behind visions and we were asking for more tools – in the mid-1990s, however, the tools surpassed the visions and the next issue was to renew the vision and create ways of using the new tools (Ericsson, 1996, 2003). E-logistics was launched to provide a framework for using the new tools of logistics, process management and ICT – and the opportunities created by the interplay between them. E-logistics is the enabler of increased collaboration in the supply chain and it also creates opportunities for true consumer orientation.

New tools are continuously developing, while old ones change focus and use. For example, the concept of quick response is not new, but it has a new and deeper meaning when used to give customer orientation in fast-moving industries. New ICT tools – especially customer databases – improve relations with customers and enable point-of-sale and point-of-demand techniques. New tools for linking enterprise databases, applications and business systems are also developing fast.

Supply chain management

The concept of supply chain management evolved as a response to the necessity of improving and extending cooperation. The relationships in supply chains moved from arm's length, often adversarial, transactions to different levels of integration – ranging from coordination, through cooperation to collaboration. Then e-logistics, with its focus on process management, is a major enabler of both SCM and DCM.

There are several ways of defining processes in business (Cooper, Lambert and Pagh, 1998). I have chosen to distinguish between three core business processes: time-to-cash, time-to-market, and customer creation and retention. The time-to-cash process includes the total materials, information and payment flows. Time-to-market is the total process for creation, development and improvement of products and services. The customer creation and retention process creates and retains customer relations all the way from the first contact, via after-sales, follow-up and continuous improvement (Ericsson, 2003).

The difference between logistics and SCM becomes clear if we take these processes as the starting point. Both concepts focus on the flow from raw materials to ultimate user. MA/logistics has its main focus on the materials flow and its connected information flows. In other words, it is focused on the time-to-cash process. The SCM concept also considers the other two core processes – time-to-market and customer creation and retention. Hence, the SCM concept is broader than the MA/logistics concept. It focuses on the integration and synchronization of inter-organizational relations and processes. This explicitly changes the focus from the individual company to the supply chain as a whole. SCM developed as a remedy for reoccurring problems at the interfaces between entities in the chain. It was important to 'get the entities to act as one', which was apparent when the fact that competition takes place more between supply chains than between individual companies started to be recognized and accepted (Christopher, 1992).

However, in practice, it still was very much 'us' against 'them' both inside supply chains and in relation to outside customers. Everyone talked about consumer-centric approaches, but they were not being implemented. This creates increasingly severe problems when the locus of power shifts down the supply chain to the final customer. Global competition, increased volatility and decreasing product life cycles accentuated the problems. It became clear that there was a need for a new business model.

The evolution of a new business model

> We need a completely new way of thinking in order to solve the problems we have created by using the old way of thinking.
>
> (Albert Einstein)

The evolution of the DCM concept is, maybe, the first step towards a major rethinking. The transition from yesterday's business model into tomorrow's is shown in Figure 8.4, which illustrates that we are moving from a push to a pull approach – from an SCM to a DCM. We are moving from yesterday's model based on independent, inventory-based entities aiming for low-cost production to tomorrow's model with information-based virtual networks aiming for creation of perceived consumer value. Supplier-driven mass production and mass marketing are replaced by market-driven mass customization and one-to-one marketing.

If we believe in this description it is quite clear where we are and where we are heading. The question is how to get there. The first step is to make some internal as well as external adaptations and alignments.

Internal alignments

There is clearly a need for closer integration of logistics/SCM and relationship marketing (Ericsson, 2003). The concept of relationship marketing has evolved into customer relationship management (CRM), which allows a business to target customers more closely and implement one-to-one marketing strategies where appropriate, and which makes the alignment with SCM even more important. The key is to knit together the knowledge and expertise from SCM with the knowledge of marketing/sales and buyer behaviour. Internally, this is a question of getting a common demand chain strategy that is based on both

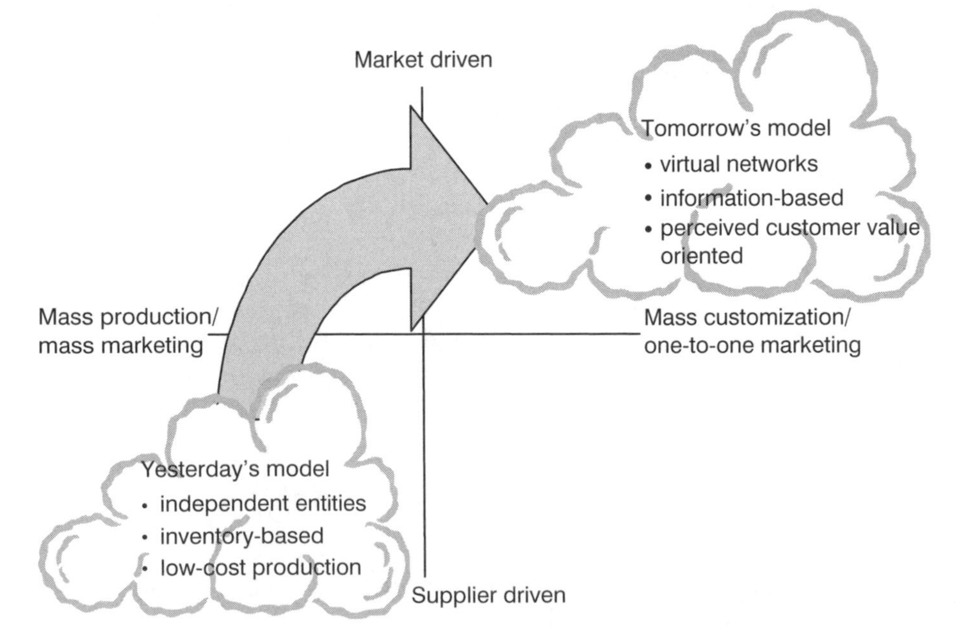

Figure 8.4 The business model of the future

the marketing/sales and logistics/SCM strategies. Demand creation has to be synchronized with demand fulfilment. In theory, this is obvious, but there still is a long way to go before this is implemented in practice.

External alignments

Externally, processes and systems must also be aligned and synchronized:

1. Perceived customer values and the market segments have to be defined to answer the question, 'What are the explicit and implicit demands and requirements of the customer?'
2. Value chain processes are defined to answer the question, 'What processes should be synchronized in order to fulfil the needs and demands in the value segments?'
3. The network structure of the customized supply chain (the value chain) must be defined, answering the question, 'Who are the key value chain members with whom to link processes?'
4. Value chain management components are defined based on the question, 'What level of integration and management should be applied for each process link?' (Cooper, Lambert and Pagh, 1998).

Most contemporary DCM research focuses on interfaces in the commercial channel, ie on B2B relations, but the interface between the commercial channel and the consumer is the most important one. Because of the direct demand, the consumer's wants, desires and needs are of a different nature. The focus on consumer insight and deep knowledge of consumer needs and wishes is the major difference between demand-driven SCM and DCM.

Demand chain management

In recent years, there has been intense discussion of SCM and DCM. Is there a choice of either one or the other? Should DCM replace SCM? Is DCM just another name for demand-driven supply chain or is it completely new? My conclusion is that DCM is a natural next step in the evolution of the SCM concept based on the necessity for adaptation to changing external and internal conditions and the availability of new tools. It is a matter of adapting to changing circumstances and creating and using the right tools.

Responsiveness is the key to the new global economy – and also to the DCM approach. 'Customer ecstasy – at a profit' is the battle-cry of the new global economy (Ericsson, 2003). The key is to create value to the consumer, but in a cost-effective and efficient way. This is, in a nutshell, the mission of the DCM approach.

From a theoretical point of view, DCM is a logical way of refocusing and creating a new business model for the digital and global society. Intensified competition and the availability of new tools push for a change of focus. The question is can we see any sign of a new model in practical applications – or is the concept just another academic fad?

Practical applications

There is some evidence of DCM emerging in business. Over the years, power in the distribution channel has moved from the manufacturer to the wholesaler and retailer. Today, the power rests with the consumer. This makes direct contact between the manufacturer and the consumer a vital ingredient in creating competitive strength. Dell has solved this problem with close collaboration with suppliers and customers. However, most companies cannot bypass intermediaries, so relationships with retailers are crucial, as they form the main interface with consumers.

The car industry has been trying to handle this problem for some time and has used all types of electronic tools. However, in 2001, an industry analyst stated that 'The business model for the car industry is broken' (*USA Today*, 2001). GM had already started to create a new model for the car industry, and they launched a project for 'Building a digital loyalty network through demand and supply chain integration' – with the purpose of benefiting from closer integration of purchasing/SCM, marketing and ICT.

On the retail side, Wal-Mart is often cited for its intelligent use of information and for running the entire organization on the basis of consumer demand. This allows it automatically to delist products from a group of stores after only two days of performing badly. IKEA's ability to move goods quickly from its suppliers, through warehouses and on to stores is impressive. Products are packaged and sold to consumers in a way that facilitates speed through the chain. IKEA measures total logistics costs for products in terms of transportation, storage and investment in inventory. The capital cost is especially important, and the company often works with double sourcing – one regional supplier and a low-cost supplier in Asia – with the control system making it possible to switch source quickly depending on sales.

Today, the fashion industry is an archetype of the new business model, and the Spanish company Zara is maybe the best example. In the volatile world of fashion, where trends go in and out of style very quickly, Zara is efficient at minimizing obsolescent stock and bringing new products to shops very quickly.

Conclusions

What, then, can we learn about the development of management concepts? We can certainly see that history repeats itself – as concepts come and go and reappear in a slightly modified and refined shape. For example, consumer orientation was stressed in the 1950s as the key to success in 'the new marketing concept'. Today, it is the key to success in the DCM approach – with consumer insight going deeper and having more tools available than the old customer orientation. However, it is evident that implementation will be just as bothersome as it was with the marketing concept, and it still takes time.

Unlearning is more difficult than learning – so a change of tools is easier and swifter than a transition of mindsets. The change process has to be based on a vision and a consistent frame of reference, which is based on earlier experience. Implementation has to be well planned and systematic, and a common language must be established within the change network. Training and education are the key!

A conceptual model for the implementation of the DCM concept

> By trying to do the impossible, you will reach the highest degree of what is possible.
>
> (August Strindberg)

If we summarize lessons from the development of major management concepts and add recent thinking regarding DCM, we come up with some cornerstones and recommendations for the transition from SCM to DCM.

Consumer insight

The first cornerstone is that we have to focus on the consumer and define not only explicit but also implicit needs, wishes and desires. So consumer insight gets more and more important. For example, Zara has fashion scouts who try to identify emerging fashion trends. Ericsson has a 'consumer and enterprise lab', which carries out several thousand interviews a year all over the world, with results reported directly to top management. Electrolux has 'the spark process' (which we discuss below).

Consumer insight is the starting point for product creation, shorter-term actions in marketing/sales and logistics, and the creation of effective and efficient demand flows. So processes in the whole chain are based on direct knowledge of consumer needs and wishes.

Value segments

The definition of value segments, based on knowledge deriving from consumer insight, is the second cornerstone. The segments reflect different perceived consumer values. Consumers are identified and classified into segments, which are used as targets for product innovation and development of value chains. Value streams are designed to fit specific segments.

Product innovation

The third cornerstone is product innovation, which grows more and more important with increasing competition. There are three strategies a company can choose to avoid being trapped in the commodity corner – to be the operational leader with the lowest costs in the industry, to be the product leader with the most innovative products, or to be the leader in terms of customer care (Treacy and Wiersema, 1995). Each of those strategies requires a different supply chain solution.

Internal alignments

The fourth cornerstone has internal alignment to create a holistic view of product flows. Perceived customer values form the starting point for focusing internal resources. Marketing and sales departments are supposed to have the best knowledge of customers, and it is important to integrate their knowledge of demand creation with logistics knowledge about demand fulfilment. One of the most important issues is to improve internal cooperation between these two.

External alignments

When the internal value-adding system is in order, the next step is to structure the value chains and the network and continuously improve relationships. This is a normative description of what to do to move a company from a business model based on traditional SCM to a business model based on DCM. How does this fit a practical situation? Swedish industry has always been an early adopter of new business concepts, and today Electrolux is one of the pioneers of the DCM concept. So we can look at Electrolux to see how management concepts can be implemented.

Case in demand flow leadership – the Electrolux Way

Background

The Electrolux Group is the world's largest producer of appliances. The logistics complexity is illustrated by the fact that around the world two people a second buy a product from the group – and in Europe a railway wagon is loaded with Electrolux products every four minutes.

Electrolux is working in an increasingly competitive industry characterized by:

- intense competition, increased global product standardization, and shorter product life cycles;
- manufacturing and sourcing being moved to low-cost countries;

- consolidation and globalization of the retail industry, leading to price decline, with cost savings passed on to retailers and consumers.

Electrolux – in common with most other companies – notices that:

- Customers have different wants and expectations, so they need different customer offers in terms of physical products, services and communication. This, in turn, requires customized logistics solutions.
- Customer perceptions of the Electrolux brand are influenced by the logistics performance.
- Electrolux has to find out more about customers and the whole demand chain.

In this situation Electrolux has chosen to 'sell products the consumers are willing to pay for, to build a strong brand image, and to put a lot of effort into the innovation process'.

Consumer insight

A DCM approach starts with the consumer, but the traditional type of customer orientation is not sufficient. A lot of companies do consumer research and use consumer panels – so this level of consumer service is a required minimum. Consumer insight has to go deeper. It has to identify wants and requirements and also the latent needs of the consumer – demands that consumers cannot really express.

Electrolux takes consumer insight as the starting point for product innovation and its 'demand flow process'. The purpose is to find out where and what the real needs and requirements are, and how consumers perceive problems. The Electrolux vision states that it should be consumer insight driven, ie focusing on consumer needs, wants and desires when setting strategies, developing products and launching them. To achieve this, thousands of scouts from Electrolux visit people's homes around the world to analyse how washing, cleaning and vacuuming are actually performed.

One observation was that a lot of people have the vacuum cleaner in the sitting room – because, when children come home dirty, it is better to clean up right away before dirt is spread to the rest of the home. This observation triggered the 'instant clean' segment and a wireless vacuum cleaner that sells very well in 40 countries.

Electrolux calls this approach 'the spark process', which identifies needs, ensures that a sufficient number of consumers share the same problem (so that there is a market for a product) and develops a solution to solve an identified, specific need. Keys to the spark process are two evaluation stages where consumers are interviewed in depth about the ideas, and where prototypes of the suggestions are made and tested.

The CEO, Hans Stråberg, says:

> From the 1960s on consumer durables were sold on technical specifications such as '500 watt, 40 decibel, 50 litre'. Today, this does not appeal to consumers. That is why Electrolux is positioned as a 'life style brand'. We are back to consumer focus – that is, not to sell what we can produce, but produce what we can sell. It is a vital distinction.
>
> (Forsman, 2005)

Value segments

The next step in the Electrolux process is to map and classify consumer needs and wishes, to create a number of consumer segments with different perceived values. Matrices are developed where, for example, one dimension is 'type of consumers' and the other dimension could be themes or trends. Every new product aims for a specific segment, with Electrolux almost doubling the number of product introductions since 2002.

Product innovation

The increase of raw material costs and the price squeeze from low-cost countries are reducing margins for Electrolux. By more focused product development, Electrolux is hoping to increase profitability – while sales are increasing. 'The strategy really delivers results', says Stråberg. 'Profit during the third quarter of 2005 has increased by 20 per cent. All divisions show profitability, increasingly because of the launching of new and innovative products.'

Globalization and the opening up of new markets have caused serious competition from low-cost countries. The Electrolux alternative is to sell products that consumers are willing to pay for, to strengthen the brand, and to put a lot of effort into innovation. They stress design, saying that 'A company without good design is a company without a vision' – and they use creative students from all over the world to spark ideas. The best ideas are presented to top management and properly rewarded. This means that design is much more than stylistic changes – it is the process that transforms ideas into products for consumers, and it has a strategic role that impacts the entire chain.

Internal and external alignments

At corporate level, a group of 15 people help the whole organization with education and training in consumer insight. The responsibility for implementation, however, rests with the different product lines. Within the product lines, product flow managers have the mission to increase growth by, among other things, focusing innovation. One of the new managers, Christina Lindstedt, says, 'My task is to take responsibility for the whole chain – from the cradle to the grave. What is new is the focus on the entire chain. Earlier the responsibility was divided between functions. There has not been a clear allocation of responsibility for profitability within the product line' (Hedelin, 2005).

On the external side, the key is the understanding that every retailer's demand is different. Some retailers have warehouses, while others carry minimal stock. Some retailers sell upper-end products, while others deal in low-end products. Understanding which retailers sell which products and how their business model works sets the stage for defining the total demand picture for the retailer. From there, a supply chain solution for satisfying the retailer's need can be developed. A supply chain solution is a combination of a supply method (reflecting the production system capabilities) and a delivery method (reflecting delivery system capabilities).

'The Electrolux Way'

To compete effectively, Electrolux has embarked upon a major change process called 'The Electrolux Way', which focuses six major processes: brand, product creation, demand flow, purchasing, people and business support. 'Demand flow leadership' is part of this rethinking and consists of four steps:

1. Change the mindset and create an understanding of:
   - new possibilities in the digital economy, and the necessity and opportunities of a new business model;
   - the needs and wishes of consumers, retailers and suppliers;
   - the value segments based on consumer insight and perceived consumer value.
2. Define interfaces and relationships in the processes – and systems and logistics solutions needed to satisfy consumer needs.
3. Develop ICT systems and tools for data sharing and collaboration.
4. Improve and strengthen relationships between partners continuously.

Changing the mindset may be the most important – and also most difficult – step. Most contemporary thinking is based on efforts to achieve efficiency through leanness. This implies a value stream that eliminates all waste – and this means a level schedule, stability, high volumes, low variability and low variety. The digital society, on the other hand, is based on agility to handle flexibility, low volumes, high variability and high variety. Agility is the key to consumer responsiveness, based on a network that enables exploitation of profitable opportunities in a volatile market. This uses marketing and consumer knowledge in a proactive way – with a mindset change from one of solely focusing cost efficiencies to one of also highlighting revenue and margin enhancement.

Electrolux establishes the link between logistics and value creation by saying 'There is no value in a refrigerator until it is in the hands of the consumer.' Torkel Elgh, head of Global Logistics, stated, 'Our ability to serve customers with excellent logistics is a competitive advantage in mature markets and this ability is built on competence.'

Conclusion

By focusing on the management of entire value chains, demand chain management has gained increasing popularity both in management research and in practical application – and also in the teaching of global businesses. The 'theory' creates the background for implementation that can take companies to great heights; lack of attention can draw companies close to peril.

References

Borsodi, R (1929) *The Distribution Age*, Appleton, New York

Christopher, M (1992) *Logistics and Supply Chain Management*, Financial Times/Pitman, London

Cooper, MC, Lambert, DM and Pagh, JD (1998) Supply chain management: implementation issues and research opportunities, *International Journal of Logistics Management*, **9** (2), pp 1–19

Ericsson, D (1969a) *Industrial Marketing*, Beckmans, Stockholm

Ericsson, D (1969b) *Material Administration/Logistik*, Hermods, Malmo

Ericsson, D (1969c) *The Purchasing Function: Goals and methods*, Hermods, Malmo

Ericsson, D (1981) *Materials Administration: A top management responsibility*, Liber, New York

Ericsson, D (1990) Business resource management: a framework for strategic management of the materials flow, in *Handbook of Logistics and Distribution Management*, ed J Gattorna, Gower, London

Ericsson, D (1996) *Virtual Integration*, Unisource, Norcross, GA

Ericsson, D (2003) Supply/demand chain management: the next frontier for competitiveness, in *Global Logistics and Distribution Planning*, 4th edn, ed D Waters, Kogan Page, London, pp 117–36

Forsman, L (2005) Innovation as a driving force, *Teknikforetagen*, December

Green, M (1989) *The Evolution of the Swedish Concept of Materials Administration from a Conceptual Perspective to an Established Discipline*, CTH, Stockholm

Hedelin, J (2005) New products are speeding up the white goods giant, *Dagens Industri*, **15**, November

Keith, RJ (1959) *An Interpretation of the Marketing Concept*, American Marketing Association, Chicago, IL

Shaw, AW (1915) *Some Problems in Market Distribution*, Harvard University Press, Cambridge, MA

Towill, DR (1997) Successful business systems engineering, *IEEE Engineering Management Journal*, **7** (1), February, pp 55–64

Treacy, M and Wiersema, F (1995) *The Discipline of Market Leaders*, Addison Wesley, Reading

USA Today (2001) Editorial, December

9

Using services marketing strategies for logistics customer service

David Grant, Heriot-Watt University

The customer is the immediate jewel of our souls. Him we flatter, him we feast, compliment, vote for, and will not contradict views.

(Ralph Waldo Emerson)

Introduction

The term 'logistics' comes from militaristic roots and is not readily associated with the non-tangible notion of customer service. And yet customer service represents the output of a firm's business logistics system and the physical distribution or 'place' component of its marketing mix (see Figure 9.1). Thus, customer service is the interface between logistics activities and the demand creation process of marketing, and it measures how well a logistics system functions in creating time and place utility for customers (Pisharodi and Langley, 1990).

Initially, physical distribution or logistics and marketing were linked; early writings in marketing related to distributive trade practices due to the increasing significance of middlemen who were performing more functions between producers and consumers (Weld, 1915). Middleman specialization

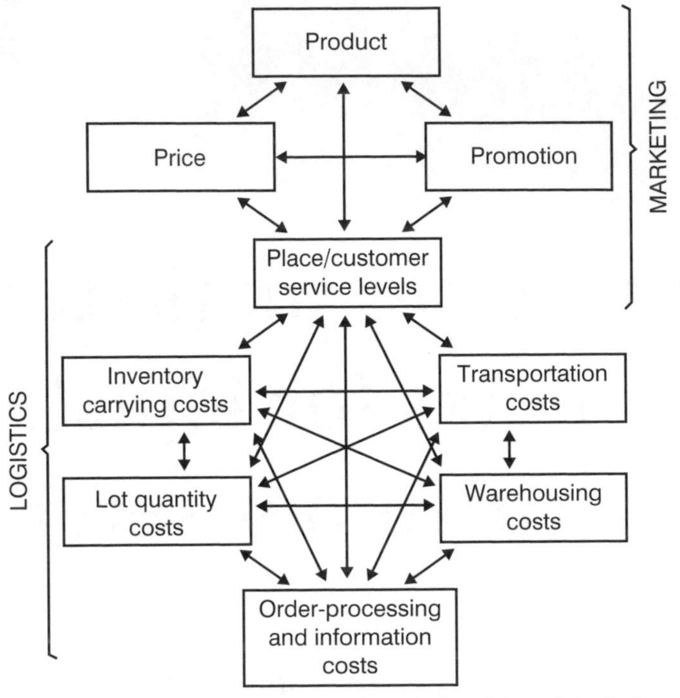

Marketing objective: allocate resources to the marketing mix to maximize the long-run profitability of the firm.
Logistics objective: minimize total costs given the customer service objective where:
Total costs = Transportation costs + Warehousing costs + Order-processing and information costs + Lot quantity costs + Inventory carrying costs.

Source: Grant *et al*, 2006

Figure 9.1 Marketing and logistics customer service costs trade-off model

included activities still prevalent today such as assembling, storing, risk bearing, financing, rearrangement, selling and transporting. Such activities provide place and time utility, ie products in the right place through movement and at the right time through availability. Conversely, manufacturing provides for utility of goods through making tangible products from raw materials while other marketing activities such as credit and quantity discounts provide possession utility. The operative instrument for such middlemen is the channel of distribution (Grant *et al*, 2006).

A disintegration or segregation of physical distribution from the other three marketing mix variables of product, price and promotion began in the 1950s with the introduction of the marketing concept. Physical distribution activities were reduced to only physical supply and distribution functions and the notion of physical distribution customer service was misplaced (Bartels, 1982).

However, a move to reintegrate physical distribution and marketing began in the 1970s when writers argued they belonged together in terms of theoretical progress and applications because of their strong historical linkages and conceptual developments. Such a rediscovery stemmed from the need to focus on customers in a changing environment (Sharman, 1984) and the realization that firms that did so would obtain additional business and profits from leveraging their distribution operations (Shapiro, 1984).

Further, customers have become more sophisticated and demanding during the last 30 years and their expectations of suppliers' abilities to meet their needs have subsequently increased. Accordingly, many suppliers, retailers and service organizations have striven to improve logistics customer service processes to establish or maintain a competitive advantage. Desired outcomes are satisfied customers, increased customer loyalty, repeat and increased purchases, and improved corporate financial performance (Daugherty, Stank and Ellinger, 1998).

But what exactly is customer service, particularly in a logistics or supply chain context? Johns (1999) noted that there are 30 definitions for the word 'service' in the dictionary; thus the concept of service in a business context may be elusive or confusing. Service can mean an industry or organization (eg government services), an outcome that has different perspectives to both service provider and customer (eg on-time delivery), product support (eg after-sales service), or an act or process (Johns, 1999).

La Londe and Zinszer (1976) initiated a refocus on logistics customer service, which they defined as:

> a process which takes place between buyer, seller and third party. The process results in a value added to the product or service exchanged... the value added is also shared, in that each of the parties to the transaction or contract is better off at the completion of the transaction than they were before the transaction took place. Thus, in a process view, customer service is a process for providing significant value-added benefits to the supply chain in a cost effective way.

The notion of process suggests that logistics activities are more like services than goods. There are distinct differences between services and goods within the marketing mix category of product, and Hoffman and Bateson (1997) describe the four important characteristics that distinguish services as:

> intangibility as services cannot be seen, smelt, felt, tasted or otherwise sensed similar to goods; inseparability of production and consumption as most services involve the customer in the production function; heterogeneity or inconsistency of the service from the perspective of the service delivery and customer experience; and perishability of the service if it is not consumed at the moment in time it takes place, ie, the service cannot be inventoried.

Primary logistics activities include transportation, warehousing, inventory management and order processing, and usually do not physically transform or affect goods. Logistics activities can certainly be heterogeneous, eg order cycle time variability and consistency, and are also intangible, eg the storage or delivery of a good, and perishable, eg a lorry leaving on its delivery route.

What is less clear is how inseparable logistics activities are as regards the customer. The customer is involved in the ordering and receiving stages but is relatively passive throughout the provision of the logistics activities, provided the variability is within accepted bounds. Nevertheless, logistics activities generally encompass characteristics and classification of services, ie benefits received by a customer such as time, place and possession utilities are provided by way of a service or enhanced product offering from logistics activities rather than from attributes of a basic product.

Products and prices are relatively easy for competitors to duplicate. Promotional efforts also can be matched by competitors, with the possible exception of a well-trained and motivated sales force. A satisfactory service encounter, or favourable complaint resolution, is one important way that a firm can really distinguish itself in the eyes of the customer. Logistics can therefore play a key role in contributing to a firm's competitive advantage by providing excellent customer service.

Thus, logistics customer service would be well served by the use of evaluation and analysis and tools from the services marketing area. However, theories and techniques from marketing have been slow in finding application in logistics research – notwithstanding calls for reintegration with logistics (Harris and Stock, 1985) and calls for other interdisciplinary applications in logistics (Stock, 1997).

The foregoing raise practical questions regarding logistics customer service and its application within firms. For example, what is the state of play in logistics customer service today? What are important elements of logistics customer service? And how can firms establish appropriate customer service strategies and policies? These issues are explored in the following sections.

Logistics customer service today

Logistics costs such as inventory, warehousing, transportation, and information/order processing can be considered as a firm's expenditure on customer service. Figure 9.1 illustrates the cost trade-offs and considerations required to implement an integrated business logistics system. The objective for the firm is to maximize profits and minimize total logistics costs over the long term, while maintaining or increasing customer service levels.

Such an objective is difficult and firms must carefully choose among the various trade-offs to satisfy customers' needs and maximize profits, while minimizing total costs and not wasting scarce marketing mix resources. Thus, there is a necessity to evaluate trade-offs between the additional customer service features sought by customers and the costs incurred to provide them.

However, customer service levels may be higher than customers would set themselves, and firms should 'banish the costly misconception that all customers seek or need improved service' (Sabath, 1978). However, choosing when to meet and when to exceed customer expectations is a key factor. Not all service features are equally important to each customer, and most customers will accept a relatively wide range of performance in any given service dimension (Markham and Aurik, 1993).

Further, most firms in the supply chain do not sell exclusively to end users. Instead, they sell to other intermediaries who in turn may or may not sell to the final customer. For this reason, it is difficult for these firms to assess the impact of customer service failures, such as stock-outs, on end users. For example, an out-of-stock situation at a manufacturer's warehouse does not necessarily mean an out-of-stock product at the retail level. However, the impact of stock-outs on the customer's behaviour is important.

Recent research has found that an average out-of-stock rate for fast-moving consumer goods retailers across the world is 8.3 per cent, or an average on-shelf availability of 91.7 per cent. Consumer responses to stock-outs are: buy the item at another store (31 per cent), substitute a different brand (26 per cent), substitute the same brand (19 per cent), delay the purchase until the item becomes available (15 per cent) and do not purchase any item (9 per cent). Thus, 55 per cent of consumers will not purchase an item at the retail store, while 50 per cent of consumers will substitute or not purchase the manufacturer's item (Corsten and Gruen, 2003).

One way to establish a desirable customer service level at the retail level is to take into account such consumer responses to stock-outs. When a manufacturer is aware of the implications of stock-outs at the retail level, it can make adjustments in order cycle times, fill rates, transportation options, and other strategies that will result in higher levels of product availability in retail stores.

These observations reinforce the notion that firms must adopt a customer-orientated view and seek out customer needs. Firms also have to ask customers the right questions to ensure important and relevant criteria are captured. For example, one food manufacturer maintained a 98 per cent service level, which necessitated large inventories in many warehouse locations. However, this practice often resulted in shipping dated merchandise, and customers, therefore, perceived this practice as evidence of low quality and poor service (Sabath, 1978).

Quality in logistics means meeting agreed customer requirements and expectations (Byrne, 1992). Suppliers need to develop and deliver service offerings more quickly in the light of the many changes to distribution that have emerged, such as the technological advances of efficient consumer response and just-in-time delivery. However, the notion of pleasing the customer at every turn regardless of cost has undergone a re-evaluation such that suppliers or shippers are now attempting to accommodate customers while optimizing the supply chain.

This tactic requires suppliers to negotiate with the customer and possibly share costs with other actors in the supply chain (Richardson, 1998). Such negotiations may be difficult to implement as there is little evidence that logisticians and suppliers have developed sufficient customer interest in logistics activities (Blanding, 1992). This may be indicative of suppliers not properly determining customer needs when they establish customer service policies and trade-offs.

Despite 30 years of research and application of logistics customer service, this attitude still appears to be the case. Van Hoek (2005), in examining barriers to establishing an agile supply chain, argued that many firms are not considering the customer's point of view or are they measuring customer service in a non-meaningful way. Figure 9.2 presents these pitfalls relative to flows in an agile supply chain.

The foregoing suggests that a customer's product and service needs, and subsequent supplier selection criteria for logistics services, extend beyond usual business-to-business criteria such as product quality, technical competence and competitive prices. Customer evaluation of logistics suppliers may include a number of intangible factors related to the service being provided as the customer seeks added value or utility from it. An example is whether customer service representatives are on call 24 hours a day. A firm must, therefore, have the ability to recognize and respond to customer needs if it is to have any chance of satisfying them and achieving the benefits of loyalty and profitability. But to do that it must initially determine what the customers' needs are, both from its own perspective and from that of the customers.

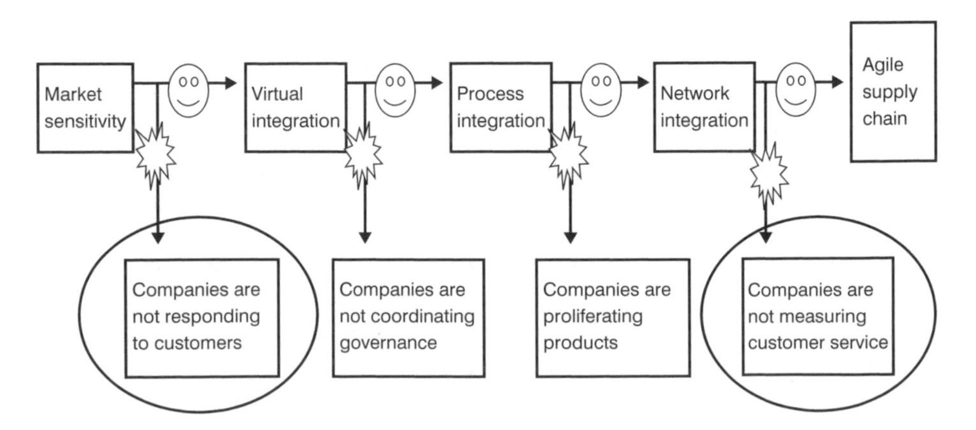

Source: van Hoek, 2005

Figure 9.2 Pitfalls in logistics customer service

Elements of logistics customer service

A first step in understanding a customer's service requirements or needs is to audit existing customer service policies (Christopher, 2005). This will allow the firm to see what they presently offer and determine how important employees believe these logistics customer service elements are to customers. Different industrial sectors will of course have different emphases regarding such elements; however, the basic groupings should be similar.

La Londe and Zinszer (1976) proposed that logistics customer service contains three distinct dimensions: pre-transaction, transaction and post-transaction, which reflect the temporal nature of a service experience. They also proposed various elements within these dimensions, as shown in Figure 9.3.

Although La Londe and Zinszer's work was conducted 30 years ago, a more recent study (Grant, 2004) from the customer's perspective (as opposed to the supplier's perspective) found similar elements and dimensions of logistics

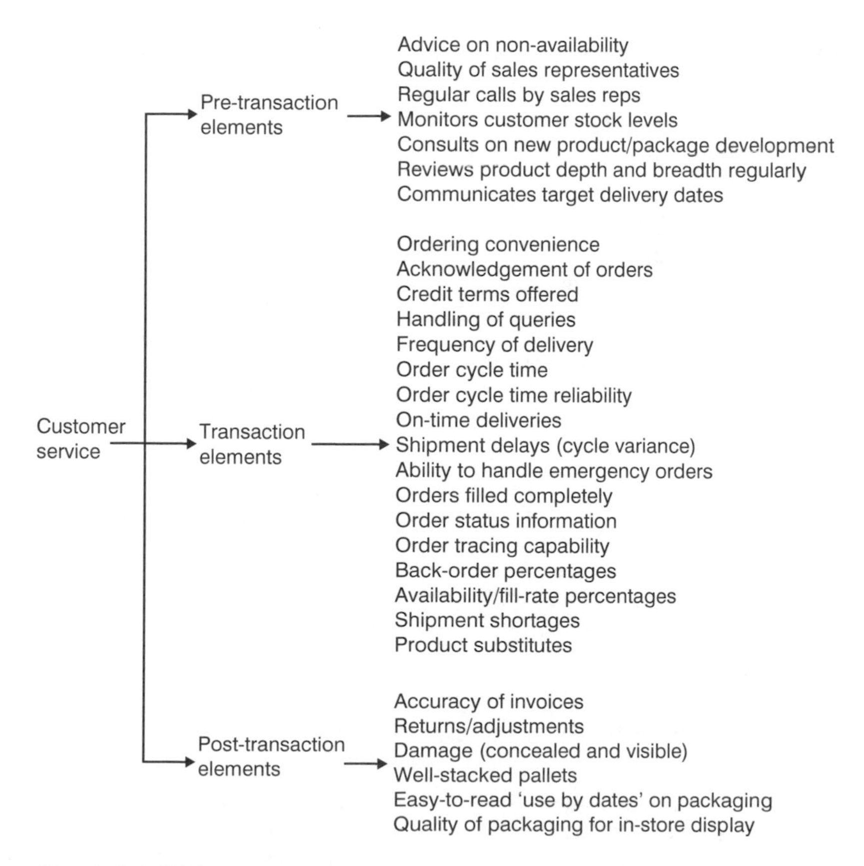

Source: Grant *et al*, 2006

Figure 9.3 Elements of logistics customer service quality

customer service. The post-transaction dimension also includes elements of relationships, and the entire set is shown in Figure 9.4.

Both studies provide a list of elements that firms can use to develop their own customer service features. These lists are by no means exhaustive but do provide a starting point for firms to develop their logistics customer service strategies. Firms will probably have to add or delete some elements to service their own sectoral and local requirements.

These studies also confirm that firms should categorize customer service elements into dimensions related to pre-transaction, transaction and post-transaction events when facilitating operations design and customer service planning. This categorization will enable firms to determine critical events in their service and allow them to monitor and follow up on service failures.

Strategies for logistics customer service

The impetus to develop logistics customer service strategies can be either proactive or reactive or a combination of both. A proactive impetus follows from a firm's desire to satisfy its customer's needs, while a reactive impetus results from a service failure. Figure 9.5 illustrates this dichotomy and presents possible customer service techniques related to each impetus.

Construct	Variable name
Pre-order (Pre-transaction)	Availability Appropriate OCT Consistent OCT
Order service and quality (Transaction)	Accurate invoices On-time delivery Complete orders Products arrive undamaged Accurate orders Consistent product quality Products arrive to specification
Relationship service (Post-transaction)	After-sales support Delivery time Helpful CSRs Customized services
Relationship quality (Post-transaction)	Trust Commitment Integrity
Global satisfaction (The outcome...)	Overall supplier quality Feelings towards suppliers Future purchase intentions

Figure 9.4 Elements of logistics customer service and relationships

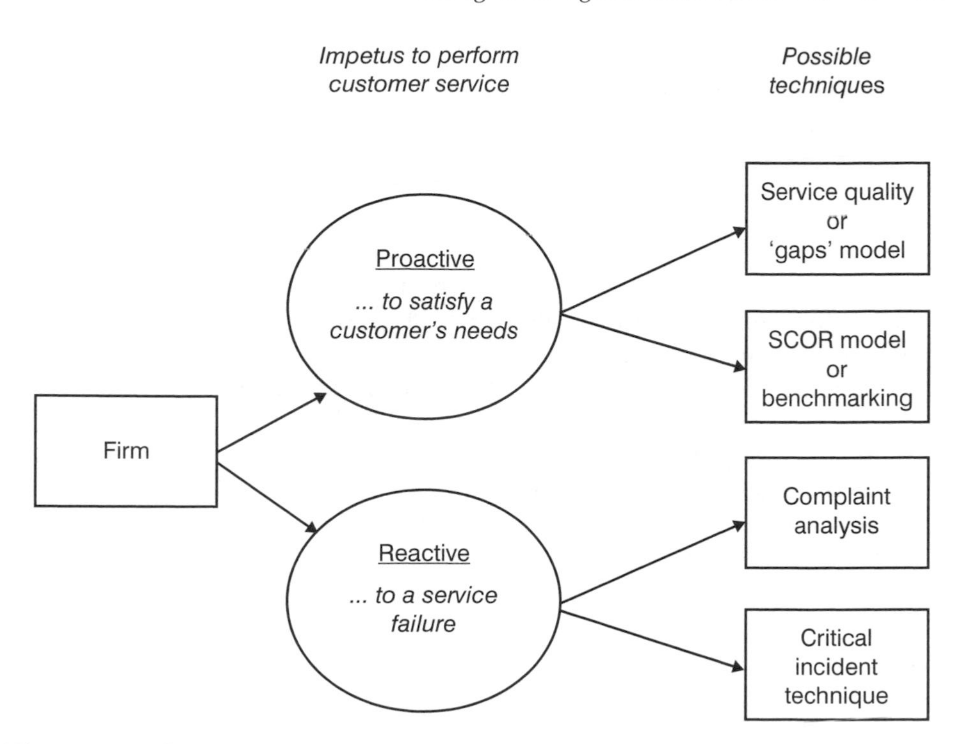

Figure 9.5 Customer service strategy process

Reactive techniques

Understanding and obtaining information about customer requirements necessitate an exchange of information between customers and firms. Complaint analysis is one such exchange concerning perceived customer dissatisfaction resulting from a customer service experience or critical incident. Complaints derive from a 'moment of truth' between supplier and customer that is considered a critical incident. Critical incidents are defined as:

> any observable human activity that is sufficiently complete in itself to permit inferences and predictions to be made about the person performing the act. To be critical, an incident must occur in a situation where the purpose or intent of the act seems fairly clear to the observer and where its consequences are sufficiently definite to leave little doubt concerning the effects.
>
> (Flanagan, 1954)

Thus, a critical incident is a moment of truth that becomes representative in the mind of a customer (Lewis, 1993).

The critical incident technique (CIT) was developed as a process to investigate human behaviour and facilitate its usefulness for solving practical problems. CIT procedures consist of collecting and analysing qualitative data to investigate and understand facts behind an incident or series of incidents. Some uses of CIT applicable to business include training, equipment design, operating procedures, and measurement of performance criteria or proficiency.

Complaint handling is significantly associated with both trust and commitment (Tax, Brown and Chandrashekaran, 1998). These concepts are important for supplier–customer relationship development. Complaint analysis thus has a role as part of a post-transaction process but is not a complete form of information for firms when used in isolation.

Such information does not provide an understanding about what customer service features actually provide customer satisfaction. Thus, whilst it 'might be an effective way to fix yesterday's problems', it is 'a poor way to determine today's (or tomorrow's) customer requirements' (Markham and Aurik, 1993).

Complaint analysis has also been called a defensive strategy since its focus is directed at aggressively protecting existing customers rather than searching for new ones (Lapidus and Schibrowsky, 1994). Therefore, firms using only complaint analysis or CIT techniques might find it difficult to determine current and future success factors and establish a competitive advantage.

Proactive techniques

It is important that a firm establish customer service policies based on customer requirements and that they are supportive of the overall marketing strategy. What is the point of manufacturing a great product, pricing it competitively and promoting it well if it is not readily available to the consumer? At the same time, customer service policies should be cost-efficient, contributing favourably to the firm's overall profitability. A proactive customer service strategy allows a firm to consider all these factors.

One popular method for setting customer service levels is to benchmark a competitor's customer service performance. One major question is what to benchmark, and the Supply Chain Council's supply chain operations reference (SCOR) model provides a framework to analyse internal processes – plan, source, make, deliver and return (Christopher, 2005).

There are several issues about the effectiveness of benchmarking. For example, it might promote imitation rather than innovation; best-practice operators might refuse to participate in any benchmarking exercise; it focuses on particular activities and thus there is a failure to allow for interactivity trade-offs; and there is difficulty in finding well-matched comparators (Santhouse, 1999).

Further, while it may be interesting to see what the competition is doing, this information has limited usefulness. In terms of what the customer requires, how does the firm know if the competition is focusing on the right customer service elements? Therefore, competitive benchmarking alone is insufficient. Competitive benchmarking should be performed in conjunction with customer surveys that measure the importance of various customer service elements.

Opportunities to close differences between customer requirements and the firm's performance can be identified and the firm can then target primary customers of competitors and protect its own key accounts from potential competitor inroads. The service quality model developed from the services marketing discipline and presented in the next section enables a firm to identify such differences and follows the call to use more interdisciplinary techniques in logistics customer service.

The service quality model

Customers evaluate services differently from goods owing to their different characteristics. One popular method of investigating such evaluations is the service quality or gaps model (Parasuraman, Zeithaml and Berry, 1985). Customers develop a-priori expectations of a service based on several criteria such as previous experience, word-of-mouth recommendations, or advertising and communication by the service provider. Once customers experience a service they compare their perceptions of that experience to their expectations. If their perceptions meet or exceed their expectations they are satisfied; conversely, if perceptions do not meet expectations they are dissatisfied. The difference between expectations and perceptions forms the major gaps to be investigated.

Figure 9.6 presents this model and includes the customer's and firm's positions. The expectations and perceptions gap is affected by four other gaps related to the firm's customer service and service quality activities that are for the most part invisible to the customer.

Firstly, the firm must understand the customer's expectations for the service. Gap 1 is the discrepancy between consumer expectations and the firm's perception of these expectations. Secondly, the firm must then turn the customer's expectations into tangible service specifications. Gap 2 is the discrepancy between the firm's perceptions of consumer expectations and the firm's establishment of service quality specifications. Thirdly, the firm must actually provide the service according to those specifications. Gap 3 is the discrepancy between the firm's establishment of service quality specifications and its actual service provision. Lastly, the firm must communicate its intentions and actions to the customer. Gap 4 is the discrepancy between the firm's actual service provision and external communications about the service to customers.

Gap 5 is associated with a customer's expectations for a service experience compared with the customer's perceptions of the actual event, and is the sum of the four gaps. The firm must minimize or eliminate each discrepancy or gap that it has control over in order to minimize or eliminate the customer's discrepancy or gap related to the service experience. Using the service quality model forces a firm to examine what customer service and service quality it provides to customers in a customer-centric framework.

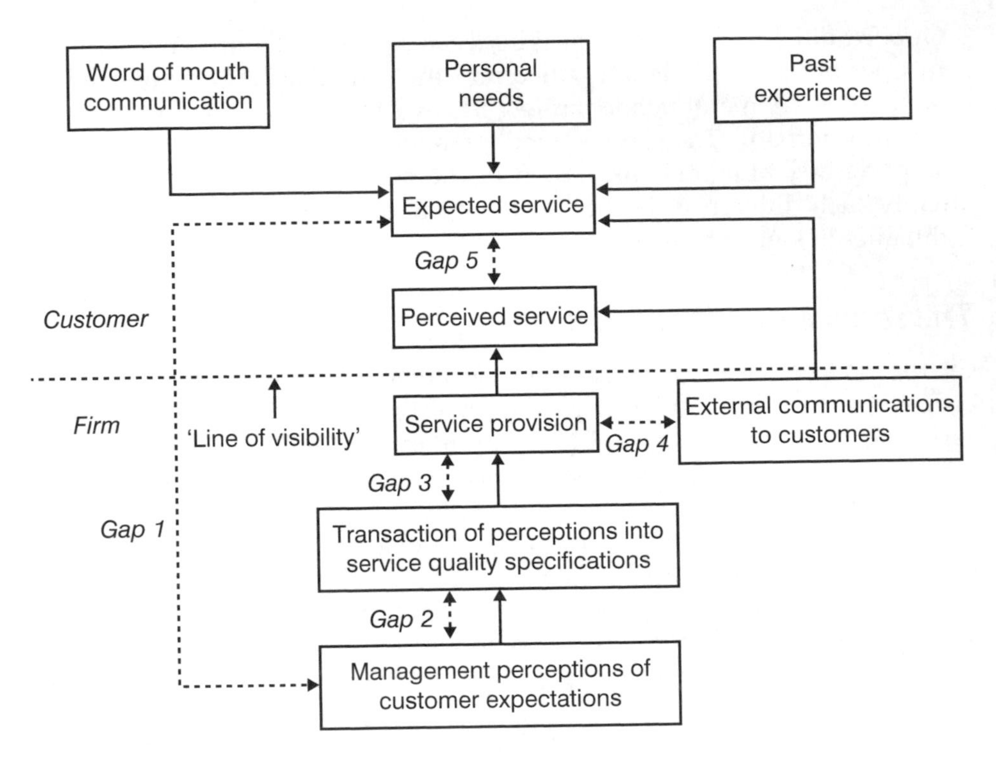

Source: Grant *et al*, 2006

Figure 9.6 Service quality or 'gaps' model

Summary

Customer service is a necessary requirement in logistics activities and is affected by various environmental factors shaping today's marketplace. Logistics customer service has its roots in the marketing discipline, and logisticians can use and learn from marketing techniques and methodologies to investigate customer service.

A strategy for logistics customer service requires a basic trade-off between costs incurred and enhanced profit received. Each industrial sector will also have its own unique needs and issues that further complicate such considerations. However, while the importance of individual customer service elements varies among firms, there is a common set of elements presented above that should provide a useful starting point for most firms.

A global perspective focuses on seeking common market demands worldwide rather than cutting up world markets and treating them as separate entities with very different product needs. However, different parts of the world have different customer service needs such as information availability, order completeness, and expected lead times. Local infrastructure, communications and time differences may make it impossible to achieve high levels of customer service. Also, management styles in different global markets may be different than those prevalent in the firm's home environment.

Although customer service may represent the best opportunity for a firm to achieve a sustainable competitive advantage, many firms still do not implement logistics customer service strategies or do so by simply duplicating those implemented by competitors. The service quality framework discussed above can be used by firms to collect and analyse customer information, determine what is really important to customers and thus enhance their customer service initiatives. Globally, customer services provided by the firm should match local customer needs and expectations to the greatest degree possible. The successful output of such customer service considerations will be a satisfied customer, which then should lead to increased profitability for the firm.

References

Bartels, R (1982) Marketing and distribution are not separate, *International Journal of Physical Distribution and Materials Management*, **12** (3), pp 3–10

Blanding, W (1992) Customer service logistics, in *Logistics: The strategic issues*, ed M Christopher, pp 179–93, Chapman & Hall, London

Byrne, PM (1992) Global logistics: improve the customer service cycle, *Transportation and Distribution*, **33**, June, pp 66–67

Christopher, M (2005) *Logistics and Supply Chain Management: Creating value-adding networks*, 3rd edn, FT Prentice Hall, London

Corsten, D and Gruen, T (2003) Desperately seeking shelf availability: an examination of the extent, the causes, and the efforts to address retail out-of-stocks, *International Journal of Retail and Distribution Management*, **31** (12), pp 605–17

Daugherty, PJ, Stank, TP and Ellinger, AE (1998) Leveraging logistics/distribution capabilities: the effect of logistics service on market share, *Journal of Business Logistics*, **19** (2), pp 35–51

Flanagan, JC (1954) The critical incident technique, *Psychological Bulletin*, **51**, July, pp 327–58

Grant, DB (2004) UK and US management styles in logistics: different strokes for different folks?, *International Journal of Logistics: Research and applications*, **7** (3), pp 181–97

Grant, DB *et al* (2006) *Fundamentals of Logistics Management*, European edn, McGraw-Hill, Maidenhead

Harris, WD and Stock, JR (1985) Marketing and distribution: coming back together at last!, in *Distribution Research and Education: Today and tomorrow*, ed MC Cooper and JR Grabner, pp 48–67, Ohio State University, Columbus, OH

Hoffman, KD and Bateson, JEG (1997) *Essentials of Services Marketing*, Dryden, Orlando, FL

Johns, N (1999) What is this thing called service?, *European Journal of Marketing*, **33** (9/10), pp 958–73

La Londe, BJ and Zinszer, PH (1976) *Customer Service: Meaning and measurement*, National Council of Physical Distribution Management, Chicago, IL

Lapidus, RS and Schibrowsky, JA (1994) Aggregate complaint analysis: a procedure for developing customer service satisfaction, *Journal of Services Marketing*, **8** (4), pp 50–60

Lewis, BR (1993) Service quality measurement, *Marketing Intelligence and Planning*, **11** (4), pp 4–12

Markham, WJ and Aurik, JC (1993) Shape up and ship out, *Journal of European Business*, **4** (5), pp 54–57

Parasuraman, A, Zeithaml, VA and Berry, LL (1985) A conceptual model of service quality and its implications for future research, *Journal of Marketing*, 49, Fall, pp 41–50

Pisharodi, RM and Langley, CJ (1990) A perceptual process model of customer service based on cybernetic/control theory, *Journal of Business Logistics*, **11** (1), pp 26–48

Richardson, HR (1998) Must you meet all customer demands?, *Transportation and Distribution*, **39**, June, pp 55–59

Sabath, RE (1978) How much service do customers really want?, *Business Horizons*, **21** (2), pp 26–32

Santhouse, D (1999) Benchmarking, in *Global Logistics and Distribution Planning: Strategies for management*, 3rd edn, ed D Waters, pp 193–202, Kogan Page, London

Shapiro, RD (1984) Get leverage from logistics, *Harvard Business Review*, **62**, May–June, pp 119–27

Sharman, G (1984) The rediscovery of logistics, *Harvard Business Review*, **62**, September–October, pp 71–79

Stock, JR (1997) Applying theories from other disciplines to logistics, *International Journal of Physical Distribution and Logistics Management*, **27** (9/10), pp 515–39

Tax, SS, Brown, SW and Chandrashekaran, M (1998) Customer evaluations of service complaint experiences: implications for relationship marketing, *Journal of Marketing*, 62, April, pp 60–76

van Hoek, R (2005) Mitigating the minefield of pitfalls in creating the agile supply chain, in *International Logistics and Supply Chain Management: Proceedings of the Logistics Research Network Conference*, ed J Dinwoodie *et al*, pp 473–78, University of Plymouth, Plymouth, UK

Weld, LDH (1915) Market distribution, *American Economic Review*, **5** (1), pp 125–39

10

Supply chain management: the challenge of systems

Philip Schary, Oregon State University

Supply chain management has become a primary business process (Hammer, quoted in Quinn, 1999). It introduced the concept of product flow through a series of hitherto autonomous organizations – from originating suppliers to final customers. As it developed, it introduced inter-functional coordination within the firm and later extending across suppliers and customers. The supply chain reduces organizational boundaries through collaboration, linking the process of material and product movement with information for control. The central task of supply chain management is the control of this process, across organizational boundaries, utilizing communication and computers, with automated procedures supplemented by selected human interventions. It serves as a prototype for business operations in the 21st century, combining human and computer-based decision making and execution.

The setting

The management task is daunting. The span of activities far exceeds the span of direct management control (Gereffi, Humphrey and Sturgeon, 2005).

Their nature exposes the supply chain to multiple decision points, as well as turbulence at many different levels and with multiple dimensions. Further, the nature of the supply chain is systemic; decisions in one area have ramifications in other areas, often requiring trade-offs balancing the local objectives of one organization with those of another. The sheer complexity of the supply chain as a system adds problems.

Any system will fail because of 'normal accidents' (Perrow, 1984). The combination of increasing pressures to meet volatile customer demands and simultaneously reducing costs brings consequences that may be unanticipated. A sense of direction, however, may reduce their impact – or more optimistically lead to new opportunities.

The vision of product flow by itself is, however, not enough. Fine (1998) describes it in terms of capabilities: 'A company is its chain of continuously evolving capabilities – this is its own capabilities, plus the capabilities of everyone it does business with.' Beyond the present task and system performance, he asks what this organization can do to contribute to its future. For the supply chain, this shifts the focus from the immediate task to a larger perspective – with the implied question 'Where is the supply chain going?' But future direction becomes submerged when immediate problems require so much attention; a focus on operations neglects a higher role for management, in anticipating structure, organization and strategy.

The task ahead

In this chapter, I consider supply chain management organization issues. The discussion focuses on two promising concepts: *networks* and *complex adaptive systems* (CAS). This treatment is qualitative (with a mathematical perspective available in Surana *et al*, 2005). Networks provide guidance for management structure and connections – saying where organizations and managers fit within the supply chain as a system. CAS provides a strategic perspective by describing the dynamics of responding to a continuously changing environment. The relationship between the two involves the complexity of management, connecting links between decision makers, and their response to environmental issues. The argument is speculative; the questions have no immediate answers, but it is important to begin the discussion.

The problem

The supply chain is a meta-organization, a system of connections transcending organizational boundaries and recognizing interdependence among individual enterprises. The immediate objective is to deliver products and services matched to identified customer requirements, following specific parameters of time and product characteristics, and accompanied by relentless pressures for lower cost. The supply chain at an operational level is a directed system, where management strives for increased performance and reduction in cost through hierarchical control over operations. Improvement comes not only from within organizations but through balancing the trade-offs between functional and organizational centres. The objective becomes whole-system – rather than organizational – optimization.

Management specifies objectives, tasks and assignments – but how is it possible to manage a supply chain spanning many tiers of suppliers? Current tools rely heavily on information systems and automated processes for operational coordination. Higher decisions use teams, matrix management, supplier associations and informal contact. None of these provide complete answers, but they work for local issues involving parts of the chain. There is a question, however, about how far hierarchical management can go in directing a system as complex as a supply chain with multiple tiers and a multitude of environmental conditions.

One solution has been to establish matrix organizations, organized around a process but with members reporting to both a task manager and a specific functional area. This forms a basis for managing process-oriented organizations – and supply chains (Hammer, quoted in Quinn, 1999). This can be extended to give three-dimensional matrices as a management solution to global corporations, with geographic location providing the extra dimension (Hedlund, 1986). However, matrix organizations are unsatisfactory because they automatically incorporate potential conflict between process and functional areas – with divided loyalties and time commitments. And they often produce poor decisions.

Teams probably offer the most successful approach to date – with task unit members consisting of those immediately involved in a specific task or problem area. They can be flexible, task-oriented and often informal – with a life extending only to the duration of the task. The absence of permanence assumes an underlying organizational guidance – otherwise, their role is to solve short-term problems. But the missing element in teams is leadership.

Leadership derives from access to knowledge, resources and position within the network. In a supply chain, however, there are limits to control because of organizational boundaries. Supply chain members may resist change when it interferes with their own domains of authority. Concepts such as lean processes take away management authority in favour of higher efficiency, reducing managers' ability to respond individually to changes outside of their immediate domains. Lean operations take resources away from inventory and capacity that could otherwise provide a buffer against adverse circumstances.

The fundamental problem of supply chain management is the conflict between hierarchy to control a processing system, and flexibility to respond to change, both internal and external. Decisions come originally from the top. These may be modified by local managers to meet specific local requirements. In turn, the collective weight of these local decisions causes the system to drift and take on new characteristics. There is little protection against error – or catastrophe. Traditional hierarchical organizations can be successful when external conditions change slowly, functional tasks are well defined, there is little inter-functional coordination, and local responsibility can be delegated. They are insufficient when task units must coordinate with each other to accomplish the objectives of the organization in a context of change and volatility. They are also inadequate to deal with problems in new settings, requiring new rules.

The product initially defines the task of the supply chain. But it must bond to operations capabilities, and determine whether suppliers, distributors and service providers have the capability and capacity to deliver to the final customer. Fine (1998) argues for a three-dimensional approach built around the capabilities of the supply chain. And while products initially define the supply chain, processing and operations in the supply chain should in turn influence the product configuration.

At higher levels, the supply chain is exposed to environmental factors, some favourable, others detrimental. There are many examples of high-level corporate intervention for supplier failures, interruption of sources, or disruption of transportation routes (Sheffi, 2005). A catalogue would include natural disasters, changes in products and markets, infrastructure, global political issues such as monetary exchange, and technology. The question is how to respond? Technological change, for example, manifested in information systems, offers frequent opportunities for competitive advantage. Early adoption can, however, be disruptive, requiring substantial organizational changes and new investment. Specific applications may take time to become established, reducing performance. Delays in realization may result in the loss of dominant positions, translatable into losses of markets and profits. Further, the advent of this new technology may change not only the system but supplier relationships, competitive positions and even the structure of an industry. Seemingly small events may unleash strong forces for change that can spin out of control.

Further, the supply chain is embedded in a larger marketplace network of global supply chains in competition with each other, but with suppliers and customers in common (described as 'co-opetition' by Brandenburger and Nalebuff, 1996). This introduces pressures at the least to standardize data codes and interfaces, and possibly convert products and components into modules that can be sold in a commodity marketplace.

Some supply chains encourage suppliers to seek outside business to remove them from complete dependency on the buyer, provide assurance that the supplier's product is competitive and introduce new innovative stimulus. Changeable products and markets force the supply chain to upgrade suppliers – or even to reconstruct itself by changing members and processes. Changes in technology also force new buyer–seller relationships.

If there is a common theme for management, it is that it must adapt to a continuously changing environment. A supply chain that becomes too ordered and insulated from change will find it difficult to respond to new environments and requirements. At the same time, new requirements from a supply chain conflict with an extended hierarchically managed process. So we must ask how a supply chain can balance a process orientation with the new requirements for organizational agility.

Networks

The new dynamism requires re-examination of the whole supply process. So it is worth examining networks from a theoretical view – recognizing that a supply chain is a network of organizations and relationships. There are two distinct perspectives on networks. One considers networks from an abstract, sometimes mathematical, perspective. The other is sociological in orientation, dealing with networks within organizations.

Network theory as a distinct body stems originally from mathematical topology, but is now emerging as a separate field of investigation (Buchanan, 2003a, 2003b). The field focuses on networks as distinct but pervasive phenomena with often randomly formed structures. Abstract networks have limited direct relevance to the supply chain – because network theory describes randomly formed networks, while supply chain networks are formed by intentional design. Some properties, however, suggest potential application.

Supply chains have an approximate metaphor in abstract networks of nodes and connectors. Nodes can be individuals or organizations – suppliers, customers, carriers, information providers or any point where decisions take place that affect other nodes. Links between nodes involve communication as well as physical movement. There is a tendency for nodes that attract the most connectors to become still larger. This is the Power Law that describes the concentration of power in a few nodes, with this concentration increasing over time. Centrality, as a property of networks, becomes a source of power. The parallel in the supply chain is the lead or dominant firm, or the e-hub that provides portals for internet transactions. Competing centres may exhibit a rivalry such as a dominant supplier challenging the supply chain leader for control.

The other basis for networks is rooted in communication and organizational behaviour, summarized by Monge and Contractor (2001). Their definition is straightforward: 'Communications networks are the patterns of contact between communication partners that are created by transmitting and exchanging messages through time and space.' Networks can include individuals, organizations, sources of influence or even types of institutions, depending on specific contexts. Most research is intra-organizational, but there is some limited reference to systems of organizations. The emphasis is on relations to create communications among entities – either people or organizations – as knowledge, guidance or command.

Networks as organizations use 'flexible, dynamic communication links to connect multiple organizations into new entities that can create products or services' (Monge and Contractor, 2001). Their connections become their strength. The denser the connections, the more potentially effective the network can become. However, it becomes more difficult to manage with increasing information available to network members, which encourages members to make more independent decisions. On the other hand, members can become overloaded with excess information, limiting their productivity.

Networks and organization

Networks offer a different form of organization from hierarchy. As Monge and Contractor (2001) describe them, 'network organizations are created out of complex webs of exchange and dependency among multiple organizations. In a sense, the network organization becomes a supra-organization whose primary function is linking many organizations together and coordinating their activities.' Their connections permeate the entire organization, establishing relationships and communication among firms, contributing value to the whole. Their characteristics include information sharing and cooperation to produce and distribute the final product to the customer. They can operate in stable structures, flat and devoid of hierarchy, or with modules in virtual organizations. There is also an increasing reliance on information technology.

They hold a balance between the opposing forces of hierarchical structure and markets (Powell, 1990). Structure establishes the position of each individual node in relationship to other nodes, ie its expected role in the network, such as a distribution centre in relation to a manufacturing plant.

Supply chain networks use management information networks to coordinate and direct the physical operations of delivering products, although the networks may take different paths (Bovet and Martha, 2000). Information networks provide control, but operating networks provide feedback on feasibility and capacity. Further, networks are not necessarily static structures, but can be dynamic and respond to specific needs.

Networks in the supply chain can take several forms. Supply chains can be linear, where material and products flow through successive tiers of suppliers, processors and distributors. They incorporate specialized complementary networks for transport, information technology, supply links and social relationships, utilizing forward loops for anticipating the future such as forecasting, and backward feedback loops for control. They can be centralized into star configurations, with information flows on the internet between a lead firm e-hub and satellites, or a buyer and multiple suppliers. Networks can also be dense clusters with high degrees of interconnection among nodes.

Relevant characteristics

One relevant feature in discussing network organization is the tendency of networks to cluster – sometimes referred to as a *small world network*. In clusters, information is restricted to small groups of decision makers, to the point of becoming insular, as in management groups. Influence extends only to nearby nodes, with a dense set of internal connections. External information becomes essential to the cluster's survival, but it requires continuous effort to acquire. The solution lies in links outside the cluster to other relevant nodes, to provide information about the industry and its environment. These are described in social networks as strong ties (clusters) and weak ties (outside links). The role of weak ties lies in supplying new information and perspectives to the cluster (Granovetter, 1982). Close collaboration between a supplier and lead firm, leading to joint product development, would be considered strong ties. However, a set of strong ties might also limit awareness of other developments. A solution would maintain ties to other organizations, such as alternative suppliers. This also reinforces procurement practices of second sourcing for critical components, or maintaining lines of communication to final customers, beyond immediate distribution partners.

Networks also tend to concentrate linkages around key nodes, enhancing positions as centres of power – ultimately to single, central nodes as a base of power. Centralization, however, is vulnerable to failure, as eliminating dominant nodes from a network will ultimately make it collapse. As nodes are removed, additional loads are placed on the remaining nodes, leading to cascading failures. Networks with distributed centres, on the other hand, have redundant paths between nodes and are less prone to failure. But too many centres creates complexity. And connectivity places upper and lower bounds on the numbers of links between nodes. Too few leads to isolation and a loss of internal energy; too many leads to excessive information and instability. Thompson (2004) argues that network structure should be managed and that most connections should be loosely coupled to local hubs, so that information coordinating the system would flow from only a limited number of sources.

One solution describes a hierarchical organization with limited lines of communication between system management and operating units. While the organization can manage under stable conditions, it would soon become overloaded under abnormal circumstances. To relieve this communication congestion, operating units with mutual interdependence would coordinate through lateral networks. By controlling communication to upper levels, managers are then freer to deal with strategic issues.

Network evolution

Historically, discussion of supply chain management organization has relied on organization within the firm, such as hierarchy. The classic Toyota keiretsu model followed this pattern by establishing dyadic relationships through a chain of supplier associations extending toward initial sources of supply. Later, Sabel (2005) observed a different form of flexible specialization by individual firms in a closely coordinated, but informal, group passing production and distribution of products in an organized sequence of stages. Later, a third way reflected the intensification of knowledge work, with small groups within an organization connecting as needed for collaboration to other problem-solving groups within an organization.

Sabel (2005) further extends this idea more directly to inter-firm relations in the supply chain, with a form of federalism among independent but cooperating firms. Firms collaborate, with both internal and external partners and organizational units, modifying the original goals and direction through internalized debate. There must be overall direction, but the direction of effort comes through negotiation at operating levels. Federalist networks differ from hierarchy in that the major flows of information and decision making are between and across organizational units and organizational boundaries. Hierarchy in contrast operates vertically, controls information and defines tasks.

Complex adaptive systems

Supply chains are systems, but there has been a profound change in how we understand the idea of systems. Cybernetic systems and system thinking are well established in the management literature, and they involve management in setting goals and developing tools to achieve them. They are basically rule-based with varying degrees of organizational learning to give feedback and guide the system toward its objectives. However, they are limited in scope to the defined boundaries of the system and by the perspectives of management. Cybernetic systems operate at the level of basic processes that are relatively undisturbed. Systems thinking comes into play through organizational learning when there is substantial change in processes. However, neither can deal with major environmental turbulence, even though they are eminently useful in dealing with routine processes and actions. Real dynamic systems are too complex to manage in a traditional manner.

Complex adaptive systems (CAS) deal with potential disruption and adaptation by the system to an environment that is necessarily turbulent. New connections to the environment may suddenly appear as emergent systems, influencing the behaviour of the established system. The unpredictable results are often expressed in the expression 'It just happens' (Marion, 1999). It is non-linear, meaning that cause cannot be directly identified with results; events are beyond the ability to predict. It can only be understood in terms of a larger context.

The roots of CAS are based on chaos theory, dissipative theory and physical systems. Chaos theory is oriented to discover complex patterns from random data. Parker and Stacey (1994) say that 'Clearly chaos is more than simply a mathematical or scientific curiosity. A common feature of its application is that it reveals the essentially unknowable future of creative systems.'

Chaos itself is a misnomer. It is an intricate mixture of order and disorder, regularity and irregularity, with patterns of behaviour that are recognized as broadly repetitive. It can be a source both of disruption and of creation. Dissipative structures are derived from fluid mechanics, and deal with positive feedback, meaning that they can evolve suddenly without warning – a process known as bifurcation.

CAS as a field of study evolved through discussion of physical systems – particularly in the biological sciences – describing how they evolve in response to environmental changes. More recently, discussion has taken on social systems and management (Dooley, Johnson and Bush, 1995; Dooley, 1997, 2002; Brown and Eisenhardt, 1998; Marion, 1999; Choi, Dooley and Runtusanatham, 2001; Choi and Krause, 2006). The direct fit is tenuous, but the message is clear: management control is limited in the face of a shifting environment. Further, while the short term is knowable and can be controlled (to a point), the long term is unknowable in advance because of the parallel evolution of systems and their environments, which both influence each other.

CAS characteristics relevant to this discussion include:

- Order within seemingly random data comes through self-organization.
- Non-linear results, ie a lack of predictability.
- Effects are not additive as in linear systems, but combine in ways that cannot be predicted in advance.
- Small events can trigger major changes.
- When systems pass a critical point of disturbance, they may be pushed far from equilibrium to create new structures.

Self-organization means that new systemic relationships can arise spontaneously without management direction. They can be either creative, in the sense of innovation, or potentially destructive by disturbing the present system. The introduction of new technologies, for example, can lead to changes in organization, relationships and other forms of orientation. These become systems that are ultimately not under control but establish a new stability. Non-linearity means that the ability to control results is limited, and that there can be more than one result from a single input – that seemingly small differences may provoke major changes in the state of the system. Finally, systems may appear to be stable but suddenly change to establish new system structures.

The result of self-organization is to create systems with effects that extend beyond visible connections and proportional response to outside stimuli, becoming unpredictable and non-linear in their effect. Systems evolve in parallel with their environments, adapting and creating response, as in competitive markets. Thompson (2004) notes: 'Its [CAS] distinctive feature is a world as a system in construction, a dynamic formulation encouraging the notion of a continual process of spontaneous emergence.' In effect, we cannot know our future, except in the short term. A seemingly minor change in information technology – such as RFID or web-based data processing – may shift the entire orientation of the supply chain. A corresponding adaptation to either internal operating changes or pressures external to the supply chain may induce a further shift in the environment. The point to emphasize is that CAS describes a parallel evolution changing both the supply chain and its environment interactively, without direction or control.

CAS and the supply chain

The foundation of CAS in the supply chain lies in organizational complexity: 'the amount of differentiation within different elements constituting the organization' (Dooley, 2002). The theme of complexity characterizes both organizations and their environments. Supply chains have a high density of connections, containing information and signals to coordinate operations. Environments have complexity stemming from technologies, economic turbulence and other influences. Organizations are complex not only because of their own technologies, but also because individual decision makers within the supply chain acting on simple information create a system with complex behaviour. CAS also adds the dimension of time to system discussion because it portrays a dynamic system able to respond to a new stimulus. It incorporates negative feedback loops that seek to stabilize systems, and positive feedback loops that tend to unstabilize them and drive them into disorder.

Organizations react and adapt to contingencies stemming from their environment. One rule of system behaviour, the Law of Requisite Variety (Ashby, 1952), emphasizes that organizations must match the variety in their environment (originating from volatility in demand, customers, suppliers, competitors, the economy and institutional settings) with equal variety. Simple supply chains would change only slowly over time, and operate by rule and formalized procedures. Complex supply chains deal with rapid change and high degrees of connection, and incorporate complex subsystems. It is necessarily complex because it deals with multiple environments.

Adaptation defines the requirements for organizational learning. Simple systems under stable conditions do not require learning; complex systems facing complex environments do. Organizations undergo three stages of learning (Argyris and Schön, 1978; Senge, 1990). First-order learning is basically fine-tuning of an ongoing system, a limited adjustment to change. Second-order learning requires reordering, recognizing a need to change the assumptions for operation. Third-order learning is the most challenging, essentially learning how to learn. This complex scenario suggests a radically changing set of circumstances, in which identifying knowledge itself becomes uncertain. Small changes with only incremental improvements over standard practice may be less successful than major changes because they force the supply chain to re-examine its previously held positions as a form of second-order learning.

Management with CAS is a delicate balance between preserving operational stability and responding to environmental forces. It requires extreme sensitivity to the unknowable. It may include both competition and cooperation between nodes. There is no consistent pattern of change resulting from CAS. It may be slow or rapid, linear (proportional to inputs) or non-linear (disproportionate), exhibit stable or abrupt change, consume few or many resources, and produce no effects on the system or a need for radical adjustment (Dooley, 1997).

The link between CAS and networks

The relationship between networks and CAS comes from two concepts that we have discussed – small world networks and weak ties. Small world networks describe closely coordinated management groups that normally have limited access to outside information. Weak ties provide this access by reaching new sources outside normal group awareness. The organizational arrangements to make this happen appear to be informal, reaching outside the established structure.

The inherent conflict within management is a struggle between order, as exemplified in the hierarchical structure of directing the supply chain as a sequential series of tasks oriented to process flow, and disorder within a turbulent environment with its need to respond. Houchin and MacLean (2005) describe this problem: 'Complexity theory makes it difficult to avoid confronting the fundamentally paradoxical nature of management in which managers must employ a rational loop within a shared mental process when they are close to certainty, and use other processes that generate instability if they are to bring about organizational transformation.'

Management has choices, whether to respond, or to protect the system against change. Thompson (1967) suggests buffering to enhance efficiency, but buffering also brings insularity. Galbraith (1977) divides response strategies into two camps: those reducing the need for information, and those increasing capacity for information processing. Reducing the need for information takes the form of either controlling the immediate task environment or buffering with slack resources such as inventory or processing capacity. The alternative requires increasing investment in information systems and collaboration. For supply chains, more intensive use of information technology and emphasis on collaboration point to increasing connections. It also suggests that there will be an increasing number of points for decision, with increasing complexity in order to achieve collective movement for the system as a whole.

Collaboration is becoming more important, developing customized products in conjunction with suppliers. Much current product development appears to follow this path. Communication is intensified, making the system more complex, and ultimately less predictable. Sabel and Zeitlin (2004) argue for a balance, utilizing relational contracting. Benchmarking, simultaneous design, concurrent engineering and collaboration broaden the scope of innovation, while still managing to divide development into task modules of effort.

Management structure

Choi, Dooley and Runtusanatham (2001) have linked the application of CAS to supply chain management. Supply chains that share processes among members, that are able to adapt rapidly to change and that are more aware of activities across the supply chain will be more effective than those that do not. Control – however it is enforced – comes at a price: less freedom for members to pursue innovation independently. A combination of control and adaptation is preferable for survival to the use of either alone.

CAS fits into an evolutionary conceptual chain proceeding from internal operations to dyads to external relationships to networks (Mills, Schmitz and Frizelle, 2004). In a dynamic perspective, managers can either seek to preserve current relationships or establish new configurations (Chandrashekar and Schary, 1999; Franke, 2002). The future appears to demand flexibility to meet rapid changes in markets, supply and technologies.

The concept of management in CAS is simple; the practice is difficult. Visualize an organization as an island of stability surrounded by chaos. Recognizing that stable organizations will stagnate and become vulnerable to competition and other changes, management must encourage and respond to change. To move away from stability is to move toward chaos. The imperative in the metaphor of Brown and Eisenhardt (1998) is to 'manage at the edge of chaos', balancing between stability and chaos, where the emergent system finds a new point of equilibrium. There are pressures for continuous change in supply chains, and this needs continuous experimentation to probe the future, to connect present practice to future options.

The current approaches to supply chain management organization have limits. When management has to span boundaries – typically with buyer–seller relationships – a number of arrangements have proved useful, including formal contracts, partnerships, supplier associations, joint ownership, and shared employees. But none of these can see beyond the immediate relationship to encompass the whole chain.

Information systems provide that ability. At the operating level, enterprise resource planning (ERP) and customer relationship management (CRM) pass the flow of orders from customer to supplier through the system. However, even ERP has limitations of ties to single firms – although forecasting can extend a signal to other members. Product life cycle management offers more visibility, extending product material requirements to suppliers. Nevertheless, even here, limited vision presents a problem that must be overcome. Information systems also require conformity – if not in procedure and software, then in data coding and assumptions. At the moment, information systems limit flexibility in changing partners within the system, unless the industry agrees in advance on protocols and data definitions.

Management must also deal with flexibility. At an operating level, strategies for agility – including product modularity, postponement, and inventory positioning – provide some degree of manoeuvrability. Their success, however, depends on confining adjustment within prescribed boundaries. Major strategic changes depend on the flexibility of the information system. We have become used to thinking of supplier relationships in terms of markets and hierarchies (Malone, Yates and Benjamin, 1987). White, Daniel and Mohdzain (2005) say that changes in technology point toward a third way. In their view, information and communication standards permit modularization of processes, making it easier to switch connections and thus reorganize the supply structure to meet new requirements. This information flexibility is further enhanced by web-based application service providers to manage computational and information processing over the web.

In Table 10.1, I have endeavoured to capture the elements of this discussion. Six levels of management start with reviews of the broad environment and end with narrow transactions. For each, there are five categories of system cognition: decision action, management emphasis, system direction, connection levels and openness. Descending through the management hierarchy, openness to new environmental pressures declines as decision choice becomes narrower. The

Table 10.1 The supply chain management organization

Management level	Decision action	Management emphasis	System direction	System connection	System openness
Environment	Adapt	Recognition	Complex adaptive systems	Loosely connected	Yes
Strategy	Objectives	Direction	Vision, tasks	Loose	Yes
Partnering	Selection	Capabilities	Definition	Loose	Yes
Coordination/ collaboration	Inter-organization	Partnerships, linkage	Relationships, communication	Loose	Yes, within limits
Planning	Optimization	Trade-offs	Limited control	Tight links	Tight
Transaction	Operations	Process	Data and physical links	Tight links	Tight

management emphasis also becomes more constrained. The key to outside influence is the number of connections that also become more limited, resulting ultimately in limited access to external influences.

Management in a CAS becomes a balance between open response and buffering to protect the system from outside disturbance (Choi, Dooley and Runtusanatham, 2001). Buffering establishes the boundaries, protects efficiency and protects against potentially disruptive influences. At the same time, emergent properties, the creation of new configurations and processes, are not limited to the upper reaches of management. Open organizations become strong sources for internal innovation. This raises a question of how much change to allow within a system. Further, if there is to be change, how do we manage it – given the inherent characteristics of the supply chain, with operations crossing organizational boundaries, at least quasi-independent organizations, and a need for precise coordination?

Conclusion

In this discussion, we have linked supply management to networks and complex adaptive systems. We emphasize that process is only the beginning. The supply chain itself becomes an organization that plays a crucial role in the corporation and in the economy at large. Yet we have little sense of how strategic decisions are made for the supply chain as a whole.

At this point, discussion becomes conjecture. The obvious statement is that we need to examine supply chains as they undergo transitions, to see how emergent systems exert change within the chain. We become concerned not necessarily with extension of theory, but with how supply chain management can direct a complex system as a form of meta-organization. The guidelines for organizational discussion so far have come from study of individual organizations. The contemporary reality of the supply chain lies in inter-organizational relationships. How it will evolve in the future will depend on its response to a changing environment.

References

Argyris, C and Schön, D (1978) *Organizational Learning: A theory of action perspective*, Addison-Wesley, Reading, MA

Ashby, WR (1952) *Design for a Brain*, Wiley, New York

Bovet, D and Martha, J (2000) *Value Nets*, Wiley, New York

Brandenburger, AM and Nalebuff, BJ (1996) *Co-opetition*, Harvard Business School Press, Boston, MA

Brown, S and Eisenhardt, K (1998) *Managing at the Edge of Chaos*, Harvard Business School Press, Boston, MA

Buchanan, M (2003a) *Nexus: Small world and the groundbreaking theory of networks*, WW Norton, New York

Buchanan, M (2003b) *Small World: Uncovering nature's hidden networks*, Orion, London

Chandrashekar, A and Schary, P (1999) Toward the virtual supply chain, *International Journal of Logistics Management*, **10** (2), pp 27–39

Choi, F and Krause, DR (2006) The supply base and its complexity: implications for transaction costs, risks, responsiveness and innovation, *Journal of Operations Management*, in press

Choi, TY, Dooley, KJ and Runtusanatham, M (2001) Supply networks and complex adaptive systems: control versus emergence, *Journal of Operations Management*, **19**, pp 351–66

Dooley K (1997) A complex adaptive systems model of organization change, *Non-Linear Dynamics, Psychology and Life Sciences*, **1** (1), pp 69–97

Dooley, K (2002) Organizational complexity, in *International Encyclopedia of Business and Management*, ed M Warner, pp 5013–22, Thomson Learning, London

Dooley, K, Johnson, T and Bush, D (1995) TQM, chaos and complexity, *Human Systems Management*, **14** (4), pp 1–16

Fine, C (1998) *Clockspeed*, Perseus Books, Reading, MA

Franke, U (ed) (2002) *Managing Virtual Web Organizations in the 21st Century*, Idea Group Publishing, Hershey, PA

Galbraith, JR (1977) *Organizational Design*, Addison-Wesley, Reading, MA

Gereffi, G, Humphrey, J and Sturgeon, T (2005) The governance of global value chains, *International Review of Political Economy*, **12** (1), February, pp 78–104

Granovetter, AM (1982) The strength of weak ties, *American Journal of Sociology*, **91**, pp 485–510

Hedlund, G (1986) A hypermodern MNC, *Human Resources Management*, **25**, Spring, pp 9–35

Houchin, K and MacLean, D (2005) Complexity theory and strategic change, *British Journal of Management*, **16**, pp 149–66

Malone, TW, Yates, J and Benjamin, RI (1987) Electronic markets and electronic hierarchies, *Communications of the ACM*, **30** (6), June, pp 484–97

Marion, R (1999) *The Edge of Organization*, Sage, Thousand Oaks, CA

Mills, J, Schmitz, J and Frizelle, G (2004) A strategic review of 'supply networks', *International Journal of Production and Operations Management*, **24** (10), pp 1012–36

Monge, PR and Contractor, NS (2001) Emergence of communication networks, in *The New Handbook of Organizational Communication*, ed FM Jablin and LI Putnam, Sage, Thousand Oaks, CA, pp 440–502

Parker, D and Stacey, R (1994) *Chaos, Management and Economics*, Institute for Economic Affairs, London

Perrow, C (1984) *Normal Accidents*, Basic Books, New York

Powell, WW (1990) Neither market nor hierarchy: network forms of organization, in *Research in Organizational Behavior*, 12, ed LL Cummings and B Straw, pp 295–336, JAI, Greenwich, CT

Quinn, FJ (1999) Reengineering the supply chain: an interview with Michael Hammer, *Supply Chain Management Review*, Spring, pp 20–26

Sabel, CF (2005) Firm collaboration in the new economy, *Enterprise and Society*, **5** (3), September

Sabel, CF and Zeitlin, J (2004) Neither modularity nor relational contracting: inter-firm collaboration in the new economy, *Enterprise and Society*, **5** (3), pp 388–403

Senge, B (1990) *The Fifth Dimension*, Currency Doubleday, New York

Sheffi, Y (2005) *The Resilient Enterprise: Overcoming vulnerability for competitive advantage*, MIT Press, Cambridge, MA

Surana, A *et al* (2005) Supply-chain networks: a complex adaptive systems perspective, *International Journal of Production Research*, **43** (20), October, pp 4235–65

Thompson, GF (2004) Is all the world a complex network?, *Economy and Society*, **13** (3), August, pp 411–24

Thompson, JD (1967) *Organizations in Action*, McGraw-Hill, New York

White, A, Daniel, EM and Mohdzain, M (2005) The role of emergent information technologies, *International Journal of Information Management*, **25**, pp 396–410

11

Information systems and information technologies for supply chain management

Xinping Shi and Simon Chan, Hong Kong Baptist University

Introduction

Data, information and knowledge are critical assets to the performance of logistics and supply chain management (SCM), because they provide the basis upon which management can plan logistics operations, organize logistics and supply chain (SC) processes, coordinate and communicate with business partners, conduct functional logistics activities, and perform managerial control of physical flow of goods, information exchange and sharing among SC partners.

Information systems (IS) are the effective and efficient means to manage those critical assets, and to provide sustainable competitive advantages. As far as SCM is concerned, information technology (IT) consists of telecommunication, networking and data-processing technologies – and is narrowly regarded here as the technological tools used to develop IS, capture or collect data, perform data analysis for generating meaningful information, and exchange and share this information with SC partners. Therefore, IT is an important enabler for the achievement of SCM effectiveness and efficiency (Simchi-Levi, Kaminsky and Simchi-Levi, 2003; Bowersox, Closs and Cooper, 2006). Effective IS/IT adoption is now thought to be an essential SCM resource.

In this chapter, we explore the functionality of IS/IT in SCM, as well as IS/IT contributions to SCM, and then describe the IS/IT development for SCM within a framework of IS/IT evolution. Finally, we discuss the theories related to IS/IT adoption, and a strategic framework and strategies for IS/IT adoption in SCM are provided.

Functionality of IS/IT in SCM

Efficiency-oriented IS/IT

From an information management perspective, IS/IT is conventionally utilized in the applications of efficiency-oriented SCM to increase productivity and reduce operational costs. Specifically, IS/IT is used to:

- capture and collect data on each product and service at a specific logistics activity, such as purchasing, to provide accurate, reliable and real-time raw facts;
- store collected data in a specific IS in predetermined categories and formats, such as a customer database management system;
- analyse stored data to generate meaningful information for management decision making in response to SCM events, and to evaluate SCM performance for cost reduction and productivity enhancement;
- collaborate and communicate with SC partners, to reduce information time lag and misunderstanding, and make the data resources available and visible to all SC partners;
- standardize logistics operations and data retrieval procedure, and develop generalized and rigorous information management policies, regulations and control measures; and
- apply transaction cost theory to SCM to gain economies of scale and implement low-cost strategies.

Effectiveness-oriented IS/IT

Nowadays, IS/IT is widely applied in the areas of effectiveness-oriented SCM to enhance SC competitive advantages, value-added SCM and globalized operations. In particular, IS/IT is deployed to:

- enhance core competence and positioning of a focal SC organization through designing and controlling the information sharing and flows;
- re-engineer SC operations and eliminate duplicated facilities or activities – such as vendor-managed inventory (VMI) instead of physical warehouses;

- manage marketing, customer, product and service knowledge or expertise developed (accumulated) in SCM, and share this with suppliers and partners – such as collaborative planning, forecasting and replenishment (CPFR);
- manage partner and customer relationships through resource-based and relational views, to stabilize SC structure and enhance relations with adjacent upstream and downstream partners; and
- deploy SC resources and capabilities to compete with other SCs at worldwide level, and through international sourcing and offshore manufacturing.

There are two main driving forces for organizations to invest in IS/IT, develop technological advantages in SCM and push the development of IS/IT applications in SCM. These are business environmental change and technological advancement. Business environmental change demands a growing capacity for data and information management in SCM; thus it continuously pulls organizational IS/IT investment. Technological evolution supplies the tools and systems to facilitate and satisfy the demands of data and information processing and transmission, and delivers innovative technology, such as wireless technology and radio frequency identification (RFID).

IS/IT development for SCM

The development and applications of IS/IT in SCM can be divided into four main levels: the first level is IS/IT in logistics functional areas – a *transaction support system*. Here typical IS/IT is bar-coding technology in a point-of-sale (POS) system, order process and inventory management, a warehouse management system (WMS), a transportation management system (TMS), etc. The second level is IS/IT for controlling information flows in integrated logistics operations' cross-functional areas in an organization – an *intranet system*, such as enterprise resources planning (ERP), a groupware system, and distribution requirement planning (DRP). The third level is IS/IT used for information exchange and sharing between organizations – an *extranet system*. The system is a structured and standard communication system, and it is used to exchange logistics information among SC partners in certain transactions, such as ordering and trading information. Two of the most widely adopted extranet systems are electronic data interchange (EDI) and CPFR. The fourth level is an *SCM system*, or inter-organizational information system (IOS) – an internet or network system for SC partners to exchange information and co-ordinate SC and logistics activities. Compared with an extranet system, an internet system is much more flexible and powerful in information distribution and conducting logistics transactions. Typical applications are electronic banking, electronic portals, electronic procurement, and customer relationship management (CRM).

The differences between intranet, extranet and internet lie in who is allowed to access and use the IS/IT. An intranet is authorized only to internal members in an organization to use; an extranet system is specified to those users who perform predefined logistics activities and transactions among two or more organizations; and internet systems allow unlimited users to access and use the system functions available and facilitate SCM information sharing.

Level one: transaction support IS/IT

At this level, IS/IT is mainly used as an efficient tool for supporting logistics operations, and the main concerns are whether IS/IT can provide reliable, accurate and real-time operation data and information to support core logistics activities. From an IS perspective, a database management system is the core technique. From an IT perspective, bar-coding and scanner technology is the core technology to capture real-time sales data and convert them into information through the POS and then produce receipts for customers – and to track storekeeping units to provide accurate inventory status information and facilitate inventory replenishment. A WMS helps to maximize the turnover of warehouse space, utilization of equipment, and productivity of labour, and to minimize the movement of goods, store time, and the lead time in responding to shipment and distribution scheduling.

Through data and information processing, a TMS provides transportation planning, freight payment auditing, carrier selection and performance monitoring. It also performs administrative tasks, reviewing transportation bills and management carrier relationships. Together, these transaction support systems support SCM to execute low-cost strategies and provide better customer services. However, although they provide regional optimal solutions in processing logistics data and information, they are often not integrated with other IS in the organization, may not be aligned with overall organizational objectives and may be inconsistent with SC partners' IS/IT when information exchange is required.

Level two: integrated organizational IS/IT

Integrated organizational IS/IT gives intranet systems that facilitate data, information and communication within an organization, among widely dispersed logistics departments and locations. For example, an intranet system is used to share order processing, inventory and shipping status, and customer credit and accounting information within a firm. The characteristics of intranet systems are that they standardize organization-wide data and information structure and format, integrate isolated transactional support systems and allow data and information sharing.

ERP is the most widely deployed intranet system. It integrates logistics transaction modules with a common, standard and consistent database or data warehouse – and provides multiple interfaces to logistics functional users. It digitalizes logistics operational procedures, regulations, organizational policies and industrial standards into an integrated system, and also contains some advanced managerial support functions like data mining, decision support and executive report functions. Essentially, ERP uses the local area network and client-server technologies to implement an organization-wide information and communication framework, and to integrate functional logistics IS such as WMS and POS.

Level three: information sharing and exchange IS/IT

An extranet system is designed to control and coordinate the flow of logistics data and information for sharing with SC partners. The system creates an effective and formal communication channel between the SC focal organization and its upstream suppliers and downstream customers, and the information flow is structured in standard business documents with standard formats. With a resource-based view, organizations in an SC become more interdependent when one organization accesses information owned by other organizations and when uncertainty affects the supply of resources. When the business environment changes and shifts power downstream in the SC, those organizations with richer information of markets and customers gain an advantage over other SC partners.

EDI is the most widely deployed extranet system for inter-firm information exchange. La Londe and Cooper (1989) have addressed EDI as one of the most important changes to affect SCM, and 'it is the glue that binds long-term relationship, and plays an important coordinating role in managing the interfaces between firms as business processes go beyond the boundaries of the firm' (Mentzer, 2001). The main benefits from using EDI are: upstream SC partners can access timely and accurate information from markets and customers, and incorporate this into planning and scheduling; downstream SC partners can provide better customer services, responding to market changes and customer demands; all SC partners can reduce paperwork and enjoy quality communication. Other derived benefits from deployment of EDI are increased productivity, cost saving, accurate billing and improved tracing and expenditure.

CPFR is also an extranet system developed for sharing logistics management processes with suppliers, and it enhances VMI and continuous replenishment by incorporating joint forecasting. SC partners exchange information about past sales, promotions, forecasts and customer behaviour – and even less structured opinions and suggestions. The system contributes to SC partners by focusing on their core business values and allowing them to benefit from each other. Like EDI, CPFR can also improve SC efficiency, increase sales and timely responsiveness to markets and customers, and reduce fixed asset investment and inventory costs.

Level four: internet-based SCM systems

The internet is increasingly becoming the most useful business communication and information exchange system. The system will eventually replace EDI because all information flows performed by EDI can be carried out through the internet, with low access costs and consistent transfer standards. Further, it can synchronize information from all SC participants – including worldwide customers. Perhaps the most outstanding feature of the internet is that it changes the information exchange from one to one, to one to many, and many to many. Then traditional business partnerships can be changed into an SC organization with many alternative SC partners simultaneously, and the stability and trust of conventional SC relationships become unstable, and the development of virtual relationships challenges all existing theories and empirical findings.

Organizations increasingly use advanced IS/IT for manipulating information flows in SCM. However, current IS/IT may not reflect organizational real needs for timely information control, information quality and visibility, reduced information costs and excellent service. The roles of IS/IT in SCM have changed dramatically in the past few decades – and will continue to change with IT advancement in the future. This raises a series of strategic issues.

Strategic issues of IS/IT in SCM

SCM and IS/IT address information flow from different perspectives. SCM focuses on developing tightly integrated SC linkages or relationships with an organization's suppliers and customers; IS/IT focuses on the technology for developing a comprehensive system or sophisticated platform, often regardless of the context. Users, organizations and IS managers are overwhelmed with the media hype and are unsure about how – if at all – to migrate from their existing real SCM processes to digitalized or virtual SCM operations. We discuss this movement from the perspective of three stakeholders – SC users, the SC focal organization and IS/IT managers.

Users' perspective

Users are the digitalized SCM operators, who are concerned about the processes, relationships with SC partners, and costs of using IS/IT for daily operations. Some strategic issues are:

- Does IS/IT fit organizational SCM strategies and core competence?
- Is IS/IT adoption compatible with current philosophies and practices?
- What business process and SC structure change will take place?
- How will existing suppliers and relationships be affected by the new IS/IT?
- What costs will be incurred during and after IS/IT adoption?

Just-in-time manufacturing and efficient consumer response in retailing have brought significant changes to SC practices. SCM attempts to achieve cycle time reduction and faster inventory turnover by establishing tight linkages with suppliers – and to move from pure efficiency orientation to greater co-ordination and integration of business processes in functional areas including product design and development, market research, production planning, etc. A high level of trust and extensive information sharing are required for successful implementation of these initiatives. But a focus on individual transactions and price reduction by IS/IT may be inconsistent with the SC philosophies of trust and long-term relationships. So IS/IT may jeopardize an organization's existing relationships with its long-term suppliers. Since the adoption of new IS/IT takes significant effort and time, organizations should check that there is alignment with current SCM strategies. The worst scenario is that the introduction of IS/IT will be inconsistent and create confusion among suppliers. Change management, both internal and external, is critical, as there are many instances of good IS/IT not producing the desired results owing to faulty implementation. For example, Nike had a major problem with production and distribution after introducing an advanced production planning system. They found later that their problem was not the software, but the quality of data input to the system.

Focal organization perspective

Some strategic issues concerning the SC focal organization are:

- Shall we build our own IS/IT or jointly develop IS/IT with SC partners?
- What strategic approach shall we take to develop IS/IT for all SC partners?
- How does the developed IS/IT impact on our current SC operations?
- What will happen to existing long-term and arm's-length relationships with key customers?
- Will the IS/IT adoption consolidate our leading SC position and enhance the competitiveness of our products?

A critical SCM decision is how to develop and introduce IS/IT, and still maintain trustworthy, long-term relationships with key SC partners. While long-term relationships and contracts provide stability, they reduce the flexibility of exploring alternative markets and the possibility of faster growth or increasing profits in some markets. The focal organization needs clear objectives and strategic planning, collaboration with other SC partners to share the risks and benefits, and a careful analysis of the impacts of new IS/IT.

IS/IT managers' perspective

Some strategic issues confronting IS/IT managers are:

- How do we migrate from dyadic EDI platforms to the advanced SCM systems?
- How do we integrate our ERP or other functional systems with SCM systems?
- What internal and external IT infrastructure has to be developed with our suppliers/users?
- What are the system and data compatibility issues in interacting with non-standardized systems?

Naturally, IS/IT managers pay more attention than others to technological issues in the development of new IS/IT, because there are usually internal legacy systems that work with EDI middleware to communicate with their trading partners. EDI provides a standardized data format for two computers to communicate automatically without any manual intervention. This brings a high level of transaction efficiency, but it is not very useful for communication of unstructured information, evaluation, and negotiation processes. Migration to new IS/IT may require interacting with different web applications and non-standardized data formats that may create problems with organizational intranet systems. For example, getting demand forecast information from multiple customers and incorporating it into intranet systems would require individually visiting customers' websites, retrieving information, checking their data formats and re-entering them in internal systems. This may be a step backward in technology for retailers unless interfaces are developed to retrieve the information automatically from the websites into intranet systems.

An integrated SCM system that links all the SC partners may be the ultimate solution for IS/IT managers. While communication incompatibilities are relatively easy to overcome through XML and related technologies, data incompatibilities are harder to handle. Unless there is a significant benefit in moving from existing EDI-based systems to an SCM system, IS/IT managers will be reluctant to make the migration.

IS/IT adoption for SCM

The strategic importance of IS/IT in SCM means that its introduction needs careful planning with SC partners to guarantee a successful implementation. In this section, we present the theories underpinning IS/IT adoption in an SCM context; then we discuss likely strategies for guiding an SC organization to implement an SCM system.

Theories for IS/IT adoption

Four theories – resource-based view, relational view, transaction cost theory and resource dependence theory – provide theoretical foundations for IS/IT adoption in SCM. Table 11.1 presents a review of the theoretical foundation of

Table 11.1 Theories for IS/IT adoption in an SCM context

	Resource-based view	**Relational view**	**Transaction cost theory**	**Resource dependence theory**
Unit of analysis	Individual firm	Pair/network firms; electronic dyads	Hierarchical and market transaction	Dyadic parnters/ firms
IS/IT nature	Functional or corporate-wide systems	Value/SCM system	Monopolies, dyads, and multilateral SCM system	Pooled information; resources of SCM system
Core theoretical concepts	Scarce tangible and intangible resources; capabilities and activities	Partnerships; relational specific assets; knowledge, information exchange; complementary scarce resources and capabilities; relationship mechanisms	Cost of transaction for the choice of an optimal governance structure; costs of setting up, operating and maintaining SC relationships	SC linkage; socio-political influences; political and behavioural partner relationships; social exchange
Managing SC relationships	Controlling and exploiting organizational strategic resources manifested in assets and capabilities	SC strategy; joint creation of unique products, services, know-how and technologies; joint learning; lower transaction costs	Cost structure and distribution; transaction efficiency; cost minimization; vertical integration	Resource dependence; securing access to strategic resources; controlling necessary external resources; using political and social pressures
Normative consequence	Control resource scarcity; resource values; inimitable; non-substitutable asset stock	Network barriers to imitation; time compression; SC assets stock; partner scarcity; resource indivisibility	Economic aspects and market transactions; static analysis; existence of optimal structure	Holistic approach; knowledge and skills in using external mechanisms

Table 11.1 *continued*

	Resource-based view	Relational view	Transaction cost theory	Resource dependence theory
Role of IS/IT	Resource control; manipulating information; organizational IS/IT and operations; functional system management, eg bar code, POS, MRP, ERP, intranet	Establishing and keeping electronic partnership; leveraging SC knowledge and information sharing, exchange and creation; SCM system with organizational systems, eg EDI, SCM, CRM, e-business systems	Transaction costs control; improving data and information utilization; virtual integration; operations in functional areas, eg inventory management and quality control	Leveraging organizational information resources; connecting with external standard; responding to/ putting pressure on competitors
Key references	Wernerfelt (1984); Barney (1991); Eisenhardt and Schoonhoven (1996)	Oliver (1990); Hamel (1991); Dyer (1997); Dyer and Singh (1998)	Williamson (1975, 1985, 1991)	Thompson (1967); Benson (1975); Pfeffer and Salancik (1978)

inter-organizational relationships (IOR) and SCM related to IS/IT adoption. Adoption is defined as the development of the 'first' successful IS/IT using a new information-process technology in an organizational process or products. In Table 11.1, five theoretical attributes are defined as follows: *unit of analysis* refers to the level of theory application to a specific social unit for analytic interpretation; the *core theoretical concepts* specify the conceptual contributions of a theory; *managing SC relationships* identifies the functions and influences of the core concepts on the IOR (eg partner relationships in SCM); the *normative consequence* refers to the anticipated outcomes of the theory when applied to IOR; and the *role of IS/IT* articulates the functionalities of adopted IS/IT in manifesting IOR and partnerships.

Resource-based view and transaction cost theory

An organization is a bundle of assets (resources) and capabilities, and the firm's competitive advantage is derived from the possession of unique strategic resources and capabilities. These resources are: value, rareness, imperfect imitability and lack of substitutability (Wernerfelt, 1984; Barney, 1991). In this vein, IS/IT adoption is a strategic investment in the organizational capability of utilizing information resources – and leverages the value of information to increase the firm's competitive advantages. Studies show that IT is deployed to develop organizational IS, to manipulate organizational information and operational effectiveness (Mata, Fuerst and Barney, 1995; Santhanam and Hartono, 2003).

Transaction cost theory mainly focuses on the market governance structures of supplying relationships (Williamson, 1985, 1991). The core concept is that, in a perfect market, a firm will optimize its supply of materials from specialized suppliers (or make its own). Firms engage in repeated and contract-based transactions with suppliers.

In cases where the resources or products are highly supplier-specific, time-specific and complex in nature, this is an appropriate approach. The transaction costs of managing the relationships and interactions with the suppliers – including searching, negotiating and monitoring execution of the transactions – are high. By reducing the transaction costs, IS/IT – especially SCM systems – allows a high level of coordination and increases the value of coordinated resources through economies of scale, vertical integration or virtual hierarchies (Johnston and Lawrence, 1988; Clemons and Row, 1991; Holland, 1995).

Resource-based view and transaction cost theory provide sound foundations for an SCM system. According to these theories, it can be predicted that adoption and diffusion of IS/IT can optimize a firm's internal and arm's-length market resources, and integrate vertical business operations with the firm's suppliers at lower transaction costs and higher efficiency. However, the theories focus on organizational resource utilization rather than IOR, and more inter-firm coordination rather than SC partners' cooperation and resource sharing. Thus, the vertical integration or virtual hierarchy is a focal firm-specific, economic-oriented and contract-based relationship; and the relationship may suffer from long-term instability when economic and market mechanisms change (Premkumar and Ramamurthy, 1995; Dyer, 1997).

Relational view and resource dependence theory

A relational view offers a theoretical understanding of the sources of inter-organizational competitive advantage from inter-organizational alliances – SC partnerships or IOR (Oliver, 1990; Dyer and Singh, 1998). Relational view asserts that SC competitive advantage comes from: 1) the relation-specific assets of IOR; 2) substantial knowledge-exchange routines, joint learning and partner-specific absorptive capabilities; 3) the synergistic effect of the endowments of complementary and distinctive resources and capabilities among SC partners; and 4) the ability to employ an informal self-enforcement relationship governance mechanism (Dyer and Singh, 1998; Kanter, 1994; Zhara and George, 2002).

In line with social exchange theory authors (Emerson, 1962; Blau, 1964; Benson, 1975), Pfeffer and Salancik (1978) postulated a resource dependence theory, where resource dependence is based on an organization's ability 1) to control resources needed by other firms, and 2) to reduce their dependence on others for resources. That is, an organization must gain control over resources that are critical to its operations, and must reduce uncertainty in the acquisition of these resources.

Much research has been conducted into the perspective of resource dependence (Gaski and Nevin, 1985; Provan and Skinner, 1989; Oliver, 1990). Organizational power – a firm's capacity to control, the actual act of control, and the impact of an organization's perception of dependence on its partners – has been intensively studied to reveal its influence on IOR. In addition, analysis of four dimensions – goal compatibility, domain consensus, evaluation of accomplishment, and norms of exchange – has made significant contributions to the understanding of the environmental influence of IOR. It is found that a favourable transaction climate gives more cooperation and better information flows and decision making (Williamson, 1975; Reve and Stern, 1986).

Compared with resource-based view and transaction cost theory, relational view and resource dependence theory give much attention to external resources and collaboration. Relational view focuses on a fair investment of relation-specific assets, and development and governance of routines for collaboration, while resource dependence theory puts emphasis on asymmetric resource distributions in social and political settings, and how a powerful organization can employ the dependency of others to accomplish its objectives. Therefore, relational view is trust-based, and resource dependence theory is power-based.

Using the power, positions and role differences, a focal organization in SC may exercise its coercive influence to control scarce and strategic resources, such as privileged information, knowledge and expertise, technology competence, etc. The organization may force its dependent SC partners to adopt innovative IS/IT, such as an SCM system, that serve mainly its own interests (Pfeffer and Salancik, 1978). Evidence of coercive behaviour has been suggested when adopting EDI (Webster, 1995; Hart and Saunders, 1997). Wal-Mart is a typical example of resource dependence theory, in the way it mandates its top 100 suppliers to use RFID labels. Suppliers that cannot satisfy this mandatory requirement endanger their business transactions and relations with Wal-Mart.

Strategic framework of IS/IT adoption in SCM

Based on these theoretical foundations for IS/IT adoption, we have developed a strategic framework (Figure 11.1) to specify strategies for IS/IT adoption.

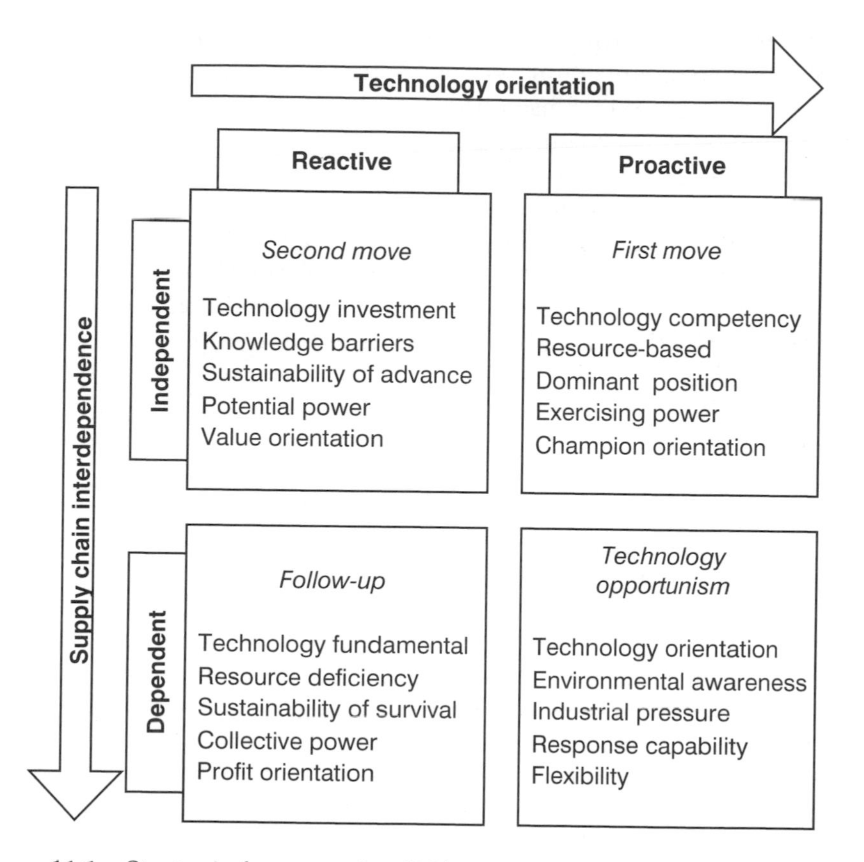

Figure 11.1 Strategic framework of IS/IT adoption in SCM context

Within the framework, the horizontal dimension – technology orientation – refers to organizational and inter-organizational technology capabilities, and ability to develop products, services and operation processes that contribute to SC competitiveness. Facing an innovative IS/IT, the focal SC organization has two broad options: proactive and reactive. With a proactive approach an organization holds positive attitudes toward IS/IT, is motivated by IS/IT adoption opportunities, devotes resources to understand and evaluate, and is willing to initiate IS/IT adoption. On the other hand, with a reactive approach an organization shows less interest in new IS/IT, holds back from the system or technology, carefully investigates implications and impacts of a new system or technology, does tentative trials of IS/IT, closely monitors trends of IS/IT among SC partners and industries, and controls the timing of IS/IT adoption.

The vertical dimension – supply chain interdependence – refers to the IOR in the SC context, and it reflects the relational view of mutual influence, exchange, interactions, knowledge and information sharing, coordination, cooperation, and integration (Oliver, 1990; Hart and Estrin, 1991; Dyer and

Singh, 1998). The interdependence has positions. One is independent, suggesting that an organization has a powerful position in an SC network and has more decision-making discretion and a strong influence on other SC partners, that the firm's resources and operations are independent of its SC partners and that SC partners are heavily dependent upon the organization. The other is dependent, suggesting that an organization in an SC network has limited resources, influence, ability to change the SC structure and process, decision making, bargaining for privileged information, and favourable treatment. And there are potential substitute firms in the marketplace, competing to join the SC network with the dominant firm and replace dependent organizations.

The framework shows that there are four strategies for focal organizations to adopt:

1. *First move strategy.* This is an aggressive and self-motivated strategy driven by intrinsic organizational demand for advancement, privilege and advantages over SC partners. A firm using this strategy clearly recognizes the benefits of IS/IT, and initiates changes for the firm and SC as a whole. Through adopting IS/IT, the firm can further consolidate its SC position and enhance its influence. However, this strategy is expensive, and needs high technology competence and resources; it also presents a higher risk and lower measurable return of investment than other strategies. Further, deployment of this strategy may require the firm to exercise its power to force any unwilling SC partners to accept and use IS/IT accordingly. (Otherwise, IS/IT is only adopted in the focal organization, with substantially reduced benefits.)

   Dos Santos and Peffers (1995) found that banks that took the first move strategy with ATM machines were able to increase market share and income – with the gains remaining over the long term. This empirically justifies a first move strategy for those capable firms that can lead technological change. Another attractive feature of this strategy for the SC dominant firm is that successful IS/IT adoption will build competitive barriers and define the rules and norms of the game in its own SC.
2. *Second move strategy.* This is a conservative strategy, and is driven by the focal organization's management style and policies – and stakeholders' interests – rather than potential opportunities from the IS/IT adoption. A firm deploying this strategy has organizational resources, technology capability, SC position and influence – but it may regard IS/IT adoption as an investment, with evaluation focusing on the return on investment and risk management. The firm may strive to be a competent technology user, but not a pioneer of IS/IT or SCM systems, because its core values and assets may not be derived from technological innovation. When facing innovative IS/IT change, the firm may have knowledge barriers, and will hold back and take a 'wait and see' attitude.

The advantages of this strategy lie in its value orientation – and its rationale is in transaction cost theory. A firm does not invest resources in uncertain projects without obviously added value. Only when the investment environment is favourable, the IS/IT is approaching maturity and the value-add from investment in IS/IT is achievable and accountable will the firm take a positive view towards IS/IT adoption. So it mainly uses IS/IT to enhance operational efficiency and cost-effectiveness – but cannot fully utilize the strategic benefits of IS/IT. The disadvantage of the strategy is obvious, as delayed adoption of IS/IT cannot give technology leadership and it cannot establish competitiveness based on an SCM system.

3. *Follow-up strategy.* This is a passive strategy for those SC partners that do not have an initiative for active IS/IT adoption. It is adopted by organizations that have limited resources, small-scale operations and little influence on their SC partners. For firms taking this strategy, the theoretical foundations are transaction cost theory and resource dependence theory – and their business transactions are largely dependent upon the dominant organization in the SC network. These firms generally adopt some nearly outdated IS/IT to support their business operations, to connect with the dominant firm and to process essential business information – with EDI adoption in small businesses being a typical example. These firms may regard investment in new IS/IT as a waste, or at least a luxury, and they hardly achieve technology competency, using technology to satisfy leading business partners' requirements and business procedure.
4. *Technology opportunism strategy.* This is defined as a sense-and-respond capability for proactive IS/IT adoption, responding to new opportunities in ways that do not violate the principle of fairness (Srinivasan, Lilien and Rangaswamy, 2002). There are two components of technology opportunism: technology sensing and technology response. Sensing is a firm's ability to scan internal and external innovations, acquire knowledge about and understand new technology and then provide innovative products and services derived from, utilizing or deploying the technology. Response is an organizational willingness and ability to respond to new technologies, re-engineer business strategy and explore opportunities (Miles and Snow, 1978).

A firm using a technology opportunism strategy strongly believes that new IS/IT can create a substantial opportunity, so it proactively scans technological opportunities and seeks to capitalize on them. The firm is not restricted to traditional principles and experience, but understands, analyses and utilizes new IS/IT technology for developing innovative products and services. It is a strategy for ambitious and strongly self-motivated firms. The firm may be small or dependent on the dominant firm in the SC context, but it wants to be powerful by using IS/IT. It may actively cooperate with the dominant SC firm to adopt IS/IT and create unique value for the firm itself and its SC partners. Microsoft's growth experience in the 1980s is an excellent example of a firm taking a technology opportunism strategy and successfully changing its position in the operating systems and software industry.

This strategy is particularly useful for small firms, and requires flexibility in managerial mindset and operations, and technological competence. Top management direct the firm, while operational flexibility and efficiency speed up organizational change. Of course, this strategy needs a risk-taker mentality, but the benefits of success are far great than failure costs.

Table 11.2 summaries the four strategies in 12 strategy evaluation scales that measure an organization's strategic readiness for IS/IT adoption. The scales cover organizational, inter-organizational and technological issues, and suggest the theory deployment in strategy selection for IS/IT. The scales can also be used as a checklist to help an organization make a strategy choice and evaluate whether it is ready to take a proactive strategy.

IS/IT utilization in SCM

The utilization of IS/IT in SCM can have an effect on performance, but how can an organization make sure that IS/IT is fully utilized? We suggest the following considerations for fulfilling organizational and SC performance requirements:

1. It is reasonable to have a detailed understanding of customer and supplier requirements, as well as all SC partners' concerns. IS/IT adoption should be flexible and adaptable, depending on specific needs and how the needs are satisfied. Performance criteria for IS/IT adoption and utilization include regular reviews of the usage of SC partners.
2. IS/IT advancement has been moving away from logistics functional areas towards a process and SC orientation. Emphasis on the latter ensures a more meaningful measurement of relevant processes and ensures more timely and accurate process feedback and coordination.
3. To grasp IS/IT adoption opportunities it is vital to integrate the knowledge of logistics managers, IS/IT managers and knowledgeable SC partners. Logistics managers need to know more IS/IT – and information specialists must develop greater insight into SCM.
4. Financial resources are needed to ensure a smooth IS/IT implementation. Employees' cooperation and use of systems are also critical.
5. Managerial experience and expertise in managing SC relationships and IS/IT adoption also play a critical role in the implementation of the SCM system – and if management keeps a proactive attitude, encourages organizational learning and works together with SC partners, then SCM system adoption among all partners is close to success.

Table 11.2 Factors for strategic evaluation of IS/IT adoption

	First move	Second move	Follow-up	Technology opportunism
Organization size	Large	Large	Medium/small	Small
Strategic importance of IS/IT adoption	Very high	Unclear	Not necessary	Ultimate
Leadership motivation of IS/IT adoption	High	Moderate	Low	Very high
Organization readiness for IS/IT adoption	High	Hold back	No	High
Pressure of SC competition for IS/IT adoption	Medium	Medium	Low	High
Pressure of SC partners for IS/IT adoption	Low	Low	High	Medium
Perceived SC needs of IS/IT adoption	Strongest	Strong	Neutral	Strongest
Relation of IS/IT adoption to SC core business	High	Medium	Unclear	High
Firm's mandatory power over SC partners	Strong	Moderate	None	Occasional
Perceived technology radicalness of IS/IT	Acceptable	High	Hardly acceptable	Appreciated
Propensity to IS/IT adoption risks	Risk taking	Avoiding	Risk averting	Aggressive risk taking
Technological slack for IS/IT initiation	Sufficient	Adequate	Lack	Specializing in RFID

Summary

In this chapter, we show how IS/IT can make significant contributions to efficient and effective SCM. We discuss the development of IS/IT at four levels, reflecting the advancement of IT and the involvement of IS/IT in SCM. IS/IT development and adoption in SCM are complicated, and organizations have to take many strategic factors into account. For those facing such a tough challenge, we provide a literature review of IS/IT adoption, and reveal the theories underpinning IS/IT adoption. We provide theoretical guidance – a framework of strategy adoption – and identity the conditions and resources for organizations to initiate IS/IT adoption.

Effective SCM requires SC partners collaboratively to develop a plan for coordinating the flows of goods and services, with timely information to ensure these are delivered at the right time, to the right place and at the right price. IS/IT plays an important role in achieving SCM objectives. To utilize IS/IT potential fully, organizations need an effective strategy that fits the organizational resources and relationships with SC partners – and they need to work together with SC partners to share the risk and costs of IS/IT development and to enjoy the benefits derived from SCM systems.

References

Barney, J (1991) Firm resources and sustained competitive advantage, *Journal of Management*, **17** (1), pp 99–120

Benson, JK (1975) The interorganizational network as a political economy, *Administrative Science Quarterly*, **20** (2), pp 229–49

Blau, PM (1964) *Exchange and Power in Social Life*, Wiley, New York

Bowersox, D, Closs, DJ and Cooper, MB (2006) *Supply Chain Logistics Management*, 2nd edn, McGraw-Hill International, New York

Clemons, E and Row, M (1991) Sustainable IT advantage: the role of structural differences, *MIS Quarterly*, **15** (3), pp 275–92

Dos Santos, BL and Peffers, K (1995) Rewards to investors in innovative information technology applications: first movers and early followers in ATMs, *Organization Sciences*, **6** (3), pp 241–59

Dyer, JH (1997) Effective interfirm collaboration: how firms minimize transaction costs and maximize transaction value, *Strategic Management Journal*, **18** (7), pp 535–56

Dyer, JH and Singh, H (1998) The relational view: cooperative strategy and sources of interorganizational competitive advantage, *Academy of Management Review*, **23** (4), pp 660–79

Eisenhardt, K and Schoonhoven, CB (1996) Resource-based view of strategic alliance formation: strategic and social effects in entrepreneurial firms, *Organization Science*, **7** (2), pp 136–50

Emerson, RM (1962) Power dependence relations, *American Sociological Review*, **27** (1), pp 31–41

Gaski, JF and Nevin, JR (1985) The differential effects of exercised and unexercised power source in a marketing channel, *Journal of Marketing*, **22** (2), pp 130–42

Hamel, G (1991) Competition for competence and inter-partner learning within international strategic alliance, *Strategic Management Journal*, 12, Winter Special Issue, pp 83–104

Hart, P and Estrin, D (1991) Interorganizational networks, computer integration, and shifts in interdependence: the case of the semiconductor industry, *ACM Transactions on Information Systems*, **9** (4), pp 370–417

Hart, P and Saunders, C (1997) Power and trust: critical factors in the adoption and use of electronic data interchange, *Organizational Science*, **8** (1), pp 83–103

Holland, CP (1995) Cooperative supply chain management: the impact of interorganizational information systems, *Journal of Strategic Information Systems*, **4** (2), pp 117–33

Johnston, R and Lawrence, PR (1988) Beyond vertical integration: rise of the value-adding partnership, *Harvard Business Review*, **66** (4), July–August, pp 94–101

Kanter, RM (1994) Collaborative advantage: the art of alliance, *Harvard Business Review*, **72** (4), pp 96–108

La Londe, BJ and Cooper, MC (1989) *Partnerships in Providing Customer Service*, Council for Logistics Management, Oak Brook, IL

Mata, FJ, Fuerst, WL and Barney, JB (1995) Information technology and sustained competitive advantage: a resource-based analysis, *MIS Quarterly*, **19** (4), pp 487–506

Mentzer, JT (2001) *Supply Chain Management*, Sage, Thousand Oaks, CA

Miles, RE and Snow, CC (1978) *Organizational Strategy, Structure and Process*, McGraw-Hill, New York

Oliver, C (1990) Determinants of interorganizational relationships: integration and future directions, *Academy of Management Review*, **15** (2), pp 241–65

Pfeffer, J and Salancik, G (1978) *External Control of Organizations: A resource dependence perspective*, Harper & Row, New York

Premkumar, GP and Ramamurthy, K (1995) The role of interorganizational and organizational factors on the decision mode for adoption of interorganizational systems, *Decision Sciences*, **26** (3), pp 303–36

Provan, KG and Skinner, S (1989) Interorganizational dependence and control as predictors of opportunism in dealer–supplier relations, *Academy of Management Journal*, **32** (1), pp 202–12

Reve, T and Stern, LW (1986) The relationship between interorganizational form, transaction climate, and economic performance in vertical interfirm dyads, in *Marketing Channels: Relationships and performance*, ed L Pellgrini and S Raddy, Lexington Books, Lexington, MA

Santhanam, R and Hartono, E (2003) Issues in linking information technology capability to firm performance, *MIS Quarterly*, **27** (1), pp 125–53

Simchi-Levi, D, Kaminsky, P and Simchi-Levi, E (2003) *Design and Managing the Supply Chain: Concepts, strategies and case studies*, 2nd edn, McGraw-Hill, New York

Srinivasan, R, Lilien, GL and Rangaswamy, A (2002) Technological opportunism and radical technology adoption: an application to e-business, *Journal of Marketing*, **66** (3), pp 47–60

Thompson, JD (1967) *Organizations in Action*, McGraw-Hill, New York

Webster, J (1995) Networks of collaboration or conflict? Electronic data interchange and power in the supply chain, *Journal of Strategic Information Systems*, **4** (1), pp 31–42

Wernerfelt, B (1984) A resource based view of the firm, *Strategic Management Journal*, **5** (2), pp 171–80

Williamson, OE (1975) *Markets and Hierarchies: Analysis and antitrust implications: a study in the economics of internal organization*, Free Press, New York

Williamson, OE (1985) *The Economic Institutions of Capitalism*, Free Press, New York

Williamson, OE (1991) Comparative economic organization: the analysis of discrete structural alternatives, *Administrative Science Quarterly*, **36** (2), pp 269–96

Zhara, S and George, G (2002) Absorptive capability: a review, reconceptualization and extension, *Academy of Management Review*, **27** (2), pp 185–203

12

Outsourcing: the result of global supply chains?

Stephen Rinsler, Bisham Consulting

Background

There can be no doubt that outsourcing has become big business. From early beginnings in the mid- to late 1970s, many companies have travelled the outsourcing road, and as technology and accessibility to shared electronic data have increased so has the range of services offered by outsourcing companies.

In the past few years the UK government has openly encouraged outsourcing, which the Private Finance Initiative (PFI) and other deals have spawned. Not all the outsourcing arrangements in the private or the public sector have been successful. There is a steady but small stream of processes being taken back in-house, and there have been some high-profile failures in the press.

We will explore why outsourcing takes place and how to avoid some of the pitfalls that undoubtedly can occur. We have tried to place outsourcing in the context of the more recent moves to source manufacture from overseas, particularly the Far East.

Definition

Outsourcing describes the deliberate movement of a series of connected business processes to a third party, which manages them on behalf of the company. The classic processes were IT, warehousing and distribution, facilities management, and payroll – and to these can now be added call centres, manufacturing, web development, home shopping, credit cards, and even merchandising and design. In these movements the commercial risk and assets are usually passed to the outsourcing company.

However, not all companies refer to the process of business process management transfer as outsourcing – for some they are just buying a service or a series of products. In this case the transfer of assets is unlikely.

The definition of outsourcing does not imply abdication of responsibility.

Examples

Some retailers over the years became very vertically integrated. They would manufacture their own goods, own and run their stores, own and run their warehousing and distribution to stores – and some even ran their own store loyalty schemes, including the Co-op's stamps. Now many retailers outsource all their manufacturing, they do not own and run their stores, they have outsourced their warehousing and distribution, a bank runs their store cards, and some have outsourced their design, packaging design and merchandising by franchising their floor space to design or cosmetic houses and niche labels.

For others, including manufacturing companies and distribution companies, the accounts function is outsourced.

Reasons for outsourcing

You may have heard these reasons:

- 'We do not have the management expertise.'
- 'We need to jump the learning curve.'
- 'We want to move fast.'
- 'The area requires major re-engineering.'
- 'We do not have the management resources.'
- 'We pay too much to do it ourselves.'
- 'It is not core.'
- 'The business is going through major change and needs to make more areas variable cost.'
- 'We need to focus our resources for training, investment, time, etc.'

However, some of the strategic reasons above are overshadowed by the personal objectives of the management involved. Some like to follow a trend and, therefore, encourage outsourcing; some, when joining a company where that department has been outsourced, start the process of reintegration to enlarge their role.

The reasons for outsourcing can be structured into five groups:

- financial;
- technology;
- resource management;
- managerial;
- personal.

Financial reasons for outsourcing

Companies have to declare in their statutory accounts – and to many stock exchanges – the value of assets leased and the methodology used by their businesses to access their markets, but it is still the case that some companies have limited access to investment funds and see the need to leave the raising of cash to their outsourcing partners. Sometimes the outsourcing provider can borrow at a better rate than the company since the provider's operation has a lower risk through better focus; sometimes the additional borrowing costs are worth the flexibility.

Flexibility of use of resources is also an important factor. If the company's use of resources can be pooled with that of others – creating better scale and better marginal costs – then using an outsourcer ensures some independence of management of those resources, and releases the company from having to manage the other users of the facilities.

Another facet of outsourcing in the past five years has been the pensions factor. Whilst many larger companies have seen their pension deficits soar, the companies to which they outsource often do not have final salary benefit schemes. Thus outsourcing crystallizes the deficit at the point of transfer, but it only does so for those people who transfer under TUPE arrangements (Transfer of Undertakings (Protection of Employment) Regulations). There is constant churn and, while those people who did transfer can freeze their pensions, new people do not create the same pension deficit, as they join defined benefit schemes based on personal pensions. Thus the deficit will decline with time and the actuaries can take that into account at the point of the company sale or merger.

Technology

Technology half-lives have fallen dramatically over the last 20 years, and the predictions are that they will fall faster still. Competitive edge comes from the rapid integration of new technologies into the company (if they are relevant). Consider the board looking at the choice of investing in the skills necessary to sell to its clients, or the skills needed to operate the latest technology in its delivery vans or the warehouse. If resources need to be rationed, better to concentrate on the sales skills and the sales systems!

Many manufacturers maintain their own machinery completely. Current technology comes often in black boxes that are replaced on failure and the skills of the supplier used to renew them. The UK utility companies have agreed the outsourcing of maintenance, since engineering companies have better skills, the latest training and the latest diagnostics. The company acts as the voice of the consumer in this instance.

Health and safety legislation and the tighter requirements of the insurance industry are leading to some companies outsourcing operations, since specialization of knowledge and service leads to lower risk and costs.

In addition, the role of IT and the necessity for robust, integrated systems have moved business in two directions. First, they purchase integrated systems and outsource the systems analysis and implementation to IT consultancies; second, they supplement their IT support staff with analysts and programmers often through a consultancy to which they delegate the resource provision to create the company's own software.

Resource management

One facet of the management of a company never changes: managers forecast resource requirements – and the forecasts are never right. Their allowance for risk and resource investment is, therefore, either too high or too low.

By focusing on core resource business areas you can probably match investment and requirements more closely than in other business areas. Then in periphery areas either you have to apply the same focus as to the core areas to manage your resources, or you will not optimize those areas. Given that many of these areas are likely not to use your core skills, the likelihood of optimizing them and achieving good service levels and costs is lower than outsourcing to a specialist. Furthermore, the outsourcing company can act as an independent manager for your resources should you wish, to pool your resources with others and spread the fixed costs.

Management skills

The point has been made that businesses are better to concentrate their management and training skills in those areas in which they can make a real difference – or they should find partners to help them.

Remember, you own the vision and strategy that are part of the management and entrepreneurial skills you need to run a successful business. Maximizing your selling and procurement skills, ensuring you have the right products and services to sell to your clients, and ensuring pricing provides the cash return you need for investment and paying for services bought should be the management skills you provide.

However if outsourcing is the answer, then there are important new skills to develop, namely the skills of choosing your partners and managing them.

Personal

It is rare for managers to have totally altruistic motives when deciding to in-source (take back an outsourcing contract) or to outsource a series of business processes. Unless there are clear strategic reasons for a change to be made, bringing back processes can often be to enlarge their role, just as pushing for outsourcing can be to ensure a job move.

In the past, strange decisions have been made. For example, a major retailer started to backload goods that were delivered by manufacturers to reduce costs by raising the utilization of its fleet. But ex-works prices were required, which under EU laws had to be offered to its competitors. Then it was found that the primary movements from regional distribution centre to store were being delayed, as the fleet was not returning at regular times, as both the extra running and the pick-ups compounded to increase the round trip time variability. The fleet was enlarged to cope with that. It is probably not known whether the final cost model was more or less expensive than the original model. The question that was not asked was whether the fleet was required in the first place.

Current relevance

Given the pace of globalization, it is inevitable that outsourcing will take place. It is not usually sensible for manufacturers to set up their own manufacturing plants in the Far East. Some have, particularly if the products can be sold for internal consumption as well as for exports. But, in the main, retailers and manufacturers are taking only part of the output of a Far East plant and, therefore, the manufacture, the distribution to the port and the customs clearance tend to be outsourced. It is not always economic to have one's own management in place in China or Taiwan or Indonesia, etc. There are specialist skills in arranging consolidated shipments from a port, and the use of freight forwarders to ensure the shipping is booked and the goods are customs-cleared in the UK is normal.

These extended supply chains have risks like any other supply chain, but we will discuss the amplification of the risks later.

How different is the public sector from the private sector with regard to outsourcing?

There are some fundamental differences between the public and private sectors – as public businesses are about cost containment rather than long-term profit sustainability. And public finances do not differentiate between capital expenditure and costs and, therefore, the driver is often to remove all expenditure from the public borrowing figures. Investments to reduce costs are far easier in the private sector where a return over time can be benchmarked against the internal rate of return for the company.

Now the pensions factor is the same for the public and private sectors, with the additional facet that in the UK the civil service retire at 60, whilst most in the private sector retire later. If the new owning company does not have a final salary scheme, then the pensions cost declines with time as the people who replace the original transferees who leave or retire join the new pension arrangements.

It is probably the experience of government trying to build its own systems that has led to the level of IT and business process outsourcing that is currently being progressed. Government wishes to distance itself from the day-to-day management of projects and it is trying to move the risk of overrun expenditure to its contractors. Politically that is understandable, but as we will see later it is crucial that organizations outsourcing business processes continue to keep a close eye on the efficiency of any interfaces and the delivery of the strategy.

The other major difference is that of the stakeholder community. The private sector includes customers, employees, shareholders, regulatory bodies and suppliers (and for many the local community and press should also be included). The public sector has customers, employees, regulatory bodies and suppliers, but also Parliament, ministers, voters, the civil service and a much closer media scrutiny.

The pitfalls in outsourcing

Given that outsourcing arrangements are about two companies joining together to provide a service or a range of products, then the pitfalls become fairly easy to list when viewed dispassionately by a third party. They are, in the main, caused by differences in strategy, objectives, culture and – at a basic level – how the two sets of management work together on a daily basis, trust and respect each other.

From the start, managers need to look at how well any tender document is detailed, how well the tasks are described and how open the client management are about their ongoing strategy and their reasons for outsourcing. Any hiding of real facts at this stage, and the contract is likely to end in considerable difficulties.

Similarly, any over-expectations raised by the outsourcing company – particularly in terms of timing, complexity and the level of cost savings the client might enjoy – will also ensure the contract flounders quite early in its life.

Major initial questions that must be addressed

The board – and it must be at that level for major outsourcing arrangements – must review the following questions with care. They are designed to highlight the strategic changes needed to accept outsourcing:

- What are the company's current strengths, weaknesses, opportunities and threats?
- Does outsourcing resolve some of the weaknesses and threats and open up opportunities to build 'new' – or consolidate current – strengths?
- What should the partner look like?
- What will the company be depending on the partner for?
- Who should drive the outsourcing project at board level? Who should be the 'project manager'?

With these questions answered honestly, the job of writing the tenders and evaluating the outsourcing companies' responses will be much easier.

Once outsourcing has been agreed as part of the strategy, the major questions to be answered by the client company to avert the outsourcing pitfalls are:

- What is our current strategy and what strategic changes are we looking for?
- What are the boundaries to our outsourcing?
- How will we evaluate the tenders?
- How will success and failure be judged in the contract itself?
- How will we remunerate and reward the other company?
- How will we link the organizations?
- How can we reduce internal frictions and the feelings that the other company is just another supplier?

Strategy and the changes needed

Outsourcing is about dovetailing other companies' expertise and focus into your company to improve competitiveness and customer service. You must keep control of the strategy: you cannot outsource that. However, your outsourcing partner will also have a strategy, and the marrying of the two strategies is an important part of the early meetings between the companies and should form part of the selection process.

Partners with diverging strategies cannot work together for long – and outsourcing can never be a two-minute wonder. The time period for an outsourcing contract should reflect the life of the underlying assets supporting the contract and the time and effort required to tender, renegotiate and implement a new contract.

The outputs from the strategy that your stakeholders can see need to be defined (for example, customer service levels, return on investment, etc). These should be discussed with your outsourcing partner only if its input to your business processes has an effect on these outputs.

What are the boundaries to outsourcing?

There needs to be a board process that challenges the added value that in-house processes contribute to the overall success of the company. This is part of the input into the company SWOT analysis. The in-house picture then needs to be compared with that provided by outsourcing some of the business processes. The changes to the SWOT analysis need to be tracked. Of importance are the threats or risks that change between the two pictures – and these must be analysed carefully. Risks in global supply chains are discussed a little later.

How will success and failure be judged?

Many outsourcing arrangements start without clarity to this question – the key performance indicators (KPIs) have not been agreed, the measurement methodology is not clear and reporting arrangements have not been agreed. This does not allow the two partners to have the same vision of the operation, and the lack of clarity will inhibit either side learning how to improve the service, etc. In many ways, if the first question on strategy has not been answered, then it is likely that this one will remain cloudy.

The indicators of success and failure – and the rewards and redress required – need to be fully laid out in the contract before the operation starts. The KPIs can include customer service measured in customer terms, budget performance, savings, damages, stock losses, accident rates, productivity measures, etc. So when looking at the remuneration of the partner, bonuses for beating customer service targets and a sharing of the budget savings are good ways of incentivizing the partnership. Sharing the losses and penalties for poor customer service are other powerful ways of ensuring the correct behaviours.

Tender process

The tender process deserves a chapter in its own right – but what is important strategically for successful outsourcing is that there is sufficient detail in the tender about the current operations, a clear statement of the key performance requirements, and a strategic vision that is shared with the prospective partners. Without the detail, without a clear pro forma of the response required, it will be difficult to evaluate the various replies. Honesty will provide better answers and build better relationships – both of which are needed if the operation is to be successful over time.

Company linkage and reducing internal friction

The outsourcing of a number of business processes implies that the processes outsourced need to communicate, and to link with the rest of the company's business processes. Thus not only are there data linkages that need to be forged, but the management and administration of the two companies need to be joined as well.

A lot of time and care must be taken to ensure a high degree of efficiency about the interfaces. Slow, inefficient interfaces will cost money, increase friction between the two groups and, in the end, result in poorer customer service and lost sales.

Thus, a good strategic board will ensure that teams are built across the interface. The outsourcing company must not be treated at complete arm's length, with face-to-face meetings not accepted as part of the contract's life. The managers working the interfaces must be compatible; they must work together and respect each other. Attempts must be made to ease any cultural differences.

This does not mean that both sides should not challenge each other. When there is no challenge, there is no creativity and an operation will slowly fossilize – but challenge must be constructive. Any internal assassins to the process of outsourcing must be dealt with.

Summary

Most of the pitfalls experienced by companies outsourcing are down to management issues – and down to not being open about strategy or other market or business factors that are germane to the evaluation of the activities the outsourcer will perform.

Additional problems can be caused by a failure to gain the buy-in of the company management during the tender process.

Outsourcing can only work with the active cooperation of both sides.

Global supply chains and the outsourcing risks

Global supply chains, somehow, have brought the promise of better margins, and both retailers and manufacturers have rushed to move the source of manufacture and some services to Eastern Europe, India and the Pacific Rim, including China.

Whilst manufacturing costs have undoubtedly fallen, not all commodity costs have fallen as well – and shipping costs, for example, have risen as the laws of supply and demand have remained true.

It should be noted that the new extended supply chain hides a number of potential risks that, if not properly accounted for, could have a severe effect on profits. Boards need to have identified and evaluated the costs of these risks in order to judge the real business case for overseas sourcing. The fact that some companies are now considering sourcing from countries that are geographically closer to the UK means that the balance may be shifting away from very extended supply chains.

What are these important risks? They fall into the following four groups:

- supply chain risks;
- management risks;
- financial risks;
- political risks.

Supply chain risks

These arise through the new geography that is a backdrop to the outsourcing arrangements. The factory is no longer in the UK or nearby in Europe. Many of the problems are the same as in the original supply chain, but the risk of not resolving the issues increases with distance and the language and culture divide. Good examples are problems with quality, specifying exactly what you want after the first proofing runs, and tying the supplier into your business.

You now have lower costs because you have agreed a single long-run production slot with your supplier – but the slot is usually not very flexible. Thus changes to quantity and timing are much harder to arrange. Under-order stock and ask for a smaller, more expensive additional run to be slotted into the production schedule, and you may have to have products sent by air-freight for them to be on the shop floor in time for the sales period. Realizing this additional cost, you may feel forced deliberately to over-order stock at the start. Many retailers now have higher stocks than they used to have – and this requires larger warehouses and results in lower warehouse productivity. Then the sales forecasts are not met, and clearing unnecessary stock through the sales channel generally requires heavy discounting – which means a reduction in profits.

Then there is the quality of goods on arrival. As they have been packaged, often badly, in the container, you now have an extensive new operation of repairing, improving, finishing and sometimes pricing, which has to be done in the UK to make the merchandise look shop-ready. Who pays for the stock as it sits in customs awaiting clearance?

Your extended supply chain is forcing you to make decisions on fabrics, design and colours earlier and earlier in the process. Because the product range needs to be specified so far in advance, there is the real risk of getting it wrong.

Many of the above are judgemental risks that supply chain or merchandising managers have to take – but there are also the physical, environmental risks in the supply chain. Hurricanes, earthquakes and typhoons all play a part in the equatorial climate and geography; they are risks that must be quantified, and sourcing strategies and contingencies should take the results into account.

Management risks

The longer the supply chain, the greater the number of nodes, the greater management time that is required to achieve a smooth result. This resource will be more than the company currently has, and even if functions are outsourced there will be the need to coordinate the outsourcing partnerships.

The greatest concern in this area for most retailers is quality. It can be difficult to oversee the accreditation and auditing of suppliers and manage proofing runs over a long distance. Once product is agreed, production schedules have to be monitored – and this requires time, personnel and particular skill sets.

Outsourcing requires regular contact between the various parties to make it work. The question to bear in mind is: has the cost of the additional merchandising and quality management been taken into account?

Outsourcing is not about abdication: you still need to control the strategy, and you need to spend time integrating the outsourced service. The more central the activity is to the heart of the company, the more time that is required to really ensure the outsourced operation is integrated. How the organizations are linked is one of the keys to the success of outsourcing.

The other management risks are that you did not define what the strategic changes that you are looking for are, and you may not have shared them with the prospective partner. You may not have decided how success and failure will be judged and therefore have not decided whether any form of gain share is appropriate to the contract.

Another risk that needs to be dealt with is the risk of poor internal communication about the potential to outsource and once the contract is implemented communicating the successes.

Financial risks

Your suppliers like hard currency, quite often US dollars, and thus a significant proportion of your costs will be exposed to the fluctuations of that currency. If the dollar strengthens and your margins decrease as you are connected to UK price competition, you are forced to try to reduce the purchase price, which may result in reduced product quality and greater finishing costs.

It is possible to hedge the dollars by buying in advance, of course, but there is a cost to these transactions. You might buy stock in pounds sterling, but if there is currency movement against the supplier it must in the long run recover lost margin or refuse to do business with you, resulting in time and expenditure accrediting a new supplier.

Shipping costs increase markedly as routes become more popular, resulting in a reduction of your margins. If the price of oil increases, so will your shipping surcharges. Were these potential costs taken into account in the budget?

Your extended supply chain requires you to offset the supply risk by receiving the stock earlier and because the stock is produced in one run, shipping costs can be minimized by shipping the whole quantity together. But this will result in extra warehousing and financing costs. What must also be taken into account is the cost of the additional write-down of unsold stock. Financial information systems will be required that allow all the various costs to be posted against each product in the range so the real margin can be reviewed.

Political risks

These are very hard to assess but we have had some examples recently, including EU trade quotas, instability in some countries, and suppliers having very different working conditions to those in European plants. These risks can directly affect your ability to trade, and can become consumer relations issues that affect your brand.

Risk analysis

The risk analysis required is a detailed review of each step in the extended supply chain, starting with ranging and supplier selection and following the course of the product and information flows through the supply chain. At each stage the possible failures (the risks) to the process need to be understood and assessed. The classic quadrant (see Figure 12.1) needs to be populated. Once done, contingency plans need to be detailed and agreed. These could include sourcing alternative suppliers and additional stocks, starting the next season early, putting in place better systems and management controls, etc.

High value: Low impact	High value: High impact
Low value: Low impact	High value: Low impact

Figure 12.1 Risk analysis

Risk analysis should also cover the contingency requirement, should it be decided or necessary, to take the outsourcing back in-house or move the management of the processes to a new company.

Summary

The benefits from overseas, global sourcing need careful analysis both before starting the transfer and at regular intervals thereafter. The analysis requires the whole cost of acquisition of each product to be determined to allow comparison with cost in other countries, including the UK. What is most important is that the analysis must be conducted dispassionately and that the interests of consumers and the shareholders remain the most important consideration.

'Getting it wrong' is not hard; losing control of the strategy is all too easy. Outsourcing requires continual effort to harness the outsourcer – but such management resource is at a very different level from running the whole operation internally. A company that harnesses the skills and resources of an outsourcing company – and provides products and services at a lower cost and higher added value than its competitors as a result of letting experts run some of its operations – will be more profitable than its competitors and quite possibly more flexible.

13

Risk in the supply chain

Lars Stemmler, BLG Consult GmbH

Introduction

Risk management is an established tool in the financial environment of the business world. The same holds true for logistics and the concept of supply chain management. The increased level of integration and cooperation along supply chains leads to new risk categories. Risk management might help in the understanding of the key risk drivers of supply chains and enable the partners to optimize their internal risk management system – at least developing an understanding of supply chain risks.

This chapter suggests an expansion of risk management into the scope of the supply chain. The objective is to provide arguments to actively pursue risk management as a planning tool. The chapter is written from the perspective of a non-financial firm such as a logistics service provider. This will highlight also the practical perspective of risk management.

Risk management and the supply chain – a new perception!

The identification, assessment and control of risks are inherent to managing commercial undertakings. Risk management was developed in the financial services industry before it spread to other sectors. However, in many companies risk management is just considered a legal obligation following the introduction of the Sarbanes–Oxley Act in the United States. The statutory requirement to establish a formal risk management system also took hold in

Europe. For example, the German commercial code stipulates the development of a reconnaissance system in order to identify risks that threaten the existence of the company at an early stage.

The perspective of such a system is principally financial. Concerned shareholders and an equally anxious public domain drove the introduction of risk management. Owing to the perceived character of risk management as a statutory obligation for companies, it is in many cases associated with additional non-value-adding costs to the enterprise. The task of managing risks constituted just another source of costs – an opportunity for planning was clearly missed.

However, a number of companies have realized the potential of risk management to improve planning processes and help to mitigate potential and actual sources of risk. It is not just banks that actively pursue risk management. Companies of other sectors are increasingly becoming aware of the potential added value of an integrated risk management. The fate of Ericsson is just one example:

> The effect on Ericsson, a Swedish mobile-phone company, of a fire in a New Mexico chip-making plant belonging to the Dutch firm Philips, has become a legend. The fire, in March 2000, started by a bolt of lightning, lasted less than 10 minutes but it caused havoc to the super-clean environment that chip-making requires. Ericsson, unable to find an alternative source of supply, went on to report a loss of over USD 2 billion in its mobile-phone division that year, a loss that left it as an also-ran in an industry where it had once been a leader.
>
> (*Economist*, 2005)

The Ericsson example highlights a necessary shift in perception regarding risk management. This shift is driven by logistics; the case comfortably sets out the framework for this new perception of risk management:

- The logistics function provides a clear competitive advantage to a company regardless of which strategy it pursues. With either of Porter's (1980) strategies of cost leadership or differentiation, logistics helps to fulfil the company's objectives and to deliver added value to the customer. The example of Ericsson of a disrupted supply chain is clearly the tip of the iceberg, and quality problems of Robert Bosch AG, a major supplier to a German car manufacturer, in 2004 are just another example.
- Supply chain management aims at integrating partners along the supply chain, reducing interfaces and smoothing the flow of material, information and finance. However, the higher the level of integration, the higher the probability of dependency on single partners. In addition, global sourcing adds a further dimension of uncertainty in terms of long transport legs, unstable political environments and different levels of commitment to quality and reliability.
- A closely knit international supply chain results in complex processes of coordinating and administering the partners along the chain. Different

levels of accountability of staff and partners have to be taken into account. The focus of risk management necessarily shifts from an enterprise-only to a supply chain perspective.

These developments clearly have an impact on the scope and functionality of a company-focused risk management system. However, the concept of risk management can be actively employed along a supply chain. It enables all partners contributing to a supply chain to limit adverse risks to the chain. For this objective to be achieved, risk management along the supply chain has to address the following issues:

- all three flows – material, information and finance – along a supply chain and its associated processes;
- the boundaries of the system, which have to be pushed beyond the organization to cover the full length of the chain;
- the challenge to cover not only the strategic but also the operational level, turning the risk management system from a statutory reporting function into a planning function.

Figure 13.1 illustrates the scope of risk management in a supply chain management context.

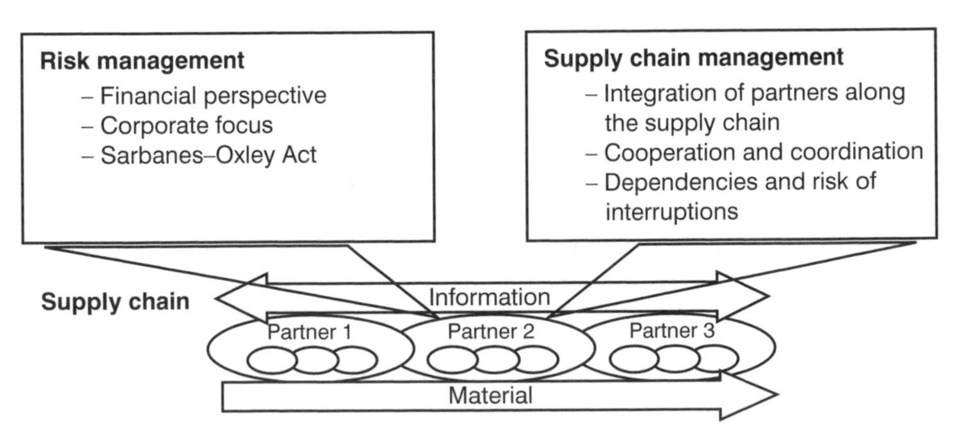

Figure 13.1 Risk management in the supply chain – a new perception

Objective and process of risk management

What do we associate with the term 'risk'? Risk denotes the chance of danger, loss or injury. In a commercial environment the chance of a good bargain must also be summarized under the term. Risk is to be differentiated from the term 'uncertainty'. Whereas risk assumes that the probabilities of the possible results of an event are known, this is not the case with uncertainty. Hence, risk is measurable uncertainty.

Risk management includes activities to identify, analyse and assess, and communicate, as well as control, risks (Müller, 2003). In an ideal case, risk management is directly assigned to the top management, providing continuous support to ensure the company's ability to survive in the marketplace (Burger and Buchhart, 2002). Risk management is governed by the internal risk policy, making the enterprise in extreme cases either a risk taker or a risk avoider.

The risk management process describes systematically the framework and methods from initially identifying the risks to finally controlling them (Holzbaur, 2001). The first activity is to identify and describe all actual and future sources of risk – at this stage of the argumentation – to the company (see Figure 13.2). In a second step the risks are assessed. When determining the exposure of a company, risks are characterized through the quantification of the probability of the occurrence and the extent of the potential damage or gain. The risk exposure can be illustrated by means of a risk map or risk portfolio, leading to a segmentation of risks into commonly three categories. Category A risks represent risks that have a potentially disastrous impact on the company, in terms of both high probability of occurrence and high

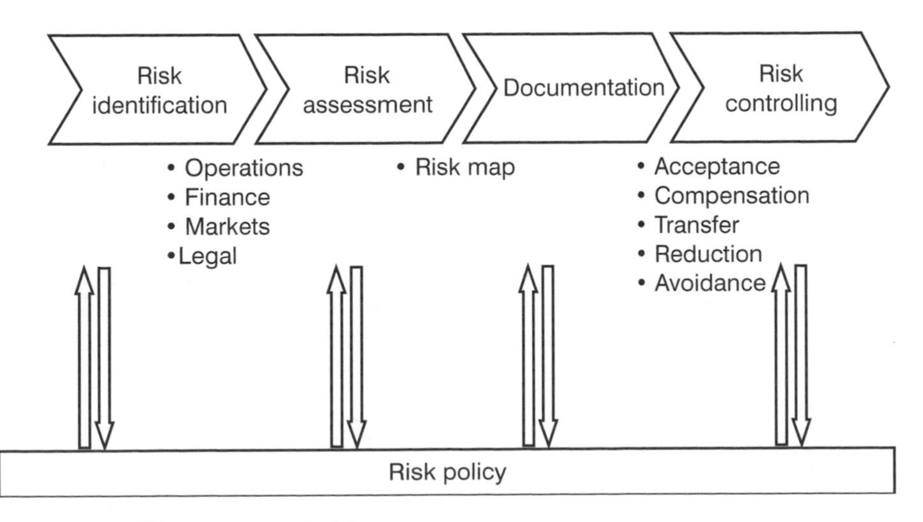

Figure 13.2 The process of risk management

damage potential (with only adverse risks normally included in the analysis). On the basis of this analysis, appropriate measures can be taken in order to control risks. Measures are taken in accordance with the stipulations of the risk management policy. A feedback loop is obligatory to ensure the effectiveness of the measures.

In theory, the risk management process looks consistent and straightforward. However, practical experience shows that not only does the quantification pose considerable problems to line managers but also the identification of risks in the first place poses an almost insurmountable challenge for line managers. The quantification, estimating both probabilities of occurrence and the monetary level of impact, is limited through the lack of data of past experiences of similar events in other companies. Further, the identification of risks is often subject to managers' reluctance of not being prepared to admit the existence of risks in their fields of responsibility: admitting to the presence of risks is considered a sign of weakness. But the effort should be made to come up with a meaningful risk portfolio.

From an enterprise perspective to the supply chain perspective

Having outlined the risk management process, let us now focus on how to incorporate the requirements of a sophisticated supply chain management into risk management, and answer the question of what benefits are produced for whom.

Ensuring supply chain integrity

Supply chain management can be described as a holistic management approach to integrating and coordinating the material, information and financial flows along a supply chain (Handfield and Nichols, 1999). Further, this includes the management of the interfaces between the partners involved in this chain, particularly from an information management and technology point of view (Schary and Skjøtt-Larsen, 2001).

A supply chain is basically a sequence of processes – however, the processes are owned and managed by different legal entities. This requires inter-organizational cooperation. Conflicting interests due to the legal and economic independence of the supply chain partners need to be aligned to a single supply chain objective. If successful, the competitive advantage of these partners increases considerably.

There are a number of implications of supply chain management on risk management. As already said, risk management is an important tool in ensuring the economic integrity of an organization. This holds particularly true if the boundaries of the organization are clearly set, for example by means of arm's-length transactions. In a supply chain management environment these boundaries become blurred, which does not mean that they no longer exist legally, but operations-wise it becomes very difficult to identify the separating line between the two companies. Just consider employees of a logistics provider doing packaging work on the premises of the shipper. The implications on the risk management system arc obvious – the scope of traditional risk management is to be extended to integrate a supply chain. At the same time, having to ensure process quality, risk management evolves into logistics.

Parallel to an expansion of the scope of managing a supply chain, risk management has to grow in responsibility as well (see Figure 13.3). The higher the degree of integration along a supply chain is, the larger the required scope of risk management becomes. And the concept of supply chain risk management is raised.

Martin Christopher (2002) suggests defining supply chain risk management as 'the integration and management of risks within the supply chain and risks external to it through a co-ordinated approach amongst supply chain members to reduce supply chain vulnerability as a whole'. The vulnerability of the chain stems from external and internal risks to it. The objectives of supply chain risk management are clearly laid out by Kajüter (2003). He sees risk management in the supply chain as 'a collaborative and structured approach to risk management, embedded in the planning and control processes of the supply chain, to handle risks that might adversely affect the achievement of the supply chain goals'.

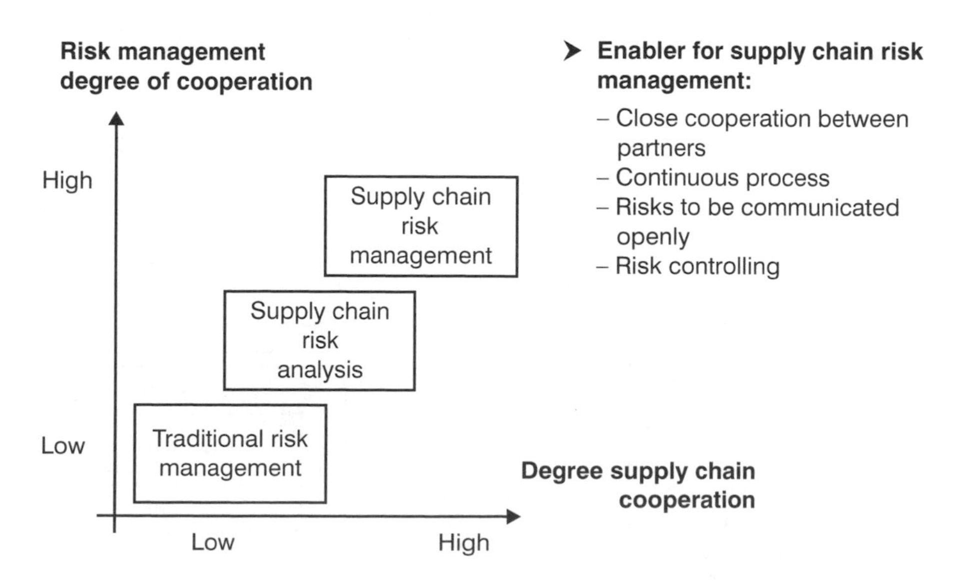

Source: Kajüter, 2003

Figure 13.3 Supply chain integration to be supported by risk management

Practitioners can agree to these definitions and clarifications, and they will clearly see the need for an inter-organizational management of risks. As with organizational or company-specific risk management, identifying the relevant risks is the first task to master in the process of supply chain risk management. It is here that the first challenges are encountered. The following section focuses on developing a framework for risk identification and assessment along a supply chain.

Risk assessment and control along the supply chain

The process of supply chain risk management is similar in all respects to the process of company-specific risk management. A preparatory step is to define a risk management policy. Along a supply chain, companies with different industry backgrounds, sizes and ownership structures have to work together to achieve a common goal. Their differing interests have to be merged in a consistent risk management policy.

Having clarified how much risk the partners are prepared to take, the identification of supply chain risks is the next step. Figure 13.4 illustrates the two different types of risks inherent to a supply chain: exogenous and endogenous risks. The former result from the interaction of the supply chain with its environment, whereas the latter stem from the interaction of the supply chain partners (Chapman *et al*, 2002).

The endogenous risks can be divided into the categories of organizational risks (those of individual partners) and specific risks from integrating, coordinating and cooperating along the supply chain. Company-specific risks are

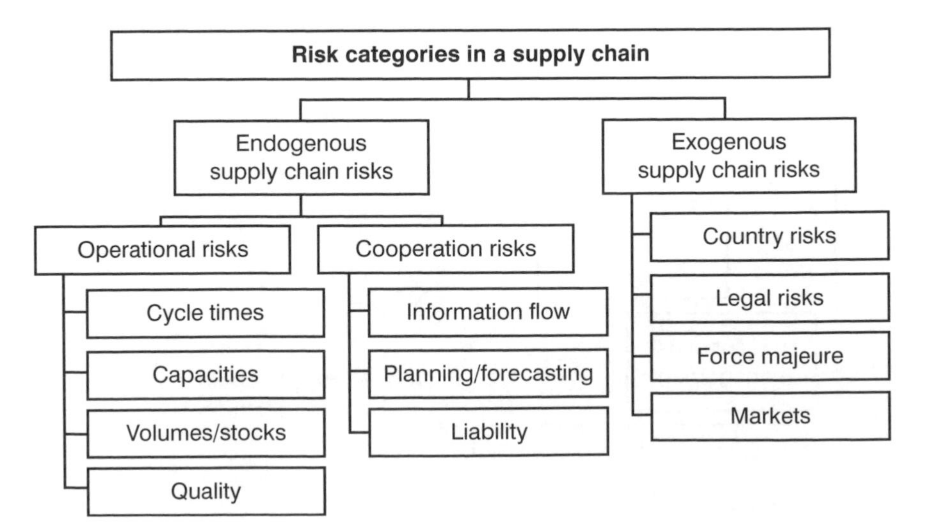

Figure 13.4 Risk categories' identification into supply chain-specific risks

adequately described in traditional risk management maps. Specific supply chain risks can now be identified, for example risks from the sharing of information on integrated platforms (integration), risks of a high level of interdependence amongst the partners (cooperation) and risks stemming from interwoven processes (coordination).

The prime objective of supply chain risk management is to identify those risks posing a major threat to the supply chain. A measurement tool is needed here to help transfer (existing) company-specific risk maps into a supply chain risk map and to integrate the supply chain-specific plus the endogenous risks. How this can be done is illustrated in Figure 13.5. The company-specific risk portfolios form the basis for an ABC classification of these risks, ideally after an inter-organizational risk-controlling process. The ABC classification leads a two-dimensional matrix showing the probability of the risk-relevant event and the net impact (after company-specific risk management) of this event (level of damage in monetary terms). The product of the two gives the expected value of the risk.

Following this step, managers have to decide which of these risks have what implication on the supply chain. Each risk in the ABC classification is assigned a high-, medium- or low-impact category, leading to the supply chain risk map. Into this map the supply chain-specific risks as well as the endogenous risks are integrated. The latter two categories are evaluated using an expected value. Regarding the impact on the partners along the supply chain an aggregated figure for possible damages has to be found.

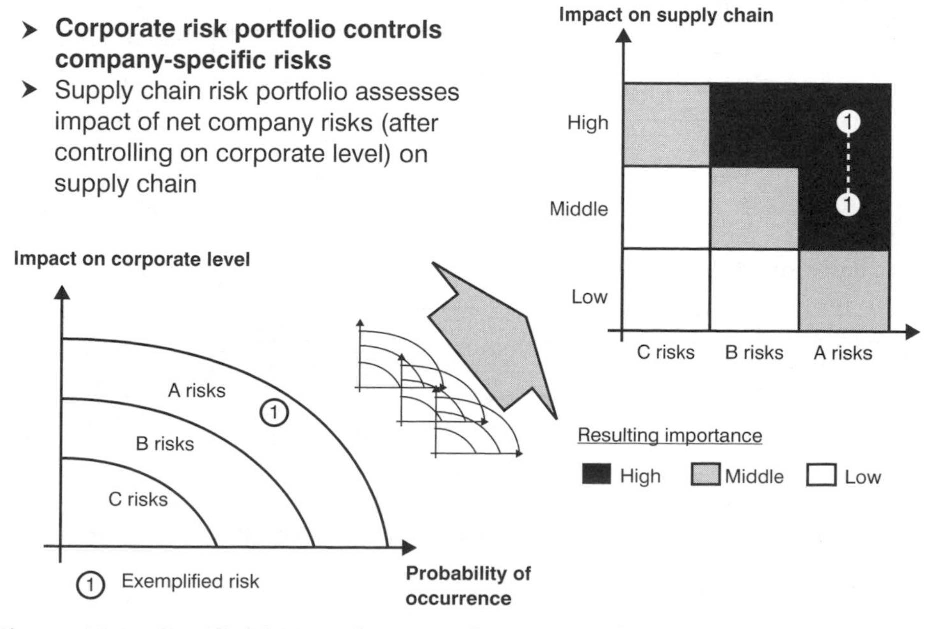

Figure 13.5 Supply chain risk assessment

As with traditional risk management, the phase of risk controlling concludes the overall process of risk management. Accepting the risk or avoiding it are the poles between which risk controlling takes place. Avoiding the risk might mean doing no business at all (see Figure 13.6). Accepting the risk means in the last instance simply living with it. In between there is an array of measures to control risks. These measures can be summarized under the categories of risk compensation, risk transfer and risk reduction.

The ability to reduce business risks is to be preferred over other measures. On a supply chain level, risk reduction includes a particular focus on interfaces. Risk transfer – although comparatively easy to achieve in traditional risk management, for example by means of buying insurance – is by definition a difficult approach for a supply chain, as we are obliged to look not at individual companies but at the whole chain. Risk compensation along a supply chain – on a company level achieved through provisions or hedging – manifests itself in rules governing cooperation between the partners. One partner is obviously not prepared to compensate another one monetarily. However, compensation can be initiated through behaviour. Partners might agree on defined actions to be taken on a mutual basis.

Risk compensation in terms of mutual rules is to be delimited from risk transfer measures, for example outsourcing or vendor-managed inventory (VMI). The latter measures feature a far more institutionalized contractual basis. Whereas in rules-based risk compensation schemes each partner takes

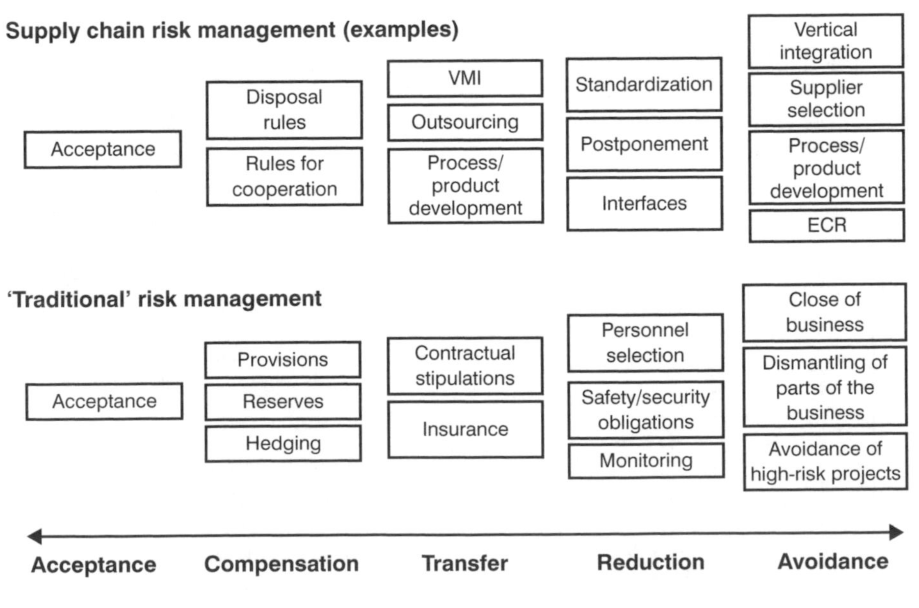

Source: Inderfurth, 2002

Figure 13.6 Risk controlling between avoidance and acceptance

risks (close to risk acceptance), transferring risks amongst the partners means selecting those partners that are willing to take a risk from another. In a supply chain perspective this only contributes to an indirect reduction of risks, as the risk is transferred to the partner that can manage it better than the other.

What becomes apparent when discussing risk controlling is that risk management does not mean simply reacting to emergencies along the supply chain but pursuing an active approach anticipating supply chain risks. Having looked into the toolbox of risk controlling it becomes further apparent that deciding on suitable measures is a complex task in terms of decision making and implementation amongst the partners – even assuming that there is a consistent risk policy in place.

The latter issue is worth exploring in some more detail, bearing in mind that we would like to pursue a practitioner's view in this chapter. The following section sheds some light on obstacles to profound supply chain risk management.

Implementation in practice

Obstacles to implementation

The necessity and the theoretical framework of supply chain risk management sound convincing. Parallel to the development of supply chain management, which introduces a high degree of integration, cooperation and coordination amongst supply chain partners, the company-specific risk management systems have to keep up, and need to expand from the traditional financial perspective into logistics – as well as focusing on supply chain risks. No doubt, there are specific supply chain risks to be addressed. However, implementing risk management that focuses on the supply chain might end in a 'prisoner's dilemma'. Let us look at the most commonly observed obstacles to implementing risk management on a company level:

- *Risk identification.* Risks are collated in a risk map and subsequently reported to top management. Hence, at middle management level or in operating units of an organization, managers tend to hide risks by simply denying their existence.
- *Risk identification is not done through neutral eyes.* External help is expensive, so that risk identification is carried out internally, resulting in a different perception of certain risks. For example, if carried out by accounting staff, operational risks are either not understood or are considered more severe compared to financial risks (zur Horst and Leisten, 2002).
- *Required quantification lacks understanding.* A basic requirement of sound risk management is to quantify the potential loss or damage and to estimate the probability of occurrence. If a process fails, the company loses sales in the

amount of the damaged lot size. What if a customer deems this company as no longer reliable and holds back future orders? Regarding the probabilities, estimating the failure rate seems simple, but what about political risks?

Assuredly, any risk management system should be implemented under the auspices of the company's auditors. However, obstacles multiply with a supply chain perspective:

- *Admitting the risks.* Drawing a supply chain risk map implies that any risk with a potential impact on the complete chain needs to be disclosed by its 'owner'. You run into a problem here if there is a dominant player along the chain, for example a manufacturer in the automobile industry. A supplier or logistics provider cannot simply admit that there is a risk. On the contrary, there is a strong tendency towards risk transfer from the manufacturer to the partner up and down the chain (Kendall, 1998).
- *Putting effort into risk management.* How much effort are companies prepared to put into a concept that potentially is a risk in itself, ie the risk of being blacklisted as a result of disclosing risks?
- *Relying on the risk map.* Bearing in mind the hidden risks as discussed here, can each partner rely on the input of other partners, or does risk controlling become mere 'risk engineering'?

An option for avoiding these issues is to use a 'bottom-up' approach, rather than the traditional 'top-down'.

Bottom-up instead of top-down

Risk management must provide tangible benefits to managers, particularly on an operational level. Coming back to our initial example of Ericsson, simply insisting on an answer to the question of what ensures business contingency is too broad an approach. Unfortunately, risk management – in the traditional sense – is a 'top-down' management tool imposed by regulation and law. Trying the opposite way and going 'bottom-up' might be part of a solution.

Admittedly it is far more cumbersome, as a bottom-up approach starts with a process model of the supply chain. This is where the supply chain operations reference (SCOR) model might be useful. Alternatively, many companies already have quality managers in place and process charts to hand, which include detailed descriptions that are amended by the stochastic information (see Figure 13.7). Simulating the processes under different, risk-oriented parameters and putting the know-how of security managers into the simulation results in a robust picture of a risk map. The focus is first of all operational: how well do our processes and those of the supply chain work?

More strategic issues come in when looking at the materials flows and the stock levels at the links and nodes of the supply chain. These links and nodes

➤ Using value/cash flow at risk models from the financial sector
➤ Simulation of a value corridor of a variable whose thresholds are not crossed with a given probability

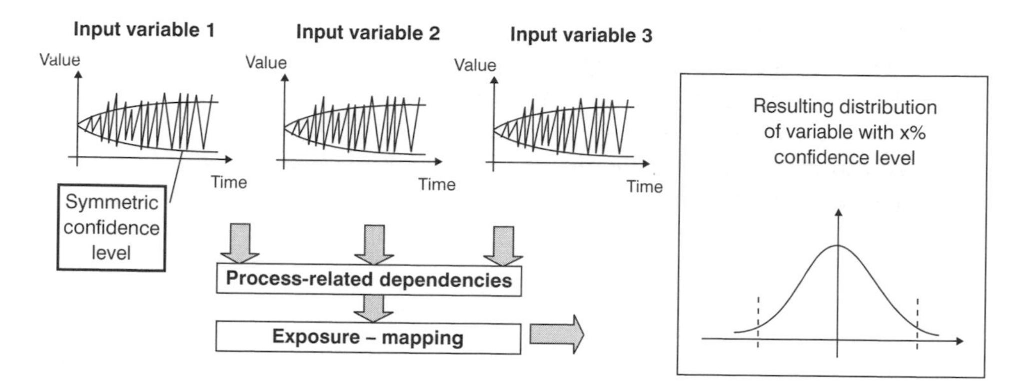

Source: Wiedemann and Hager, 2003

Figure 13.7 Random walks with 'at-risk' models

can also be modelled as processes and subsequently simulated, bearing in mind different performance and cost levels. By aggregating those processes, a company – and then a supply chain – risk map emerges.

Conclusions

The concept of supply chain management brings additional risks to the supply chain, which – in accordance with the objective of SCM of increasing the level of integration and coordination amongst the supply chain partners – should be addressed jointly. Those risks include the endogenous risks of a supply chain, such as operational and cooperation risks. A supply chain risk portfolio is suggested to initiate the risk management process along the supply chain, leading to a toolbox of risk-controlling measures on a strategic and operational level.

This is the opportunity for risk management to expand from the financial and corporate perspectives respectively into the field of logistics and inter-organizational cooperation. However, easy as it sounds, problems that have to be addressed include:

- the challenge of turning risk management from a mere statutory obligation into a planning tool;
- the identification of hidden risks and overcoming dominant players in the supply chain;
- the quantification of probabilities and damage levels;

- the pursuance of a bottom-up approach for supply chain risk management to avoid the overload of top management as in the case of a top-down approach.

An elegant, but complex, task might be to simulate (parts of) the supply chain by means of stochastic modelling in order to support the risk mapping and to evaluate the influence of variations in different risk parameters.

Despite the efforts needed, supply chain partners should develop a sound understanding of how well the processes along their chain work and what the key risk drivers in the structure are.

References

Burger, A and Buchhart, H (2002) *Risiko-Controlling* [Risk controlling], Oldenbourg, Munich

Chapman, P *et al* (2002) Identifying and managing supply chain vulnerability, *Journal of the Institute of Logistics and Transport*, **4** (4), May, pp 59–64

Christopher, M (2002) Supply chain vulnerability, Executive Report, Cranfield University, Cranfield

Economist (2005) 29 October, p. 71

Handfield, RB and Nichols, EL (1999) *Introduction to Supply Chain Management*, Pearson, Upper Saddle River, NJ

Holzbaur, U-D (2001) *Management*, Kiehl, Ludwigshafen

Inderfurth, K (2002) Risikomanagement in der Supply Chain [Risk management in the supply chain], in *Wissenschaftssymposium Logistik der BVL*, ed Bundesvereinigung Logistik, Tagungsband, Munich

Kajüter, P (2003) Risk management in supply chains, in *Strategy and Organization in Supply Chains*, ed SA Seuring *et al*, Springer-Verlag, Heidelberg

Kendall, R (1998) *Risk Management for Executives*, FT Prentice Hall, London

Müller, S (2003) *Management-Rechnungswesen: Ausgestaltung des externen und internen Rechnungswesens unter Konvergenzgesichtspunkten* [Management accounting: developing a convergent management accounting system], Gabler, Wiesbaden

Porter, ME (1980) *Competitive Strategy*, Free Press, New York

Schary, PB and Skjøtt-Larsen, T (2001) *Managing the Global Supply Chain*, 2nd edn, Copenhagen Business School Press, Copenhagen

Wiedemann, A and Hager, P (2003) Messung finanzieller risiken mit cash-flow-at-risk/earnings-at-risk-verfahren, ccfb, Eitorf

zur Horst, A-D and Leisten, R (2002) Supply Chain Controlling: Vertrauen ist gut – Controlling ist noch besser! [Supply chain controlling], in *Forum Forschung 2002/2003*, GMU Duisburg, Duisburg

14

Supply chain vulnerability, risk and resilience

Helen Peck, Cranfield University

Introduction

Few areas of management interest have risen to prominence in recent years as rapidly as supply chain vulnerability. In only a handful of years the subject has been transformed from a truth that dare not speak its name to one of the most fashionable disciplines of the decade. This chapter looks first at the factors and events behind the rise of the field. Next it tackles the thorny issues of supply chain definitions and dissonance within supply chain management, before moving on to see how they pan out when competing concepts of risk and risk management come into play. How, when and why the different concepts from risk management fit with some elements of the supply chains but not others are explained, positioning each within a multi-level framework, based on a simple exploded model of a supply chain. It provides a holistic overview of supply chain vulnerability, and explains why supply chain resilience is perhaps a more appropriate concept in this context. In conclusion the chapter draws on earlier writings in open systems theory to explain why supply chains should be viewed as open societal systems as well as engineered processes.

Supply chain vulnerability: an idea whose time had come

At the dawn of the new century, industry and policy makers waited to see whether efforts to contain the Y2K 'millennium bug' had been successful. Happily for most organizations, the year 2000 arrived without a hitch. Y2K made everyone aware of how IT-dependent our societies had become, but its legacy was to leave managers sceptical about the need to spend scarce time and resources warding off supply chain disruptions that might never occur. In government the event was viewed differently. Business continuity planning (BCP) had successfully averted an economic meltdown.

The UK fared less well the following September when a small number of protestors managed to blockade oil refineries, causing chaos at the petrol pumps and serious economic disruption. The outbreak of foot-and-mouth disease in the national livestock herd only months later sent government searching for ways to improve the national resilience to all manner of disruptive challenges. Few realize that it was these events – together with BSE (mad cow disease) in the 1990s – and not terrorism that prompted a major review of UK emergency planning doctrine and sowed the seeds of the Civil Contingencies Act (2004). It was because these events were so different from the 'sudden onset' emergencies – bombing accidents or natural disasters – that national emergency planners had hitherto focused upon that such a revision was deemed necessary. For a start, these were not site-specific as a bombing might be. They had many sites or none at all. Moreover these crises tended to build slowly at first (often almost unnoticed at a national level) and then escalate quickly, causing enormous economic damage and social disquiet. In each instance it was industry and government, not the emergency services, that found themselves in the unfamiliar role of first responders. These creeping crises were remarkable in one other respect – they represented *systemic supply chain disruptions*, hinting that there might be a dark side to the ever increasing efficiency of contemporary supply chains. Nevertheless, the whole notion of supply chain vulnerability remained deeply unfashionable until 11 September 2001.

The international terrorist attacks on New York and Washington marked the beginning of a change in attitude towards the whole notion of supply chain vulnerability. In general terms the attacks put a supercharger behind the business continuity industry, and all aspects of security management. It is now widely recognized that the terrorist attacks did not themselves cause any significant disruption to global supply chains or even North American industry. But the reaction of the US authorities did. The closure of US borders and grounding of transatlantic flights caused massive disruptions following an outpouring of press articles (mainly in the United States) highlighting the terrorist threat and the frailty of international supply chains.

Post-9/11, new security measures were hurriedly introduced at US borders, ports and airports, affecting inbound cargos to the United States. The new measures – including the Container Security Initiative (CSI) and Customs–Trade Partnership (C–TPAT) – employed principles and approaches borrowed from the application of total quality management in manufacturing supply chains. They demanded much more rigorous and earlier electronic presentation of manifests, as well as documentation and validation of security policies and procedures from the companies involved. Compliant companies could then, it was suggested, become approved 'known shippers', thereby ensuring speedier customs clearance. Inevitably, the measures slowed down 'abnormal' shipments or those coming in from non-approved shippers. Moreover the programme required all inbound shipments to the United States to be vetted at designated approved overseas ports, thereby displacing much of the cost of compliance and subsequent congestion to the ports and airports of departure. Around the world, national or supranational customs authorities adopted similar mindsets and soon tabled rafts of similar measures.

Meanwhile, back in the 'business as usual' world of corporate profitability, the Enron Corporation, once held up as a model of best-practice corporate risk management, wobbled and collapsed, taking international auditors Arthur Andersen with it. Another North American giant, WorldCom, quickly followed. In Europe, Dutch retailer Royal Ahold and Italian dairy conglomerate Parmalat Finanziara did the same.

Financial markets, like supply chains, rely on confidence. In a bid to protect shareholders – and ultimately the well-being of the financial markets – regulators hurried to bring in their own more rigorous reporting requirements. The international banking community had faced the same stark realities only a few years earlier, when the unchecked activities of 'rogue trader' Nick Leeson led to the collapse of London-based Barings Bank, threatening irreparable damage to Singapore's reputation as a financial centre. These scandals highlighted the need for more diligent corporate governance in general and the appetite for measures to monitor, manage and control operational risk (ie internal threats to organizational well-being) in particular. The Basel Accords in International Banking (1998, 2004) and the introduction in the United States of the Sarbanes–Oxley Act (2002) formalized the requirements.

Sarbanes–Oxley (SOX), mentioned in the previous chapter, has been a particularly potent force in raising the profile of all aspects of corporate risk management. It focused the minds more directly than ever before by making jail sentences a realistic possibility for negligent chief executives. It did so by removing the opportunity to claim ignorance of wrongdoing as a defence. SOX demanded disclosure of all potential risks to corporate well-being, including those that might once have been considered beyond the legal boundaries of the firm. Section 401 demands that organizations declare all 'material off-balance sheet transactions' including 'contingent obligations' and 'interests transferred to an unconsolidated entity'. These clauses encompass some inter-organizational risk sharing and risk transfer activities. For example, fixed-volume shipping service contracts are guarantee contracts; VMI and outsourcing agreements – sometimes used to hedge risk and place retained assets off-balance sheet – must also be declared. SOX also requires that providers of outsourced services (including logistics service suppliers) must be able to demonstrate the existence of appropriate internal process controls. Finally, it demands that consideration be given to other possible externally induced disruptions. Externally induced disruptions include disruptions to transport and communications. SOX was rolled out in successive waves, beginning with US quoted companies, but later extending to their US-based suppliers, and then to those in other countries in 2003.

All of the factors described so far have raised the profile of supply chain-related risk and vulnerabilities, and attitudes have changed dramatically in just a handful of years. Being concerned with matters of supply chain vulnerability has become the epitome of good corporate governance and the socially responsible thing to do. Clearly, supply chain managers should be part of those discussions, but it is also important to recognize that managers from many disciplines now need to have a clear understanding of what supply chains are and how they fit in with their own responsibilities and risk management concerns.

Supply chain risk management: a recipe for confusion

The term 'supply chain' lingers on despite the near-universal recognition that supply chains are not simply linear processes. They are in fact complex systems of interlocking networks. Beyond that there is no commonly agreed definition of 'supply chain'. Several different definitions are given within this book, and for the purpose of this chapter two are included here. Both emerged in the late 1990s. Aitken (1998) proposed: 'a network of connected and interdependent organizations, mutually and co-operatively working together to control, manage and improve the flow of material and information from suppliers to end users'. Shortly afterwards, Christopher (1998) adopted a value-based variation on the theme, defining a supply chain as 'the network of organisations that are linked through upstream and downstream relationships in the different processes and activities that produce value in the form of products and services in the hands of the ultimate customer'.

Thus supply chains comprise flows of materials, goods and information (including money), which pass within and between organizations, linked by a range of tangible and intangible facilitators, including relationships, processes, activities, and integrated information systems. They are also linked by physical distribution networks, and the national/international communications and transport infrastructures. In their totality, supply chains link organizations, industries and economies.

Notwithstanding the different interpretations of what constitutes a supply chain, understanding supply chain vulnerability is complicated by two other distinct problems. The first is confusion over the scope of supply chain management. The second (which deserves a volume in its own right) is the nature of 'risk'.

The confusion surrounding the scope of supply chain management is well documented, not least its ambivalent relationship with logistics (Larson and Halldorsson, 2004). The term 'supply chain management' (SCM) first appeared in the early 1980s when Oliver and Webber (1992) used it to describe an amalgamation and relabelling of established functions – notably 'logistics' (integrated transport, warehousing and distribution) and manufacturing-based 'operations management' (elements of purchasing, order and inventory management, production planning and control as well as customer service). Though the title was new, many of the fundamental assumptions, such as the sharing of information – to allow the substitution of information for inventory – and systems integration across organizational boundaries, had been around for decades (Forrester 1958, 1969; La Londe, 1984).

The SCM agenda has unquestionably broadened in recent times to include aspects of marketing, new product development, order management and payment (Cooper *et al*, 1997). According to Stock and Lambert (2001) it had become 'the integration of key business processes, from end user through original suppliers that provides products, services and information that add value for customers'. Christopher (1998) adopts a more relational value-adding perspective, when he describes SCM as 'the management of upstream and downstream relationships with suppliers and customers to deliver superior customer value at less cost to the supply chain as a whole'. However, closer examination shows that these and other writers are actually conceptualizing SCM in several different ways, eg as a management philosophy, the implementation of a management philosophy, or a set of management processes (Mentzner *et al*, 2001). In short, SCM is used to describe at least two quite different concepts. One is the functional scope of SCM, encompassing the tactical management of those elements of logistics and the many other supply chain processes, across functions and between businesses. The other is a philosophy demanding strategic-level recognition of the need for coordination and collaboration throughout the supply chain, which must be present across three or more adjacent firms.

For the practitioner, academic arguments about the nature of supply chains or scope of supply chain management are probably viewed as just that – academic. In the real world, functional legacies and assumptions remain and resurface regularly in writings on the subject. In much of that literature, 'risk' is simply the commercial consequence of failure to implement functional best practice, be it in purchasing, materials management or manufacturing process controls. However, if supply chain management is indeed the interdisciplinary, inter-organizational, globe-spanning concern it purports to be, then these characteristics should be recognized and reflected in both our understanding of supply chain vulnerability and our approaches to risk management.

Given that supply chains comprise many different elements, and supply chain management embraces many different functions, it is perhaps useful first to ask the question 'What is it that is vulnerable, ie *at risk*?' Is it the performance of a process or specific activities, or the well-being of an organization, a trading relationship or the wider networks as a whole? Or is it the vulnerability of one or more of these to some external malevolent force that should be the focus of our consideration? In fact, supply chain vulnerability takes in all of these. What seems to muddy the water is when concepts of risk and risk management come into the equation.

Risk: the great divide

The starting point for many discussions of risk is in classical decision theory (Borge, 2001). Here risk is a measure of the possible upside and downside of a single rational and quantifiable (financial) decision. In a seminal paper on managerial perceptions of risk and risk taking, March and Shapira (1987) define risk – from a decision theory perspective – as 'variation in the distribution of possible outcomes, their likelihoods and their subjective values'. However, they go on to observe that this interpretation has been under attack for many years, particularly by those studying financial markets. The problem is that research has shown that it does not reflect how managers see risk, nor does it reflect their behaviours or the social norms that influence them (MacCrimmon and Wehrung, 1986; Shapira, 1986). Studies show that managers adopt and apply only selected elements of the total risk equation. They pay little attention to uncertainty surrounding positive outcomes, viewing risk in terms of dangers or hazards with potentially negative outcomes. Moreover, it is the scale of the likely losses associated with plausible outcomes, rather than the range of possible outcomes, that focuses managerial minds. Underlying March and Shapira's (1987) observations about dissonance between how people are supposed to behave and how they do behave is a wider debate on the nature of risk that has been gathering momentum for over 20 years.

In 1983, scientists and engineers of the Royal Society in London produced a report that presented risk as 'the probability that a particular adverse event occurs during a stated period of time, or results from a particular challenge. As a probability in the sense of statistical theory, risk obeys all formal laws of combining probabilities'. The report reflected the prevailing international orthodoxy of the time and was widely accepted as a definitive document in the field. It made a clear distinction between 'objective risk', as determined by experts applying quantitative scientific means, and 'perceived risk' – the imprecise and unreliable perceptions of the laity. This 'objective' position, combined with the Society's definition of 'detriment' as 'the numerical measure of harm or loss associated with an adverse event', reflects the compound measure of risk widely encountered within the engineering, health and safety literature.

In 1992, the Royal Society revisited the subject of risk, this time inviting a group of social scientists – psychologists, anthropologists, sociologists, geographers and economists – to add their expert opinions. Only the economists supported the earlier stance of their colleagues from the physical sciences. The other social scientists took an opposing position, arguing that objective and perceived risk are in practice inseparable, particularly where people are involved. They argued that risk is not a discrete or objective phenomenon, but an interactive culturally determined one that is inherently resistant to objective measurement. The essential problem is that people modify their behaviour and thereby their likely exposure to risk in response to subjective perceptions of that risk, subtly balancing perceived costs and benefits. Writers such as Adams (1996), therefore, contend that these unquantified or unquantifiable changes in exposure invariably defeat all attempts to measure risk outside the casino, where odds can be mechanically controlled. The outcome of the Royal Society's 1992 study was discord within the Society and a descent into 'uncertainty' within the risk management discipline.

Risk and uncertainty are terms that in practice are often used interchangeably, but back in the 1920s Knight (1921) made a helpful distinction: 'If you don't know for sure what will happen, but you know the odds, that's risk and if you don't even know the odds, that's uncertainty.' Uncertainty is, according the Knight, 'the realm of judgement'. Nevertheless, as Adams (1996) points out, 'Virtually all the formal treatments of risk and uncertainty in game theory, operations research, economics and management science require that the odds be known, that numbers be attachable to the probabilities and magnitudes of possible outcomes'. In these disciplines, risk management still strives to identify, quantify, control and where possible eliminate specific narrowly defined risks. Similarly, most of the tools, techniques and concepts used for identifying, evaluating and estimating risk remain rooted in the thinking of scientific management. Consequently they fail to consider that failures and accidents may be emergent properties arising from the wider system as a whole (White, 1995). Even in enterprise risk management, it is clear to some that risk management models have failed to keep pace with the realities of our networked world. They have failed to account for operational interdependencies between firms brought about by the trend to outsource and the reality of supply chain networks, thereby underestimating the range and severity of risks faced by a company (Starr, Newfrock and Delurey, 2003).

Why this all matters from a practical supply chain risk management perspective is that, if supply chains are seen only from a business process engineering and control perspective, then a selective (downside only) version of a variance-based view of risk sits quite well. However, if we also accept that supply chains involve relationships that link organizations sharing a common philosophy and purpose, then there is an equally persuasive argument that supply chains should be viewed as open interactive societal systems. Organizations are, whether we like it or not, socially constructed, managed and populated by people, imbued with all the fallibility of human nature and its good common sense. Moreover, if we also accept that these may be global supply chains, then those culturally determined perceptions of risk could vary greatly from one country to another. Along the way the forces of nature can easily demonstrate just how far removed from the controlled environment of the casino this all might be.

Supply chain resilience: a holistic view

Mindful of the need for more holistic approaches to risk management, this section looks not only at risks in terms of specific vulnerabilities and hazards, but at what that means for the resilience of the supply chain as an integrated system. In this context, the term 'resilience' refers to the ability of the system to return to its original (or desired) state after being disturbed. However, keeping our feet in the real world, it is important to remember that no one person manages a whole supply chain. Many people are responsible for the management of activities, functions, processes or other aspects of these complex dynamic networks. Each will be viewing supply chain risk through the lens of his or her own performance measures. The upshot is that, in practice, supply chain risk management is likely to be a patchwork of sometimes complementary, but often conflicting or competing, efforts. Figure 14.1 shows a supply chain broken down into its component parts, hopefully without losing the sense of dynamic interaction. Looking at supply chains in this way enables the inclusion of many different functional and hierarchical perspectives and their respective interpretations of risk, as well as an opportunity to position some of the management tools and techniques currently available.

Process engineering and inventory management

Level 1 in Figure 14.1 concentrates on a process engineering or inventory management perspective. It focuses on what is being carried – work and information flows – and process design within and between organizations. This perspective underlies lean operations and the 'end-to-end' perspective required for the 'agile' supply chain, where reliable, responsive processes and inventory management concerns remain central themes. Risk management is largely about improved visibility (of demand and inventory), velocity (to

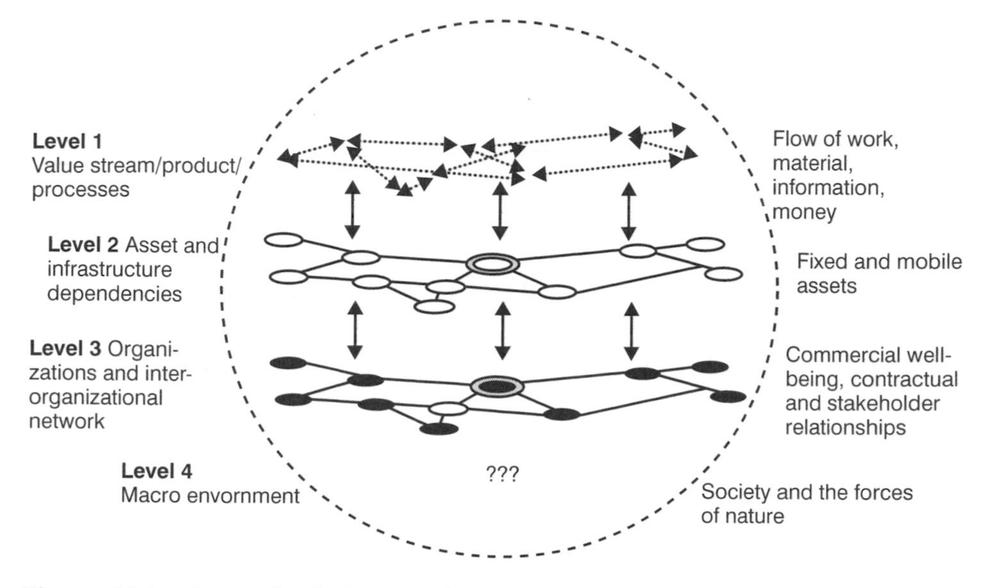

Figure 14.1 A supply chain as an interactive system

reduce the likelihood of obsolescence and optimize asset utilization) and control. If processes are tightly monitored and controlled, then non-conformance to plan can be quickly detected. Risk reduction tools are often borrowed from total quality management. Related process improvement and control methodologies such as Six Sigma are also favoured by some, as are automated event management systems, which readily alert managers to deviations from plan and minimize human intervention.

In the ideal world of scientific management, mastery of process control methodologies would facilitate the identification, management and elimination of risk. Unfortunately, we do not live in an ideal world, so Levels 2, 3 and 4 of the model bring in a host of other factors that regularly intervene.

Assets and infrastructure dependencies

Level 2 considers the fixed and mobile assets used to source, produce or carry the goods and information flows addressed at Level 1. When viewed at this level, nodes in the networks may be farms, factories, distribution centres, commercial retail outlets, or public service delivery points such as schools or hospitals. Alternatively, they may be facilities housing IT servers and call centres. Links in the network are the transport and communications infrastructure, ie roads, railways, flight paths and sea lanes, pipelines and grids, plus mobile assets – boat, trains, trucks and planes. The transport and communications networks have their own nodes too – ports, airports, satellites, etc.

Well-known asset-based approaches to risk management, developed in insurance, are appropriate and commonly used in this context. They tend to define risk as the probability of a given event multiplied by the severity (negative impact) should it occur. They draw on plentiful historical data to provide some indication of the likelihood of fire, flood and many other eventualities affecting the insured asset. In a wider vein it is helpful to explore the impact on operations of the loss of links or nodes in the production/distribution and infrastructure networks, through network modelling.

Mitigating the impacts of potential disruptions to nodes and links is where business continuity planning (BCP) has a place. As a discipline, BCP is gradually moving beyond asset-based approaches to risk management, to a wider remit of maintaining 'mission critical activities'. In practice, though, efforts are still first and foremost concerned with safeguarding against the loss of IT systems, or loss of a particular facility, whether that be due to accident, attack or natural disasters. However, more often than not, disruptions at this level are not the result of catastrophic failures caused by the phenomena that have exercised generations of actuaries. The disruptions are just as likely to be the results of poorly managed IT upgrades or physical network reconfigurations (Peck *et al*, 2003). Planned site closures, relocations or indiscriminate outsourcing of activities are often to blame. Nevertheless, it is worth noting that cross-sector surveys undertaken in recent years suggest that loss of key skills is actually a more frequent problem than either loss of site or loss of IT systems (Peck and Jüttner, 2002).

Level 2 is the territory of unglamorous 'trucks and sheds' logistics – an early candidate for outsourcing in most manufacturing and retail organizations. Within Europe, manufacturing has migrated eastwards. Globally, it has headed for China, which means that for much of the world the transport element of supply chain management and the associated resource requirements are increasing. HGV driver shortages are a familiar problem to companies in the UK, while shortages of shipping capacity from the Far East at certain times of the year have been causing problems for some retailers in Western Europe.

In terms of monitoring mobile assets, we see radio frequency identification (RFID) used in consignment tracking systems. Of course, technological solutions need appropriately trained people, though this simple fact is often overlooked. RFID was used to some extent during the 2003 invasion of Iraq – but nobody informed front-line troops, who had no idea what the tags were or what should be done with them when they reached their destination. As a result many were simply unclipped and thrown into buckets. The people part of the equation was also overlooked in the C–TPAT and CSI anti-terrorism initiatives. Automated solutions seemed to offer a way forward, but insufficient customs personnel were available to undertake the necessary validation checks to admit those applying to be 'known shippers' on to the programme. Thus the measures are regarded by many as increasing the difficulties faced by organizations already struggling to keep pace with a dramatic increase in volumes of global shipments.

Organizations and inter-organizational networks

Level 3 looks at supply chain risk at the strategic level of organizations and the inter-organizational network. These are the organizations that own or manage the assets and infrastructure that make or carry the goods and information flows. At this level, risk is likely to be perceived as the financial consequences of an event or decision for an organization – particularly its impact on budget or shareholders. This is where strategic management concerns and corporate governance requirements really kick in. It is also where conflicts of interest in risk management become most evident.

From a purely supply chain management perspective, risk at this level is the downside financial consequences of a specific event. The loss of a sole supplier or customer is the most obvious danger here. The trading relationships that link organizations and power dependencies between them should also be watched carefully. Low margins are likely to encourage consolidation within the industry, changing power balances and reversing dependencies. They also herald network reconfigurations and the associated disruptions described at Level 2. Partnering, dual sourcing and outsourcing are likely to be put forward as risk management solutions, backed up by contractual obligations. However, anecdotal evidence abounds to suggest that in times of shortage contractual guarantees become unreliable, with suppliers diverting scarce resources to their largest customers, regardless of contractual requirements. Indeed software is now available that allows companies to divert supplies automatically to service their most valuable accounts.

Best-practice strategic management and corporate governance tend to see things a little differently. Here risk retains the upside as well as the downside connotations of decision theory. Strategic management is likely to encourage 'big bets' to maintain competitive advantage. High-risk big bets are likely to be offset by a requirement for lower risk taking in non-core activities. This line of logic encourages strategists and corporate risk managers (few of whom have operational supply chain management experience) to attempt to transfer risks associated with non-core activities off-balance sheet to suppliers. One pitfall associated with this reasoning is that the definition of what is, and is not, a core capability may be too narrowly drawn, with key elements of supply chain management falling by the wayside. Outsourcing and contractual means are nevertheless seen as legitimate methods employed to reduce exposure to financial risk. The option is even more tempting if short-term cost saving can be realized. However, when liability for risk management is transferred in this way, the operational consequences of failure remain.

The industrial relations battle between the Swiss-based, North American-owned airline catering company Gate Gourmet and its UK workforce in the summer of 2005 illustrated the point. The Gate Gourmet dispute was a landmark case in that it marked the return of secondary industrial action, not seen in the UK for decades. It also illustrates why supply chains should also be viewed as interactive social systems. Gate Gourmet was sole supplier of in-flight catering services to British Airways (BA). The staff had been BA workers until a cost reduction programme prompted the airline to outsource the activity. The move had been financially beneficial to BA, which, in a competitive environment, had continued to pursue further cost reductions through its supply chain. A dispute involving catering staff did not, on the face of it, represent a significant threat to BA, as the airline could operate its core business without in-flight meals. However, when around 670 BA ground staff – many with family ties to sacked catering workers – decided to walk out in sympathy, the consequences for BA were unavoidable. The four-day strike halted BA flights out of Heathrow, costing an estimated £40 million in cancelled flights, and additional costs of food and accommodation for 70,000 stranded passengers.

The macro environment

The fourth and final level of analysis is the macro environment, within which the assets and infrastructure are positioned and organizations do business. The PEST (political, economic, social and technological) analysis of environmental changes, used in strategic management, is useful here. Sometimes environmental and legal/regulatory changes are included in the basic analysis or given separate treatment. Socio-political factors – such as action by pressure groups (eg environmentalists or fuel protestors) or supposedly unrelated industrial disputes – should be picked up by routine 'horizon scanning' using specialist or general media sources, allowing measures to be put in place to mitigate the impact. Geo-political factors (eg war) should not come as a surprise, but the extent to which they can influence demand for all manner of goods and services should not be underestimated. The 2003 invasion of Iraq coincided with a drop in business confidence, leading to a drop in advertising and a marked reduction in demand for high-quality paper – with the reverse impact on oil prices.

Far from our controlled casino environment, there are also the forces of nature – metrological, geological and pathological – to contend with. Most are likely to be far beyond the control of supply chain managers, so risk avoidance and contingency planning are appropriate courses of action. However, one category of pathogens – ie contaminants and diseases – is worth particular attention here. Whether it is BSE, foot-and-mouth, avian flu, or the computer viruses that mimic them, what makes pathological factors so dangerous is that they are mobile. They have the ability to hitch a ride with the flows of goods and information that supply chain managers speed around the globe. Once inside the system, they have the potential to bring it down from within. The creeping crises referred to at the beginning of this chapter are all Level 4 disruptions – but it would be wrong to regard them only as external threats to the supply chain. Their potency as disruptive challenges is a reflection of our interconnected, interdependent societies and the efficiency of our supply chains.

Supply chains and wicked problems

Having run through the levels of the model, examining the perspectives and risk management methods prevalent at each, it is important to reiterate the fact that managers at every level see risk first and foremost through the lens of their own performance measures. The snag here is that efforts to optimize performance (and thereby reduce risk) in one dimension will often have unexpected and undesirable consequences for others. Whilst this notion may sit uncomfortably with objective approaches to risk management and prevailing wisdom in supply chain management, it comes as no surprise to some complex systems thinkers. That is because supply chain risk is technically a 'wicked problem'.

The term was coined in the early 1970s by Rittel and Webber (1973), whose paper on 'Dilemmas in a general theory of planning' is not an obvious source of enlightenment for those charged with the management of supply chain risk. Nevertheless, their contribution was to produce a lucid explanation of why societal problems are inherently different from the problems that scientists and some engineers tackle. Scientists and engineers tend to deal with discrete, identifiable problems, where the desired outcome is known, providing clarity of mission and an easily recognizable desired end state. But Rittel and Webber (1973) argued that the assumption of discrete problems did not reflect the reality of societal dilemmas – including most public policy issues. These are complex 'wicked problems'. Societal problems invariably encompass the interests of multiple stakeholders who rarely share a single definitive common goal. The absence of a definitive common interest means that the clarity of mission is also absent, and there is unlikely to be a definitive universal solution. Personal interests and value sets invariably come into play. Moreover, once implemented, any solution will probably generate consequences elsewhere in the system, often over an extended period of time. The term 'wicked' is not used in the sense that something is ethically deplorable, but in the sense that it is vicious, displaying the characteristics of a vicious circle. Moreover, attempts to solve wicked problems are quite likely to result in malignant side-effects.

It is clear that some threats to supply chains (eg Y2K) do fall into the discrete problem category, but there are many other problems facing managers of supply chain risk that do not – including creeping crises and counter-terrorism. Given the nature of wicked problems, searching for a one-time definitive optimal solution is not the way forward. Instead Rittel and Webber (1973) observed it is better to ask the right questions about the consequences of actions, within the context of multiple frameworks, recognizing social processes as the links tying open systems into larger interconnected networks of systems. This chapter concurs with that advice, and has put forward just such a framework, addressing supply chain vulnerability at many levels and risk from multiple perspectives – but all within the context of an integrated supply chain system.

Engineering perspectives do have a well-deserved place in that framework, as does lean thinking and least-cost efficiency, but the notion that everyone can minimize risk (however that is construed) and optimize performance simultaneously is far from realistic. Compromises do have to be made. Resilience requires redundancy or slack in terms of time, capacity and capability within and preferably throughout the system, which means that suboptimal efficiency for someone is inevitable. In the ideal world of collaborative supply chain management, all parties should be willing and able to share the risks – benefits and cost burdens – for the greater good of all. In practice, human nature and short-term financial pressures give a distinct possibility that, instead of everyone carrying slack, no one will carry it. All will be hoping that just over their network horizon someone else will be doing the right thing or that market forces can be relied upon to ensure that resources will always be there, ready and waiting, just in case they are needed. They might be but, in an emergency, would you be willing to bet on it?

References

Adams, J (1996) *Risk*, Routledge, London

Aitken, J (1998) Supply chain integration within the context of a supplier association, PhD thesis, Cranfield University, Cranfield

Borge, D (2001) *The Book of Risk*, John Wiley & Sons, New York

Christopher, M (1998) *Logistics and Supply Chain Management: Strategies for reducing costs and improving services*, Pitman Publishing, London

Cooper, MC *et al* (1997) Supply chain management: more than a new name for logistics, *International Journal of Logistics Management*, **8** (1), pp 1–13

Forrester, JW (1958) Industrial dynamics: a major breakthrough for decision makers, *Harvard Business Review*, **38**, July–August, pp 37–66

Forrester, JW (1969) *Principles of Systems*, Wright Allen Press, Cambridge, MA

Knight, F (1921) *Risk, Uncertainty and Profit*, Harper & Row, New York

La Londe, BJ (1984) A recognition of logistics systems in the 80's: strategies and challenges, *Journal of Business Logistics*, **4** (1), pp 1–11

Larson, PD and Halldorsson, A (2004) Logistics versus supply chain management: an international survey, *International Journal of Logistics: Research and applications*, **7** (1), pp 17–31

MacCrimmon, KR and Wehrung, DA (1986) *Taking Risks: The management of uncertainty*, Free Press, New York

March, JG and Shapira, Z (1987) Managerial perspectives on risk and risk taking, *Management Science*, **33** (11), pp 1404–18

Mentzner, JT *et al* (2001) *Supply Chain Management*, Sage, Thousand Oaks, CA

Oliver, RK and Webber, MD (1992) Supply chain management: logistics catches up with strategy, in *Logistics: The strategic issues*, ed M Christopher, Chapman & Hall, London

Peck, H and Jüttner, U (2002) Risk management in the supply chain, *Logistics and Transport Focus*, **4** (11), December, pp 17–22

Peck, H *et al* (2003) Supply chain resilience, Final report on behalf of the Department for Transport, Cranfield University, Cranfield

Rittel, HWJ and Webber, MM (1973) Dilemmas in a general theory of planning, *Policy Sciences*, **4**, pp 155–69

Royal Society (1983) *Risk Assessment: A study group report*, Royal Society, London

Royal Society (1992) *Risk: Analysis, perception and management*, 2nd edn, Royal Society, London

Shapira, Z (1986) Risk in managerial decision making, Unpublished manuscript, Hebrew University, cited in JG March and Z Shapira (1987) Managerial perspectives on risk and risk taking, *Management Science*, **33** (11), pp 1404–18

Starr, R, Newfrock, J and Delurey, M (2003) Enterprise resilience: managing risk in the networked economy, Booz, Allen and Hamilton, McLean, VA

Stock, JR and Lambert, DM (2001) *Strategic Logistics Management*, 4th edn, McGraw-Hill, Boston, MA

White, D (1995) Applications of systems thinking to risk management: a review of the literature, *Management Decision*, **33** (10), pp 35–45

15

Delivering sustainability through supply chain management

Kirstie McIntyre, Hewlett-Packard

Supply chains span industry groups, cross industry boundaries, have a wide geographical spread and are an excellent vehicle for improving the environmental, social and economic performance of companies and industry sectors over the long term. Supply chain management functions are analysed for their potential impacts on the performance of a company. Practical examples from many industry sectors show the steps that can be taken to improve sustainability for the environment, for society and for the business. Specifically, the European Waste Electrical and Electronic Equipment (WEEE) Directive will have a significant and long-reaching effect on the supply chain. From purchasing decisions to reverse logistics, the whole supply chain will be reshaped by this new environmental law.

Background

Sustainability has traditionally been a concept that is difficult to sell to senior management because it describes a state in the future that has never been experienced, rather than a specific process or methodology of how to get there. Theoretically, the concept makes sense, but translating it into actionable steps has proved a significant stumbling block for a organizations (Preston, 2001). The concept of sustainability or sustainable development has been around for a while, but is a very recent customer requirement and one that many companies are trying to grapple with. Sustainability is a difficult concept to grasp in an industrial context, as shown by the definition (DETR, 2000):

Sustainable development is:

- social progress which recognizes the needs of everyone;
- effective protection of the environment;
- prudent use of natural resources; and
- maintenance of high and stable levels of economic growth and employment.

When a company considers what the above elements mean, it seems impossible to continue to do business and be sustainable. But sustainability is not just about being altruistic about the environment and workers' rights. It is also about ensuring the long-term viability of a business model and company. Shareholders, customers, suppliers and employees all want to see a future in their businesses. The functions that the supply chain organization manages are an ideal place for a company to begin putting together the actionable steps and investments that will demonstrate positive progress towards sustainable development.

Waste electrical and electronic equipment is one of the priority waste streams identified by the European Commission alongside batteries, tyres, vehicles and packaging. The directive has been written as part of the 'producer responsibility' set of laws, which demonstrates a shift in focus from process- to product-oriented environmental legislation. In the past, environmental legislation has focused on industrial emissions and air and water quality – but, owing to increasing waste generation and reducing disposal capacity, waste is now one of the top environmental issues in Europe. EU and UK waste policies increasingly involve the private sector. Producer responsibility legislation aims to increase product recycling by making producers financially responsible for their products at end of life.

WEEE has been specifically chosen as a priority waste stream for a number of reasons. There are perceived problems with the current state of waste management. Growing quantities of WEEE mean a higher contribution of WEEE to pollutants in municipal waste streams – and underdeveloped recycling technologies and infrastructure mean that there are limited ways of dealing with this. Diverging national legislation does not support a single European market or the ease of doing business in Europe. Therefore the general objectives of the WEEE legislation are to improve waste management processes, eliminate hazardous substances, increase recycling capacity and introduce harmonizing legislation.

Supply chain management has risen high on the corporate agenda as companies recognize the potential that it offers for creating sustainable competitive advantage in an increasingly turbulent business environment (Christopher and Lambert, 2001). Customers' requirements are becoming more stringent and companies aim to be increasingly customer-focused – and it is often the supply chain that is able to provide the added value that customers are looking for. The 6th Business in the Environment Index of Corporate Environmental Engagement (BiE, 2002) identified the integration of environmental risk into supply chain management as a real challenge for many companies. Supply chain aspects of sustainable development resulted in the lowest management score, with 17 out of 38 industry sectors scoring below 50 per cent. There is a need to look strategically beyond the immediate environmentally driven aspects of supply chain management. With all stakeholders giving attention to the quality of management and corporate governance – demonstrated through supply chains and sustainability – this is an ideal time to look at combining the best of both disciplines. This chapter takes each of the major supply chain functions (shown in Figure 15.1) and discusses their ability to improve sustainability in terms of environmental, social and economic impacts.

Purchasing or procurement

Purchasing is often the first place that companies start to integrate environmental issues into their management processes. This is especially true for

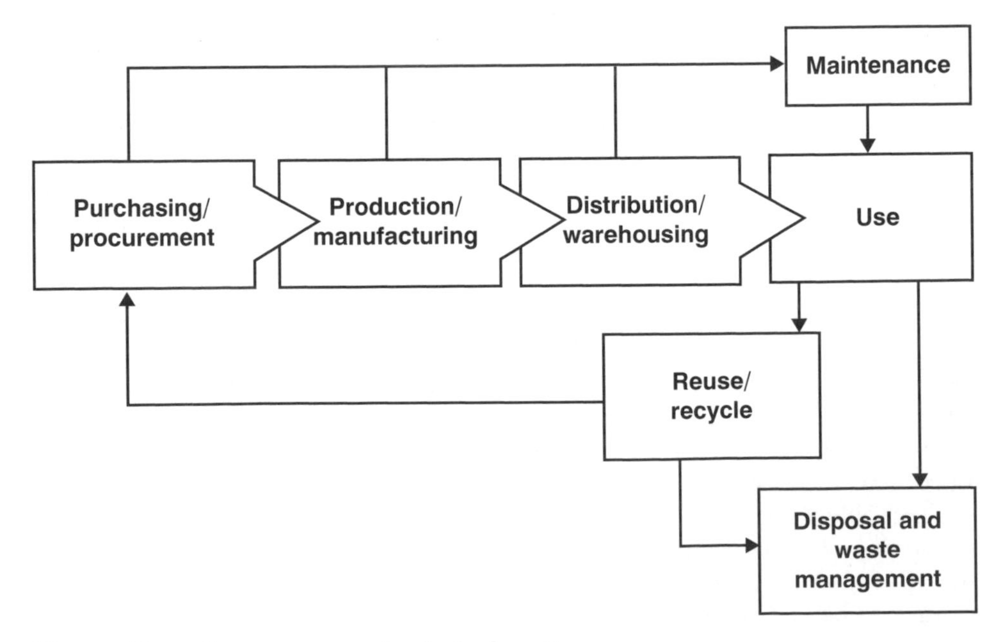

Figure 15.1 Common supply chain functions

service companies. Such companies often do not have large environmental impacts themselves – but the operations that use their services are frequently the area where there is a significant scope for improvement. Environmental performance is certainly now integrated into the procurement function of many large companies, whether for services or for raw materials. These large companies affect whole supply chains and cross many industries with their requirements for improved environmental performance. Some of this is being driven by environmental management systems (ISO 14000 or EMAS) and some is being driven by consumer pressure or even market differentiation. Toyota first laid out its goal of becoming an industry leader in environmental performance in 1992 with its Earth Charter. It is now imposing the same standards on its suppliers in its Green Supplier Guidelines – which are not so much guidelines as mandates. Toyota in North America demanded that all suppliers implement an environmental management system that conforms to ISO 14001 by the end of 2003. Suppliers must also obey a ban on 450 chemicals as well as comply with hazardous materials transport rules. Many of Toyota's suppliers welcome the tough standards as it brings them to the forefront of environmental performance in their own industries. Toyota has further environmental aspirations with long-term energy reduction and greenhouse gas and zero landfill targets (Zachary, 2001). Such strictures can apply a lot of pressure on suppliers, but Toyota's suppliers appear to have embraced the challenge and feel that they have gained from doing so. Toyota itself has improved its environmental performance by leveraging the effort of its suppliers. This seems an increasingly popular way of improving environmental and social performance, particularly by customer-facing organizations such as car manufacturers and retailers.

A growing number of European retail chains are developing their own safety initiatives by banning chemicals in their products. Many retailers are asking suppliers of own-label products to withdraw or phase out chemicals that have been put on priority lists for further research by the European Commission, national governments or environmental monitoring organizations. Fewer organizations have been successful at incorporating social issues into their procurement processes. However, with recent media attention on Nike and Gap over child-labour issues in their supply chains, the clothing retailers have taken a much more proactive approach to supplier assurance. Nike and Gap both have corporate compliance and monitoring teams who audit contract factories for fulfilment of stated aims and objectives. Many British retailers have joined the Ethical Trading Initiative (ETI), which identifies and promotes good practice in the implementation of codes of labour practice (see the ETI website, www.ethicaltrade.org). It is reasonable to expect more retailers to take these approaches to managing social impacts in their supply chain.

B&Q has been in the forefront of action in this area since the early 1990s when it realized that – as a DIY retailer – the majority of its environmental and social impacts came from its products and suppliers. The company uses both questionnaires and auditors to track environmental and social issues in its supplier base, and has decided that this approach is preferable to requiring an environment management system (B&Q, 1995). It submitted to suppliers, chemical companies and environmental groups a list of chemicals it wanted to ban in its products so that it could declare itself toxic-free by 2005. Some of the chemicals are among the 15 hazardous substances pinpointed for priority action by the Ospar convention, responsible for protecting the marine environment of the north-east Atlantic. Homebase, another DIY retailer, is going even further by planning to ban all the chemicals on the Ospar list – even though the governments that defined the list set a deadline of 2020 for ending these emissions.

The pressure to green the procurement function does not come only from companies; governments are also leveraging their purchasing power. The UK government has for some time produced a *Green Government Handbook*, which advises central and local departments on environmentally sound goods and services. The European Commission (2001) has recently issued guidelines that clarify the extent to which environmental criteria may be used in the public procurement process and still remain in line with procurement directives that regulate freedom of movement, competition and best value. A *Green Public Procurement Handbook* is being developed. The drivers for this are that the achievement of sustainable development requires that economic growth supports social progress and respects the environment, that social policy underpins economic performance, and that environmental policy is cost-effective. Public purchasing represents 14 per cent of EU GDP, and member states should consider how to make better use of public procurement to favour environmentally friendly products and services. The guidance goes beyond differentiating between products and services, and suggests that there are other possibilities for integrating environmental considerations into public purchases, notably when defining the technical specifications, the selection criteria and the award criteria of a contract. This means that public procurement departments may have the ability to change the way that goods are produced or manufactured or the supplies that service providers use.

Changing methods of public procurement are also being used to drive sustainability into goods and services purchased from the private sector. The construction sector in the UK has discovered that new procurement methods such as private finance initiatives (PFIs) and Prime Contracting (an MOD initiative) have long-term outlooks and responsibilities (25 years in the case of PFI), which means that designing, building and maintaining sustainable facilities become key to the successful tendering and managing of contracts.

Production or manufacturing

The primary output of today's production processes is waste. Across all industries, less than 10 per cent of everything that is extracted from the earth (by weight) becomes usable products. The remaining 90 per cent becomes waste from production (Senge, Carstedt and Porter, 2001). Resource efficiency – or doing more with less – is the first place to start in improving sustainability performances. Through its 'waste-free factories' programme, Xerox has reduced landfill by over 75 per cent since 1993. Cornwell Parker Furniture's timber minimization programme has saved £250,000 per year and reduced waste by 20 per cent. Cornwell has also overhauled coating procedures, saving a further £180,000 per year, and cut solvent use by 21 tonnes per year. Instead of sending wood waste to landfill, a wood-fired incinerator with energy recovery has been installed. Although this cost £480,000, the reduction in landfill tax and heating fuel gives a payback period of four to five years (Envirowise, 2002). British Airways and its waste management contractor, Grundon, have created a strategic partnership to deal with waste arising from aircraft, engineering facilities and offices. The partnership means that, instead of being presented with an opaque final bill for services, BA receives a detailed breakdown of Grundon's waste handling costs. This has enabled both parties to identify opportunities for cost savings and then share in those savings (ENDS, 2002a).

Many argue that what we need is a different way of looking at products. Firms such as Dow Chemical, Carrier and IKEA believe that higher profits will come from providing better solutions, rather than selling more units. This creates a potential alignment between what is sound economically and what is sound environmentally. A company's business model no longer requires designed-in obsolescence to push customers into buying new products. Instead, producers have an incentive to design for longevity, efficient servicing, improved functioning and product take-back. Such design maintains relationships with customers by continually ensuring that products are providing the services that people desire, at the lowest cost to the producer.

The shift from valuing 'stuff' to valuing the service that the 'stuff' provides leads to a radical change in the concept of ownership. In the future, producers may own their products for ever and, therefore, will have strong incentives to design products to be disassembled and remanufactured or recycled, whichever is more economical. Owning products for ever would represent a powerful step toward changing companies' attitudes about product discard. When the production function is considered to be a part of the supply chain, there is obviously much that can be done to improve environmental and social performance at this stage. The environmental performance of manufacturing activities has been improving now for many years, much of it driven by easy cost savings.

Social impact assessments are common for large infrastructure projects (roads, pipelines, etc) but are not yet a common part of manufacturing activities. However, many companies forget that social impacts include the health and safety of employees and neighbours, community relations or noise and congestion abatement processes. Many of these impacts are already part of environmental management systems. Human resource management processes also play a role in identifying and improving social performance – training, fair pay, equality and diversity activities all contribute to a company's sustainability performance.

The case of Scandic Hotels shows, firstly, that sustainable strategies and practices can be just as useful in service operations as in manufacturing and, secondly, that such strategies and practices can support a corporate turnaround. In the early 1990s, Scandic Hotels was turned from collapse by a new value system, embodied in the concept of sustainable development, which linked customers and employees. Through employee training programmes, environmental information systems and innovative collaborations with suppliers, Scandic was revived as a profitable corporation (Goodman, 2000).

Distribution and warehousing

Cooper, Browne and Peters (1991) maintain that the transport and storage of goods are at the centre of any logistics activity, and these are areas where a company should concentrate its efforts to reduce its environmental impacts. The authors claim that 24-hour transport is less environmentally damaging, as fuel consumption is more efficient with less congestion, and that just-in-time operations raise fuel consumption, as smaller lorries consume more fuel per tonne of goods moved than larger vehicles. This is an important point with the exponential growth of e-commerce and home deliveries. The use of combined transport options such as containers using road and rail links is advocated for environmental improvement. To begin the improvement process, the authors suggest a three-stage approach: an environmental audit of the logistics operation, a listing of actions to reduce impacts and a priority ranking of these actions. The problem with these recommendations is that they are not stakeholder-focused, but look only at fuel consumption and economic cost. Improving the efficiency of fuel consumption will indeed reduce environmental impact, but local community issues may become more important when using large lorries in a 24-hour operation.

Supermarkets are only just beginning to take into account the miles travelled by food from its country of origin to our plates. Consumer demand for fresh fruit and vegetables all year round and the falling costs of freight transport have not provided retailers with an economic incentive to reduce the transport associated with their products. However, climate change levies may change this as transport emissions are counted as part of a company's carbon dioxide burden. Drinks manufacturer HP Bulmer has identified that the second-biggest source of carbon dioxide and other air pollutants is transport – with outbound goods accounting for some 85 per cent of its total transport emissions. Currently 100 per cent of the company's transport is by road, but it has been testing ways of putting some back on the railway. A partial switch to rail appears to be cost-neutral and results in environmental benefits, with carbon dioxide emissions per tonne-kilometre reduced by 80 per cent. Such initiatives allowed Bulmer to set a target of reducing the environmental impacts of its transport operations by 75 per cent in 2004 (ENDS, 2002b).

Transport is often viewed as an activity with a negative environmental impact, yet the transport sector represents 7 per cent of the GDP of Western Europe and employs 7 per cent of the workforce. On the other hand, the cost to society in terms of congestion, pollution and accidents has been estimated to be 5 per cent of the GDP. The energy consumption of the transport sector is one-third of all the energy consumed by EU industry, and 85 per cent of this is used by road transport. Unfortunately, the recent troubles of Railtrack in the UK have done nothing to encourage goods to move from road to rail. And the sector is fragmented, very competitive and disinclined to act in concert to find solutions to its problems (Howie, 1994). Congestion is inflationary and decreases productivity through delays, stock-outs or over-stocking. So, there is a dilemma between reducing environmental impact and increasing financial cost. To some extent, this can be overcome by intermediaries like consolidators (organizations that ship many companies' products together to maximize loading efficiencies).

Warehouse management is another key social and environmental factor in distribution. The siting of warehousing and distribution centres can be a major issue for local communities because of noise and congestion. The energy consumption or health and safety record in a poorly managed, temperature-controlled warehouse can eclipse all the other efforts that a company may make, yet it is often an overlooked function of the supply chain. Packaging and waste management are also important processes, often based at warehouse locations, which can have far-reaching impacts on the environment. The Packaging Waste Directive (94/62/EC) and national packaging laws now include all types of packaging in aggressive recovery and recycling targets for companies using over 50 tonnes of packaging a year. Anheuser-Busch, the US food processor, is looking at both in- and outbound materials to see how suppliers can improve the company's environmental performance as well as its bottom line. Suppliers have played a major role in its packaging programme, which has resulted in a reduction of aluminium use, saving $250 million per year. The company has also worked with materials-recovery suppliers to increase recycling rates as well as the quality of collected aluminium beverage containers. It is now the world's largest recycler of used aluminium drinks containers, currently recycling 130 per cent of the amounts it ships in the USA. Overall, the company has reduced the amount of solid waste to landfill by 68 per cent since 1991, saving $19 million. Such efforts take several years, require collaboration with suppliers and need to be integrated into existing quality programmes and new business initiatives (*Purchasing*, 2001).

Use and maintenance

As many life cycle analyses have proved, it is the 'use' phase of a product or service that often creates the biggest environmental and social impact (McIntyre *et al*, 1998). It is also the use phase that many companies are recognizing as key to customer relationship management. As Volvo discovered years ago, when a company is selling cars its relationship with the customer ends at the purchase; when the company is providing customer satisfaction, the relationship just begins with the purchase. By interacting with the producer, the consumer can become a co-creator of value or, in some cases, a destroyer of value (Senge, Carstedt and Porter, 2001). Xerox found that it was not the electricity that its equipment consumed that caused the biggest environmental impact, but the consumption of paper and toner and the visits from the service engineer in a van (McIntyre, 1999). This indicated to Xerox that designing greater reliability into machines and then providing more training to customers would substantially mitigate the environmental impacts of its supply chain. Cooperating with paper and toner suppliers to reduce energy consumption at the production stage would result in greater cost savings and less environmental damage.

BASF's premise is that its products will have commercial advantage if they deliver environmental benefits as well as performing at the same level as the competition. The company examines all of its major products and processes every three years and assesses how they can be made more profitable or more environmentally friendly or, where necessary, replaced. The company has now undertaken more than 100 eco-efficiency analyses. One example introduced plastic fuel tanks for cars as being more eco-efficient than metal ones (because they are lighter and will reduce energy use and, therefore, cost to customers). Collaborations between BASF and its customers have become increasingly important in making choices about materials (Scott, 2001).

The examples above show that product stewardship is the key issue in the use phase of products and services. It is a key issue for a number of reasons, not only environmental and social impact, but also as added value to the customer. Corporate governance, ensuring that stated policies are adhered to and maintained, is also being extended by some companies into product stewardship. It is not enough for them to have products disappear on to the next stage in the chain: they are concerned about how their products are being used.

It may be difficult for service sectors to internalize product stewardship, but in practice 'service stewardship' can be applied equally. Understanding the environmental and social impacts that occur through the lifespan of a service is the first step to a reduction of those impacts. The hotel industry, for example, has understood that laundering towels is one of its biggest impacts. Many hotels now have a green hotel charter, which asks guests to consider whether they need clean towels on a daily basis. Although it is still the customer's choice, the hotel is using its relationship with its customers to mitigate environmental impacts from detergent, water and energy consumption.

Dispose or reuse and recycle?

Other organizations have focused their environmental efforts on the other end of the supply chain with recycling issues. Equipment is returned from the customers of companies such as IBM, Nokia, BMW and Xerox (Hopfenbeck, 1993: 139–73). These companies either recondition the old equipment or reclaim the materials they are made from, reprocessing them into raw materials. Logistics is well qualified to deal with cradle-to-grave issues because of its focus on the control of materials from suppliers, through value-added processes and on to the customer. The interface between logistics and the environment is embedded in the value-adding functions it performs (Wu and Dunn, 1995). To minimize total environmental impact, it must be evaluated from the total system perspective and reverse logistics may be the answer to improving the environmental impact of the supply chain by improving material use (Giuntini, 1996).

The requirements of the WEEE Directive emphasize that industry and governments should be driving towards individual producer responsibility, away from the collective responsibility of dealing with historical WEEE waste. This means that each producer would be responsible for only its own products, not a share of all WEEE within its market category. The aim of this is to achieve environmental benefits through encouraging innovative design and recycling technologies driven by producers. For example, Hewlett-Packard (2005) has been designing products for a number of years using the concept of extended producer responsibility. It is equally concerned about the design impacts on the cost of recycling the product at the end of its life as it is about the energy consumption and hazardous materials content. HP therefore assumes that its products will be easier and cheaper to recycle than its competitors' products and that it will be able to pass on this cost advantage to its customers.

The challenge for the supply chain is clear in this scenario. In order for HP to realize its cost advantage, it needs to recover and recycle only its own products. In these days of underdeveloped recycling infrastructure and technologies, it is difficult to see how this can happen without large amounts of manual handling to sort through piles of IT WEEE and select only HP branded products. Studies in the UK and other countries have shown that a significant proportion of WEEE returned by householders is unrecognizable or has no brand name left on it. This issue may be resolved with the advent of radio frequency identity (RFID) tagging, but this would require significant investment by producers to incorporate it into products, and by the recycling industry to invest in the sorting machinery needed to make the system efficient. However, it is only through producers being able to realize the benefits of eco-design at the end of life of products that the WEEE Directive will achieve one of its primary objectives – preventing so much electronic waste being generated in the first place.

The construction industry in the United Kingdom consumes around 6 tonnes of material per person per year and about 10 per cent of national energy consumption is used in the production and transport of construction products and materials. Some 250–300 million tonnes of material are quarried in the UK each year for use as aggregates, cement and bricks. Approximately 13 million tonnes of construction materials are delivered to site and thrown away unused every year (DETR, 2004). The construction industry produced an estimated 73 million tonnes of construction and demolition waste in 1999, representing 18 per cent of the total waste produced in the UK. Only 12–15 million tonnes of materials (less than 20 per cent) are recycled per year, as hardcore and landscaping fill. Using these materials more effectively, through reclamation and higher-grade recycling, would reduce the use of aggregates, save energy and reduce pressures on landfill sites (Vivian, 2001). For example, in 10 demonstration projects MACE, Laing Homes, AMEC Capital, Wren & Bell, Schal, Scottish Executive, Try Construction, the Environment Agency and Carillion have all worked with CIRIA to minimize waste. Examples of waste minimization on these sites include (CIRIA, 2001):

- the recovery of 500,000 roof tiles for reuse in housing developments, saving £80,000;
- a house builder saving £600 waste disposal costs per housing unit built;
- a reduction in over-ordering by using just-in-time deliveries;
- the minimization of waste at the design stage of an office refurbishment;
- the segregation of waste on-site, saving 20 per cent on disposal costs; and
- better control of waste by the use of rigorous procurement and contractual measures.

Managerial and financial sustainability

What about all the support structures around supply chains, such as financial decisions, management systems and governance? Certain preconditions are necessary before an environmentally oriented value chain can be created.

These include an environmentally oriented system of corporate management, a culture that allows learning, and a top-down principle with bottom-up support. Development and change aimed at the target audience are more likely to result in the environment (or sustainability) being considered from the beginning of the process (Steger, 1996).

Much of the influence on sustainability comes from outside the firm. Many in the fund management community probably think that sustainable development has little relevance to their decision making – but what about the energy company that is ignoring the rising tide of pollution legislation, or an automotive stockist that has not considered the implications of forthcoming vehicle recycling directives (Belsom, 2001)? When the cost of emitting climate-change gases is incorporated into the tax regime through the UK climate change levy, then the economics of doing business will change. The Society of Motor Manufacturers and Traders estimate that the extra cost for each new UK car after the implementation of the End of Life Vehicle Directive will be between £115 and £300. These uncertainties reduce the earnings from companies' stock and so their performance on the stock market.

Socially responsible investment aims to influence companies to adopt policies that benefit the environment and society at large. As investors, socially responsible investment funds have a great deal of influence over the way in which a company conducts business (CIS, 2002). An EIRiS/NOP (1999) survey found that over 75 per cent of UK adults think their pension scheme should operate an ethical policy, if it can do so without reducing the level of financial return. Of these, 39 per cent said their pension should operate an ethical policy even when it might reduce the size of their final pension. The growing prominence of ethical issues is also reflected in the spectacular growth in numbers and size of available funds that apply ethical criteria. Research by the Social Investment Forum indicates that, in 1999, more than $2 trillion was invested in ethical funds in the United States, up 82 per cent from 1997 levels.

Socially responsible investment is a growing trend and there are a large number of rating organizations that assess and screen companies to provide information on their operations. These rating organizations scrutinize factors like environmental impacts and solutions, sustainability issues, management and external focus – and companies will need to consider the strategic responses in these areas (Walker and Farnworth, 2001).

Reputation and governance of a company and its supply chain are also key issues. Shell appeared very badly when it decided to sink an ageing oil platform, Brent Spar, even though it transpired that its solution for disposal was well researched and advised. Shell was unable to recover its corporate reputation and has since attracted more unwanted attention over its operations in Nigeria. Public and pressure group perception of a product is also important in laundry detergents. Suppliers of phosphates and linear alkyl benzene sulfonate (LAS) for laundry detergents in Europe are having mixed success in their fight to gain environmental support for their products. Denmark's environmental authorities are taking such a determined stance over LAS that Procter & Gamble has decided to stop marketing detergents with the surfactant in that country. It is not good for the image of its brands for the company to be seen to be opposing local authorities, even though research indicates that LAS is more biodegradable than the alternatives (*Chemical Market Reporter*, 2001).

BP looks at the challenge of sustainable development as a business opportunity. 'There are good commercial reasons for being ahead of the pack when it comes to environmental issues', says John Brown, BP's chairman. Business can play a leadership role in changes, with change driven through market innovation being easiest for our society to understand. The challenge is to develop sustainable business that is compatible with the current economic reality. Dell, Sun Microsystems and Cisco Systems have all identified supply chains as strategic differentiators, using them to forecast and plan future products and services by building trusting relationships through collaboration. As supply chains evolve from linear supplier–customer links to dynamic networking organizations, all members become involved in defining the processes and contributing to the value of the finished product or service. Innovative business models and products must work financially, or it will not matter how good they are ecologically or socially.

Conclusion

This chapter has shown that the pressures to be a more sustainable company in terms of the environment, economics and social responsibility are increasing. It has also shown that many companies have already started on the long road to sustainable development, some with huge success. Sustainable development is here to stay as a customer requirement, and the processes of supply chain management are ideally placed to respond to that requirement. However, meeting customer and market expectations, improving market access and increasing cost savings represent baseline expectations and are important simply to environmentally responsible companies remaining competitive. Control of the social and environmental aspects of supply chains will lead to better understanding of the supply chain as a whole. This in turn can lead to cost savings and better relationships between partners.

There are many challenges for the supply chain in the WEEE legislation in Europe. For some operators, little will change; for others, there will be a complete sea change. There are opportunities in data management, traceability and assurance, and in the potential development of interim sorting centres or platforms, for retailers and producers. The division of responsibility and accurate reporting is a challenge for members of specific product supply chains. Those parts of the supply chain that can respond to sustainability issues such as WEEE will generally be more proactive and able to meet changing customer requirements and market forces. By taking sustainability one step at a time – early in business planning – it is indeed possible to differentiate and innovate to create value. Supply chain management processes are an ideal place to start.

References

B&Q (1995), *How Green Is My Front Door?*, July, B&Q, Eastleigh

Belsom, T (2001) Unsustainable investors, *Global Investor*, 142, May, p 142

Business in the Environment (BiE) (2002) *Sustaining Competitiveness*, 6th Annual Index of Corporate Environmental Engagement, 26 February, BiE, London

Chemical Market Reporter (2001) Phosphate and LAS eco profiles under siege in Scandinavia, *Chemical Market Reporter*, 259, 11 June, p 259

Christopher, M and Lambert, D (2001) The challenges of supply chain management, Cranfield School of Management online conference, www.supplychainknowledge2001.com

CIRIA (2001) www.ciria.org.uk

Cooper, J, Browne, M and Peters, M (1991) *European Logistics: Markets, management and strategy*, Blackwell, London

Co-operative Insurance Society (CIS) (2002), *Sustainability Pays*, Report by Co-operative Insurance and Forum for the Future, CIS, Manchester

Department of Environment, Transport and the Regions (DETR) (2000) *A Better Quality of Life: A strategy for sustainable development for the United Kingdom*, CM4345, DETR, London

DETR (2004) *UK Statistics*, DETR, London

EIRiS/NOP (1999) *Survey of Pension Scheme Members*, EIRiS/NOP Solutions, London

ENDS (2002a) BA's 'shared savings' scheme with waste firm, *ENDS Report*, 324, January

ENDS (2002b) HP Bulmer: a ferment of sustainability ideas, *ENDS Report*, 324, January

Envirowise (2002) *Furniture Workbook*, GG308, DETR, London

European Commission (2001), *Commission Interpretative Communication on the Community Law Applicable to Public Procurement and the Possibilities for Integrating Environmental Considerations into Public Procurement*, COM(2001) 274 final, 4 July, European Commission, Brussels

Giuntini, R (1996) An introduction to reverse logistics for environmental management: a new system to support sustainability and profitability, *Total Quality Environmental Management*, Spring, pp 81–87

Goodman, A (2000) Implementing sustainability in service operations at Scandic Hotels, *Interfaces*, **30** (3), May/June, pp 202–14

Hewlett-Packard (2005) *Design for Environment Programme Description*, www.hp.com
Hopfenbeck, W (1993) *The Green Management Revolution: Lessons in excellence*, Prentice Hall, London
Howie, B (1994) Environmental impacts on logistics, in *An International Review of Logistics Practice and Issues*, ed G Brace, pp 53–55, Logistics Technology International, London
McIntyre, K (1999) Integrated supply chains and the environment: establishing performance measurement for strategic decision making application – the case of Xerox Ltd, Engineering doctorate thesis, University of Surrey, January
McIntyre, K *et al* (1998) Environmental performance indicators for integrated supply chains: the case of Xerox Ltd, *Supply Chain Management*, **3** (3), pp 149–56
Preston, L (2001) Sustainability at Hewlett-Packard: from theory to practice, *California Management Review*, **43** (3), Spring, pp 26–37
Purchasing (2001) Anheuser-Busch 'greens' its supply chain for cost savings, *Purchasing*, 17 May
Scott, A (2001) BASF aligns R&D with sustainable development, *Chemical Week*, **163** (12), March, pp 39–40
Senge, P, Carstedt, G and Porter, P (2001) Innovating our way to the next industrial evolution, *MIT Sloan Management Review*, **42** (2), Winter, pp 24–38
Social Investment Forum (1999), *Report on Socially Responsible Investing Trends in the United States*, www.socialinvest.org
Steger, U (1996) Managerial issues in closing the loop, *Business Strategy and the Environment*, **5** (4), December, pp 252–68
Vivian, S (2001) Opportunities from environmental management, Paper given at the Institution of Highways and Transportation, June, Cambridge
Walker, J and Farnworth, E (2001) Rating organisations: what is their impact on corporate sustainable strategy?, Business Strategy and the Environment conference, Sept, ERP Environment
Wu, H-J and Dunn, S (1995) Environmentally responsible logistics systems, *International Journal of Physical Distribution and Logistics Management*, **25** (2), pp 20–38
Zachary, K (2001) Toyota prods suppliers to be green, *Ward's Auto World*, **37** (7), July

16

Performance measurement and management in the supply chain

Alan Braithwaite, LCP Consulting

Introduction

> If you cannot measure it, you cannot improve it.
>
> (Lord Kelvin, 1824–1907)

The measurement of business performance is deeply grounded in the backward-looking accounting disciplines of recording profit. As a means to enhance future profits, management now measures and reports on a wide range of business performance from customer perception to strategy consistency and adherence. At the operational level of customer service, the supply chain is the kernel of the business. Indeed, the potential from supply chain thinking and practice is founded in realigning operations through the chain to reduce total cost and maximize service and return on assets. So measurement is a core discipline and capability to provide a framework for defining realignment and reporting progress as to its attainment.

The supply chain is a complex system with many interfaces and dynamic interactions. It is a significant challenge to define the measures at each point in the chain that are appropriate and consistent with the overall desired results. In addition, the desired outcomes in terms of profit, service, stock, assets and costs cannot be managed directly; while there is a general expectation that sales growth will drive profits, the connections to stock, service and cost are less direct.

Performance management in the supply chain is about setting goals within and between functions that will lead to the desired results with balance and without conflict. Ideally, these goals are then embedded in the fabric of the management measurement and reporting of the functions of the firm and its customers, suppliers and service providers. Each function is responsible for delivering its part of the chain to the performance objectives; and when things do not work as planned, the requirement is for failures to be identified and recovery actions mounted. Learning organizations will take the lessons of actual performance and the experience of failure and recovery to adjust the goals across the chain, acting as 'stewards' of the supply chain. This stewardship role is a key responsibility for supply chain managers, since they often do not have functional responsibility for all the chain, albeit they are judged and rewarded on its overall performance.

There are two requirements of performance measurement in the supply chain: 1) understanding and embedding the value and importance of measurement in a strategic framework for supply chain management; and 2) creating a predictive framework of supply chain risk.

Keeping score – a basic management principle

> Revenue is vanity, profit is sanity, and cash is reality.
>
> (Anon)

The essence of business is to generate profits and cash from satisfying customers through its investment in assets and capabilities. Compared with investing deposits in a bank, investors seek a premium return on investment that reflects the additional risk of trading with the assets as compared with the relative safety of the bank. Investors can mitigate risk by holding a number of investments in a portfolio – since some investments will go up while others may go down. Investors generally cannot run the businesses in which they participate so they appoint management to do this for them. They therefore want information on the financial health – or otherwise – of the business so that they can make judgements on the management and the prospects of the investment. Banks want the same information in order to assess the viability of making loans, and governments want information so that they can exact the tax due.

The requirement for compilation and disclosure of performance, in terms of financial health, is therefore vital for the stakeholders. For quoted companies there is an industry of financial analysis that picks over the reported results and attempts to forecast the prospects. Accounting standards bodies such as the Securities and Exchange Commission in the United States and the Accounting Standards Authority in the UK regulate the preparation of company information. The trend has been to require increasing disclosure – not just financially but also in respect of subjects such as equal opportunities and environmental compliance achievement.

The importance of trust and integrity in the preparation of financial statements has been brought into sharp focus with the exposures of corporate catastrophe and financial deceit at Enron, WorldCom and Parmalat. The scale of these cases was unprecedented, but there have always been such cases – with Maxwell Communications and Atlantic Computers being UK examples from the last 20 years. Setting aside these high-profile scandals, there are two major difficulties with financial reporting. The first is that even financial reports prepared with absolute integrity can stretch the notion of 'profit' to meet the aspirations of management and option holders, or to defer tax liabilities. The second is that reported performance is historical and has been likened to driving down a highway steering through the rear-view mirror.

Performance measurement, reporting and management, therefore, need to come closer to the reality of serving customers and the operational demands of day-to-day decision making. In the context of both business direction and the detail of the supply chain, the task of measuring performance unpacks into many layers of detail; it is a subject in its own right.

The balanced scorecard – the standard for goal setting and measurement

Since neither historical performance nor company budgets can be assured to bear directly on a business's long-term strategic objectives, a considerable effort in the development of models and theories has been dedicated to this problem. Amongst these are the Deming Prize (Isixsigma, 2006a), the Malcolm Baldrige Award (Isixsigma, 2006b), the European Foundation of Quality Management's business excellence model (EFQM, 2006) and the balanced scorecard (Kaplan and Norton, 1996). In addition, theories such as the learning organization (Senge, 1990) and knowledge management (Snowden, 2000) devote much energy to similar issues. All these models have strengths, depending on the purpose for which they are being used. However, the balanced scorecard offers a contained and comprehensive approach to strategic direction and control issues; it is the reference for many corporations and it fits especially well with supply chain thinking.

A balanced scorecard provides a picture of a business by combining financial measures with assessments for customer satisfaction, key internal processes and organizational learning and growth (see Figure 16.1). It requires specific goals for customers in terms of time, quality, performance, service and cost as

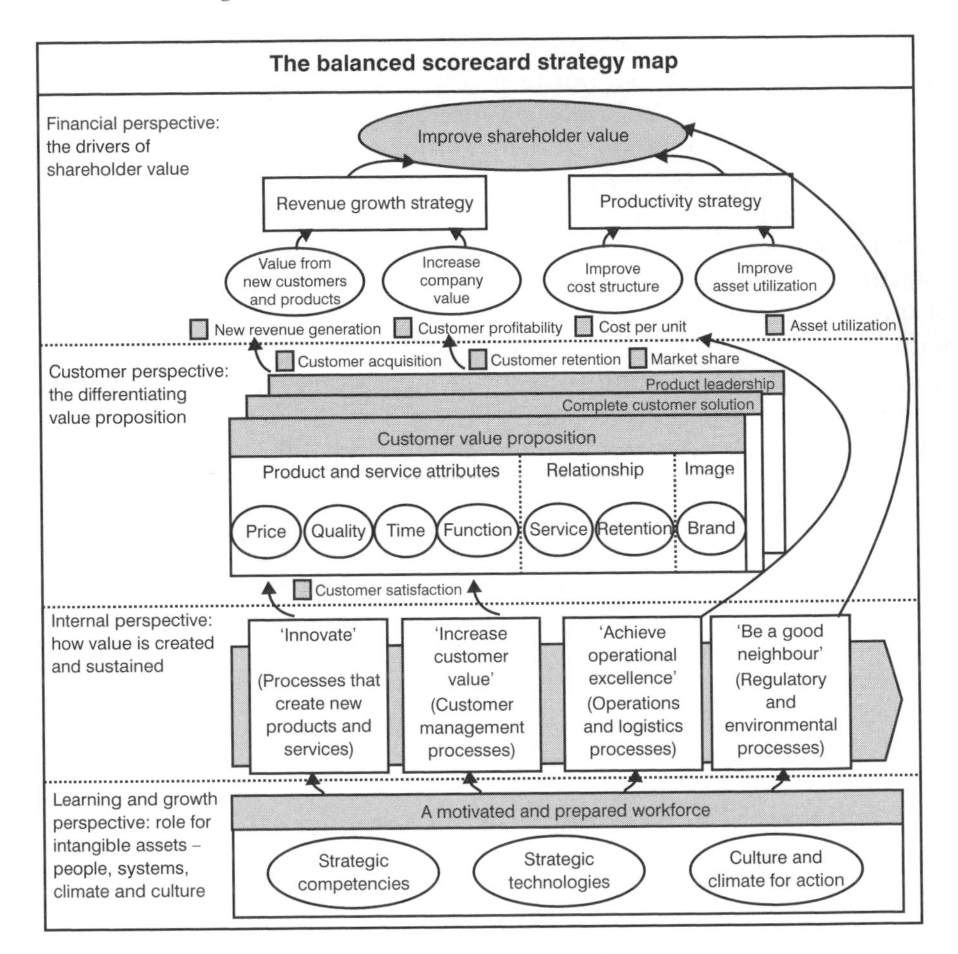

Figure 16.1 Kaplan and Norton's balanced scorecard framework

well as relationship, brand and product leadership. The internal perspective provides focus on the core competencies, processes, decisions, and actions that have the greatest impact on attaining customer satisfaction. The learning and growth perspective measures continual improvements to people, systems and processes. Sitting above this framework are the financial measures, which are essential for showing whether executives have correctly identified and constructed their measures in the three preceding areas.

Fundamentally a balanced scorecard should have a balance between output measures (financial and customer) and input measures (performance drivers, such as value proposition, internal processes, learning and growth). Every measure selected for a scorecard should be part of a link of cause-and-effect relationships, ending in financial objectives that represent a strategic theme for the business. Kaplan and Norton (1992) outline four key processes that the balanced scorecard relies on to connect short-term activities to long-term objectives:

1. *Translating the vision.* Managers are required to translate their vision into actual measurements linked directly to the people who will realize the vision.
2. *Communicating and linking.* The scorecard indicates what the organization is trying to achieve for both shareholders and customers. The high-level strategy map is translated into business unit scorecards and eventually personal scorecards so that individuals understand how their personal goals and performance support the overall strategy.
3. *Business planning.* Once the performance measures for the four perspectives have been agreed, the company identifies the key drivers of the desired outcome and defines the milestones that mark progress towards achieving their strategic goal.
4. *Feedback and learning.* This allows for regular performance reviews to enable continuous improvement of the strategy and its execution.

In summary, the scorecard puts strategy and vision, not control, at the centre. The measures are designed to pull people toward the overall vision. This methodology is consistent with the approach of supply chain management by helping managers overcome traditional functional barriers and ultimately leads to improved decision making and problem solving.

Fundamental concepts of supply chain management and measurement

There are countless definitions of logistics and supply chain management in circulation, with the two terms broadly interchangeable – but there is not a consistent view of what SCM really is or should be (Cooper, Lambert and Pagh, 1997). Generally, SCM transcends firms, functions and business – with a working definition of 'A process orientation to managing business in an integrated way that transcends the boundaries of firms and functions, leading to cooperation, through-chain business process synchronization, effective ranging and new product introduction, as well as managing the entire physical logistics agenda'.

The mechanism by which the network of entities, which together make up the supply chain, works is through shared information and closely aligned processes. The vision for these networks is that they are characterized by high levels of communication and transparency supported by synchronous operations and performance measurement and management. This brings us to:

- improved customer service experience;
- reduced inventories;
- lower operating costs; and
- improved use of fixed assets.

The ultimate benefit is improvement in a mix of profitability, shareholder value and market share – depending on the strategic priorities of the firm. The implication is that the potential of supply chain management can transform a company in terms of its performance; the leverage through the combination of many small (albeit radical in their conception) improvements in the economic structure of a company can be remarkable.

The big idea that sits behind the supply chain concept is a move from function to process; the principle is that effectiveness of the chain is enhanced dramatically by optimizing across functions and through the whole chain compared with the accumulation of optimized functions. Striking a balance between functional and total business is a crucial dimension of SCM, although breaking down the barriers between functions to improve supply chain integration is not a substitute for functional excellence. Companies need to secure both dimensions – retaining and improving their competence in all the functions in the supply chain.

Optimizing individual functional performance can prevent the achievement of the most cost- and service-effective supply chain (Braithwaite and Wilding, 2004). Not only that, but it will also most likely insert further undesirable volatility and actually increase cost. Traditional functional methods of planning will never lead to breakthrough thinking in supply chain design and, indeed, are a cause of organizational problems. So the requirement is for the corporation to measure the end-to-end cost-to-serve – at least internally, but preferably looking inside both its customers' and its suppliers' operations – to enable a fundamental rebalancing on a holistic basis that will deliver the required service at the lowest total cost (see Figure 16.2).

Performance measurement and management are a critical component of this rebalancing effort and a fundamental part of the supply chain concept. They require balance and overall goal setting. Supply chain performance measurement and management are the operational microclimate of the balanced scorecard of Kaplan and Norton.

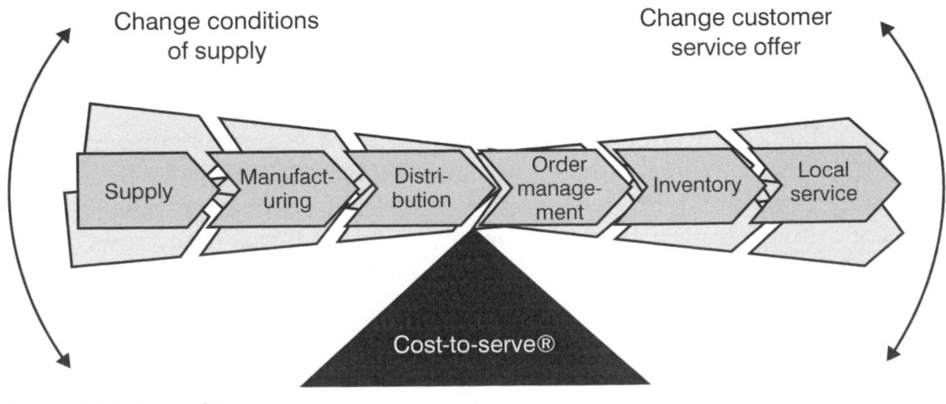

Source: LCP Consulting

Figure 16.2 Balancing the supply chain

Mastering the complexity of supply chain and logistics performance management

Supply chain management at this microclimate level is complex in its detail. The biggest challenge in setting up measurement and management programmes is mastering that complexity, to create an internally consistent framework of goals that reflect the true relationships of cause and effect.

Figure 16.3 shows a framework of cost and performance based on structural determinants and management determinants. The idea of structural and management determinants – and the distinction between them – is important. Structural determinants relate to the 'business we are in' expressed as products and customers. Here the choices for management are limited; if you are in the fertilizer or seeds business you have farmers and merchants as customers and deliver to farms. The characteristics of the product are well defined and the nature of demand is broadly local and national. In contrast, microchip manufacturers operate on an international scale using airfreight and with billions of dollars invested in plant. The fundamental difference in the products is driven home by the cost per tonne of microchips being more than $500,000, whereas the cost per tonne for fertilizer is typically less than $300.

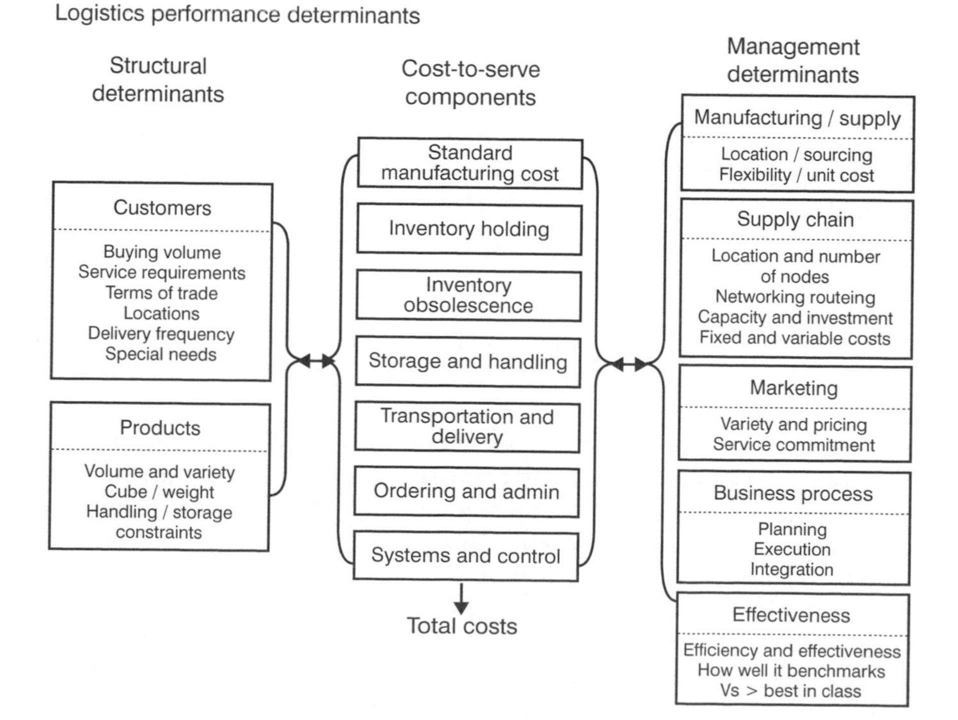

Figure 16.3 The complexity of supply chain and logistics, viewed through determinants

Management determinants reflect the areas where management has choices to make within the constraints of the nature of the business. There are big strategy decisions to be made here in relation to sourcing, capacity investment and characteristics, marketing positioning and service levels, business process design and operational effectiveness. These choices interact with each other and the structural determinants to drive the end-to-end cost and performance. The scale and degree of interaction across the various areas of cost and performance are multivariate and complex. The challenge that emerges for performance measurement and management in the supply chain is to define correctly the relationships and key drivers in the context of the choices that the company has made in its markets. From the definition of these relationships arises the precise specification of the measures to be used and the values to be set as goals for the individual functional managers.

The principle of input and output measures

The definition of cause and effect is important. The nature of the complexity illustrated in Figure 16.3 is such that the measures of effect are driven by the structure of the business and the key choices and designs that management make.

The implications of this observation are that the ultimate performance measures on which the stakeholders judge the business are not open to direct action. For example, we cannot act directly on:

- sales revenue and the economies that go with scale without dealing with the levels of customer satisfaction that are achieved in terms of inventory availability and service turnaround;
- inventory levels in the chain without dealing with processes such as forecasting accuracy and forecasting frequency and horizon, and inventory record accuracy;
- cost-to-serve by product and customer without having designed the network for sourcing and fulfilment.

These points make the distinction between input and output measures. Of course we need both to see if the actions taken have achieved the desired result. But there is limited value in just measuring the outputs without having first identified the cause-and-effect relationships, and the input measures that are likely to generate the desired change.

Figure 16.4 illustrates a simple example of input and output measures. The input measures reflect the major changes that were effected in a company, and the output measures were the consequences of these actions, and illustrate the shareholder value that was created. The strategic nature of the input measures is immediately clear, as is the improvement that was attained in this manufacturing business. All of these improvements were achieved through a long-term

Measure	Start	Finish
Input measures		
Forecast accuracy	Poor	Improved but less important
Manufacturing change time	8 hours	15 minutes
New product introduction	Months	Weeks
Logistics structure	3 depots	Single national site
Output measures		
Sales		+10%
Customer service (OTIF)	96%	99%
Stock	12 weeks	2 weeks
Obsolescence	High	Minimal
Distribution costs	14% of turnover	9% of turnover
Manufacturing unit cost		Reduced by 20%

Figure 16.4 Input and output measures in a performance improvement case

commitment to measurement, stock policy adherence and stewardship, leading to the rebalancing of the company's supply chain.

Setting goals across the chain through service level agreements

The question most often asked in relation to performance measurement is 'How should functional goals be set in the chain to secure the potential?' And there is a further series of sub-questions arising from this major question:

- How does a function see its role and contribution to improving the whole supply chain?
- What levels of visibility should be given, between functions, of the goals and attainment by others?
- How does a function influence the performance of other members in the chain that can impact its own performance but are out of its direct control?
- Who sets the measures of performance across the chain?

The idea of inter-functional service level agreements (SLAs) is designed to resolve the first three of these questions. SLAs create a framework in which the various functions within a company and between organizations – both customers and suppliers – are measured against meaningful objectives that will generate overall performance improvement.

The first big idea embedded in such SLAs is that they are not just sequential between players in the physical chain, but also recognize the obligations of every member of the team to the others, whether or not they are next in line.

The second big idea is that SLAs create a team environment; all players know their places in the side, the contribution that they make and the dependencies they have with other positions.

Figure 16.5 shows the standard conceptual framework of a sequential chain that, by this definition of SLAs, is incomplete; it also shows an example matrix of the SLAs that really need to exist. Each box in the SLA framework needs to be populated with input measures as they reflect the relationship that the functions have with each other. The entries are not symmetrical, as the obligations of the functions in the context of the overall goals are not mutual. So, for example, the relationship between sales and marketing and production planning is that sales and marketing must produce a forecast on time and to the agreed level of accuracy, while production planning's commitment to sales and marketing is to turn that forecast into available product through the creation of timely and economic schedules. Equally, manufacturing will have commitments to the business, including sales and marketing, that relate to adherence to schedule, yield and quality performance; but in return manufacturing is entitled to expect acceptable levels of demand volatility and schedule stability from sales and marketing and demand planning.

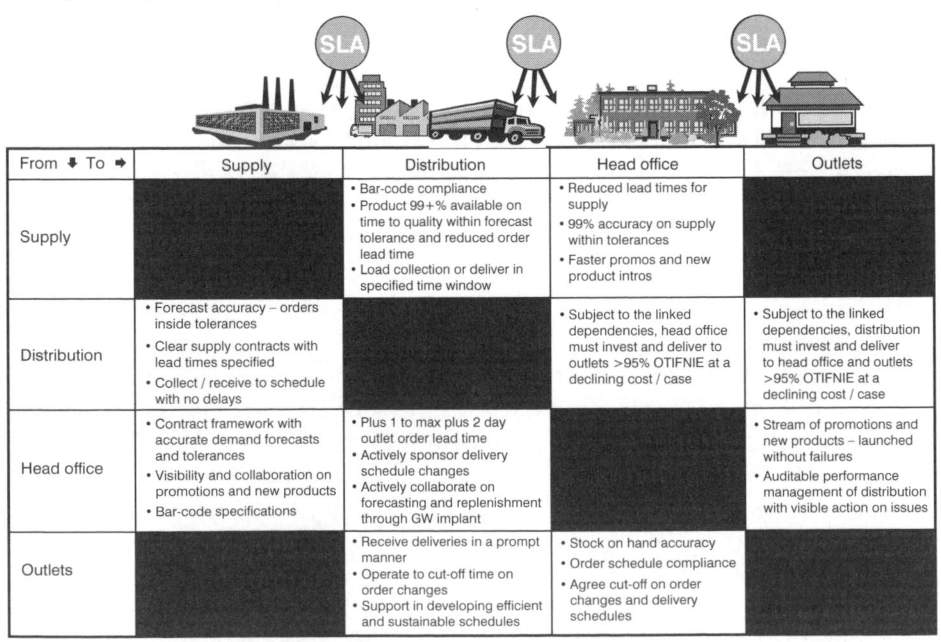

From ⬇ To ➡	Supply	Distribution	Head office	Outlets
Supply		• Bar-code compliance • Product 99+% available on time to quality within forecast tolerance and reduced order lead time • Load collection or deliver in specified time window	• Reduced lead times for supply • 99% accuracy on supply within tolerances • Faster promos and new product intros	
Distribution	• Forecast accuracy – orders inside tolerances • Clear supply contracts with lead times specified • Collect / receive to schedule with no delays		• Subject to the linked dependencies, head office must invest and deliver to outlets >95% OTIFNIE at a declining cost / case	• Subject to the linked dependencies, distribution must invest and deliver to head office and outlets >95% OTIFNIE at a declining cost / case
Head office	• Contract framework with accurate demand forecasts and tolerances • Visibility and collaboration on promotions and new products • Bar-code specifications	• Plus 1 to max plus 2 day outlet order lead time • Actively sponsor delivery schedule changes • Actively collaborate on forecasting and replenishment through GW implant		• Stream of promotions and new products – launched without failures • Auditable performance management of distribution with visible action on issues
Outlets		• Receive deliveries in a prompt manner • Operate to cut-off time on order changes • Support in developing efficient and sustainable schedules	• Stock on hand accuracy • Order schedule compliance • Agree cut-off on order changes and delivery schedules	

Figure 16.5 The conventional sequential supply chain relationship and the SLA matrix

It is important to note that the SLAs are entirely about input measures such as adherence to schedule, quality and lead time. It is changes to these measures and improvements in performance that drive value through the company's supply chain and its output measures of profit and value.

The creation of this matrix, even in the most rudimentary form, and making it available to the entire business – together with published current performance and future targets – answer the first two of the sub-questions.

The process of setting up the SLA matrix and populating the targets and the performance actually achieved is the way that the functions can start to resolve the tensions relating to the impact they may have on each other. This is a crucial organizational process – correctly represented at board level – and it is this person (or small team) that sets the matrix in conjunction with the functional heads, and then monitors attainment and institutes corrective action where necessary. This is the idea of supply chain stewardship. The steward holds the total vision for supply chain improvement for the firm and the individual functional performances that will deliver the result.

The SLA matrix needs to be maintained as a living framework that responds to external forces, actual performance and continuous learning. This is a full-time organizational role. If supply chain management also has direct functional reports, then it will need to isolate the stewardship role within its own organization to ensure that balance and impartiality are achieved.

The delivery, recovery and stewardship model

Putting the SLA matrix into action is the process and activity of tracking performance against targets and identifying opportunities for improvement, not just looking back at past performance. The focus of performance management should be the future: what do you need to be able to do and how can you do things better?

The delivery, recovery and stewardship (DRS) model is a way of institutionalizing measurement across the business. Figure 16.6 is a simple representation of the DRS model designed to illustrate the cycle of each function, measuring its delivery against its SLA in the matrix and including the cost performance goals. Reports including the identification of failures and the impact of recovery actions are produced at the functional level and then consolidated by the supply chain steward. Recovery is an important activity with the learning that comes with it. It is critically important for organizations to recognize and plan for things that go wrong. The stewardship role is to feed back to the functions the impact of overall performance and propose changes to the SLAs, delivery performance and the means of recovery.

The model is consistent with the so-called Shewhart or plan–do–check–act (PDCA) cycle, based on continuous improvement:

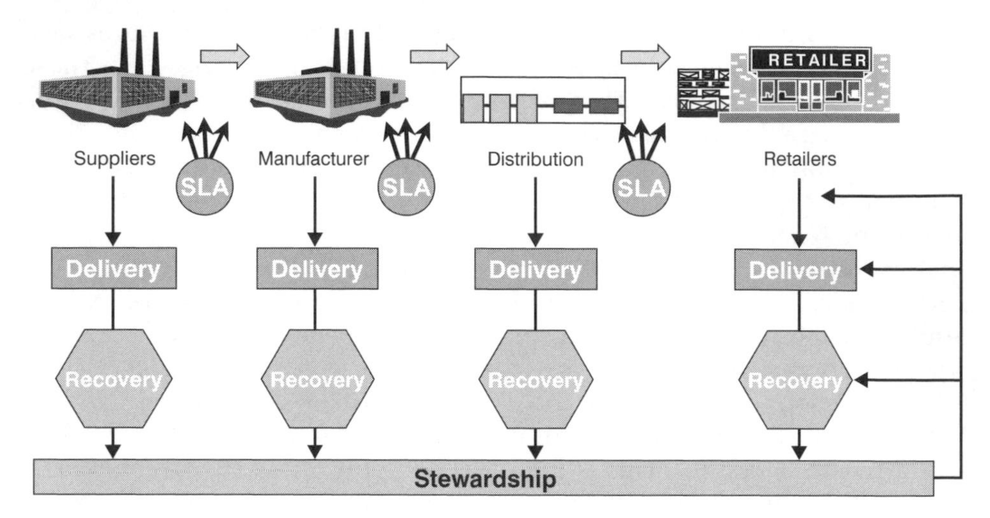

Figure 16.6 The delivery, recovery and stewardship (DRS) model

1. Business understanding and strategic directions: *plan* the process.
2. Running the operation to try to deliver in line with the plan: *do* the operation and record the results.
3. Performance reporting against plan and interpretation of results: *check* by analysis and reporting of performance according to key business drivers.
4. Tactical and strategic realignment: *act* to initiate improvement efforts based on the lessons learned from experience. These experiences feed into the new plan, since PDCA is a cyclical process.

In summary, the DRS model is a way to capture the supply chain improvement vision for the firm and to record and manage progress to its attainment. It may seem daunting and potentially complex – and if this is the case, the key is to start with the simplest possible framework and build from it as the organization learns. In other words, adopt the same principles of plan–do–check–act to the process of planning and measurement across the chain as are being applied to the chain itself.

The stewardship role as a functionally independent agent in the organization is crucial to the DRS model, and this is a difficult position to define and maintain in the organization. The person who holds the role will require vision, interpersonal skills and tenacity. The role needs the highest level of board sponsorship, and the results of DRS need to be a standard part of the board agenda. It is at this point that supply chain management and corporate strategy meet.

Defining specific metrics across the chain

The input and output measures described earlier are the high-level corporate cause-and-effect metrics for the supply chain. The measures in the SLAs are primarily about quality, compliance and time. The stewardship role requires these measures and adds cost measures to the portfolio. In this section, the specifics of the measures that can be applied across the supply chain are unpacked and described.

The supply chain and logistics professional and the corporate steward of the chain will want to develop an overview of the chain; a useful way to think about this is as a 'dashboard' or control panel for the business. This idea is illustrated in Figure 16.7, and many executives find the preparation of such diagrams valuable in identifying the performance issues in the chain and describing them to their colleagues. Measures may need to reflect both changes over time and performance across the product range of both customers and suppliers.

A further important point in relation to this overview is that, while supply chain rebalancing via SLAs will be one of the key drivers for competitive advantage, firms must also recognize that an equal and parallel emphasis should remain on attaining functional excellence. The goals of functional excellence, however, will be tempered at the margin through an understanding that such aims can lead to supply chain sub-optimization; the SLAs are developed over time to eliminate potential conflicts.

Although the measures themselves are generic for most businesses, the precise situation and issues for each firm will vary based on its competitive situation,

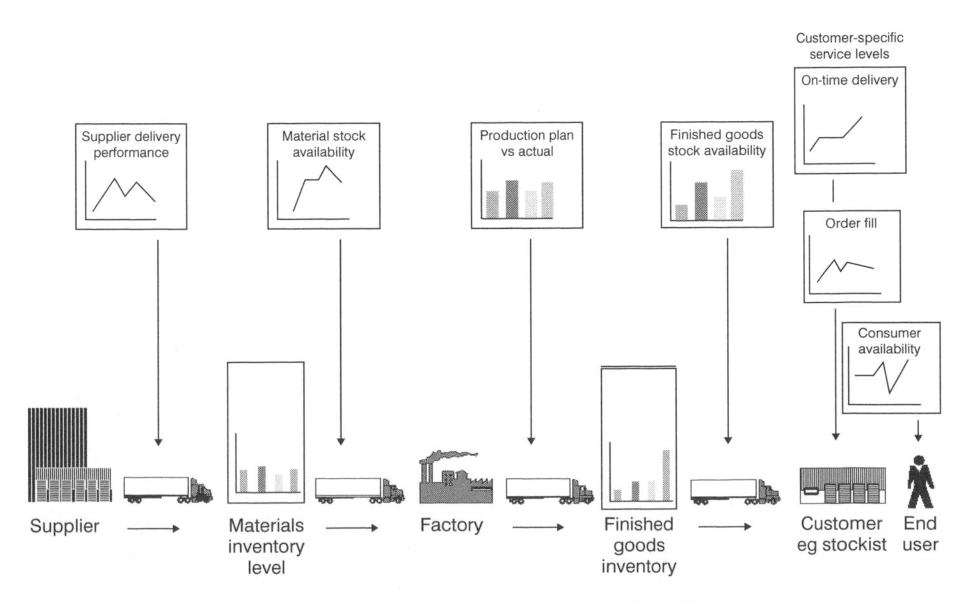

Figure 16.7 Viewing supply chain metrics across the chain

technology and product-market characteristics. It is helpful to think of a hierarchy of measures across the chain in terms of both input and output measures:

- Level 1 measures should provide headline measures for the supply chain, such as orders on time in full with no invoice errors (OTIFNIE) and stock cover set in a balanced way that supports the vision for change.
- Level 2 measures should be used to provide further insight into the results of level 1, such as quantity fill percentage, line fill percentage and invoice accuracy.
- Finally, level 3 measures should provide diagnostics for use in problem resolution and improvement processes, such as requests for credit, clear-up rate and number of days out of stock by SKU.

Figure 16.8 provides examples of level 1 and 2 performance metrics across a typical retail supply chain.

Figure 16.8 starts to provide insight into the levels of detail that are involved and can be used to challenge the connections between functions and the real drivers. So, for example, the figure shows both 'On time in full' (OTIF) and 'Order to delivery turnaround time' (TAT). It is immediately obvious that the longer the TAT, the higher should be the OTIF – since there is more time to get it right. But at the same time the longer the TAT, the lower should be the inventory, as the more time manufacturing has to respond to actual demand. TAT is therefore an input measure, and it is also one that management may want to change, as faster service is likely to be more competitive and create increased demand. In the same vein, measures of plant, distribution centre and transportation efficiency will be influenced by customer order turnaround time, forecast accuracy and plant changeover time – all of which are input measures.

Having decided on the appropriate metrics of performance, it is necessary to ensure that these individual measures are set in a balanced way to provide an overall picture of supply chain performance and support the business in moving to its goals. Figure 16.9 shows an example of a balanced set of objective measures for a fast-moving consumer goods company.

Very high service performance with low levels of stock is secured by quite high levels of forecast accuracy, very short manufacturing schedule horizons and exceptional supplier performance. High levels of accuracy are also essential, and the area sacrificed is that of distribution and freight utilization. Setting these measures consistently – having understood the relationships – is the key to avoiding functional conflicts that can cause sub-optimal performance. Examples of this are:

- Stockholding targets that are set too low will disable customer service attainment and reduce the number of orders fulfilled on time in full.
- Freight utilization and cost targets may delay shipments, leading to increased stock and a negative impact on customer service.

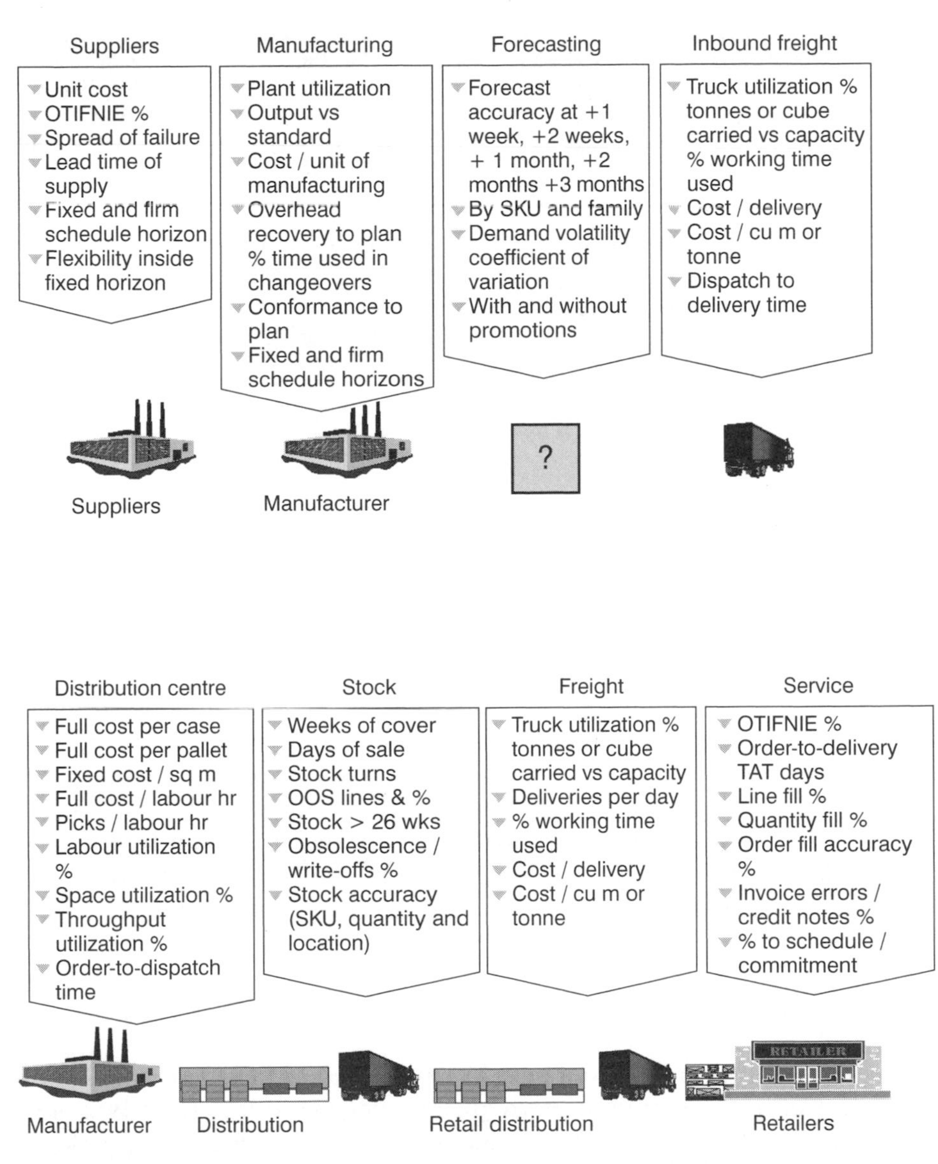

Figure 16.8 Sample level 1 and 2 metrics containing both input and output measures

- Manufacturing unit cost goals may drive up stocks and downstream distribution costs because of long production runs and infrequent line changes.

With performance metrics established, greater focus can be put on supply chain issues. This also aids in benchmarking by identifying current and best practice in companies and their supply chains before using some of the level 3 diagnostic metrics to develop an improvement programme.

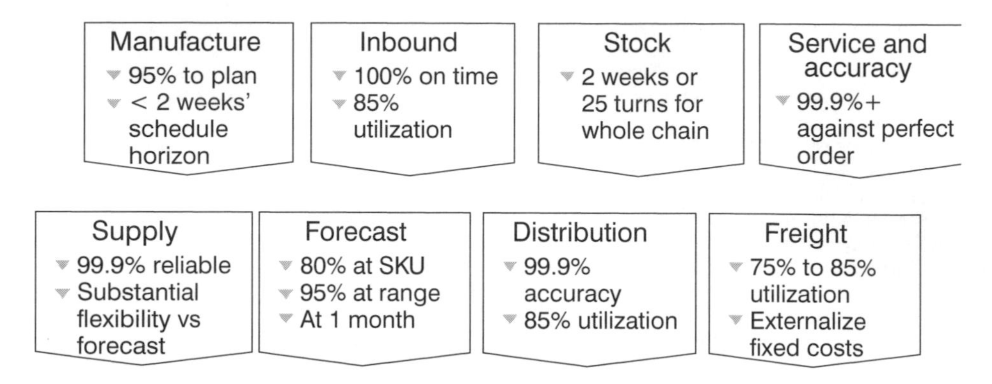

Figure 16.9 A sample logistical balanced scorecard

Two of the biggest barriers to a successful performance measurement and management programme are the compilation of data, and its analysis and interpretation. Typically this involves hundreds of thousands of transactions, many hundreds of general ledger codes, some thousands of stock-keeping units, and hundreds of customers and suppliers. All these can be linked through a number of plants and distribution centres.

Measurement and reporting used to be labour-intensive, but developments in mass data storage – often referred to as data warehousing – have provided a new platform. Changes in recent years have been revolutionary in terms of low-cost data storage, easy-to-program queries, and graphical programs to represent the outputs. Skills and experience in data warehousing are being accumulated, and new software environments are being launched to bring data together from different sources to give an end-to-end picture.

Future directions in performance measurement

The major challenges for performance measurement in the supply chain for the future rest in: 1) integrating performance management into the fabric of the organization to drive supply chain strategy development and implementation; and 2) creating predictive measurement frameworks through which the corporation can identify the levels of risk that are inherent in its supply chains. Both of these areas are 'work in progress' in terms of the development of a complete understanding and operational frameworks through which they can be applied.

The word 'integration' is overused in supply chain management, without great clarity as to its meaning and implications. The LCP strategic crystal has been used successfully to address this question by describing the elements of an integrated supply chain strategy and showing how they interact to deliver business value in terms of customer satisfaction and economic value-add. Figure 16.10 shows the crystal, with the key elements:

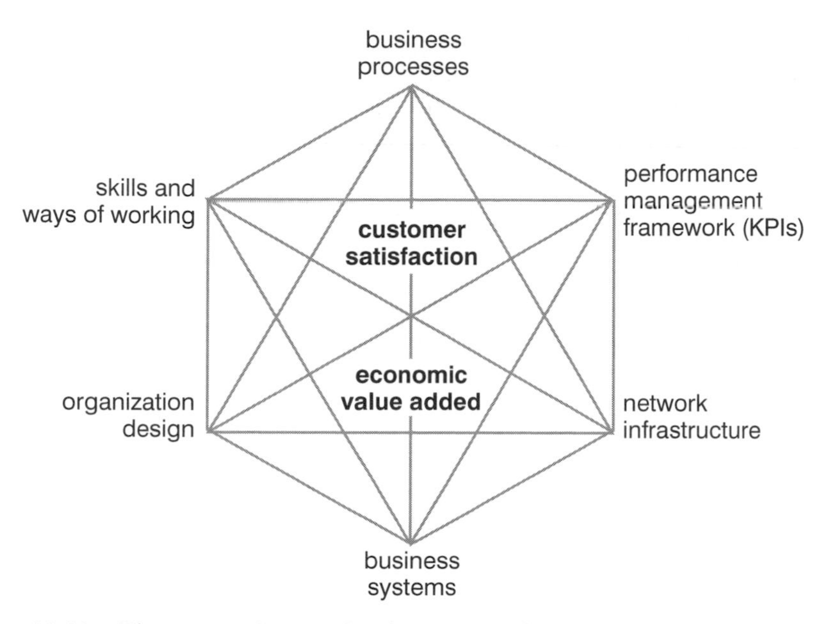

Figure 16.10 The strategic supply chain crystal

- Business processes – the processes of generating planning and execution instructions through the chain that, if correctly designed, will increase customer service and reduce inventories and capital applied. Business process redesign in supply chain management is focused on the principles of time compression and simplification. Business processes are crucially dependent on systems, organization and KPIs, three other points in the crystal. Business processes are key input measures and a major part of the SLAs.
- Business systems – the computer information systems that are applied must serve the business processes and the organization, support the network and inform the performance measurement environment.
- Network infrastucture – the supply chain network is the key to the cost performance in the chain and is enabled by the processes and systems. The organization design must align to the network to enable the lowest-cost operation.
- Performance management framework through consistent and appropriate KPIs is central to an effective supply chain strategy, as we have seen in this chapter. The process of performance management enables the organization and is dependent on the systems and the processes.
- Organization design is a most under-represented area of supply chain strategy. An organization that is aligned to the strategy and is served by the systems, processes and KPIs is central to realizing supply chain value. As businesses move from a functional to a process orientation, the boundaries of traditional functional power are challenged and tensions are exposed. The SLA approach can help resolve these tensions since functional control

is not required under that model. However, the stewardship role is mandatory and, as discussed earlier, it must be positioned in the organization with both power and independence.

- Skills and ways of working are the final facet of the crystal and, like organization, are under-represented. The skills and behaviours to move to a supply chain ethic, from function to process, are profoundly different from those that have been trained into management over many years.

Another major challenge in performance management is for boards to recognize the risk that is endemic in their supply chains. Singhal and Hendricks (2000) have shown that supply chain catastrophes are common and that they destroy shareholder value by an average 20 per cent. With companies' supply chains being run ever more leanly, there is less room for unexpected errors. The requirement exists to evaluate the risk in a corporation's supply; Figure 16.11 shows a conceptual model (Braithwaite, 2003).

The underlying principle is that there are external determinants of risk that relate to the business environment, and there are internal determinants that relate to how the organization is aligned to its external environment. As an example of how this model works, it should be immediately clear that a company with a volatile market and supplies on long lead times with extended planning, scheduling and manufacturing processes and a poor record of performance management is riding for a fall. In contrast, a company operating in a market where demand is stable and competition well defined can accommodate longer lead times from suppliers and more rigid internal processes.

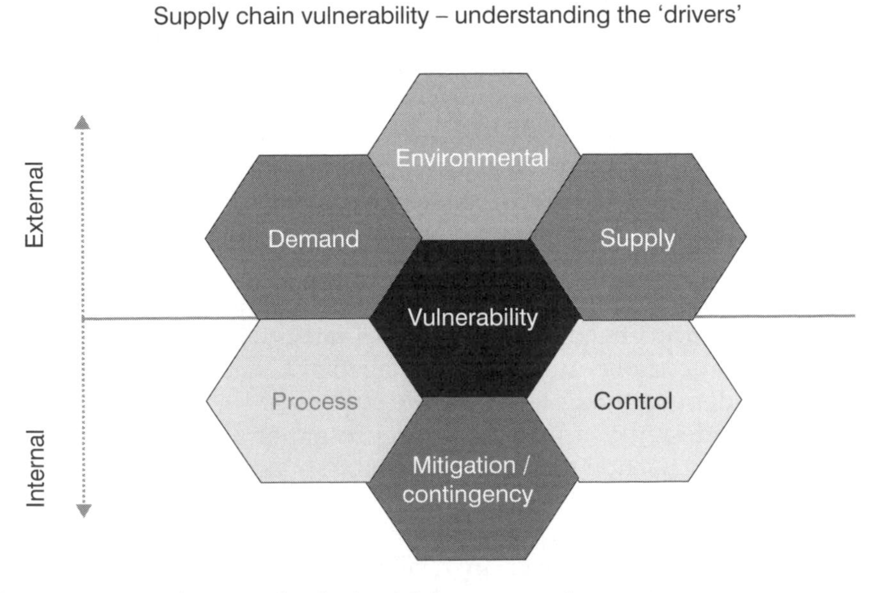

Figure 16.11 The supply chain risk honeycomb

Risks external to the corporation can be summarized as follows:

- *Demand risk* relates to disturbances to the flow of product, information and cash emanating from within the network, between the focal firm and its market. In particular, it relates to the processes, controls, asset and infrastructure dependencies of the organizations downstream.
- *Supply risk* is the upstream equivalent of demand risk; it relates to disturbances to the flow of product or information emanating within the network upstream of the focal firm.
- *Environmental risk* is the risk associated with external and, from the firm's perspective, uncontrollable events.

Risks internal to the corporation relate both to how the firm addresses the external risks and to its competences to plan and execute its own business:

- *Processes* are the sequences of value-adding activities undertaken by the firm. The execution of these processes is dependent on internally owned or managed assets and on a functioning infrastructure. Process risk relates to disruptions to these processes.
- *Controls* are the assumptions, rules, systems and procedures that govern how an organization exerts control over the processes – and in the supply chain they may be order quantities, batch sizes, safety stock policies, etc. Control risk is the risk arising from the application or misapplication of these rules.
- *Mitigation* is a hedge against risk built into the operations and, therefore, the lack of mitigating tactics is a risk in itself. *Contingency* is the existence of a prepared plan in the event of a risk being identified.

Conclusion

The potential for improvement through the development of performance management metrics across the supply chain is a key differentiator of change capability and organizational agility. Firms that develop supply chain measurement, as a core business competence associated with strategic objectives, will have a strong foundation for defining realignment internally and with both customers and suppliers.

The combined use of supply chain performance metrics, balanced scorecards, and the delivery, recovery and stewardship framework provides the capability to report on improvement, understand the factors that are driven by the change and identify supply chain management best practice.

There are six key points to hold in focus when developing a supply chain performance management framework:

- No single measure defines supply chain performance – there are many dimensions to measure.
- Measures can be in conflict – accentuating rather than breaking functional differences.
- The need is to obtain balance throughout the supply chain and be prepared to change.
- Measuring the overall performance at input and output levels is a key first step to making improvements.
- This requires considerable investment of time and commitment.
- Measurement and its interpretation are valuable and difficult skills that organizations should develop and nurture.

Organizations that have persevered with supply chain measurement and management have experienced sustained improvements in business performance.

References

Braithwaite, A (2003) Supply chain vulnerability self-assessment workbook, Cranfield School of Management on behalf of the Department for Transport, March, pp 249–59

Braithwaite, A and Wilding, R (2004) Laws of logistics and supply chain management, in *The Financial Times Handbook of Management*, 3rd edn, ed E Crainer and D Dearlove, Pearson, London

Cooper, MC, Lambert, DM and Pagh, JD (1997) Supply chain management: more than a new name for logistics, *International Journal of Logistics Management*, **8** (1), pp 1–4

European Foundation of Quality Management (EFQM) (2006) *European Quality Awards*, EFQM, wwwefqm.org

Isixsigma (2006a) *The Deming Prize Check List*, www.isixsigma.com

Isixsigma (2006b) *Malcolm Baldrige National Quality Award*, www.isixsigma.com

Kaplan, RS and Norton, DP (1992) The balanced scorecard: measures that drive performance, *Harvard Business Review*, January–February 70(1), pp 71–79

Kaplan, RS and Norton, DP (1996) *Translating Strategy into Action: The balanced scorecard*, Harvard Business School Press, Cambridge, MA

Senge, PM (1990) *The Fifth Discipline*, Doubleday, New York

Singhal, VR and Hendricks, K (2000) *Report on Supply Chain Glitches and Shareholder Value Destruction*, December, Dupree College of Management, Georgia Institute of Technology

Snowden, D (2000) *Liberating Knowledge*, Institute of Knowledge Management, Toronto

17

Road transport optimization

Alan McKinnon, Heriot-Watt University

In an ideal world all trucks would run fully laden on every kilometre travelled. If this could be achieved the economic and environmental costs of road freight movement would be substantially reduced. Large potential benefits can therefore accrue to individual companies and the wider community from initiatives that improve the utilization of vehicle capacity.

In this chapter we will examine the various ways in which vehicle utilization can be assessed, consider the reasons why so many trucks run empty or only partially loaded and outline a series of measures that companies can take to attain higher levels of vehicle fill.

Assessing the utilization of vehicle fleets

Different indices can be used to measure the utilization of vehicle fleets, each giving a different impression of transport efficiency.

Tonne-kilometres per vehicle per annum

This index generally presents the trucking industry in a positive light. It is essentially a productivity indicator, measuring the average amount of work done annually by trucks. In the UK, for instance, it increased fivefold between the early 1950s and late 1990s, mainly as a result of companies taking advantage of increases in maximum truck weight and running their vehicles for more hours of the day (see Figure 17.1). This productivity measure, however, takes no account of the proportion of the available carrying capacity actually used during the year. A vehicle with greater capacity could record higher productivity despite having inferior utilization (see Table 17.1). This important difference between productivity and utilization is discussed in detail by Caplice and Sheffi (1994).

Weight-based loading factor

This is generally expressed as the ratio of the actual weight of goods carried to the maximum weight that could have been carried on a laden trip. When this ratio is plotted through time, a less rosy picture emerges of transport efficiency. In the UK, for example, average load factors (for trucks with gross weights over 3.5 tonnes) declined from 63 per cent in 1990 to 57 per cent in 2004. This load factor is only a partial measure of vehicle utilization, however. As it is an exclusively weight-based measure it takes no account of the use of vehicle space/deck area or the proportion of vehicle-kilometres run empty.

Space utilization

Many low-density products fill the available vehicle space (or 'cube out') long before the maximum permitted weight is reached. In sectors characterized by

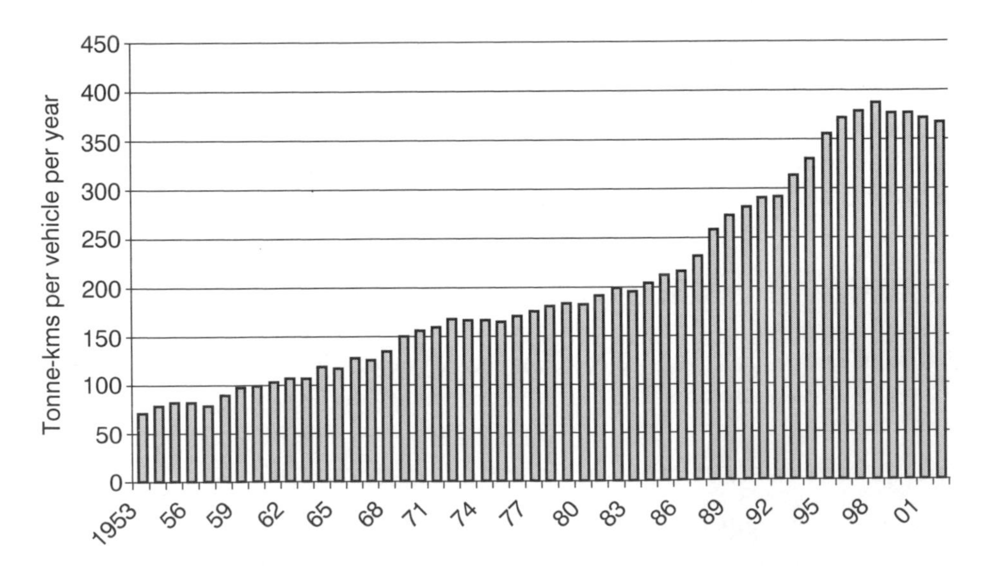

Source: Department for Transport, 2005b

Figure 17.1 Increase in truck productivity in the UK 1953–2003

Table 17.1 Comparison of vehicle productivity and utilization measures

Gross weight	Max payload (tonnes)	Annual distance travelled	Average load (tonnes)	Productivity (tonne-kms/ vehicle/year)	Capacity kms/utilization (actual tonne-km/max tonne-km
32 tonnes	20	100,000	16	1,600,000	80%
40 tonnes	26	100,000	18	1,800,000	69%

low-density products, weight-based load factors tend to underestimate the true level of utilization. Where there are tight limits on the stacking height of the product, loading is usually constrained much more by the available deck area than by the cubic capacity. This deck area, for example, can be covered with pallets stacked to a height of 1.5 metres, leaving a metre or more of wasted space above them.

Very little research has been done on the space utilization of vehicles, and few attempts made to collect volumetric data on road freight flows. In a study conducted in the Netherlands and Sweden, Samuelsson and Tilanus (1997) asked a panel of industry experts to estimate the average utilization of trucks, engaged in less-than-truckload deliveries, with reference to a series of space-related indices. This revealed that cube utilization was typically very low at around 28 per cent. On average, however, just over 80 per cent of deck area was occupied and 70 per cent of the available pallet positions filled. It was therefore mainly in the vertical dimension that space was being wasted, with average load heights reaching only 47 per cent of the maximum. A survey of 53 fleets, comprising roughly 3,500 vehicles, in the UK food supply chain in 2002 found that, on loaded trips, an average of 69 per cent of the deck area and 76 per cent of the available height was utilized, corresponding to a mean cube utilization of 52 per cent (McKinnon and Ge, 2004).

Empty running

The most obvious form of vehicle underutilization is empty running. Typically around a third of vehicle-kilometres are run empty, though this proportion varies with length of haul, type of vehicle, industrial sector and the nature of the delivery operation (McKinnon, 1996). Empty running generally occurs when operators are unable to find a return load. Unlike passengers, who usually return to their starting point, most freight only travels in one direction. In some countries, such as the UK, the proportion of truck-kilometres travelled empty has been declining. In Britain, for example, it fell from 33 per cent in 1980 to 27 per cent in 2004, yielding significant economic and environmental benefits. Other things being equal, if the empty running percentage had remained at its 1980 level, road haulage costs in 2004 would have been £1.2 billion higher and an extra 1 million tonnes of carbon dioxide would have been emitted by trucks (McKinnon, 2005).

Factors constraining vehicle utilization

The dominant constraints on vehicle utilization are as follows:

- *Demand fluctuations.* Variability of demand over daily, weekly, monthly and seasonal cycles is one of the main causes of the underutilization of vehicle capacity. Vehicles that are acquired with sufficient space or weight to accommodate peak loads inevitably spend much of their time running with excess capacity. Companies subject mainly to seasonal fluctuations can hire additional vehicles or outsource more of their transport at peak periods, allowing them to carry a regular base-load of traffic on their own vehicles during the year. For those exposed to demand volatility on a daily basis, the efficient management of transport capacity presents a much greater challenge. Figure 17.2, for example, shows fluctuations in the daily demand for trucks imposed on a major distributor of steel products over the period of a month. The average daily requirement was for 150 vehicles, but on particular days it varied between 96 and 190 vehicles. The company in question was often only informed at 4 pm on day 1 how many vehicles would be required for deliveries by noon on day 2. It is clearly very

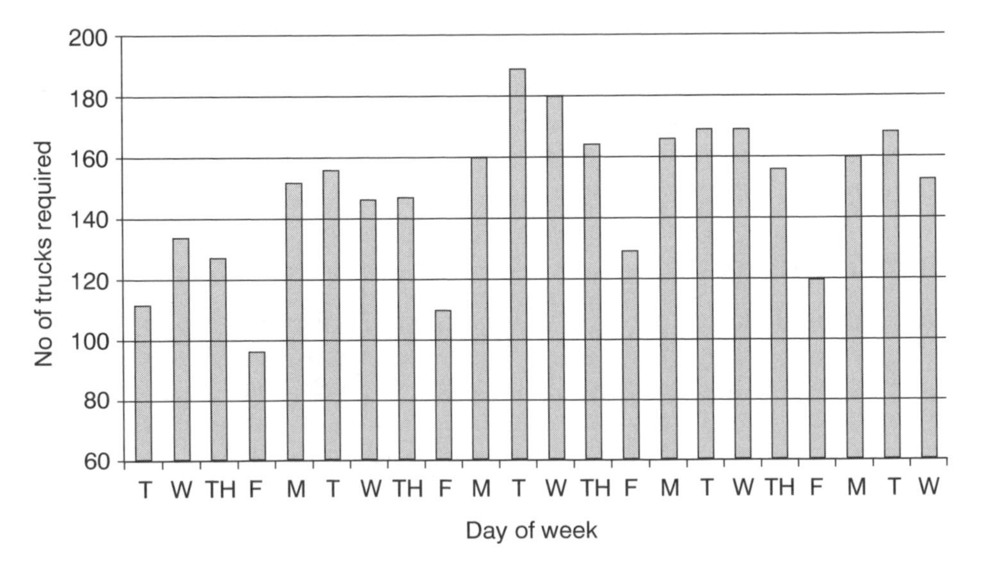

Figure 17.2 Variations in daily demand for trucks from a major steel distributor

difficult to maintain high load factors across a vehicle fleet subject to this degree of demand variability. Such variability is common in industries characterized by just-in-time replenishment.

- *Just-in-time (JIT) delivery.* The replenishment of supplies in smaller quantities more frequently within shorter lead times has tended to depress vehicle load factors. Companies have often been prepared to accept lower vehicle utilization and higher transport costs in return for large reductions in inventory and other productivity benefits resulting from JIT. There is, nevertheless, disagreement in the literature over the extent to which JIT has impaired transport efficiency. Simulation modelling work by Swenseth and Buffa (1990), for example, suggested that transport costs were inflated by JIT, whereas Ansari and Heckel (1987) claim that, in practice, they were reduced. By reconfiguring their inbound logistics, companies can mitigate the adverse effects of JIT on transport efficiency as illustrated by the Nissan car company (Energy Efficiency Best Practice Programme, 1998a).
- *Unreliability of delivery schedules.* Where schedules are unreliable, transport managers are naturally reluctant to arrange backhauls or more complex collection and delivery routes within which higher degrees of load consolidation can be achieved. Companies understandably prioritize outbound distribution to customers and fear that a vehicle engaged in backhauling may not be repositioned in time to handle the next delivery. Available survey evidence suggests that the probability of a delivery being delayed can be relatively high. The 2002 transport KPI survey in the UK food supply chain, for instance, found that roughly 29 per cent of the 15,600 journey legs monitored were subject to a delay and that these delays averaged 45 minutes (McKinnon and Ge, 2004). Just under a third of these delays were caused mainly by traffic congestion on the road network. Most of the delays, however, occurred at the reception bays of factories, distribution centres (DCs) and shops, where 'back-door congestion' increases the average length and variability of loading and off-loading times. In other countries characterized by much longer journey length and transit times, delays of this magnitude would be unlikely to deter back-loading and consolidation initiatives, particularly as the potential rewards would be much greater.
- *Vehicle size and weight restrictions.* As noted above, some loads reach the maximum weight limit before all the space in the vehicle is occupied. Conversely, some low-density loads exhaust the available space before the legal weight limit is reached. This results in underutilization of the vehicle in terms of either volume or weight.
- *Handling requirements.* Many companies sacrifice vehicle utilization for handling efficiency. For example, by using roll-cages rather than wooden pallets supermarket chains can substantially reduce handling times and costs but at the expense of around 15–20 per cent lower space utilization in shop delivery vehicles.

- *Incompatibility of vehicles and products.* It is clearly not possible to transport a return load of bulk liquids in a box van or to consolidate part-loads of fertilizer and hanging garments. The need for specialist handling and/or refrigeration and rules governing cross-contamination restrict the proportion of the truck fleet that can be used for particular loads.
- *Health and safety regulations.* The weight and dimensions of loads are partly constrained by health and safety regulations designed to ensure the welfare of employees.
- *Capacity constraints at company premises.* Often the size of load is constrained by the available storage capacity at either the origin or the destination of the trip – more commonly the latter. Tanks and silos at farms or factories, for example, may not be able to hold a full truckload, while many retailers have compressed back-storeroom areas to maximize the front-of-shop sales floor. Warehouse racking systems, particularly in the fast-moving consumer goods (FMCG) sector, have a standard slot height for pallets of 1.6 metres. This limits pallets to a height significantly below the vertical clearance of at least 2.4 metres in most articulated trucks.
- *Lack of knowledge of backloading and load consolidation opportunities.* Many of these opportunities are missed because carriers are simply unaware of them. It is hardly surprising, therefore, that roughly half the return loads carried by road in the UK are generated internally from within the same company (Lex Transfleet, 2002). Companies have traditionally relied on informal methods of finding external backloads, most commonly word of mouth.
- *Poor coordination of the purchasing, sales and logistics functions.* Opportunities for backloading are seldom discussed in the context of trade negotiations between companies. Purchasing departments typically regard inbound delivery as the responsibility of the supplier and fail to explore with logistics managers possible synergies with the transport operations of vendor companies. Sales staff, on the other hand, have a habit of making delivery commitments to customers that entail transporting part-loads often at short notice.

These constraints relate to five general factors: regulatory, market-related, inter-functional, infrastructural and equipment-related. Figure 17.3 maps the links between the constraints and the five factors, recognizing that the same factor can inhibit vehicle utilization in different ways. Physical infrastructure, for example, can affect reliability, the maximum size and weight of the vehicle and storage capacity at the delivery point. Figure 17.3's network diagram illustrates the underlying complexity of the problem.

One of the most pervasive and influential factors is the inter-functional relationship between transport and other activities such as production, procurement, inventory management, warehousing and sales. Companies often quite rationally give these other activities priority over transport

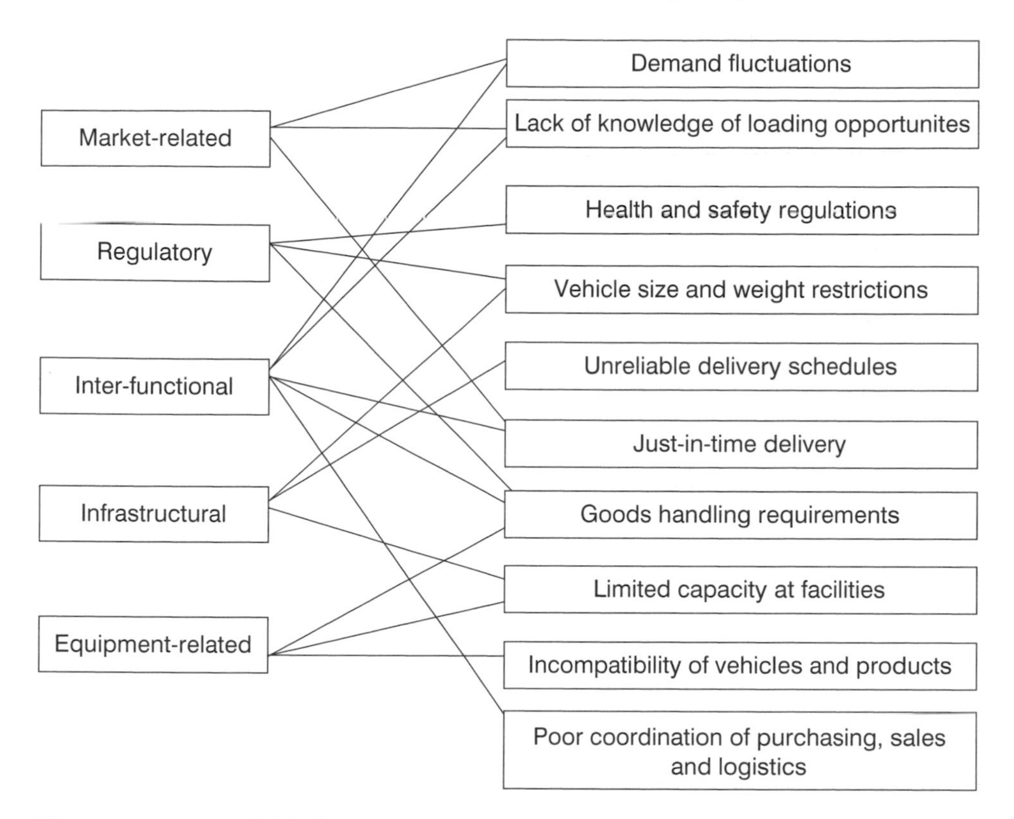

Figure 17.3 Fivefold classification of the constraints on vehicle utilization

efficiency. For example, inventory savings from JIT replenishment or reductions in handling costs accruing from the use of roll-cages may exceed the additional cost of running a truck only part-loaded. It can also be economically justifiable to deliver small orders to important customers in an effort to secure their longer-term loyalty.

Much underutilization of vehicle capacity, however, is not based on careful analysis of logistical cost trade-offs and explicit calculations of any related sales benefits. It is often unplanned and reflects the relatively low status given to transport within corporate hierarchies dominated by production, marketing and sales. The most that a logistics manager can do is to optimize transport within the targets and constraints set by other departments (McKinnon, 2003). This may not be in the best interests of the company, however. It would be preferable if the cost of reduced vehicle utilization were objectively weighed against the benefits from the other activities that regularly impair transport efficiency.

Measures to improve vehicle utilization

This section reviews a series of measures that companies can adopt, individually and in combination, to make better use of vehicle capacity.

Increase return loading

There are several ways in which companies can increase the level of backloading:

- *Logistical initiatives.* There have been numerous examples in recent years of companies introducing initiatives to increase backloading. For example, Britain's largest supermarket chain, Tesco, has implemented 'supplier collection' and 'onward delivery' schemes. In the case of supplier collection, a returning shop delivery vehicle collects goods from a supplier's factory and carries them to the retailer's distribution centre. Onward delivery occurs where a supplier's vehicle offloads goods at the retailer's distribution centre and backloads with supplies destined for one of the retailer's shops. This is delivered on the way back to the factory, usually with minimal deviation from the direct route. Tesco estimated that, over a five-year period, these schemes saved around 4.8 million truck-kilometres (Energy Efficiency Best Practice Programme, 1998b). The company has since assumed control of most of the primary distribution of supplies from factories to distribution centres by establishing 'factory gate pricing' arrangements with suppliers. This has enabled it to increase the proportion of inbound supplies collected on a backload basis (Potter *et al*, 2004).
- *Use of freight procurement services.* Load matching agencies have existed for several decades, providing road hauliers with a 'clearing house' service for potential backloads. They relied on market knowledge, personal networking and the telephone to broker deals between shippers and carriers. With the advent of the internet, a new generation of freight exchanges has emerged, providing web-enabled tendering, online auctions and bulletin boards for road haulage services (Lewis, 2002). This is making it easier to match loads with available vehicle capacity across much larger 'communities' of shippers and carriers on both a short- and a medium-term basis. Freight exchange websites contain case studies of clients that have achieved significant reductions in empty running (eg www.freighttraders.co.uk and www.teleroute.co.uk). To date, however, there has been no systematic assessment of their net effect on empty running.
- *Installation of vehicle tracking systems.* Advances in IT and telematics are facilitating the backloading of trucks (Department for Transport, 2003). They allow vehicle schedules and routes to be replanned in real time while the vehicle is on the road. Operators are then able to exploit backloading and load consolidation opportunities that arise at short notice. Also, by

making transport operations more 'visible', telematics can give both shippers and carriers greater confidence in delivery schedules, helping to overcome one of the traditional obstacles to backloading.

- *Reverse logistics.* An increasing proportion of products is travelling back along the supply chain for repair, reuse, recycling or remanufacture. The growth in the recovery of waste packaging and life-expired product is partly the result of government regulations and directives. This is creating new opportunities for backloading in some industrial and retail sectors (Anderson, Browne and Allen, 1999).

Statistical evidence that around 30 per cent of truck-kilometres are run empty can give the impression that there is huge inefficiency in road haulage and enormous potential for increasing backloading. A retrospective analysis of just under 9,000 road deliveries in the British food supply chain over a period of 48 hours, however, revealed relatively few opportunities for backloading after allowance was made for a series of operational constraints (McKinnon and Ge, 2006). It may not be possible to extrapolate this result to other sectors and countries, though it does cast doubt on claims that empty running can be drastically reduced.

Maximize the available carrying capacity

Very few loads simultaneously reach vehicle weight and volume limits. Most fill out the vehicle space before the weight limit is reached or vice versa. Increasing the weight limit or the physical dimensions of the vehicle can, therefore, result in greater consolidation of loads:

- *Maximum vehicle weight.* Within the EU, trucks engaged in cross-border transport have a weight limit of 40 tonnes. For domestic road haulage within member states, weight limits vary from 40 to 60 tonnes. In 2001, the UK government decided to increase the maximum weight of a six-axle truck from 41 to 44 tonnes, following a study that suggested that the resulting consolidation of loads in heavier vehicles could benefit both the economy and the environment. An impact study conducted three years after the implementation of this measure confirmed that significant savings in vehicle-kilometres, cost and emissions have been achieved, with the greatest benefits enjoyed by industrial sectors producing and distributing dense products, such as coal, drinks, petroleum products and timber (McKinnon, 2005). Over the past 25 years a series of major studies of truck size and weight limits has been conducted in the United States (Transportation Research Board, 2002). These have tried to determine the optimum size and weight, taking account of vehicle operating costs, infrastructural requirements, road safety issues, the effect on general traffic flow and a range of other factors.

- *Vehicle size and design.* It is generally acknowledged that the average density and 'stackability' of freight are declining. The box at the end of this section lists the major reasons for these trends. This is partly reflected in the increasing use of taller 9-foot 6-inch containers in deep-sea container operations and of drawbar-trailer combinations in European road haulage. Truck dimensions are constrained by the geometry of road layouts, bridge heights and loading bays and by the height of bridges and tunnels. Where the transport infrastructure permits an increase in vehicle height, the insertion of an extra deck can allow firms to make more effective use of vehicle space. In the UK, where most roads have height clearances of 5 metres (mainly to accommodate double-deck buses), there are several thousand high-cube trailers, most of which have a second deck (McKinnon and Campbell, 1997). One major UK retailer demonstrated the benefits of double-decking by comparing operating parameters for deliveries using a double-deck vehicle and two single-deck vehicles with similar capacity. Unit delivery costs, vehicle-kilometres and carbon dioxide emissions were all around 48 per cent lower (Department for Transport, 2005a).

Vehicles can be redesigned in other ways to permit greater load consolidation. The compartmentalization of trucks has enabled grocery retailers and their contractors to combine the movement of products at different temperatures on a single journey. This form of 'composite distribution', for example, enabled the UK retailer Safeway to reduce the average number of vehicle trips required to deliver 1,000 cases from five in 1985 to one in 1995 (FTA, 1995).

It is also possible to increase the maximum carrying capacity of a truck within legal restrictions on gross weight, by reducing the weight of the empty vehicle (or 'tare' weight). Use of lighter materials and fittings can substantially cut the tare weight. For example, a survey of trucking operations in Germany revealed that the average empty weight of trucks with a maximum 40-tonne gross weight was 14 tonnes, but the minimum only 11 tonnes (Leonardi and Baumgartner, 2004). The main performance indicator used in this study, the 'efficiency of vehicle usage' (E), made allowance for differences in the vehicle tare weights:

$$E = \text{tonne-kilometres} / (\text{vehicle tare weight} + \text{load weight}) \times \text{distance travelled}$$

If the lightest truck were used and fully laden, a theoretically optimal E value of 0.725 could be achieved. The best-practice operator in the survey had an average E value of 0.56, while across the entire sample the mean value was only 0.36. There was therefore considerable scope for efficiency improvement, with much of the potential gain coming from the use of lighter vehicles.

Reasons for the declining density and 'stackability' of road freight

- *Change in the nature of the products.* Many consumer products have become lighter through time, as plastic and other synthetic materials have increasingly replaced metal, wood and leather.
- *Increase in packaging.* As packaging is relatively light, increases in the ratio of packaging volume to product volume reduce the average density of freight consignments.
- *Greater use of unitized handling equipment.* This handling equipment takes up space in the vehicle and reduces the average weight/volume ratio for the overall payload.
- *Declining rigidity.* In some sectors the increasing fragility of the product and weakening of packaging material are limiting the height to which it can be stacked. In the food and drink industry, for instance, cans have become thinner, and rigid cardboard, plastic or even wooden boxes been replaced by cardboard trays, which offer little vertical support.
- *Order picking of palletized loads at an earlier stage in the supply chain.* The mixed pallet-loads that this produces tend to be lower, have an irregular profile and offer less opportunity for stacking.
- *Tightening health and safety regulations.* These regulations have restricted the height to which pallets can be stacked to minimize the risk of injury to operatives during loading and unloading.

Use more space-efficient handling systems and packaging

The efficiency with which the cubic capacity of a vehicle is used partly depends on the nature of the packaging and handling equipment. Companies must reconcile the desire to maximize vehicle fill with the need to protect products from damage in transit and to minimize handling costs. The following examples illustrate the effects that handling and packaging changes can have on the transport operation:

- *Choice of loading method.* A large mail-order company managed to improve vehicle cube utilization and cut vehicle-kilometres by 6 per cent by loading parcels loose rather than in bags.
- *Pallet dimensions.* It has been estimated that standardizing on a more efficient size and shape of pallet in the European grocery supply chain could cut transport costs by the equivalent of 0.25 per cent of sales revenue (AT Kearney, 1997).
- *Stacking height.* It was estimated in 1997 that if pallet-loads made full use of the 'vehicle inner heights', the European grocery distribution system

would have required 15 per cent fewer trucks (AT Kearney, 1997). Often the maximum height of these loads, however, is constrained by the slot height in warehouse racking systems (typically 1.7 metres), while articulated trailers commonly have internal heights of 2.4 metres.

- *Modular loads.* A French food manufacturer was able to improve vehicle fill by 35–41 per cent by packing orders into modules of varying heights (University of St Gallen, 2000).
- *Shape and dimensions of product packaging.* If cans of food were square, rather than round, space utilization in vehicles, warehouses and shop shelves could be raised by 20 per cent (Buckley and Hoyle, 2005).

Employ computer-based planning tools

A wide range of software tools is available to help companies optimize the use of vehicle capacity. Over the past quarter-century, computerized vehicle routeing and scheduling (CVRS) software has vastly improved in terms of functionality, flexibility, applicability, user-friendliness and the efficiency of the solutions it yields. While the quality of the product has dramatically improved, the real cost of the software and associated hardware has sharply declined. CVRS helps companies to optimize the use of vehicle assets with respect to various metrics, including distance travelled, driving time, vehicle loading and cost. It is difficult to estimate the average gain in transport efficiency from the use of CVRS, as this depends on the complexity and variability of the delivery operation and the performance attained by the previous system of manual route and load planning. Transport cost savings of 10–15 per cent are not atypical, however (Department for Transport, 2003).

Over the past six to eight years, a new generation of higher-level modelling tools has been developed to optimize freight transport networks (rather than the multiple-drop delivery rounds to which CVRS packages are normally applied). Particular demand for such packages has come from large retailers that have integrated their systems of primary (factory to DC) and secondary (DC to shop) distribution and are trying to maximize truck utilization across the entire network. This has presented a formidable analytical challenge. Currently available packages perform reasonably well, though the development of new software tools incorporating genetic algorithms should yield even more efficient solutions.

Adopt more transport-efficient order cycles

The nature of the order-fulfilment process can have a significant impact on the efficiency of the transport operation. There are ways in which this process can be modified to allow firms to increase the degree of load consolidation and hence improve transport efficiency:

- *Nominated day delivery system (NDDS).* Firms operating this system achieve much higher levels of transport efficiency by encouraging customers to adhere to an ordering and delivery timetable. Customers are informed that a vehicle will be visiting their area on a 'nominated' day and that, to receive a delivery on that day, they must submit their order a certain period in advance. The advertised order lead time is thus conditional on the customer complying with the order schedule. By concentrating deliveries in particular areas on particular days, suppliers can achieve higher levels of load consolidation, drop density and vehicle utilization. Some sales managers oppose this system, however, on the grounds that it will weaken their company's competitive position and probably result in sales losses in excess of the transport cost savings. The experience of many of the businesses that have applied NDDS contradicts this view.
- *Abandoning the monthly payment cycle.* Many companies invoice their customers at the end of each month, giving them an incentive to order at the start of the month and thereby obtain a longer period of interest-free credit. This can induce wide monthly fluctuations in freight traffic levels, making it difficult for firms to manage their vehicle capacity efficiently. By relaxing the monthly payment cycle and moving to a system of 'rolling credit', where customers are still granted the same payment terms but from the date of the order rather than the start of the month, suppliers could significantly improve the average utilization of logistics assets. This, however, 'would require a fundamental change in corporate culture and a relaxation of long-established traditions in sales and finance departments' (McKinnon, 2004).

Collaborate with other users and providers of transport services

There is a limit to how much any individual company can do to improve the utilization of vehicle capacity. To reach high levels of utilization it is often necessary to collaborate with other companies. This collaboration can be in two dimensions – horizontal and vertical.

Horizontal collaboration

This occurs where companies at the same level in a supply chain combine their freight transport demands to increase average consignment size or create additional backloading opportunities. The need for such collaboration is well illustrated by an analysis undertaken by a large British FMCG manufacturer. It was concerned about the effects of JIT pressures in the retail supply chain on the efficiency of delivery operations. The company estimated that to be able to provide daily delivery of full truckloads to a retailer's distribution centre it would need to supply the DC with approximately 750,000 cases annually. As Britain's main supermarket and grocery wholesale chains have a total of roughly 70 distribution centres, this would require an annual distribution throughput of approximately 50 million cases. Only a small group of very large FMCG manufacturers have annual sales volumes as large as this. To maintain full load deliveries on a daily basis, other manufacturers would have to combine their loads.

Several mechanisms exist for integrating different companies' delivery operations. Firms can merge their logistics operations at a shared distribution facility. For example, Unilever and Kimberly-Clark channel products for the Dutch retail market through a distribution centre in Raamsdonksveer operated for them by a logistics service provider (LSP). As a result of this collaboration the companies have been able to cut their logistics costs by 12–15 per cent while responding to retailers' demands for faster and more frequent delivery. Many LSPs now operate 'primary consolidation centres' at which manufacturers can consolidate their orders for onward delivery to retailers' distribution centres in full loads. It has been estimated that the number of 'shared supplier consolidation centres' in the UK grocery supply chain increased from 11 in 1998 to over 100 in 2003 (Potter *et al*, 2003). Multi-company load consolidation also occurs at the secondary distribution level (between distribution centre and shop). Exel, for instance, operates a retail consolidation centre for shops located at Heathrow Airport. It was estimated that when fully implemented this retail consolidation scheme would cut the number of shop delivery vehicles visiting the terminal by 75 per cent and raise vehicle load factors 90 per cent (Energy Efficiency Best Practice Programme, 2002).

To take advantage of horizontal collaboration, many companies must change the basis on which they outsource their transport. During the 1980s and 1990s, there was a sharp increase in the proportion of trucking services provided on a dedicated basis for individual clients. Dedication denies carriers the opportunity to perform their traditional 'groupage' role and, as a result, carries a vehicle utilization penalty. Many users of dedicated services have now granted LSPs the freedom to carry other firms' traffic in their vehicles. Several company-sponsored studies in the UK of the potential benefits of shared-user services in the automotive, consumer electrical and clothing sectors, in each case replacing four or five separate dedicated services, have indicated that this can reduce truck-kilometres by around 20 per cent.

Vertical collaboration

This involves collective action by trading partners at different levels in a supply chain, often with the assistance of LSPs. It can help to ease the first two constraints on vehicle utilization listed earlier, namely demand fluctuations and JIT pressures. In the United States, the term 'collaborative transportation management' (CTM) has been used to describe a formal initiative to encourage collaboration and the sharing of information between manufacturers, retailers and carriers to cut transport costs while improving service quality (Murphy, 2003). This is an extension of collaborative planning, forecasting and replenishment (CPFR), which has focused on the management of inventory across the supply chain. Key features of CTM are the sharing of demand information with carriers and the closer involvement of carriers in the replenishment process. As Browning and White (2000) explain, 'CTM… re-engineers the whole process so that the carrier is now part of the larger, more focused buyer/seller team.' By giving carriers an 'extended planning horizon' some have been able to increase the utilization of their regional truck fleets in the United States by between 10 and 42 per cent, mainly as a result of improved backloading (Esper and Williams, 2003).

Another initiative relating to the management of product flow through the vertical channel is vendor-managed inventory (VMI). This gives suppliers control over the replenishment process, enabling them to phase the movement of products in a way that makes more efficient use of vehicle capacity. Simulation modelling has been used to demonstrate the potential transport benefits of VMI over a 'traditional supply chain' (Disney, Potter and Gardner, 2003). Sometimes it is also necessary to increase storage capacity at the customer's premises to accommodate the delivery of supplies in full truckloads. This applies particularly to the movement of bulk commodities in process industries.

Conclusion

'Transport optimization' is the term now being widely used in business circles to describe efforts to maximize vehicle utilization. It is partly a reaction to the JIT trend that has swept through manufacturing and retailing over the past quarter-century. In the headlong rush to cut inventory, many companies were prepared to sacrifice transport efficiency. Now that low-inventory strategies are firmly in place, attention is shifting to freight transport operations to see what can be done to improve their efficiency. This is being reinforced by mounting concern about fuel costs, driver shortages, traffic congestion and the environmental impact of logistical activity, particularly on climate change.

Transport will inevitably be optimized within a range of constraints. This chapter has examined these constraints and the series of measures that companies can take to ease or overcome them. If properly implemented, these measures can yield a combination of economic and environmental benefits and help to make logistics more sustainable in the longer term.

References

Anderson, S, Browne, M and Allen, J (1999) Logistical implications of the UK packaging waste regulations, *International Journal of Logistics: Research and applications*, **2** (2), pp 129–45

Ansari, A and Heckel, J (1987) JIT purchasing: impact on freight and inventory costs, *Journal of Purchasing and Materials Management*, **23** (2), pp 24–28

AT Kearney (1997) *The Efficient Unit Loads Report*, ECR Europe, Brussels

Browning, B and White, B (2000) *Collaborative Transportation Management: A proposal*, White Paper, Logility, Atlanta, GA

Buckley, C and Hoyle, B (2005) Is this really the shape of tins to come?, *Times*, 30 March

Caplice, C and Sheffi, Y (1994) A review and evaluation of logistics metrics, *International Journal of Logistics Management*, **5** (2), pp 11–28

Department for Transport (2003) *Telematics Guide*, Good Practice Guide 341, Stationery Office, London

Department for Transport (2005a) *Focus on Double Decks*, Transport Energy Best Practice report, Stationery Office, London

Department for Transport (2005b) *Transport Statistics Great Britain*, Stationery Office, London

Disney, S, Potter, A and Gardner, B (2003) The impact of VMI on transport operations, *Transportation Research*, part E: *Logistics and transportation*, **39**, pp 363–80

Energy Efficiency Best Practice Programme (1998a) *Efficient JIT Supply Chain Management: Nissan Motor Manufacturing (UK) Ltd*, Good Practice Case Study 374, AEA Technology Environment, Harwell

Energy Efficiency Best Practice Programme (1998b) *Energy Savings from Integrated Logistics Management: Tesco plc*, Good Practice Case Study 364, AEA Technology Environment, Harwell

Energy Efficiency Best Practice Programme (2002) *Heathrow Airport Retail Consolidation Centre*, Good Practice Case Study 402, AEA Technology Environment, Harwell

Esper, TL and Williams, LR (2003) 'The value of collaborative transportation management (CTM): its relationship to CPFR and information technology, *Transportation Journal*, **42** (4), Summer, pp 55–66

Freight Transport Association (FTA) (1995) JIT: time sensitive distribution, *Freight Matters*, 1/95, FTA, Tunbridge Wells

Leonardi, J and Baumgartner, M (2004) CO_2 efficiency in road freight transportation: status quo, measures and potential, *Transportation Research*, part D, **9**, pp 451–64

Lewis, CN (2002) Freight exchanges: how are the survivors faring?, *e.logistics magazine*, 16

Lex Transfleet (2002) *The Lex Transfleet Report on Freight Transport 2002*, Lex Transfleet, Coventry

McKinnon, AC (1996) The empty running and return loading of road goods vehicles, *Transport Logistics*, **1** (1), pp 1–19

McKinnon, AC (2003) Influencing company logistics management, in *Managing the Fundamental Drivers of Transport Demand*, European Conference of Ministers of Transport, pp 60–74, OECD, Paris

McKinnon, AC (2004) *Supply Chain Excellence in the European Chemical Industry*, European Petrochemical Association, Brussels

McKinnon, AC (2005) The economic and environmental benefits of increasing maximum truck weight: the British experience, *Transportation Research*, part D, **10** (1), pp 77–95

McKinnon, AC and Campbell, J (1997) *Opportunities for Consolidating Volume-Constrained Loads in Double-Deck and High-Cube Vehicles*, Christian Salvesen Logistics Research Paper no 1, School of Management, Heriot-Watt University, available at http://www.sml.hw.ac.uk/logistics/s1.html

McKinnon, AC and Ge, Y (2004) Use of a synchronised vehicle audit to determine opportunities for improving transport efficiency in a supply chain, *International Journal of Logistics: Research and applications*, **7** (3), pp 219–38

McKinnon, AC and Ge, Y (2006) The potential for reducing empty running by trucks: a retrospective analysis, *International Journal of Physical Distribution and Logistics Management*, **36** (forthcoming)

Murphy, J (2003) CTM: collaborating to weed out transportation inefficiency, *Global Logistics and Supply Chain Strategies*, November

Potter, A *et al* (2004) Modelling the impact of factory gate pricing on transport and logistics, in *Transport in Supply Chains*, ed C Lalwani *et al*, Cardiff Business School, Cardiff

Potter, M *et al* (2003) *ECR UK Transport Optimisation: Sharing best practices in distribution management*, Institute of Grocery Distribution, Letchmore Heath

Samuelsson, A and Tilanus, B (1997) A framework efficiency model for goods transportation, with an application to regional less-than-truckload distribution, *Transport Logistics*, **1** (2), pp 139–51

Swenseth, SR and Buffa, FP (1990) Just-in-time: some effects on the logistics function, *International Journal of Logistics Management*, **1** (2), pp 25–34

Transportation Research Board (2002) *Regulation of Weights, Lengths and Widths of Commercial Motor Vehicles*, Special Report 267, Transportation Research Board, Washington, DC

University of St Gallen (2000) *The Transport Optimisation Report*, ECR Europe, Brussels

18

Retail logistics

John Fernie, Heriot-Watt University

The principles behind logistics and supply chain management are not new, but it is only in the last 10 to 15 years that logistics has achieved prominence in companies' boardrooms. This is primarily because of the impact that the application of supply chain techniques can have on a company's competitive position and profitability. Retailers have been in the forefront of applying best-practice principles to their businesses, with UK grocery retailers being acknowledged as innovators in logistics management. This chapter discusses:

- the evolution of the logistics concept;
- QR/ECR and managing supply chain relationships;
- the application of supply chain concepts in different international markets;
- future trends, including the impact of e-commerce upon logistics networks.

The evolution of the logistics concept

The starting point for any discussion of logistics invariably centres around Drucker's (1962) description of 'the economy's dark continent', which suggested that distribution was one of the last frontiers of business to be 'discovered'. He noted that distribution was viewed as a low-status activity by managers, yet major cost savings could be achieved by managing this function more effectively. His ideas stimulated much debate, and most of the early research emanated from the United States as techniques developed in the context of military logistics began to gain acceptance in the commercial sector.

By the 1970s and 1980s, the supply chain was still viewed as a series of disparate functions – with materials management dealing with the 'back end' of the supply chain and physical distribution management focusing upon the flow of product from manufacturers to their customers (retailers and wholesalers). As a result, the literature on the subject has developed along two distinct routes: one pertaining to industrial and the other to consumer markets. The materials management literature has its roots in the management strategies of the Japanese and the application of total quality management, just-in-time (JIT) production and supplier associations. More recently, the 'Europeanization' of the concepts includes 'lean supply' and 'network sourcing'.

The 'front end' of the supply chain achieved greater prominence from the 1970s, initially as physical distribution management (PDM) but more recently as supply chain/logistics management. Initial work focused upon manufacturers' distribution systems, but as retailers centralized their distribution and began to exert control over the retail supply chain, most research focused upon retailers' logistics strategies. In both industrial and retail logistics research, the emphasis since the 1990s has been on viewing the supply chain as an integrated whole rather than a series of disparate parts. There is no point in taking cost out of one part of the supply chain, only to add costs somewhere else in the chain!

In the context of retail logistics, several authors have sought to explain the transformation of logistics practices since the 1970s. McKinnon (1996) identified six trends to account for this:

- retailers increasing their control over secondary distribution (warehouse to shop) – in the UK this process is complete in most sectors;
- restructuring of retailers' logistical systems through the development of 'composite distribution' and centralization of certain commodities into particular supply chain streams;
- adoption of quick response techniques to reduce lead times through the implementation of information technology, especially electronic data interchange (EDI), electronic point of sales (EPOS) and sales-based ordering (SBO);
- rationalization of primary distribution (factory to warehouse) and attempts to integrate this and secondary distribution into a single 'network system';
- introduction of supply chain management and efficient consumer response (ECR);
- increasing return flow of packaging material and handling equipment for recycle or reuse.

Fernie, Pfab and Marchant (2000) have built upon the work of Whiteoak, who charted the evolution of UK grocery distribution from the 1970s to the early 1990s, and identify four stages:

1. supplier control (pre-1980);
2. centralization (1981–89);
3. just-in-time (1990–95);
4. relationship (1995 onwards).

The first stage, supplier control, is widespread in many countries today, and was the dominant method of distribution to UK stores in the 1960s and 1970s. Suppliers manufactured and stored products at the factory or numerous warehouses throughout the country. Direct store deliveries (DSDs) were made on an infrequent basis (7 to 10 days), often by third-party contractors that consolidated products from a range of factories. Store managers negotiated with suppliers and kept this stock in 'the back room'.

The second stage, centralization, is now becoming a feature of retail logistics in many countries and was prominent in the UK in the 1980s. The grocery retailers took the initiative at this time in constructing large, purpose-built regional distribution centres (RDCs) to consolidate products from suppliers for onward delivery to stores. This stage marked the beginning of a shift from supplier to retailer control of the supply chain, with clear advantages for retailers:

- reduced inventories;
- lead times at stores reduced from weeks to days;
- 'back-room' areas released for selling space;
- greater product availability;
- 'bulk discounts' from suppliers;
- fewer invoices and lower administrative costs;
- better utilization of staff in stores.

Centralization, however, required much capital investment in RDCs, vehicles, material handling equipment and human resources. Centralization of distribution also meant centralization of buying, with store managers losing autonomy as new headquarter functions were created to manage this change. This period also witnessed a boom in the third-party contract market, as retailers considered whether to invest in other parts of the retail business rather than logistics. All of the UK's 'big four' grocery retailers – Sainsbury, Tesco, Asda and Safeway – contracted out many RDCs to logistics service providers in the mid- to late 1980s.

In stage 3, the just-in-time phase, major efficiency improvements were achieved as refinements to the initial networks were implemented. The larger grocery chains focused upon product-specific RDCs, with most temperature-controlled products being channelled through a large number of small warehouses operated by third-party contractors. By the early 1990s, temperature-controlled products were subsumed within a network of composite distribution centres developed by superstore operators.

Composites allowed products of all temperature ranges to be distributed through one system of multi-temperature warehouses and vehicles. This allowed retailers to reduce stock in store as delivery frequency increased. Furthermore, a more streamlined system not only improved efficiency but reduced waste in short-shelf-life products, giving a better-quality offer to the customer.

Initial projects were also established to integrate primary with secondary distribution. When Safeway opened its composite in 1989 at Bellshill in Strathclyde, it included a resource recovery centre that washed returnable trays and baled cardboard from its stores. It also established a supplier collection programme, which saved the company millions of pounds during the 1990s. Most secondary networks were established to provide stores with high customer service levels; however, vehicle utilization on return trips to the RDC were invariably poor, and it was efforts to reduce this empty running that led to initiatives such as return trips with suppliers' products to the RDC, or equipment or recycling waste from stores.

Although improvements to the initial networks were being implemented, RDCs continued to carry two weeks or more of stock of non-perishable products. To improve inventory levels and move to a just-in-time system, retailers began to request more frequent deliveries from their suppliers in smaller order quantities. Whiteoak, who represented Mars and therefore suppliers' interests, wrote in 1993 that these initiatives gave clear benefits to retailers at the expense of increased costs to suppliers. In response to these changes, consolidation centres have been created upstream from RDCs to enable suppliers to improve vehicle utilization from the factory.

The final stage, the relationship stage, is ongoing but is crucial if further costs are going to be taken out of the supply chain. In the earlier, third, stage, Whiteoak had noted that the transition from a supplier- to a retail-controlled network had given cost savings to both suppliers and retailers *until* the just-in-time phase in the early 1990s. By the mid-1990s, retailers had begun to appreciate that there were no more 'quick wins' to improve margins. If another step change in managing retail logistics was to occur, it had to be realized through supply chain cooperation.

ECR initiatives launched throughout the 1990s have done much to promote the spirit of collaboration. Organizations are having to change to accommodate and embrace ECR and to dispel inherent rivalries that have built up over decades of confrontation. The UK has been in the vanguard of implementing ECR, with Tesco and Sainsbury claiming to have saved hundreds of millions of pounds. The key to the relative success of UK companies has been their willingness to share EPOS data with their suppliers through internet-based information exchanges.

Logistics and competitive strategy in retailing

Many of the current ideas on supply chain management and competitive advantage have their roots in the work of Porter (1985), who introduced the concept of the value chain in relation to competitive advantage. These ideas have been further developed by academics such as Christopher (1997). Now we have a supply chain model (Figure 18.1) where each stage of the chain adds value to the product through manufacturing, branding, packaging, display at the store and so on. At the same time, at each stage cost is added in terms of production, branding and overall logistics costs. The trick for companies is to manage this chain to create value for the customer at an acceptable cost.

According to Christopher there are three dimensions to time-based competition that must be managed effectively if an organization is going to be responsive to market changes:

- *time to market:* the speed of bringing a business opportunity to market;
- *time to serve:* the speed of meeting a customer's order;
- *time to react:* the speed of adjusting output to volatile responses in demand.

He uses these principles to develop strategies for lead-time management. He argues that, if the lead times of the integrated web of suppliers necessary to manufacture a product are understood, a 'pipeline map' can be drawn to represent each stage in the supply chain process from raw materials to customer. In these maps it is useful to differentiate between value-adding time (manufacture, assembly, in-transit, etc) and non-value-adding time (when nothing is happening, but products and materials are standing as inventory).

It was in fashion markets that time-based competition had most significance, because of the short time window for changing styles. In addition, the prominent trend in the last 20 years has been to source products offshore,

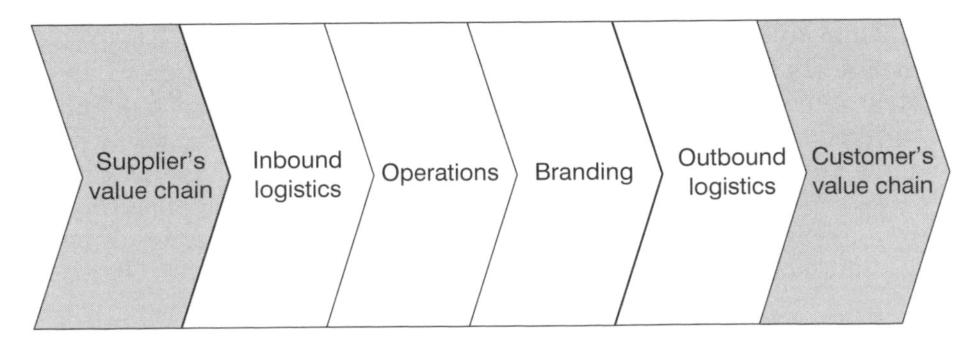

Figure 18.1 The extended value chain

usually in low-cost Pacific Rim nations, which lengthened the physical supply chains. These factors combined to illustrate the trade-offs that have to be made in supply chain management and the need to develop closer working relationships with supply chain partners. Christopher has used the example of The Limited in the United States to illustrate his accelerating 'time to market'. The company revolutionized the apparel supply chain philosophy in the United States by designing, ordering and receiving products from South-East Asia to stores in a matter of weeks rather than the months of its competitors. New lines were test-marketed in trial stores, and orders communicated by EDI to suppliers, which used CAD/CAM technology in modifying designs. The products, already labelled and priced, were consolidated in Hong Kong, where chartered 747s air-freighted the goods to Columbus, Ohio, for onward dispatch to stores. The higher freight costs were easily compensated for by lower markdowns and higher inventory turns per annum.

Quick response

The term 'quick response' (QR) was coined in the United States in 1985 (Fernie, 1994; Hines, 2001) when Kurt Salmon Associates (KSA) recognized deficiencies in the fashion supply chain. According to KSA, only 11 weeks out of the 66-week lead time were spent on value-adding processes, and the rest were wasted in the form of WIP and finished inventories at various stages of the complex system (Christopher, 1997, 1998; KSA, 1997; Christopher and Peck, 2003). The resultant losses arising from this were estimated at $25 billion – due to stocking too large an inventory of unwanted items and too small an inventory of the fast movers.

In response to this situation, the US textiles, apparel and retail industries formed the Voluntary Interindustry Commerce Standards Association (VICS) in 1986 as their joint effort to streamline the supply chain and make a significant contribution in getting the in-vogue style at the right time in the right place (Fernie, 1994, 1998) with increased variety (Lowson, 1998; Lowson, King and Hunter, 1999; Giunipero *et al*, 2001) and inexpensive prices. This is done by applying an industry standard for information technologies (eg bar code, EDI, shipping container marking, roll ID, etc) and contractual procedures among the supply chain members (Ko, Kincade and Brown, 2000). QR adopts an IT-driven systematic approach (Hunter, 1990; Forza and Vinelli, 1996, 1997, 2000; Riddle *et al*, 1999) to achieve supply chain efficiency from raw materials to retail stores – and each member of the supply chain shares the risks and the benefits of the partnership on an equal basis to realize the philosophy of 'the whole is stronger than the parts'.

QR, in principle, requires the traditional buyer–supplier relationship, which is too often motivated by opportunism, to transform into a more collaborative partnership. In this QR partnership, the objectives of the vendor are to develop the customer's business. The benefit to the vendor is the likelihood that it will be treated as a preferred supplier. At the same time, the costs of serving that customer should be lower as a result of a greater sharing of information, integrated logistics systems and so on (Christopher and Jüttner, 2000).

The last, and perhaps one of the most important, of the tenets of the original proposition of the QR concept sees it as a survival strategy of the domestic manufacturing sector in the advanced economies against competition from low-cost imports (Finnie, 1992; MITI, 1993, 1995, 1999; METI, 2002).

With the basic fashion category, relatively steady demand is a feature of the market; therefore the US-born QR concept places much focus on the relationship between retailers and the apparel manufacturers. The eventual benefits to both parties are detailed in Table 18.1. Giunipero *et al* (2001) summarize the hierarchical process of QR adoption (Table 18.2). This model – most appropriate for the apparel–retail linkage in basic clothing – has become a role model for QR programmes in other advanced economies.

Having achieved many of the QR goals, VICS implemented a collaborative planning, forecasting and replenishment (CPFR) programme, to synchronize market fluctuations and the supply chain in more real time. Through establishing firm contracts among supply chain members and allowing them to share key information, CPFR makes the forecasting, production and replenishment cycle ever closer to the actual demands in the marketplace (VICS, 1998). While US practices have played a leading role in QR initiatives in the apparel industry, much of their success is in the basic fashion segment – where the manufacturing phase is normally the first to be transferred offshore. In this sense, the philosophy of QR as the survival strategy of fashion manufacturing in the industrial economies has not been realized.

QR in Japan

The US fashion industry essentially produces for the international market that is mostly controlled by the largest retailers – which are the real promoters and the first to profit from QR (Taplin and Ordovensky, 1995; Scarso, 1997). Japanese apparel firms have forged their success on flexible specialization in a

Table 18.1 Retailers' and suppliers' QR benefits

Retailers' QR benefits	Suppliers' QR benefits
Reduced costs	Reduced costs
Reduced inventories	Predictable production cycles
Faster merchandise flow	Frequency of orders
Customer satisfaction	Closer ties to retailers
Increased sales	Ability to monitor sales
Competitive advantage	Competitive advantage

Source: Quick Response Services, 1995

Table 18.2 Technological and organizational QR development stages

Stage 1	**Introduction of basic QR technologies** SKU level scanning JAN (standard) bar code Use of EDI Use of standard EDI
Stage 2	**Internal process re-engineering via technological and organizational improvement** Electronic communication for replenishment Use of cross-docking Small amounts of inventory in the system Small lot size order processing ARP (automatic replenishment programme) JIT (just-in-time) delivery SCM (shipping container marking) ASN (advance shipping notice)
Stage 3	**Realization of a collaborative supply chain and win–win relationship** Real-time sales data sharing Stock-out data sharing QR team meets with partnerships MRP (material resource planning)

Source: Giunipero *et al*, 2001; KSA, 1997

subcontracting network of process specialists (Piore and Sabel, 1984; Azuma, 2001). Harsh competition from offshore, and stagnant domestic consumption have come to highlight the costly structure and the lack of partnership in the Japanese fashion supply chain. This led to the formation of the Quick Response Promotion Association (QRPA) in 1994, as a joint endeavour to regain competitiveness of the domestic industry, and effectively and efficiently serve ever-changing customer needs.

Since the introduction of the first QR initiative in the Japanese fashion industry, a series of programmes have been implemented from 1) the retail–textiles, 2) the textiles–apparel, to 3) the apparel–sewing interfaces (see Figure 18.2). With an increasing adoption of industry-standard platforms for EDI, department stores and apparel firms have achieved some of the expected QR benefits. Elsewhere in the supply chain, however, there are fewer QR initiatives – and QR initiatives have not necessarily worked throughout the domestic apparel sector.

Benetton and Zara

The importance of supply chain integration cannot be overstated; however, much depends on the degree of control a company has over the design, manufacture, marketing and distribution of its supply chain. Two of the most

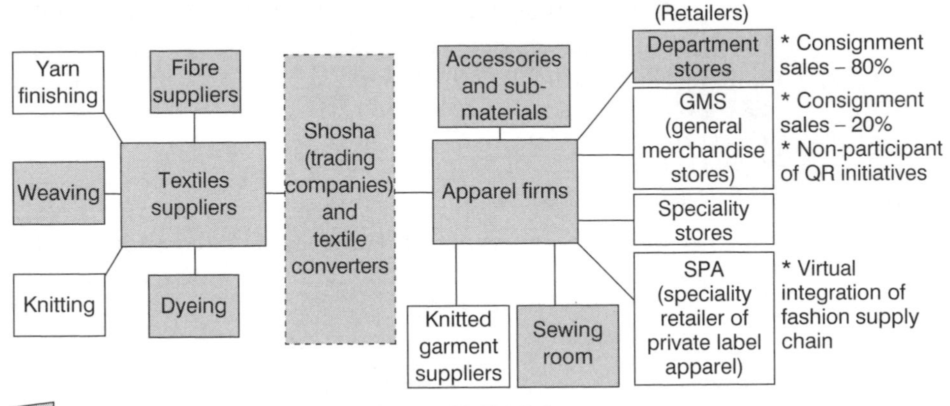

Figure 18.2 The structure of the Japanese fashion industry

successful fashion retailers in Europe – Benetton and Zara – illustrate how an integrated supply chain can enhance the retail offer. Both companies draw heavily on lean production techniques developed in Japan. Their manufacturing operations are flexible, involving a network of subcontractors and, in the case of Benetton, suppliers in close proximity to the factory. Benetton was one of the first retail companies to apply the 'principle of postponement' to its operations, whereby semi-finished garments were dyed at the last possible moment when colour trends for a season became apparent from EPOS data at the stores. So rather than manufacture stock to sell, Benetton could manufacture stock to demand.

Zara's operation has similarities with The Limited in the United States in that the company scours the globe for new fashion trends prior to negotiating with suppliers to produce specific quantities of finished and semi-finished products. Only 40 per cent of garments – those with the broadest appeal – are imported as finished goods from the Far East; the rest are produced in Zara's automated factories in Spain. The result of its supply chain initiatives is that Zara has reduced its lead-time gap for more than half of the garments it sells to a level unmatched by any of its European or North American competitors.

Benetton, Zara and The Limited – as the latter's name suggests – have narrow product assortments for specific target markets. This streamlines and simplifies the logistics network. For general fashion merchandisers, the supply chain is more complex, with thousands of suppliers around the globe. Nevertheless, quick response concepts are being applied to these sectors in an effort to minimize markdowns due to out-of-season or unwanted stock in stores.

Although grocery retailers are more orientated to their national or super-regional markets – such as the EU – than their clothing counterparts are, the internationalization of grocery retailers and their customers has led to changing sourcing patterns. Furthermore, the increased competition in grocery markets, with the resultant pressure on profit margins, has acted as a spur to companies to improve supply chain performance.

Efficient consumer response

ECR emerged in the United States partly through the joint initiatives between Wal-Mart and Procter & Gamble, in response to recession and increased competition in the grocery industry in the early 1990s. Kurt Salmon Associates were again commissioned to analyse the supply chain of a US industrial sector, and they found similar features to those identified in their earlier work in the apparel sector – excessive inventories, long uncoordinated supply chains and an estimated potential savings of $30 billion, 10.8 per cent of sales turnover (see Table 18.3).

ECR programmes commenced in Europe in 1993, and a series of projects and pilot studies were commissioned – for example, a Coopers & Lybrand (1996) survey of the grocery value chain estimated potential savings of 5.7 per cent of turnover. Since then ECR has been adopted in countries around the world.

Table 18.3 Comparison of scope and savings from supply chain studies

Supply chain study	Scope of study	Estimated savings
Kurt Salmon Associates (1993)	US dry grocery sector	10.8% of sales turnover (2.3% financial, 8.5% cost). Total supply chain $30 billion; warehouse supplier dry sector $10 billion. Supply chain cut by 41% from 104 days to 61 days.
Coca-Cola supply chain collaboration (1994)	127 European companies. Focused on cost reduction from end of manufacturer's line. Small proportion of category management.	2.3%–3.4% of sales turnover (60% to retailers, 40% to manufacturer).
ECR Europe (1996, ongoing)	15 value chain analysis studies (10 European manufacturers, 5 retailers). 15 product categories. 7 distribution channels.	5.7% of sales turnover (4.8% operating costs, 0.9% inventory cost). Total supply chain saving of $21 billion. UK savings £2 billion.

Source: Fiddis, 1997

The European ECR initiative defines ECR as a 'global movement in the grocery industry focusing on the total supply chain – suppliers, manufacturers, wholesalers and retailers, working closer together to fulfil the changing demands of the grocery consumer better, faster and at least cost' (Fiddis, 1997). Despite the apparent emphasis on consumers, early studies focused on the supply side of ECR. Initially reports sought efficiencies in replenishment and the standardization of material-handling equipment to eliminate unnecessary handling through the supply chain. The Coopers & Lybrand report in 1996 and subsequent reprioritizing towards demand management – especially category management (McGrath, 1997) – have led to a more holistic view of the supply chain. Indeed, the greater cost savings attributed to the Coopers study compared with that of Coca-Cola can be attributed to their broader perspective of the value chain.

The main focus areas addressed under ECR are category management, product replenishment and enabling technologies. Figure 18.3 breaks these down into 14 further areas where improvements can be made to enhance efficiency.

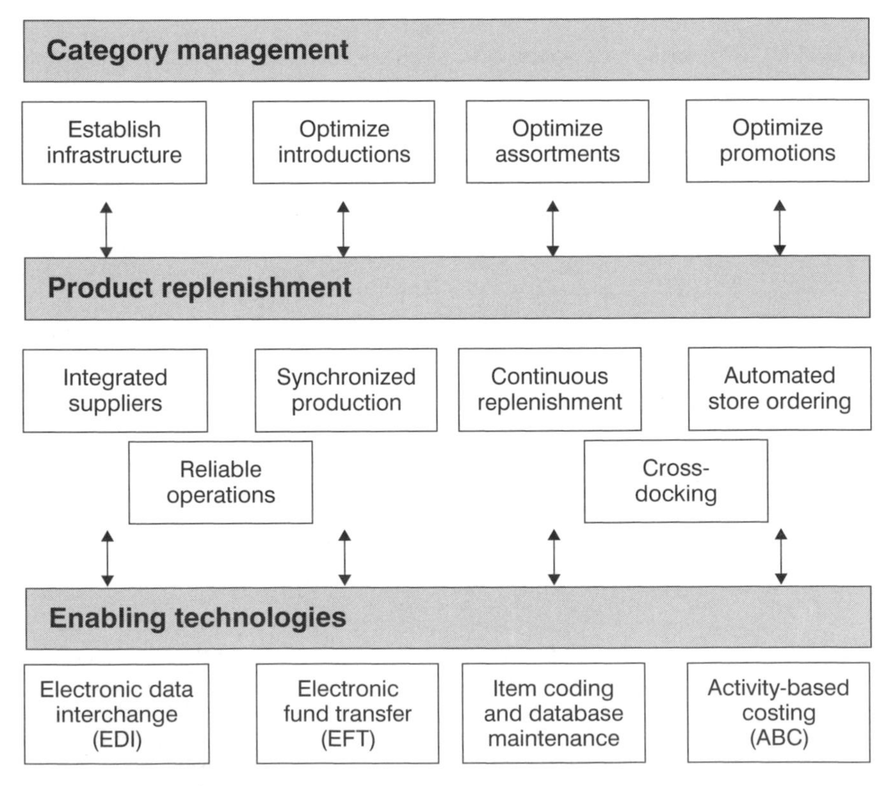

Source: Coopers & Lybrand, 1996

Figure 18.3 ECR improvement concepts

After the success of ECR Europe's annual conferences from 1996, a series of initiatives encouraged much greater international collaboration. ECR movements began to share best-practice principles, most notably the bringing together of different versions of the 'scorecard' that was used to assess the performance of trading relationships. These relationships were measured under four categories – demand management, supply management, enablers and integrators (see Figure 18.4). Comparing this with Figure 18.3 shows how ECR has developed in recent years to accommodate changes in the market environment. Retailers are becoming more sophisticated in their approach to demand and supply management, and there has been considerable progress in moving from traditional 'bow tie' relationships between retailers and their suppliers to a multi-functional team structure (see Figures 18.5 and 18.6).

Although logisticians would prefer a consistent flow of product through the supply chain, tactical promotions remain a feature in many retailers' marketing strategies. Research by Hoch and Pomerantz (2002) on 19 food product categories in 106 supermarket chains in the United States shows that price sensitivity and promotional responsiveness are much greater with high-frequency, staple purchases. These staple products benefited from range reduction, compared with more specialist niche products where greater variety and range built store traffic.

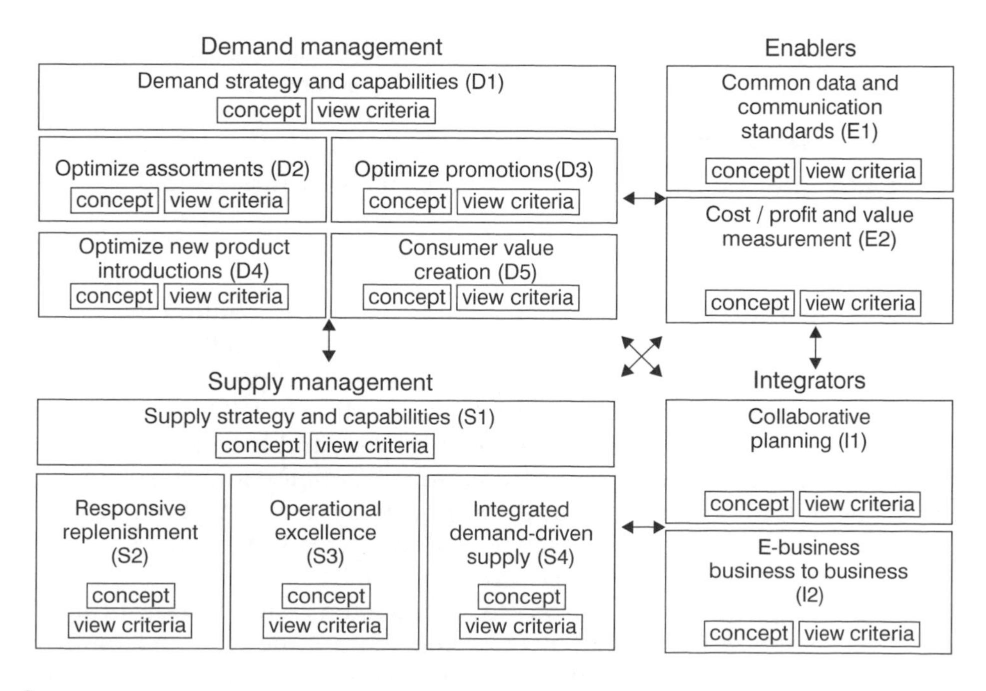

Source: www.ecr-sa.co.za

Figure 18.4 ECR concepts

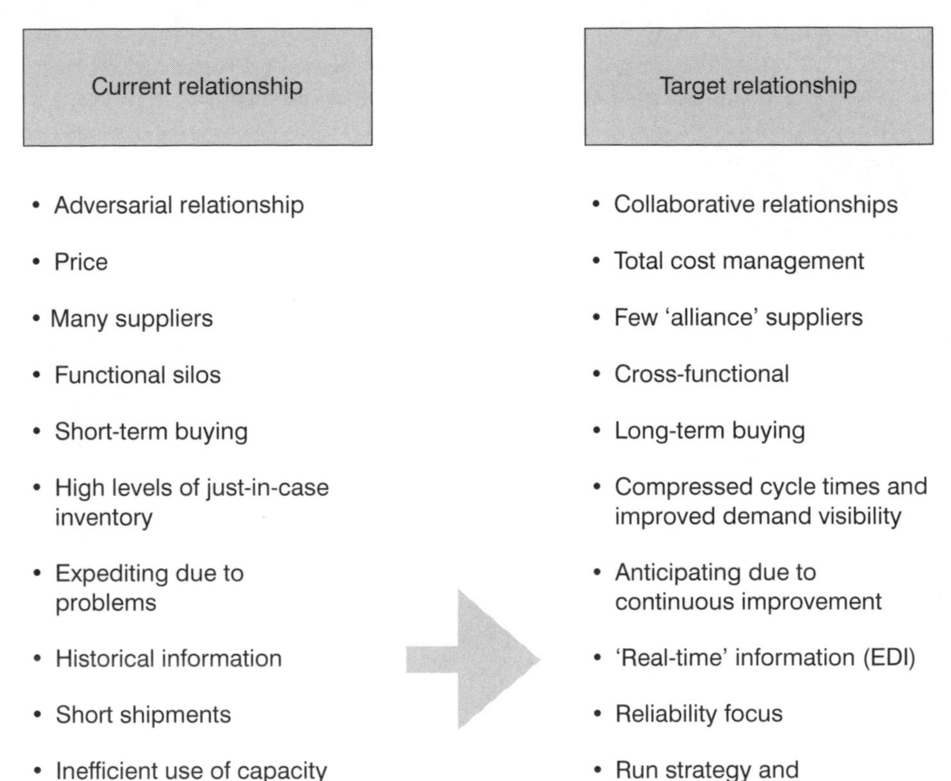

Source: Coopers & Lybrand, 1996

Figure 18.5 Changing relationships between manufacturers and their suppliers

In order to integrate this demand-side planning with continuous replenishment, collaborative planning is necessary. The main catalyst for this was the VICS initiative on CPFR, which drew its primary support from US non-food retailers and their suppliers until the late 1990s when the grocery sector embraced the CPFR model. For example, Wal-Mart and Warner-Lambert are usually cited as key partners in sales forecast collaboration in the early to mid-1990s. The shift into grocery is hardly surprising in view of Wal-Mart's move into food through its supercentres in the United States and its overseas acquisitions of grocery businesses such as Asda in the UK.

By the late 1990s, VICS had produced a nine-step generic model bringing together elements of ECR initiatives – the development of collaborative arrangements, joint business plans, shared sales forecasts and continuous replenishment from orders generated. Although the tenets of CPFR have been established, the implementation of the model remains patchy and,

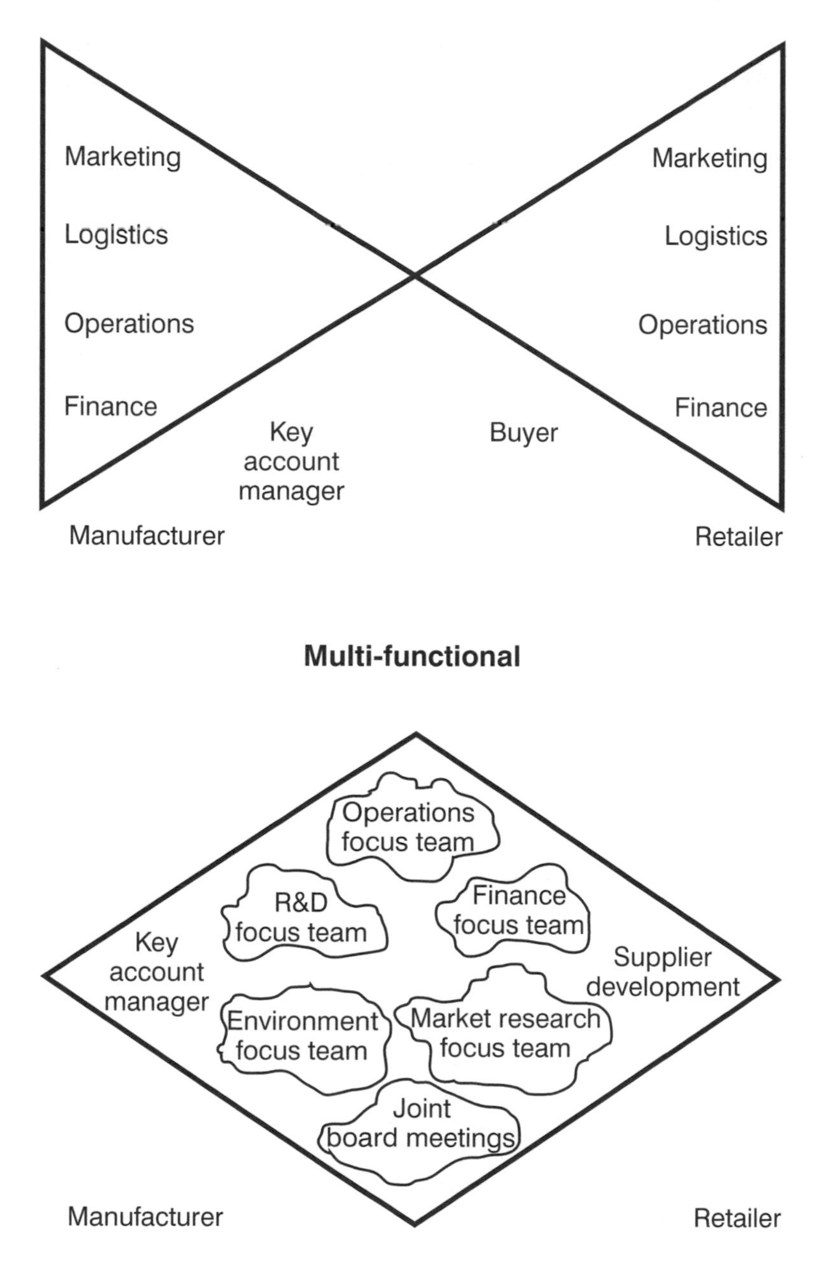

Source: Fiddis, 1997

Figure 18.6 Transformation of the interface between manufacturer and retailer

like ECR initiatives, tends to focus on 'quick wins' where measurable profit enhancement or cost savings can be achieved. Most pilot schemes have involved a handful of partners dealing with specific categories. Companies come from a variety of technical platforms and cultures of collaboration. Indeed, the likes of Wal-Mart, Tesco and Sainsbury with their own intranet exchanges could actually impede more universal adoption of common standards!

To implement CPFR, it is a prerequisite that a close working relationship has been fostered between trading partners, in order to invest the necessary human resources to develop joint plans to generate real-time forecasts. There is clearly more volatility of demand with price promotions and seasonal and event planning. CPFR generates greater benefits in these heavily promoted channels where over-stocks or out-of-stocks are more evident than in high-volume, staple, frequently purchased items where demand is more predictable.

Differences in logistics 'culture' in international markets

ECR principles have been adopted at different stages by different companies in international markets – and new entrants to a market can change the distribution culture of that market. Differences in such markets are more likely to exist in the context of fast-moving consumer goods, especially groceries, because of the greater variations in tastes that occur in both national and regional markets. The catalyst for much of the interest in these international comparisons was the revealing statistic from Kurt Salmon Associates (1997) that it took 104 days for dry grocery products to pass through the US supply chain from the suppliers' picking line to the checkout. With the advent of ECR, it was hoped to reduce this to 61 days – a figure that was still behind the lead times encountered in Europe, especially in the UK, where inventory in the supply chain averaged around 25 days (GEA, 1994).

Mitchell (1997) explains the differences between the United States and Europe in terms of trading conditions, stating that:

- The US grocery retail trade is fragmented and not as concentrated as in parts of Europe.
- US private-label development is primitive compared with that in many European countries.
- The balance of power in the manufacturer–retailer relationship is very different.
- The trade structure is different, with wholesalers playing a more important role in the United States.
- Trade practices such as forward buying are more deeply rooted in the United States than in Europe.

- Trade promotional deals and the use of coupons in consumer promotions are unique to the United States.
- Legislation, especially anti-trust legislation, can inhibit supply chain collaboration.

Fernie (1994, 1995) cites the following factors to explain these differences in trading conditions:

- the extent of retail power;
- the penetration of store brands in the market;
- the degree of supply chain control;
- types of trading format;
- geographical spread of stores;
- relative logistics costs;
- level of IT development;
- relative sophistication of the distribution industry.

Of these eight factors, the first three can be classified as relationship factors and the remainder as operational factors. Clearly there has been a significant shift in the balance of power between manufacturer and retailer during the last 20 to 30 years, as retailers increasingly take over responsibility for product development, branding, packaging and marketing. As mergers continue in Europe, retailers have grown in economic power to dominate their international branded manufacturer suppliers. While there are different levels of retail concentration at the country level, the trend is for increased concentration – especially as Southern and Eastern European markets are targeted by the major Western European retail chains.

By contrast, Ohbora, Parsons and Riesenbeck (1992) maintain that this power struggle is more evenly poised in the United States, where the grocery market is more regional in character, enabling manufacturers to wield their power. This, however, is changing as Wal-Mart develops its supercentres and acts as a catalyst for the 'consolidation wave' throughout the 1990s and early 21st century (Wrigley, 2001). Nevertheless, the immense size of the United States has meant that there has never been a true national grocery retailer.

Commensurate with the growth of these powerful retailers has been the development of distributor labels. This is particularly relevant in the UK where supermarket chains have followed the Marks & Spencer strategy of strong value-added brands that can compete with manufacturers' brands. British retailers dominate the list of top 25 own-label retailers in Europe.

The net result of this shift to retail power and own-label development has meant that manufacturers have been either abdicating or losing their responsibility for controlling the supply chain. In the UK the transition from a supplier-driven system to one of retail control is complete compared with some parts of Europe and the United States.

Of the operational factors identified by Fernie (1994), the nature of trading format has been a key driver in shaping the type of logistics support to stores. For example, in the UK the predominant trading format has been the superstore in both food and specialist household products and appliances. This has led to the development of large RDCs for the centralization of stock from suppliers. In the grocery sector, supermarket operations have introduced composite warehousing and trucking whereby products of various temperature ranges can be stored in one warehouse and transported in one vehicle. This has been possible because of the scale of the logistics operation – namely large RDCs supplying large superstores. Further upstream, primary consolidation centres have been created to minimize inventory held between factory and store. The size and spread of stores will, therefore, determine the form of logistical support to retail outlets. Geography also is an important consideration in terms of the physical distances products have to be moved in countries such as the UK, the Netherlands and Belgium compared with the United States and, to a lesser extent, France and Spain. Centralization of distribution into RDCs was more appropriate to urbanized environments, where stores could be replenished regularly. By contrast, in France and Spain some hypermarket operators have widely dispersed stores, often making it more cost-effective to hold stock in store rather than at an RDC.

The question of a trade-off of costs within the logistics mix is, therefore, appropriate at a country level. Labour costs permeate most aspects of logistics – and not surprisingly dependence on automation and mechanization increases as labour costs rise. Scandinavian countries have been in the vanguard of innovation here because of high labour costs – and similarly it can be argued that UK retailers have been innovators in ECR because of high inventory costs, caused by high interest rates, in the 1970s and 1980s. This also is true of land and property costs. In Japan, the United Kingdom and the Benelux countries, the high cost of retail property acts as an incentive to maximize sales space and minimize the carrying of stock in store. In France and the United States, the relatively lower land costs lead to the development of rudimentary warehousing to house forward-buy and promotional stock.

In order to implement ECR, there are 'enabling technologies' (Coopers & Lybrand, 1996) but their implementation is patchy both within and between organizations. For example, McLaughlin, Perosio and Park (1997) comment that 40 per cent of order fulfilment problems in US retailers are a result of miscommunications between retail buyers and their own distribution centre personnel. In Europe, Walker (1994) showed that EDI usage was much greater in the UK than in other European countries – notably Italy with its high cost of telecommunications, lack of management commitment and insufficient critical mass of participants. Since then, widespread ECR initiatives have led to greater use of 'enabling technologies', including web-based technologies, to enhance collaboration.

One area of collaboration that is often overlooked is that between retailer and logistics contractors. The provision of third-party services to retailers varies markedly by country according to the regulatory environment, the competitiveness of the sector and other logistics culture factors. For example, in the UK the deregulation of transport occurred in 1968, and many of the companies that provide dedicated distribution to RDCs today are the same companies that acted for suppliers when they controlled the supply chain 20 years ago. Retailers contracted out because of the opportunity cost of opening stores rather than RDCs, the cost was 'off-balance sheet', and there was a cluster of well-established professional companies available to offer the service. The situation is different in other markets. In the United States, third-party logistics is much less developed, warehousing is primarily run by the retailer, and transport is invariably contracted out to local hauliers. Deregulation of transport markets has been relatively late in the United States, leading to more competitive pricing. Similarly, the progressive deregulation of EU markets is breaking down some nationally protected markets.

The internationalization of logistics practices

The transfer of 'know-how' proposed by Kacker (1988) can be applied to logistics practices. Alternatively, companies can pursue an organic growth strategy by building up a retail presence in target markets before rolling out an RDC support function. For example, Marks & Spencer's European retail strategy initially was supported from distribution centres in southern Britain. As French and Spanish markets were developed, warehouses were built to support these stores in Paris and Madrid respectively. Another dimension to the internationalization of retail logistics is the internationalization of logistics service providers, many of whom were commissioned to operate sites on the basis of their relationship with retailers in the UK. With Marks & Spencer, Exel was the contractor operating the RDCs in France and Spain.

The expansion of the retail giants into new geographical markets is leading to internationalization of logistics. The approach to knowledge transfer is largely dependent upon the different models of globalized retail operations utilized by these mega-groups. Wrigley (2002) classified these retailers into two groups: one following the 'aggressively industrial' model, the other the 'intelligently federal' model (see Table 18.4). In the former model, to which Wal-Mart and to a lesser extent Tesco can be classified, the focus is upon economies of scale in purchasing and strong implementation of the corporate culture and management practices.

In the UK, Wal-Mart's impact on Asda's logistics has been mainly in enhancing IT infrastructure and reconfiguring its distribution network to supply the increase in non-food lines. By 2005, 20 supercentres had been opened, with 50 per cent of their space devoted to non-food items – and

Table 18.4 Alternative corporate models of a globalized retail operation

'Aggressively industrial'	'Intelligently federal'
Low format adaptation Lack of partnerships/alliances in emerging markets	Multiple/flexible formats Parnerships/alliances in emerging markets
Focus on economies of scale in purchasing, marketing and logistics	Focus on back-end integration, accessing economies of skills as much as scale, and best-practice knowledge transfer
Centralized bureaucracy, export of key management and corporate culture from core	Absorb, utilize/transfer, best local management acquired
The global 'category killer' model	The umbrella organization/corporate parent management acquired model

Source: Wrigley, 2002

existing stores will release more space for these with the release of space from enhanced IT systems. Project Breakthrough introduced new EPOS and stock data systems from 2000, and their retail link system has allowed greater co-ordination of information from till to supplier, reducing costs and enhancing product availability.

Ahold, by contrast, adheres to the intelligently federal model. It has transformed logistics practices through retail alliances, and through synergies developed with its web of subsidiaries. In the United States, for example, it has retained the local store names post-acquisition and adopted best practice across subsidiaries.

Another method of transferring 'know-how' is through retail alliances, a large number of which exist throughout Europe, most of which are buying groups (Robinson and Clarke-Hill, 1995). However, some of these alliances have been promoting a cross-fertilization of logistics ideas and practices. In the case of the European Retail Alliance, Safeway in the UK has partnered with Ahold of the Netherlands and Casino in France. Not surprisingly, the exploitation of UK retail logistics expertise has enabled distribution contractors to penetrate foreign retail markets, not only in support of British retail companies' entry strategies but also for other international retailers. Harvey (1997), chairman of Tibbett and Britten, argued that the success of his company – and other UK logistics specialists – is derived from the success of fast-moving consumer goods, but, as with UK retailers, success for the future lies with global opportunities.

The future

Clearly there has been a transformation of logistics within retailing during the last 25 years. Centralization, new technologies, ECR, QR and CPFR, and the implementation of best-practice principles have resulted in logistics becoming a key management function within retailing. But what of the future? With the exception of e-tail logistics, there is a feeling of déjà vu about the concerns expressed by senior logistics managers on the key issues to be addressed. Product availability – or the 'last 50 yards' issue – is of prime concern. It is somewhat alarming that on-shelf availability for some of our major grocery retailers is no better than it was 30 to 40 years ago for many key value items (KVIs). In the 1960s and 1970s, customers could easily go to the nearest store to pick up a manufacturer's brand unavailable at their preferred store. In the days of car-orientated supermarkets it would seem that store switching is less likely than in the days when a greater number of outlets and companies prevailed. Continual non-availability of key items can be a major factor in diminishing store loyalty. It is not surprising, therefore, that much of the focus of CPFR initiatives is not only on promotional items but also on KVIs to enhance on-shelf availability. In order to sell in-store, replenishment times need to be reduced so that the overall supply chain is more flexible to meet changing consumer demands.

In many ways this is a rerun of issues originally raised in the 1970s and 1980s. The main difference now is that retailers have a range of tools that allow massive supply chain savings to be realized. The problem is that the infrastructure changes required and the systems enhancement needed involve massive capital investment at a time when competition is fierce and achieving sales growth is difficult. All of these initiatives are also resource-hungry in terms of management time, and have considerable implications for the relationships amongst people, processes and technology. In retailing, competitive advantage is invariably achieved on the successful implementation of initiatives that are available to all – but only realized by companies with the quality of management to achieve results.

Tesco has been particularly innovative in seeking new solutions to improve on-shelf availability and reduce stockholding levels. Shock stock-outs in the 1970s emphasized the importance of supply chain management to the company and drove recognition that the supply chain was an integral part of company strategy. In the 1980s Tesco was in the forefront in creating composite distribution centres, and in the 1990s it implemented ECR and CPFR. Since the late 1990s much of Tesco's management philosophy has been linked to 'lean thinking', and further improvements are ongoing. One initiative that has created a high degree of controversy has been the advent of factory gate pricing. Although backhauling and consolidation of loads was a feature of the previous decades, this was organized on a fairly ad hoc manner with a series of bilateral transport contracts between logistics service providers and retailers and manufacturers. Now the larger grocery retailers are sourcing products 'ex-works', thereby managing the entire transport operation from factory to consumer.

The concept of factory gate pricing is not just being applied to the grocery sector. Similar principles are being adopted in non-food, and especially the fashion sector. Instead of FOB, retailers are seeking to source ex-works, liaising with LSPs to consolidate loads and prepare floor-ready merchandise to minimize handling at the downstream part of the supply chain. The fashion sector has a longer and more complex supply chain than groceries, but lead times to the EU can be reduced (relative to Pacific Rim sources) by sourcing from the Middle East and Eastern Europe. As Marks & Spencer has acknowledged, however, the quest for low-cost sourcing is only one solution to competing in highly competitive pricing markets. Other developments in fashion have seen time-based competition become more critical, with retailers such as Zara emerging and competing successfully, in part on supply chain speed and excellence.

Advances in information systems over the last two decades have acted as enablers facilitating supply chain efficiency. Bar codes, EDI, ERP systems and internet-based exchanges have all reduced the administrative costs of communication amongst supply chain partners. The next potential major technological breakthrough that will have a significant impact upon supply chain costs is RFID technology. Potential benefits to retailers are claimed to be immense. RFID could lead to the effective tracking of goods from factory to the home. Issues of cost and concerns over consumer privacy threaten the implementation of RFID, but it may also be that proponents have minimized some of the management and data use implications.

It is probable that the technology will be rolled out in stages, focusing on obvious issues and bottlenecks in supply chains. Initially the focus will be on tracking pallets, dollies and bins as they move from picking to the back room of the store. This will give cost savings in labour through greater automation of tracking and more visibility. Shrinkage (which costs retailers 1–2 per cent of sales a year) and stockholding levels should be reduced. As the costs of tags reduce – and if fears over consumer privacy are addressed – RFID tags will be used at the item level and implemented at store level. For retailers seeking to maximize on-shelf availability, this should give up-to-date information on sales and in-store inventory, with consequent supply chain benefits.

E-tail logistics is one area where activity is considerable – though perhaps not yet at the level anticipated by most commentators. Major changes may still occur, particularly when the e-tailing sector achieves greater stability. In the last few years a shake-out of the dot.com sector has occurred. In the non-food sector, a well-established delivery system is now in place and this system is being refined to accommodate the multi-channel strategy that is being adopted by most successful retailers. Traditional catalogue retailing incurred a high rate of 'returns' through the logistical network. This is being reinforced by online retailing, where around one-third of non-food products delivered to the home are returned. The reverse logistics task of retrieval, repackaging and returning or re-routeing merchandise is complex enough from home to warehouse, but web shoppers are also returning merchandise to their nearest store. 'Bricks and clicks' may increase customer spend and enhance loyalty but it also adds to costs. The need to invest in systems and infrastructure to accommodate such changes is leading to the formation of alliances amongst retailers to share these costs and build upon their relative expertise in supply chain functions.

E-grocery logistics has posed more formidable challenges. The initial 'hype' associated with the dot.com boom led to much investment into dedicated picking centres. In retrospect this was a flawed strategy based on unrealistic demand projections. Store-based fulfilment offered a more risk-averse approach to e-grocery, with demand met from existing assets and the e-grocer able to refine its systems and customer service as it gained experience. Nevertheless, there are questions about the long-term sustainability of such a model if online grocery sales continue to grow at current rates. The sharing of the same inventory between store and online shopper could aggravate the on-shelf availability problem and ultimately lead to poor customer service levels for both. As the market matures, investment in 'stand-alone' picking centres will be necessary in specific geographical markets, and the market leader, Tesco, intends to open such a centre in Croydon, near London, in 2006.

Regardless of the fulfilment model used, the 'last mile' problem is far from being resolved. Customers prefer narrow time slots for attended delivery; retailers prefer to utilize their transport assets around the clock. Ideally, the unattended delivery option is best for most parties, as customers are not constrained by delivery times, retailers can reduce their transport costs, and local authorities can reduce van congestion with 24-hour deliveries. But will customers invest in home reception facilities or be willing to pick up groceries in communal reception boxes? Initial reactions to such proposals have been lukewarm to say the least, leaving key problems to be overcome.

References

Azuma, N (2001) The reality of quick response (QR) in the Japanese fashion sector and the strategy ahead for the domestic SME apparel manufacturers, *Logistics Research Network 2001 Conference Proceedings*, pp 11–20, Heriot-Watt University, Edinburgh

Christopher, M (1997) *Marketing Logistics*, Butterworth-Heinemann, Oxford

Christopher, M (1998) *Logistics and Supply Chain Management*, 2nd edn, Financial Times, London

Christopher, M and Jüttner, U (2000) Achieving supply chain excellence: the role of relationship management, *International Journal of Logistics: Research and application*, **3** (1), pp 5–23

Christopher, M and Peck, H (2003) *Marketing Logistics*, Butterworth-Heinemann, London

Coopers & Lybrand (1996) *European Value Chain Analysis Study: Final report*, ECR Europe, Utrecht

Drucker, P (1962) The economy's dark continent, *Fortune*, April, pp 265–70

Fernie, J (1994) Quick response: an international perspective, *International Journal of Physical Distribution and Logistics Management*, **24** (6), pp 38–46

Fernie, J (1995) International comparisons of supply chain management in grocery retailing, *Service Industries Journal*, **15** (4), pp 134–47

Fernie, J (1998) Relationships in the supply chain, in *Logistics and Retail Management*, ed J Fernie and L Sparks (eds), Kogan Page, London

Fernie, J, Pfab, F and Marchant, C (2000) Retail logistics in the UK: planning for the medium term, *International Journal of Logistics Management*, **11** (2), pp 83–90

Fiddis, C (1997) *Manufacturer–Retailer Relationships in the Food and Drink Industry: Strategies and tactics in the battle for power*, FT Retail and Consumer Publishing, Pearson Professional, London

Finnie, TA (1992) *Textiles and Apparel in the U.S.A.: Restructuring for the 1990s*, Special Report 2632, Economist Intelligence Unit, London

Forza, C and Vinelli, A (1996) An analytical scheme for the change of the apparel design process towards quick response, *International Journal of Clothing Science and Technology*, **8** (4), pp 28–43

Forza, C and Vinelli, A (1997) Quick response in the textile-apparel industry and the support of information technologies, *Integrated Manufacturing Systems*, **8** (3), pp 125–36

Forza, C, and Vinelli, A (2000) Time compression in production and distribution within the textile-apparel chain, *Integrated Manufacturing Systems*, **11** (2), pp 138–46

GEA Consultia (1994), *Supplier–Retailer Collaboration in Supply Chain Management*, Coca-Cola Retailing Research Group Europe, London

Giunipero, LC *et al* (2001) The impact of vendor incentives on quick response, *International Review of Retail, Distribution and Consumer Research*, **11** (4), pp 359–76

Harvey, J (1997) International contract logistics, *Logistics Focus*, April, pp 2–6

Hines, T (2001) From analogue to digital supply chain: implications for fashion marketing, in *Fashion Marketing: Contemporary issues*, ed P Hines and M Bruce, Butterworth-Heinemann, Oxford

Hoch, SJ and Pomerantz, JJ (2002) How effective is category management?, *ECR Journal*, **2** (1), pp 26–32

Hunter, A (1990) *Quick Response in Apparel Manufacturing: A survey of the American scene*, Textile Institute, Manchester

Kacker, M (1988) International flows of retail know-how: bridging the technology gap in distributions, *Journal of Retailing*, **64** (1), pp 41–67

Ko, E, Kincade, D and Brown, JR (2000) Impact of business type upon the adoption of quick response technologies: the apparel industry experience, *International Journal of Operations and Production Management*, **20** (9), pp 1093–111

Kurt Salmon Associates (KSA) (1997) *Quick Response: Meeting customer needs*, KSA, Atlanta, GA

Lowson, B (1998) *Quick Response for Small and Medium-Sized Enterprises: A feasibility study*, Textile Institute, Manchester

Lowson, B, King, R and Hunter, A (1999) *Quick Response: Managing the supply chain to meet consumer demand*, John Wiley & Sons, New York

McGrath, M (1997) *A Guide to Category Management*, Institute of Grocery Distribution, Letchmore Heath

McKinnon, AC (1996) The development of retail logistics in the UK: a position paper, Technology Foresight's Retail and Distribution Panel, Heriot-Watt University, Edinburgh

McLaughlin, EW, Perosio, DJ and Park, JL (1997) *Retail Logistics and Merchandising: Requirements in the year 2000*, Cornell University Press, Ithaca, NY

Ministry of Economy, Trade and Industry (METI) (2002) *Seni Sangyo no Genjo to Seisaku Taiou* [The current status of the Japanese textile industry and the political responses], METI, Tokyo

Mitchell, A (1997), *Efficient Consumer Response: A new paradigm for the European FMCG sector*, FT Retail and Consumer Publishing, Pearson Professional, London

Ministry of International Trades and Industries (MITI) (1993) *Seni Vision* [Textile vision], MITI, Tokyo

MITI (1995) *Sekai Seni Sangyo Jijo* [MITI world textile report], MITI, Tokyo

MITI (1999) *Seni Vision* [Textile vision], MITI, Tokyo

Ohbora, T, Parsons, A and Riesenbeck, H (1992) Alternative routes to global marketing, *McKinsey Quarterly*, **3**, pp 52–74

Piore, MJ and Sabel, CF (1984) *The Second Industrial Divide: Possibilities for prosperity*, Basic Books, New York

Porter, ME (1985) *Competitive Advantage*, Free Press, New York

Quick Response Services (1995) *Quick Response Services for Retailers and Manufacturers*, Quick Response Services, Richmond, CA

Riddle, EJ *et al* (1999) The role of electronic data interchange in quick response, *Journal of Fashion Marketing and Management*, **3** (2), pp 133–46

Robinson, T and Clarke-Hill, CM (1995) International alliances in European retailing, in *International Retailing Trade and Strategies*, ed PJ McGoldrick and G Davies, Pitman, Harlow

Scarso, E (1997) Beyond fashion: emerging strategies in the Italian clothing industry, *Journal of Fashion Marketing and Management*, **1** (4), pp 359–71

Taplin, IM and Ordovensky, JF (1995) Changes in buyer–supplier relationships and labor market structure: evidence from the United States, *Journal of Clothing Technology and Management*, **12**, pp 1–18

Voluntary Interindustry Commerce Standards Association (VICS) (1998) *Collaborative Planning, Forecasting, and Replenishment Voluntary Guidelines*, VICS, Lawrenceville, NJ

Walker, M (1994) Supplier–retailer collaboration in European grocery distribution, Paper presented at the IGD Conference on Profitable Collaboration in Supply Chain Management, London

Whiteoak, P (1993) The realities of quick response in the grocery sector: a supply viewpoint, *International Journal of Retail and Distribution Management*, **21** (8), pp 3–10

Wrigley, N (2001) The consolidation wave in US food retailing: a European perspective, *Agribusiness*, **17**, pp 489–513

Wrigley, N (2002) The landscape of pan-European food retail consolidation, *International Journal of Retail and Distribution Management*, **30** (2), pp 81–91

19

Internet traders can increase profitability by reshaping their supply chains

Robert Duncan, B & C Business Services

Internet trading is forecast to account for a quarter of all purchases in 2006

The volume of internet trading grew significantly in the final years of the last century. It continued to grow in the early years of this century and is forecast to grow even further in the next few years. Forrester (2001a) forecast that global online trade, a combination of both business-to-business (B2B) and business-to-consumer (B2C) sales, will account for 18 per cent of all sales by 2006. Furthermore (Forrester, 2001b), two-thirds of the $12.8 trillion expenditure will be accounted for by purchases in the United States, representing 27 per cent of all their goods and services purchased. It is estimated that this increase will add 1.7 per cent to US transport service revenues. The US Department of Commerce reported continuing growth in 2004 with e-commerce sales up 21 per cent for the year. The growth is forecast to continue. US internet retail sales are predicted to grow at a compound annual rate of 14 per cent a year until 2010 (Forrester, 2005b). It is recognized that the United States leads the way in most e-commerce-driven initiatives and, therefore, the scale of increases in the United States is likely to be seen in other developed countries shortly – followed by less developed countries. The UK reported a 30 per cent increase in year-on-year e-retail sales in the third quarter of 2004 (GVA, 2004). The level of sales during the first half of 2004 reflected a fivefold increase in the level experienced in 2001. The route to market, particularly with the introduction of broadband, is seen as so important that in the United States it is forecast that, by 2010, 8 per cent of all advertising spend will be directed at internet advertising in various forms (Forrester, 2005c). This sum will rival that being spent on cable and satellite TV and radio.

Customer satisfaction is less than satisfactory

Such growth predictions lie against a background of dissatisfied customers, press reports that many internet traders do not fully understand their order fulfilment costs, and transport service providers complaining that their customers tend to be cost- rather than service-driven. This leads them to suggest that their customers do not fully understand the complexity of home delivery – or B2C operations – and consequently the added value that they provide. This background has been created by internet traders trying to operate effectively utilizing traditional distribution methods and networks. There has been a tendency to concentrate too much effort on websites, and not pay enough attention to the business processes needed to integrate order capture with other business systems and order fulfilment.

Dissatisfaction in the mind of the customer can be created in a number of ways. Late delivery, damaged goods, poorly handled financial transactions and bad-tempered delivery people are just a few. It is generally accepted that because the placing of an order via the internet is extremely quick, simple and in many cases pleasurable, the expectation in the mind of the customer is that all aspects of the transaction will be of a similar nature. Customer expectation has been heightened. The ordering process was slick and customers, not unreasonably, expect the rest of the process to be undertaken with the same efficiency. Under these circumstances, it is more likely that the customer will not be fully satisfied unless particular steps are taken to ensure that the level of service provided meets the heightened level of expectations. It is all too easy to undo the excellent work done by the website in winning the customer – and the order – by inadequate business processes and order fulfilment procedures.

Integration of business processes has not always received enough attention

Many organizations are now realizing – often too late – that they should have paid as much attention to their internal business processes, their order fulfilment resources and systems, and the integration of these processes and systems with those of their suppliers and order fulfilment services as they did to their customer-facing website. The need is for a seamless, end-to-end 'order-to-cash' process incorporating the website, the business's accounting systems and the delivery mechanism. The accounting needs should embrace, as a minimum, accounts payable, accounts receivable, inventory, purchase orders, invoicing and credit control.

In many organizations, when internet trading is added to the traditional market offering the delivery mechanisms cannot cope with the requirement for a large number of small orders that require, to all intents and purposes, instant shipping. They may historically have been shipping relatively large orders to a few intermediate supply chain points with a two- to three-day lead time. The business processes – and perhaps more importantly the business systems that are required to manage a large number of small orders – are different from those required to manage the traditional business. The potential for making mistakes is high when an organization attempts to manage the internet business in the same way as the traditional business. And all the effort and resources that went into winning the business are wasted by losing that business due to the inadequate processes and systems to support order fulfilment.

Moving away from traditional supply chains adds complexity but provides an opportunity for profit

The situation is made even more complex by the fact that the rise in internet trading has provided the potential to restructure traditional distribution networks, supply chains and product flows. Much of the thinking to date relates to the traditional ways of moving products from manufacturers to customers. In the B2C area this has reflected traditional mail-ordering concepts as typified by those organizations selling products such as books and music CDs. In simple terms, rather than ordering from a catalogue received in the mail and posting their order back to their suppliers, customers are placing their order via the internet. Their products are delivered to them in much the same way as they were with traditional mail order. The key differences are that the ordering process has been shortened and the manufacturers' order capture and processing costs have been reduced. Food retailers offering home-delivery services typically rely on the order that has been received via the internet being printed in the branch nearest to the customer, picked from the shelves in that branch and delivered, by a branch-based vehicle, to the home of the customer.

Internet trading has enabled improved supply chains

Recent supply chain trends have reflected changes made possible by the internet as a means of communicating between buyers and sellers. When the simple scenario described above is related to books, it no longer requires a supply chain involving the printer and publisher, an intermediate stockholding location and an organization to promote the offer, capture the order and execute the delivery. Potential customers can place their orders using either their own PC at home or a terminal in the branch of a high-street book retailer specifically provided for browsing and order capture. The order is then transmitted to the relevant publisher – not an intermediate stockholding point – for picking, packing and shipping directly to the customer.

Books and CDs lend themselves ideally to this type of trade as, apart from some minor exceptions, they can easily be shipped across borders and they do not require particular shipping conditions in terms of temperature control. The situation for foodstuffs is very different. A single customer order may be relatively heavy, consist of a number of different-size cartons and bottles, require a range of temperature regimes and need to be delivered within a tightly defined time-frame. As volumes increase, the industry is beginning to introduce home-delivery picking and delivery depots located away from the prime retail sites. Such facilities enable the use of sophisticated warehouse techniques, made possible by the automatic entry of customer orders into the warehouse system. The advantages created by customers ordering over the internet include more effective picking operations in a depot rather than a branch, improved product availability through monitoring the particular purchasing patterns of internet shoppers, lower delivery costs as the increased volumes allow sophisticated routeing and scheduling techniques, and less congestion in the branches.

The monitoring of individuals' consumption patterns – and the retailers' websites both prompting and reminding their regular customers of those patterns as they go through the ordering process – could further extend the concept.

Such changes could be introduced into other market sectors

The two examples above – books and CDs – suggest modifications of current practices and adjustment to supply chains that result from the ability to place orders over the internet. The concepts could be used by other manufacturers not currently fully embracing the potential of electronically capturing orders and shipping customer orders directly to them. Figure 19.1 shows a general supply chain for the distribution of prescription drugs from a manufacturer to a patient.

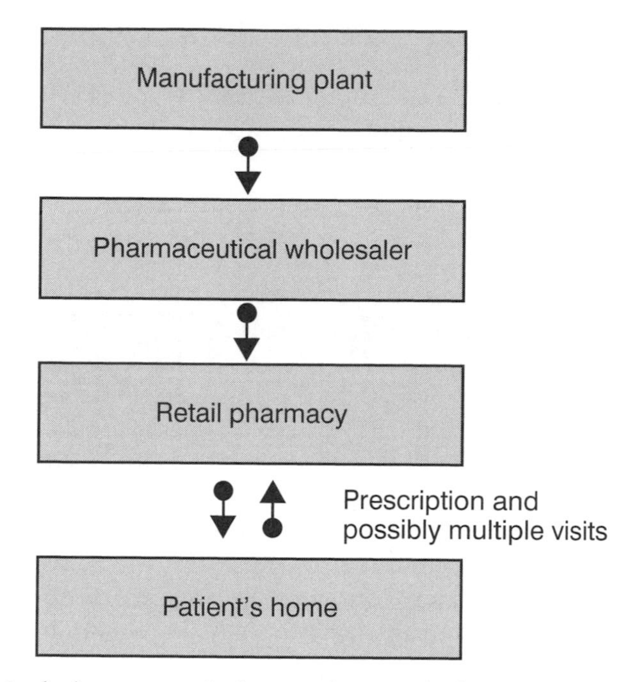

Figure 19.1 A typical pharmaceutical manufacturer's distribution network

The main characteristic is the use of wholesalers and retailers to make the delivery to the patient once a doctor has prescribed the particular drug. In the case of hospitalized patients, there is usually another stockholding point in the hospital's pharmacy, between the manufacturer and the patient. Large hospitals using large amounts of particular drugs receive deliveries directly from the manufacturers, but these are the exception rather than the rule.

The level of service provided is extremely high, with wholesalers making multiple deliveries a day to retailers to ensure that particular drugs – from the plethora potentially available – are delivered to the patients as soon as possible. However, patients often have to return to the pharmacy for either all or part of their requirements once they have presented their prescription. Owing to the nature of the products, the flows are highly regulated, and some form of control is obviously necessary. However, a more streamlined approach could be envisaged using the internet as the means of communication. Figure 19.2 illustrates a possible use of the internet to facilitate the order fulfilment of prescription drugs.

The scenario starts with the doctor prescribing the drugs in an electronic format and sending details via the internet to the manufacturer once the consultation with the patient has finished. The manufacturer simply picks, packs and ships the products to the patient's home. The shipping process would utilize the best means available to suit the characteristics of the product. Small and light packets of tablets, for example, could be shipped

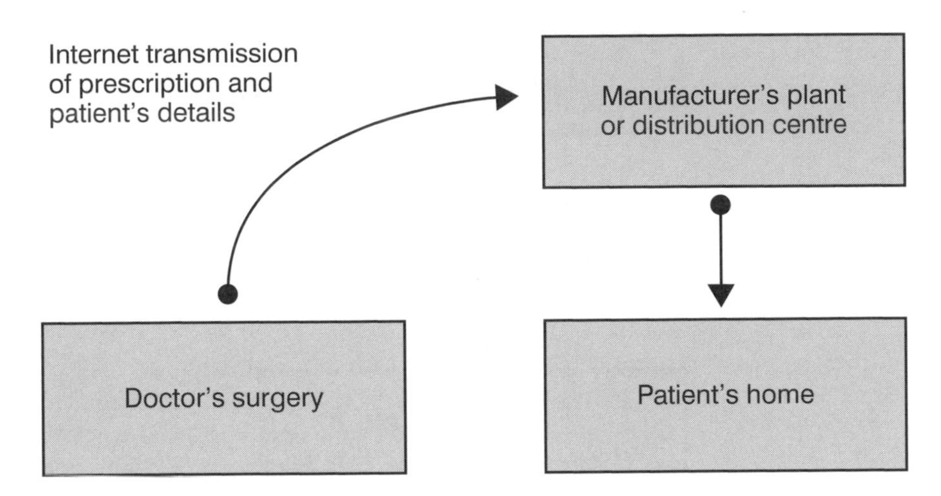

Figure 19.2 A possible pharmaceutical manufacturer's distribution network

using conventional postal services; more sophisticated products requiring careful handling may use specialist express parcels services. A less radical version of the concept may result in the wholesalers providing the home-delivery service on a regional basis. In each case, the distribution supply chain is simplified and the patient does not have to go to the retail outlet, sometimes more than once, to obtain his or her medication. This is particularly advantageous for elderly and infirm patients.

Many retail pharmacists have introduced a prescription collection and delivery service, but their aim is not to simplify the supply chain, but to maintain the status quo. The supply chain change outlined not only provides an improved service to customers and a reduction in the complexity of the manufacturers' supply chains, but also helps overcome some of the issues associated with the parallel importing of pharmaceuticals. Pharmaceuticals are sold at varying prices around the world, so traders can buy cheaply in some areas, ship the products to areas of high selling prices and make a profit. Pharmaceutical companies experience lower sales in those areas with high selling prices, reduced profit levels – and, therefore, potentially lower research budgets. The proposed supply chain change gives pharmaceutical companies greater control through disintermediation, with less buying and selling of product by third parties, and less cross-border movements. The use of RFID technology, effectively electronically 'tagging' products, will also assist with the control of pharmaceuticals from the manufacturing plant to the point of use by the patient. This will increase service levels, reduce costs and sustain pharmaceutical research and development in the future.

The concept can also be applied in the B2B context

The B2B area also provides opportunities to restructure traditional supply chains. For many years, supply chain organizations have exchanged information electronically regarding production schedules, raw material and component stock levels and forecast levels of demand and production capacity. Suppliers and buyers, particularly in the automotive sector, have practised just-in-time techniques relying on electronic communication. They have developed and introduced order fulfilment techniques reshaping the structure of the distribution supply chains, enabling minimal inventories to be maintained through line-side delivery and rapid communication.

Other organizations have centralized their storage operations as a result of being able to communicate rapidly and fulfil orders using efficient transport services. The emergence of cost-effective and reliable, high-speed transport services has played an important role in achieving the ambitions of those players embarking upon an internet trading journey. The systems used by such organizations enable their customers to track their own shipments. This is essential in the early stages of using a changed network to give customers – both internal and external to the organization – the confidence that the remote operation will provide the required levels of service. More importantly, the systems enable carriers themselves to be proactive on the rare occasion that some corrective action is needed.

The impact will not be as large in all industry sectors

The reshaping of the supply chain as a result of internet trading and the emergence of reliable and cost-effective rapid-transport service providers will not affect all industry sectors to the same extent. While communications may improve – a worthwhile end in itself – it is difficult to envisage the network for bulk building supplies (such as sand, ballast and cement) changing significantly. The biggest impact is likely to be in the order fulfilment of those products that are relatively high in value and easily transported. The B2B environment is more stable than B2C, with a more defined customer base and a better understanding of demand patterns. The traditional distribution supply chain of an industrial company is shown in Figure 19.3. It is characterized by the direct delivery of large orders from factory to customer and the use of distributors, agents or wholesalers for the delivery of small orders to customers on a geographic basis.

The internet can capture and process orders more cheaply and quickly, so manufacturers are beginning to consider reducing the number of middlemen that they use to fulfil customers' orders. Companies that supply consumables to other companies for use in their manufacturing can provide monitoring devices that send material usage statistics to them, via the internet, triggering automatic replenishment orders. Once a history of usage has been established,

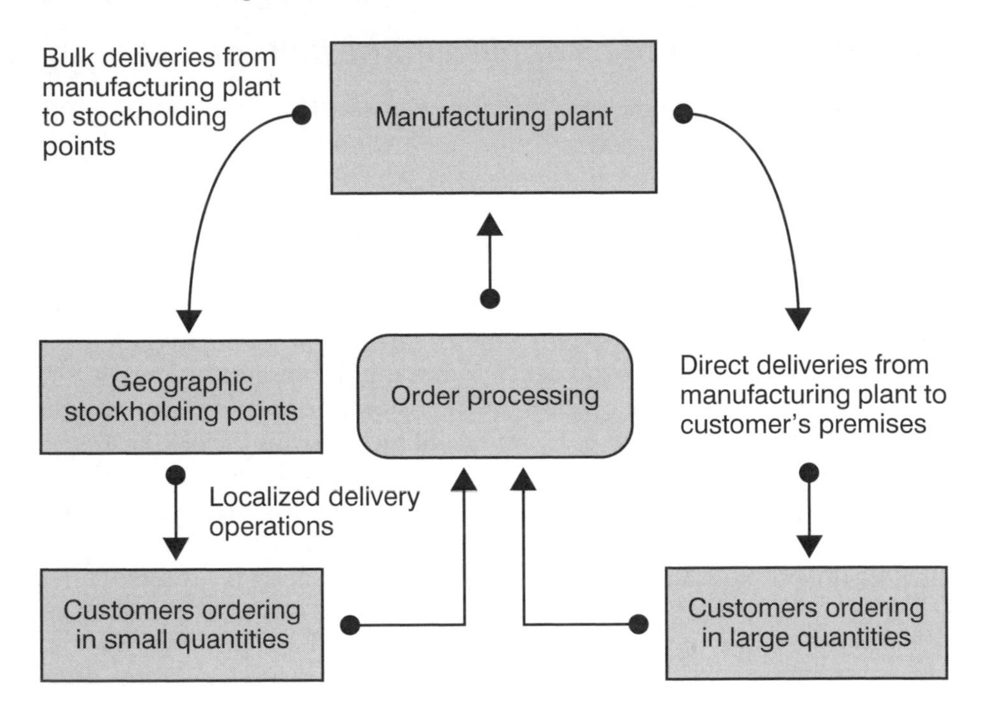

Figure 19.3 A traditional industrial supplier's distribution network

order fulfilment can be achieved more cost-effectively, with better planning to minimize the effects of peaks in demand. The customer does not need to maintain a purchasing function to place orders, and the supplier does not need to incur the costs of an order processing department – a 'win–win' scenario.

There is likely to be an increase in centralized operations

The biggest changes in order fulfilment infrastructure as a result of internet trading are likely to be in the area of centralized operations. Establishing a small number of order fulfilment centres – with associated software to integrate the website ordering process with the organization's business systems – is likely to be more cost-effective than the establishment of a larger number of local operations. Although transport costs are likely to increase as a result, they will be more than offset by lower order processing costs, inventory-related costs and warehouse facility costs. At constant volume, increased margins will be attainable or lower prices can be charged to increase market share and enhance profitability.

In Europe, organizations that typically operated on a national basis are establishing more regionalized operations. Products that are of relatively high value and easily transported tend to support larger regions than those that have low value and require specific transport resources. For example, companies with spare-part operations tend to centralize activities, as field engineers and customers can communicate with a central point via the internet, and inventory control is much simpler with a central stock than several stockholding locations. The enlarged membership of the EU has resulted in many organizations revisiting their infrastructure and designing regionalized structures.

As the infrastructures change and the traditional role of intermediaries declines, a new group of internet traders is emerging offering purchasing function services. In general terms, they negotiate prices with a range of suppliers and offer, over the internet, a one-stop service for the products of those suppliers to their customers. Once they have taken an order from a customer it is converted to an order with a supplier. That supplier then fulfils the order in the conventional manner. The benefits of this scenario are that the customers obtain better prices, the suppliers do not have the costs of the customer-facing activities and the internet trader makes money by providing an added-value service to both customer and supplier without stocking and handling the products.

The challenge is becoming greater

The growth in internet trading has not been accompanied by tales of delighted customers or order fulfilment processes to match the heightened customer expectation. Early experience suggested that organizations were not particularly good at integrating their website order capturing activities with their internal business systems and those of their order fulfilment service provider. And many organizations did not realize the potential of the internet for streamlining their supply chains. Changing business processes and introducing the necessary systems to trade over the internet provided a challenge within existing business relationships and infrastructures. The challenge is being made all the more difficult as business relationships and the physical infrastructure within which those relationships operate are changing.

How can internet traders take advantage of opportunities?

In this ever-changing world not all of the potential internet-driven supply chain changes will be appropriate for all internet traders. Even within an industry sector, patterns will emerge, but the same solution may not be suitable for all of the players in that sector. There are, however, four activities that all internet traders can complete as a starting point for optimizing their benefits:

1. *The establishment of a vision of the future:* 'Where are we going and what is it going to be like when we get there?'
2. *The definition of the partnering arrangements needed for success:* 'Who is going to help us get to where we are going and how are we going to manage them?'
3. *The reviewing of their business processes and electronic systems:* 'Can our processes and systems enable us to achieve our long-term objectives?'
4. *The undertaking of trade-off calculations:* 'What options are open to us and how much will they cost?'

These four activities form the key steps of an overall route to success outlined in Figure 19.4.

The establishment of a vision of the future

It is perhaps a little obvious to say that an organization must be able to define the direction in which it intends to go. This vision of the future is not a loose

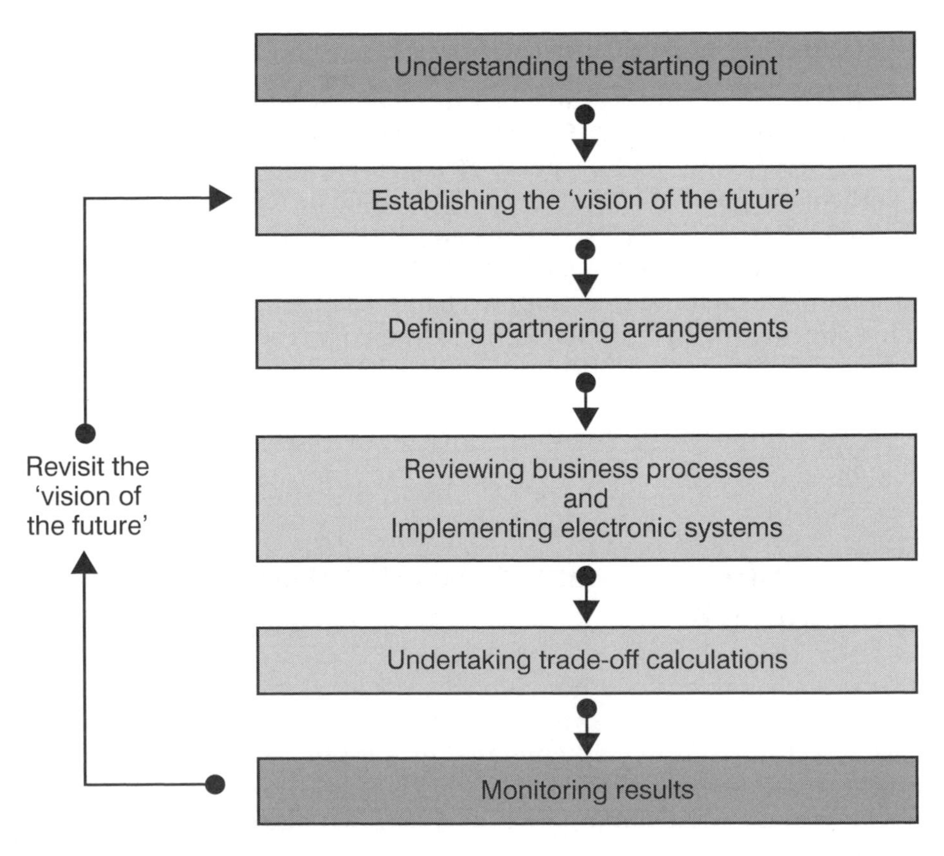

Figure 19.4 A route to success

collection of statements amounting to little more than a wish list. It is, however, several statements describing – in quantifiable terms – the nature of the business at some point in the future. That point will vary depending upon the nature of the marketplace in which the organization is operating. In the high-tech sector, the foreseeable future may be only a few months, or a year at the most. In traditional industry sectors that do not expect a significant percentage of their business ever to be undertaken over the internet, the vision may take several years to come to fruition.

The statements should cover the total volume of business both in terms of value and in physical terms, the share that is undertaken over the internet, the size of both the customer and the supplier bases, the profitability of the internet business, the costs associated with order fulfilment, and the delivery profile in terms of order numbers and the amount in each order size band appropriate to the business. Any individual organization will have many other metrics particular to its industry sector and product range. The key issue is that they should be measurable. They will be used to establish key performance indicators (KPIs) for the business. These KPIs will be monitored, and the organization can establish the extent to which it is achieving its vision and reaping the rewards from the changes it has made.

The definition of the partnering arrangements needed for success

Organizations wanting to trade over the internet, with a few exceptions, are unlikely to have all of the required skills in-house to establish the website effectively, integrate it with their business systems, and manage the order fulfilment activities. Partners are, therefore, essential for the vast majority of organizations. A number of options are available to potential electronic traders:

- *A single 'one-stop shop' able to deliver the website, integration with a commerce platform, and order fulfilment.* This gives the advantages of a single point of contact for the management team, and an organization that manages all of the difficult interfaces. Until recently, such organizations have been few and far between. This made selecting partners and a successful outcome something of a lottery – with service providers often developing a formula that worked for their original customer, and being reluctant to change it to meet the needs of new entrants. Such is the pace of change that this does not provide as large a barrier to progress as it did a few years ago. The investment in IT by a number of major value-adding order fulfilment contractors is now beginning to manifest itself, and they have the skills, resources, hardware and software that allow them to offer a single end-to-end service. The second wave of internet commerce in 2004 saw an increase in the demand for hosted or outsourced e-commerce solutions

(Forrester, 2005a). Vendors, including internet service providers, have responded with a range of offerings addressing the supply chain in either its entirety or its component parts.

- *Partnerships with a number of specialist service providers to source all of the services that they require.* To achieve this successfully, project management and outsourcing management skills need to be in abundance in the organization. While the individual elements of website design, systems integration and order fulfilment may be readily available in the market, the required in-house skills of project and outsourcing management may not. With a trend to more outsourced resources, this issue will gain in significance for many organizations.
- *An organization that has already done all the hard work, but is not in competition with the market entrant.* It is likely that potential partners are traditional 'bricks and mortar' traders that have extended their offering to include an electronic commerce element. Perhaps niche players could partner with major players in their own industry to provide a wider offering to the major players' customers. In the past, small niche players would not have attempted to partner the major industry players, as they would have regarded them as competitors – and unequal partners. For example, the online market for books is dominated by mega-sites such as Amazon and Barnes & Noble. Alibris, a small organization specializing in used and hard-to-find books, now works with the major organizations as a supplier of titles that are not their mainstream business – to the mutual benefit of all of the supply chain partners (Internet.com, 2003).

Thus, there are many ways of developing a partnership. An organization that expects a rapid growth in volume over a short period may favour an added-value service provider, as it could overwhelm a traditional business that currently has only a small part of its business handled by the internet. Organizations that are hoping to move into new markets and/or geographies are likely to favour the added-value service provider. Organizations that see a relatively slow but steady growth may favour managing the situation themselves or partnering with an organization that has already made the leap to internet trading.

The reviewing of their business processes and electronic systems

When reviewing in-house systems, internet traders should include both electronic software systems and the business processes. In terms of the electronic software, the simplest questions include:

- 'Can our systems cope with a significant increase in transactional volume?'
- 'Can our systems interface with modern websites?'

- 'Can our systems interface with those of our suppliers of both goods and services?'
- 'Can our systems enable us to deliver the required level of customer service?'

A few years ago, some of these questions would have sent shivers down the spines of would-be internet traders. Thankfully, modern systems do not generally present significant difficulties with interfacing, and extra capacity is no longer the hugely expensive item that it was in the past. However, the critical area for most organizations is not the software systems and supporting hardware networks, but their business processes. Will any of the order processing, credit checking, inventory allocation, manufacturing, warehousing, shipping, invoicing and cash collection processes within the overall order-to-cash process negatively affect the requirements of the internet business?

If an organization is a true middleman and does not expect to hold stock, but converts a sales order from a customer into a purchase order for a supplier, its internal processes will need to be able to cope with this. It may be necessary to have a different process for internet trade from that used for conventional business in organizations handling both routes to market. The questions needing to be answered under these circumstances include:

- 'Who will design the required processes to ensure that all customers' requirements are met?'
- 'What will be the impact of those new processes on existing processes and the consequent risk to our traditional business?'
- 'Will we achieve the predicted levels of economies of scale employing two or more order-to-cash processes?'

These questions will be easier to answer if a clear understanding of the business direction has been established. When the internet business is seen to grow steadily but will never be a significant part of the business, the duplicated process route may be the easiest way of dealing with matters. Alternatively, if the internet business is expected to grow rapidly and both the conventional and the internet trades become significant elements of the total business, a single process route would have merit.

Trade-off calculations

Analyses of the overall network and the options available to achieve the required levels of customer service are essential. To undertake the trade-off calculations associated with changing supply chains and distribution networks in order to select the best route to market for any individual internet entrepreneur, a full knowledge of the current and potential operating costs is needed. Again, the importance of a vision of the future can readily be appreciated. While having that vision is important, understanding the starting point is also extremely important. Key questions to be answered include:

- 'What volumes are being dispatched?'
- 'What levels of service are being achieved?'
- 'What costs are being incurred?'
- 'Do we feel that we are obtaining value for money from the resources being employed?'

The vision will be able to provide answers to the questions about future volumes and expected margins. The internet trader must then define a number of options for delivering the future volumes within the required customer service level constraints. They are likely to be network models with decentralized or centralized, direct delivery or delivery via distributors, and stockless or inventory-holding themes. A number of evaluation criteria – in addition to those that are strictly cost-related – will be required to establish the most appropriate solution for each particular trader. While industry sectors may find similar solutions, an individual organization in that sector will be driven by its vision of the future and its culture in achieving that goal.

Opportunity waiting to be exploited

Internet trading is here to stay and, if recent experience is any guide, volumes are set to grow significantly in the very near future. Given the growth predictions, suppliers to both the consumer and the business markets have a tremendous opportunity. They are setting out on the journey against a background of heightened customer expectation and a history of failure to meet those expectations. The winners will be those organizations that take the opportunity afforded by the internet to change the manner in which they capture and fulfil their customers' orders.

To date, many traders have implemented an internet 'front end' to their existing business processes. Consequently, the initial limited volumes have been treated in the same way as their mainstream volumes. Those customers ordering via the internet have different customer service level needs and expectations from most traditional customers – hence the levels of disappointment expressed.

The internet allows for different trading relationships and physical networks to be established. Those traders that develop a vision of the future incorporating the available potential, enter into partnering arrangements to enhance their internal skill base, review their business processes to meet their customers' needs, implement electronic systems to support those new business processes, and undertake the trade-off calculations to identify the most appropriate ways of meeting all of their customers' needs will reap the benefits. Newcomers can learn from those organizations that are acknowledged industry leaders and advance quickly up the learning curve.

The opportunity is real. The winners will be those that grasp the opportunity by using the internet as a means of gaining competitive advantage, rather than continue to use it as a bolt-on extra to existing traditional operating methods.

References

Department of Commerce (2004) *Ecommerce-guide.com: E-commerce business is booming*, November, US Department of Commerce, Washington, DC

Forrester (2001a) *Techstrategy Brief*, December, Forrester Research, Cambridge, MA

Forrester (2001b) *Techstrategy Report: eBusiness propels productivity*, November, Forrester Research, Cambridge, MA

Forrester (2005a) *A Buyer's Guide to Hosted eCommerce Solutions*, January, Forrester Research Paper, Cambridge, MA

Forrester (2005b) *US eCommerce, 2005 to 2010*, September, Forrester Research Paper, Cambridge, MA

Forrester (2005c) *US Online Marketing Forecast, 2005 to 2010*, May, Forrester Research Paper, Cambridge, MA

GVA (2004) *Retail Trends*, Third Quarter, Grimley Research, London

Internet.com (2003) *Case Study: Alibris*, August

Global sourcing and supply

Alan Braithwaite, LCP Consulting Ltd

Background

Global sourcing and supply is now a central part of many companies' business strategies. It has proved essential to sustaining marketplace competitiveness and maintaining net margins. Indeed, global sourcing and supply is probably both the biggest economic trend of the last 20 years and a key ingredient for corporate survival; it takes advantage of low-cost and available labour, cheap international logistics, and less regulated operating environments than in mature economies.

The adoption of low-cost sourcing and supply areas has displayed an exponential trend, which is forecast to continue. However, the dynamics of this new way of operating are only just being understood and have not been documented extensively. Global sourcing implies long-distance supply chains, multiple hand-offs and extended lead times. As companies move to increase their share of global sourcing beyond the current entry levels, there will be major implications for how these extended chains are managed; security of supply, demand responsiveness and product life cycle management all take on greater significance.

This chapter describes the landscape of global sourcing and supply and the dimensions that companies need to address to ensure a stable operational and business base. Global sourcing is an established geopolitical and economic fact of life. It is now a market-driven trend. But the challenge for every individual corporation is to implement it in a way that secures a sustainable advantage. This means organizing to manage risk alongside commercial and competitive advantage. All of the principles of supply chain management still apply; the specifics of global sustainability have many additional dimensions that are not experienced in more conventional local chains.

Growth in global trade

The expansion of global trade in manufactured goods has been one of the most pronounced and remarkable economic trends of the last 40 years. It has both fuelled and enabled the growth in the GDP of most developed countries, exporting jobs to countries with large pools of increasingly skilled and low-cost labour. The capacity of the labour pool in developed countries is being released to higher-value or essentially local activities and the service sector. The scale of this shift is shown in Figure 20.1.

This growth shows no sign of abating. It has been reinforced by the reduction in tariff barriers and the expansion of low-cost international logistics in the form of container freight. The importance of global trade is illustrated in Figure 20.2, which shows the strong correlation between import

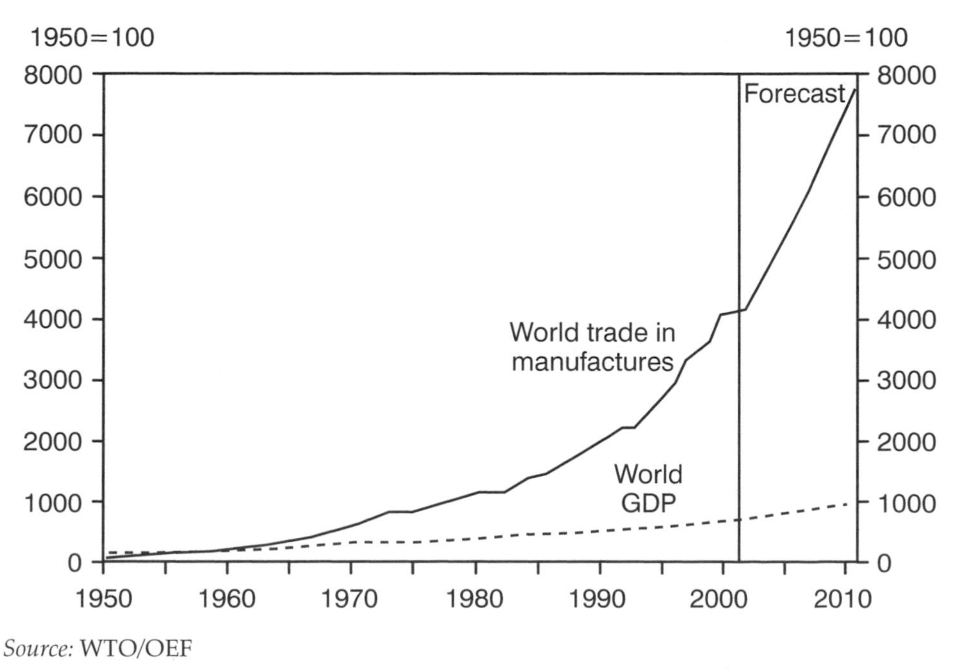

Source: WTO/OEF

Figure 20.1 Growth in global trade in manufactures

Exports and imports ranked by export growth 2002–03

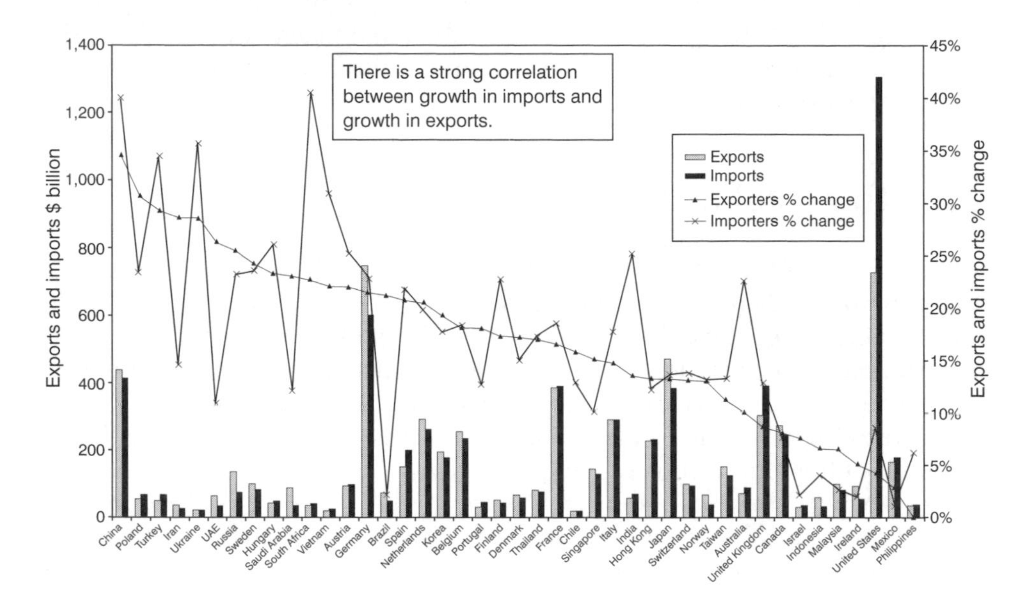

Figure 20.2 Correlation of import and export growth showing the country scale of activity

and export growth. This also demonstrates that there is no correlation with growth and the absolute scale of imports and exports. This means that the opportunity of global trade is an economic benefit to both mature and emerging economies. If we set aside the natural tensions of self-interest that have been evident in recent world trade negotiations, it is clear that there are enormous benefits for buyers and sellers alike.

China has been posting GDP growth of 8 to 9 per cent a year and this has recently been described as an underestimate. It refers to itself with pride as the 'factory to the world'. No one can ignore this trade potential, and global sourcing is now a matter of board strategy for all businesses in developed economies.

Statements in relation to planned increases in this trend are a regular feature of annual reports and analyst briefings. Wal-Mart, the world's largest retailer, made the trend to direct international sourcing a key feature of its 2002 annual report, saying:

> We also are making exciting strides in… global procurement. Last year we assumed responsibility of global procurement from a third party. This allowed us to better co-ordinate the entire global supply chain from product development to delivery. In addition, our global procurement program allows us to share our buying power and merchandise network with all our operations throughout the world.

Dyson closed its entire manufacturing in the UK and moved to Asia as a key element of its entry strategy for the US market. New origins for the garment trade are Turkey and Morocco, where companies can still leverage low-cost labour, but without full Far East sacrifices on lead time and flexibility.

Figure 20.3 shows the critical contribution of the automotive industry, engineering and electronics to globalization. In reality, companies like Wal-Mart are only catching up and this will probably be at the expense of both importers and local manufacturers.

The WTO (2005) predicts that global supply is the future. Indeed, it is an irreversible trend, since capacity is leaving developed markets because it cannot compete with low-cost imports. This global sourcing dimension of strategy is now a cornerstone of companies' plans to generate value for customers and shareholders alike. Few can envisage a sustainable future without an increasing level of global supply.

Given this landscape of major change, this chapter brings together some key dimensions of the practice of global sourcing. It reviews the 'layer and pillar' model (Figure 20.4), which proved useful as a means to describe the multifaceted nature of global supply chain management (Liang, 2005). Supply chain management in global sourcing must address all of the layers. Best practice is bound together by a requirement to understand and manage through a structured approach to risk and through the total Cost-to-Serve®.

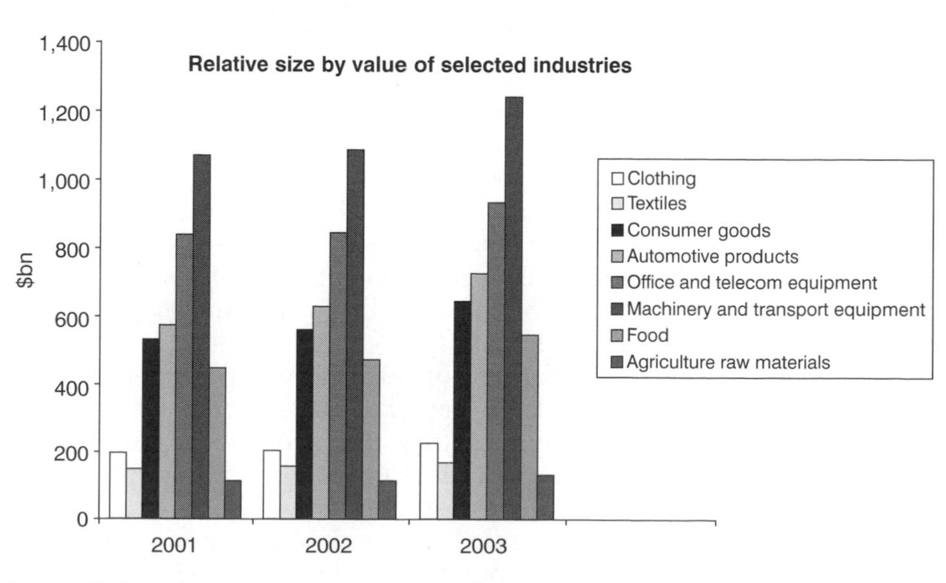

Source: WTO, 2005

Figure 20.3 Global trade growth by product category

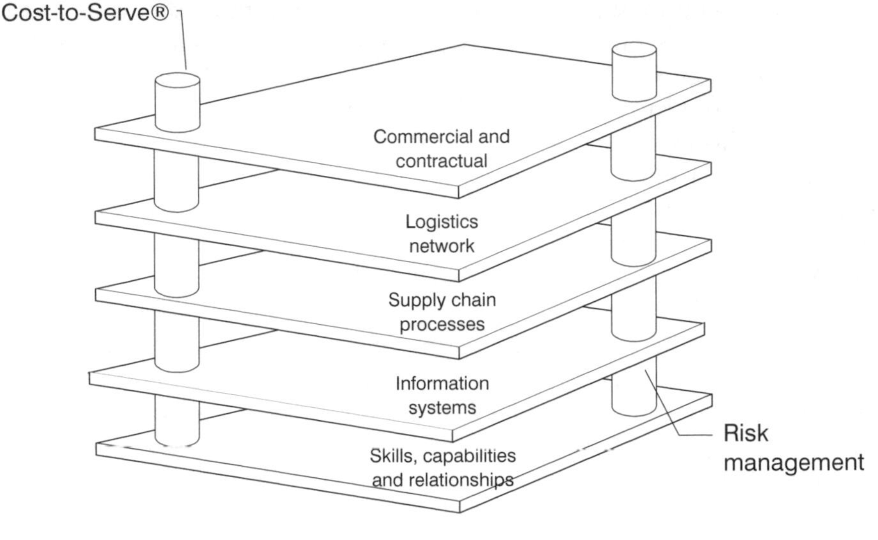

Figure 20.4 The layers and pillars of global sourcing best practice

Cost-to-Serve, which is a registered mark of LCP Consulting, is a supply chain costing methodology that can quickly capture the true logistics cost drivers, and identify activities that are intrinsically uneconomic.

Global sourcing as a way to change business strategy

The central role of global sourcing in transforming business strategies can be understood by comparing the relative wage rates in regions of the world. Because of difficulties with exact comparisons, these figures are indicative rather than definitive. For skilled labour per hour in Germany the cost is $18 to $25; in the Czech Republic it is $3 to $5; in the United States it is $9 to $15; in Asia and India it is often less than $1. The cost of support services, construction, capital investment and management are in proportion, which means that the cost of an equivalent article made in an emerging economy can be as little as half of that sourced locally.

Traders have been taking advantage of this arbitrage potential for many years and have used their local relationships, buying skills and logistics know-how to make a margin. That margin was their return for taking risk, including quality, financing and marketing. The ultimate price differentials were reduced to 10 to 20 per cent to the end customer.

The surge in growth of global trade is the result of more companies going into markets to deal direct – cutting out the middleman. The effect of this has been to increase margins and also to increase the buyer's risk. The business strategy has been to plough back the margin benefit into lower prices, which in turn has increased volumes and market share. The trick has been – and will be – to exploit the elasticity of demand by just enough to get more volume than the margin that has been conceded. Getting this right makes both sales and profits grow.

Across industry as a whole, the trend has been for lower real prices as value is passed on to customers. The open question is the extent to which this trend is now played out. The next step in global sourcing will involve another doubling of activity levels and this will require improved levels of control and integration. The skills of supply chain management will become increasingly central.

Identifying and selecting sources

The practice of sourcing depends on the commodity and product. For example, chemicals display different supply characteristics from clothing, which in turn is different from microelectronics. Entering a new sourcing arrangement is a moment of risk and there are many factors to be considered. These include the following:

- *Quality is a key issue.* Vendors are increasingly able to deliver to quality – but this ability cannot be taken for granted. The implications of a long-distance quality failure are much greater than a local one, as the problem may not be discovered soon enough to avoid serious disruption. Increasingly, companies are insisting on more comprehensive quality control at vendors, alongside detailed specification and engineering integration.
- *Ethical supply.* The marketing and PR impacts of the use of child labour and the environmental conditions surrounding production are now important for consumers. Media disclosures can damage a brand with consumers and shake investor confidence. Increasingly, companies are conducting regular audits and inspections of their sources to make sure that they do not get surprises that damage their reputation.
- *Patent protection.* The leaking of design and technology advantage has become a common experience. Companies have outsourced to places where respect for patents and know-how is rather less than the standard they would expect. Often designs, ideas and products reappear through different channels and can erode markets and price levels. This risk requires a very careful approach to ensure that key differentiators are protected and that contractual guarantees are obtained that can be enforced.
- *Operational excellence.* Vendors' capabilities can vary widely and it is crucial to understand the extent to which they will be able to perform to expectation. For example, late new product introductions can significantly affect the buying and marketing organization, and there is evidence of share price erosion when international chains fail.

These points require a higher level of due diligence and ongoing management than many might expect. Dealing across cultural boundaries is a major part of this challenge – and the word 'yes' in many languages cannot be taken as an unequivocal agreement.

Commercial models

Global trade is by definition more remote than buying locally. A problem with local supply can prompt a whole range of quite simple actions, including refusing to pay and taking legal action. With global sourcing and supply these actions are more difficult, since the goods may already have been paid for, and legal action is less likely to be successful. Commercial models are, therefore, a key part of supply chain design. These are about the point of payment for the various activities along the chain, where the risk is taken, and the margin that is taken or conceded for that risk and credit period. These terms can vary enormously by both sector and companies' preferences. Traditionally traders took title to the goods at the side of the ship and paid with a currency instrument (letter of credit) that was guaranteed by a bank and cross-guaranteed by the buyer. Then they organized their own freight and paid any duties and tariffs at the destination. This model is often called FOB (free on board) and has been adopted by retailers, which are progressively replacing their traders and agents.

Another common option is CIF (cost of goods plus insurance and freight), where the vendor charges for the cost of goods plus the insurance and freight to get them to the final destination. Any duties and taxes in this model are for the buyer to arrange to pay when the goods arrive in the country. DDP is the most equivalent option to local supply. It stands for delivered duty paid and it is where the vendor takes total responsibility for all costs until the product is delivered. Financing is invariably part of this package.

These are the most common of many models that are referred to as IncoTerms. The precise selection of the right Incoterm is a critical decision for the specific trade on extended supply chains with many hidden risks and the requirement for extended financing. It will be influenced by a whole range of factors, including the buyer's balance sheet, the vendor's financial capacity, the risk in the trade, and the relative cost of financing and operating the chain under the different models.

International logistics

The importance of international logistics cannot be overemphasized. The flexibility of container freight to make efficient, shared capacity available to many users has been a huge driver of global trade. But with scale in global trade have come new issues that require new approaches.

Even with container freight, traditional methods of managing international logistics can involve as many as 10 to 12 hand-offs in movement and documents. If just one or two of these fail, with no effective way of putting them right, the unreliability of global logistics becomes the reality that is often a subject of comment and complaint.

With scale and growth, inbound management at the destination now requires central coordination. Correspondingly, management at the origin also needs to be controlled to ensure the right flow at the destination and to enable the buyer to take advantage of the scale of its activities. The management of documentation, customs clearance and compliance can also benefit from a single centralized administrative and forwarding set-up.

Finally, the question of security against terrorism is now a major concern in international trade. There are onerous requirements for certification of cargoes, especially into the United States, under the C–TPAT (Customs–Trade Partnership against Terrorism) scheme. Failure to comply can lead to cargoes being refused carriage or blocked for lengthy inspection and clearance.

The result of these factors is that major buyers are tending to appoint a global 'lead logistics service provider' (LLP). These are often offshoots of the container shipping lines or international freight forwarders that have extended their services, and are especially appropriate where a buyer is maintaining many trading relationships. In companies where there are a smaller number of very large trading relationships, the tendency is to adopt an in-house forwarder.

In all circumstances, the operational need is for integrated management of many remote origins, providing information visibility, certification, and the capability to respond to factors in the supply chain.

Flow management

Flow management and control is often executed, but seldom planned, by the LLP. Someone, generally the buyer, has to make the planning, forecasting and ordering decisions. The key feature of global sourcing is that chains become extended, with longer lead times and less agility to respond to changes in the actual marketplace. This needs improved forecast accuracy and more integrated supply chain planning. The consequences of poor planning are a combination of service failures and increased cost from emergency deliveries and associated expediting.

Global best practice is to introduce a sales and operations planning process, part of which is to identify the products whose demand characteristics make them particularly vulnerable during extended lead times. With these products there is generally the potential to implement supply chain strategy options such as postponement, capacity booking or switch sourcing:

- *Postponement* is where the product is made and shipped in a generic form so that it can go into a number of different final products. The generic parts are then localized in the final market to meet real customer orders (HP and

Dell are renowned for using this approach).

- *Capacity booking* is where a vendor is 'booked' to provide capacity on a fixed cycle; the exact mix of product to be made is decided at the last minute. This reduces lead times and ensures that the product made is the one that is most needed.
- *Switch sourcing* is where the initial quantity is made in the lowest-cost source and, if demand forecasts are exceeded, any patterns or moulds are transferred to higher-cost sources where the product can be made and shipped with a much shorter lead time.

Organization design

The organization of global sourcing is a major issue, with companies that use global sourcing creating organizations in their main origins that now seem disconnected from the core organization at the destination. The dilemma seems to be whether the offices in the origins are buying functions, logistics functions, technical functions – or some combination of these. Each of these relates to different functions in the parent organization – and ownership and control appear to become an issue. Furthermore, the relationship of the origin offices and capabilities with the main organization is inevitably challenged by distance, communications, systems issues and – most of all – goals and KPIs.

It is clear that the next stage of maturity in global sourcing and supply will require a greater definition of the organizational lines and responsibilities than exists in many businesses today. This will most likely be based on team-based structures working on categories, technologies and product life cycle projects as appropriate; it will be fully integrated with the core business at the right points and work actively to overcome the barriers of geography and culture.

Information technology

Extended chains require information technology that can manage the long-distance 'purchase-to-pay' cycle and all the steps along the way. The key is to make available a single version of the order and its status to every point along the chain. It must allow the appropriate people and organizations to make amendments, update status and provide a history of events. This is beyond ERP, as the various players along the chain (such as vendors, service providers and Customs and Excise) all have many relationships with other parties. They also have particular information needs that will not fit with the customers' ERP systems – and the attributes of the data are rather different from those in conventional ERP systems. The data architecture needs to be able to handle consignments, waybills, containers, tariffs, providers, VAT and duty as well as orders, SKUs, vendors and locations.

Data interchange between systems is essential to provide the visibility needed for flow control. Internet technology has provided the ideal platform on which many-to-many relationships can be maintained. It is low-cost and provides widely based connectivity. However, every major shipper then needs a single reference point for its international trade, and this is unlikely to be the main ERP system. Some of the major shippers and forwarders have invested heavily in such event management systems and the associated connectivity. The early versions of these systems have added considerable value, and the new generation is expected to provide another step change.

However, the systems world is full of tensions as providers compete to promote their systems and lock in their clients. It is unwise to expect that the IT world of global trade is an open and transparent one. There are many barriers, including the operational excellence (or lack of it) with which the technology is fed.

Operational excellence

With as many as 12 operational hand-offs in the extended international supply chain, there is much that can go wrong – so operational excellence is critical to a smooth supply chain. Typical issues that must be done with excellence are:

- product labelling and bar-coding – right code, right box, right quantity;
- invoicing – right product, right cost, right consignee;
- customs – right classifications;
- advanced shipping notices for right product;
- schedule and date required compliance;
- container packing accuracy;
- handling quality.

Surveys have shown very high levels of non-compliance and operational variability in global supply. Quite simply, the origin participants do not understand the requirements for supply chain management by their customers and, therefore, often do not comply. The use of an LLP can be combined with more proactive vendor management to make sure that due dates and data quality are achieved – and to impose charges when standards are missed. Case material has demonstrated the downstream value of upstream excellence. The cost is tiny in relation to the value, and the barriers to excellence are more about culture and understanding than deliberate obstruction.

Risk management

Risk management should be continuous for buyers. There is much to be concerned about, for example:

- the basics of vendor viability;
- sudden and unadvised changes in priorities by vendors and service providers;
- quality and timeliness issues;
- introduction of unauthorized materials or child labour;
- loss/leakage of technical know-how and patents;
- sudden and unexpected duty and quota constraints as a result of political and economic pressures;
- currency variations;
- sudden and unforecast changes in customer demand.

A lot of these would apply to local supply as well, but their scale and impacts would generally be less. The combination of culture, language, distance and complexity conspire to make a formal risk management process with regular checks essential. This requirement will expand further as global sourcing moves into its next phase of growth.

Critical success factors

The measures to manage global chains and mitigate risk require six capabilities. These capabilities form the critical success factors:

1. *Total acquisition cost management:* the ability to analyse and predict the total cost-to-serve from the source of supply to its final point of sale. The capability in this analysis is not simply to build up the logistics costs from freight, inventory holding, duty, applicable customs regimes and so on. It is more important to analyse and build into the costing the risk of markdown and lost sales through a market–risk–cost profile. This analysis identifies products that should never be traded on a long lead time or that should be the subject of a postponement strategy. It is also likely to show that there are some products where actions to reduce lead time and increase flexibility will justify a higher initial purchasing cost.
2. *One-touch information flow:* to avoid double entry, duplication, mistakes and inconsistency as the same transaction moves through the many points of contact in the chain. Accuracy of information is a precondition of proactive management. This capability is systems-enabled – and it is critical to have the widest view of the total chain on one information platform with the ability to recognize inconsistencies.
3. *Total product identification and compliance:* to ensure fast, accurate product and handling unit identification that feeds the 'one-touch information' requirement. The use of bar codes and RFID to the correct standards is the enabling technology.
4. *Real-time routeing through dynamic visibility:* the capability to see through the chain, know what is coming and test for events that have not happened as planned, and to interpret the implications of failures in a

proactive way and make decisions to minimize their impact. This is the 'traffic control' of a global supply chain, and it must be managed transparently and with the cooperation of all the parties in the chain.

5. *Vendor development:* the capability to understand and improve the long-term performance of vendors in terms of cycle times, timeliness, quality and accuracy. Based on the historical performance of the chain, it is possible to identify improvement programmes to develop supplier reliability. The ultimate goal is to issue orders and schedules on shorter lead times, reflecting real demand or more accurate forecasts. Understanding the underlying performance of vendors and their category of products in the marketplace is the starting point for this.
6. *Information platform to provide consistent and timely information:* the capability to put in place, operate and maintain a full supply chain visibility solution. All of the above capabilities are anchored by the operational skill to secure and maintain the information backbone, with the diverse data structures that are needed by each supply chain function.

Global sourcing – sustaining the trend

It is clear that first movers to global sourcing have gained a competitive advantage. Often these were traders that had an intimate knowledge of a supply market in terms of the vendors and their capabilities – as well as the logistics to get the product to the market. They committed to stock risk and knew where to dispose of product if the original channel did not work. For this they earned a respectable margin for the risks they took.

In the context of the explosion of global sourcing and the further potential, the conclusion is that the 'land grab' is over. Figure 20.5 suggests that we are

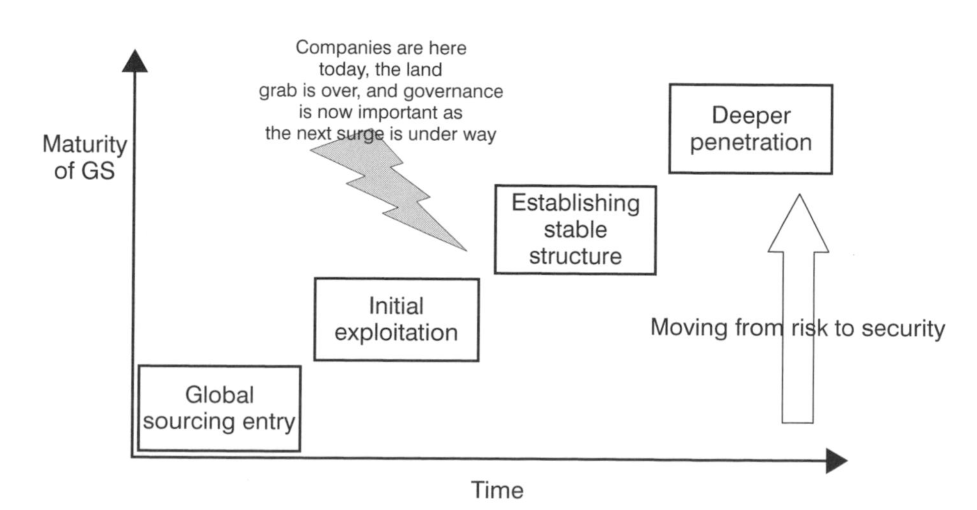

Figure 20.5 Maturity development of global sourcing

moving from initial exploitation to putting in place stable structures that can handle the next phase of growth. This will be essential as companies become more dependent on long-distance supply chains with all the risks and issues that we have identified.

The increased penetration of global sourcing will make its management a core skill and capability. This chapter has attempted to provide an initial view of the emerging landscape and issues.

References

Liang, JX (2005) Best practice in global sourcing, Unpublished MSc thesis, Cranfield School of Management, Cranfield

World Trade Organization (WTO) (2005) *International Trade Statistics*, WTO, Geneva

21

The changing supply of logistics services – a UK perspective

Colin Bamford, University of Huddersfield

In the four years since the publication of the 4th edition of this book, there has been substantial change to the supply of logistics services in the UK. This change has in part been internal to the business through a significant consolidation of provision amongst the largest companies. This has included Exel's acquisition of the Tibbett and Britten Group (2004), closely followed by Deutsche Post's takeover of the greatly expanded Exel (2005) and further consolidation with Wincanton's takeover of P and O Trans European (2003). At the same time all companies have experienced difficult trading conditions as a result of:

- uncertainties over the price of fuel and the climbdown on lorry road user charging;
- lower operating profits in many cases despite an increase in turnover;
- driver shortages and concerns over the short- and longer-term effects of the EU's Working Time Directive on logistics providers.

External change and challenges have come about through the further globalization of supply chains and the demands for a high level of customer performance from the retail and manufacturing customers of logistics providers, as well as through the long-awaited geographical expansion of the EU in May 2004 to include eight new members in Central and Eastern Europe plus Cyprus and Malta.

In short, much has happened to change the way in which logistics services are supplied to customers in the UK.

UK market trends

Table 21.1 shows general trends in the overall market since 1994 (ONS, 2005). As this indicates, in terms of goods moved, the market has been relatively static since 1998. This is slightly surprising given the unprecedented and consistent growth in real GDP over the period. It is also in contrast to the period before 1998 when the total goods moved was broadly in line with the state of the economy.

The causes of this changing pattern are not easy to explain. An obvious one is the continued de-industrialization of the British economy. The manufacturing sector has experienced continued decline over the period shown in Table 21.1. Given the derived demand for freight transport, it is clear that there is now less demand from customers in those sectors of manufacturing that have experienced structural changes due to increased competition from the rest of the world. By 2004, the manufacturing sector was responsible for less than one-fifth of GDP.

Table 21.1 Freight transport by road – goods moved by goods vehicles over 3.5 tonnes, 1994–2004 (billion tonne-kilometres)

Year	Mainly public haulage[1]	Mainly own account[2]	Total	Percentage mainly public haulage
1994	100.8	37.0	137.8	73.0
1995	106.5	37.2	143.7	74.1
1996	109.1	37.7	146.8	74.3
1997	112.2	37.4	149.6	75.0
1998	114.3	37.6	151.9	75.2
1999	110.9	38.3	149.2	74.3
2000	113.0	37.5	150.5	75.1
2001	114.7	34.7	149.4	76.8
2002	110.6	39.2	149.8	73.8
2003	114.3	37.4	151.7	75.3
2004[3]	110.8	41.4	152.2	72.8

Notes:
[1] Relates to carriage of goods owned by people other than the operator.
[2] Relates to goods carried by operators in the course of their own business.
[3] A minor reclassification means that data for 2004 are not strictly comparable with earlier years.

A second reason for change though is the improvement in logistical efficiency as a result of better road vehicle utilization. This has been evidenced in a recent study by the Department for Transport that indicated that, since 1998, the intensity of road freight activity had increased by just 2 per cent whilst the economy had grown by almost 17 per cent (DfT, 2005). The increase since 2002 reflects the increased use of 44-tonne vehicles; the average length of haul in contrast has fallen slightly. Transport efficiency has also improved through a steady fall in empty running. This decreased from around 29 per cent in 1998 to 26.5 per cent in 2004. In part this can be explained through more supplier collections and factory gate pricing contracts from major retailers especially. In contrast, lading factors (the ratio of goods carried in relation to the maximum carrying capacity of the vehicle) have fallen. This is best explained by the increased use of less dense unitized loads through the greater use of roll-cages, tote boxes and so on, again mainly by the major retailers.

Table 21.1 also shows that, although there are minor annual variations, the 'mainly public haulage' sector, which includes third-party logistics providers (3PLs), has remained more or less static at around three-quarters of the total market. A tentative conclusion could be that this sector has more or less reached saturation level relative to the 'mainly own account' sector. If this is the case, it supports the view that the supply of logistics services through 3PLs has become even more competitive.

The arguments in favour of businesses using a 3PL are well documented (see Chapter 17, for example). This sector in the past has seen most of the growth of activity in goods moved. Although the data are not strictly comparable, in total terms, the own account sector would appear to be holding its own. This should not in any way undermine the importance of 3PLs (and in some cases advice from a fourth-party logistics provider, or 4PL) in offering a full range of supply chain management services to clients. As well as offering the usual transport and warehouse management services, 3PLs can provide for the assembly and management of inventory and the integration of business IT systems.

With a relatively static market, there are clear signs of increasing segmentation, particularly on the part of middle-sized operators, which are increasingly vulnerable to competition from the top tier of providers in the market. Typical segments are automatic parts, food services and home deliveries, to add to the more traditional ones of fuel oils and chemicals. The top-tier operators tend to have interests in most segments: primary and secondary distribution, temperature-controlled as well as ambient.

The annual round of contracts awarded attracts considerable attention in the trade press (see, for example, *Motor Transport* magazine). As market growth has slowed, the market has become even more competitive. The uncertainty over fuel prices, given their importance in contract terms, and the need to be price-competitive have meant that most providers have had a difficult time in maintaining margins. In 2005, for example, Analytica reported that around half of the main European providers in 2004 had experienced a small decline in operating margins (Analytica, 2005). This list included Exel, Wincanton, Christian Salvesen, TDG and GIST.

A crucial issue in any contract renegotiations is whether service levels are being met. It has been clear for some time that businesses invariably compete on the efficiency of their supply chains – getting it right is vital for business success, in the retail sector more than ever.

In a difficult marketplace, the challenge for the top logistics providers has been to meet the needs of supply chain globalization, whilst integrating the services that they are able to provide. As the Analytica study stated, 'This enables logistics providers to benefit from scale, creating competitive advantage and a greater breadth of expertise, both of which results in benefits to their customers... customer service must come first. This is the only true base upon which a fully integrated service can be built.'

A further insight into outsourcing and globalization has questioned whether the former really is a magical solution in cases where businesses have sought to benefit from lower unit labour costs in Eastern Europe and Asia (Sweeney, 2005). It is argued that this has resulted in a shift away from controlling the supply chain through ownership to one based on management and control through effective supply chain relationship management. In some cases, the outcome has been a disaster. In other cases, particularly in clothing, textiles and hi-tech manufacturing, many companies have gained significant benefits from outsourcing various supply chain services. The key to success is to see outsourcing as part of an integrated approach to managing the supply chain, a task that increasingly is best carried out by one of the top tier of global logistics providers.

The need for customers to have strategies to exploit the global market is one that is increasingly being carried out by 3PLs. In some cases, this might be a 4PL, an outside organization that has the task of assembling and integrating supply chain capabilities for clients. Our largest 3PLs now see themselves as 4PLs, usually ensuring that much of the supply chain management function for clients produces an appropriate amount of business for themselves.

Market structure – continuing consolidation and globalization

The term 'market structure' is one that is used by economists to describe the way in which a market is organized. In distinguishing market structures, there are two key variables, namely the number of firms and the extent of barriers to entry for new firms seeking to join the market. The significance of these is that they determine the degree of competition in a market. The smaller the number of firms and the higher the barriers to entry, then in theory the less competitive the market will be.

In some markets such as grocery retailing, vehicle production and certain branches of food processing, the level of industrial concentration has been high. In others, such as road freight and distribution, the existence of thousands of small firms has meant that historically this has been a very competitive, low-concentration market. The continuing consolidation amongst the big players, particularly since 2000, has resulted in this market showing increasing signs of being an oligopoly (see Sloman, 2003).

What has happened over the past six years or so is that the 3PL market especially has become increasingly concentrated in the hands of a small number of very powerful providers. The experience of Exel and to a lesser extent Wincanton is typical of the behaviour of firms in an oligopolistic market. Exel, for example, merged with MSAS Global Logistics in 2000, took over the Tibbett and Britten Group in 2004 and was itself acquired by Deutsche Post World Net (DPWN) in 2005. In theory, an oligopolistic market has some or all of the following characteristics:

- a market leader that often takes the lead in pricing decisions;
- interdependence in so far as the actions of one firm can often determine the reactions of others;
- a strong brand image;
- although illegal, the possibility of collusion, for example to squeeze out would-be competition.

So, to what extent is the 3PL an oligopolistic market? Table 21.2 shows the top 10 providers in the UK market in 2003–04 (*Motor Transport*, 2004). As indicated, Table 21.2 incorporates Exel's acquisition of Tibbett and Britten; it also includes Wincanton's purchase of P and O Trans European. Exel had an estimated turnover of over four times that of its leading rival and was substantially greater than any of the remaining 3PLs shown in the table. This former state-owned business has more than maintained its pole position following its privatization in 1981.

Tibbett and Britten was perceived as the rising star of the 1990s. Prior to the Exel takeover, its turnover had increased tenfold since 1990. It had also led the way amongst 3PLs in establishing a strong foothold in intermodal distribution, both for international and for domestic movements, and in the way it had tackled the challenge of providing 3PL services to clients in the emerging Central and Eastern European markets.

Wincanton, unlike Exel and Tibbett and Britten, has traditionally concentrated its growth in the domestic market. Its acquisition of P and O Trans European was its first successful venture into the wider European market. Equally, there have been casualties. TDG, for example, has lost market share as the market has grown and, in late 2005, TNT announced that its logistics business was to be sold in order to allow it to concentrate its business activities on its mail and courier/express services. Although the reasons behind these

Table 21.2 The UK's leading 3PLs, 2003–04

Company	Financial year end	Turnover[1] (£m)	Percentage change on previous year	Employees
Exel[2]	Dec 03	6,749	+44.2	104,200
Wincanton	Mar 04	1,681	+68.4	25,000
Hays Logistics[3]	Dec 03	854	–3.0	n/a[4]
Christian Salvesen	Apr 03	846	–3.6	n/a[4]
Autologic Holdings	Dec 03	701	+4.8	4,380
TDG	Dec 03	541	–4.5	7,990
TNT Logistics UK[5]	Dec 03	500	+32.5	8,000
GIST	Sept 03	292	+10.2	5,750
Kuehne & Nagel	Dec 03	276	+32.8	832
Securicor Omega Logistics	Sept 03	215	n/a	1,700

Notes:
[1] Total turnover from UK market and elsewhere for UK companies only.
[2] Includes recently acquired Tibbett and Britten Group.
[3] Now ARC Logistics.
[4] Data not available for the logistics side of these companies.
[5] Estimates.

changes must be complex, a simple conclusion is that both companies have been victims of the increasingly competitive market.

At a European level, as Table 21.3 indicates, in 2004 Exel became the largest single provider of logistics services (Analytica, 2005). As with all of the major players, its business is truly global. The acquisition of Tibbett and Britten gave Exel additional business in 13 countries, including Austria, Poland, Romania and Slovakia, where it had previously no involvement. The growth in its contracts logistics business has been particularly strong in Europe, the Middle East, Africa and the Americas. In the Asia Pacific region, the provision of air and sea freight services accounted for 75 per cent of its turnover. Growth prospects for contract logistics in this region remain healthy. As in Europe, though, operating margins remain subject to external pressures such as the rising price of fuel (Exel, 2005).

The consolidation and integration of the logistics sector has brought substantial business benefits to global European players. These benefits include:

- Economies of sale. As a business increases in scale, it can put pressure on its supply partners to reduce longer-term average costs when purchasing fuel, vehicles, shipping capacity and so on. There are also financial and risk-bearing economies.
- Gaining competitive advantage through not only offering a wider range of services but also concentrating activities in key market segments such as clothing and textiles, automotive, retail, electronics and so on.

Table 21.3 Europe's leading logistics providers, 2004

Company	Turnover in 2004 (£m)	Change in turnover in 2003 %
Exel	8,961	25.2
Schenker	8,042	17.3
NYK	7,976	7.1
Kuehne & Nagel	7,432	21.2
Deutsche Post World Net	6,786	15.4
Logista	4,406	8.0
TNT Logistics	4,082	9.3
Panalpina	3,965	14.1
Ryder	3,776	7.2
Geodis	3,371	4.8
Wincanton	2,438	2.7

- Providing a fully integrated supply chain management service for global clients.

Analytica's recent research, though, adds a clear warning with respect to the last point in stating that 'Integration is not a licence to win new customers... a "one size fits all" solution may not be acceptable to all global manufacturers. This sends out a clear message that customer service must come first.'

Finally, in September 2005, it was announced that Exel's shareholders had agreed a massive £3.6 billion takeover bid from DPWN. The logistics arm of Exel would be DHL, with Exel as a sub-brand (*Daily Telegraph*, 2005). At the time it was estimated that the combined Deutsche Post and Exel group would have between 6 and 7 per cent of the European logistics market.

The only concern about the takeover was whether it would be blocked by the European Commission on the grounds that it would impede effective competition in the European logistics market. Although total market share is small compared to other sectors of business, a dominant firm like DPWN/Exel could be against the interests of customers of logistics services. After only a brief period of investigation, the Commission approved the merger.

On the face of it, this deal is about logistics. Underneath, though, there would seem to be a very serious threat to the UK's Royal Mail, which in January 2006 saw its traditional postal business opened up to full competition. Deutsche Post is already a competitor to the Royal Mail in the bulk mail market. Its marriage with Exel's logistics expertise must surely enhance its opportunities to make further inroads into the UK postal market.

The EU25 – new market opportunities and threats

Given the nature of the degree of change analysed in the last section, one might conclude that UK 3PLs have a strong hold over the domestic market and that they have little to fear from operators based elsewhere in the EU. This conclusion might also naively be made from the conclusions of research by the Institute of Grocery Distribution (IGD), which once again recognized that UK 3PL operators are the most efficient within the whole of the EU (IGD, 2005). This may well be the case, in particular for the retail grocery market, but in other sectors 3PLs from the rest of the EU and elsewhere are having an increasing share of the UK market.

Table 21.4 shows some such operators (*Motor Transport*, 2004). Most have particular strengths in the automotive and clothing sectors. In addition, the strength of companies such as DHL and UPS, both of which are major players in the express parcels and document sectors, should be recognized.

The geographical enlargement of the EU in May 2004 has presented increased market opportunities for 3PL operators, including those based in the UK. Prior to the formal accession of the eight countries in Central and Eastern Europe (CEE) plus Cyprus and Malta, various UK operators such as Exel (including in particular Tibbett and Britten) and P and O Trans European (now part of Wincanton) had penetrated the market in Central and Eastern Europe. All have recognized the considerable market opportunities in Poland, the Czech Republic and Hungary.

In these countries there are two main types of opportunity for UK 3PLs. These are

1. *Non-food.* Unit labour costs in the joining countries are substantially lower than elsewhere in the EU. Consequently, automotive manufacturers such as VW Audi and Suzuki have established assembly plants in these countries

Table 21.4 Non-UK-owned hauliers in the UK market

Company	Turnover 2003–04 (£m)	Change from previous year %
Autologic Holdings[1]	701.7	+4.8
Kuehne & Nagel	275.7	+32.8
DFDS Transport	157.0	+12.1
UK subsidiaries:		
TNT Logistics (UK)	500	+32.5
NYK Logistics (UK) MIR	135	+23.5
Gefco UK	110	+0.5

Note:
[1] Includes Walon, Ansa and Acumen.

and ship finished vehicles into the rest of the EU. Other typical manufacturers are those involved in chemicals, electronics and textiles. As well as producing for export, the domestic market in these countries is growing as local consumers become more affluent.

2. *Retail distribution.* This has been an obvious area of development. EU retailers such as Tesco, Metro, Carrefour and so on now have a strong presence in Poland, Hungary and the Czech Republic. It seems logical for them to follow the same logistics practices as in their domestic markets. In some cases, their 3PLs have moved into the market with them.

Getting a foothold in the CEE market is a risky and uncertain business. Some 3PLs have bought transport and warehousing companies in these countries, Tibbett and Britten being a particularly good example. An alternative means of entry is to go it alone and set up a brand new operation. This outcome, of course, is much less certain to succeed.

Realistically, UK companies may have the logistical expertise to make substantial inroads into the expanding CEE market. Geographically, though, German operators are far better placed to know the market and the opportunities that may be available. This is a major threat to UK operators.

Transport policy issues

Businesses supplying logistics services are required to operate within a policy and regulatory framework that is increasingly laid down by the EU. It is beyond the scope of this chapter to look at recent issues in depth. It is, though, useful to indicate those that have been and remain of particular concern to UK 3PLs, for example:

- The Working Time Directive. From April 2005, all operators governed by drivers' hours regulations (excluding self-employed) must comply with these new rules (European Commission, 2002). Driver working time is now limited to an average 48-hour week over a reference period. No more than 60 hours can be spent working in any single week. Complying has raised fundamental problems of driver shortages, although last-minute concessions on 'periods of availability' have helped some operators.
- Drivers from new EU countries. The accession of eight new CEE member states to the EU has opened up the opportunity for drivers and warehouse operatives from these countries to work in the UK. This may help companies in places where there is a labour shortage, although there are concerns over the rates of pay that are being offered. Whether the current wave of activity by recruitment consultants becomes a flood remains to be seen.
- The comparative price of diesel fuel between the UK and the rest of the EU remains a major concern to all UK operators, not only those involved in

international work. Given the importance of fuel costs in relation to total operating costs, any marked variation in fuel prices between the UK and the rest of the EU must damage the competitiveness of UK operators.

Conclusions

It should be clear from this chapter that the market for 3PL logistics services is subject to ongoing change. Demand-side influences – a highly competitive domestic market and opportunities in the CEE – require UK companies to become increasingly efficient to maintain pole position in the European market.

Simultaneously, supply-side factors have seen major changes in ownership, with increasing concentration in the top tier of operators. This has coincided with concerns over the impact of EU regulations on UK operators, although in context these are unlikely to halt the process of market consolidation and globalization.

References

Analytica (2005) *Profitability in European Logistics*, Analytica, London
Daily Telegraph (2005) Exel snapped up in £3.6bn takeover, 19 September
Department for Transport (DfT) (2005) *Continuing Survey of Road Goods Transport*, DfT, London
European Commission (2002) Working Time Directive, 2002/15/EC
Exel (2005) Delivering value across the supply chain, *Annual Report*, Exel
Institute of Grocery Distribution (2005) *Retail Logistics*, IGD, Watford.
Motor Transport (2004), 30 September
Office for National Statistics (ONS) (2005) *Transport Statistics, Great Britain*, ONS, London
Sloman, J (2003), *Economics*, Prentice Hall, New York
Sweeney, E (2005) Outsourcing – a managerial solution?, *Logistics Solutions*, **8** (1)

22

Developments in Western European logistics strategies

Michael Browne, Julian Allen and Allan Woodburn,
University of Westminster

Introduction

Several political initiatives have taken place since 1990 that have had major implications for logistics services throughout Western Europe:

- Border controls and customs arrangements within the EU were lifted following the creation of the Single European Market (SEM) under the Treaty of Maastricht in January 1993.
- In 1999, the euro was launched as an electronic currency and became legal tender in 2002. It was implemented in 12 EU states, which represent the 'eurozone' (Austria, Belgium, Finland, France, Germany, Greece, Ireland, Italy, Luxembourg, the Netherlands, Portugal and Spain). The European Central Bank is responsible for the monetary policy within the eurozone.
- Ten more countries (Cyprus, the Czech Republic, Estonia, Hungary, Latvia, Lithuania, Malta, Poland, Slovakia and Slovenia) joined the EU in 2004, bringing the total to 25. These 10 members increased the surface area of the EU by a quarter, and its population to 450 million. Bulgaria, Romania and Croatia are expected to join the EU in the next few years.

Central to the logic of creating the European Union free from unnecessary trading restrictions has been the desire to encourage the development of European companies able to compete on a global basis. It is often claimed that fragmented national economies within Europe have resulted in too many small companies in certain key industrial sectors. Dismantling barriers to trade and opening up new market opportunities allow companies to grow and become more competitive. Inevitably this is also likely to result in the relocation of certain economic activities as some companies become larger and others fail. The collapse of communism in the former Soviet Union and the countries of Central and Eastern Europe, and the subsequent reorientation of these countries towards the free market, has also opened up new avenues of trade that extend beyond the borders of the EU.

This chapter addresses the ways in which company business strategies and operations have been developing within Europe during this time of political and economic change, and the effect that this is having on the demand for logistics services, and the corresponding supply.

Changes in the demand for logistics services

An enlarged and more integrated Europe has influenced the demand for logistics services. Indeed, markets for goods and services in Europe have become much less fragmented over the past 10 years and at the same time, for many companies, there has been a discernible shift away from a mainly national approach to a more unified European strategy. In general, companies increasingly regard the EU as their home market rather than having their trading horizons restricted to a single country. This in turn has important implications for logistics services. For example, increased trade between member states creates new demands for logistics services such as transport and warehousing. However, the transition to a European pattern of operation has not been as smooth as many commentators expected and in some cases the benefits have been slow to emerge.

Market developments and retailer/manufacturer strategies

Increasing market integration enables large companies to pursue a number of strategies designed to take advantage of their size. The scope to concentrate production at a small number of carefully selected locations is one that has a special importance within Europe. Until recently the strategy followed by many companies was based on production for separate national markets. The requirement to produce product variants for different markets, the complexity of border crossing formalities and the added costs of international trade transactions led, typically, to a rather fragmented approach to production. Although for many companies the changes in strategy have been part of a broader response to growing global opportunities and increased international competition, the abolition of border controls and the simplification of trading procedures have undoubtedly encouraged plant and warehouse rationalization.

Since the business ambitions of many companies are not confined to the existing EU, the scope for inventory rationalization has grown as Europe becomes more commercially integrated. Dismantling trade barriers has allowed firms to reduce the number of warehouses within their logistics systems, which in turn has important longer-term implications for transport patterns. Instead of looking at Europe on a country-by-country basis, firms have been able to consider more natural market demand patterns and adapt their warehousing accordingly. Significantly, these developments are not confined to the EU – many firms have already adopted a very wide definition of Europe in developing their logistics strategies. For example, Bosch-Siemens (manufacturers of domestic appliances with a head office in Munich) took its first steps in cross-market distribution by rationalizing its Scandinavian warehousing operations and consolidating stocks for Finland, Norway and Sweden in one regional centre located between Stockholm and Malmo, distributing to other Scandinavian countries from that single location (O'Laughlin, Cooper and Cabocel, 1993). There are many examples of this type of initiative as companies have changed their traditional views about the best way to serve markets. The sports equipment firm Nike has adopted a completely centralized strategy for storage within its European supply chain despite increasing diversity of sourcing and continued demands for fast response to customer requirements (Kemp, 1997). Geest, the prepared food company, announced plans to consolidate production in 2001, with dressed salads being produced at one rather than two sites (*European Logistics Management*, 2001b). The French food group Danone also announced a restructuring plan for its biscuit production business in 2001, in which six of its 36 factories in Europe would be closed, with production levels increasing at the remaining factories (*European Logistics Management*, 2001a). The trend to centralization has taken a firm hold on management thinking and there are still many companies seeking further opportunities to reduce the number of stockholding points. Whether these initiatives can be justified against a background of pressure to develop more sustainable logistics strategies remains to be seen.

Many large companies now take a supply chain view when considering new ways 1) to integrate their own operations and then 2) to seek to extend this integration to their supply chain partners. Growing integration has profound implications for the role of external service providers since in many cases the physical flow of materials is one of the first areas of change when a supply chain view becomes more clearly developed. When companies start the process of considering the supply chain as a whole it often becomes evident that there is scope to rationalize the number of service providers, in much the same way as it may become possible to reduce the number of stock-holding points.

A survey of logistics costs has been carried out by the European Logistics Association (ELA) and AT Kearney Logistics five times during the past 20 years and indicates that costs as a proportion of sales fell by approximately 50 per cent for Western European companies between 1987 and 2003 (see Figure 22.1). This has been achieved at the same time that customer service has been rising. However, the survey results indicate that cost reductions were limited between 1998 and 2003, and respondents' forecasts about likely logistics costs in 2008 suggest that they will remain at approximately 6 per cent of sales revenue. More than 100 companies in 14 European countries responded to the survey, which indicates that transportation is the single largest component of logistics cost, representing 43 per cent of total logistics costs in 2003.

Market concentration has been occurring in the vast majority of European retail and manufacturing markets in recent years. In grocery retailing, for example, the market share of the top five national retailers in several European countries including the UK, the Netherlands, Belgium, Germany and France is between 50 per cent and 70 per cent (Mintel, 2002). However, it is important to recognize that the degree of market concentration varies significantly between industries in any one country, and that the general degree of market concentration varies from one country to another.

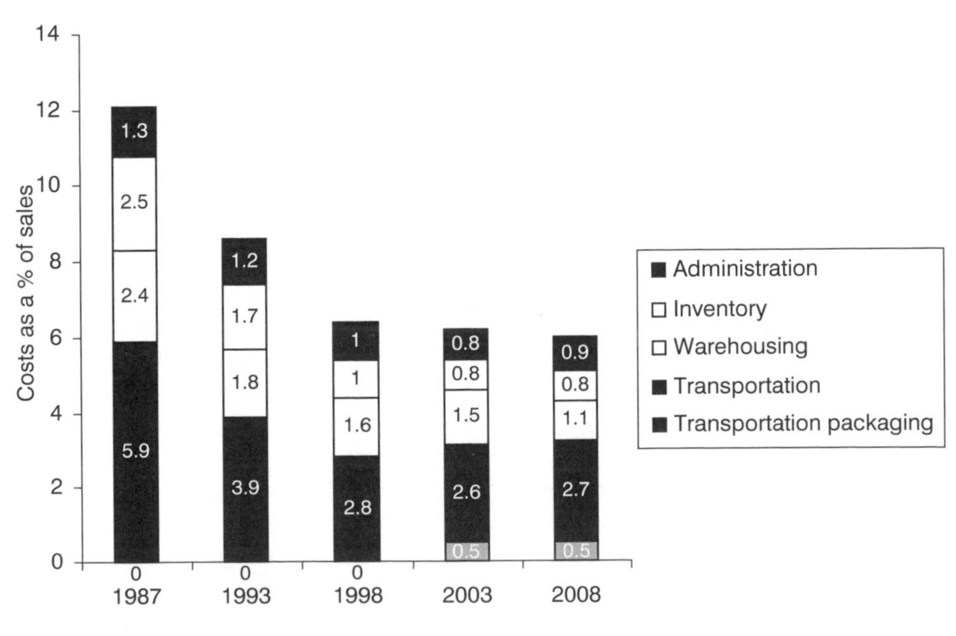

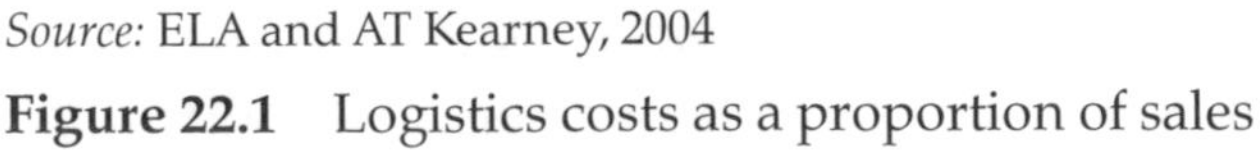
Source: ELA and AT Kearney, 2004

Figure 22.1 Logistics costs as a proportion of sales

Limitations on European integration

Despite growing similarities, there are still many differences between European countries; retailing is a case in point. The retail format used in different European markets varies significantly between countries, with very large stores playing the biggest role in some countries (eg hypermarkets selling food and non-food in France and out-of-town supermarkets in the UK) and small food stores and traditional grocers far more common in others (such as Spain and Italy). As a result of these different retail formats, the numbers of stores operated by retailers varies between European countries; for example, there are approximately 120,000 grocery stores in Italy compared with only 33,000 in the UK (WARC, 2002). In addition, patterns of consumption also vary widely between European countries for a range of cultural, demographic and economic reasons. If one argues that we are now operating within an integrated European marketplace, this ignores the special distinguishing features of Europe and, in particular, the complexity, size and maturity of the market, the density of population spread, the number of separate nation-states, and the many languages. It must be acknowledged that in many cases these factors have acted as a brake on the introduction of European-wide supply chains and logistics systems to serve them.

However, many companies will continue to strengthen their European initiatives, resulting in further examples of corporations making dramatic changes to their European logistics networks – which in turn places new demands on logistics managers and logistics services. We need to be aware that there are often conflicting tensions within large organizations and, in some instances, initiatives to implement changes on a European scale will be overtaken by the desire to have in place a framework allowing global coordination of supply chains. Changing priorities can make it difficult to determine the most appropriate way to develop logistics management structures and this in turn has implications for the relationship with service providers (Hindson, 1998).

Eastern Europe and distribution centre locations

Alongside the move towards centralization noted earlier has been a move eastwards within European manufacturing and distribution. As Lenders (2005) notes, an increasing number of manufacturers are relocating from Western Europe towards Eastern Europe. Since most raw material shipments are arriving at ports in Western Europe, the logistics flows that follow from this change in strategy are potentially important. In turn there is a strong expectation that European distribution functions will also move eastwards from their present concentration in the Netherlands. This has led some to predict a new location for distribution 'hot spots' within Central and Eastern Europe (Lloyd, 2004). While it would be wrong to exaggerate the speed of this trend, it is nevertheless clear that this type of development reinforces the need for a more Europe-wide approach to the selection of European logistics services. In addition, from a policy perspective it poses some major challenges for existing European transport infrastructure.

Market structure of logistics service providers

Recent changes in the demand for logistics services in Europe pose a problem for logistics service providers (LSPs), as they are working with a range of companies all moving at different speeds towards what may well be rather varied objectives. Out of this challenge comes the advantage for the bigger organization that can match these requirements across and within different markets.

Company size and response to international opportunities

European deregulation, the abolition of internal frontiers, harmonization of fiscal and technical standards and the introduction of the euro have all helped to boost trade within an enlarged EU – and made it simpler for all LSPs to participate in that activity. Many factors influence the response of logistics companies to these opportunities. Among the most important are:

- company culture and background (for example, the size of the company and its ability to absorb the financial and management consequences of rapid change);
- customer profile (industry, and speed of reaction to European opportunities);
- customer culture (for example, the customers of the LSP could purchase services either at the European level or purely on a national basis).

Company size is likely to have a special significance in determining the response to the opportunities created by an enlarged EU. Larger logistics providers can continue internationalizing their activities to provide full national distribution services in more than one country. For smaller companies the impact of an enlarged EU are far more limited. There are, for example, many small road freight companies that operate at a local level and expect to go on working in this way. Although these smaller companies predominate in terms of numbers, it is the larger companies that dominate the market in terms of the total vehicle fleet and capacity. In the United Kingdom, for example, 7 per cent of hire or reward companies operate 56 per cent of the vehicles, and this is a trend that can be identified right across the EU (Reed Business Information, 2002).

Internationalization among larger carriers

One way in which LSPs can enter into foreign markets is through the establishment of operating centres in other countries and gradually increasing their networks. However, rather than follow this evolutionary and somewhat slow route to growth, some firms prefer the prospect of mergers, takeovers or strategic trading alliances with operators based in other European countries as a means of becoming more international.

The growing internationalization of business has forced companies providing logistics services to consider their own strategies to meet these new needs. Service providers need to determine the extent to which they can meet all the service requirements of a European business or whether they can realistically only meet part of those needs. In many cases there remains a potential mismatch between the logistics demands of European companies and the ability of any single service provider to meet these demands. This often results in disappointment when a manufacturer decides to rationalize its logistics network and reduce the number of service providers it deals with – only to find that there is no LSP that wishes to take on the commitment of handling all its European activities (*Distribution*, 2002).

Providers of logistics services need to be concerned with two dimensions to their activities in the first instance: geographical scope and range of services. A consideration of these two dimensions highlights how challenging it really is for the logistics service company to be able to provide 'one-stop shopping' for a European company. Some companies already provide what can be described as European services in the sense that they are the long-distance links in a network used by manufacturing companies. This provision of services is evident in the case of airlines, shipping lines, freight forwarders and integrators. It is clearly at the level of local and national distribution that Europeanization of service provision has been slowest to develop.

Freight transport and warehousing services have been widely available for many decades, together with associated documentation services, but in recent years LSPs have begun to offer an ever expanding range of services, such as final assembly of products, inventory management, product and package labelling, product tracking and tracing along the supply chain, order planning and processing, and reverse logistics systems (which tackle the collection and recovery of end-of-life products and used packaging in the supply chain).

Despite a period of uncertainty about the benefits of scale for LSPs, there have been some important developments in the last few years. Larger LSPs have grown mainly through merger and acquisition and appear to be committed to developing more European and global capabilities:

- Deutsche Post World Net (DPWN) is the former state department responsible for German postal services. In 1995 it became a private company owned by government, and it was partly privatized in 2000. It has pursued a strategy of extending its geographical coverage in the mail and express sectors as well as expanding the range of logistics services offered. The aim of the company is to become an international player capable of offering an extensive range of mail, express and logistics services, and thereby providing one-stop shopping for national and international customers. Most of its growth has been achieved through acquisitions (Harnischfeger, 2002), including express companies (DHL, Securicor Distribution, and Ducros) and distribution companies (such as Danzas, ASG, AEI and Nedlloyd ETD). The most recent major acquisition is Exel plc, which Deutsche Post acquired in 2005, making it the largest logistics provider in the world, with 500,000 employees and €55 billion in annual sales (Deutsche Post, 2005).

- Exel had itself been involved in a major merger with Ocean Group in 2000, creating the largest logistics service provider in the UK and one of the largest in the world. The merger was viewed as highly appropriate, bringing together the contract logistics capabilities of Exel Logistics with the freight-forwarding strengths of Ocean Group. Both of these companies had been active in the acquisition market over recent years, which had led to Exel Logistics' presence in several European countries and to Ocean's services in both Europe and the United States (Datamonitor, 2002).
- Kuehne & Nagel has 40,000 employees based at approximately 600 locations in more than 100 countries. Traditionally the company was a significant presence in the sea- and airfreight markets, and recently it has been expanding its contract logistics expertise through acquisition. An alliance with SembCorp Logistics of Singapore increased Kuehne & Nagel's presence in Asia. The acquisition in 2001 of USCO, a large logistics service provider in the United States, increased the company's strengths, with warehousing and distribution becoming part of its service offering (King, 2002). The acquisition of the overseas logistics division of French group CAT in 2004 facilitated the expansion of forwarding activities in France as well as in Mexico and Belgium (Kuehne & Nagel, 2004). In 2005, the company acquired the contract logistics group ACR Logistics, a major contract logistics provider in Europe. This acquisition increases the number of employees to 40,000 – and the logistics services offered now include supply chain management, distribution and transport management, factory support, and value-added services (eg call centre management and repair management), as well as managing approximately 3 million square metres of warehouse space (Kuehne & Nagel, 2005).
- TNT NV is a global provider of mail, express and logistics services, employing over 161,000 people in 63 countries, with sales of €12.6 billion (TNT, 2006). The company announced in 2005 that it was going to change its strategic focus to its core competency of providing mail and express

network services. As a result, TNT decided to sell its logistics business, which was producing €3.4 billion in annual revenues. This focus on its delivery networks would allow simplified operations, with the company retaining only a limited amount of the logistics activities that clearly fitted its core network strategy (TNT, 2005). TNT achieved much of its growth through acquisition – but it is itself now subject to a possible takeover bid (10 per cent of shares in TNT are still owned by the Dutch government) (Manners Bell, 2005).

Transportation in Europe

European freight activity

The changing demand for logistics services in Europe has had a significant impact on transportation patterns and activity. Europe's economic growth has gone hand in hand with a growing flow of goods. The growth in freight transport in Western European countries between 1970 and 2002 is shown in Figure 22.2. During this same period there has been an ongoing shift towards road transport and, to a slightly lesser extent, short-sea shipping within and between Western European countries (see Table 22.1). These data relate to the

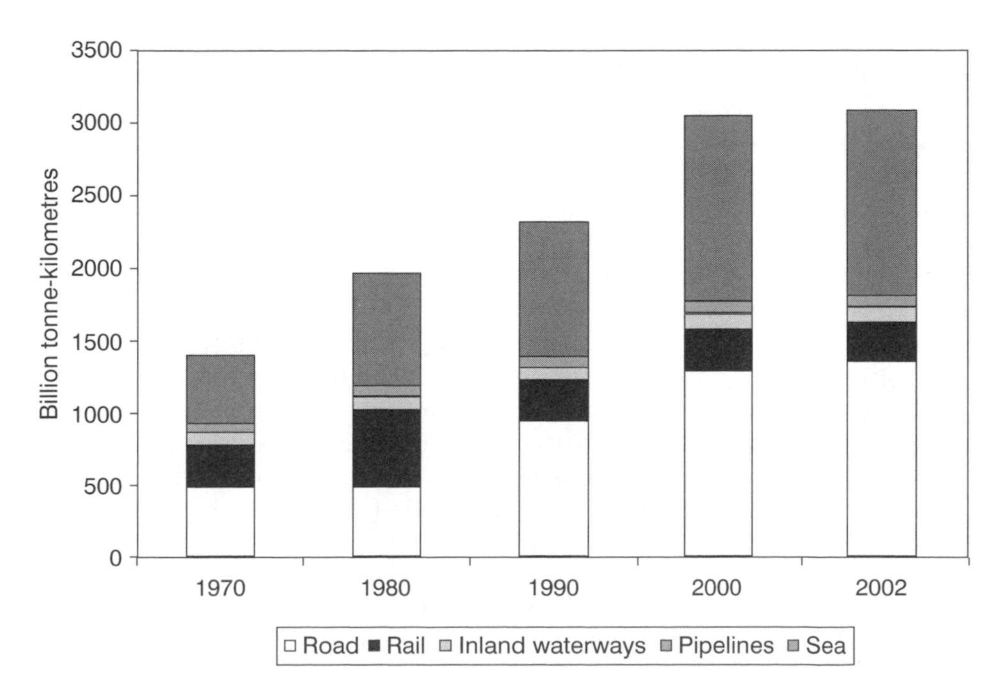

Figure 22.2 Growth in freight transport in Western Europe (EU15) (billion tonne-kilometres)

Table 22.1 Trends in market share of freight transport modes, EU15 (tonne-kilometres)

	1970 %	1980 %	1990 %	2000 %	2002 %
Road	35	36	42	43	45
Rail	20	15	11	8	8
Inland waterways	7	5	5	4	4
Pipeline	5	4	3	3	3
Sea	33	39	40	42	41
Total	100	100	100	100	100

Source: European Commission, 2004

15 member states of the European Union prior to its enlargement in 2004. Although there are some important differences between individual countries, it is evident that road freight dominates the inland movement of goods within Europe and that road freight has increased in recent years. Short-sea shipping services have also grown in importance and account for almost as much freight activity as road. Rail, inland waterways and pipeline have all lost market share, though the decline has slowed in more recent years.

There is also an integration effect – for example, the EU countries trade four times more foodstuffs than other countries with identical production and consumption levels – and this has important implications for logistics demands. As already discussed, the prospect of a Europe free from internal borders spurred many companies to review and then reconfigure their logistics systems (Cooper, Browne and Peters, 1994). This has resulted in a rationalization of both production and stockholding sites among some large companies, thereby increasing the demand for national and, especially, international transport services. At the same time there has been a trend to reduce stock levels by managing production more carefully and implementing just-in-time operations. Both of these have led to an increase in the consumption of transport services within the supply chain – as a result of either increasing trip length (with concentration of production and storage) or greater frequency of deliveries (with just-in-time systems). In addition, there is greater pressure on transport services to achieve high levels of reliability.

Many developments in modern logistics tend to increase road transport (see Table 22.2). The growth in international trade and sourcing as well as the relevance of new business strategies will make policies aimed at reducing road transport difficult to implement. It is still not clear whether the concentration of production and warehousing will in fact open up new opportunities for rail and inland shipping – although in theory this should happen.

At the same time as this growth in road freight activity across Europe, most countries have also experienced significant growth in car traffic, resulting in

Table 22.2 Developments in logistics and the impact on transport and traffic

Main development	Impact on transport and traffic
Modal shift towards road	More road vehicle trips
Spatial concentration of production and warehousing	Longer distances; increase in transport volumes on key routes
Adoption of JIT in manufacturing	Smaller shipments; faster transport (road); decrease in load factors
Adoption of quick response and ECR in retail distribution	Smaller shipments; faster transport (road); decrease in load factors
Wider geographical sourcing of supplies	Raw materials and components transported over greater distances
Wider geographical distribution of finished product	Finished products transported over greater distances
Supply chain integration	Decrease in number of suppliers and transport providers; increased road transport in the case of more outsourcing
Decrease in order cycle time	Demand-driven flows leading to increased number of trips; decrease in transport efficiency
Increase in assortments	Smaller shipments; increased number of trips
Reverse logistics	Additional transport of waste materials and end-of-life products
Retail market concentration	Fewer, larger out-of-town stores, encouraging the use of car journeys for shopping

Source: Adapted from NEA, quoted in Dutch National Spatial Planning Agency, 1997; and Technical University of Berlin *et al*, 2001

increasingly congested urban and inter-urban road networks. Freight transport costs and operational efficiency are ever more affected by this road congestion.

Policy measures affecting logistics and transport in Europe

European Commission White Paper on Transport

The European Commission White Paper on Transport published in 2001 has identified many potential policies that if introduced, would have significant effects on freight transport and logistics services. It identified the lack of fiscal and social harmonization in the transport market as leading to several key problems:

- Unequal growth in different modes of transport. This reflects that not all external costs have been included in the cost of transport as well as the fact that some modes have adapted better to the needs of a modern economy than others.
- Congestion on the main road and rail routes, in urban areas and at airports. Growth in the demand for goods transport is due to the shift from a 'stock' economy to a 'flow' economy.
- Harmful effects on the environment and public health.

In the view of the European Commission, 'sustainable development offers an opportunity, not to say lever, for adapting common transport policy. This objective, as introduced by the Treaty of Amsterdam, has to be achieved by integrating environmental considerations into Community policies' (European Commission, 2001: 14). The White Paper proposes 60 specific measures to be taken at Community level as part of the transport policy, grouped under four main objectives. The measures that are likely to have the greatest impact on freight movement are incorporated into the following themes:

- Shifting the balance between modes of transport, addressing a wide range of issues such as: infrastructure charging; capacity utilization; regulations and enforcement; inter- and intramodal competition; taxation; and integration of the different modes to achieve the best outcome in economic, social and environmental terms.
- Eliminating bottlenecks, particularly through the development of the trans-European network and its corridors, with priority for freight together with traffic management plans for major roads.
- Managing the effects of transport globalization, particularly the improvement of access to remote areas and the incorporation of the new European Union member states into the existing transport networks and operations.

Policies encouraging the use of rail, inland waterways and short-sea shipping

The European Union anticipates considerable further growth in freight transport, but is developing policies to ensure that as much of this growth as possible is by non-road modes. It hopes to achieve higher shares for these modes through a combination of measures to achieve two key objectives: regulated competition between modes, and the integration of modes for successful intermodality. The policies essentially seek to ensure that the different modes of transport account for their true costs and compete on an equal basis, while investment is made in the infrastructure to support rail and waterborne traffic to ensure that the capacity exists to increase their share of the freight transport market.

At the international level, the European Union is implementing its Trans-European Network (TEN-T) programme (European Commission, 2005). This originated in the 1990s and by 2005 a total of 30 key projects were either completed, under way or being developed. By 2020, the Network should include 89,500 kilometres of roads and 94,000 kilometres of railways, 11,250 kilometres of inland waterways (including 210 inland ports), 294 seaports and 366 airports. The majority of new or enhanced infrastructure will be for modes other than road. A number of the TEN-T key projects are wholly or significantly focused upon rail and inland waterway freight transport, including:

- international intermodal (rail) corridors (eg the Iberian peninsula to France);
- the Betuwe railway line from Rotterdam to the German border;
- the Rhine/Meuse–Main–Danube inland waterway axis;
- the Seine–Scheldt inland waterway.

Significant capacity exists in the seas around Europe, and this can be exploited subject to sufficient port capacity being available. The European Union is, therefore, promoting the concept of 'motorways of the sea' (European Commission, 2006). Four corridors have been identified for projects to:

- develop more efficient, more cost-effective and less polluting freight transport;
- reduce road congestion at major bottlenecks across Europe;
- provide better-quality, more reliable connections for Europe's peripheral regions;
- assist in making Europe's economy stronger and more sustainable.

The four corridors are the Baltic Sea, Western Europe (Atlantic Ocean–North Sea/Irish Sea), South-Western Europe (western Mediterranean Sea) and South-Eastern Europe (Adriatic, Ionian and eastern Mediterranean seas). It is intended that these sea corridors link with other modes of transport – particularly non-road ones – to encourage intermodal flows.

The European Union is also concerned with the charging of access to the transport infrastructure for different modes, since freight users do not always pay for the costs that they impose on others. Policies are being developed to integrate external costs into the charging regimes and to harmonize fuel taxation. It is widely expected that these policies will favour rail and water-borne modes, with their rates becoming more competitive relative to road haulage.

Particular issues exist for rail freight operations, which have been slow to adapt to the Single European Market. As a result, policies have been developed to encourage rail freight to become more competitive. These include open and non-discriminatory access to infrastructure for rail freight service providers to stimulate competition, transparent pricing, interoperability between national transport networks, the development of priority rail freight corridors, and quality assurance standards for freight services. Since railway privatization in Great Britain in the mid-1990s, rail freight's mode share of the total road and rail market has increased from 9 per cent to 12 per cent, representing an absolute increase in rail volumes of 45 per cent. Many factors have led to this increase, though the development of competition between an increasing number of operators is an important contributory factor. This British experience contrasts sharply with that in many other Western European countries, where liberalization of the rail network has tended to be much slower.

Policies concerning goods vehicles in urban areas

Goods vehicles operating in urban areas are subject to a growing number of policy measures. These measures are being implemented by policy makers in response to congestion, pollution and safety issues, and include:

- time-of-day access and loading restrictions (including night deliveries);
- vehicle size and weight restrictions for urban logistics work;
- congestion charging systems;
- the development of urban freight consolidation centres;
- the use of alternative vehicle fuels and quieter vehicles (through the promotion of appropriate technologies and compulsory restrictions);
- the promotion of information systems and telematic applications with scope to improve logistics efficiency in urban areas;
- establishing partnerships between different retailers, transport and logistics operators, and local government to put in place measures to achieve greater efficiency and reduce negative impacts in freight activity in urban areas.

Time and vehicle weight and size restrictions have been used for many decades to control the use of goods vehicles in urban areas. However, these restrictions are being applied in more urban areas in Western Europe, especially in central business districts and retailing areas – and often accompany pedestrianization schemes. There have also been trials to see if night deliveries are feasible, with delivery and collection at times when urban areas are quieter and pedestrians are not present (Browne *et al*, 2005a).

Congestion charges were introduced in central London in 2003 to address road congestion. This is an area-based scheme – approximately 5 kilometres from east to west and 4 kilometres from north to south – for vehicles that are in the area between 7 am and 6.30 pm on weekdays. All vehicles entering the zone (except alternatively fuelled and electrically powered goods vehicles that attain very strict emission standards) are subject to the charge of £8 (€12). Since the introduction of charges, the total volume of traffic entering the zone during charging hours has fallen by 18 per cent and there has been a 30 per cent reduction in delays. Transport for London research suggests that congestion charging has had a broadly neutral impact on business performance in the charging zone. However, some retailers believe they have been adversely affected. Other urban authorities have shown interest in the London congestion charging scheme but none have implemented a similar scheme so far.

The aim of urban consolidation centres (UCCs) is to avoid the need for goods vehicles to deliver part-loads into busy urban areas. This can be achieved by providing facilities for consolidating deliveries into the urban area in an appropriate vehicle with a high load utilization. UCCs have been studied, trialled, and established in urban areas in several Western European countries including France, Germany, Italy, the Netherlands, Spain, Sweden and the UK. The approach has differed between these countries in terms of the organization of the UCC (ie the extent of private and public sector involvement), whether it is a compulsory or voluntary scheme, and the types of logistics operators it is aimed at (either small or large logistics operators). Many early UCCs have since closed, especially in Germany. However, new schemes in Italy, Sweden and the UK suggest that UCCs are likely to continue and may well become more popular (Browne et al, 2005b).

Greater use of alternative vehicle fuels and quieter vehicles is being achieved by national and urban authorities through a combination of research and promotion, as well as through compulsory vehicle operating schemes. In the Netherlands, the PIEK research programme has studied and disseminated information about vehicle and associated delivery noise (PIEK, 2003). In the UK, the Freight Best Practice Programme produces guidance for operators about a wide range of vehicle design and fuel issues, as well as information systems and telematic applications to improve logistics efficiency in urban areas. Meanwhile, in some urban areas, low-emission zones (LEZs) have been introduced. The LEZ concept reduces emission levels by restricting goods vehicle (and potentially other vehicle) access to those vehicles that meet certain emission criteria. Such zones already exist in some Dutch and Swedish cities and are planned for London (Browne, Allen and Anderson, 2005).

Partnerships have been established between retailers, transport and logistics operators, and local government to agree measures for greater efficiency and reduce negative impacts in freight activity in urban areas. Examples of such schemes are the work carried out by Platform Stedelijke Distributie (PSD, or the Forum for Physical Distribution in Urban Areas) in the Netherlands, and freight quality partnerships (FQPs) in the UK (Browne *et al*, 2004).

Other policy measures affecting road freight transport

There are two other policy measures that are having a significant impact on road-based freight and logistics services in the EU, and may also affect the location of logistics and other industrial activities. These are 1) the EU Working Time Directive and 2) road user charging for goods vehicles.

The EU Working Time Directive (WTD) was applied to the freight transport sector in all EU states in 2005. These regulations introduce limits on weekly working time, and the amount of work that can be done at night. Under the new regulations, working time for goods vehicle drivers must not exceed: 1) an average 48-hour week, 2) 60 hours in any single week, and 3) 10 hours in any 24-hour period, if working at night (DfT, 2005). This represents a reduction in the total number of hours that goods vehicle drivers can work in a week, with an overall reduction from 55 hours to 48 hours in the UK (Pott, 2001). This creates a need for companies to employ more drivers to maintain the same level of distribution activity.

Time- or distance-based road user charging for goods vehicles relates the charge to the usage of the vehicle, and better reflects the costs that users impose when using roads. Time-based road user charges already exist in Belgium, Luxembourg, the Netherlands, Denmark and Sweden. Switzerland currently uses a distance-based road user charge. In 2005, a new toll system was introduced on the 12,000 kilometres of German autobahn for all trucks weighing 12 tonnes and more. This toll taxes trucks on the basis of the distance driven, the number of axles and the emission category of the truck – with an average charge of €0.12 per kilometre (roadtraffic-technology.com, 2005). An extension to this scheme will allow the government to add other roads to the toll network (m.logistics, 2005). The British government planned a distance-based lorry road user charge by 2008, which would have ensured that truck operators from overseas paid their fair share towards the cost of using UK roads (HM Treasury, 2002). However, the government announced in 2005 that it would not proceed with the scheme, and national road pricing for cars and goods vehicles is unlikely to be introduced before 2015.

Opportunities and pressures for logistics providers in a new Europe

It is evident that many multinationals are rationalizing the number of LSPs they deal with across Europe – in much the same way as they have rationalized their production and warehousing operations (there is, of course, a link between these developments). This, together with the growth in intra-European trade, is leading to greater demand for transport and logistics services. Political changes have opened up new geographical markets, both for production and for consumption. Devising and implementing the right logistics strategies lie at the heart of successfully capitalizing on these commercial opportunities. Many of these changes are of significance to LSPs, especially those concerned with international markets.

The very different nature of European markets means that logistics providers wishing to provide for this growing demand for services adopt suitable and appropriate approaches for different markets. International transport companies engaged in cross-border work already understand that strategies need to be tailored to the particular country of operation.

Naturally, what is right for one company will not be right for all. In particular there are important differences between the sort of strategies and initiatives that need to be devised by larger companies and by smaller ones.

Strategies for larger LSPs

In deciding how to take advantage of the new European opportunities, LSPs need to be clear about which of the following strategies they wish to adopt (shown in Figure 22.3):

- *a pan-European strategy:* providing a Europe-wide service offering *distribution both within and between a number of European countries;*
- *a multi-domestic strategy:* providing national services that are in several European countries;
- *Eurolinkers:* providing a network (or part of a network) of mainly international services between major European markets.

Clearly the most ambitious strategy is to provide a truly pan-European service. Several major LSPs are working towards achieving this – but it is a challenging goal. The foundations for the multi-domestic strategy lie in the successful duplication of domestic services – adapted as required – in other countries.

Strategies for small- and medium-sized service providers

The smallest LSPs tend either to operate at a local level or to work for a few companies. The scope for these companies to develop strategies to take advantage of European opportunities is rather limited. For medium-sized companies – and especially those already operating in the international marketplace – there are undoubtedly ways in which they could take advantage of the growing opportunities in the EU. However, many multinationals are seeking to rationalize the number of logistics providers that they deal with and, therefore, medium-sized providers should find ways to tie their operations into those of their customers so that they become a vital part of their customers' distribution operation.

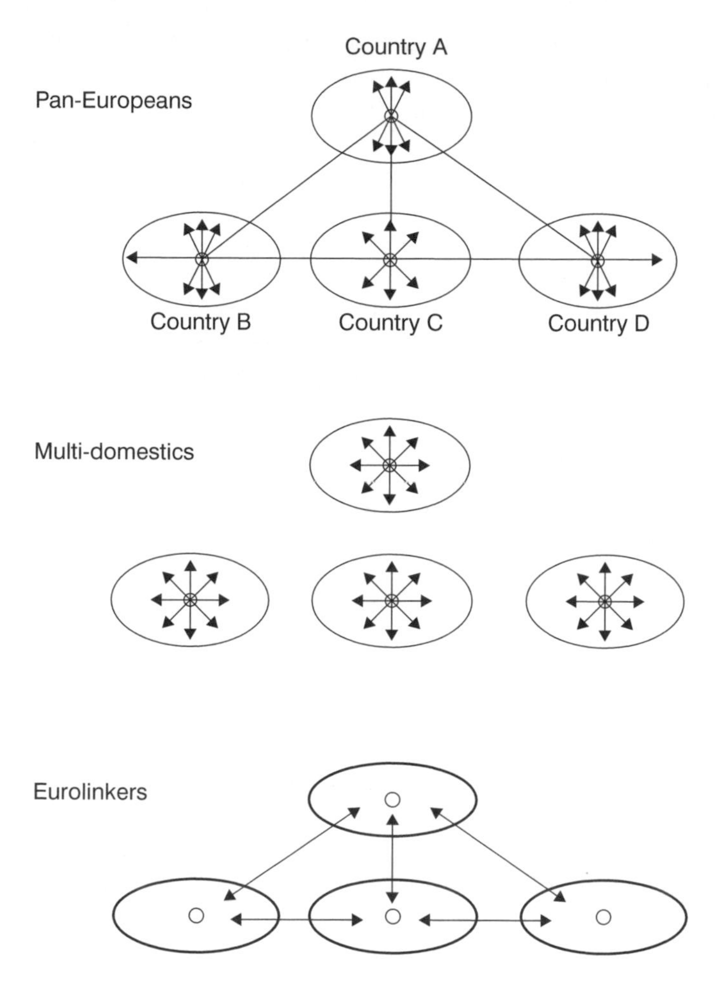

Source: Browne and Allen, 1994

Figure 22.3 Strategy options for providers of logistics services

Concluding remarks

Cost-effective systems of goods distribution are often argued to be an essential prerequisite for competing in international markets and for delivering a good standard of living at a national level. Efficient distribution of goods and services influences market diversity, consumer choice, jobs and prosperity. So logistics becomes as critical to economic success as manufacturing, retailing and service industries, contributing to economic growth by: 1) extending market reach, thereby giving firms access to a wider range of raw materials and supplies and providing access to a wider market; and 2) reducing waste – concepts such as just-in-time have a significant impact on reducing stock held within supply chains.

Logistics management and supply chain strategies play a critical role in the competitiveness of firms. Indeed, it has been argued that competition is increasingly between supply chains rather than between individual enterprises. Within logistics, the role of transport is an important one and is frequently the aspect of logistics most affected by policy interventions (for example, deregulation of transport markets or decisions about infrastructure expenditure).

A number of logistics developments have tended to increase the consumption of transport services within the supply chain. This can either increase trip length (with the concentration of production and storage locations) or give greater frequency of deliveries (with JIT).

However, there are also many positive logistics initiatives that combine both environmental and commercial benefits. Clearly, companies at the leading edge already enjoy the benefits of this and contribute to sustainability. There is much to be gained by improving the efficiency of companies that are not at the forefront of these initiatives. Therefore, ways must be found to encourage more companies operating in Europe to improve logistics and ensure that those approaches that contribute to sustainability become more widely disseminated.

References

Browne, M and Allen, J (1994) Logistics strategies for Europe, in *Logistics and Distribution Planning: Strategies for management*, ed J Cooper, Kogan Page, London, pp 122–134

Browne, M, Allen, J and Anderson, S (2005) Low emission zones: the likely effects on the freight transport sector, *International Journal of Logistics: Research and applications*, **8** (4), pp 269–81

Browne, M *et al* (2004) Urban freight movements and public–private partnerships, in *Logistics Systems for Sustainable Cities*, ed E Taniguchi and R Thompson, pp 17–35, Elsevier, Oxford

Browne, M *et al* (2005a) Night-time delivery restrictions: a review, Paper presented at the third International Conference on City Logistics, 25–27 June, Madeira, Portugal

Browne, M *et al* (2005b) *Urban Freight Consolidation Centres*, Report to the UK Department for Transport, University of Westminster, London

Cooper, J, Browne, M and Peters, M (1994) *European Logistics: Markets, management and strategy*, 2nd edn, Blackwell Publishers, Oxford

Datamonitor (2002) *Consolidation in the European Logistics Industry*, June, Datamonitor, London

Department for Transport (DfT) (2005) *Road Transport (Working Time) Guidance*, March, DfT, London

Deutsche Post (2005) Deutsche Post World Net completes acquisition of Exel, Press release, 14 December, Bonn/London

Distribution (2002) Europe yet to become a single entity, interview with Steve Allen, managing director of Securicor Omega Logistics, *Distribution*, **15** (3), June, p 17

Dutch National Spatial Planning Agency (1997) *Spatial Patterns of Transportation: Atlas of freight transport in Europe*, Dutch National Spatial Planning Agency, The Hague

European Commission (2001) *European Transport Policy for 2010: Time to decide*, White Paper, Office for Official Publications of the European Communities, Luxembourg

European Commission (2004) *European Union: Energy and transport in figures 2004*, Directorate-General for Energy and Transport, Brussels

European Commission (2005) *Trans-European Transport Network: TEN-T priority axes and projects 2005*, Directorate-General for Energy and Transport, Brussels

European Commission (2006) *Motorways of the Sea: Shifting freight off Europe's roads*, Directorate-General for Energy and Transport, Brussels

European Logistics Association (ELA) and AT Kearney (2004) *Excellence in Logistics*, ELA, Brussels

European Logistics Management (2001a) Danone's plan to revamp biscuit business includes closure of six manufacturing sites, 17 April, p 9

European Logistics Management (2001b) Geest accelerates French acquisition, 19 February, pp 9–10

Harnischfeger, U (2002) Deutsche Post out to prove its gusto, *Financial Times*, 20 September, p 30

Hindson, D (1998) The pressure for pan-European logistics, Pan-European Logistics Conference, 20–21 January, London

HM Treasury (2002) *Modernising the Taxation of the Haulage Industry*, Progress Report One, April, HM Treasury, London

Kemp, D (1997) Competitive supply chain structure: Nike – a case study, World Logistics Conference, December, London

King, M (2002) We can be king of the jungle, *International Freighting Weekly*, 1 April, p 7

Kuehne & Nagel (2004) Expanding integrated logistics in France, *World Magazine*, 1, p 21

Kuehne & Nagel (2005) The quantum leap: the acquisition of ACR Logistics marks a new era in contract logistics for Kuehne & Nagel, *World Magazine*, 2, p 22

Lenders, R (2005) European DCs on the move, *Capgemini Supply Chain and Procurement Newsletter*, November

Lloyd, S (2004) Europe's DC hot spots, *Logistics Europe*, April, pp 38–42

Manners Bell, J (2005) Market monitor November 2005, *Logistics Europe*, November, p 16

Mintel (2002) *Food Retailing in Europe*, Mintel, June

m.logistics (2005) Telematics – they work if you let them, m.logistics, 17, May/June

O'Laughlin, K, Cooper, J and Cabocel, E (1993) *Reconfiguring European Logistics Systems*, Council of Logistics Management, Oak Brook, IL

PIEK (2003) Technical final assessment PEAK multi-annual programme, PIEK project, Utrecht

Pott, R (2001) Working time: part one, *Croner's Road Transport Operation Bulletin*, 53, May

Reed Business Information (2002) *Road Transport Market Survey 2001*, Reed Business Information, prepared by NOP Research Group, London

roadtraffic-technology.com (2005) *LKW-MAUT Electronic Toll Collection System for Heavy Goods Vehicles, Germany*, http://www.roadtraffic-technology.com/projects/lkw-maut/

Technical University of Berlin *et al* (2001) SULOGTRA: analysis of trends in supply chain management and logistics, SULOGTRA Deliverable Report D1, Workpackage 1

TNT (2005) TNT announces initiatives to sharpen strategic focus, TNT press release, 6 December

TNT (2006) TNT and Malherbe conclude deal for the sale of the remaining activities of Logistiques Nicolas, TNT press release, 27 January

World Advertising Research Centre (WARC) (2002) *The Retail Pocket Book 2002*, WARC, Henley

23

Logistics strategies for Central and Eastern Europe

Grzegorz Augustyniak, Warsaw School of Economics

Introduction

The fall of communism in Central and Eastern Europe (CEE) at the turn of the 1990s began a fascinating period of systemic transition. This period of transformation has coincided with unprecedented economic integration in Europe that, on the one hand, creates enormous opportunities and advantages, but, on the other, needs great – often painful – changes. Since 2004, eight former Soviet-bloc countries have joined the European Union (the Czech Republic, Estonia, Hungary, Latvia, Lithuania, Poland, Slovakia and Slovenia), another two (Bulgaria and Romania) may join the EU in 2007 and most of the remaining ones strive to do so in the future. Both the new members of the Community and the candidates must follow or adapt quickly to EU standards at a time of slow economic growth in Western Europe, and intense competition resulting from globalization and the lifting of trade barriers within WTO member countries. The scale of changes in CEE countries, inherited gaps in infrastructure and limited access to financial resources make the implementation of logistics strategy – or any strategy – in this region very difficult.

When analysing the situation in CEE countries we should not forget that despite their numerous similarities – resulting from their common fate as

Soviet satellites – each is significantly distinct. The most often quoted differences between them include:

- the size of the respective markets (measured by population and per capita income);
- the size of territories and their geographical configuration (determining their logistics systems);
- different starting positions for reforms (determined, for example, by ownership and industry structures, foreign indebtedness, etc);
- cultural and historical differences;
- different ways, degrees and effectiveness of reforms implemented (from a shock-therapy approach, through evolutionary progress, to almost giving up);
- different levels of salaries, productivity and price indexes (which in turn differentiate them from their richer partners in the West, as indicated in Table 23.1);
- degree of integration with NATO and the EU, with new EU members from CEE in a favourable position because of EU financial support for less developed regions and structural funds.

For these reasons, this description of logistics strategies for CEE is focused on those countries that are the most advanced in the transition process, and whose logistics strategies are the most similar. This primarily refers to the Czech Republic, Hungary and Poland. Just recently, Slovakia joined the team, with a high increase in investments due to favourable conditions for foreign investors and a flat, transparent tax system. These four countries share similar

Table 23.1 Comparison of salaries, labour standards and price indexes in selected cities (Zurich, Berlin and capitals of new EU members representing CEE)

City (country)	Salary index	Working hours per year	Vacations (days per year)	Price index
Zurich (Switzerland)	100	1,872	23	100.0
Berlin (Germany)	64	1,666	28	75.0
Lubljana (Slovenia)	21.2	1,830	22	55.0
Budapest (Hungary)	16.6	2,012	23	56.0
Warsaw (Poland	13.0	1,901	26	50.7
Riga (Latvia)	12.6	1,862	20	43.0
Tallin (Estonia)	12.4	1,826	21	50.0
Prague (Czech Republic)	11.8	1,943	22	40.3
Vilnius (Lithuania)	11.2	1,833	26	49.0
Bratislava (Slovakia)	9.7	1,881	19	38.3

Source: Eurostat, 2005; Dudzik, 2004

political strategies that are based on integration with NATO (as new members accepted in 1999), development within the European Union (since 2004), and joining the eurozone no later than 2011.

While focusing on those three, we should not forget that EU membership also affects other CEE and Baltic states that have recently joined the Community. All of these are similar in size but differ in per capita GDP, with Slovenia being the richest of all CEE countries. When talking of NATO enlargement we should mention states that are less advanced in reforms, but becoming strongly Western-oriented, such as Bulgaria and Romania, which aspire to join the EU in 2007. Such aspirations are also expressed by other Balkan states and Ukraine.

In other words, the CEE region constitutes a mosaic that is struggling with internal logistics problems, while aiming at integration of its logistics systems with both the EU and within CEE.

It would be hard to overestimate the impact of this integration on the countries' logistics strategies. However, the current conditions determining the development of logistics in CEE are to a large extent the result of the communist legacy, so it is necessary to take a brief overview of the 'old' system of working practices.

Conditions of economic development of CEE countries before 1990

After the Second World War, the economic development of CEE countries focused on their reconstruction. This was accompanied by rapid industrialization based on heavy industry and mining. However, this industrial structure did not reflect the real needs of the economies but was rather dictated by the prevailing 'Cold War' doctrine. As a result, in the 1960s, while the West was experiencing its first consumer revolution, Comecon countries were still developing enormous industrial potential, with almost complete disregard for actual consumer needs. The problems were exacerbated by the measures of organizational effectiveness. The most common was based on the maximization of assets employed. In other words, the more you use resources (ideally, the entire amount assigned by the relevant central plan) the better. When economies were faced by shortages of supplies, the focus was shifted towards maximization of output – but abandoning any measures of quality. Other measures of performance were meaningless, since permanent shortages of consumer products – sold at fixed prices – gave producers absolute powers in the market. The ways of doing business in CEE countries stimulated waste and corrupted workers, whose intuitive efforts at rationalization were not only ignored but were, in many ways, punished (Kisperska-Moron, Kapcia and Piniecki, 1996).

Paradoxically, the wave of Western credit in the 1970s, when East–West relations were relaxed, deepened the economic crisis in CEE countries. Money was wrongly spent or consumed, and this resulted in huge indebtedness. Moreover, industrial plants built on Western technology made countries dependent on imports of spare parts, and when these became too expensive they could only be replaced by low-quality substitutes produced locally. Consequently, the efficiency and life span of production lines were significantly reduced. Further attempts at reform in the 1980s brought nothing but economic slump. Soon, the political system collapsed, and since 1989 CEE countries, one after another, have moved towards market economies.

The logistics system of CEE before 1989

In centrally planned economies, knowledge of logistics and other modern management concepts and techniques was practically useless. The only exceptions were found in those companies whose export orientation exposed them to operations in the West. In other companies, monopolistic producers, whose distribution was also in the hands of monopolies, dominated the quasi-market. The government set prices for products and services (with few exceptions where higher prices were allowed) and fixed the currency exchange rates. In these circumstances, the only business goal was to exist – at the expense of the state, which covered any loss.

The only concern of logistics was to obtain scarce resources from suppliers to secure the execution of centrally set plans (which meant that the logistics in CEE had a very strong supply orientation) and to deliver goods produced to customers. This sounds similar to the tasks of logistics in the West, but with the significant difference that the logistics system was not focused on quality. None of the logistics systems objectives (well known from the '7 Rs' definition) had to be fulfilled, and both effectiveness and customer satisfaction could be ignored without penalty. Ineffectiveness was officially explained by 'objective reasons' – or sometimes by firing or imprisoning selected managers, employees or 'speculators'. This approach led to enormous waste and technological obsolescence of companies, which treated investments and customer service as costs to be avoided rather than sources of potential improvement and revenue.

These facts indicate that the logistics system of CEE countries was extremely expensive, especially because of high transportation and inventory carrying costs. The transportation system consisted of a relatively dense, but low-quality, infrastructure serviced by obsolete and inefficient fleets. Another major factor contributing to the high cost of transportation was the commercially ridiculous (but politically motivated) location of production plants and other logistics facilities. The criteria for location were based on a theory of balanced development for all regions in a country. This meant that a factory could be erected anywhere, regardless of its proximity to suppliers or consumers, existing transportation, telecommunication infrastructure and the profile of the labour force available. In practice, every investment of this kind required huge investments in new roads and social infrastructure, eg workers' hotels, heating plants, sewage systems, etc. This was rarely shared with any other local facilities. To make matters worse, the lack of money often meant that new infrastructure was incapable of serving the needs of the facility. The result of these poor locations – and supporting infrastructure – decisions was that distances travelled by transport were far greater than necessary, for both supply and distribution. This often had an impact on the quality of goods carried – while the fixed cost of investment was very high, the system generated a lot of pollution, and other environmental threats were totally ignored. Another major drawback for CEE countries lay in the poor telecommunication infrastructure, which came with a lack of incentive to improve information flows.

Shortages of supplies, combined with inefficient transportation, forced all companies in CEE to carry huge amounts of inventory to secure smooth production. This meant that inventory was treated more like an investment than a necessary evil. The quality aspect again had no impact on the system, since eventual waste was added into the cost of production. Final product defects did not harm the producers, since chronic shortages meant that customers were forced to accept any products they could find.

Overall, the 1990s found CEE countries with inefficient, fragmented and out-of-date logistics systems that did not meet their requirements as they moved towards market economies. The system was generally characterized by:

- a lack of customer focus;
- the underdevelopment of a transportation and telecommunication infrastructure;
- poorly located, ineffective and obsolete industrial plants and related logistics infrastructure (especially low-standard warehouses);
- a lack of specialized, integrated logistics services;
- inadequate and poor management education, especially in logistics and quality management across all levels;
- a lack of reverse logistics systems – as there were no environmental policies for, say, the reuse and recycling of packaging and hazardous waste;
- low employee morale and job satisfaction.

The clear conclusion is that the logistics system inherited from communism was a fundamental barrier to the transformation of these economies and their subsequent competitiveness. This is supported by an analysis of the cost of logistics of these countries – which is estimated at up to 30 per cent of GDP, perhaps twice as high as typical values in the West. Thus, poor logistics is a major counterbalance for the few advantages of the region, such as:

- a low-cost and technically well-educated workforce;
- incentives for investment in selected regions;

- the relatively low cost of land acquisition;
- favourable geographical conditions (part of the EU market and its transit location);
- the size of the market and its potential, accompanied by rapid economic growth.

Logistics has a huge potential for significant improvements and savings, and successful transformation in this area might be a key to success for CEE countries (especially those that have recently joined the EU) and investors.

Development of logistics in the period of transition and after joining the EU

At the beginning of reforms, all CEE countries suffered from similar problems – though on different scales. Their major effort in the early 1990s concentrated on stabilizing the macroeconomic condition, focusing on curbing inflation (or hyperinflation, as it was in Poland), high unemployment (a term that never existed in centrally planned economies) and social security. Simultaneously removing most barriers and curbs on entrepreneurship – accompanied by privatization of government-run industries – led to the rapid, but also chaotic, development of market economies. Government efforts to gain some sort of control over these changes were made on a trial-and-error basis. In general – regardless of the many limitations, mistakes and high social costs – those CEE countries that followed more radical approaches to reforms have become leaders in the transition to market economies.

Soon, the development of market economies and the need to compete globally raised new challenges for politicians and entrepreneurs, who realized that:

- the transition into market economies means that CEE markets will gradually adopt Western patterns;
- the relaxation or abandonment of trade barriers forces these countries radically to improve their productivity;
- the major impediments to the transition will be the underdeveloped banking, telecommunication and transportation systems that are heavily dependent on the state or are hard to privatize.

Unfortunately, the shaky political situation in CEE countries (both during the creation of democratic institutions and habits, and caused by changing governments) coupled with the need to pursue tough financial policies (based on IMF guidelines) was a major obstacle in implementing reforms. These problems were magnified by the sudden fall of production and replacement of local products by imports. This created an unfavourable trade balance with the West that could not be compensated for by trade with the East, since the Comecon system no longer existed and internal ties had been broken. Lower incomes for governments and inherited indebtedness (despite substantial reductions) limited their scope for investment in logistics infrastructure. While it was not a major problem at the beginning of transition, after a few years of rapid development the state of the deteriorating – or at best very slowly improving – transport and logistics infrastructure became the major obstacle for future development. To understand better the reasons for this, it is worth considering the major factors that stimulated the rapid growth in logistics and related areas, which include:

- the rapid growth of trade;
- productivity improvements, especially in inventory management;
- deregulation and liberalization in some modes of transportation;
- development of telecommunication and information infrastructure;
- development of management education;
- accession to the EU.

Developing trade

The general area of 'trade' was the first to adapt itself fully to the market economy, the main reason being that the consumer market was the weakest element of the previous system and attempts to deregulate it were implemented before the systemic changes of the 1990s. Trade was also the first area in which private capital was invested and entrepreneurship appeared. Growth of the sector was especially high in the retail industry. In Poland, the number of retail outlets (mostly small shops) tripled between 1989 and 1995, excluding the number of pedlars and market stalls that covered the streets of cities and villages. Of course, this growth reflected the great underdevelopment of these services during communist times.

Along with retail trade, wholesaling companies were reorganized and many new ones entered the market. At the beginning these were local firms or family business units. But they were soon confronted with aggressive competition from large wholesaling and retailing companies from the West (including large supermarket chains like Casino, Carrefour, Tesco and Metro), which also brought new technology. For these companies CEE is now one of the major markets (with hundreds of hyper- and supermarkets), with further expansion planned into Ukraine and Russia.

These new entrants had an inherent advantage, since the collapse of the old system caused paralysis in the former centralized and state-owned companies, but there is still some space for expansion.

Another sign of the gradual unification of CEE markets with the West is a behavioural change among consumers, who now prefer shopping at large supermarkets and department stores at the weekend (Rutkowski, 1996). This, in turn, has forced small shops to search for consolidation opportunities to enable them to compete with the large hyper- and supermarket chains. Another strategy, implemented by local grocery shops, is to make a transition into convenience stores that operate longer hours, offer wider ranges of products and improve customer service and shop layout.

Significant improvements in customer service, along with better consumer legal protection (increasingly matching EU standards), encourage more sophisticated systems of delivery, often aimed at achieving just-in-time, quick response (QR) and efficient consumer response (ECR). Joining the EU removed another significant obstacle that ruined many logistics strategies and lowered the attractiveness of the region: this was congestion at borders, which reduced vehicle performance by 15 per cent or more.

Among other positive changes in CEE logistics systems is the rationalization of costs, with significant improvements to stock levels and turnover, which have reduced the average costs of inventory by more than 20 per cent. The biggest improvement is in food products and other perishable items. This was achieved despite – as is typical in an emerging market – shifts of inventory from distributors and retailers to producers. Now, the producers are adopting innovative approaches to production and distribution, including flexible manufacturing and advanced management concepts.

Warehousing is also a dynamically developing area. There was an initial fall in numbers resulting from the bankruptcy of old, multi-storey and small warehouses. But then many companies, both local and foreign, started to develop modern and well-equipped warehouses, and provide services that go beyond the standard stockholding. The first state-of-the-art logistics platforms were created at the end of the 1990s, with many new logistics production centres already completed. In 2005, total modern warehousing and logistics space reached 1.2 million square metres, and the capacity of the recently planned logistics centre in Piotrków Trybunalski in central Poland is 500,000 square metres. In the Czech Republic, 110,000 square metres of new space is added annually (mostly around Prague and seven other major cities). In Hungary there are already around 200 industrial parks providing logistics services to manufacturing and service companies. Most of these centres are run by large, well-known companies, which start to consider them not only as centres for further expansion to the East (into Ukraine, Belarus and Russia) but also as logistics centres for Central Europe including some 'old 15' EU member states. Such platforms not only improve services, but also create new employment opportunities. Logistics becomes a vital element of the whole economy, and the demand for logistics specialists – as a new profession in CEE – is very high.

As in the West, logistics centres have added activities, including final production activities outsourced by large manufacturers. These developments – along with a growing inflow of foreign investments, growth of local markets and exports – have created a basis for rapid growth in advanced logistics services. Third-party logistics services became a reality in CEE, and the introduction of fourth-party logistics is only a question of time. Another positive sign of change into more sophisticated contracts is the rising number of companies integrating their whole supply chains.

It is also worth mentioning that there has also been a rapid development of management and logistics education, both at university level and as a part of in-company training. This is also reflected in the growing number of professional logistics associations and clubs, and the many professional magazines popularizing logistics theory and practice.

Road transport

All these developments in logistics require parallel development of the transport network and services. After decades of state monopoly, transportation became a hot topic during liberalization, with road transport being the first mode to be substantially deregulated.

Domestic services were offered by almost anybody who held a driver's licence and registered the activity. In terms of international transport, some restrictions applied, but after joining the EU the market reopened, giving transport companies new opportunities of offering services between EU states. The liberalization of road transport led to the establishment of thousands of small, private carriers – and the prices for these services decreased significantly, taking most business away from the railways. However, this created some negative impact on safety, environmental protection and the profitability of the sector. The rush to attract more and more orders for transport services and the maximization of loads resulted in widespread violation of transport procedures – especially for the rest time of drivers and overloading trucks. The dynamically developing and deregulated road transport industry left government agencies unable to control safety standards. This gap, especially in Poland, forced the authorities to take radical measures to reorganize the system by investing in more truck weigh stations (including mobile ones) and the creation of a specialized agency – Road Transport Inspection – empowered to penalize any deviation from technical, legal and humanitarian (such as the movement of livestock) standards.

After joining the EU the regulations got stricter and forced many transport companies to reorganize and modernize their fleet and management systems. Of course, opening new markets created new opportunities for transport companies in CEE, but they also faced new and fierce competition from companies in other EU countries. This again resulted in a drastic reduction in profitability, and eventually the lowering of service standards. But now companies had begun to quit the 'cheapest-and-nearest' approach to carrier selection and looked for more integrated, dedicated services offered by respected and well-established logistics companies. Some of these are still independent and local – but the leading ones are country-wide, with long experience of international transport, or have emerged from forwarding agencies that are part of global companies like Schenker, P&O, etc.

Despite concentration, small, private transport companies can still modernize themselves and succeed in market niches. They are obviously more vulnerable to competition, but prospects are good, since road transport remains the dominant mode (except in Estonia and Latvia, where sea transport is dominant) and there is no strong competition from other modes.

These changes are associated with a programme of construction of new roads and motorways supported by the EU. Unfortunately, progress still lags behind the growing transport needs, and the density of motorways is far behind that in former EU15 states (3 metres per square kilometre in CEE against 17 metres in EU15). Motorway construction in Poland attempts to use private–public partnership, but this appears to be ineffective, slow and very costly – both in construction and in use by motorists (because of high tolls). This in turn means that new motorways do not attract enough traffic to give a return on investment. More progress in this area has been made in the Czech Republic, Slovakia and Hungary, but it does not change the overall picture of a growing infrastructure gap between EU15 and new members. For example, the planned density of motorways in the Czech Republic in 2008 (12.8 kilometres per 1,000 square kilometres) is still below the EU15 average in 1999 (15.8 kilometres per 1,000 square kilometres). The situation requires more action both at the EU and at the local levels, since further deepening of this gap may adversely affect the investment attractiveness of CEE countries – and ultimately the development of Eastern markets.

Rail transport

Railways in CEE countries are still run by the state, and the restructuring process is not as advanced as other modes. Each country is searching for the best route to eventual privatization, but owing to large numbers of employees and the high cost of modernization the transformation changes are only gradually being implemented. In Poland, for example, the first step was to separate all services (such as maintenance facilities, construction companies, etc) from the railways. This has already allowed a few non-state-run railway companies to act as carriers, paying for the use of the track – and hopefully fostering competition and allowing better allocation of resources for modernization and upgrades. But substantial modernization to allow heavier loads and higher speeds of transport will require enormous additional financial resources.

More progress has been made in separating cargo and passenger operations. At the moment, some local connecting passenger services are being closed, while vital commuter lines in cities are managed by local authorities alone, or in cooperation with the former monopoly. Fully owned state railways usually focus on intercity connections.

The major obstacle to restructuring comes from the trade unions, which realize that applying market principles will mean track closures and further reductions in employment (at a time when unemployment is high, reaching 18 per cent in Poland). The need for such a reduction paradoxically reflects the relatively high density of rail track (with the majority of the network electrified – 60 per cent in Poland, 45 per cent in Hungary, but only 30 per cent in the Czech Republic, compared to a 52 per cent average for EU15). But much of this is used exclusively for commuter passenger services, or has minimal use because of competition from road transport. It is also important to note that, to comply with AGC and AGTC European agreements, most of the existing tracks need to be upgraded for high-speed transport, higher axle load, and clearance profile of cargo movement.

Most CEE railways offer limited intermodal services – so there is a major opportunity for them to compete with road transportation (or to support its transit traffic) provided there are financial resources to finance such programmes. A good example is in Hungary, where intermodal carriages account for 7 per cent of all operations done by MAV (Hungarian state railways). Another initiative is to put more commuter carriages on to tracks by limiting or eliminating competition on such routes. And the European Commission's investigation of the true cost of transport and its strategy of supporting 'greener' modes of transport may encourage more cargo and passengers on to rail.

We should also note that the climate around railway privatization – influenced by the poor results from the UK – is not encouraging. We should expect more efforts towards the commercialization of state-owned railways, rather than their privatization, especially in larger CEE countries.

Air transport

Ownership changes in the turbulent air transport industry are also slow, but the modernization process is well advanced. Former flag carriers are still major players in this slowly deregulating market, but their share is substantially lower than a few years ago – largely because of the arrival of low-cost airlines. The response of full-service airlines is further restructuring of fleet and services, deeper cooperation with alliances (LOT Polish Airlines with Star Alliance, and CSA Czech Airlines with SkyTeam) and the creation of low-cost carriers (like Centralwings, which is a joint venture between LOT and Germanwings). All major CEE carriers started to replace Soviet-built aircraft with Western products in the 1980s, and when this process was completed it brought dramatic increases in passenger service quality and cargo capacity. CEE airlines continue to keep among the most modern and newest of aircraft fleets.

After 9/11 all CEE airlines have been exposed to enormous turbulence but, fortunately, few disappeared. Financial reports from 2005 show profits, but the situation – as in the whole airline industry – is still shaky. Uncertain economic conditions in the region and the threat of terrorism have slowed the rate of privatization – but not the investments and improvements in CEE airline operations. These actions are essential, so – despite higher productivity and an increased number of passengers – extra revenues are largely spent on tighter security in the airports and on planes.

Along with airline modernization, the air traffic control infrastructure is undergoing radical changes. New passenger and cargo terminals have been built, and air traffic control systems have been upgraded to improve safety and services in the increasingly crowded skies of the region. Some of these projects are supported by EU structural financial aid and the European Bank for Reconstruction and Development.

Other modes

The pipeline system is also expanding to deal with new sources of natural gas and crude oil. Conversely, there is a general decline in sea and inland water transportation because it is not being used to its full potential. This is largely due to the lack of proper terminals and underdevelopment of waterways, especially in Poland. However, in the Baltic States modern container terminals are being built, and the increase in operations exceeds 20 per cent a year. The rising costs of fuel revitalize many projects to integrate European waterways, especially on the River Danube.

Some progress has taken place in the development of telecommunication and information networks. In Hungary, the Czech Republic and Poland, the monopolistic service providers have already been privatized, but in other countries the networks are still under the control of the state. Economic recession and over-optimism about the uptake of the latest technology have slowed the rate of privatization, but recent changes in ownership (for example, Hungarian Matav sold to Deutsche Telecom) may indicate a return to previous policy.

Large investments in the latest communications technology – along with customer relationship management (CRM) strategies – have dramatically increased service levels. Increasing competition and anti-monopoly measures have resulted in lower tariffs, so prices may soon be at the same level as those in EU15. Unfortunately, consumer perception of telecoms is still of low quality at a high price (compared with salary levels), so access to the internet is still much lower than in EU15. There is a different situation in the mobile phone market, where there is more competition. The underdevelopment of landlines, along with the greater availability and lower prices of mobile services, make CEE one of the most dynamically developing regions. But even here, there are signs of saturation that are forcing mobile network companies to focus on effectiveness and more diversified services. To some extent (but not as obviously as in some Western companies), the financial position of mobile service providers has worsened due to investment in UMTS technology concessions. These were, however, relatively cheap, and government regulatory agencies were flexible about its introduction. Another clear trend in the mobile industry is the replacement of local brands by global logos – leading to the unification of marketing and service strategies across Europe.

The use of information networks – particularly fibre optics – is also increasing, and the first applications of electronic data interchange (EDI) in accordance with UN/EDIFACT standards are being introduced. In addition, more companies are using integrated management information systems – but with mixed results. This is not unique to CEE – but value for money seems to be lower here, and it requires more advanced management systems to use the technology as a support tool and not a solution in itself.

Summarizing

Regardless of the economic transformation and improvements in logistics infrastructure, statistical data – supported by everyday experience – show that logistics in CEE still requires rapid modernization. The gap with the West in the case of road infrastructure is still 10–20 years, but the accession to the EU should help gradually to close this. There are both advantages and disadvantages of the current situation. The advantages include:

- increasing recognition and application of modern logistics solutions in both manufacturing and services;
- increasing efficiency and effectiveness of logistics systems in companies;
- more investment in modern logistics infrastructure;
- the advent of logistics services providers (mainly from the West) promoting state-of-the-art logistics solutions; and
- significant progress in customer service and rapid development of the service sector.

A separate group of advantages results from the recent accession of some CEE countries to the EU:

- lifted border and customs barriers (accompanied by dynamic development of border infrastructure with non-EU neighbours);
- adoption of EU regulations and even greater access to the common European market;
- higher logistics productivity due to increasing competition and modernization;
- greater access to capital and financial support for logistics investment.

The disadvantages include:

- too slow development of a new transport infrastructure (especially roads) to upgrade the existing, and often very poor, system;
- financial instability and organizational weakness of companies (especially SMEs);
- the too-high cost of logistics activities (a result of the conditions described earlier), which lowers the attractiveness of CEE for potential foreign investors in industries requiring effective logistics;

- low demand for integrated logistics services (despite quite impressive supply of such operations); and
- fragmentation of logistics activities (resulting in constant sub-optimization of decisions) and not fostering a holistic approach to supply chains as the result of a complex and slow process of implementation of modern management concepts.

A full understanding of the problems and their causes is a key requirement for the design and successful implementation of logistics strategies in these countries. Despite the continuing process of assimilation of EU standards, this awareness is especially important to potential investors in the region, for whom the experience and challenges of CEE countries may still be new.

Logistics strategies in CEE countries

The description of the existing logistics system in selected CEE countries indicates that it is affected by:

- the dynamics of their economic growth and the inflow of foreign investments (slowed down because of the recent global economic downturn and the threat of terrorism);
- development of the economic and political situation, mostly within the EU – the major trade partner of all CEE countries;
- the progress of CEE countries in utilizing their membership of the EU, and the process of opening up other EU markets to the new members;
- global trends;
- a focus on environment protection.

Obviously, all these factors are dependent on one another but the aim is clear: the logistics system of CEE has to adapt and be close to EU15 standards. It will be a long process – but inevitable for the creation of an integrated and pan-European logistics system that is ready to compete globally.

CEE countries enjoy higher economic growth than EU15 – partially boosted by accession – and the defective infrastructure and social conditions inherited from the communist system will be removed. Further inflows of modern technology and management methods give improving productivity and competitiveness – supported by the advantages of low-cost labour, which should continue for the next decade. But the high cost of logistics is a major constraint on the development of CEE economies. So investment in logistics – improving infrastructure and developing the logistics services market and logistics education – should be one of the major priorities of economic policies. The key objectives for developing logistics strategies are determined by the major challenges that exist in the region at the beginning of the 21st century, namely:

- further development of integrated supply chains;
- implementation of modern tools for forecasting and designing logistics systems in companies;
- a focus on achieving further synergy between cost reduction and customer service levels, especially in delivery times, reliability and flexibility;
- development of agile logistics systems based on transformation of companies' management systems to give process orientation and adoption of relevant information technology;
- acceleration of the development of transport, information, banking and customs infrastructure;
- integration of CEE logistics systems with those of other EU countries;
- recognition and development of logistics in service industries, especially in health care, banking, telecommunications and tourism – which all have potential for growth and expansion.

Successfully meeting these challenges will be a major test for CEE members' ability to capitalize on EU membership. The reality is that the willingness of EU15 to support the integration of the new members is lower than it was at the time of the accession of Spain, Greece or Ireland. Another fact is that logistics investments have to compete with other important reforms of administration, education, health care and pension schemes – as well as restructuring heavy industry, agriculture and so on. The economic growth that CEE enjoys at the moment is also too slow for a satisfactory rate of progress. In such complex situations, the logistics strategy implemented by the state should:

- focus on key investments that the private sector is unable to make;
- create a favourable climate for other investments to improve the logistics system;
- work out a joint strategy with NATO and the EU aimed at directing more structural aid for the development and integration of CEE logistics systems with the rest of Europe;
- limit or eliminate monopolistic practices, unfair treatment, corruption and bad practices in the logistics sector – which is the major threat expressed by SMEs in CEE.

This is why the logistics strategy at the macroeconomic level should focus on:

- expanding the liberalization and deregulation processes in logistics in accordance with EU regulations;
- finishing the privatization processes in the banking and telecommunication sectors, complementary to the proper organization of material and services flows;
- more active involvement of CEE governments in the construction of motorways and bypasses, along with modernization of border infrastructure;

- actively supporting environmental solutions in logistics by enacting the relevant legislation and incentives for companies dealing with reverse logistics and intermodal transport systems.

At the micro level, logistics strategies should reflect global trends and focus on:

- orientation towards, development of and participation in supply chains – aimed at continuously improving performance and similar to those that meet customer needs in the West;
- investment in modern management education that emphasizes the development of human resources and knowledge-based management;
- implementation of outsourcing strategies for logistics, as the development of owned operations is too expensive and risky;
- development of agile logistics in manufacturing and services;
- further investments in information technology linked with radical changes in managing the company towards process-oriented structures.

All these strategies have to be implemented simultaneously to bring maximum effect and significantly improve the ability of these countries to become strong and attractive partners in a united Europe. Any further delay in this sphere may destroy the whole effort and waste the sacrifices made during the transition process, especially in those countries that will still remain for some time outside the EU.

Conclusions

CEE countries are at different stages in their move towards market economies, but they are all still a long way from their desired targets. Logistics and the related infrastructure were the most neglected elements of the previous system. To upgrade and develop modern logistics systems, CEE countries must use a significant part of their financial and human resources. They must realize that, after fixing the financial system, the second step is significantly to improve logistics. This would give enormous savings to help the economies of CEE gain further momentum in their development. Such reforms seem to be gaining support from countries already experiencing the negative aspects of underdeveloped logistics infrastructures.

Another important element of successful reforms concerns the development of human resources – and the change of 'inherited' thinking. The emerging market economies inspired individualism and entrepreneurship, but the simplest ways of improving productivity in the region have been almost exhausted. Further development requires more teamwork, a holistic view of enterprise and better education. Changes must be implemented in a smart way, so that capital will be acquired and used in the most efficient and effective way. Modern logistics, along with developed management concepts, offers a variety of solutions.

These challenges have now been recognized in CEE countries. Logistics associations have reached maturity – and more universities and companies offer logistics training and consultation. In technology, state-of-the-art solutions are becoming available, and companies are making better use of them. These initiatives are a prerequisite for the rapid development of both the internal markets and the external environment. Only effective implementation of the presented strategies will ensure that this region becomes an attractive platform linking the West with the East.

Finally, it is worth emphasizing that – regardless of some criticisms and real problems faced by the region on its path to joining the EU – enormous progress has already been made. Even when politicians prefer short cuts and focus on the elimination of symptoms rather than causes, effort and resources have shifted towards the future – towards better infrastructure and management of resources.

Not all the countries have used their time of transition equally well, and new EU members fall below some standards (as was the case with Spain, Greece, Portugal and Ireland), but they are attractive places for investment, with most of the market rules and institutions already functioning. It is a stable region that more companies should discover. And, in turn, major companies from CEE can expand into the established markets of the West.

We hope that progress in CEE logistics systems and their unification into a pan-European logistics network will allow us to stop discussing the legacy of communism and focus on the discovery of Central and Eastern Europe as a good place to develop business.

References

Dudzik, M (2004) Magiczna data 1 maja 2004? [1 May 2004 – a magic date?], *Gospodarka Materialowa i Logistyka*, 5

Eurostat (2005) *Euro-Indicators*, Statistical Office of the European Communities, Brussels

Kisperska-Moron, D, Kapcia, B and Piniecki, R (1996) Badanie kwalifikacji kadry logistycznej w polskich firmach [Evaluation of logistics staff qualifications in Polish enterprises], *Zeszyty Naukowe*, 5, TNOiK Poznan, pp 117–24

Rutkowski, K (1996) Tendencje rozwojowe logistyki w Polsce – od dezintegracji do integracji [Logistics development trends in Poland – from fragmentation to integration], 3rd International Conference, Logistics 96, on Logistics Systems as Key to Economic Development, Polish Logistics Association, Poznan

24

Logistics in China

James Wang, University of Hong Kong

Introduction

China started its transition in 1978 from a centrally planned economy to a market economy. Since then, the country has witnessed a fast and relatively consistent growth: an average of 10 per cent growth in GDP, and 18 per cent in trade from 1980 to 2005. The growth in fact has accelerated since 2001 when China became a member of the World Trade Organization (WTO). By the end of 2005, China was ranked as the fourth-largest economy in terms of total GDP, following the United States, Japan and Germany. With such a background, China's logistics sector has been experiencing a significant expansion never seen before.

Wuliu, the word for 'logistics' in Chinese, has become very popular, although it was very confusing when it began to appear in the 1990s. Literally, *wuliu* means 'material [*wu*] flow [*liu*]'. Many, including some officials in charge of the sector, took the term as being similar to 'transportation'. Suddenly, large numbers of companies such as home movers renamed themselves as *wuliu* firms, in order to take advantage of any government policies or incentives aimed at encouraging the sector.

Indeed, government policies have been critical in nurturing the development of the logistics sector in China, as the state machine, including all levels of government, is still the most influential power in driving and shaping changes in the economy, and the logistics sector is not an exception. Two recent developments show this power. First, central government decided to promote producer service industries and logistics activities in China's 10th Five-Year Plan commencing in 2001. Because of that, each level of government

– from county and city to province – needed to work out schemes and plans to boost the logistics sector. Second, China committed at the time of joining the WTO in November 2001 to open its logistics market fully to the world within three years (see Table 24.2), indicating the strong willingness of the state to accelerate the reforms of its logistics sector by introducing pressure from outside.

China has been left behind the most developed countries in logistics, which can be seen by examining the efficiency of logistics activities as revealed by the ratio of logistics spending to GDP. A report by the State Development and Planning Commission (SDPC) (2006) shows that, in 2000, the logistics sector spending, including transportation, inventory storage, and loss and breakage, amounted to about 20 per cent of China's total GDP. Such a proportion was much higher than those of the United States (10 per cent) and Japan (14 per cent) (see Table 24.1). The three major cost components, transportation, inventory storage and management cost, contribute roughly 57 per cent, 29 per cent and 14 per cent respectively of the total.

Despite the target of the central government to increase the efficiency of its logistics sector and reduce its proportion of the national GDP, the reality has been the opposite. China's logistics industry grew at an annual rate of 15–30 per cent during 2000–04 – much faster than the national economic growth of 8–9 per cent annually for the same period of time. The total logistics cost accounted for 21.4 per cent of GDP in 2003 and 21.3 per cent in 2004, both in fact higher than that of 2000 (20 per cent). Interestingly, specialist third-party suppliers handled only 18 per cent of raw material logistics, 16 per cent of semi-finished product distribution and 17.6 per cent of final product distribution in 2000. In other words, more than 80 per cent of the logistics activities were conducted by producers themselves. This indicates that China is in an early stage of industrialization. At this stage, there is a huge potential market for logistics. Therefore, market expansion, rather than raising efficiency, is – and will continue to be – the focus of most logistics firms.

Logistics operators in China come from five different backgrounds. The first group comprises former subsidiaries of relevant ministries, for example Sinotrans from the Ministry of Foreign Trade. These firms are generally large

Table 24.1 Proportion of logistics spending to GDP, 2000

Country/region	Logistics spending as percentage of GDP %
China	20
Japan	14
European Union	10–13
United States	10.3

Source: SDPC, 2006

in size and have some 'natural' connections or *guanxi* advantages stemming from their previous freight-forwarding or distribution networks. The second group comprises the foreign logistics firms or freight forwarders such as DHL and APL Logistics. With the power and reputation of their brand names, they entered the China market earlier than many others. They enjoy an advantageous position owing to regulations that favour foreign investors with a large registered capital. The third group consists of the logistics departments of certain large conglomerates that expand their logistics operations to serve both their parent companies and some others in the same or a similar industrial sector. Annto Logistics from the Midea Group is an example. It was once the logistics department of the Midea Group, responsible for national distribution of Midea air conditioners, and now extends its services to many other producers of home appliances. The fourth group basically consists of the transportation firms that have developed vertically to have their own agents doing freight forwarding and warehousing, such as China Railway Express Co. The last group consists of many private firms. Unlike firms from the other four groups, firms in this group tend to be small in size and usually have their special coverage or focus of business. These small, private firms make a very important contribution in fitting into market niches and helping avoid monopoly. For example, Hercules Logistics in Shenzhen provides special logistics services between the fast-growing Special Economic Zone next to Hong Kong and Siberian cities in the far east of Russia.

Major areas of improvement

Infrastructure development

Development of the market for logistics in China has two prominent features – infrastructure development and the prevalence of outsourcing activities with international players.

Regarding the infrastructural development, a total of 728.3 billion yuan (about US $88 billion) was invested in fixed assets for the logistics industry in 2004, a growth of 24 per cent from the previous year (CFLP, 2004). Of this, transport amounted to 604 billion yuan (US $73 billion), or 82 per cent of the total (see Figure 24.1). This shows that the Chinese government has been placing huge emphasis on developing the transport sector. Most of these investments have gone to projects of new railways, highways, deep-water berths and civilian airports. However, the country still lacks a fully integrated transport network for intermodal transportation. For example, all the major ports such as Shanghai and Shenzhen – ranking third and fourth respectively in the world in container throughput – move less than 1 per cent of their containers from or to the railways. This compares with 7–15 per cent in major

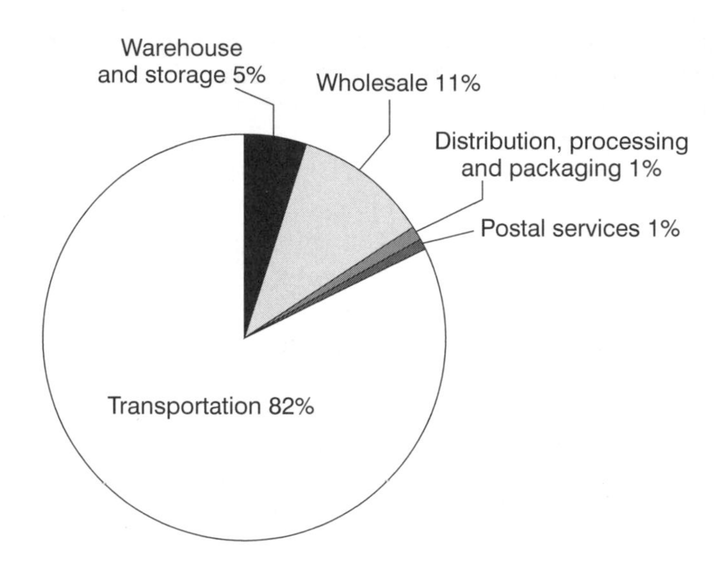

Source: Li & Fung Centre for Supply Chain Management and Logistics, Chinese University of Hong Kong, 2004

Figure 24.1 China's logistics industry – composition of total fixed asset investment in 2004

European and US ports – keeping in mind that China is a huge country and its railway network plays a much bigger role than that of other modes of transport in its economy.

Another major area of investment has been the construction of logistics parks. As the sector has been largely pushed by government policies, building logistics parks is regarded as an important measure to promote and upgrade the sector. Starting from Shenzhen, the Special Economic Zone next to Hong Kong, every major city in China has several logistics parks, which were planned and quickly constructed in the past few years through special incentives such as land rent exemption or deduction. These newly built logistics parks can be categorized into three types by their expected roles: 1) serving gateway facilities such as airports and ports for international and national trade; 2) regional distribution centres, which are normally located near railway stations or highway junctions; and 3) local services centres for city logistics. From an operational perspective, not many of these parks are running as well as expected for the following reasons:

- *Positioning their role wrongly.* Some cities set up their logistics parks aiming at high-value-added logistics activities for regional or international distribution, but the reality is that, for cities with an export-oriented processing industry, there is little need for regional or domestic distribution. The real logistics activities surrounding their ports, for example, are things such as empty container depots and truck parks.

- *Lack of a proper regulatory environment for borderless logistics.* In a transitional period from a centrally controlled economy, customs is a key body of central government that monitors imports and exports at all the local gateways where international logistics occur. When local governments try to reform their systems, with deregulation to create a true international environment such as a real free trade zone, they need not only the permission of the State Council, but also local cooperation from customs. This often requires much longer to achieve than constructing a logistics park.
- *Abuse of the concept of logistics parks.* As China is the country with the world's largest population, urban land in cities with large logistics activity potential is definitely scarce. Some companies have taken advantage of government incentives for logistics parks by packaging commercial or residential property development into a 'logistics development project' to occupy the logistics parks.
- *Misinterpretation and poor location of logistics parks.* In some cities, it was expected that, when a logistics park was set up somewhere in the city, other logistics firms would also come and work together to achieve some sort of economies of scale. The reality, however, is that, because of the different needs of their own supply chains, firms behave differently and do not move to the same location, even when some incentives are provided.

Prevalence of outsourcing and foreign logistics operators entering China

The economic reforms and open-door policy since the 1980s have made China a world factory for both domestic and foreign enterprises. The growing marketization and internationalization have led to huge demands for outsourcing activities and third-party logistics (3PL), particularly after China's entry to the WTO. Many foreign logistics service providers have established joint ventures with domestic enterprises or wholly foreign-owned enterprises – such as APL Logistics, Exel, Kerry Logistics and SembCorp Logistics, which formed joint ventures with Legend Group Holdings, Sinotrans, Beijing Holdings and St-Anda respectively. These ventures offer 3PL services to most major cities in China.

China's accession to the WTO in 2001 created many deadlines for opening its logistics markets (see Table 24.2). This further opening of markets is very tempting to foreign logistics enterprises, since the country is now in a stage of fast economic development and urbanization. On one hand, the GDP growth rate was 10.3 per cent on average from 1979 to 2004 and is expected to

Table 24.2 Post-WTO accession regulations in China

	By 2002	By 2003	By 2004	By 2005	By 2006	By 2007
Shipping and freight forwarding	–	Majority ownership by foreign firms	–	–	Wholly owned subsidiaries. No limit on foreign firms to international freight business	
Maritime cargo handling, customs clearance	–	Majority	–	–	–	–
Rail transport	Foreign–PRC joint venture permitted	–	Majority ownership	–	–	Wholly owned subsidiaries
Road transport	Minority ownerships/ joint ventures	Majority ownership	–	Wholly owned subsidiaries	–	–
Warehousing and storage	Minority ownerships/ joint ventures	Majority ownership	–	Wholly owned subsidiaries	–	–
Courier	Minority ownerships/ joint ventures	Majority ownership	–	–	Wholly owned subsidiaries	–

Source: Accenture, 2002

continue at a rate of at least 6 per cent for another decade or two, and its foreign trade volume grows even faster (35.7 per cent in 2004) as the economy depends more on the global market. This means that more global supply chains have their first links or production bases inside China. On the other hand, as there will be about half a billion of the population moving from countryside to urban regions to work in the next 10 years – and 10 million people becoming 'middle-income class' by world standards every year from 2005 to 2010 – a huge market for domestic consumption is in the making. This is leading to a rapid expansion of China's retail sector and ample room for further development of its logistics industry – and 3PL in particular. Major transnational retail chains such as Wal-Mart, Carrefour, KFC, McDonald's and Starbucks are already setting up more retail stores – and major 3PLs and integrators such as FedEx, UPS, DHL and AT&T are opening offices and cargo-collecting points in as many cities as possible. Some are even moving or establishing their Asian distribution centres in China as well.

Challenges to developing modern logistics

Huge geographical variations

The first and probably most challenging reality is the enormous variations within China. When talking about China as a world factory, often people are thinking of the entire China – a country of 96 million square kilometres of land and 1.3 billion people. In fact, it is not really true. Geographically speaking, the real world factory is just the coastal part of China, consisting of 332 cities and counties. Statistics in Table 24.3 show that the coastal provinces, mainly their port cities, have become more and more important in the global market, as their contribution to China's external trade keeps increasing. Up to 2004, 94 per cent of the total value of Chinese foreign trade was made in the coastal region of 11 provinces. More than 83 per cent of foreign direct investment to China has concentrated in these cities as well. The country is thus divided clearly by the level of international trade and transport connectivity with the outside world. Production in the coastal area is highly associated with the global economy, while that of the inland is still largely for the domestic market. As this trend has been reinforced rather than weakened in the past two decades (as shown in Table 24.3), one can see that logistics development

Table 24.3 China: international trade by origin/destination in China (1998–2004)

	1998 US$'000	1999 US$'000	2000 US$'000	2001 US$'000	2002 US$'000	2003 US$'000	2004 US$'000
National total	324,033,642	360,649,443	474,308,185	509,768,127	620,768,077	851,207,294	1,154,791,620
Coastal provinces	287,290,620	321,688,892	430,176,402	463,222,811	567,871,428	778,312,733	1,069,529,407
Inland	36,743,022	38,960,551	44,131,783	46,545,316	52,896,649	72,894,561	85,262,213
Proportion	%	%	^{3}%	^{3}%	^{3}%	^{3}%	^{3}%
Coastal	88.7	89.2	90.7	90.9	91.5	91.4	92.6
Inland	11.3	10.8	9.3	9.1	8.5	8.6	7.4

Source: China Customs, 1998–2004

in China is currently a dual-track system. On one hand, there is a fast track in its coastal region, where ports are equipped with the most up-to-date equipment and operate with the highest efficiency of any world top-class container terminal operators. On the other hand, one rarely sees a container truck driving in an inland province, and competition in transport and logistics often comes by overloading trucks or vessels for unit-cost saving. The domestic markets of most products are still largely production-driven rather than buyer-driven.

As a result of such huge unbalanced development, either domestic or international logistics enterprises may need to have local strategies to deal with the situation. For example, Wal-Mart has decided not to have regional distribution centres in China, considering that inland transportation, including railways and highways, is not reliable enough for time-definite delivery. Haier, the top brand name and largest producer of electric home appliances in China (and probably in the world by 2006), has been doing logistics on its own rather than contracting out, as it sees that none of the 3PLs can do a better job than itself.

Absence of a fully integrated national transport network

Despite the fact that some efforts have been made by the Chinese government in developing the logistics infrastructure for the entire nation, bottlenecks in transport hamper logistics efficiency. Among major transport modes, railways are the key links between the inland cities and the gateway port cities, and they started to operate unit-trains for containers in the late 1990s. But by 2005, less than 1 per cent of container throughputs at major Chinese ports were associated with railway services. Upgrading railway systems for containerized transport is not easy, since the double-deck trains that are commonly used in the United States are not feasible for most routes in China, which is a mountainous country. Waterborne transport is not as feasible as in some European countries, as only in a very few places are there rivers that are navigable by barges. As a result, highways have become the backbone of land surface containerization. The economic distance of trucking is thus forming an invisible division between container-accessible coastal regions and the rest of China – the former being served by modern transport and logistics that match international standards, while the latter is served by conventional means. The gap in transport and logistics provision is contributing to social inequity in the country, so the question of how to improve it becomes a critical issue not only for the logistics firms, but also for the various levels of government.

Multiple jurisdictions and local protectionism

The third challenge in developing modern logistics systems in China is from the local governments. The essence of logistics services is the efficiency of getting things and information through supply/demand chains and over space. Strong intervention from governments for local interests has become probably the most difficult obstacle to overcome. Often improvement of logistics is regarded by many local governments as an instrument to help generate more GDP within their own jurisdictions, rather than a way to improve the efficient flow of cargo across them. Individual municipal governments are motivated to compete for logistics hubs regardless of their geographical locations – and none of them is willing to see firms with home bases in their cities set up distribution centres in other jurisdictions. Consequently, there is duplicated construction of regional logistics parks and distribution centres – and even airports in neighbouring cities are common. One scheme by logistics firms serving the nationwide market is to register the firm at a city that charges the lowest tax – but locate the operations wherever best fits the network needs. This may mislead, statistically, the governments of both jurisdictions and cause more duplication of investment in infrastructure.

Absence of trust for the domestic 3PL

Although most regulatory regimes have changed to facilitate the growth of 3PL, it is still very tough for 3PLs to be successful in the real world, or even to survive. Many enterprises that say they use 3PL are really transport operators themselves with their own fleets of trucks, vessels or both. They operate more as transport firms; for example, China Merchants Logistics in Shenzhen relies on its transport business – including a fleet of taxis. The major reason, as stated by Mr Chan, the director of Hercules Logistics, a leading private domestic logistics firm in China, is that 'If we do not have our own transport means, people will never trust us and we will not get any good deals.' He adds: 'People consider a real 3PL user [ie without its own fleet of transportation] as "tae kwon do" [a Japanese martial art: fighting without any other weapon than one's own bare hands].' Such an absence of trust is partly due to the lack of any established brand names in the field, which may take time to build. At the current stage, the challenge to those that are working hard to be one of the brand names in the future is how to keep their transport operations running on a less than economic scale, while surviving and developing their core business. Alternatively, they may seek help or support from international investors – particularly those with brand names in the field – which will eventually result in merging or buying out.

Old-fashioned wholesale marketplaces remain competitive

Associated with the trust problem discussed above is the prosperity of conventional wholesale marketplaces in many cities and city regions where the low-end products are traded, and transport and logistics are often taken care of by the buyer. For example, in Foshan, a city near Guangzhou, Canton, there is a huge wholesale market for furniture that is 9.5 kilometres long and 150 metres wide along each side of Highway 305. Each day, thousands of individual consumers – such as new home owners in the nearby cities – or groups come to the Le Cong Furniture Market to do a day's shopping. Most of them buy their furniture and truck it back home using their own means of transport. Le Cong has contributed to the local economy for more than 10 years and employed significant numbers of people, and many local governments wonder if the same success could be achieved in their own town. As a result, many wholesale marketplaces (or 'professional markets' as they are called in China) have been set up to boost the competitiveness of the local economy by enhancing the logistics and distribution systems. However, since logistics services in China have been developed to different stages of maturity for different types of products, some of these marketplaces have had very short lives before fading away.

New government policies and future prospects

The Ministry of Commerce – together with other related ministries and commissions – released a communiqué on 5 August 2004, 'Notice on promoting the development of China's modern logistics'. This covers various areas such as administration, management, taxation, financing and market opening, etc. Major policy initiatives suggested in the document include:

- standardizing registration and approval procedures of logistics enterprises;
- promoting the opening up of the logistics market and adjusting administrative procedures – reducing to a minimum the entry requirements for domestic railway freight-forwarding agencies, marine freight-forwarding agencies and other intermodal transport agencies;
- simplifying the taxation on all logistics enterprises;
- improving the current practices in regulations to establish a competitive, fair and regulated market environment.

All the above initiatives aim at encouraging more foreign participation and more consolidation of the logistics industry in China. Although the economic growth of this country is expected to slow down from an average of 8.1 per cent for the 25 years from 1980 to 2004, the momentum of growth is still high and will probably continue for another decade or two. In this period, it is expected that the following trends in development will appear:

- *More penetration by foreign logistics enterprises.* DHL, FedEx Express, Maersk, and Exel Logistics are investing more in China. The penetration of these transnationals takes different forms. FedEx, for example, has committed itself to move its Asian hub from Subic Bay in the Philippines to Guangzhou by 2008. Exel Logistics has invested in Sinotrans, in order to take advantage of its partnership with this leading Chinese logistics firm. Foreign firms may also follow APL Logistics and set up wholly foreign-owned enterprises. For example, FedEx Express announced in 2006 that it would acquire all the shares of its partner DT Logistics in Tianjin to turn their joint venture into a wholly foreign-owned enterprise.

- *Consolidation and upgrading of domestic logistics firms.* Except for Sinotrans, most leading domestic logistics firms are currently more or less dependent on their parent firms. For example, Annto Logistics (a leading logistics firm established in 2000) was originally a subsidiary of the Midea Group (one of China's largest conglomerates, with a focus on household appliances). Annto Logistics still considers Midea as its most important client, and its home base is in Shunde, where the headquarters of Midea is located. This is going to change in the near future when Annto's network expands nationwide and its status is recognized by more clients. This will eventually lead the firm – and others of this kind – towards real 3PL operations.
- *Highly efficient intermodal logistics/transport corridors.* To narrow the development gap in logistics services between the coastal and the inland regions, intermodal corridors linking major inland cities should be the first requirement. According to the State Council, such initiatives should encourage more inland cities to open their airports to international connections, with the Ministry of Railways forced to operate fixed-schedule trains for container shipments along major national corridors, even if such operations are not profitable in the short term.
- *More free trade zones opened at major ports and airports.* An important new policy initiative from the State Council is called 'zone port interaction'. From the beginning of 2005, eight major port cities in China started a trial of this. The policy aims at establishing an integrated space within which there is a free trade zone together with some terminals for international transactions. Within these spaces, cargo can be handled as if it is outside customs, although it is physically present within the territory of China. This policy intends to set up several 'mini Hong Kongs' to facilitate international logistics – including trans-shipment, consolidation and even exhibitions.
- *More advanced e-platforms and technologies.* The late 1990s was an embarrassing period for China when it started to introduce new technologies such as electronic data interchange to potential users. After spending a lot of time and resources in human resource training and installation of equipment, most of the EDI systems did not work. Eventually, by the time everything was ready, the systems were out of date and not compatible with the newer systems employed by major international organizations and government departments. Recognizing this problem of compatibility, China is now putting more effort into standardizing and upgrading e-platforms among government departments – such as the General Customs and their local offices – in order to improve the efficiency of logistics services, including documentation handled at all international gateways.

Web-based platforms for freight forwarding and cargo monitoring are becoming popular. The country is also trying to catch up with the developed world by designing and introducing the most advanced technologies in logistics, such as radio frequency identity (RFID).

Concluding remarks

Being a fast-growing economic giant, China is at a stage where advanced technologies and management in logistics coexist with backward and conventional ones – the former being employed in its global trading sector, while the latter are largely for its domestic market. A bifurcation is also found between the transnational logistics companies and local firms: the former are penetrating from individual major coastal cities to regional or inland markets, while the latter are upgrading themselves from transport provider to true 3PL or even 4PL.

Governments at all levels are keen to develop modern logistics, since it is widely believed in China that the logistics sector is one of the key sectors for the country and for the competitiveness of individual provinces or cities in today's globalizing economy. Interestingly enough, however, the major obstacles for better provision of logistics services in China also come largely from governments of various levels. They are putting too much effort into manipulating the sector, with over-investment in logistics parks, and protection of local interests through discriminatory regulations against non-local firms.

The injection of high-quality logistics services by international providers after China's accession to the WTO seems to be regarded as an effective means of raising the quality of logistics services. But this strategy becomes problematic when tensions grow between Chinese firms and transnational companies. After all, perhaps, a more fundamental and long-term solution is to nurture a better market environment, with fair play between domestic and foreign firms, and between the inland and coastal regions. For such a solution, improvements in infrastructure and governance are equally important.

References

Accenture (2002) *On the Edge: The changing pace of supply chain management in China*, Accenture, New York

China Customs (1998–2004) *China Trade Statistics*, China Customs, Beijing

China Federation of Logistics and Purchasing (CFLP) (2004) Circular released by CFLP

State Development and Planning Commission (SDPC) (2006) *National Statistics*, China SDPC, Beijing

25

Logistics in North America

Garland Chow and Trevor Heaver,
University of British Columbia

Introduction

There is increasing similarity in logistics strategies and practices among the developed industrial regions of the world. The geographical spread of manufacturing by global companies and the development of global supply chains are bringing competitive pressures and global competencies to bear on logistics systems. The rapid growth of sourcing products in Asia, Eastern Europe and Mexico has been associated with comparable issues for buyers in all developed regions. The increasing application of communication and information systems across supply chain members is also facilitating the rapid evolution of similar practices and standards. Nevertheless, important differences in logistics conditions exist among regions.

Table 25.1 shows estimates of logistics costs as a percentage of GDP for 1997 and 2002. These estimates suggest that outside of North America improvement in logistics performance since 1997 has at best been patchy. It has generally not improved in developing countries, where logistics costs also tend to be highest because of the average of lower-valued and denser products. Performance in North America has continued to improve. In general, logistics costs are affected by the contrasted geographic, economic and institutional circumstances of countries and regions.

Table 25.1 Estimated logistics costs as a percentage of GDP, 1997 and 2002, by region

Region	1997 %	2002 %
Europe	12.2	13.3
France	12.0	11.6
Germany	13.1	16.7
UK	10.1	11.3
Pacific Rim	14.5	15.7
China	16.9	17.9
India	15.4	17.4
Japan	11.4	11.4
South America	14.3	15.7
Brazil	15.0	15.0
North America	11.0	9.9
Canada	12.1	11.9
Mexico	15.3	15.0
United States	10.5	9.3

Source: Rodrigues, Bowersox and Calantone, 2005

This chapter deals first with the distinctive characteristics of North America that affect logistics, followed by the trends, challenges and opportunities for logistics in the region. Dominant logistics strategies in the region are described prior to some concluding comments.

Special features of North America for logistics

Three aspects of North America warrant highlighting as background to the logistics conditions. These are: the size of the region and the characteristics of its transport system, the North American Free Trade Agreement; and the roles of international trade and globalization.

The size of the region and the characteristics of its transport system

The geographic size of the region and the size of the economy have implications for the structure and growth of transport and logistics services. Major features of scale are shown in Table 25.2.

Table 25.2 The scale of North America

	Canada	Mexico	United States
Population estimate (millions) for July 2005	32.8	106.2	295.7
Gross domestic product (purchasing power parity) (trillion US$)	1.08	1.07	12.37
Area (millions of square kilometres)	9.9	2.0	9.6

Source: US Central Intelligence Agency, 2006

The United States is not only the largest national economy in the world, but it is also a large country from which have flowed two characteristics relevant to logistics. First, the country has enjoyed a high level of economic self-sufficiency, which has resulted in a limited role for freight forwarding in comparison with Europe. On the other hand, the size of the economy gives rise to large national corporations – for example, Wal-Mart – that have been important in the evolution of global supply chain management. Second, the size of the United States and Canada necessitated efficient rail freight transport, which has facilitated the development of intermodal transport services. The ownership of the Class I railways in North America is in nine companies; in 2004, they had a combined operating revenue of US $47.4 billion, of which US $8.0 billion was from Canadian railways and US $1.3 billion from Mexican (Association of American Railroads, 2005). Major revenue traffic is in bulk commodities, especially coal, but intermodal traffic has had sustained growth over the last decade. Overseas traffic has been the major contributor to this growth. Intermodal traffic accounts for approximately 20 per cent of the revenue of US Class I railroads. However, in spite of the substantial role of rail freight about 80 per cent of transportation freight revenue in the United States is earned by trucking. As elsewhere, this is the result of the convenience and reliability of truck service and its lower cost for short-haul and low-volume movements.

North American Free Trade Agreement

Canada, Mexico and the United States entered into the North American Free Trade Agreement (NAFTA) in 1993. The adoption of NAFTA reflects the prior success of trade liberalization between Canada and the United States under the Auto Pact of 1965 and the Canada–US Free Trade Agreement (FTA) of 1989. When Mexico and the United States were to enter free trade discussions, it was in Canada's interest to participate, to ensure that its interests were protected and that improvements might be made relative to the FTA. The interest of Mexico was part of a changing policy to integrate more fully into the global economy.

NAFTA effects were most significant for Mexico because of the previous relative isolation of its economy. The only closely integrated businesses between Mexico and the United States were the maquiladora, established in border communities after the agreement with the United States in 1989, that imported goods duty-free for processing and exported them without tariffs.

NAFTA is a rules-based agreement that facilitates trade. It does not seek to impose the harmonization of industrial and government practices required for a single market. Similar transport regulation policies have been followed in Canada and the United States and later were adopted by Mexico. Encouraging open and competitive markets in transport (and generally) have required and enabled more efficient and, therefore, better-integrated services within and between countries. At the insistence of the United States, NAFTA does not apply to water transport. Only specialized air services came under NAFTA. Other air services fell under bilateral agreements that have been gradually liberalized separately. Under NAFTA, foreign-owned trucking and rail companies may be established in the United States to provide transport and logistics services domestically, employing persons with the right to live and work in the country. Cabotage is reserved for national companies.

Because of the numerous simultaneous factors affecting the North American economy since 1994, quantification of the effects of NAFTA with aggregate data is difficult. While in aggregate NAFTA merely accelerated the integration of the three economies – particularly the US and Mexican – its effects were differentiated among commodities. Romalis (2005) shows a significant sensitivity of trade on a commodity basis to differences in tariff levels between NAFTA partners and other countries. There has been a diversion of trade to within NAFTA for certain sectors of the economy. The growth in trade was largely in commodities groups in the trade mix prior to NAFTA (Hillberry and McDaniel, 2002). NAFTA encouraged businesses to pursue North American strategies that led to the promotion of north–south commerce, thereby shifting the pattern of demands for transport and logistics services. The efficiency of border crossings as stricture points in the flow of traffic has become an important issue, especially with the escalated concern for security from terrorism. (Significant congestion at seaports is a more recent phenomenon.)

The effects of NAFTA on logistics have been felt mainly through the encouragement to the rationalization of industrial location and the greater – but not free and complete – integration of transport and logistics services. NAFTA advances three strategies in the redesign of continental supply chains. The first is strategy to close certain plants. This strategy applies especially to companies with branch plants – for example, in Canada – to avoid duties. Companies that closed plants for this reason included Bilt-Rite Upholstery, Florsheim Shoes and Gillette. The second strategy is to have plants that specialize in products for continental or global markets, as had been done in the automotive industry between Canada and the United States for a number of years. For example, prior to NAFTA, Upjohn operated a multi-product pharmaceutical plant in Ontario to serve the Canadian market. After NAFTA, that plant specialized in medium-volume sterile products for the Canadian and US markets. US plants specialized in high-volume sterile products, and Puerto Rican plants specialized in non-sterile products destined for both Canadian and US markets. Campbell's Soup, General Electric, Whirlpool, Avon and Dupont followed an almost identical strategy. The third strategy is to consolidate manufacturing or distribution, often close to the border. The product will now flow from one central stocking or manufacturing point instead of from two, and cross-border traffic increases (Taylor and Closs, 1993). The balance of cost and service considerations affects location decisions. Industries in which customer service is important are likely to maintain a local market presence. The low value of the Canadian dollar favoured Canadian locations, but this advantage is now diminishing.

The roles of international trade and globalization

Foreign trade has always been important to Canada, as a relatively small economy. In 1971, foreign trade and services accounted for just over 40 per cent of gross domestic product. It exceeded 80 per cent for the years 1998–2001 and was over 70 per cent in 2004. However, a high proportion of this trade is with the United States: in 2004, over 80 per cent of exports went to, and just under 70 per cent of imports came from, the United States (Antweiler, 2006).

Foreign trade has played a much lesser role in the US economy. The rapid growth of trade is now one of the important pressures on logistics in the United States. In the period 1970–2004, the average annual growth in US trade was nearly double the pace of GDP growth, 6.2 per cent versus 3.2 per cent (Office of the US Trade Representative, 2005). The value of goods and services as a percentage of GDP has increased from 11 per cent in 1970 to 22 per cent in 1994 and to 25 per cent in 2004.

Table 25.3 shows the faster growth of US imports over exports. This has important consequences not only for the balance of payments but also for the balance of freight in international transport. Canada is still the major national trading partner of the United States, leading in imports and exports. Mexico has increased to second place in US exports but, after rising to second place in US imports, it has slipped to third place because of the rapid growth of imports from China. Trade with China grew rapidly in anticipation of, and then subsequent to, China's accession to the World Trade Organization in 2001. The size of the trade imbalance with China and the presence of imbalances with other Asian countries are reflected strongly in the freight imbalance faced by trans-Pacific container services. There has also been more than a doubling of US imports from the EU. The small change in the trade with Japan is remarkable, a reflection of the stalled Japanese economy and the manufacture of Japanese-brand cars in North America. The NAFTA countries accounted for 29 per cent of the increase in US imports between 1994 and 2004. China accounted for 20 per cent (but much of it since 2000) and the EU 19 per cent.

Table 25.3 US trade in goods for selected countries, 1994 and 2004

	1994 $ billion	2004 $ billion	Change %
US exports to			
Total	502.9	818.8	62.8
Canada	114.4	189.9	66.0
European Union (EU15)	107.8	168.6	56.4
Japan	53.5	54.2	1.3
Mexico	50.8	110.8	118.1
China	9.3	34.7	273.1
Asia Pacific, excluding Japan and China	85.0	121.0	42.3
US imports from:			
Total	668.7	1,469.7	119.8
Canada	128.4	256.4	99.6
European Union (EU15)	119.5	272.4	127.9
Japan	119.2	129.8	8.9
Mexico	49.5	155.9	214.9
China	38.8	196.7	407.0
Asia Pacific, excluding Japan and China	103.2	166.7	61.6

Sources: Office of the US Trade Representative, 2005; US Census Bureau, 2004

Thirteen per cent of total US imports were sourced from China in 2004, up from 6 per cent in 1994. However, when imports from China, Japan and the other Asian–Pacific Rim countries are considered together, the region's share of US imports has actually declined from 39 per cent in 1994 to 33 per cent in 2004. Much of the US imports from China are low-value-added consumer goods; they made up 54 per cent of the imports in 2004 (Office of the US Trade Representative, 2005). The potential continued high rate of growth of imports, particularly from China, is a major concern for the adequacy of transport infrastructure and, therefore, the functioning of the logistics system in the future.

The increased role of foreign trade in a country's economy is just one aspect of the international nature of the economy. The growth in the size and in the number of multinational corporations and the extent of foreign direct investment (FDI) are also significant. In transport and logistics (and some other businesses), the global expansion of companies is linked to the desire of shippers to deal with fewer companies in their logistics network. Transport and logistics firms often see international growth as a means to achieve system-wide cost reductions and to participate more fully in the growth of international transport and logistics.

Table 25.4 US business logistics costs in 2004

Carrying costs $1.493 trillion		$ billion	%
Interest		23	2
Taxes, obsolescence, depreciation, insurance		227	22
Warehousing		82	8
	Subtotal	332	33
Transportation costs			
Motor carriers:			
Intercity		335	33
Local		174	17
	Subtotal	509	50
Other carriers:			
Railroads		42	4
Water (international 22, domestic 5)		27	3
Oil pipelines		9	1
Air (international 9, domestic 22)		31	3
Forwarders		18	2
	Subtotal	127	12
Shipper-related costs		8	1
Logistics administration		39	4
Total logistics costs		1015	100

Source: Wilson, 2005

Trends, opportunities and challenges for logistics in North America

Logistics performance in North America has continued to improve, although affected annually by specific factors such as the effects of interest rates on inventory costs. Table 25.4 shows the latest estimate of logistics costs in the United States. The evolution of logistics practices accounts for the excellent performance, with important trends – and associated challenges and opportunities – discussed in the following sections.

Supply chain management vision

The supply chain management vision has led to improved strategic coordination across traditional business functions within companies and across businesses that share the goal of meeting consumer expectations. Supply chain management is thus a corporate philosophy that has considerable implications for logistics (Mentzer, 2001).

The management of a supply chain has moved from relationships that are separate, sequential and transaction-based to ones that emphasize collaboration-based strategies that link cross-enterprise business operations under a shared vision (Bowersox, 1997). The efficient management of a supply chain does not preclude the existence of certain transaction-based relationships as conditions warrant – but, in general, the management of supply chains has resulted in greater reliance on long-term relationships among fewer participants.

At the same time, global sourcing has become more important, driven initially by opportunities for cost reduction. US firms were faster to adopt global sourcing strategies in Asia than Japanese firms (McCann, 1998; McKendrick, Doner and Haggard, 2000). However, firms must follow flexible global supply chain strategies. As the skill and wage levels of workers in locations change and as the logistics needs of products change as they move through their development cycle, so shifts occur in supply chains. Proximity and short lead times are important during periods of product innovation, but reliable, low-cost logistics is appropriate during a mass-production phase. The need to save time to reduce costs is important in industries such as fashion clothing (Abernathy, 2001) and fad toys (Johnson, 2001) that are characterized by highly uncertain demands and high product seasonality. Abernathy finds strong evidence that the growth of Mexican and Caribbean apparel exports to the United States can be attributed to the increasing importance of shorter and more reliable times for logistics functions. This accounted for the greatest growth being in apparel items requiring frequent replenishment. (The same phenomenon works to the benefit of ex-communist Europe serving Western Europe (*Economist*, 2005)).

Logistics outsourcing and third-party logistics

Fuelled by pressures to decrease cost and maximize return on assets, many firms have reduced their activities to those processes that they regard as strategic and as giving them a competitive advantage. This focus on core processes or strengths has resulted in increased outsourcing of non-core logistics processes. However, the characteristics of outsourcing logistics have changed over time. Up to the deregulation era in transportation, most outsourcing involved a single logistics service, such as transportation or warehousing, and was primarily for the physical performance of the service. Today, third-party logistics companies (TPLs, 3PLs) offer an array of bundled logistics services, including operational and strategic planning as well as monitoring and control of the logistics processes.

The attractiveness of outsourcing is evidenced by the rapid growth of the third-party logistics industry. This sector was a $10 billion industry in 1992, more than doubling to $25 billion by 1996. Since 2000, the North American TPL sector has grown 83 per cent, with a 16 per cent increase to $103.7 billion in 2005 (Armstrong & Associates, 2005). Total logistics expenditures increased much less, for example only 1 per cent from 2000 to 2004 in the United States (Wilson, 2005). By 2004, the North American TPL market was earning $89.4 billion or 7 per cent of total logistics expenditures in North America.

Armstrong & Associates (2005) report that 64 per cent of domestic Fortune 500 companies use 3PLs for logistics and supply chain functions. Lieb and Bentz's (2005: 5–15) survey of manufacturers shows that at least 80 per cent used 3PL services and it was the eighth consecutive year that two-thirds or more of the respondents were 3PL users. The 2005 Third-Party Logistics Annual Study (Langley *et al*, 2005) found that 78, 79 and 80 per cent of the North American respondents reported using 3PL services in 2003, 2004 and 2005 respectively. The largest 3PL expenditures by industry are for automotive, retailing and technology (Armstrong & Associates, 2005).

Recent surveys continue to find transportation and warehousing as the most frequently outsourced logistics processes (Armstrong & Associates, 2005; Langley *et al*, 2005; Lieb and Bentz, 2005: 5–15). Other logistics processes that are frequently outsourced or for which outsourcing is growing are value-added services, international 3PL services, customs clearance and brokerage, freight forwarding, cross-docking and shipment consolidation, order fulfilment and distribution.

In spite of only marginal increases in the percentage of firms outsourcing logistics, logistics outsourcing expenditures have risen significantly as firms outsourcing logistics increased their expenditures significantly. For example, BMW Manufacturing initially outsourced the basic delivery of parts to the production line. In 2002, it used TNT to provide inbound supply chain management, including inbound material control and transportation from suppliers to plant. In 2004, the management of finished parts from its supplier network to its parts distribution centres was also turned over to TNT (Harps, 2004). Similarly, what began as a basic pallet-in/pallet-out warehousing arrangement between the Robert Bosch Corporation and Standard Corporation grew into a full-service logistics outsourcing relationship.

Companies that have outsourced successfully have gained more confidence in their relationships with third-party providers. Their experience has led them to expand the scope of the logistics services outsourced and shift from tactical to strategic relationships with more value-added managerial and information technology services provided. Langley *et al* (2005) note that, although users are generally satisfied with their 3PL providers, the providers are continually pressured to expand their service offerings. Finally, as firms expanded into global markets, a market was created for comprehensive, global TPL services, which further fuelled the growth of the TPL sector.

Shippers traditionally outsourced transportation because of economies of scale, utilization and specialization. However, the value of a knowledge base is seen as increasingly important as information technology plays an ever greater role in supply chain integration. Langley *et al* (2005) find that 89 per cent of North American respondents agreed that IT capabilities are necessary for 3PL providers, 80 per cent indicate that having the right software is a major competitive advantage and 34 per cent of the North American respondents rely on 3PL providers for IT leadership. This is particularly true in the provision of transportation management systems (TMS) and warehouse management systems (WMS) information technology. The 3PL can leverage its expertise and spread out fixed costs of utilizing such technology over multiple clients. However, the Langley *et al* (2005) survey reveals that only 53 per cent of North American companies use TPL-provided transportation management systems, compared with 80 per cent in Europe.

Flexibility and responsiveness are another reason why North American firms have increased their outsourcing of logistics. In 2002, Canadian apparel manufacturer and retailer Roots was handling licensed USA-logo Olympic wear during the Winter Games in Salt Lake City. With patriotism in those post-11 September days spurring on demand for Team USA apparel, expectations of 100 calls per day into the Roots customer service centre were well below the actual 1,500 per day peak. The company was forced to open a separate web-based ordering channel and revamp its entire distribution strategy on the fly. With the help of a third-party call centre and fulfilment provider, it added two US-based call centres, moved distribution to Memphis and changed delivery carriers (*Logistics Today*, 2004).

During the initial development of third-party services, successful North American firms developed the business from an asset base, such as trucking fleets and warehousing facilities. Non-asset third-party logistics services dominate the market today. Armstrong & Associates (2005) segment the TPL sector into four main groups, as shown in Table 25.5.

Table 25.5 Revenues and profitability by segment, 2005

3PL segment	Gross revenue $ billion	Net revenue $ billion	Net revenue % growth	Net income % margin
Domestic transportation management	30.3	4.8	18.3	12.1
International transportation management	38.2	14.0	13.6	6.3
Dedicated contract carriage	9.9	9.9	10.2	4.6
Value-added warehouse/ distribution	22.3	18.6	9.5	4.0
Total	100.7	47.3	11.7	5.6

Note:
Total gross revenue for the 3PL industry in the United States is estimated at $103.7 billion; $3 billion is included for the logistics software segment.

Source: Armstrong & Associates, 2005

The largest segment by gross revenues is international transportation management, composed of North American firms that have expanded into international 3PL services and international firms, some of which were traditional freight forwarders. This business and that of the domestic transportation management sector are largely no-asset-based. They pass on the costs incurred for purchasing and managing transport and logistics services on behalf of their clients. Large firms with significant transportation volumes may have 3PLs manage their transportation at a tactical level but may directly identify, select and negotiate their own transportation contracts with carriers. This is the dominant pattern for international shipping. The dedicated contract carriage sector supplies tractors, drivers and management as a direct alternative to the client operating its own fleet. Value-added warehouse/distribution is provided by 3PLs normally providing long-term contract warehousing or distribution centre operations with a host of value-added services.

Of course, not all outsourced service arrangements work out as hoped. However, the growth of outsourced logistics services will continue, as 3PLs provide the expertise and responsiveness needed for firms to compete in rapidly shifting and increasingly competitive markets. As the 3PL industry matures and more experience is gained, and existing relationships grow into true partnerships, outsourcing will become an even more viable and less risky option to more firms.

Large firms can afford to diversify their base of logistics services. Armstrong & Associates (2005) report that General Motors, Daimler Chrysler and Wal-Mart each use 30 or more 3PLs, and at least 30 other firms were found to use eight or more TPLs. Langley *et al* (2005) report that 64 to 82 per cent of the respondents to their survey use one to five 3PL providers, and smaller percentages used larger numbers, in some instances over 50 providers. However, there has been a trend to reduce the number of 3PLs used. Langley *et al* observe that approximately half of their respondents agreed that they were 'moving to rationalize or reduce the number of third parties we use'. Lead logistics providers (LLPs) and fourth-party logistics providers (4PLs) are another alternative. They have broad supply chain expertise with deep industry and consultative skills, advanced technology capability and integration, and are recognized for innovation and continual improvement. For example, Nortel Networks selected Kuehne & Nagel to be its 4PL in 2002 to manage its global logistics operations including 3PLs, carriers and parcel movers (*Inbound Logistics*, 2003). In 2001, General Motors and Menlo Logistics formed Vector SCM to act as the LLP managing and coordinating the activities of approximately 20 core 3PLs in North America as well as redesigning GM's global supply chain (Armstrong, 2004). Despite these high-profile examples, there are very few true LLP or 4PL partnerships, as the concept still needs to be proven and only the largest firms have the complexity problem of multiple 3PLs.

Foreign-owned freight forwarders once dominated international logistics services in North America. Foreign 3PLs such as Tibbett and Britten, and Exel have also been significant. This has changed slowly with the expansion of domestic firms. Some of the best-known examples have been carriers that have developed logistics services.

US shipping companies were among the leaders of carriers developing logistics services. They commenced by providing freight consolidation services to meet the needs of US retail stores buying in Asia. Sea-Land and APL developed separately branded and run consolidation services in Asia: American Consolidation Services of APL, and Buyers of Sea-Land. Subsequently, these services have grown and been rebranded to the names of the shipping lines, APL Logistics and Maersk Logistics, of which they are now a part (see Heaver, 2002.)

UPS is another example. UPS started out as a company specializing in small shipment services in the United States. Geographic growth was inhibited by regulations: UPS only obtained authority to serve the contiguous 48 states in 1975. It started limited services in Canada in 1975 and in Germany in 1976. International air service with Europe was not commenced until 1985. UPS then expanded rapidly internationally. UPS branched out into related logistics services with the formation in 1995 of the UPS Logistics Group. An even wider range of services is provided by the formation of UPS Supply Chain Solutions in 2002. Acquisitions of firms in the logistics sector have been a vital part of the service expansion strategy. UPS now has courier services to over 200 countries. In 2004, 26 per cent of package revenue came from international services, up from 17 per cent in 2000 (UPS, 2006).

The management of global logistics has become a much greater part of logistics management. This is reflected in the orientation of the logistics service industry. A survey in 2005 of 3PL executives shows that in North America the increased pressure to internationalize service offerings was perceived as the most important industry dynamic. In Europe, this pressure was ranked behind downward pressure on pricing and the recent expansion of EU membership (Lieb and Bentz, 2005, 2006).

Supply chain integration through collaboration, strategic alliances and partnerships

To realize a supply chain's full competitive and market potential, companies need to link their organization with other participants in the supply chain, creating an extended team or 'interprise'. These 'partners' include suppliers, vendors, distributors and customers, where suppliers can be suppliers of logistics services as well as products.

Sharing of risks and gains, long-term commitments, and co-mingling of operations and information characterize cooperative relationships. These actions can result in customer service enhancement and cost reduction from redesigning processes across the whole supply chain instead of one part of it, from specialization building on each partner's strengths, and from better planning resulting from increased information flow among the partners. Communication and information sharing characterize successful partnerships, allowing all participants to plan and coordinate their operations more effectively.

A number of collaborative strategies and tactics have been developed and applied, including information sharing, vendor-managed inventory, just-in-time II, collaborative production and forecasting replenishment, and collaborative transportation management to name a few. Many of these techniques were pioneered in the 1990s, but their use has continued to accelerate. In 2002, Capital Consulting & Management concluded that only 1 to 5 per cent of US manufacturing companies had reached the stage of optimized planning where the most substantial supply chain benefits existed (CCMI, 2002). Similarly, a survey of 150 senior executives of Fortune 1000 companies by Accenture indicated that many companies are lagging in terms of true collaboration – despite a compelling business case for achieving it (Bowman, 2002). The 2002 Ohio State University Survey of Career Patterns in Logistics study found substantial increases in the percentage of the respondents using strategic partnerships with key suppliers and key consumers. This finding was confirmed by a 2005 Accenture survey, which found that 'Collaboration levels have increased dramatically in the past three years' (Matchette and Seikel, 2004).

Vendor-managed inventory (VMI) is a tactic where the supplier rather than the customer generates orders based on stocking information, typically accessed using EDI. It is often considered a first step towards more advanced supply chain collaboration, and has been used for many years in North America in a variety of industry sectors, but it rose to prominence in the efficient consumer response (ECR) era because it achieved results. Labelled continuous replenishment, it enjoyed one of its most successful applications with Campbell's Soup, where 31 participating grocery chains obtained significant improvement in inventory turns and a reduction in stock-outs (Lee, Clark and Tam, 1999). Similar successes across North America are reported in a variety of industry sectors. VMI Projects at Dillard Department Stores, JC Penney and Wal-Mart have shown sales increases of 20 to 25 per cent, and 30 per cent inventory turnover improvements.

Of course, there have been failures. After 12 months of their VMI programme, Spartan Stores decided to halt the programme. Inventories did fall, but it was because small orders were being placed at more frequent intervals. A root problem was that Spartan and their VMI vendors did not come up with an effective way to deal with promotions planning and pricing. As a result, the vendor's decision makers could not all do as effective a job as Spartan's own buyers.

One mechanism for communication is just-in-time II. JIT II has vendor-managed operations taking place within a customer's facility, and was popularized by the Bose Corporation. Supplier representatives – called 'in-plants' – place orders to their own companies, relieving the customer's buyers of this task. Many also become involved at a deeper level, such as participating in new product development projects and manufacturing planning.

Collaborative production and forecasting replenishment (CPFR) uses available internet and EDI-based technologies to collaborate from operational planning through to execution. CPFR is recognized as a breakthrough business model for planning, forecasting and replenishment, and was originally developed by Wal-Mart and Warner-Lambert in 1995. It has been formalized into a nine-step process that is adjusted to fit specific trading partner relationships and capabilities. Numerous pilot and full implementations have proven the benefits, but this has been generally confined to the retail and consumer package goods industry (Suleski, 2001). In 1998, Wegmans Food Markets and Nabisco, Inc began a CPFR project on Planters Nuts items and gained service level increases and an 18 per cent inventory reduction. In 1999, Canadian Tire shared with 10 suppliers information such as statistical forecasts, promotional life forecasts, dealer order holdings, purchase orders, planned orders and on-hand inventory levels, resulting in service increases, DC stock reduction, increased stock turnover and reduced supplier delivery cycle. A CPFR survey conducted in 2000 found that 70 per cent of the respondents were actively researching, undergoing pilots or preparing to roll out CPFR programmes (Saha, undated), but 'its adoption however remains sluggish'. To date, most CPFR implementations have been limited to near-exclusive relationships between a single large manufacturer and a single retailer for a specific set of products (Fraser, 2003).

Collaborative transportation management (CTM) is an extension of CPFR that involves converting order forecasts developed via CPFR into shipment forecasts and collaboratively ensuring their accurate fulfilment (Esper and Williams, 2003). For example, the dense network efficiency model of Transplace improves vehicle utilization through the development of continuous movement routeings that minimize empty miles, circuitry and dwell time for truckers. Similarly, the NISTEVO alliance illustrates collaboration across competitors. Under the NISTEVO programme, the transportation needs of each participant are sent in advance to a neutral third party (NISTEVO), which utilizes advanced routeing software to optimize routeing and vehicle utilization across the shippers and the carriers. The matching process improves asset utilization. Its effectiveness is increased by the large volume of traffic aggregated from high-volume shippers and because the matching process begins before vehicles are dispatched rather than after they have been put on the road. Dollar savings are estimated to be in the range of 5 to 18 per cent.

The 3PLs are often enablers for collaboration. For example, in Ontario, Canada, Excel Logistics operates distribution centres for a cereal manufacturer and a soup manufacturer delivering products to the same or closely located grocery stores. As canned soup products have a high density and cereal products have low density, Excel is able to fully utilize vehicles' weight and cubic capacity by combining the freight of both clients, reducing the total number of vehicle trips that would have been required if the products had been shipped separately. Lieb and Bentz observe that increasingly the 3PL users in their surveys report that their major vendors and customers are also served by their primary 3PL provider (Lieb and Bentz, 2004). 'Clearly, one would expect this development to facilitate further supply chain integration.'

While many success stories can be cited, there are also many failures. Nix *et al* (2004) found that approximately 29 per cent of 477 respondents indicated their collaboration was unsuccessful. Collaboration requires a relationship often characterized as a partnership or alliance to be successfully implemented. While many surveys may indicate that firms are participating in partnerships, deeper inquiry often finds that 'truly synergistic relationships are very rare'. These relationships 'represent only a small fraction of supply chain management relationships – typically 5 per cent or less' (Fawcett, Magnan and McCarter, 2005). Fawcett, Magnan and McCarter (2005) sum up the situation in North America well when they conclude:

> Companies today are much more aware of opportunities to improve organizational competitiveness through closer, partnership relationships and have moved away from the adversarial model that dominated buy/seller relations for much of the 1900s. However few managers have completely abandoned the notion that channel power can and should be used to advance their companies' positions. The result is that more collaboration is taking place in modern supply-chain relationships but is taking place in a very selective basis.

By remaining opportunistic, most managers are 'limiting their ability to build truly cohesive, mutually advantageous supply chain teams'.

In summary, the supply chain concept recognizes that, for optimum efficiency, logistics needs to be designed and managed in the context of the whole supply chain, including internal and external aspects. Collaborative decision making among partners in a supply chain is a new business model characterized by the building of relationships, shared knowledge, more certainty, less guessing and ultimately better planning. The 3PLs are facilitating collaboration and integration among their clients, and information technology is improving communication linkages. However, to collaborate effectively, supply chain management requires partnerships and alliances. North American firms recognize the benefits of collaboration and have selectively embraced the concept, but there is a long way to go with respect to developing the relationships that make collaboration successful.

Evolving supply chain process design – from push to pull

Reducing inventory investment and associated costs through cycle time reduction has become a primary thrust for many firms. This has led to a movement from 'push' to 'pull' systems where the ultimate objective is to 'make what the company has sold' rather than 'sell what the company has made'. 'Demand driven', 'just-in-time', 'quick response', 'build or assemble to order' and 'continuous replenishment' are some of the labels used to describe various applications and types of pull systems. Suppliers and logistics service providers are required to be more responsive as demand drives logistics transactions and products can bypass traditional storage and holding processes and go directly to the retail store or customer. These products are often mixed with other freight for immediate delivery in cross-dock facilities by truck. Dell is considered the defining demand-driven business and is well described elsewhere (Magretta, 1998). However, there are numerous examples of firms and supply chains successfully re-engineering their processes from push to pull in North America. Pilot implementation is usually not an option as the transformation required is both systems-wide and strategic.

Pull systems are desirable for goods with high inventory costs. This applies not only to high-value and high-obsolescence products but also to high-cubic items, such as beds. Bedford Furniture Industries and Sears Canada developed a quick response partnership after Bedford re-engineered its production process from make to stock to assemble beds within days (Chow, 1995). The result was a virtual elimination of inventory and subsequent reduction in warehouse space required the substitution of substantially less cross-docking space for the storage space, reduced handling and more efficient transportation delivery patterns. Similar pull systems have been established for bed supply chains in the United States and for appliance manufacturers. Arntzen and Shumway (2002) describe the changes in demand planning, material supply, manufacturing scheduling and order management introduced by NMS Communications and its manufacturing subcontractor, STMC Manufacturing, to create a high-speed, demand-driven supply chain. Despite the many high-profile examples of successful pull supply chain strategies, most observers still view the migration from manufacturing-based 'push' logistics systems to 'pull' networks as an emerging trend. Ross, Holcomb and Mandrodt (2004) indicate that much work remains to be done to develop adaptive supply chains. Much of the current logistics environment appears to be a 'blended model': one that incorporates elements of both push and pull systems. Industries where the economics of large production batches is overwhelming, such as in the chemical industry, have seen only limited application of pull logistics systems for their line of industrial and consumer products. For example, in Dupont's industrial chemicals and compounds supply chain, the overwhelming economics of large production batches has led the company to forward-place product inventories (generally in multiple railcar quantities) at customer sites. Similar batch economies exist for many of Dupont's industrial chemical customers. This field inventory allows Dupont to provide its customers with consistent and timely replenishment.

The development of pull systems has increased the utilization of a number of best practices, including vendor-managed inventory (discussed above), cross-docking, just-in-time supply, supplier hubs and merge in transit. Strategies to reduce inventory have also encouraged the location of supplier factories close to manufacturing facilities. This is not new, particularly in the automobile and other mass-production industries. In industries where relocation of production is not possible, vendor or supplier hubs have been developed to improve the efficiency of local just-in-time delivery. Supplier hubs are quite common in the PC and electronics manufacturing sector (Dell calls them 'logistics supply centres'). In 2003, about 30 suppliers provided 75 per cent of Dell's direct material purchase spend, and most of them maintained 8 to 10 days of inventory in the nearby logistics supply centre (Blanchard, 2003). The supplier hub operation maximizes vehicle load factors by consolidating components for delivery, which also reduces dock congestion at plants by reducing the number of vehicles making daily deliveries. Toyota has consolidated the majority of inventory in the Toyota supply chain into regional parts distribution centres, reducing inventory across the system. However, frequent small deliveries of parts to the dealers and overnight courier deliveries are increased. The cost trade-off is judged to favour this inventory centralization.

The JIT concept has been adapted to serve the retail, grocery and health care sectors in the form of quick response, continuous replenishment and stockless inventory respectively. The tools used to implement these approaches include bar-coding of product, point-of-sale capture of sales information, electronic data interchange and vendor-managed inventory. Pioneers like Procter & Gamble (P&G) and Wal-Mart lead the way with systems geared to quick response and continuous replenishment. The firms use real-time sales data available through robust information systems to take time and, therefore, inventory out of the supply chain. Quick response emphasizes the speed of delivery while continuous replenishment focuses on the small but frequent lot size dimension. Most of these inbound logistics networks still utilize the retailer's distribution centre, and the impact on inbound truck trips is typically minimal. For example, P&G supplies multiple products at a time instead of sending large batches of single commodities infrequently. Suppliers and customers alike benefit from levelled production and delivery of product, which reduces inventory requirements at both ends of the supply chain.

The next step involves bypassing the retailer's distribution centre (DC) either by direct store delivery or by cross-docking. Direct delivery to retail stores from manufacturers is frequently uneconomical for major suppliers unless full loads can be built. One way to build full loads is to use cross-docking. Cross-docking is a process that prevents products from coming to rest as static inventory at the retailer's DC. The manufacturer makes up individual store orders and delivers this store-ready merchandise to the retailer, which simply offloads it at the DC and cross-docks it to awaiting delivery trucks already scheduled for delivery to stores. Retailers like Wal-Mart, which are able to 'pull' their products, are able to cross-dock a larger percentage of their product directly to their stores. However, few retailers have been able to achieve anything close to true cross-docking, as it requires incredibly complex planning and coordination. Perhaps its greatest weakness is that few manufacturers are equipped to create store order quantities efficiently. Dell and Cisco utilize a variation of cross-docking, merge in transit, where the cross-docked components from different suppliers are merged with stored goods. Blanchard (2003) reports that Maytag maintained 41 cross-dock facilities, which store no inventory. Maytag covers 70 per cent of the US population from a cross-dock facility no more than 125 miles away, enabling high fill rates and short lead times.

In summary, many North American firms seek to become more demand-driven and move towards pull supply chains, but this is still an emerging practice despite the high-profile examples. To be sure, there are many industry sectors and specific businesses where supply lead times and production economies will more than justify the traditional forecast-driven supply chain, but just as certain is the need to be responsive to declining product life cycles and customer order lead times. The trend by many North American retailers and manufacturers to source offshore makes it more difficult to develop fast and reliable supply chains necessary for a pull strategy. This requires mixed strategies with a combination of the two systems and, often, a relocation of distribution centres.

Information technology and visibility

Information technology is a key enabler in the North American logistics and supply chain management practices highlighted in this chapter. It is crucial to the upstream visibility of supply and the downstream visibility of demand essential to effective logistics and supply chain management. Information technology plays an ever greater role in supply chain integration because it is the availability of the right information at the right place at the right time at the right level of granularity and detail that enables decisions across supply chain partners to be coordinated and integrated.

The need to achieve visibility has been spurred by many factors, some unique to the United States, others relevant worldwide (Abbot, Mandrodt and Moore, 2005). The terrorist attack of 11 September 2001 has made information systems an important tool in security initiatives. Measures have been led by the United States and have global consequences. The US Customs Service introduced the Container Security Initiative to screen for high-risk containers at overseas ports, and the Customs–Trade Partnership against Terrorism (C–TPAT) under which companies can reduce the likelihood of their containers being inspected by participating in the C–TPAT programme. Advance notice requirements for goods being shipped to the United States have advanced the application of information processes to facilitate security, but to the benefit of logistics, as it requires collecting information farther back (upstream) in the supply chain. There are some benefits to offset the costs that security measures impose. To facilitate trade within NAFTA, the three countries have an interest in compatibility of security measures.

The United States has introduced new requirements in business practices as a result of the fraud scandals of Enron, WorldCom and others. The Sarbanes–Oxley Act (SOA) was passed to make sure that there are internal controls in businesses that govern the information related to financial statements. This has implications for contractual relationships including outsourced supplies and logistics services. The need to report the financial implications of contracts, including the consequences of breaches of contracts, adds new dimensions to the logistics manager's tasks and further links with the financial processes of companies. The logistics job is more complicated.

Installing an enterprise resource planning (ERP) system is an important driver for companies of a centralized data repository to collect, store, organize and cross-reference data across applications, processes and functions. This is a major corporate undertaking, so that for logistics many firms utilize the information system capabilities of 3PLs. Shippers and carriers are now looking to adopt new technologies to track assets and products, such as radio frequency identification devices (RFID) and mobile or satellite communications.

Abbot, Mandrodt and Moore (2005) found that RFID was the most frequently added software capability in 2004. RFID has the potential not only to automate manual processes but to provide cost-effective visibility in the supply chain down to the item level. Wal-Mart, which drove the adoption of bar codes throughout retail nearly 20 years ago, is the leader in adopting RFID by requiring its suppliers, numbering into the tens of thousands, to implement RFID tagging on all pallets and cases. It also required the 100 biggest suppliers to have implementation plans in place by February 2004. Only a few years earlier, the retail giant endorsed the EDI-INT AS2 standard and directed 10,000 mid-size suppliers to adopt those communication protocols as a way of sending and receiving transactional data. Its adoption of the UCCnet standard in 2001 provided much-needed momentum throughout the consumer packaged goods industry to embrace data synchronization. This has spurred other sectors in the supply chain community to act as well. Suppliers to Wal-Mart will have the same RFID capabilities to offer to their other customers. Lieb and Bentz found that two-thirds of the manufacturing companies identified as 3PL users in their 2004 survey are either currently committed to the use of RFID technology in their logistics operations or are actively considering its use (Lieb and Bentz, 2005: 5–15). The 3PLs and other logistics service providers will have to respond with their own ability to read and utilize RFID tags, which could eventually supplant many bar-coding applications.

Growing challenges to the logistics system

The growth and globalization of commerce rely on efficient transport and logistics services – and this poses two substantial challenges for the future. The first is to ensure that sufficient capacity exists in the infrastructure system, and the second is to develop and operate with a greater consideration for environmental consequences.

Capacity constraints

The rapid growth of international trade means that congestion pressures arise because this traffic moves through a limited number of gateways at border crossings, airports and seaports. However, two conditions have pushed capacities to their limits. The first is the need for heightened security measures that effectively reduce capacity, especially at trans-border locations. In spite of increased spending on staff and facilities, including information technology, major congestion exists at busy crossings such as the crossing of the Detroit River, which sees heavy traffic serving the integrated auto industry. Delays in border crossing and uncertainties about the continuity of reliable service now make trans-border logistics a less attractive strategy than previously.

The second condition has been the unexpectedly high rates of growth in trade, especially with China. The efficiency of the overseas container logistics system has been of concern for some time; in the United States, the ability of ports to serve larger vessels, the adequacy of terminal capacity, and the quality of the land-side access have been of concern. In 2000, shippers and carriers on the West Coast formed a West Coast Waterfront Coalition to help address challenges there. In February 2003, the group became a national organization and dropped 'West Coast' from its name. Its existence could not prevent the severe congestion of 2004. The congestion threatened the ability of firms to meet their business plans and brought home the importance of seaports in the North American economy.

In 2005, the Waterfront Coalition (2005b) issued a call to action, which reflected that the level of congestion experienced in 2004 was the result of many factors, including the failures of shippers and carriers 'collaboratively to share information concerning expected cargo volumes' and the inadequacy of many operating practices. (See also Damas, 2005; Damas and Kulisch, 2005.) The problems for shippers and expectations of continuing high rates of trade growth have resulted in revisions to perceptions and strategies, some of which were evident during 2005. They include immediate and long-term initiatives:

- Spreading the peak by shipping earlier and using more ports, including shipping from South Asia to the Atlantic coast.
- The development of more inland terminals to receive goods directly from ports by rail, for example in Kansas City (KC Smartport, 2005).
- Increased efforts to improve the integration of port terminals and inland carriers, for example the launch of PierPass in Los Angeles and Long Beach as a means to reduce the congestion of drayage trucks (Waterfront Coalition, 2005a; PierPass Inc, 2006). The working of PierPass may also have contributed to the 25 per cent increase in rail moves off the terminals in Los Angeles in 2005 (Seaports Press Review, 2006).
- The interest of major shippers and major terminal management companies in the development of new container terminals, including those in Mexico, for example at Lazaro Cardenas and, possibly, Punto Colonet, and in Canada at Prince Rupert.

Two important dimensions of the transport capacity problem in North America are the need for more infrastructure capacity and the need for better methods of integration among all participants in supply chains. The ability of infrastructure to serve the growth of international traffic is tight. The rail industry, in particular, has progressed through 25 years of capacity rationalization and service improvement under the pressures of market competition. It is faced with more urgent needs for capacity expansion than formerly. Ports and highways serving international trade require expansion to meet trade growth. However, a part of the capacity problem arises from the ways in which logistics has been managed. Capacity has been assumed to be available. Strategies to reduce peak demands have been given too little attention in logistics and supply chain decisions. The port–inland interface provided by drayage services has not been managed effectively as a part of the logistics system. It has too often been ignored or fallen through the gap at the transfer of responsibility between shipping lines and shippers or their representatives. The result is that the Waterfront Coalition now recognizes the need to ensure a system that provides drayage services with adequate financial returns.

Unfortunately, ideas on paper take a long time in their acceptance for action and then their implementation. Traffic forecasts based on expected rates of growth in China (and then India, Brazil and other developing countries) and the rate of expansion of Chinese (and other) port facilities cast serious doubts on the adequacy of the North American infrastructure. The capacities of port terminals, of city highways and of the rail system are all potential real bottlenecks. The rate at which capacities may be expanded are constrained by many factors: institutional factors when public and private participation is necessary or appropriate; the availability of resources; and the environmental considerations.

Environmental considerations

There is now heightened awareness of the consequences of economic growth for the environment. Transport and, therefore, logistics services are affected because of the effects of fuel consumption on air quality and economic growth generally on land uses. Recognition of the need to address environmental concerns has led to environmental approval processes that can be lengthy and are often large parts of critical paths for new facilities, such as port terminals. Ports face particular problems because of sensitivity of the marine as well as the land environments and because ships, generally an energy-efficient way to move goods, are a major source of urban air pollution. Further, the concentration of trucks on routes to and from terminals, often already heavy with urban traffic, can be problematic. In general, congestion is a major source of environmental damage.

Providing increased logistics capacity to meet the growing needs of commerce and, particularly, of international trade faces new challenges because of the need for greater attention to the environmental consequences of economic growth. Proactive approaches are increasingly common, welcomed by many environmentalists but treated cynically by others.

Concluding comments

The development of logistics strategies in North America over the last decade has followed well-established paths. Logistics has become a more important and better-integrated part of corporate strategy, and supply chain management has been associated with increased outsourcing globally. The success of North American enterprises in improving logistics performance is evident in the low level of logistics costs compared with other regions.

Developments in information technology have played an important role in improved performance in the past and hold new opportunities for improvements in the future. However, success brings challenges. Traffic growth is putting pressure on the capacity of transport infrastructure. Transport and logistics services face new challenges in the design and operation of their systems in the light of capacity conditions. Security requirements place new demands on procedures and facilities. Greater awareness of the effects of economic activities on the environment is placing new constraints and requirements on transport and logistics infrastructure and services.

The success of logistics in North America in the past has been its ability to facilitate domestic and international trade with improved service levels and lower costs. To achieve these results in the future will require further innovation in technologies and strategies.

References

Abbot, J, Mandrodt, KB and Moore, P (2005) *From Visibility to Action: Year 2004 report on trends and issues in logistics and transportation*, Capgemini, Paris

Abernathy, FH (2001) Globalization in the apparel and textile industries: what is new and what is not, Harvard University, Center for Textile and Apparel Research, mimeo

Antweiler, Werner (2006) *Canada's International Trade and Investment Profile*, http://strategy.sauder.ubc.ca/antweiler/ [accessed 14 February 2006]

Armstrong & Associates (2005) *5th Annual Analysis of Third-Party Logistics Provider (3PL) Customers Trends and Market Segments*, www.3plogistics.com/news.htm

Armstrong, E (2004) Site visit – Vector SCM and Menlo Worldwide, 16 November

Arntzen, BC and Shumway, HM (2002) Driven by demand: a case study, *Supply Chain Management Review*, Jan/Feb, pp 34–41

Association of American Railroads (2005) www.aar.org/PubCommon/Documents/AboutTheIndustry/Statistics.pdf

Blanchard, D (2003) 10 best supply chains, *Logistics Today*, December

Bowersox, DJ (1997) Integrated supply chain management: a strategic imperative, *Council of Logistics Management Annual Conference Proceedings*, pp 181–90

Bowman, RJ (2002) Collaboration: desired by most, practiced by a precious few, *Global Logistics and Supply Chain Strategies*, November

Capital Consulting & Management (CCMI) (2002) CCMI outlines current state of supply chain collaboration, Press release, 8 July

Chow, G (1995) Logistics trends and strategies: implications for carrier strategies, in *TPW Policy Perspectives '94*, ed M Nyathi and J Schmitzer, pp 143–61, March, Institute of Transport Studies, University of Sydney, Sydney

Damas, P (2005) Too many cooks in part capacity decisions, *American Shipper*, May, pp 88–90

Damas, P and Kulisch, E (2005) Shippers, politicians sound off on transport bottlenecks, *American Shipper*, August, pp 66–69

Economist (2005) The rise of nearshoring, 3 December, pp 65–67

Esper, TL and Williams, LR (2003) The value of collaborative transportation management (CTM): its relationship to CPFR and information technology, *Transportation Journal*, Spring, pp 55–65

Fawcett, S, Magnan, GM and McCarter, MW (2005) Supply chain alliances and reality, Working paper, www.business.uiue.edu/Working_Papers/papers/05-0116.pdf

Fraser, J (2003) CPFR – status and perspectives: key results of a CPFR survey in the consumer goods sector and updates, in *Collaborative Forecasting and Replenishment: How to create a supply chain advantage*, ed D Seifert, pp 70–93, American Management Association, New York

Harps, LH (2004) From tactical to strategic: the 3PL continuum, *Inbound Logistics*, July

Heaver, TD (2002) Supply chain and logistics management: implications for liner shipping, in *Maritime Economics and Business*, ed Costas Grammenos, pp 375–96, Lloyds of London Press, London

Hillberry, R and McDaniel, C (2002) *A Decomposition of North American Trade Growth since NAFTA*, USITC Working Paper 2002-12-A, US International Trade Commission, Washington, DC

Inbound Logistics (2003) Outsourcing globally from the inside out, January

Johnson, E (2001) Learning from toys: Lessons in managing supply chain risk from the toy industry, *California Management Review*, **43** (3), pp 106–24

KC SmartPort (2005) *America's Inland Port Solution*, http://www.kcsmartport.com/sec_about/section/StrategicPlan.htm [accessed 3 March 2006]

Langley, JC *et al* (2005) *2005 Third-Party Logistics: Results and findings of the 10th annual study*, Capgemini, Paris

Lee, HG, Clark, T and Tam, KY (1999) Can EDI benefit adopters?, *Information Systems Research*, **10** (2), pp 186–95

Lieb, R and Bentz, BA (2004) 3PL CEO perspectives, North America, *American Shipper*, December, pp 46–54

Lieb, R and Bentz, BA (2005) *Third Party Logistics Services by Large American Manufacturers: The 2004 survey*, Spring, Capgemini, Paris

Lieb, R and Bentz, BA (2006) European 3PL CEO perspectives, *American Shipper*, January, pp 58–64

Logistics Today (2004) 10 best supply chains of 2004, www.logisticstoday.com

McCann, Philip (1998) *The Economics of Industrial Location: A logistics-costs approach*, Springer, Berlin, p 228

McKendrick, DG, Doner, RF and Haggard, S (2000) *From Silicon Valley to Singapore*, Stanford University Press, Stanford, CA

Magretta, J (1998) The power of virtual integration: an interview with Dell Computer's Michael Dell, *Harvard Business Review*, March–April, pp 72–84

Matchette, J and Seikel, A (2004) How to win friends and influence supply chain collaboration, *Logistics Today*, December

Mentzer, JT (2001) Defining supply chain management, *Journal of Business Logistics*, **22** (2), pp 1–26

Nix, N *et al* (2004) Keys to effective supply chain collaboration, Special report from the Collaborative Practices Research Program, Executive summary, 15 November, The Neeley School of Business, Fort Worth, Texas

Office of the US Trade Representative (2005) *Trade Policy Agenda*, www.ustr.gov/assets/Document_Library/Reports_Publications/2005 [accessed 17 February 2006]

Ohio State University (2002) Ohio State Survey of Career Patterns in Logistics, Ohio State University, Ohio

PierPass Inc (2006) *PierPASS Offpeak Program Diverts a Million Truck Trips from Daytime Los Angeles Traffic*, 6 January, http://www.pierpass.org/files/million_trucks_jan_6_06_final.pdf [accessed 3 March 2006]

Rodrigues, AM, Bowersox, DJ and Calantone, RJ (2005) Estimation of global and national logistics expenditures: 2002 data update, *Journal of Business Logistics*, **26** (2), pp 1–15

Romalis, John (2005) *NAFTA's and CUSFTA's Impact on International Trade*, National Bureau of Economic Research, Working Paper 11059, January 2005

Ross, T, Holcomb, MC and Mandrodt, KB (2004) *Operations Excellence: The transition from tactical to adaptive supply chains – Year 2003 report on trends and issues in logistics and transportation*, Capgemini, Paris

Saha, P (undated) *Factors Influencing Broad Based CPFR Adoption*, www.vics.org/committees/cpfr/academic_papers/Factors_Impacting_CPFR_Adoption_(VICS).pdf

Seaports Press Review (2006) *Port of Los Angeles Reports Record 25% Increase in On-Dock Rail Usage for 2005*, http://www.seaportspr.com/viewportnews.cgi?newsletter_id=45&article_id=2087 [accessed 13 February 2006]

Suleski, J (2001) Beyond CPFR: retail collaboration comes of age, *AMR Research Report*, 1 November, www.cpfr.org

Taylor, JC and Closs, DJ (1993) Logistics implications of an integrated US–Canada market, *International Journal of Physical Distribution and Logistics Management*, **23** (1), pp 3–11

UPS (2006) http://www.ups.com [accessed 21 February 2006]

US Census Bureau, *US International Trade in Goods and Services*, Annual revision for 2004, http://www.census.gov/foreign-trade/Press-Release/2004pr/final_revisions/index.html#goods [accessed 20 February 2006]

US Central Intelligence Agency (2006) *The World Fact Book*, www.cia.gov/cia/publications/factbook/index.html [accessed 13 February 2006]

Waterfront Coalition (2005a) *Marine Terminals in So Cal Launch PierPass*, http://portmod.org/HOT%20TOPICS/hot%20topics.htm [accessed 3 March 2006]

Waterfront Coalition (2005b) *The National Marine Container Transportation System: A call to action*, www.portmod.org/news/press/White%20Paper.htm [accessed 3 March 2006]

Wilson, R (2005) 16th annual state of logistics report: security report card – not making the grade, Council of Supply Chain Management Professionals Conference, 27 June, Washington, DC

Index